THE JUDICIAL CODE

AND

RULES OF PROCEDURE

IN THE

FEDERAL COURTS

WITH EXCERPTS FROM THE CRIMINAL CODE

Compiled by

HENRY M. HART, JR.
Late Dane Professor of Law, Harvard University

and

HERBERT WECHSLER
Harlan Fiske Stone Professor of Constitutional Law Emeritus,
Columbia University

STUDENTS' EDITION
1984 REVISION

Mineola, New York
THE FOUNDATION PRESS, INC.
1984

ISBN 0-88277-166-3

Hart & Wechsler F.P. '84 Pamph.

PREFATORY NOTE

When the late Professor Henry M. Hart, Jr., and I originally planned this compilation, we had in mind primarily the utility of such a supplement to our casebook on *The Federal Courts and the Federal System.* It was designed, however to meet a need that exists also in courses in judicial remedies and procedure which focus upon federal practice. Successive editions, of which the last appeared in 1981, have sought to keep pace with the rapid rate of change in this surprisingly dynamic field. The publication in 1973 of a second edition of the casebook, prepared by Professors Paul M. Bator, Paul J. Mishkin, David L. Shapiro and myself, with supplements in 1977 and 1981, and the prospect of a third edition before long, afford a continuing incentive to keep this pamphlet up to date. There has been sufficient change upon important points within the last two years to call for a revision now.

Statutes and regulations are useful principally for reference. But the good ordering of the basic materials on the federal courts —the Judicial Code and the rules of civil and criminal and appellate procedure—gives to each of them a further value not often achieved by enacted law: that of a connected and intelligible exposition which can be profitably read as a whole. Each of them, therefore, should be available to students as a whole, rather than distributed through a casebook in disjointed excerpts.

Partly to preserve this advantage and partly to make possible a compact and easily manageable volume, the code and the various rules have been printed as they stand from time to time, without annotation or parallel printing of previous versions.

The revised rules of the Supreme Court, the Supplemental Rules for Certain Admiralty and Maritime Claims, the Rules of Procedure for United States Magistrates, the Rules of Procedure of the Judicial Panel on Multidistrict Litigation and the Supreme Court's Rules and Forms governing proceedings under 28 U.S.C. §§ 2254 and 2255 have also been included.

The present edition incorporates amendments to the statutes and the rules as of August 1, 1983.

As was the case with the six previous editions, I am indebted to Doris Wechsler for bearing the major burdens of this revision of the compilation.

HERBERT WECHSLER

New York City
August 4, 1983

*

TABLE OF CONTENTS

JUDICIAL CODE (TITLE 28, UNITED STATES CODE)

PART IV—Continued

RULES AND FORMS GOVERNING PROCEEDINGS IN THE UNITED STATES DISTRICT COURTS UNDER SECTION 2254 AND SECTION 2255 OF TITLE 28, UNITED STATES CODE—Continued

TITLE 28

UNITED STATES CODE

As enacted in Public Law 773, 80th Congress, Second Session, and as amended to August 1, 1983

Editorial Note:

Revised Title 28 of the United States Code, Judiciary and Judicial Procedure, approved June 25, 1948 and effective September 1, 1948, is the fourth comprehensive revision of the statutes relating to the federal courts. It is the third of the four revisions to be formally enacted into law.

The First Judiciary Act of 1789, 1 Stat. 73, provided a framework around which successive enactments affecting the federal courts might have been systematically arranged. But in this as in other matters Congress followed a practice of piecemeal legislation. New provisions were occasionally enacted as amendments to the Judiciary Act but more often as independent measures or as parts of statutes changing the substantive law. Thus the statutes affecting the federal courts, like all federal statutes, rapidly became a formless and confused mass.

The Revised Statutes of 1873 were the first great effort to deal with this problem. Enacted in 1874, they codified all laws of a general and permanent nature in force on December 1, 1873, and repealed prior statutes outright. This was not only the first but the last occasion on which Congress has thus enacted as law a revision of all the permanent statutes of the United States. The judiciary title of the Revised Statutes was Title XIII, comprising 563 sections.

The judiciary title of the Revised Statutes was in turn revised, and the revision enacted into law, by the Judicial Code of 1911, 36 Stat. 1087. This revision was the work of a commission which had originally been appointed in 1897 to revise and codify the criminal and penal laws of the United States. The duties of the Commission were extended in 1899 to include the laws concerning the jurisdiction and practice of United States courts, and in 1901 to include all laws of a general and permanent nature. Having enacted the Criminal Code in 1909, 35 Stat. 1089, and the Judicial Code in 1911, Congress, however, rejected the rest of the Commission's work.

The next great effort at comprehensive revision of the federal statutes culminated in the adoption of the United States Code on June 30, 1926, 44 Stat. 1. Warned by the numerous errors discovered in previous codifications, Congress this time refused to enact the Code as law. Section 1 declares the intention of Congress "to embrace the laws of the United States, general and permanent in their nature," in a single volume. But Section 2 says that the matter set forth in the Code "shall establish prima facie" what such laws are, "but nothing in this Act shall be construed as repealing or amending any such law, or as enacting as new law any matter contained in the Code." Successive supplements to the Code have included the same provision. Thus Title 28 of the original Code, the judiciary title, never acquired the statutory force of the Revised Statutes and the Judicial Code.

In the 1948 revision Congress again singled out the judiciary title (and at the same time, Title 18, the Criminal Code) for special treatment. The revision is enacted as law and includes a comprehensive schedule of prior enactments which are repealed.

The progress of codification has never put an end to the practice of Congress of enacting, on occasion, provisions relating to the courts as parts of statutes changing the substantive law rather than as amendments to the Judicial Code. Nor have the revisers ever succeeded in extracting all these provisions from the general body of the statutes and incorporating them in the Code. For example, Chapter 83 of the present revision, dealing with the jurisdiction of the courts of appeals, includes none of the numerous provisions for review in these courts of the orders of various federal administrative agencies. Similarly, Chapter 85, dealing with the jurisdiction of the District Courts, does not incorporate many specific jurisdictional provisions enacted in the course of legislating on particular subjects, which may narrow or enlarge jurisdiction that would otherwise obtain under § 1331. To be sure of finding all the applicable statutes on jurisdiction and procedure in a federal case, therefore, it remains necessary to examine not only Revised Title 28 but the substantive statutes involved.

Revised Title 28 was embodied in Public Law 773, 80th Congress, Second Session, approved June 25, 1948, which also includes additional material reprinted here. The revised title (together with Revised Title 18) was extensively amended to correct minor errors by Public Law 72, 81st Congress, First Session, approved May 24, 1949, and has been further amended from time to time since. As amended up to August 1, 1983 it is reproduced here in its entirety, with the exception only of Sections 81 to 131, inclusive, of Chapter 5, which divide the several states into judicial districts and many of the districts in turn into divisions, and § 376, dealing with Judges' survivors' annuities.

The Bankruptcy Reform Act of 1978 (Pub.L. 95–598, Nov. 6, 1978, 92 Stat. 2549) includes substantial amendments to Title 28, some of which took effect on October 1, 1979, but many of which do not take effect until April 1, 1984. Only those amendments which have taken effect are included in this edition.

AN ACT

To revise, codify, and enact into law title 28 of the United States Code entitled "Judicial Code and Judiciary".

Be it enacted by the Senate and House of Representatives of the United States of America in Congress assembled, That:

Title 28 of the United States Code, entitled "Judicial Code and Judiciary" is hereby revised, codified, and enacted into law, and may be cited as "Title 28, United States Code, section —", as follows:

TITLE 28

JUDICIARY AND JUDICIAL PROCEDURE

PART I—ORGANIZATION OF COURTS

CHAPTER 1—SUPREME COURT

§ 1. Number of justices; quorum

The Supreme Court of the United States shall consist of a Chief Justice of the United States and eight associate justices, any six of whom shall constitute a quorum.

§ 2. Terms of court

The Supreme Court shall hold at the seat of government a term of court commencing on the first Monday in October of each year and may hold such adjourned or special terms as may be necessary.

§ 3. Vacancy in office of Chief Justice; disability

Whenever the Chief Justice is unable to perform the duties of his office or the office is vacant, his powers and duties shall devolve upon the associate justice next in precedence who is able to act, until such disability is removed or another Chief Justice is appointed and duly qualified.

§ 4. Precedence of associate justices

Associate justices shall have precedence according to the seniority of their commissions. Justices whose commissions bear the same date shall have precedence according to seniority in age.

§ 5. Salaries of justices

The Chief Justice and each associate justice shall each receive a salary at annual rates determined under section 225 of the Federal Salary Act of 1967 (2 U.S.C. §§ 351–361), as adjusted by section 461 of this title.

§ 6. Records of former court of appeals

The records and proceedings of the court of appeals, appointed previous to the adoption of the Constitution, shall be kept until deposited with the National Archives of the United States in the office of the clerk of the Supreme Court, who shall furnish copies thereof to any person requiring and paying for them, in the manner provided by law for giving copies of the records and proceedings of the Supreme Court. Such copies shall have the same faith and credit as proceedings of the Supreme Court.

CHAPTER 3—COURTS OF APPEALS

§ 41. Number and composition of circuits

The thirteen judicial circuits of the United States are constituted as follows:

Circuits	Composition
District of Columbia	District of Columbia.
First	Maine, Massachusetts, New Hampshire, Puerto Rico, Rhode Island.
Second	Connecticut, New York, Vermont.
Third	Delaware, New Jersey, Pennsylvania, Virgin Islands.
Fourth	Maryland, North Carolina, South Carolina, Virginia, West Virginia.
Fifth	District of the Canal Zone, Louisiana, Mississipi, Texas.
Sixth	Kentucky, Michigan, Ohio, Tennessee.
Seventh	Illinois, Indiana, Wisconsin.
Eighth	Arkansas, Iowa, Minnesota, Missouri, Nebraska, North Dakota, South Dakota.
Ninth	Alaska, Arizona, California, Idaho, Montana, Nevada, Oregon, Washington, Guam, Hawaii.
Tenth	Colorado, Kansas, New Mexico, Oklahoma, Utah, Wyoming.
Eleventh	Alabama, Florida, Georgia.
Federal	All Federal judicial districts.

§ 42. Allotment of Supreme Court justices to circuits

The Chief Justice of the United States and the associate justices of the Supreme Court shall from time to time be allotted as circuit justices among the circuits by order of the Supreme Court. The Chief Justice may make such allotments in vacation.

A justice may be assigned to more than one circuit, and two or more justices may be assigned to the same circuit.

§ 43. Creation and composition of courts

(a) There shall be in each circuit a court of appeals, which shall be a court of record, known as the United States Court of Appeals for the circuit.

(b) Each court of appeals shall consist of the circuit judges of the circuit in regular active service. The circuit justice and justices or judges designated or assigned shall also be competent to sit as judges of the court.

§ 44. Appointment, tenure, residence and salary of circuit judges

(a) The President shall appoint, by and with the advice and consent of the Senate, circuit judges for the several circuits as follows:

Circuits	Number of Judges
District of Columbia	11
First	4
Second	11
Third	10
Fourth	10
Fifth	14
Sixth	11
Seventh	9
Eighth	9
Ninth	23
Tenth	8
Eleventh	12
Federal	12

(b) Circuit judges shall hold office during good behavior.

(c) Except in the District of Columbia, each circuit judge shall be a resident of the circuit for which appointed at the time of his appointment and thereafter while in active service. While in active service, each circuit judge of the Federal judicial circuit appointed after the effective date of this Act, and the chief judge of the Federal judicial circuit, whenever appointed, shall reside within fifty miles of the District of Columbia.

(d) Each circuit judge shall receive a salary at an annual rate determined under section 225 of the Federal Salary Act of 1967 (2 U.S.C.A. §§ 351–361), as adjusted by section 461 of this title.

§ 45. Chief judges; precedence of judges

(a)(1) The chief judge of the circuit shall be the circuit judge in regular active service who is senior in commission of those judges who—

(A) are sixty-four years of age or under;

(B) have served for one year or more as a circuit judge; and

(C) have not served previously as chief judge.

(2)(A) In any case in which no circuit judge meets the qualifications of paragraph (1), the youngest circuit judge in regular active service who is sixty-five years of age or over and who has served as circuit judge for one year or more shall act as the chief judge.

(B) In any case under subparagraph (A) in which there is no circuit judge in regular active service who has served as a circuit judge for one year or more, the circuit judge in regular active service who is senior in commission and who has not served previously as chief judge shall act as the chief judge.

(3)(A) Except as provided in subparagraph (C), the chief judge of the circuit appointed under paragraph (1) shall serve for a term of seven years and shall serve after expiration of such term until another judge is eligible under paragraph (1) to serve as chief judge of the circuit.

(B) Except as provided in subparagraph (C), a circuit judge acting as chief judge under subparagraph (A) or (B) of paragraph (2) shall serve until a judge has been appointed who meets the qualifications under paragraph (1).

(C) No circuit judge may serve or act as chief judge of the circuit after attaining the age of seventy years unless no other circuit judge is qualified to serve as chief judge of the circuit under paragraph (1) or is qualified to act as chief judge under paragraph (2).

(b) The chief judge shall have precedence and preside at any session of the court which he attends. Other circuit judges of the court in regular active service shall have precedence and preside according to the seniority of their commissions. Judges whose commissions bear the same date shall have precedence according to seniority in age. The circuit justice, however, shall have precedence over all the circuit judges and shall preside at any session which he attends.

(c) If the chief judge desires to be relieved of his duties as chief judge while retaining his active status as circuit judge, he may so certify to the Chief Justice of the United States, and thereafter the chief judge of the circuit shall be such other circuit judge who is qualified to serve or act as chief judge under subsection (a).

(d) If a chief judge is temporarily unable to perform his duties as such, they shall be performed by the circuit judge in active service, present in the circuit and able and qualified to act, who is next in precedence.

§ 46. Assignment of judges; panels; hearings; quorum

(a) Circuit judges shall sit on the court and its panels in such order and at such times as the court directs.

(b) In each circuit the court may authorize the hearing and determination of cases and controversies by separate panels each consisting of three judges, at least a majority of whom shall be judges of that court, unless such judges cannot sit because recused or disqualified, or unless the chief judge of that court certifies that there is an emergency including, but not limited to, the unavailability of a judge of the court because of illness. Such panels shall sit at the times and places and hear the cases and controversies assigned as the court directs. The United States Court of Appeals for the Federal Circuit shall determine by rule a procedure for the rotation of judges from panel to panel to ensure that all of the judges sit on a representative cross section of the cases heard and, notwithstanding the first sentence of this subsection, may determine by rule the number of judges, not less than three, who constitute a panel.

(c) Cases and controversies shall be heard and determined by a court or panel of not more than three judges (except that the United States Court of Appeals for the Federal Circuit may sit in panels of more than three judges if its rules so provide), unless a hearing or rehearing before the court in banc is ordered by a majority of the circuit judges of the circuit who are in regular active service. A court in banc shall consist of all circuit judges in regular active service, or such number of judges as may be prescribed in accordance with section 6 of Public Law 95–486 (92 Stat. 1633), except that any senior circuit judge of the circuit shall be eligible to participate, at his election and upon designation and assignment pursuant to section 294(c) of this title and the rules of the circuit, as a member of an in banc court reviewing a decision of a panel of which such judge was a member.

(d) A majority of the number of judges authorized to constitute a court or panel thereof, as provided in paragraph (c), shall constitute a quorum.

§ 47. Disqualification of trial judge to hear appeal

No judge shall hear or determine an appeal from the decision of a case or issue tried by him.

§ 48. Terms of court

(a) The courts of appeals shall hold regular sessions at the places listed below, and at such other places within the respective circuit as each court may designate by rule.

Circuits	Places
District of Columbia	Washington.
First	Boston.
Second	New York.
Third	Philadelphia.
Fourth	Richmond, Asheville.
Fifth	New Orleans, Fort Worth, Jackson.
Sixth	Cincinnati.
Seventh	Chicago.
Eighth	St. Louis, Kansas City, Omaha, St. Paul.
Ninth	San Francisco, Los Angeles, Portland, Seattle.
Tenth	Denver, Wichita, Oklahoma City.
Eleventh	Atlanta, Jacksonville, Montgomery.

Circuits	Places
Federal	District of Columbia, and in any other place listed above as the court by rule directs.

(b) Each court of appeals may hold special sessions at any place within its circuit as the nature of the business may require, and upon such notice as the court orders. The court may transact any business at a special session which it might transact at a regular session.

(c) Any court of appeals may pretermit, with the consent of the Judicial Conference of the United States, any regular session of court at any place for insufficient business or other good cause.

(d) The times and places of the sessions of the Court of Appeals for the Federal Circuit shall be prescribed with a view to securing reasonable opportunity to citizens to appear before the court with as little inconvenience and expense to citizens as is practicable.

§ 49. Assignment of judges to division to appoint independent counsels

(a) Beginning with the two-year period commencing on the date of the enactment of this section, three judges or justices shall be assigned for each successive two-year period to a division of the United States Court of Appeals for the District of Columbia to be the division of the court for the purpose of appointing independent counsels.

(b) Except as provided under subsection (f) of this section, assignment to such division of the court shall not be a bar to other judicial assignments during the term of such division.

(c) In assigning judges or justices to sit on such division of the court, priority shall be given to senior circuit judges and retired justices.

(d) The Chief Justice of the United States shall designate and assign three circuit court judges or justices, one of whom shall be a judge of the United States Court of Appeals for the District of Columbia, to such division of the court. Not more than one judge or justice or senior or retired judge or justice may be named to such division from a particular court.

(e) Any vacancy in such division of the court shall be filled only for the remainder of the two-year period in which such vacancy occurs and in the same manner as initial assignments to such division were made.

(f) Except as otherwise provided in chapter 39 of this title, no member of such division of the court who participated in a function conferred on the division under chapter 39 of this title involving a[n] independent counsel shall be eligible to participate in any judicial proceeding concerning a matter which involves such independent counsel while such independent counsel is serving in that office or which involves the exercise of such independent counsel's official duties, regardless of whether such independent counsel is still serving in that office.

CHAPTER 5—DISTRICT COURTS

§ 132. Creation and composition of district courts

(a) There shall be in each judicial district a district court which shall be a court of record known as the United States District Court for the district.

(b) Each district court shall consist of the district judge or judges for the district in regular active service. Justices or judges designated or assigned shall be competent to sit as judges of the court.

(c) Except as otherwise provided by law, or rule or order of court, the judicial power of a district court with respect to any action, suit or proceeding may be exercised by a single judge, who may preside alone and hold a regular or special session of court at the same time other sessions are held by other judges.

§ 133. Appointment and number of district judges

The President shall appoint, by and with the advice and consent of the Senate, district judges for the several judicial districts, as follows:

Districts	Judges
Alabama:	
Northern	7
Middle	3
Southern	2
Alaska	2
Arizona	8
Arkansas:	
Eastern	3
Western	1
Eastern and Western	2
California:	
Northern	12
Eastern	6
Central	17
Southern	7

Districts	Judges
Colorado	6
Connecticut	5
Delaware	3
District of Columbia	15
Florida:	
Northern	3
Middle	9
Southern	12
Georgia:	
Northern	11
Middle	2
Southern	3
Hawaii	2
Idaho	2
Illinois:	
Northern	16
Southern	3
Eastern	2
Indiana:	
Northern	4
Southern	5
Iowa:	
Northern	1
Southern	2
Northern and Southern	1
Kansas	5
Kentucky:	
Eastern	4
Western	3
Eastern and Western	1
Louisiana:	
Eastern	13
Middle	2
Western	5
Maine	2
Maryland	9
Massachusetts	10
Michigan:	
Eastern	13
Western	4
Minnesota	5
Mississippi:	
Northern	2
Southern	3

Districts	Judges
Missouri:	
Eastern	4
Western	5
Eastern and Western	2
Montana	2
Nebraska	3
Nevada	3
New Hampshire	2
New Jersey	11
New Mexico	4
New York:	
Northern	3
Southern	27
Eastern	10
Western	3
North Carolina:	
Eastern	3
Western	3
Middle	3
North Dakota	2
Ohio:	
Northern	9
Southern	6
Oklahoma:	
Northern	2
Eastern	1
Western	3
Northern, Eastern, and Western	2
Oregon	5
Pennsylvania:	
Eastern	19
Middle	5
Western	10
Puerto Rico	7
Rhode Island	2
South Carolina	8
South Dakota	3
Tennessee:	
Eastern	3
Middle	3
Western	3
Texas:	
Northern	9
Southern	13
Eastern	4
Western	6

Districts	Judges
Utah	3
Vermont	2
Virginia:	
Eastern	8
Western	4
Washington:	
Eastern	2
Western	5
West Virginia:	
Northern	1
Southern	3
Northern and Southern	1
Wisconsin:	
Eastern	4
Western	2
Wyoming	1

§ 134. Tenure and residence of district judges

(a) The district judges shall hold office during good behavior.

(b) Each district judge, except in the District of Columbia, shall reside in the district or one of the districts for which he is appointed.

(c) If the public interest and the nature of the business of a district court require that a district judge should maintain his abode at or near a particular place for holding court in the district or within a particular part of the district the judicial council of the circuit may so declare and may make an appropriate order. If the district judges of such a district are unable to agree as to which of them shall maintain his abode at or near the place or within the area specified in such an order the judicial council of the circuit may decide which of them shall do so.

§ 135. Salaries of district judges

Each judge of a district court of the United States shall receive a salary at an annual rate determined under section 225 of the Federal Salary Act of 1967 (2 U.S.C. §§ 351–361), as adjusted by section 461 of this title.

§ 136. Chief judges; precedence of district judges

(a)(1) In any district having more than one district judge, the chief judge of the district shall be the district judge in regular active service who is senior in commission of those judges who—

(A) are sixty-four years of age or under;

(B) have served for one year or more as a district judge; and

(C) have not served previously as chief judge.

(2)(A) In any case in which no district judge meets the qualifications of paragraph (1), the youngest district judge in regular active service who is sixty-five years of age or over and who has served as district judge for one year or more shall act as the chief judge.

(B) In any case under subparagraph (A) in which there is no district judge in regular active service who has served as a district judge for one year or more, the district judge in regular active service who is senior in commission and who has not served previously as chief judge shall act as the chief judge.

(3)(A) Except as provided in subparagraph (C), the chief judge of the district appointed under paragraph (1) shall serve for a term of seven years and shall serve after expiration of such term until another judge is eligible under paragraph (1) to serve as chief judge of the district.

(B) Except as provided in subparagraph (C), a district judge acting as chief judge under subparagraph (A) or (B) of paragraph (2) shall serve until a judge has been appointed who meets the qualifications under paragraph (1).

(C) No district judge may serve or act as chief judge of the district after attaining the age of seventy years unless no other district judge is qualified to serve as chief judge of the district under paragraph (1) or is qualified to act as chief judge under paragraph (2).

(b) The chief judge shall have precedence and preside at any session which he attends.

Other district judges shall have precedence and preside according to the seniority of their commissions. Judges whose commissions bear the same date shall have precedence according to seniority in age.

(c) A judge whose commission extends over more than one district shall be junior to all district judges except in the district in which he resided at the time he entered upon the duties of his office.

(d) If the chief judge desires to be relieved of his duties as chief judge while retaining his active status as district judge, he may so certify to the Chief Justice of the United States, and thereafter, the chief judge of the district shall be such other district judge who is qualified to serve or act as chief judge under subsection (a).

(e) If a chief judge is temporarily unable to perform his duties as such, they shall be performed by the district judge in active service, present in the district and able and qualified to act, who is next in precedence.

§ 137. Division of business among district judges

The business of a court having more than one judge shall be divided among the judges as provided by the rules and orders of the court.

The chief judge of the district court shall be responsible for the observance of such rules and orders, and shall divide the business and assign the cases so far as such rules and orders do not otherwise prescribe.

If the district judges in any district are unable to agree upon the adoption of rules or orders for that purpose the judicial council of the circuit shall make the necessary orders.

§ 138. Terms abolished

The district court shall not hold formal terms.

§ 139. Times for holding regular sessions

The times for commencing regular sessions of the district court for transacting judicial business at the places fixed by this chapter shall be determined by the rules or orders of the court. Such rules or orders may provide that at one or more of such places the court shall be in continuous session for such purposes on all business days throughout the year. At other places a session of the court shall continue for such purposes until terminated by order of final adjournment or by commencement of the next regular session at the same place.

§ 140. Adjournment

(a) Any district court may, by order made anywhere within its district, adjourn or, with the consent of the judicial council of the circuit, pretermit any regular session of court for insufficient business or other good cause.

(b) If the judge of a district court is unable to attend and unable to make an order of adjournment, the clerk may adjourn the court to the next regular session or to any earlier day which he may determine.

§ 141. Special sessions; places; notice

Special sessions of the district court may be held at such places in the district as the nature of the business may require, and upon such notice as the court orders.

Any business may be transacted at a special session which might be transacted at a regular session.

[§ 142. Repealed.]

§ 143. Vacant judgeship as affecting proceedings

When the office of a district judge becomes vacant, all pending process, pleadings and proceedings shall, when necessary, be continued by the clerk until a judge is appointed or designated to hold such court.

§ 144. Bias or prejudice of judge

Whenever a party to any proceeding in a district court makes and files a timely and sufficient affidavit that the judge before whom the matter is pending has a personal bias or prejudice either against him or in favor of any adverse party, such judge shall proceed no further therein, but another judge shall be assigned to hear such proceeding.

The affidavit shall state the facts and the reasons for the belief that bias or prejudice exists, and shall be filed not less than ten days before the beginning of the term at which the proceeding is to be heard, or good cause shall be shown for failure to file it within such time. A party may file only one such affidavit in any case. It shall be accompanied by a certificate of counsel of record stating that it is made in good faith.

CHAPTER 6—BANKRUPTCY COURTS

Sec.

151–160. **(Editorial note:** As noted in the introduction to Title 28, the Bankruptcy Reform Act of 1978 (Pub.L. 95–598, Nov. 6, 1978, 92 Stat. 2657) includes substantial amendments to Title 28, most of which do not take effect until April 1, 1984. Among these is a new Chapter 6, which purports to establish Bankruptcy Courts and to provide for appointment of judges (as to which see Northern Pipeline Construction Co. v. Marathon Pipe Line Company and United States, —— U.S. ——, 102 S.Ct. 2858, 73 L.Ed.2d 598 [1982]); a new Chapter 50, which provides for clerks and employees; and a new Chapter 90, which deals with jurisdiction and venue. None of these postponed provisions is included in this compilation.)

CHAPTER 7—UNITED STATES CLAIMS COURT

Sec.

§ 171. Appointment and number of judges; character of court; designation of chief judge

(a) The President shall appoint, by and with the advice and consent of the Senate, sixteen judges who shall constitute a court of record known as the United States Claims Court. The court is declared to be a court established under article I of the Constitution of the United States.

(b) The President shall designate one of the judges of the Claims Court who is less than seventy years of age to serve as chief judge. The chief judge may continue to serve as such until he reaches the age of seventy years or until another judge is designated as chief judge by the President. After the designation of another judge to serve as chief judge, the former chief judge may continue to serve as a judge of the court for the balance of the term to which appointed.

§ 172. Tenure and salaries of judges

(a) Each judge of the United States Claims Court shall be appointed for a term of fifteen years.

(b) Each judge shall receive a salary at an annual rate determined under section 225 of the Federal Salary Act of 1967 (2 U.S.C. 351–361), as adjusted by section 461 of this title.

§ 173. Times and places of holding court

The principal office of the United States Claims Court shall be in the District of Columbia, but the Claims Court may hold court at such times and in such places as it may fix by rule of court. The times and places of the sessions of the Claims Court shall be prescribed with a view to securing reasonable opportunity to citizens to appear before the Claims Court with as little inconvenience and expense to citizens as is practicable.

§ 174. Assignment of judges; decisions

(a) The judicial power of the United States Claims Court with respect to any action, suit, or proceeding, except congressional reference cases, shall be exercised by a single judge, who may reside alone and hold a regular or special session of court at the same time other sessions are held by other judges.

(b) All decisions of the Claims Court shall be preserved and open to inspection.

§ 175. Official duty station; residence

(a) The official duty station of each judge of the United States Claims Court is the District of Columbia.

(b) After appointment and while in active service, each judge shall reside within fifty miles of the District of Columbia.

§ 176. Removal from office

(a) Removal of a judge of the United States Claims Court during the term for which he is appointed shall be only for incompetency, misconduct, neglect of duty, engaging in the practice of law, or physical or mental disability. Removal shall be by the United States Court of Appeals for the Federal Circuit, but removal may not occur unless a majority of all the judges of such court of appeals concur in the order of removal.

(b) Before any order of removal may be entered, a full specification of the charges shall be furnished to the judge involved, and such judge shall be accorded an opportunity to be heard on the charges.

(c) Any cause for removal of any judge of the United States Claims Court coming to the knowledge of the Director of the Administrative Office of the United States Courts shall be reported by him to the chief judge of the United States Court of Appeals for the Federal Circuit, and a copy of the report shall at the same time be transmitted to the judge.

§ 177. Disbarment of removed judges

A judge of the United States Claims Court removed from office in accordance with section 176 of this title shall not be permitted at any time to practice before the Claims Court.

CHAPTER 11—COURT OF INTERNATIONAL TRADE

§ 251. Appointment and number of judges; offices

(a) The President shall appoint, by and with the advice and consent of the Senate, nine judges who shall constitute a court of record to be known as the United States Court of International Trade. Not more than five of such judges shall be from the same political party. The court is a court established under article III of the Constitution of the United States.

(b) The President shall designate one of the judges of the Court of International Trade who is less than seventy years of age to serve as chief judge. The chief judge shall continue to serve as chief judge until he reaches the age of seventy years and another judge is designated as chief judge by the President. After the designation of another judge to serve as chief judge, the former chief judge may continue to serve as a judge of the court.

(c) The offices of the Court of International Trade shall be located in New York, New York.

§ 252. Tenure and salaries of judges

Judges of the Court of International Trade shall hold office during good behavior. Each shall receive a salary at an annual rate determined under section 225 of the Federal Salary Act of 1967 (2 U.S.C. §§ 351–361), as adjusted by section 461 of this title.

§ 253. Duties of chief judge; precedence of judges

(a) The chief judge of the Court of International Trade, with the approval of the court, shall supervise the fiscal affairs and clerical force of the court;

(b) The chief judge shall promulgate dockets.

(c) The chief judge, under rules of the court, may designate any judge or judges of the court to try any case and, when the circumstances so warrant, reassign the case to another judge or judges.

(d) Whenever the chief judge is unable to perform the duties of his office or the office is vacant, his powers and duties shall devolve upon the judge next in precedence who is able to act, until such disability is removed or another chief judge is appointed and duly qualified.

(e) The chief judge shall have precedence and shall preside at any session which he attends. Other judges shall have precedence and shall preside according to the seniority of their commissions. Judges whose commissions bear the same date shall have precedence according to seniority in age.

§ 254. Single-judge trials

Except as otherwise provided in section 255 of this title, the judicial power of the Court of International Trade with respect to any action, suit or proceeding shall be exercised by a single judge, who may preside alone and hold a regular or special session of court at the same time other sessions are held by other judges.

§ 255. Three-judge trials

(a) Upon application of any party to a civil action, or upon his own initiative, the chief judge of the Court of International Trade shall designate any three judges of the court to hear and determine any civil action which the chief judge finds: (1) raises an issue of the constitutionality of an Act of Congress, a proclamation of the President or an Executive order; or (2) has broad or significant implications in the administration or interpretation of the customs laws.

(b) A majority of the three judges designated may hear and determine the civil action and all questions pending therein.

§ 256. Trials at ports other than New York

(a) The chief judge may designate any judge or judges of the court to proceed, together with necessary assistants, to any port or to any place within the jurisdiction of the United States to preside at a trial or hearing at the port or place.

(b) Upon application of a party or upon his own initiative, and upon a showing that the interests of economy, efficiency, and justice will be served, the chief judge may issue an order authorizing a judge of the court to preside in an evidentiary hearing in a foreign country whose laws do not prohibit such a hearing: *Provided, however,* That an interlocutory appeal may be taken from such an order pursuant to the provisions of section 1292(d)(1) of this title, and the United States Court of Appeals for the Federal Circuit may, in its discretion, consider the appeal.

§ 257. Publication of decisions

All decisions of the Court of International Trade shall be preserved and open to inspection. The court shall forward copies of each decision to the Secretary of the Treasury or his designee and to the appropriate customs officer for the district in which the case arose. The Secretary shall publish weekly such decisions as he or the court may designate and abstracts of all other decisions.

CHAPTER 13—ASSIGNMENT OF JUDGES TO OTHER COURTS

Sec.

§ 291. Circuit judges

(a) The Chief Justice of the United States may designate and assign temporarily any circuit judge to act as circuit judge in another circuit upon presentation of a certificate of necessity by the chief judge or circuit justice of the circuit where the need arises.

(b) The chief judge of a circuit or the circuit justice may, in the public interest, designate and assign temporarily any circuit judge within the circuit, including a judge designated and assigned to temporary duty therein, to hold a district court in any district within the circuit.

§ 292. District judges

(a) The chief judge of a circuit may designate and assign one or more district judges within the circuit to sit upon the court of appeals or a division thereof whenever the business of that court so requires. Such designations or assignments shall be in conformity with the rules or orders of the court of appeals of the circuit.

(b) The chief judge of a circuit may, in the public interest, designate and assign temporarily any district judge of the circuit to hold a district court in any district within the circuit.

(c) The chief judge of the United States Court of Appeals for the District of Columbia Circuit may, upon presentation of a certificate of necessity by the chief judge of the Superior Court of the District of Columbia pursuant to section 11–908(c) of the District of Columbia Code, designate and assign temporarily any district judge of the circuit to serve as a judge of such Superior Court, if such assignment (1) is approved by the Attorney General of the United States following a determination by him to the effect that such assignment is necessary to meet the ends of justice, and (2) is approved by the chief judge of the United States District Court for the District of Columbia.

(d) The Chief Justice of the United States may designate and assign temporarily a district judge of one circuit for service in another circuit, either in a district court or court of appeals, upon presentation of a certificate of necessity by the chief judge or circuit justice of the circuit wherein the need arises.

(e) The Chief Justice of the United States may designate and assign temporarily any district judge to serve as a judge of the Court of International Trade upon presentation to him of a certificate of necessity by the chief judge of the court.

§ 293. Judges of the Court of International Trade

(a) The Chief Justice of the United States may designate and assign temporarily any judge of the Court of International Trade to perform judicial duties in any circuit, either in a court of appeals or district court, upon presentation of a certificate of necessity by the chief judge or circuit justice of the circuit in which the need arises.

*(b)

§ 294. Assignment of retired justices or judges to active duty

(a) Any retired Chief Justice of the United States or Associate Justice of the Supreme Court may be designated and assigned by the Chief Justice of the United States to perform such judicial duties in any circuit, including those of a circuit justice, as he is willing to undertake.

(b) Any judge of the United States who has retired from regular active service under section 371(b) or 372(a) of this title shall be known and designated as a senior judge and may continue to perform such judicial duties as he is willing and able to undertake, when designated and assigned as provided in subsections (c) and (d).

(c) Any retired circuit or district judge may be designated and assigned by the chief judge or judicial council of his circuit to perform such judicial duties within the circuit as he is willing and able to undertake. Any other retired judge of the United States may be designated and assigned by the chief judge of his court to perform such judicial duties in such court as he is willing and able to undertake.

(d) The Chief Justice of the United States shall maintain a roster of retired judges of the United States who are willing and able to undertake special judicial duties from time to time outside their own circuit, in the case of a retired circuit or district judge, or in a court other than their own, in the case of other retired judges, which roster shall be known as the roster of senior judges. Any such retired judge of the United States may be designated and assigned by the Chief Justice to perform such judicial duties as he is willing and able to undertake in a court outside his own circuit, in the case of a retired circuit or district judge, or in a court other than his own, in the case of any other retired judge of the United States. Such designation and assignment to a court of appeals or district court shall be made upon the presentation of a certificate of necessity by the chief judge or circuit justice of

* Subsection (b) is among the provisions of the Bankruptcy Act that do not become effective until April 1, 1984, and are therefore not included here.

the circuit wherein the need arises and to any other court of the United States upon the presentation of a certificate of necessity by the chief judge of such court. No such designation or assignment shall be made to the Supreme Court.

(e) No retired justice or judge shall perform judicial duties except when designated and assigned.

§ 295. Conditions upon designation and assignment

No designation and assignment of a circuit or district judge in active service shall be made without the consent of the chief judge or judicial council of the circuit from which the judge is to be designated and assigned. No designation and assignment of a judge of any other court of the United States in active service shall be made without the consent of the chief judge of such court.

All designations and assignments of justices and judges shall be filed with the clerks and entered on the minutes of the courts from and to which made.

The Chief Justice of the United States, a circuit justice or a chief judge of a circuit may make new designation and assignments in accordance with the provisions of this chapter and may revoke those previously made by him.

§ 296. Powers upon designation and assignment

A justice or judge shall discharge, during the period of his designation and assignment, all judicial duties for which he is designated and assigned. He may be required to perform any duty which might be required of a judge of the court or district or circuit to which he is designated and assigned.

Such justice or judge shall have all the powers of a judge of the court, circuit or district to which he is designated and assigned, except the power to appoint any person to a statutory position or to designate permanently a depository of funds or a newspaper for publication of legal notices.

A justice or judge who has sat by designation and assignment in another district or circuit may, notwithstanding his absence from such district or circuit or the expiration of the period of his designation and assignment, decide or join in the decision and final disposition of all matters submitted to him during such period and in the consideration and disposition of applications for rehearing or further proceedings in such matters.

CHAPTER 15—CONFERENCES AND COUNCILS OF JUDGES

Sec.

§ 331. Judicial Conference of the United States

The Chief Justice of the United States shall summon annually the chief judge of each judicial circuit, and a district judge from each judicial circuit to a conference at such time and place in the United States as he may designate. He shall preside at such conference which shall be known as the Judicial Conference of the United States. Special sessions of the conference may be called by the Chief Justice at such times and places as he may designate.

The district judge to be summoned from each judicial circuit shall be chosen by the circuit and district judges of the circuit at the annual judicial conference of the circuit held pursuant to section 333 of this title and shall serve as a member of the conference for three successive years, except that in the year following the enactment of this amended section the judges in the first, fourth, seventh, and tenth circuits shall choose a district judge to serve for one year, the judges in the second, fifth, and eighth circuits shall choose a district judge to serve for two years and the judges in the third, sixth, ninth, and District of Columbia circuits shall choose a district judge to serve for three years.

If the chief judge of any circuit or the district judge chosen by the judges of the circuit is unable to attend, the Chief Justice may summon any other circuit or district judge from such circuit. Every judge summoned shall attend and, unless excused by the Chief Justice, shall remain throughout the sessions of the conference and advise as to the needs of his circuit or court and as to any matters in respect of which the administration of justice in the courts of the United States may be improved.

The Conference shall make a comprehensive survey of the condition of business in the courts of the United States and prepare plans for assignment of judges to or from circuits or districts where necessary. It shall also submit suggestions and recommendations to the various courts to promote uniformity of management procedures and the expeditious conduct of court business. The Conference is authorized to exercise the authority provided in section 372(c) of this title as the Conference, or through a standing committee. If the Conference elects to establish a standing committee, it shall be appointed by the Chief Justice and all petitions for review shall be reviewed by that committee. The Conference or the standing committee may hold hearings, take sworn testimony, issue subpoenas and subpoenas duces tecum, and make necessary and appropriate orders in the exercise of its authority. Subpoenas and subpoenas duces tecum shall be issued by the clerk of the Supreme Court or by the clerk of any court of appeals, at the direction of the Chief Justice or his designee and under the seal of the court, and shall be served in the manner provided in rule 45(c) of the Federal Rules of Civil Procedure for subpoenas and subpoenas duces tecum issued on behalf of the United States or an officer or any agency thereof. The Conference may also prescribe and modify rules for the exercise of the authority provided in section 372(c) of this title. All judicial officers and employees of the United States shall promptly carry into effect all orders of the Judicial Conference or the standing committee established pursuant to this section.

The Conference shall also carry on a continuous study of the operation and effect of the general rules of practice and procedure now or hereafter in use as prescribed by the Supreme Court for the other courts of the United States pursuant to law. Such changes in and additions to those rules as the Conference may deem desirable to promote simplicity in procedure, fairness in administration, the just determination of litigation, and the elimination of unjustifiable expense and delay shall be recommended by the Conference from time to time to the Supreme Court for its consideration and adoption, modification or rejection, in accordance with law.

The Attorney General shall, upon request of the Chief Justice, report to such conference on matters relating to the business of the several courts of the United States, with particular reference to cases to which the United States is a party.

The Chief Justice shall submit to Congress an annual report of the proceedings of the Judicial Conference and its recommendations for legislation.

§ 332. Judicial councils of circuits

(a)(1) The chief judge of each judicial circuit shall call, at least twice in each year and at such places as he may designate, a meeting of the judicial council of the circuit, consisting of—

(A) the chief judge of the circuit, who shall preside;

(B) that number of circuit judges fixed by majority vote of all such judges in regular active service; and

(C) that number of district judges of the circuit fixed by majority vote of all circuit judges in regular active service, except that—

(i) if the number of circuit judges fixed in accordance with subparagraph (B) of this paragraph is less than six, the number of district judges fixed in accordance with this subparagraph shall be no less than two; and

(ii) if the number of circuit judges fixed in accordance with subparagraph (B) of this paragraph is six or more, the number of district judges fixed in accordance with this subparagraph shall be no less than three.

(2) Members of the council shall serve for terms established by a majority vote of all judges of the circuit in regular active service.

(3) The number of circuit and district judges fixed in accordance with paragraphs (1)(B) and (1)(C) of this subsection shall be set by order of the court of appeals for the circuit no less than six months prior to a scheduled meeting of the council so constituted.

(4) Only circuit and district judges in regular active service shall serve as members of the council.

(5) No more than one district judge from any one district shall serve simultaneously on the council, unless at least one district judge from each district within the circuit is already serving as a member of the council.

(6) In the event of the death, resignation, retirement, or disability of a member of the council, a replacement member shall be designated to serve the remainder of the unexpired term by the chief judge of the circuit.

(7) Each member of the council shall attend each council meeting unless excused by the chief judge of the circuit.

(b) The council shall be known as the Judicial Council of the circuit.

(c) The chief judge shall submit to the council the semi-annually reports of the Director of the Administrative Office of the United States Courts. The council shall take such action thereon as may be necessary.

(d)(1) Each judicial council shall make all necessary and appropriate orders for the effective and expeditious administration of justice within its circuit. Each council is authorized to hold hearings, to take sworn testimony, and to issue subpoenas and subpoenas duces tecum. Subpoenas and subpoenas duces tecum shall be issued by the clerk of the court of appeals, at the direction of the chief judge of the circuit or his designee and under the seal of the court, and shall be served in the manner provided in rule 45(c) of the Federal Rules of Civil Procedure for subpoenas and subpoenas duces tecum issued on behalf of the United States or an officer or agency thereof.

(2) All judicial officers and employees of the circuit shall promptly carry into effect all orders of the judicial council.

(3) Unless an impediment to the administration of justice is involved, regular business of the courts need not be referred to the council.

(e) The judicial council of each circuit may appoint a circuit executive from among persons who shall be certified by the Board of

Certification. The circuit executive shall exercise such administrative powers and perform such duties as may be delegated to him by the circuit council. The duties delegated to the circuit executive of each circuit may include but need not be limited to:

(1) Exercising administrative control of all nonjudicial activities of the court of appeals of the circuit in which he is appointed.

(2) Administering the personnel system of the court of appeals of the circuit.

(3) Administering the budget of the court of appeals of the circuit.

(4) Maintaining a modern accounting system.

(5) Establishing and maintaining property control records and undertaking a space management program.

(6) Conducting studies relating to the business and administration of the courts within the circuit and preparing appropriate recommendations and reports to the chief judge, the circuit council, and the Judicial Conference.

(7) Collecting, compiling, and analyzing statistical data with a view to the preparation and presentation of reports based on such data as may be directed by the chief judge, the circuit council, and the Administrative Office of the United States Courts.

(8) Representing the circuit as its liaison to the courts of the various States in which the circuit is located, the marshal's office, State and local bar associations, civic groups, news media, and other private and public groups having a reasonable interest in the administration of the circuit.

(9) Arranging and attending meetings of the judges of the circuit and of the circuit council, including preparing the agenda and serving as secretary in all such meetings.

(10) Preparing an annual report to the circuit and to the Administrative Office of the United States Courts for the preceding calendar year, including recommendations for more expeditious disposition of the business of the circuit.

All duties delegated to the circuit executive shall be subject to the general supervision of the chief judge of the circuit.

(f) The standards for certification as qualified to be a circuit executive shall be set by a Board of Certification. These standards shall take into account experience in administrative and executive positions, familiarity with court procedures, and special training. The Board of Certification shall consist of five members, three of whom shall be elected by the Judicial Conference of the United States, and at least one of these three shall be selected from among persons experienced in executive recruitment and selection. The additional two members shall be the Director of the Administrative Office of the United States Courts and the Director of the Federal Judicial Center. The members of the Board elected by the Judicial

Conference shall each serve for three years except that upon appointment of the first members, one member shall serve for one year, one for two years, and one for three years. The Board shall consider all applicants who apply for certification, shall certify qualified applicants, shall maintain a roster of all persons certified, and shall publish the standards for certification. A person's name shall be removed from the roster after three years unless he is recertified. Three members of the Board shall constitute a quorum for purposes of fixing standards and for certifying applicants, but no action of the Board shall be taken unless three of the members are in agreement. The Director of the Administrative Office of the United States Courts shall provide staff assistance in support of the operation of the Board. Expenses of the Board of Certification shall be borne by the travel and miscellaneous expense funds appropriated to the Federal judiciary. Any member of the Board who is an officer or employee of the United States shall serve without compensation. Other members shall receive the daily equivalent of the rate provided for GS–18 of the General Schedule contained in section 5332 of title 5, United States Code, when actually engaged in service for the Board.

Each circuit executive shall be paid at a salary to be established by the Judicial Conference of the United States not to exceed the annual rate of level V of the Executive Schedule pay rates (5 U.S.C. § 5316).

The circuit executive shall serve at the pleasure of the judicial council of the circuit.

The circuit executive may appoint, with the approval of the council, necessary employees in such number as may be approved by the Director of the Administrative Office of the United States Courts.

The circuit executive and his staff shall be deemed to be officers and employees of the judicial branch of the United States Government within the meaning of subchapter III of chapter 83 (relating to civil service retirement), chapter 87 (relating to Federal employees' life insurance program), and chapter 89 (relating to Federal employees' health benefits program) of title 5, United States Code.

§ 333. Judicial conferences of circuits

The chief judge of each circuit shall summon annually the circuit, district, and bankruptcy judges of the circuit, in active service, to a conference at a time and place that he designates, for the purpose of considering the business of the courts and advising means of improving the administration of justice within such circuit. He shall preside at such conference, which shall be known as the Judicial Conference of the circuit. The judges of the United States District Court for the District of the Canal Zone, the District Court of Guam, and the District Court of the Virgin Islands shall also be summoned annually to the conferences of their respective circuits.

Every judge summoned shall attend, and unless excused by the chief judge, shall remain throughout the conference.

The court of appeals for each circuit shall provide by its rules for representation and active participation at such conference by members of the bar of such circuit.

§ 334. Institutes and joint councils on sentencing

(a) In the interest of uniformity in sentencing procedures, there is hereby authorized to be established under the auspices of the Judicial Conference of the United States, institutes and joint councils on sentencing. The Attorney General and/or the chief judge of each circuit may at any time request, through the Director of the Administrative Office of the United States Courts, the Judicial Conference to convene such institutes and joint councils for the purpose of studying, discussing, and formulating the objectives, policies, standards, and criteria for sentencing those convicted of crimes and offenses in the courts of the United States. The agenda of the institutes and joint councils may include but shall not be limited to: (1) The development of standards for the content and utilization of presentence reports; (2) the establishment of factors to be used in selecting cases for special study and observation in prescribed diagnostic clinics; (3) the determination of the importance of psychiatric, emotional, sociological and physiological factors involved in crime and their bearing upon sentences; (4) the discussion of special sentencing problems in unusual cases such as treason, violation of public trust, subversion, or involving abnormal sex behavior, addiction to drugs or alcohol, and mental or physical handicaps; (5) the formulation of sentencing principles and criteria which will assist in promoting the equitable administration of the criminal laws of the United States.

(b) After the Judicial Conference has approved the time, place, participants, agenda, and other arrangements for such institutes and joint councils, the chief judge of each circuit is authorized to invite the attendance of district judges under conditions which he thinks proper and which will not unduly delay the work of the courts.

(c) The Attorney General is authorized to select and direct the attendance at such institutes and meetings of United States attorneys and other officials of the Department of Justice and may invite the participation of other interested Federal officers. He may also invite specialists in sentencing methods, criminologists, psychiatrists, penologists, and others to participate in the proceedings.

(d) The expenses of attendance of judges shall be paid from applicable appropriations for the judiciary of the United States. The expenses connected with the preparation of the plans and agenda for the conference and for the travel and other expenses incident to the attendance of officials and other participants invited by the Attorney General shall be paid from applicable appropriations of the Department of Justice.

CHAPTER 17—RESIGNATION AND RETIREMENT OF JUSTICES AND JUDGES

§ 371. Resignation or retirement for age

(a) Any justice or judge of the United States appointed to hold office during good behavior who resigns after attaining the age of seventy years and after serving at least ten years continuously or otherwise shall, during the remainder of his lifetime, continue to receive the salary which he was receiving when he resigned.

(b) Any justice or judge of the United States appointed to hold office during good behavior may retain his office but retire from regular active service after attaining the age of seventy years and after serving at least ten years continuously or otherwise, or after attaining the age of sixty-five years and after serving at least fifteen years continuously or otherwise. He shall, during the remainder of his lifetime, continue to receive the salary of the office. The President shall appoint, by and with the advice and consent of the Senate, a successor to a justice or judge who retires.

§ 372. Retirement for disability; substitute judge on failure to retire; judicial discipline

(a) Any justice or judge of the United States appointed to hold office during good behavior who becomes permanently disabled from performing his duties may retire from regular active service, and the President shall, by and with the advice and consent of the Senate, appoint a successor.

Any justice or judge of the United States desiring to retire under this section shall certify to the President his disability in writing.

Whenever an associate justice of the Supreme Court, a chief judge of a circuit or the chief judge of the Court of International Trade, desires to retire under this section, he shall furnish to the President a certificate of disability signed by the Chief Justice of the United States.

A circuit or district judge, desiring to retire under this section, shall furnish to the President a certificate of disability signed by the chief judge of his circuit.

A judge of the Court of International Trade desiring to retire under this section, shall furnish to the President a certificate of disability signed by the chief judge of his court.

Each justice or judge retiring under this section after serving ten years continuously or otherwise shall, during the remainder of his lifetime, receive the salary of the office. A justice or judge retiring under this section who has served less than ten years in all shall, during the remainder of his lifetime, receive one-half the salary of the office.

(b) Whenever any judge of the United States appointed to hold office during good behavior who is eligible to retire under this section does not do so and a certificate of his disability signed by a majority of the members of the Judicial Council of his circuit in the case of a circuit or district judge, or by the Chief Justice of the United States in the case of the Chief Judge of the Court of International Trade, or by the chief judge of his court in the case of a judge of the Court of International Trade, is presented to the President and the President finds that such judge is unable to discharge efficiently all the duties of his office by reason of permanent mental or physical disability and that the appointment of an additional judge is necessary for the efficient dispatch of business, the President may make such appointment by and with the advice and consent of the Senate. Whenever any such additional judge is appointed, the vacancy subsequently caused by the death, resignation, or retirement of the disabled judge shall not be filled. Any judge whose disability causes the appointment of an additional judge shall, for purpose of precedence, service as chief judge, or temporary performance of the duties of that office, be treated as junior in commission to the other judges of the circuit, district, or court.

(c)(1) Any person alleging that a circuit, district, or bankruptcy judge, or a magistrate, has engaged in conduct prejudicial to the effective and expeditious administration of the business of the courts, or alleging that such a judge or magistrate is unable to discharge all the duties of office by reason of mental or physical disability, may file with the clerk of the court of appeals for the circuit a written complaint containing a brief statement of the facts constituting such conduct.

(2) Upon receipt of a complaint filed under paragraph (1) of this subsection, the clerk shall promptly transmit such complaint to the chief judge of the circuit, or, if the conduct complained of is that of the chief judge, to that circuit judge in regular active service next senior in date of commission (hereafter, for purposes of this subsection only, included in the term "chief judge"). The clerk shall simultaneously transmit a copy of the complaint to the judge or magistrate whose conduct is the subject of the complaint.

(3) After expeditiously reviewing a complaint, the chief judge, by written order stating his reasons, may—

(A) dismiss the complaint, if he finds it to be (i) not in conformity with paragraph (1) of this subsection, (ii) directly related to the merits of a decision or procedural ruling, or (iii) frivolous; or

(B) conclude the proceeding if he finds that appropriate corrective action has been taken.

The chief judge shall transmit copies of his written order to the complainant and to the judge or magistrate whose conduct is the subject of the complaint.

(4) If the chief judge does not enter an order under paragraph (3) of this subsection, such judge shall promptly—

(A) appoint himself and equal numbers of circuit and district judges of the circuit to a special committee to investigate the facts and allegations contained in the complaint;

(B) certify the complaint and any other documents pertaining thereto to each member of such committee; and

(C) provide written notice to the complainant and the judge or magistrate whose conduct is the subject of the complaint of the action taken under this paragraph.

(5) Each committee appointed under paragraph (4) of this subsection shall conduct an investigation as extensive as it considers necessary, and shall expeditiously file a comprehensive written report thereon with the judicial council of the circuit. Such report shall present both the findings of the investigation and the committee's recommendations for necessary and appropriate action by the judicial council of the circuit.

(6) Upon receipt of a report filed under paragraph (5) of this subsection, the judicial council—

(A) may conduct any additional investigation which it considers to be necessary;

(B) shall take such action as is appropriate to assure the effective and expeditious administration of the business of the courts within the circuit, including, but not limited to, any of the following actions:

(i) directing the chief judge of the district of the magistrate whose conduct is the subject of the complaint to take such action as the judicial council considers appropriate;

(ii) certifying disability of a judge appointed to hold office during good behavior whose conduct is the subject of the complaint, pursuant to the procedures and standards provided under subsection (b) of this section;

(iii) requesting that any such judge appointed to hold office during good behavior voluntarily retire, with the provision that the length of service requirements under section 371 of this title shall not apply;

(iv) ordering that, on a temporary basis for a time certain, no further cases be assigned to any judge or magistrate whose conduct is the subject of a complaint;

(v) censuring or reprimanding such judge or magistrate by means of private communication;

(vi) censuring or reprimanding such judge or magistrate by means of public announcement; or

(vii) ordering such other action as it considers appropriate under the circumstances, except that (I) in no circumstances may the council order removal from office of any judge appointed to hold office during good behavior, and (II) any removal of a magistrate shall be in accordance with section 631 of this title and any removal of a bankruptcy judge shall be in accordance with section 153 of this title; and

(C) shall immediately provide written notice to the complainant and to such judge or magistrate of the action taken under this paragraph.

(7)(A) In addition to the authority granted under paragraph (6) of this subsection, the judicial council may, in its discretion, refer any complaint under this subsection, together with the record of any associated proceedings and its recommendations for appropriate action, to the Judicial Conference of the United States.

(B) In any case in which the judicial council determines, on the basis of a complaint and an investigation under this subsection, or on the basis of information otherwise available to the council, that a judge appointed to hold office during good behavior has engaged in conduct—

(i) which might constitute one or more grounds for impeachment under article I of the Constitution; or

(ii) which, in the interest of justice, is not amenable to resolution by the judicial council,

the judicial council shall promptly certify such determination, together with any complaint and a record of any associated proceedings, to the Judicial Conference of the United States.

(C) A judicial council acting under authority of this paragraph shall, unless contrary to the interests of justice, immediately submit written notice to the complainant and to the judge or magistrate whose conduct is the subject of the action taken under this paragraph.

(8) Upon referral or certification of any matter under paragraph (7) of this subsection, the Judicial Conference, after consideration of the prior proceedings and such additional investigation as it considers appropriate, shall by majority vote take such action, as described in paragraph (6)(B) of this subsection, as it considers appropriate. If the Judicial Conference concurs in the determination of the council, or makes its own determination, that consideration of impeachment may be warranted, it shall so certify and transmit the determination and the record of proceedings to the House of Representatives for whatever action the House of Representatives considers to be necessary.

(9)(A) In conducting any investigation under this subsection, the judicial council, or a special committee appointed under paragraph (4) of this subsection, shall have full subpoena powers as provided in section 332(d) of this title.

(B) In conducting any investigation under this subsection, the Judicial Conference, or a standing committee appointed by the Chief Justice under section 331 of this title, shall have full subpoena powers as provided in that section.

(10) A complainant, judge, or magistrate aggrieved by a final order of the chief judge under paragraph (3) of this subsection may petition the judicial council for review thereof. A complainant, judge, or magistrate aggrieved by an action of the judicial council under paragraph (6) of this subsection may petition the Judicial Conference of the United States for review thereof. The Judicial Conference, or the standing committee established under section 331 of this title, may grant a petition filed by a complainant, judge, or magistrate under this paragraph. Except as expressly provided in this paragraph, all orders and determinations, including denials of petitions for review, shall be final and conclusive and shall not be judicially reviewable on appeal or otherwise.

(11) Each judicial council and the Judicial Conference may prescribe such rules for the conduct of proceedings under this subsection, including the processing of petitions for review, as each considers to be appropriate. Such rules shall contain provisions requiring that—

(A) adequate prior notice of any investigation be given in writing to the judge or magistrate whose conduct is the subject of the complaint;

(B) the judge or magistrate whose conduct is the subject of the complaint be afforded an opportunity to appear (in person or by counsel) at proceedings conducted by the investigating panel, to present oral and documentary evidence, to compel the attendance of witnesses or the production of documents, to cross-examine witnesses, and to present argument orally or in writing; and

(C) the complainant be afforded an opportunity to appear at proceedings conducted by the investigating panel, if the panel concludes that the complainant could offer substantial information.

Any rule promulgated under this subsection shall be a matter of public record, and any such rule promulgated by a judicial council may be modified by the Judicial Conference.

(12) No judge or magistrate whose conduct is the subject of an investigation under this subsection shall serve upon a special committee appointed under paragraph (4) of this subsection, upon a judicial council, upon the Judicial Conference, or upon the standing

committee established under section 331 of this title, until all related proceedings under this subsection have been finally terminated.

(13) No person shall be granted the right to intervene or to appear as amicus curiae in any proceeding before a judicial council or the Judicial Conference under this subsection.

(14) All papers, documents, and records of proceedings related to investigations conducted under this subsection shall be confidential and shall not be disclosed by any person in any proceeding unless—

(A) the judicial council of the circuit, the Judicial Conference of the United States, or the Senate or the House of Representatives by resolution, releases any such material which is believed necessary to an impeachment investigation or trial of a judge under article I of the Constitution; or

(B) authorized in writing by the judge or magistrate who is the subject to the complaint and by the chief judge of the circuit, the Chief Justice, or the chairman of the standing committee established under section 331 of this title.

(15) Each written order to implement any action under paragraph (6)(B) of this subsection, which is issued by a judicial council, the Judicial Conference, or the standing committee established under section 331 of this title, shall be made available to the public through the appropriate clerk's office of the court of appeals for the circuit. Unless contrary to the interests of justice, each such order issued under this paragraph shall be accompanied by written reasons therefor.

(16) Except as expressly provided in this subsection, nothing in this subsection shall be construed to affect any other provision of this title, the Federal Rules of Civil Procedure, the Federal Rules of Criminal Procedure, the Federal Rules of Appellate Procedure, or the Federal Rules of Evidence.

(17) The United States Claims Court, the Court of International Trade, and the Court of Appeals for the Federal Circuit shall each prescribe rules, consistent with the foregoing provisions of this subsection, establishing procedures for the filing of complaints with respect to the conduct of any judge of such court and for the investigation and resolution of such complaints. In investigating and taking action with respect to any such complaint, each such court shall have the powers granted to a judicial council under this subsection.

§ 373. Judges in Territories and Possessions

Any judge of the United States District Court for the District of the Canal Zone, the District Court of Guam, or the District Court of the Virgin Islands, who resigns after attaining the age of seventy years and after serving at least ten years, continuously or otherwise, or after attaining the age of sixty-five years and after serving at least fifteen years, continuously or otherwise, shall continue during the remainder of his life to receive the salary he received when he relinquished office.

Any judge of any such courts who is removed by the President of the United States upon the sole ground of mental or physical disability, or who fails of reappointment, shall be entitled, upon attaining the age of sixty-five years or upon relinquishing office if he is then beyond the age of sixty-five years, (a) if his judicial service aggregated sixteen years or more, to receive during the remainder of his life the salary he received when he relinquished office, or (b) if his judicial service aggregated less than sixteen years but not less than ten years, to receive during the remainder of his life that proportion of such salary which the aggregate number of years of his judicial service bears to sixteen.

Service at any time in any of the courts referred to in the first paragraph, or in any other court under appointment by the President, shall be included in the computation of aggregate years of judicial service for the purposes of this section.

Any judge who has retired by resigning under the provisions of this section, or who is otherwise entitled to payments under this section, shall be entitled after the effective date of this Act to a cost-of-living adjustment in the amount payable to him computed as specified in section 8340(b) of title 5, United States Code: *Provided, however,* That in no case shall the salary or amount payable to such judge as increased under this paragraph exceed 95 per centum of the salary of a United States district court judge in regular active service.

§ 374. Residence of retired judges; official station

Retired judges of the United States are not subject to restrictions as to residence. The place where a retired judge maintains the actual abode in which he customarily lives shall be deemed to be his official station for the purposes of section 456 of this title.

§ 375. Annuities to widows of justices

(a) The Director of the Administrative Office of the United States Courts shall pay to the surviving widow of a justice of the United States who died on or before the date of enactment of this section, while in regular active service or after having retired or resigned under the provisions of this chapter, an annuity of $10,000.

(b) The surviving widow of a justice of the United States who is in regular active service or is retired or resigned under the provisions of this chapter on the date of enactment of this section, shall, if the justice gives written notice to the Director of the Administrative Office of the United States Courts within six months of the date of enactment of this section of his election to become subject to the provisions of section 376 of this chapter, be paid an annuity of $5,000 or an annuity in accordance with the provisions of section 376, whichever is the greater.

(c) The surviving widow of a justice of the United States who is in regular active service or is retired or resigned under the provisions of this chapter on the date of enactment of this section, shall, if the justice fails to give timely written notice of his election to become subject to the provisions of section 376 of this chapter, be paid an annuity of $5,000.

(d) The widow of a justice of the United States who is appointed after the date of enactment of this section shall be ineligible for an annuity under this section.

(e) An annuity payable under this section shall accrue monthly and shall be due and payable in monthly installments on the first business day of the month following the month for which the annuity shall have accrued. Such annuity shall commence on the first day of the month in which a justice dies, and shall terminate upon the death or remarriage of the annuitant.

§ 376. Annuities for survivors of certain judicial officials of the United States

(Editorial Note: The provisions of this section, the text of which is omitted from this compilation, were amended by Act of October 19, 1976, Pub.L. 94–554; 90 Stat. 2603, to enhance the benefits conferred, and further amended by Act of Nov. 6, 1978, Pub.L. 95–598, 92 Stat. 26.)

CHAPTER 19—DISTRIBUTION OF REPORTS AND DIGESTS

§ 411. Supreme Court reports; printing, binding, and distribution

(a) The decisions of the Supreme Court of the United States shall be printed, bound, and distributed in the preliminary prints and bound volumes of the United States Reports as soon as practicable after rendition, to be charged to the proper appropriation for the judiciary. The number and distribution of the copies shall be under the control of the Joint Committee on Printing.

(b) Reports printed prior to June 12, 1926, shall not be furnished the Secretary of the Army, the Secretary of the Navy, or the Secretary of the Air Force.

(c) The Public Printer, or other printer designated by the Supreme Court of the United States, upon request, shall furnish to the

Superintendent of Documents the reports required to be distributed under the provisions of this section.

§ 412. Sale of Supreme Court reports

The Public Printer, or other printer designated by the Supreme Court of the United States shall print such additional bound volumes and preliminary prints of such reports as may be required for sale to the public. Such additional copies shall be sold by the Superintendent of Documents, as provided by law.

§ 413. Publications; distribution to courts

Distribution of publications to Federal courts in accordance with the provisions of this chapter shall not be made to any place where such court is held in a building not owned or controlled by the United States unless such publications are committed to the custody of an officer of the United States at such building.

The Attorney General and the Director in the procurement of law books, books of reference or periodicals may exchange or sell similar items and apply the allowance or proceeds to payment in whole or in part of the cost of the items procured.

§ 414. Transmittal of books to successors

All government publications and law books furnished to justices, judges, clerks of courts, and United States attorneys of the United States and its territories and possessions, and other officers of the United States or an agency thereof shall be transmitted to their successors in office. All permanent or bound books and publications furnished under this chapter except those books furnished to the Library of Congress for international exchange shall remain the property of the United States and shall be marked plainly, "The Property of the United States".

CHAPTER 21—GENERAL PROVISIONS APPLICABLE TO COURTS AND JUDGES

Sec.

§ 451. Definitions

As used in this title:

The term "court of the United States" includes the Supreme Court of the United States, courts of appeals, district courts constituted by chapter 5 of this title, including the Court of International Trade and any court created by Act of Congress the judges of which are entitled to hold office during good behavior.

The terms "district court" and "district court of the United States" mean the courts constituted by chapter 5 of this title.

The term "judge of the United States" includes judges of the courts of appeals, district courts, Court of International Trade and any court created by Act of Congress, the judges of which are entitled to hold office during good behavior.

The term "justice of the United States" includes the Chief Justice of the United States and the associate justices of the Supreme Court.

The term "district" and "judicial district" mean the districts enumerated in Chapter 5 of this title.

The term "department" means one of the executive departments enumerated in section 1 of Title 5, unless the context shows that such term was intended to describe the executive, legislative, or judicial branches of the government.

The term "agency" includes any department, independent establishment, commission, administration, authority, board or bureau of the United States or any corporation in which the United States has a proprietary interest, unless the context shows that such term was intended to be used in a more limited sense.

§ 452. Courts always open; power unrestricted by expiration of sessions

All courts of the United States shall be deemed always open for the purpose of filing proper papers, issuing and returning process, and making motions and orders.

The continued existence or expiration of a session of court in no way affects the power of the court to do any act or take any proceeding.

§ 453. Oaths of justices and judges

Each justice or judge of the United States shall take the following oath or affirmation before performing the duties of his office: "I, ——————— ———————, do solemnly swear (or affirm) that I will administer justice without respect to persons, and do equal right to the poor and to the rich, and that I will faithfully and impartially discharge and perform all the duties incumbent upon me as ——————— according to the best of my abilities and understanding, agreeably to the Constitution and laws of the United States. So help me God."

§ 454. Practice of law by justices and judges

Any justice or judge appointed under the authority of the United States who engages in the practice of law is guilty of a high misdemeanor.

§ 455. Disqualification of justice, judge, or magistrate

(a) Any justice, judge, or magistrate of the United States shall disqualify himself in any proceeding in which his impartiality might reasonably be questioned.

(b) He shall also disqualify himself in the following circumstances:

(1) Where he has a personal bias or prejudice concerning a party, or personal knowledge of disputed evidentiary facts concerning the proceeding;

(2) Where in private practice he served as lawyer in the matter in controversy, or a lawyer with whom he previously practiced law served during such association as a lawyer concerning the matter, or the judge or such lawyer has been a material witness concerning it;

(3) Where he has served in governmental employment and in such capacity participated as counsel, adviser or material witness concerning the proceeding or expressed an opinion concerning the merits of the particular case in controversy;

(4) He knows that he, individually or as a fiduciary, or his spouse or minor child residing in his household, has a financial interest in the subject matter in controversy or in a party to the proceeding, or any other interest that could be substantially affected by the outcome of the proceeding;

(5) He or his spouse, or a person within the third degree of relationship to either of them, or the spouse of such a person:

(i) Is a party to the proceeding, or an officer, director, or trustee of a party;

(ii) Is acting as a lawyer in the proceeding;

(iii) Is known by the judge to have an interest that could be substantially affected by the outcome of the proceeding;

(iv) Is to the judge's knowledge likely to be a material witness in the proceeding.

(c) A judge should inform himself about his personal and fiduciary financial interests, and make a reasonable effort to inform himself about the personal financial interests of his spouse and minor children residing in his household.

(d) For the purposes of this section the following words or phrases shall have the meaning indicated:

(1) "proceeding" includes pretrial, trial, appellate review, or other stages of litigation;

(2) the degree of relationship is calculated according to the civil law system;

(3) "fiduciary" includes such relationships as executor, administrator, trustee, and guardian;

(4) "financial interest" means ownership of a legal or equitable interest, however small, or a relationship as director, adviser, or other active participant in the affairs of a party, except that:

(i) Ownership in a mutual or common investment fund that holds securities is not a "financial interest" in such securities unless the judge participates in the management of the fund;

(ii) An office in an educational, religious, charitable, fraternal, or civic organization is not a "financial interest" in securities held by the organization;

(iii) The proprietary interest of a policyholder in a mutual insurance company, of a depositor in a mutual savings association, or a similar proprietary interest, is a "financial interest" in the organization only if the outcome of the proceeding could substantially affect the value of the interest;

(iv) Ownership of government securities is a "financial interest" in the issuer only if the outcome of the proceeding could substantially affect the value of the securities.

(e) No justice, judge, magistrate, or referee in bankruptcy shall accept from the parties to the proceeding a waiver of any ground for disqualification enumerated in subsection (b). Where the ground for disqualification arises only under subsection (a), waiver may be accepted provided it is preceded by a full disclosure on the record of the basis for disqualification.

§ 456. Traveling expenses of justices and judges; official duty stations

(a) The Director of the Administrative Office of the United States Courts shall pay each justice or judge of the United States, and each retired justice or judge recalled or designated and assigned to active duty, while attending court or transacting official business at a place other than his official duty station for any continuous period of less than thirty calendar days (1) all necessary transportation expenses certified by the justice or judge; and (2) a per diem allowance for travel at the rate which the Director establishes not to exceed the maximum per diem allowance fixed by section 5702(a) of title 5, or in accordance with regulations which the Director shall prescribe with the approval of the Judicial Conference of the United States, reimbursement for his actual and necessary expenses of subsistence not in excess of the maximum amount fixed by section 5702 of title 5. The Director of the Administrative Office of the United States Courts shall also pay each justice or judge of the United States, and each retired justice or judge recalled or designated and assigned to active duty, while attending court or transacting official business under an assignment authorized under chapter 13 of this title which exceeds in duration a continuous period of thirty calendar days, all necessary transportation expenses and actual and necessary expenses of subsistence actually incurred, notwithstanding the provisions of section 5702 of title 5, in accordance with regulations which the Director shall prescribe with the approval of the Judicial Conference of the United States.

(b) The official duty station of the Chief Justice of the United States, the Justices of the Supreme Court of the United States, and the judges of the United States Court of Appeals for the District of Columbia Circuit, the United States Court of Appeals for the Federal Circuit, and the United States District Court for the District of Columbia shall be the District of Columbia.

(c) The official duty station of the judges of the United States Court of International Trade shall be New York City.

(d) The official duty station of each district judge shall be that place where a district court holds regular sessions at or near which the judge performs a substantial portion of his judicial work, which is nearest the place where he maintains his actual abode in which he customarily lives.

(e) The official duty station of a circuit judge shall be that place where a circuit or district court holds regular sessions at or near which the judge performs a substantial portion of his judicial work, or that place where the Director provides chambers to the judge where he performs a substantial portion of his judicial work, which is nearest the place where he maintains his actual abode in which he customarily lives.

(f) The official duty station of a retired judge shall be established in accordance with section 374 of this title.

(g) Each circuit or district judge whose official duty station is not fixed expressly by this section shall notify the Director of the Administrative Office of the United States Courts in writing of his actual abode and official duty station upon his appointment and from time to time thereafter as his official duty station may change.

§ 457. Records; obsolete papers

The records of district courts and of courts of appeals shall be kept at one or more of the places where court is held. Such places shall be designated by the respective courts except when otherwise directed by the judicial council of the circuit.

Papers of any court established by Act of Congress which have become obsolete and are no longer necessary or useful, may be disposed of with the approval of the court concerned in the manner provided by sections 366–380 of Title 44 and in accordance with the rules of the Judicial Conference of the United States.

§ 458. Relative of justice or judge ineligible to appointment

No person shall be appointed to or employed in any office or duty in any court who is related by affinity or consanguinity within the degree of first cousin to any justice or judge of such court.

§ 459. Administration of oaths and acknowledgments

Each justice or judge of the United States may administer oaths and affirmations and take acknowledgments.

§ 460. Application to other courts

(a) Sections 452 through 459 and section 462 of this chapter shall also apply to the United States Claims Court, to each court created by Act of Congress in a territory which is invested with any jurisdiction of a district court of the United States, and to the judges thereof.

(b) The official duty station of each judge referred to in subsection (a) which is not otherwise established by law shall be that place where the court holds regular sessions at or near which the judge performs a substantial portion of his judicial work, which is nearest the place where he maintains his actual abode in which he customarily lives.

§ 461. Adjustments in certain salaries

(a) Effective at the beginning of the first applicable pay period commencing on or after the first day of the month in which an adjustment takes effect under section 5305 of title 5 in the rates of pay under the General Schedule (except as provided in subsection (b)), each salary rate which is subject to adjustment under this section shall be adjusted by an amount, rounded to the nearest multiple of $100 (or if midway between multiples of $100, to the next higher multiple of $100) equal to the percentage of such salary rate which corresponds to the overall average percentage (as set forth in the report transmitted to the Congress under such section 5305) of the adjustments in the rates of pay under such Schedule.

(b) Subsection (a) shall not apply to the extent it would reduce the salary of any individual whose compensation may not, under section 1 of article III of the Constitution of the United States, be diminished during such individual's continuance in office.

§ 462. Court accommodations

(a) Sessions of courts of the United States (except the Supreme Court) shall be held only at places where the Director of the Administrative Office of the United States Courts provides accommodations, or where suitable accommodations are furnished without cost to the judicial branch.

(b) The Director of the Administrative Office of the United States Courts shall provide accommodations, including chambers and courtrooms, only at places where regular sessions of court are authorized by law to be held, but only if the judicial council of the appropriate circuit has approved the accommodations as necessary.

(c) The limitations and restrictions contained in subsection (b) of this section shall not prevent the Director from furnishing chambers to circuit judges at places where Federal facilities are available when the judicial council of the circuit approves.

(d) The Director of the Administrative Office of the United States Courts shall provide permanent accommodations for the United States Court of Appeals for the Federal Circuit and for the United States Claims Court only at the District of Columbia. However, each such court may hold regular and special sessions at other places utilizing the accommodations which the Director provides to other courts.

(e) The Director of the Administrative Office of the United States Courts shall provide accommodations for probation officers, pretrial service officers, and Federal Public Defender Organizations at such places as may be approved by the judicial council of the appropriate circuit.

(f) Upon the request of the Director, the Administrator of General Services is authorized and directed to provide the accommodations the Director requests, and to close accommodations which the Director recommends for closure with the approval of the Judicial Conference of the United States.

§ 463. Expenses of litigation

Whenever a Chief Justice, justice, judge, officer, or employee of any United States court is sued in his official capacity, or is otherwise required to defend acts taken or omissions made in his official capacity, and the services of an attorney for the Government are not reasonably available pursuant to chapter 31 of this title, the Director of the Administrative Office of the United States Courts may pay the costs of his defense. The Director shall prescribe regulations for such payments subject to the approval of the Judicial Conference of the United States.

PART II—DEPARTMENT OF JUSTICE

CHAPTER 31—THE ATTORNEY GENERAL

* [Ed.] The duplicate designations seem to represent a drafting error that apparently has not yet been corrected.

§ 501. Executive department

The Department of Justice is an executive department of the United States at the seat of Government.

§ 502. Seal

The Attorney General shall have a seal for the Department of Justice. The design of the seal is subject to the approval of the President.

§ 503. Attorney General

The President shall appoint, by and with the advice and consent of the Senate, an Attorney General of the United States. The Attorney General is the head of the Department of Justice.

§ 504. Deputy Attorney General

The President may appoint, by and with the advice and consent of the Senate, a Deputy Attorney General.

§ 504a. Associate Attorney General

The President may appoint, by and with the advice and consent of the Senate, an Associate Attorney General.

§ 505. Solicitor General

The President shall appoint in the Department of Justice, by and with the advice and consent of the Senate, a Solicitor General, learned in the law, to assist the Attorney General in the performance of his duties.

§ 506. Assistant Attorneys General

The President shall appoint, by and with the advice and consent of the Senate, ten Assistant Attorneys General, who shall assist the Attorney General in the performance of his duties.

§ 507. Assistant Attorney General for Administration

(a) The Attorney General shall appoint, with the approval of the President, an Assistant Attorney General for Administration, who shall perform such duties as the Attorney General may prescribe.

(b) The position of Assistant Attorney General for Administration is in the competitive service.

§ 508. Vacancies

(a) In case of a vacancy in the office of Attorney General, or of his absence or disability, the Deputy Attorney General may exercise all the duties of that office, and for the purpose of section 3345 of title 5 the Deputy Attorney General is the first assistant to the Attorney General.

(b) When by reason of absence, disability, or vacancy in office, neither the Attorney General nor the Deputy Attorney General is available to exercise the duties of the office of Attorney General, the Associate Attorney General shall act as Attorney General. The Attorney General may designate the Solicitor General and the Assistant Attorneys General, in further order of succession, to act as Attorney General.

§ 509. Functions of the Attorney General

All functions of other officers of the Department of Justice and all functions of agencies and employees of the Department of Justice are vested in the Attorney General except the functions—

(1) vested by subchapter II of chapter 5 of title 5 in administrative law judges employed by the Department of Justice;

(2) of the Federal Prison Industries, Inc.;

(3) of the Board of Directors and officers of the Federal Prison Industries, Inc.; and

(4) of the Board of Parole.

§ 510. Delegation of authority

The Attorney General may from time to time make such provisions as he considers appropriate authorizing the performance by any other officer, employee, or agency of the Department of Justice of any function of the Attorney General.

§ 511. Attorney General to advise the President

The Attorney General shall give his advice and opinion on questions of law when required by the President.

§ 512. Attorney General to advise heads of executive departments

The head of an executive department may require the opinion of the Attorney General on questions of law arising in the administration of his department.

§ 513. Attorney General to advise Secretaries of military departments

When a question of law arises in the administration of the Department of the Army, the Department of the Navy, or the Department of the Air Force, the cognizance of which is not given by statute to some other officer from whom the Secretary of the military department concerned may require advice, the Secretary of the military department shall send it to the Attorney General for disposition.

§ 514. Legal services on pending claims in departments and agencies

When the head of an executive department or agency is of the opinion that the interests of the United States require the service of counsel on the examination of any witness concerning any claim, or on the legal investigation of any claim, pending in the department or agency, he shall notify the Attorney General, giving all facts necessary to enable him to furnish proper professional service in attending the examination or making the investigation, and the Attorney General shall provide for the service.

§ 515. Authority for legal proceedings; commission, oath, and salary for special attorneys

(a) The Attorney General or any other officer of the Department of Justice, or any attorney specially appointed by the Attorney General under law, may, when specifically directed by the Attorney General, conduct any kind of legal proceeding, civil or criminal, including grand jury proceedings and proceedings before committing magistrates, which United States attorneys are authorized by law to conduct, whether or not he is a resident of the district in which the proceeding is brought.

(b) Each attorney specially retained under authority of the Department of Justice shall be commissioned as special assistant to the Attorney General or special attorney, and shall take the oath required by law. Foreign counsel employed in special cases are not required to take the oath. The Attorney General shall fix the annual salary of a special assistant or special attorney at not more than $12,000.

§ 516. Conduct of litigation reserved to Department of Justice

Except as otherwise authorized by law, the conduct of litigation in which the United States, an agency, or officer thereof is a party, or is interested, and securing evidence therefor, is reserved to officers of the Department of Justice, under the direction of the Attorney General.

§ 517. Interests of United States in pending suits

The Solicitor General, or any officer of the Department of Justice, may be sent by the Attorney General to any State or district in the United States to attend to the interests of the United States in a suit pending in a court of the United States, or in a court of a State, or to attend to any other interest of the United States.

§ 518. Conduct and argument of cases

(a) Except when the Attorney General in a particular case directs otherwise, the Attorney General and the Solicitor General shall conduct and argue suits and appeals in the Supreme Court and suits in the United States Claims Court or in the United States Court of Appeals for the Federal Circuit and in the Court of International Trade in which the United States is interested.

(b) When the Attorney General considers it in the interests of the United States, he may personally conduct and argue any case in a court of the United States in which the United States is interested, or he may direct the Solicitor General or any officer of the Department of Justice to do so.

§ 519. Supervision of litigation

Except as otherwise authorized by law, the Attorney General shall supervise all litigation to which the United States, an agency, or officer thereof is a party, and shall direct all United States attorneys, assistant United States attorneys, and special attorneys appointed under section 543 of this title in the discharge of their respective duties.

520. Transmission of petitions in United States Claims Court or in United States Court of Appeals for the Federal Circuit; statement furnished by departments

(a) In suits against the United States in the United States Claims Court or in the United States Court of Appeal for the Federal Circuit founded on a contract, agreement, or transaction with an executive department or military department, or a bureau, officer, or agent thereof, or when the matter or thing on which the claim is based has been passed on and decided by an executive department, military department, bureau, or officer authorized to adjust it, the Attorney General shall send to the department, bureau, or officer a printed copy of the petition filed by the claimant, with a request that the department, bureau, or officer furnish to the Attorney General all facts, circumstances, and evidence concerning the claim in the possession or knowledge of the department, bureau, or officer.

(b) Within a reasonable time after receipt of the request from the Attorney General, the executive department, military department, bureau, or officer shall furnish the Attorney General with a written statement of all facts, information, and proofs. The statement shall contain a reference to or description of all official documents and papers, if any, as may furnish proof of facts referred to in it, or may be necessary and proper for the defense of the United States against the claim, mentioning the department, office, or place where the same is kept or may be secured. If the claim has been passed on and decided by the department, bureau, or officer, the statement shall briefly state the reasons and principles on which the decision was based. When the decision was founded on an Act of Congress it shall be cited specifically, and if any previous interpretation or construction has been given to the Act, section, or clause by the department, bureau, or officer, it shall be set forth briefly in the statement and a copy of the opinion filed, if any, attached to it. When a decision in the case has been based on a regulation of a department or when a regulation has, in the opinion of the department, bureau, or officer sending the statement, any bearing on the claim, it shall be distinctly quoted at length in the statement. When more than one case or class of cases is pending, the defense of which rests on the same facts, circumstances, and proofs, the department, bureau, or officer may certify and send one statement and it shall be held to apply to all cases as if made out, certified, and sent in each case respectively.

§ 521. Publication and distribution of opinions

The Attorney General, from time to time—

(1) shall cause to be edited, and printed in the Government Printing Office, such of his opinions as he considers valuable for preservation in volumes; and

(2) may prescribe the manner for the distribution of the volumes.

Each volume shall contain headnotes, an index, and such footnotes as the Attorney General may approve.

§ 522. Report of business and statistics

The Attorney General, by April 1 of each year, shall report to Congress on the business of the Department of Justice for the last preceding fiscal year, and on any other matters pertaining to the Department that he considers proper, including—

(1) a statement of the several appropriations which are placed under the control of the Department and the amount appropriated;

(2) the statistics of crime under the laws of the United States; and

(3) a statement of the number of causes involving the United States, civil and criminal, pending during the preceding year in each of the several courts of the United States.

§ 523. Requisitions

The Attorney General shall sign all requisitions for the advance or payment of moneys appropriated for the Department of Justice, out of the Treasury, subject to the same control as is exercised on like estimates or accounts by the General Accounting Office.

§ 524. Availability of appropriations

(a) Appropriations for the Department of Justice are available for payment of—

(1) notarial fees, including such additional stenographic services as are required in connection therewith in the taking of depositions, and compensation and expenses of witnesses and informants, all at the rates authorized or approved by the Attorney General or the Assistant Attorney General for Administration; and

(2) when ordered by the court, actual expenses of meals and lodging for marshals, deputy marshals, or criers when acting as bailiffs in attendance on juries.

(b) Except as provided in subsection (a) of this section, a claim of not more than $500 for expenses related to litigation that is beyond the control of the Department may be paid out of appropriations currently available to the Department for expenses related to litigation when the Comptroller General settles the payment.

§ 525. Procurement of law books, reference books, and periodicals; sale and exchange

In the procurement of law books, reference books, and periodicals, the Attorney General may exchange or sell similar items and apply the exchange allowances or proceeds of such sales in whole or in part payment therefor.

§ 526. Authority of Attorney General to investigate United States attorneys, marshals, and trustee[s], clerks of court, and others

(a) The Attorney General may investigate the official acts, records, and accounts of—

(1) the United States attorneys, marshals, and trustees; and

(2) at the request and on behalf of the Director of the Administrative Office of the United States Courts, the clerks of the United States courts and of the district courts of the Canal Zone and the Virgin Islands, probation officers, trustees in cases under title 11, United States magistrates, and court reporters;

for which purpose all the official papers, records, dockets, and accounts of these officers, without exception, may be examined by agents of the Attorney General at any time.

(b) Appropriations for the examination of judicial officers are available for carrying out this section.

§ 527. Establishment of working capital fund

There is hereby authorized to be established a working capital fund for the Department of Justice, which shall be available, without fiscal year limitation, for expenses and equipment necessary for maintenance and operations of such administrative services as the Attorney General, with the approval of the Office of Management and Budget, determines may be performed more advantageously as central services. The capital of the fund shall consist of the amount of the fair and reasonable value of such inventories, equipment, and other assets and inventories on order pertaining to the services to be carried on by the fund as the Attorney General may transfer to the fund less related liabilities and unpaid obligations together with any appropriations made for the purpose of providing capital. The fund shall be reimbursed or credited with advance payments from applicable appropriations and funds of the Department of Justice, other Federal agencies, and other sources authorized by law for supplies, materials, and services at rates which will recover the expenses of operations including accrual of annual leave and depreciation of plant and equipment of the fund. The fund shall also be credited with other receipts from sale or exchange of property or in payment for loss or damage to property held by the fund. There shall be transferred into the Treasury as miscellaneous receipts, as of the close of each fiscal year, any net income after making provisions for prior year losses, if any.

§ 528. Disqualification of officers and employees of the Department of Justice

The Attorney General shall promulgate rules and regulations which require the disqualification of any officer or employee of the Department of Justice, including a United States attorney or a member of such attorney's staff, from participation in a particular investigation or prosecution if such participation may result in a personal, financial, or political conflict of interest, or the appearance thereof. Such rules and regulations may provide that a willful violation of any provision thereof shall result in removal from office.

§ 529. Annual report of Attorney General

Beginning on June 1, 1979, and at the beginning of each regular session of Congress thereafter, the Attorney General shall report to Congress on the activities and operations of the Public Integrity Section or any other unit of the Department of Justice designated to supervise the investigation and prosecution of—

(1) any violation of Federal criminal law by any individual who holds or who at the time of such violation held a position, whether or not elective, as a Federal Government officer, employee, or special employee, if such violation relates directly or indirectly to such individual's Federal Government position, employment, or compensation;

(2) any violation of any Federal criminal law relating to lobbying, conflict of interest, campaigns, and election to public office committed by any person, except insofar as such violation relates to a matter involving discrimination or intimidation on grounds of race, color, religion, or national origin;

(3) any violation of Federal criminal law by any individual who holds or who at the time of such violation held a position, whether or not elective, as a State or local government officer or employee, if such violation relates directly or indirectly to such individual's State or local government position, employment, or compensation; and

(4) such other matters as the Attorney General may deem appropriate.

Such report shall include the number, type, and disposition of all investigations and prosecutions supervised by such Section or such unit, except that such report shall not disclose information which would interfere with any pending investigation or prosecution or which would improperly infringe upon the privacy rights of any individuals.

CHAPTER 33—FEDERAL BUREAU OF INVESTIGATION

§ 531. Federal Bureau of Investigation

The Federal Bureau of Investigation is in the Department of Justice.

§ 532. Director of the Federal Bureau of Investigation

The Attorney General may appoint a Director of the Federal Bureau of Investigation.* The Director of the Federal Bureau of Investigation is the head of the Federal Bureau of Investigation.

§ 533. Investigative and other officials; appointment

The Attorney General may appoint officials—

(1) to detect and prosecute crimes against the United States;

(2) to assist in the protection of the person of the President; and

(3) to conduct such other investigations regarding official matters under the control of the Department of Justice and the Department of State as may be directed by the Attorney General.

This section does not limit the authority of departments and agencies to investigate crimes against the United States when investigative jurisdiction has been assigned by law to such departments and agencies.

§ 534. Acquisition, preservation, and exchange of identification records and information; appointment of officials

(a) The Attorney General shall—

(1) acquire, collect, classify, and preserve identification, criminal identification, crime, and other records;

* Pub.L. 90–351, 82 Stat. 236, as amended by Pub.L. 94–503, 90 Stat. 2427, provides that:

"(a) Effective as of the day following the date on which the present incumbent in the office of Director ceases to serve as such, the Director of the Federal Bureau of Investigation shall be appointed by the President, by and with the advice and consent of the Senate, and shall receive compensation at the rate prescribed for level II of the Federal Executive Salary Schedule.

"(b) Effective with respect to any individual appointment by the President, by and with the advice and consent of the Senate, after June 1, 1973, the term of service of the Director of the Federal Bureau of Investigation shall be ten years. A Director may not serve more than one ten-year term. The provisions of subsections (a) through (c) of section 8335 of title 5, United States Code, shall apply to any individual appointed under this section."

(2) acquire, collect, classify, and preserve any information which would assist in the identification of any deceased individual who has not been identified after the discovery of such deceased individual;

(3) acquire, collect, classify, and preserve any information which would assist in the location of any missing person (including an unemancipated person as defined by the laws of the place of residence of such person) and provide confirmation as to any entry for such a person to the parent, legal guardian, or next of kin of that person (and the Attorney General may acquire, collect, classify, and preserve such information from such parent, guardian, or next of kin); and

(4) exchange such records and information with, and for the official use of, authorized officials of the Federal Government, the States, cities, and penal and other institutions.

(b) The exchange of records and information authorized by subsection (a) (4) of this section is subject to cancellation if dissemination is made outside the receiving departments or related agencies.

(c) The Attorney General may appoint officials to perform the functions authorized by this section.

§ 535. Investigation of crimes involving Government officers and employees; limitations

(a) The Attorney General and the Federal Bureau of Investigation may investigate any violation of title 18 involving Government officers and employees—

(1) notwithstanding any other provision of law; and

(2) without limiting the authority to investigate any matter which is conferred on them or on a department or agency of the Government.

(b) Any information, allegation, or complaint received in a department or agency of the executive branch of the Government relating to violations of title 18 involving Government officers and employees shall be expeditiously reported to the Attorney General by the head of the department or agency, unless—

(1) the responsibility to perform an investigation with respect thereto is specifically assigned otherwise by another provision of law; or

(2) as to any department or agency of the Government, the Attorney General directs otherwise with respect to a specified class of information, allegation, or complaint.

(c) This section does not limit—

(1) the authority of the military departments to investigate persons or offenses over which the armed forces have jurisdiction under the Uniform Code of Military Justice (chapter 47 of title 10); or

(2) the primary authority of the Postmaster General to investigate postal offenses.

§ 536. Positions in excepted service

All positions in the Federal Bureau of Investigation are excepted from the competitive service, and the incumbents of such positions occupy positions in the excepted service.

§ 537. Expenses of unforeseen emergencies of a confidential character

Appropriations for the Federal Bureau of Investigation are available for expenses of unforeseen emergencies of a confidential character, when so specified in the appropriation concerned, to be spent under the direction of the Attorney General. The Attorney General shall certify the amount spent that he considers advisable not to specify, and his certification is a sufficient voucher for the amount therein expressed to have been spent.

CHAPTER 35—UNITED STATES ATTORNEYS

Sec.

§ 541. United States attorneys

(a) The President shall appoint, by and with the advice and consent of the Senate, a United States attorney for each judicial district.

(b) Each United States attorney shall be appointed for a term of four years. On the expiration of his term, a United States attorney shall continue to perform the duties of his office until his successor is appointed and qualifies.

(c) Each United States attorney is subject to removal by the President.

§ 542. Assistant United States attorneys

(a) The Attorney General may appoint one or more assistant United States attorneys in any district when the public interest so requires.

(b) Each assistant United States attorney is subject to removal by the Attorney General.

§ 543. Special attorneys

(a) The Attorney General may appoint attorneys to assist United States attorneys when the public interest so requires.

(b) Each attorney appointed under this section is subject to removal by the Attorney General.

§ 544. Oath of office

Each United States attorney, assistant United States attorney, and attorney appointed under section 543 of this title, before taking office, shall take an oath to execute faithfully his duties.

§ 545. Residence

(a) Each United States attorney and assistant United States attorney shall reside in the district for which he is appointed, except that these officers of the District of Columbia, the Southern District of New York, and the Eastern District of New York may reside within 20 miles thereof. The provisions of this subsection shall not apply to any United States attorney or assistant United States attorney appointed for the Northern Mariana Islands who at the same time is serving in the same capacity in another district.

(b) The Attorney General may determine the official stations of United States attorneys and assistant United States attorneys within the districts for which they are appointed.

§ 546. Vacancies

The district court for a district in which the office of United States attorney is vacant may appoint a United States attorney to serve until the vacancy is filled. The order of appointment by the court shall be filed with the clerk of the court.

§ 547. Duties

Except as otherwise provided by law, each United States attorney, within his district, shall—

(1) prosecute for all offenses against the United States;

(2) prosecute or defend, for the Government, all civil actions, suits or proceedings in which the United States is concerned;

(3) appear in behalf of the defendants in all civil actions, suits or proceedings pending in his district against collectors, or other officers of the revenue or customs for any act done by them or for the recovery of any money exacted by or paid to these officers, and by them paid into the Treasury;

(4) institute and prosecute proceedings for the collection of fines, penalties, and forfeitures incurred for violation of any revenue law, unless satisfied on investigation that justice does not require the proceedings; and

(5) make such reports as the Attorney General may direct.

§ 548. Salaries

Subject to sections 5315–5317 of title 5, the Attorney General shall fix the annual salaries of United States attorneys, assistant United States attorneys, and attorneys appointed under section 543 of this title at rates of compensation not in excess of the highest rate of GS–18 of the General Schedule set forth in section 5332 of title 5.

§ 549. Expenses

Necessary office expenses of United States attorneys shall be allowed when authorized by the Attorney General.

§ 550. Clerical assistants and messengers

The United States attorneys may employ clerical assistants and messengers on approval of the Attorney General.

CHAPTER 37—UNITED STATES MARSHALS

§ 561. United States marshals

(a) The President shall appoint, by and with the advice and consent of the Senate, a United States marshal for each judicial district.

(b) Each marshal shall be appointed for a term of four years. On expiration of his term, a marshal shall continue to perform the duties of his office until his successor is appointed and qualifies, unless sooner removed by the President.

(c) The Attorney General shall designate places within the district for the official station and offices of each marshal. Each marshal shall reside within the district for which he was appointed, except that the marshal for the District of Columbia and the Southern District of New York may reside within 20 miles thereof. The preceding sentence shall not apply to any United States marshal appointed for the Northern Mariana Islands who at the same time is serving in the same capacity in another district.

§ 562. Deputy marshals and clerical assistants

The Attorney General may authorize a United States marshal to appoint deputies and clerical assistants. Each deputy marshal is subject to removal by the marshal pursuant to civil-service regulations.

§ 563. Oath of office

Each United States marshal and deputy marshal before assuming the duties of his office shall take the following oath or affirmation:

"I, ____________ ____________, do solemnly swear (or affirm) that I will faithfully execute all lawful precepts directed to the ____________ under the authority of the United States, make true returns, take only lawful fees, and in all things well and truly, and without malice or partiality, perform the duties of the office of ____________ during my continuance in office. So help me God."

[§ 564. Repealed.]

§ 565. Vacancies

The district court for a district in which the office of United States marshal is vacant may appoint a United States marshal to serve until the vacancy is filled. The order of appointment by the court shall be filed with the clerk of the court.

§ 566. Death of a marshal

On the death of a United States marshal, his deputy or deputies shall perform the duties of the deceased marshal in his name until his successor is appointed and qualifies.

§ 567. Expenses of marshals

Under regulations prescribed by the Attorney General, each United States marshal shall be allowed—

(1) his actual and necessary office expenses;

(2) the expense of transporting prisoners, including the cost of necessary guards and the travel and subsistence expense of prisoners and guards; and

(3) other necessary expenditures in line of duty, approved by the Attorney General.

§ 568. Availability of appropriations; transfer of prisoners to narcotic farms

Appropriations for salaries and expenses of United States marshals are available for actual and necessary expenses incident to the transfer of prisoners in the custody of the marshals to narcotic farms.

§ 569. Powers and duties generally; supervision by Attorney General

(a) The United States marshal of each district is the marshal of the district court and of the court of appeals when sitting in his district, and of the Court of International Trade holding sessions in his district elsewhere than in the Southern and Eastern Districts of New York, and may, in the discretion of the respective courts, be required to attend any session of court.

(b) United States marshals shall execute all lawful writs, process and orders issued under authority of the United States, including those of the courts and Government of the Canal Zone, and command all necessary assistance to execute their duties.

(c) The Attorney General shall supervise and direct United States marshals in the performance of public duties and accounting for public moneys. Each marshal shall report his official proceedings, receipts and disbursements and the condition of his office as the Attorney General directs.

§ 570. Power as sheriff

A United States marshal and his deputies, in executing the laws of the United States within a State, may exercise the same powers which a sheriff of the State may exercise in executing the laws thereof.

§ 571. Disbursement of salaries and moneys

(a) The United States marshals, under regulations prescribed by the Attorney General, shall pay the salaries, office expenses and travel and per diem allowances of United States attorneys, their assistants, clerks and messengers of the marshals, their deputies and clerical assistants, and of the United States trustees, their assistants, staff and other employees.

(b) The United States marshals, under regulations prescribed by the Director of the Administrative Office of the United States Courts, shall pay the salaries, office expenses, and travel and per diem allowances of circuit and district judges, clerks of court and their deputies, court reporters, and other personnel of courts within their districts.

(c) On all disbursements made by United States marshals for official salaries or expenses, the certificate of the payee is sufficient without verification on oath.

(d) Appropriations for salaries, expenses, and fees of marshals are available for advances with the approval of the Attorney General.

§ 572. Collection of fees; accounting

(a) Each United States marshal shall collect, as far as possible, his lawful fees and account for the same as public moneys.

(b) The marshal's accounts of fees and costs paid to a witness or juror on certificate of attendance issued as provided by sections 1825 and 1871 of this title may not be reexamined to charge him for an erroneous payment of the fees or costs.

§ 572a. Depositing public moneys

Except for public moneys deposited under section 2041 of this title, each United States marshal shall deposit public moneys that the marshal collects into a checking account in the Treasury, subject to disbursement by the marshal. At the end of each accounting period, the earned part of public moneys accruing to the United States shall be deposited in the Treasury to the credit of the appropriate receipt accounts.

§ 573. Delivery of prisoners to successor

Each United States marshal shall deliver to his successor all prisoners in his custody.

§ 574. Delivery of unserved process to successor

All unserved process remaining in the hands of a United States marshal or his deputies shall be delivered to his successor. When a deputy marshal resigns or is removed, he shall deliver to the marshal all process in his hands.

§ 575. Practice of law prohibited

A United States marshal or deputy marshal may not practice law in any court of the United States.

* CHAPTER 39—UNITED STATES TRUSTEES

§ 581. United States trustees

(a) The Attorney General shall appoint one United States trustee for each of the following districts or groups of districts:

(1) District of Maine, District of New Hampshire, District of Massachusetts, and District of Rhode Island.

(2) Southern District of New York.

(3) District of Delaware and District of New Jersey.

(4) Eastern District of Virginia and District of District of Columbia.

(5) Northern District of Alabama.

(6) Northern District of Texas.

(7) Northern District of Illinois.

* [Ed.] See footnote to analysis of Part II, *supra*, p. 43.

(8) District of Minnesota, District of North Dakota, District of South Dakota.

(9) Central District of California.

(10) District of Colorado and District of Kansas.

(b) Each United States trustee shall be appointed for a term of seven years. On the expiration of his term, a United States trustee shall continue to perform the duties of his Office until his successor is appointed and qualifies.

(c) Each United States trustee is subject to removal for cause by the Attorney General.

§ 582. Assistant United States trustees

(a) The Attorney General may appoint one or more assistant United States trustees in any district when the public interest so requires.

(b) Each assistant United States trustee is subject to removal for cause by the Attorney General.

§ 583. Oath of office

Each United States trustee and assistant United States trustee, before taking office, shall take an oath to execute faithfully his duties.

§ 584. Official stations

The Attorney General may determine the official stations of the United States trustees and assistant United States trustees within the districts for which they were appointed.

§ 585. Vacancies

The Attorney General may appoint an acting United States trustee for a district in which the office of United States trustee is vacant, or may designate a United States trustee for another judicial district to serve as trustee for the district in which such vacancy exists. The individual so appointed or designated may serve until the earlier of 90 days after such appointment or designation, as the case may be, or the date on which the vacancy is filled by appointment under section 581 of this title.

§ 586. Duties; supervision by Attorney General

(a) Each United States trustee, within his district, shall—

(1) establish, maintain, and supervise a panel of private trustees that are eligible and available to serve as trustees in cases under chapter 7 of title 11;

(2) serve as and perform the duties of a trustee in a case under title 11 when required under title 11 to serve as trustee in such a case;

(3) supervise the administration of cases and trustees in cases under chapter 7, 11, or 13 of title 11;

(4) deposit or invest under section 345 of title 11 money received as trustee in cases under title 11;

(5) perform the duties prescribed for the United States trustee under title 11; and

(6) make such reports as the Attorney General directs.

(b) If the number of cases under chapter 13 of title 11 commenced in a particular judicial district so warrant, the United States trustee for such district may, subject to the approval of the Attorney General, appoint one or more individuals to serve as standing trustee, or designate one or more assistant United States trustee, in cases under such chapter. The United States trustee for such district shall supervise any such individual appointed as standing trustee in the performance of the duties of standing trustee.

(c) Each United States trustee shall be under the general supervision of the Attorney General, who shall provide general coordination and assistance to the United States trustees.

(d) The Attorney General shall prescribe by rule qualifications for membership on the panels established by United States trustees under subsection (a)(1) of this section, and qualifications for appointment under subsection (b) of this section to serve as standing trustee in cases under chapter 13 of title 11. The Attorney General may not require that an individual be an attorney in order to qualify for appointment under subsection (b) of this section to serve as standing trustee in cases under chapter 13 of title 11.

(e)(1) The Attorney General, after consultation with a United States trustee that has appointed an individual under subsection (b) of this section to serve as standing trustee in cases under chapter 13 of title 11, shall fix—

(A) a maximum annual compensation for such individual, not to exceed the lowest annual rate of basic pay in effect for grade GS–16 of the General Schedule prescribed under section 5332 of title 5; and

(B) a percentage fee, not to exceed ten percent, based on such maximum annual compensation and the actual, necessary expenses incurred by such individual as standing trustee.

(2) Such individual shall collect such percentage fee from all payments under plans in the cases under chapter 13 of title 11 for which such individual serves as standing trustee. Such individual shall pay to the United States trustee, and the United States trustee shall pay to the Treasury—

(A) any amount by which the actual compensation of such individual exceeds five percent upon all payments under plans in cases under chapter 13 of title 11 for which such individual serves as standing trustee; and

(B) any amount by which the percentage for all such cases exceeds—

(i) such individual actual compensation for such cases, as adjusted under subparagraph (A) of this paragraph; plus

(ii) the actual, necessary expenses incurred by such individual as standing trustee in such cases.

§ 587. Salaries

The Attorney General shall fix the annual salaries of United States trustees and assistant United States trustees at rates of compensation not to exceed the lowest annual rate of basic pay in effect for grade GS–16 of the General Schedule prescribed under section 5332 of title 5.

§ 588. Expenses

Necessary office expenses of the United States trustee shall be allowed when authorized by the Attorney General.

§ 589. Staff and other employees

The United States trustee may employ staff and other employees on approval of the Attorney General.

* CHAPTER 39—INDEPENDENT COUNSEL

Sec.

§ 591. Applicability of provisions of this chapter

(a) The Attorney General shall conduct an investigation pursuant to the provisions of this chapter whenever the Attorney General receives information sufficient to constitute grounds to investigate that any of the persons described in subsection (b) of this section has committed a violation of any Federal criminal law other than a violation constituting a petty offense.

(b) The persons referred to in subsection (a) of this section are—

(1) the President and Vice President;

(2) any individual serving in a position listed in section 5312 of title 5;

(3) any individual working in the Executive Office of the President who is compensated at or above a rate equivalent to level II of the Executive Schedule under section 5313 of title 5;

* [Ed.] See footnote to analysis of Part II, *supra*, p. 43.

(4) any Assistant Attorney General and any individual working in the Department of Justice compensated at a rate at or above level III of the Executive Schedule under section 5314 of title 5;

(5) the Director of Central Intelligence, the Deputy Director of Central Intelligence, and the Commissioner of Internal Revenue;

(6) any individual who held any office or position described in any of paragraphs (1) through (5) of this subsection during the period consisting of the incumbency of the President such individual serves plus one year after such incumbency, but in no event longer than two years after the individual leaves office;

(7) any individual described in paragraph (6) who continues to hold office for not more than 90 days into the term of the next President during the period such individual serves plus one year after such individual leaves office;

(8) the chairman and treasurer of the principal national campaign committee seeking the election or reelection of the President, and any officer of the campaign exercising authority at the national level, such as the campaign manager or director, during the incumbency of the President.

(c) Whenever the Attorney General receives information sufficient to constitute grounds to investigate that any person not described in subsection (b) of this section has committed a violation of any Federal criminal law other than a violation constituting a petty offense, the Attorney General may conduct an investigation and apply for an independent counsel pursuant to the provisions of this chapter if the Attorney General determines that investigation of such person by the Attorney General or other officer of the Department of Justice may result in a personal, financial, or political conflict of interest.

§ 592. Application for appointment of a[n] independent counsel

(a)(1) Upon receiving information that the Attorney General determines is sufficient to constitute grounds to investigate that any person covered by the Act has engaged in conduct described in subsection (a) or (c) of section 591 of this title, the Attorney General shall conduct, for a period not to exceed ninety days, such preliminary investigation of the matter as the Attorney General deems appropriate. In determining whether grounds to investigate exist, the Attorney General shall consider—

(A) the degree of specificity of the information received, and

(B) the credibility of the source of the information.

(2) In conducting preliminary investigations pursuant to this section, the Attorney General shall have no authority to convene grand juries, plea bargain, grant immunity, or issue subpenas.

(b)(1) If the Attorney General, upon completion of the preliminary investigation, finds that there are no reasonable grounds to believe that further investigation or prosecution is warranted, the Attorney General shall so notify the division of the court specified in section 593(a) of this title, and the division of the court shall have no power to appoint a[n] independent counsel.

(2) Such notification shall be by memorandum containing a summary of the information received and a summary of the results of any preliminary investigation.

(3) Such memorandum shall not be revealed to any individual outside the division of the court or the Department of Justice without leave of the division of the court.

(c)(1) If the Attorney General, upon completion of the preliminary investigation, finds reasonable grounds to believe that further investigation or prosecution is warranted, or if ninety days elapse from the receipt of the information without a determination by the Attorney General that there are no reasonable grounds to believe that further investigation or prosecution is warranted, then the Attorney General shall apply to the division of the court for the appointment of a[n] independent counsel. In determining whether reasonable grounds exist to warrant further investigation or prosecution, the Attorney General shall comply with the written or other established policies of the Department of Justice with respect to the enforcement of criminal laws.

(2) If—

(A) after the filing of a memorandum under subsection (b) of this section, the Attorney General receives additional information sufficient to constitute grounds to investigate about the matter to which such memorandum related, and

(B) the Attorney General determines, after such additional investigation as the Attorney General deems appropriate, that reasonable grounds exist to warrant further investigation or prosecution,

then the Attorney General shall, not later than ninety days after receiving such additional information, apply to the division of the court for the appointment of a[n] independent counsel.

(d)(1) Any application under this chapter shall contain sufficient information to assist the division of the court to select a[n] independent counsel and to define that independent counsel's prosecutorial jurisdiction.

(2) No application or any other documents, materials, or memorandums supplied to the division of the court under this chapter shall be revealed to any individual outside the division of the court or the Department of Justice without leave of the division of the court.

(e) The Attorney General may ask a[n] independent counsel to accept referral of a matter that relates to a matter within that independent counsel's prosecutorial jurisdiction.

(f) The Attorney General's determination under subsection (c) of this section to apply to the division of the court for the appointment of a[n] independent counsel shall not be reviewable in any court.

§ 593. Duties of the division of the court

(a) The division of the court to which this chapter refers is the division established under section 49 of this title.

(b) Upon receipt of an application under section 592(c) of this title, the division of the court shall appoint an appropriate independent counsel and shall define that prosecutorial jurisdiction. A[n] independent counsel's identity and prosecutorial jurisdiction shall be made public upon request of the Attorney General or upon a determination of the division of the court that disclosure of the identity and prosecutorial jurisdiction of such independent counsel would be in the best interests of justice. In any event the identity and prosecutorial jurisdiction of such prosecutor * shall be made public when any indictment is returned or any criminal information is filed.

(c) The division of the court, upon request of the Attorney General which may be incorporated in an application under this chapter, may expand the prosecutorial jurisdiction of an existing independent counsel and such expansion may be in lieu of the appointment of an additional independent counsel.

(d) The division of the court may not appoint as a[n] independent counsel any person who holds or recently held any office of profit or trust under the United States.

(e) If a vacancy in office arises by reason of the resignation or death of a[n] independent counsel, the division of the court may appoint a[n] independent counsel to complete the work of the independent counsel whose resignation or death caused the vacancy. If a vacancy in office arises by reason of the removal of a[n] independent counsel, the division of the court may appoint an acting independent counsel to serve until any judicial review of such removal is completed. Upon the completion of such judicial review, the division of the court shall take appropriate action.

(f) Upon a showing of good cause by the Attorney General, the division of the court may grant a single extension of the preliminary investigation conducted pursuant to section 592(a) of this title for a period not to exceed sixty days.

(g) Upon request by the subject of an investigation conducted by an independent counsel pursuant to this chapter, the division of the court may, in its discretion, award reimbursement for all or part of the attorney's fees incurred by such subject during such investigation if—

(1) no indictment is brought against such subject; and

(2) the attorney's fees would not have been incurred but for the requirements of this chapter.

* [Ed.] Probably should be "counsel."

§ 594. Authority and duties of a[n] independent counsel

(a) Notwithstanding any other provision of law, a[n] independent counsel appointed under this chapter shall have, with respect to all matters in such independent counsel's prosecutorial jurisdiction established under this chapter, full power and independent authority to exercise all investigative and prosecutorial functions and powers of the Department of Justice, the Attorney General, and any other officer or employee of the Department of Justice, except that the Attorney General shall exercise direction or control as to those matters that specifically require the Attorney General's personal action under section 2516 of title 18. Such investigative and prosecutorial functions and powers shall include—

(1) conducting proceedings before grand juries and other investigations;

(2) participating in court proceedings and engaging in any litigation, including civil and criminal matters, that such independent counsel deems necessary;

(3) appealing any decision of a court in any case or proceeding in which such independent counsel participates in an official capacity;

(4) reviewing all documentary evidence available from any source;

(5) determining whether to contest the assertion of any testimonial privilege;

(6) receiving appropriate national security clearances and, if necessary, contesting in court (including, where appropriate, participating in in camera proceedings) any claim of privilege or attempt to withhold evidence on grounds of national security;

(7) making applications to any Federal court for a grant of immunity to any witness, consistent with applicable statutory requirements, or for warrants, subpenas, or other court orders, and, for purposes of sections 6003, 6004, and 6005 of title 18, exercising the authority vested in a United States attorney or the Attorney General;

(8) inspecting, obtaining, or using the original or a copy of any tax return, in accordance with the applicable statutes and regulations, and, for purposes of section 6103 of the Internal Revenue Code of 1954, and the regulations issued thereunder, exercising the powers vested in a United States attorney or the Attorney General;

(9) initiating and conducting prosecutions in any court of competent jurisdiction, framing and signing indictments, filing informations, and handling all aspects of any case in the name of the United States; and

(10) consulting with the United States Attorney for the district in which the violation was alleged to have occurred.

(b) A[n] independent counsel appointed under this chapter shall receive compensation at a per diem rate equal to the annual rate of basic pay for level IV of the Executive Schedule under section 5315 of title 5.

(c) For the purposes of carrying out the duties of the office of independent counsel, a[n] independent counsel shall have power to appoint, fix the compensation, and assign the duties, of such employees as such independent counsel deems necessary (including investigators, attorneys, and part-time consultants). The positions of all such employees are exempted from the competitive service. No such employee may be compensated at a rate exceeding the maximum rate provided for GS–18 of the General Schedule under section 5332 of title 5.

(d) A[n] independent counsel may request assistance from the Department of Justice, and the Department of Justice shall provide that assistance, which may include access to any records, files, or other materials relevant to matters within such independent counsel's prosecutorial jurisdiction, and the use of the resources and personnel necessary to perform such independent counsel's duties.

(e) A[n] independent counsel may ask the Attorney General or the division of the court to refer matters related to the independent counsel's prosecutorial jurisdiction. A[n] independent counsel may accept referral of a matter by the Attorney General, if the matter relates to a matter within such independent counsel's prosecutorial jurisdiction as established by the division of the court. If such a referral is accepted, the independent counsel shall notify the division of the court.

(f) A[n] independent counsel shall, except where not possible, comply with the written or other established policies of the Department of Justice respecting enforcement of the criminal laws.

(g) The independent counsel shall have full authority to dismiss matters within his prosecutorial jurisdiction without conducting an investigation or at any subsequent time prior to prosecution if to do so would be consistent with the written or other established policies of the Department of Justice with respect to the enforcement of criminal laws.

§ 595. Reporting and congressional oversight

(a) A[n] independent counsel appointed under this chapter may make public from time to time, and shall send to the Congress statements or reports on the activities of such independent counsel. These statements and reports shall contain such information as such independent counsel deems appropriate.

(b)(1) In addition to any reports made under subsection (a) of this section, and before the termination of a[n] independent counsel's office under section 596(b) of this title, such independent counsel shall submit to the division of the court a report under this subsection.

(2) A report under this subsection shall set forth fully and completely a description of the work of the independent counsel, including cuting any matter within the prosecutorial jurisdiction of such independent counsel which was not prosecuted.

(3) The division of the court may release to the Congress, the public, or to any appropriate person, such portions of a report made under this subsection as the division deems appropriate. The division of the court shall make such orders as are appropriate to protect the rights of any individual named in such report and to prevent undue interference with any pending prosecution. The division of the court may make any portion of a report under this section available to any individual named in such report for the purposes of receiving within a time limit set by the division of the court any comments or factual information that such individual may submit. Such comments and factual information, in whole or in part, may in the discretion of such division be included as an appendix to such report.

(c) A[n] independent counsel shall advise the House of Representatives of any substantial and credible information which such independent counsel receives that may constitute grounds for an impeachment. Nothing in this chapter or section 49 of this title shall prevent the Congress or either House thereof from obtaining information in the course of an impeachment proceeding.

(d) The appropriate committees of the Congress shall have oversight jurisdiction with respect to the official conduct of any independent counsel appointed under this chapter, and such independent counsel shall have the duty to cooperate with the exercise of such oversight jurisdiction.

(e) A majority of majority party members or a majority of all nonmajority party members of the Committee on the Judiciary of either House of the Congress may request in writing that the Attorney General apply for the appointment of a special prosecutor. Not ney General apply for the appointment of a[n] independent counsel. Not later than thirty days after the receipt of such a request, or not later than fifteen days after the completion of a preliminary investigation of the matter with respect to which the request is made, whichever is later, the Attorney General shall provide written notification of any action the Attorney General has taken in response to such request and, if no application has been made to the division of the court, why such application was not made. Such written notification shall be provided to the committee on which the persons making the request serve, and shall not be revealed to any third party, except that the committee may, either on its own initiative or upon the request of the Attorney General, make public such portion or portions of such notification as will not in the committee's judgment prejudice the rights of any individual.

§ 596. Removal of a[n] independent counsel; termination of office

(a)(1) A[n] independent counsel appointed under this chapter may be removed from office, other than by impeachment and conviction, only by the personal action of the Attorney General and only for good cause, physical disability, mental incapacity, or any other condition that substantially impairs the performance of such independent counsel's duties.

(2) If a[n] independent counsel is removed from office, the Attorney General shall promptly submit to the division of the court and the Committees on the Judiciary of the Senate and the House of Representatives a report specifying the facts found and the ultimate grounds for such removal. The committees shall make available to the public such report, except that each committee may, if necessary to protect the rights of any individual named in the report or to prevent undue interference with any pending prosecution, delete or postpone publishing any or all of the report. The division of the court may release any or all of such report in the same manner as a report released under section 595(b)(3) of this title and under the same limitations as apply to the release of a report under that section.

(3) A[n] independent counsel so removed may obtain judicial review of the removal in a civil action commenced before the division of the court and, if such removal was based on error of law or fact, may obtain reinstatement or other appropriate relief. The division of the court shall cause such an action to be in every way expedited.

(b)(1) An office of independent counsel shall terminate when (A) the independent counsel notifies the Attorney General that the investigation of all matters within the prosecutorial jurisdiction of such independent counsel or accepted by such independent counsel under section 594(e) of this title, and any resulting prosecutions, have been completed or so substantially completed that it would be appropriate for the Department of Justice to complete such investigations and prosecutions and (B) the independent counsel files a report in full compliance with section 595(b) of this title.

(2) The division of the court, either on its own motion or upon suggestion of the Attorney General, may terminate an office of independent counsel at any time, on the ground that the investigation of all matters within the prosecutorial jurisdiction of the independent counsel or accepted by such independent counsel under section 594 (e) of this title, and any resulting prosecutions, have been completed or so substantially completed that it would be appropriate for the Department of Justice to complete such investigations and prosecutions. At the time of termination, the independent counsel shall file the report required by section 595(b) of this title.

§ 597. Relationship with Department of Justice

(a) Whenever a matter is in the prosecutorial jurisdiction of a[n] independent counsel or has been accepted by a[n] independent counsel under section 594(e) of this title, the Department of Justice, the Attorney General, and all other officers and employees of the Department of Justice shall suspend all investigations and proceedings regarding such matter, except to the extent required by section 594 (d) of this title, and except insofar as such independent counsel agrees in writing that such investigation or proceedings may be continued by the Department of Justice.

(b) Nothing in this chapter shall prevent the Attorney General or the Solicitor General from making a presentation as amicus curiae to any court as to issues of law raised by any case or proceeding in which a[n] independent counsel participates in an official capacity or any appeal of such a case or proceeding.

§ 598. Termination of effect of chapter

This chapter shall cease to have effect five years after the date of the enactment of the Ethics in Government Act Amendments of 1982, except that this chapter shall continue in effect with respect to then pending matters before a[n] independent counsel that in the judgment of such independent counsel require such continuation until that independent counsel determines such matters have been completed.

PART III—COURT OFFICERS AND EMPLOYEES

CHAPTER 41—ADMINISTRATIVE OFFICE OF UNITED STATES COURTS

§ 601. Creation; Director and Deputy Director

The Administrative Office of the United States Courts shall be maintained at the seat of government. It shall be supervised by a Director and a Deputy Director appointed and subject to removal by the Supreme Court.

§ 602. Employees

(a) The Director shall appoint and fix the compensation of necessary employees of the Administrative Office in accordance with the provisions of chapter 51 and subchapter III of chapter 53 of title 5, relating to classification and General Schedule pay rates.

(b) Notwithstanding any other law, the Director may appoint certified interpreters in accordance with section 604(a)(15)(B) of this title without regard to the provisions of chapter 51 and subchapter III of chapter 53 of title 5, relating to classification and General Schedule pay rates, but the compensation of any person appointed under this subsection shall not exceed the appropriate equivalent of the highest rate of pay payable for the highest grade established in the General Schedule, section 5332 of title 5.

(c) The Director may obtain personal services as authorized by section 3109 of title 5, at rates not to exceed the appropriate equivalent of the highest rate of pay payable for the highest grade established in the General Schedule, section 5332 of title 5.

(d) All functions of other officers and employees of the Administrative Office and all functions of organizational units of the Administrative Office are vested in the Director. The Director may delegate any of the Director's functions, powers, duties, and authority (except the authority to promulgate rules and regulations) to such officers and employees of the judicial branch of Government as the Director may designate, and subject to such terms and conditions as the Director may consider appropriate; and may authorize the successive redelegation of such functions, powers, duties, and authority as the Director may deem desirable. All official acts performed by such officers and employees shall have the same force and effect as though performed by the Director in person.

§ 603. Salaries

The salary of the Director shall be the same as the salary of a district judge. The salary of the Deputy Director shall be in the same amount as the annual rate of basic pay for positions at level V of the Executive Schedule under section 5316 of title 5.

§ 604. Duties of Director generally

(a) The Director shall be the administrative officer of the courts, and under the supervision and direction of the Judicial Conference of the United States, shall:

(1) Supervise all administrative matters relating to the offices of clerks and other clerical and administrative personnel of the courts;

(2) Examine the state of the dockets of the courts; secure information as to the courts' need of assistance; prepare and transmit quarterly to the chief judges of the circuits, statistical data and reports as to the business of the courts;

(3) Submit to the annual meeting of the Judicial Conference of the United States, at least two weeks prior thereto, a report of the activities of the Administrative Office and the state of the business of the courts, together with the statistical data submitted to the chief judges of the circuits under paragraph (a) (2) of this section, and the Director's recommendations, which report, data and recommendations shall be public documents.

(4) Submit to Congress and the Attorney General copies of the report, data and recommendations required by paragraph (a) (3) of this section;

(5) Fix the compensation of clerks of court, deputies, librarians, criers, messengers, law clerks, secretaries, stenographers, clerical assistants, and other employees of the courts whose compensation is not otherwise fixed by law;

(6) Determine and pay necessary office expenses of courts, judges, and those court officials whose expenses are by law allowable, and the lawful fees of United States Commissioners;

(7) Regulate and pay annuities to widows and surviving dependent children of justices and judges, Directors of the Federal Judicial Center, and Directors of the Administrative Office, and necessary travel and subsistence expenses incurred by judges, court officers and employees, and officers and employees of the Administrative Office, and the Federal Judicial Center, while absent from their official stations on official business.

(8) Disburse, directly or through the several United States marshals, moneys appropriated for the maintenance and operation of the courts;

(9) Establish pretrial services pursuant to section 3152 of title 18, United States Code;

(10)(A) Purchase, exchange, transfer, distribute, and assign the custody of lawbooks, equipment, supplies, and other personal property for the judicial branch of Government (except the Supreme Court unless otherwise provided pursuant to paragraph (17)); (B) provide or make available readily to each court appropriate equipment for the interpretation of proceedings in accordance with section 1828 of this title; and (C) enter into and perform contracts and other transactions upon such terms as the Director may deem appropriate as may be necessary to the conduct of the work of the judicial branch of Government (except the Supreme Court unless otherwise provided pursuant to paragraph (17)), and contracts for nonpersonal services providing pretrial services, for the interpretation of proceedings, and for the provision of special interpretation services pursuant to section 1828 of this title may be awarded without regard to section 3709 of the Revised Statutes of the United States (41 U.S.C. 5);

(11) Audit vouchers and accounts of the courts, the Federal Judicial Center, the offices providing pretrial services, and their clerical and administrative personnel;

(12) Provide accommodations for the courts, the Federal Judicial Center, the offices providing pretrial services and their clerical and administrative personnel;

(13) Lay before Congress, annually, statistical tables that will accurately reflect the business transacted by the several bankruptcy courts, and all other pertinent data relating to such courts;

(14) * Pursuant to section 1827 of this title, establish a program for the certification and utilization of interpreters in courts of the United States;

(14) * Pursuant to section 1828 of this title, establish a program for the provision of special interpretation services in courts of the United States;

(15)(A) In those districts where the Director considers it advisable based on the need for interpreters, authorize the full-time or part-time employment by the court of certified interpreters; (B) where the Director considers it advisable based on the need for interpreters, appoint certified interpreters on a full-time or part-time basis, for services in various courts when he determines that such appointments will result in the economical provision of interpretation services; and (C) pay out of moneys appropriated for the judiciary interpreters' salaries, fees, and expenses, and other costs which may accrue in accordance with the provisions of sections 1827 and 1828 of this title;

(16) In the Director's discretion, (A) accept and utilize voluntary and uncompensated (gratuitous) services, including services as authorized by section 3102 of title 5, United States Code; and (B) accept, hold, administer, and utilize gifts and bequests of personal property for the purpose of aiding or facilitating the work of the judicial branch of Government, but gifts or bequests of money shall be covered into the Treasury;

(17) Perform such other duties as may be assigned to him by the Supreme Court or the Judicial Conference of the United States.

(b) The clerical and administrative personnel of the courts shall comply with all requests by the Director for information or statistical data as to the state of court dockets.

(c) Inspection of court dockets outside the continental United States may be made through United States officials residing within the jurisdiction where the inspection is made.

* [Ed.] The duplicate designations seem to represent a drafting error that has not yet been corrected.

(d) The Director, under the supervision and direction of the conference, shall:

(1) supervise all administrative matters relating to the offices of the United States magistrates;

(2) gather, compile, and evaluate all statistical and other information required for the performance of his duties and the duties of the conference with respect to such officers;

(3) lay before Congress annually statistical tables and other information which will accurately reflect the business which has comes before the various United States magistrates, including (A) the number of matters in which the parties consented to the exercise of jurisdiction by a magistrate, (B) the number of appeals taken pursuant to the decisions of magistrates and the disposition of such appeals, and (C) the professional background and qualifications of individuals appointed under section 631 of this title to serve as magistrate;

(4) prepare and distribute a manual, with annual supplements and periodic revisions, for the use of such officers, which shall set forth their powers and duties, describe all categories of proceedings that may arise before them, and contain such other information as may be required to enable them to discharge their powers and duties promptly, effectively, and impartially.

(e) The Director may promulgate appropriate rules and regulations approved by the conference and not inconsistent with any provision of law, to assist him in the performance of the duties conferred upon him by subsection (d) of this section. Magistrates shall keep such records and make such reports as are specified in such rules and regulations.

*(f) The Director may make, promulgate, issue, rescind, and amend rules and regulations (including regulations prescribing standards of conduct for Administrative Office employees) as may be necessary to carry out the Director's functions, powers, duties, and authority. The Director may publish in the Federal Register such rules, regulations, and notices for the judicial branch of Government as the Director determines to be of public interest; and the Director of the Federal Register hereby is authorized to accept and shall publish such materials.

*(f) For each bankruptcy court, the Director shall name qualified persons to membership on the panel of trustees. The number and qualifications of persons named to membership on the panel of trustees shall be determined by rules and regulations to be adopted by the Director. An individual named to membership on the panel of trustees shall have a residency or office in the State served by the court or in any adjacent State. A corporation named to membership on the panel of trustees shall be authorized by its charter or by law

* The duplicate designations seem to represent a drafting error that has not yet been corrected.

to act as trustee and shall have an office in the State served by the court. The Director on his own initiative may at any time remove for cause a person named to a panel of trustees or remove a trustee appointed from the panel.

(g)(1) When authorized to exchange personal property, the Director may exchange or sell similar items and may apply the exchange allowance or proceeds of sale in such cases in whole or in part payment for the property acquired, but any transaction carried out under the authority of this subsection shall be evidenced in writing.

(2) The Director hereby is authorized to enter into contracts for public utility services and related terminal equipment for periods not exceeding ten years.

(h)(1) The Director shall, out of funds appropriated for the operation and maintenance of the courts, provide facilities and pay necessary expenses incurred by the judicial councils of the circuits and the Judicial Conference under section 372 of this title, including mileage allowance and witness fees, at the same rate as provided in section 1821 of this title. Administrative and professional assistance from the Administrative Office of the United States Courts may be requested by each judicial council and the Judicial Conference for purposes of discharging their duties under section 372 of this title.

(2) The Director of the Administrative Office of the United States Courts shall include in his annual report filed with the Congress under this section a summary of the number of complaints filed with each judicial council under section 372(c) of this title, indicating the general nature of such complaints and the disposition of those complaints in which action has been taken.

§ 605. Budget estimates

The Director, under the supervision of the Judicial Conference of the United States, shall submit to the Office of Management and Budget annual estimates of the expenditures and appropriations necessary for the maintenance and operation of the courts and the Administrative Office and the operation of the judicial survivors annuity fund, and such supplemental and deficiency estimates as may be required from time to time for the same purposes, according to law. The Director shall cause periodic examinations of the judicial survivors annuity fund to be made by an actuary, who may be an actuary employed by another department of the Government temporarily assigned for the purpose, and whose findings and recommendations shall be transmitted by the Director to the Judicial Conference.

Such estimates shall be approved, before presentation to the Office of Management and Budget, by the Judicial Conference of the United States, except that the estimate with respect to the Court of International Trade shall be approved by such court and the estimate with respect to the United States Court of Appeals for the Federal Circuit shall be approved by such court.

All such estimates shall be included in the budget without revision, but subject to the recommendations of the Bureau of the Budget, as provided by section 11 of Title 31 for the estimates of the Supreme Court.

§ 606. Duties of Deputy Director

The Deputy Director shall perform the duties assigned to him by the Director, and shall act as Director during the absence or incapacity of the Director or when the Director's office is vacant.

§ 607. Practice of law prohibited

An officer or employee of the Administrative Office shall not engage directly or indirectly in the practice of law in any court of the United States.

§ 608. Seal

The Director shall use a seal approved by the Supreme Court. Judicial notice shall be taken of such seal.

§ 609. Courts' appointive power unaffected

The authority of the courts to appoint their own administrative or clerical personnel shall not be limited by any provisions of this chapter.

§ 610. Courts defined

As used in this chapter the word "courts" includes the courts of appeals and district courts of the United States, the United States District Court for the District of the Canal Zone, the District Court of Guam, the District Court of the Virgin Islands, the United States Claims Court, and the Court of International Trade.

§ 611. Retirement of Director

(a) The Director may, by written election filed with the Chief Justice of the United States within six months after the date on which he takes office, waive coverage under subchapter III (relating to civil service retirement) of chapter 83, title 5, United States Code, and bring himself within the purview of this section. Such waiver and election shall not operate to foreclose to the Director, upon separation from service other than by retirement, such opportunity as the law may provide to secure civil service retirement credit for service as Director by depositing with interest the amount required by section 8334 of title 5, United States Code.

(b) Upon the retirement of a Director who has elected coverage under this section and who has served at least fifteen years and attained the age of sixty-five years the Administrative Office of the United

States Courts shall pay him an annuity for life equal to 80 per centum of the salary of the office at the time of his retirement.

Upon the retirement of a Director who has elected coverage under this section and who has served at least ten years, but who is not eligible to receive an annuity under the first paragraph of this subsection, the Administrative Office of the United States Courts shall pay him an annuity for life equal to that proportion of 80 per centum of the salary of the office at the time of his retirement that the number of years of his service bears to fifteen, reduced by one-quarter of 1 per centum for each full month, if any, he is under the age of sixty-five at the time of separation from service.

(c) A Director who has elected coverage under this section and who becomes permanently disabled to perform the duties of his office shall be retired and shall receive an annuity for life equal to 80 per centum of the salary of the office at the time of his retirement if he has served at least fifteen years, or equal to that proportion of 80 per centum of such salary that the aggregate number of years of his service bears to fifteen if he has served less than fifteen years, but in no event less than 50 per centum of such salary.

(d) For the purpose of this section, "service" means service, whether or not continuous, as Director of the Administrative Office of the United States Courts, and any service, not to exceed five years, as a judge of the United States, a Senator or Representative in Congress, or a civilian official appointed by the President, by and with the advice and consent of the Senate.

CHAPTER 42—FEDERAL JUDICIAL CENTER

Sec.

§ 620. Federal Judicial Center

(a) There is established within the judicial branch of the Government a Federal Judicial Center, whose purpose it shall be to further the development and adoption of improved judicial administration in the courts of the United States.

(b) The Center shall have the following functions:

(1) to conduct research and study of the operation of the courts of the United States, and to stimulate and coordinate such re-

search and study on the part of other public and private persons and agencies;

(2) to develop and present for consideration by the Judicial Conference of the United States recommendations for improvement of the administration and management of the courts of the United States;

(3) to stimulate, create, develop, and conduct programs of continuing education and training for personnel of the judicial branch of the Government, including, but not limited to, judges, referees, clerks of court, probation officers, and United States commissioners; and

(4) insofar as may be consistent with the performance of the other functions set forth in this section, to provide staff, research, and planning assistance to the Judicial Conference of the United States and its committees.

§ 621. Board; composition, tenure of members, compensation

(a) The activities of the Center shall be supervised by a Board to be composed of—

(1) the Chief Justice of the United States, who shall be the permanent Chairman of the Board;

(2) two active judges of the courts of appeals of the United States, three active judges of the district courts of the United States, one active judge of the bankruptcy courts of the United States elected by vote of the members of the Judicial Conference of the United States: *Provided, however*, That the judges so elected shall not be members of the Judicial Conference of the United States; and

(3) the Director of the Administrative Office of the United States Courts, who shall be a permanent member of the Board.

(b) The term of office of each elected member of the Board shall be four years. A member elected to serve for an unexpired term arising by virtue of the death, disability, retirement, or resignation of a member shall be elected only for such unexpired term.

(c) No member elected for a four-year term shall be eligible for reelection to the Board.

(d) Members of the Board shall serve without additional compensation, but shall be reimbursed for actual and necessary expenses incurred in the performance of their official duties.

§ 622. Meetings; conduct of business

(a) Regular meetings of the Board shall be held quarterly. Special meetings shall be held from time to time upon the call of the Chairman, acting at his own discretion or pursuant to the petition of any four members.

(b) Each member of the Board shall be entitled to one vote. A simple majority of the membership shall constitute a quorum for the conduct of business. The Board shall act upon the concurrence of a simple majority of the members present and voting.

§ 623. Duties of the Board

(a) In its direction and supervision of the activities of the Federal Judicial Center, the Board shall—

(1) establish such policies and develop such programs for the Federal Judicial Center as will further achievement of its purpose and performance of its functions;

(2) formulate recommendations for improvements in the administration of the courts of the United States, in the training of the personnel of those courts, and in the management of their resources;

(3) submit to the Judicial Conference of the United States, at least one month in advance of its annual meeting, a report of the activities of the Center and such recommendations as the Board may propose for the consideration of the Conference;

(4) present to other government departments, agencies, and instrumentalities whose programs or activities relate to the administration of justice in the courts of the United States the recommendations of the Center for the improvement of such programs or activities;

(5) study and determine ways in which automatic data processing and systems procedures may be applied to the administration of the courts of the United States, and include in the annual report required by paragraph (3) of this subsection details of the results of the studies and determinations made pursuant to this paragraph; and

(6) consider and recommend to both public and private agencies aspects of the operation of the courts of the United States deemed worthy of special study.

(b) The Board shall transmit to Congress and to the Attorney General of the United States copies of all reports and recommendations submitted to the Judicial Conference of the United States. The Board shall also keep the Committees on the Judiciary of the United States Senate and House of Representatives fully and currently informed with respect to the activities of the Center.

§ 624. Powers of the Board

The Board is authorized—

(1) to appoint and fix the duties of the Director of the Federal Judicial Center, who shall serve at the pleasure of the Board;

(2) to request from any department, agency, or independent instrumentality of the Government any information it deems necessary to the performance of the functions of the Federal Judicial Center set forth in this chapter, and each such department, agency, or instrumentality is directed to cooperate with the Board and, to the extent permitted by law, to furnish such information to the

Center upon request of the Chairman or upon request of the Director when the Board has delegated this authority to him;

(3) to contract with and compensate government and private agencies or persons for research projects and other services, without regard to section 3709 of the Revised Statutes, as amended (41 U.S.C. 5), and to delegate such contract authority to the Director of the Federal Judicial Center, who is hereby empowered to exercise such delegated authority.

§ 625. Director and staff

(a) The Director shall supervise the activities of persons employed by the Center and perform other duties assigned to him by the Board.

(b) The Director shall appoint and fix the compensation of such additional professional personnel as the Board may deem necessary, without regard to the provisions of title 5, United States Code, governing appointments in competitive service, or the provisions of chapter 51 and subchapter III of chapter 53 of such title, relating to classification and General Schedule pay rates: *Provided, however,* That the compensation of any person appointed under this subsection shall not exceed the annual rate of basic pay of level V of the Executive Schedule pay rates, section 5316, title 5, United States Code: *And provided further,* That the salary of a reemployed annuitant under the Civil Service Retirement Act shall be adjusted pursuant to the provisions of section 8344, title 5, United States Code.

(c) The Director shall appoint and fix the compensation of such secretarial and clerical personnel as he may deem necessary, subject to the provisions of title 5, United States Code, governing appointments in competitive service and the provisions of chapter 51 and subchapter III of chapter 53 of such title, relating to classification and General Schedule pay rates.

(d) The Director may procure personal services as authorized by section 3109 of title 5, United States Code, at rates not to exceed the daily equivalent of the highest rate payable under General Schedule pay rates, section 5332, title 5, United States Code.

(e) The Director is authorized to incur necessary travel and other miscellaneous expenses incident to the operation of the Center.

§ 626. Compensation of the Director

The compensation of the Director of the Federal Judicial Center shall be the same as that of the Director of the Administrative Office of the United States Courts, and his appointment and salary shall not be subject to the provisions of title 5, United States Code, governing appointments in competitive service, or the provisions of chapter 51 and subchapter III of chapter 53 of such title, relating to classification and General Schedule pay rates: *Provided, however,* That any Director who is a justice or judge of the United States in active or retired status shall serve without additional compensation.

§ 627. Retirement; employee benefits

(a) A Director of the Federal Judicial Center who attains the age of seventy years shall be retired from that office.

(b) The Director, the professional staff, and the clerical and secretarial employees of the Federal Judicial Center shall be deemed to be officers and employees of the judicial branch of the United States Government within the meaning of subchapter III of chapter 83 (relating to civil service retirement), chapter 87 (relating to Federal employees' life insurance program), and chapter 89 (relating to Federal employees' health benefits program) of title 5, United States Code: *Provided, however,* That the Director, upon written notice filed with the Director of the Administrative Office of the United States Courts within six months after the date on which he takes office, may waive coverage under subchapter III of chapter 83 of title 5, United States Code (relating to civil service retirement), and elect coverage under the retirement and disability provisions of this section: *And provided further,* That upon his non-retirement separation from the Federal Judicial Center, such waiver and election shall not operate to foreclose to the Director such opportunity as the law may provide to secure civil service retirement credit for service as Director by depositing with interest the amount required by section 8334 of title 5, United States Code.

(c) Upon the retirement of a Director who has elected coverage under this section and who has served at least fifteen years and attained the age of sixty-five years the Director of the Administrative Office of the United States Courts shall pay him an annuity for life equal to 80 per centum of the salary of the office at the time of his retirement.

Upon the retirement of a Director who has elected coverage under this section and who has served at least ten years, but who is not eligible to receive an annuity under the first paragraph of this subsection, the Administrative Office of the United States Courts shall pay him an annuity for life equal to that proportion of 80 per centum of the salary of the office at the time of his retirement that the number of years of his service bears to fifteen, reduced by one-quarter of 1 per centum for each full month, if any, he is under the age of sixty-five at the time of separation from service.

(d) A Director who has elected coverage under this section and who becomes permanently disabled to perform the duties of his office shall be retired and shall receive an annuity for life equal to 80 per centum of the salary of the office at the time of his retirement if he has served at least fifteen years, or equal to that proportion of 80 per centum of such salary that the aggregate number of years of his service bears to fifteen if he has served less than fifteen years, but in no event less than 50 per centum of such salary.

(e) For the purpose of this section, "service" means service, whether or not continuous, as Director of the Federal Judicial Center, and any service, not to exceed five years, as a judge of the United States, a Senator or Representative in Congress, or a civilian official appointed by the President, by and with the advice and consent of the Senate.

§ 628. Appropriations and accounting

There are hereby authorized to be appropriated such sums as may be necessary to carry out the provisions of this chapter. The Administrative Office of the United States Courts shall provide accounting, disbursing, auditing, and other fiscal services for the Federal Judicial Center.

CHAPTER 43—UNITED STATES MAGISTRATES

§ 631. Appointment and tenure

(a) The judges of each United States district court and the district court of the Virgin Islands shall appoint United States magistrates in such numbers and to serve at such locations within the judicial district as the conference may determine under this chapter. In the case of a magistrate appointed by the district court of the Virgin Islands, this chapter shall apply as though the court appointing such magistrate were a United States district court. Where there is more than one judge of a district court, the appointment, whether an original appointment or a reappointment, shall be by the concurrence of a majority of all the judges of such district court, and when there is no such concurrence, then by the chief judge. Where the conference deems it desirable, a magistrate may be designated to serve in one or more districts adjoining the district for which he is appointed. Such a designation shall be made by the concurrence of a majority of the judges of each of the district courts involved and shall specify the duties to be performed by the magistrate in the adjoining district or districts.

(b) No individual may be appointed or reappointed to serve as a magistrate under this chapter unless:

(1) He has been for at least five years a member in good standing of the bar of the highest court of a State, the District of Columbia, the Commonwealth of Puerto Rico, or the Virgin Islands of the United States, and he is a member in good standing of the bar of the highest court of the State in which he is to serve, or, in the case of an individual appointed to serve—

(A) in the District of Columbia, a member in good standing of the bar of the United States district court for the District of Columbia; or

(B) in the Commonwealth of Puerto Rico, a member in good standing of the bar of the Supreme Court of Puerto Rico, and in the Virgin Islands of the United States, a member in good standing of the bar of the district court of the Virgin Islands.

except that an individual who does not meet the bar membership requirements of the first sentence of this paragraph may be appointed and serve as a part-time magistrate if the appointing court or courts and the conference find that no qualified individual who is a member of the bar is available to serve at a specific location;

(2) He is determined by the appointing district court or courts to be competent to perform the duties of the office;

(3) In the case of an individual appointed to serve in a national park, he resides within the exterior boundaries of that park, or at some place reasonably adjacent thereto;

(4) He is not related by blood or marriage to a judge of the appointing court or courts at the time of his initial appointment; and

(5) He is selected pursuant to standards and procedures promulgated by the Judicial Conference of the United States. Such standards and procedures shall contain provision for public notice of all vacancies in magistrate positions and for the establishment by the district courts of merit selection panels, composed of residents of the individual judicial districts, to assist the courts in identifying and recommending persons who are best qualified to fill such positions.

(c) A magistrate may hold no other civil or military office or employment under the United States: *Provided, however,* That, with the approval of the conference, a part-time referee in bankruptcy or a clerk or deputy clerk of a court of the United States may be appointed and serve as a part-time United States magistrate, but the conference shall fix the aggregate amount of compensation to be received for performing the duties of part-time magistrate and part-time referee in bankruptcy, clerk or deputy clerk: *And provided further,* That retired officers and retired enlisted personnel of the Regular and Reserve components of the Army, Navy, Air Force, Marine Corps, and Coast Guard, members of the Reserve components of the Army, Navy, Air Force, Marine Corps, and Coast Guard, and members of the Army National Guard of the United States, the Air National Guard of the United States, and the Naval Militia and of the National Guard of a State, territory, or the District of Columbia, except the National Guard disbursing officers who are on a full-time salary basis, may be appointed and serve as United States magistrates.

(d) No individual may serve under this chapter after having attained the age of seventy years: *Provided, however,* That upon the unanimous vote of all the judges of the appointing court or courts, a magistrate who has attained the age of seventy years may continue to serve and may be reappointed under this chapter.

(e) The appointment of any individual as a full-time magistrate shall be for a term of eight years, and the appointment of any individuals as a part-time magistrate shall be for a term of four years, except that the term of a full-time or part-time magistrate appointed under subsection (j) shall expire upon—

(1) the expiration of the absent magistrate's term,

(2) the reinstatement of the absent magistrate in regular service in office as a magistrate,

(3) the failure of the absent magistrate to make timely application under subsection (i) of this section for reinstatement in regular service in office as a magistrate after discharge or release from military service,

(4) the death or resignation of the absent magistrate, or

(5) the removal from office of the absent magistrate pursuant to subsection (h) of this section,

whichever may first occur.

(f) Upon the expiration of his term, a magistrate may, by a majority vote of the judges of the appointing district court or courts and with the approval of the judicial council of the circuit, continue to perform the duties of his office until his successor is appointed, or for 60 days after the date of the expiration of the magistrate's term, whichever is earlier.

(g) Each individual appointed as a magistrate under this section shall take the oath or affirmation prescribed by section 453 of this title before performing the duties of his office.

(h) Each appointment made by a judge or judges of a district court shall be entered of record in such court, and notice of such appointment shall be given at once by the clerk of that court to the Director.

(i) Removal of a magistrate during the term for which he is appointed shall be only for incompetency, misconduct, neglect of duty, or physical or mental disability, but a magistrate's office shall be terminated if the conference determines that the services performed by his office are no longer needed. Removal shall be by the judges of the district court for the judicial district in which the magistrate serves; where there is more than one judge of a district court, removal shall not occur unless a majority of all the judges of such court concur in the order of removal; and when there is a tie vote of the judges of the district court on the question of the removal or retention in office of a magistrate, then removal shall be only by a concurrence of a majority of all the judges of the council. In the case of a magistrate appointed under the third sentence of subsection (a) of this section, removal shall not occur unless a majority of all the judges of the appointing district courts concur in the order of removal; and where there is a tie vote on the question of the removal or retention in office of a magistrate, then removal shall be only by a concurrence of a majority of all the judges of the council or councils. Before any order or removal shall be entered, a full specification of the charges shall be furnished to the magistrate, and he shall be accorded by the judge or judges of the removing court, courts, council, or councils an opportunity to be heard on the charges.

(j)(1) A magistrate who is inducted into the Armed Forces of the United States pursuant to the Military Selective Service Act of 1967 (50 U.S.C. App. 451 et seq.), or is otherwise ordered to active duty with such forces for a period of more than thirty days, and who makes application for a leave of absence to the district court or courts which appointed him, shall be granted a leave of absence without compensation for such period as he is required to serve in such forces. Every application for a leave of absence under this subsection shall include a copy of the official orders requiring the magistrate's military service. The granting of a leave of absence under this subsection shall not operate to extend the term of office of any magistrate.

(2) A magistrate granted a leave of absence under this subsection who—

(A) receives a certificate of service under section 9(a) of the Military Selective Service Act of 1967 (50 U.S.C. App. 459(a)), or is released under honorable conditions from the military service,

(B) makes application for reinstatement to regular service in office as a magistrate within ninety days after he is released from such service or training or from hospitalization continuing after discharge for a period of not more than one year, and

(C) is determined by the appointing court or courts in the manner specified in subsection (a) of this section to be still qualified to perform the duties of such position,

shall be reinstated in regular service in such office.

(k) Upon the grant by the appropriate district court or courts of a leave of absence to a magistrate entitled to such relief under the terms of subsection (i) of this section, such court or courts may proceed to appoint, in the manner specified in subsection (a) of this section, another magistrate, qualified for appointment and service under subsections (b), (c), and (d) of this section, who shall serve for the period specified in subsection (e) of this section.

§ 632. Character of service

(a) Full-time United States magistrates may not engage in the practice of law, and may not engage in any other business, occupation, or employment inconsistent with the expeditious, proper, and impartial performance of their duties as judicial officers.

(b) Part-time United States magistrates shall render such service as judicial officers as is required by law. While so serving they may engage in the practice of law, but may not serve as counsel in any criminal action in any court of the United States, nor act in any capacity that is, under such regulations as the conference may establish, inconsistent with the proper discharge of their office. Within such restrictions, they may engage in any other business, occupation, or employment which is not inconsistent with the expeditious, proper, and impartial performance of their duties as judicial officers.

§ 633. Determination of number, locations, and salaries of magistrates

(a) Surveys by the Director.—

(1) The Director shall, within one year immediately following the date of the enactment of the Federal Magistrates Act, make a careful survey of conditions in judicial districts to determine (A) the number of appointments of full-time magistrates and part-time magistrates required to be made under this chapter to provide for the expeditious and effective administration of justice, (B) the locations at which such officers shall serve, and (C) their respective salaries under section 634 of this title. Thereafter, the Director shall, from time to time, make such surveys, general or local, as the conference shall deem expedient.

(2) In the course of any survey, the Director shall take into account local conditions in each judicial district, including the areas and the populations to be served, the transportation and communications facilities available, the amount and distribution of business of the type expected to arise before officers appointed under this chapter (including such matters as may be assigned under section 636(b) of this chapter), and any other material factors. The Director shall give consideration to suggestions from any interested parties, including district judges, United States commissioners or officers appointed under this chapter, United States attorneys, bar associations, and other parties having relevant experience or information.

(3) The surveys shall be made with a view toward creating and maintaining a system of full-time United States magistrates. However, should the Director find, as a result of any such surveys, areas in which the employment of a full-time magistrate would not be feasible or desirable, he shall recommend the appointment of part-time United States magistrates in such numbers and at such locations as may be required to permit prompt and efficient issuance of process and to permit individuals charged with criminal offenses against the United States to be brought before a judicial officer of the United States promptly after arrest.

(b) Determination by the Conference.—Upon the completion of the initial surveys required by subsection (a) of this section, the Director shall report to the district courts, the councils, and the conference his recommendations concerning the number of full-time magistrates and part-time magistrates, their respective locations, and the amount of their respective salaries under section 643 of this title. The district courts shall advise their respective councils, stating their recommendations and the reasons therefor; the councils shall advise the conference, stating their recommendations and the reasons therefor, and shall also report to the conference the recommendations of the district courts. The conference shall determine, in the light of the recommendations of the Director, the district courts, and the councils, the number of full-time United States magistrates and part-time United States magistrates, the locations at which they shall serve, and their respective salaries. Such determinations shall take effect in each judicial district at such time as the district court for such judicial district shall determine, but in no event later than one year after they are promulgated.

(c) Changes in number, locations, and salaries.—Except as otherwise provided in this chapter, the conference may, from time to time, in the light of the recommendations of the Director, the district courts, and the councils, change the number, locations, and salaries of full-time and part-time magistrates, as the expeditious administration of justice may require.

§ 634. Compensation

(a) Officers appointed under this chapter shall receive as full compensation for their services salaries to be fixed by the conference pursuant to section 633 of this title, at rates for full-time and part-time United States magistrates not to exceed the rates now or hereafter provided for full-time and part-time referees in bankruptcy, respectively, referred to in section 40a of the Bankruptcy Act (11 U.S.C. 68(a)), as amended, except that the salary of a part-time United States magistrate shall not be less than $100 nor more than one-half the maximum salary payable to a full-time magistrate. In fixing the amount of salary to be paid to any officer appointed under this chapter, consideration shall be given to the average number and the nature of matters that have arisen during the immediately preceding period of five years, and that may be expected thereafter to arise, over which such officer would have jurisdiction and to such other factors as may be material. Disbursement of salaries shall be made by or pursuant to the order of the Director.

(b) Except as provided by section 8344, title 5, relating to reductions of the salaries of reemployed annuitants under subchapter III of chapter 83 of such title and unless the office has been terminated as provided in this chapter, the salary of a full-time United States magistrate shall not be reduced, during the term in which he is serving, below the salary fixed for him at the beginning of that term.

(c) All United States magistrates, effective upon their taking the oath or affirmation of office, and all necessary legal, clerical, and secretarial assistants employed in the offices of full-time United States magistrates shall be deemed to be officers and employees in the judicial branch of the United States Government within the meaning of subsection III (relating to civil service retirement) of chapter 83, chapter 87 (relating to Federal employees' group life insurance), and chapter 89 (relating to Federal employees' health benefits program) of title 5. Part-time magistrates shall not be excluded from coverage under these chapters solely for lack of a prearranged regular tour of duty.

§ 635. Expenses

(a) Full-time United States magistrates serving under this chapter shall be allowed their actual and necessary expenses incurred in the performance of their duties, including the compensation of such legal assistants as the Judicial Conference, on the basis of the recommendations of the judicial councils of the circuits, considers necessary, and the compensation of necessary clerical and secretarial assistance. Such expenses and compensation shall be determined and paid by the Director under such regulations as the Director shall prescribe with the approval of the conference. The Administrator of General Services shall provide such magistrates with necessary courtrooms, office space, furniture and facilities within United States courthouses or office buildings owned or occupied by departments or agencies of the United States, or should suitable courtroom and office space not be available within any such courthouse or office building, the Administrator of General Services, at the request of the Director, shall procure and pay for suitable courtroom and office space, furniture and facilities for such magistrate in another building, but only if such request has been approved as necessary by the judicial council of the appropriate circuit.

(b) Under such regulations as the Director shall prescribe with the approval of the conference, the Director shall reimburse part-time magistrates for actual expenses necessarily incurred by them in the performance of their duties under this chapter. Such reimbursement may be made, at rates not exceeding those prescribed by such regulations, for expenses incurred by such part-time magistrates for clerical and secretarial assistance, stationery, telephone and other communications services, travel, and such other expenses as may be determined to be necessary for the proper performance of the duties of such officers: *Provided, however,* That no reimbursement shall be made for all or any portion of the expense incurred by such part-time magistrates for the procurement of office space.

§ 636. Jurisdiction, powers, and temporary assignment

(a) Each United States magistrate serving under this chapter shall have within the territorial jurisdiction prescribed by his appointment—

(1) all powers and duties conferred or imposed upon United States commissioners by law or by the Rules of Criminal Procedure for the United States District Courts;

(2) the power to administer oaths and affirmations, impose conditions of release under section 3146 of title 18, and take acknowledgements, affidavits, and depositions; and

(3) the power to conduct trials under section 3401, title 18, United States Code, in conformity with and subject to the limitations of that section.

(b)(1) Notwithstanding any provision of law to the contrary—

(A) a judge may designate a magistrate to hear and determine any pretrial matter pending before the court, except a motion for injunctive relief, for judgment on the pleadings, for summary judgment, to dismiss or quash an indictment or information made by the defendant, to suppress evidence in a criminal case, to dismiss or to permit maintenance of a class action, to dismiss for failure to state a claim upon which relief can be granted, and to involuntarily dismiss an action. A judge of the court may reconsider any pretrial matter under this subparagraph (A) where it has been shown that the magistrate's order is clearly erroneous or contrary to law.

(B) a judge may also designate a magistrate to conduct hearings, including evidentiary hearings, and to submit to a judge of the court proposed findings of fact and recommendations for the disposition, by a judge of the court, of any motion excepted in subparagraph (A), of applications for posttrial relief made by individuals convicted of criminal offenses and of prisoner petitions challenging conditions of confinement.

(C) the magistrate shall file his proposed findings and recommendations under subparagraph (B) with the court and a copy shall forthwith be mailed to all parties.

Within ten days after being served with a copy, any party may serve and file written objections to such proposed findings and recommendations as provided by rules of court. A judge of the court shall make a de novo determination of those portions of the report or specified proposed findings or recommendations to which objection is made. A judge of the court may accept, reject, or modify, in whole or in part, the findings or recommendations made by the magistrate. The judge may also receive further evidence or recommit the matter to the magistrate with instructions.

(2) A judge may designate a magistrate to serve as a special master pursuant to the applicable provisions of this title and the Federal Rules of Civil Procedure for the United States district courts. A judge may designate a magistrate to serve as a special master in any civil case, upon consent of the parties, without regard to the provisions of rule 53(b) of the Federal Rules of Civil Procedure for the United States district courts.

(3) A magistrate may be assigned such additional duties as are not inconsistent with the Constitution and laws of the United States.

(4) Each district court shall establish rules pursuant to which the magistrates shall discharge their duties.

(c) Notwithstanding any provision of law to the contrary—

(1) Upon the consent of the parties, a full-time United States magistrate or a part-time United States magistrate who serves as a full-time judicial officer may conduct any or all proceedings in a jury or nonjury civil matter and order the entry of judgment in the case, when specially designated to exercise such

jurisdiction by the district court or courts he serves. Upon the consent of the parties, pursuant to their specific written request, any other part-time magistrate may exercise such jurisdiction, if such magistrate meets the bar membership requirements set forth in section 631(b)(1) and the chief judge of the district court certifies that a full-time magistrate is not reasonably available in accordance with guidelines established by the judicial council of the circuit. When there is more than one judge of a district court, designation under this paragraph shall be by the concurrence of a majority of all the judges of such district court, and when there is no such concurrence, then by the chief judge.

(2) If a magistrate is designated to exercise civil jurisdiction under paragraph (1) of this subsection, the clerk of court shall, at the time the action is filed, notify the parties of their right to consent to the exercise of such jurisdiction. The decision of the parties shall be communicated to the clerk of court. Thereafter, neither the district judge nor the magistrate shall attempt to persuade or induce any party to consent to reference of any civil matter to a magistrate. Rules of court for the reference of civil matters to magistrates shall include procedures to protect the voluntariness of the parties' consent.

(3) Upon entry of judgment in any case referred under paragraph (1) of this subsection, an aggrieved party may appeal directly to the appropriate United States court of appeals from the judgment of the magistrate in the same manner as an appeal from any other judgment of a district court. In this circumstance, the consent of the parties allows a magistrate designated to exercise civil jurisdiction under paragraph (1) of this subsection to direct the entry of a judgment of the district court in accordance with the Federal Rules of Civil Procedure. Nothing in this paragraph shall be construed as a limitation of any party's right to seek review by the Supreme Court of the United States.

(4) Notwithstanding the provisions of paragraph (3) of this subsection, at the time of reference to a magistrate, the parties may further consent to appeal on the record to a judge of the district court in the same manner as on an appeal from a judgment of the district court to a court of appeals. Wherever possible the local rules of the district court and the rules promulgated by the conference shall endeavor to make such appeal expeditious and inexpensive. The district court may affirm, reverse, modify, or remand the magistrate's judgment.

(5) Cases in the district courts under paragraph (4) of this subsection may be reviewed by the appropriate United States court of appeals upon petition for leave to appeal by a party stating specific objections to the judgment. Nothing in this paragraph shall be construed to be a limitation on any party's right to seek review by the Supreme Court of the United States.

(6) The court may, for good cause shown on its own motion, or under extraordinary circumstances shown by any party, vacate a reference of a civil matter to a magistrate under this subsection.

(7) The magistrate shall determine, taking into account the complexity of the particular matter referred to the magistrate, whether the record in the proceeding shall be taken, pursuant to section 753 of this title, by electronic sound recording means, by a court reporter appointed or employed by the court to take a verbatim record by shorthand or by mechanical means, or by an employee of the court designated by the court to take such a verbatim record. Notwithstanding the magistrate's determination, (A) the proceeding shall be taken down by a court reporter if any party so requests, (B) the proceeding shall be recorded by a means other than a court reporter if all parties so agree, and (C) no record of the proceeding shall be made if all parties so agree. Reporters referred to in this paragraph may be transferred for temporary service in any district court of the judicial circuit for reporting proceedings under this subsection, or for other reporting duties in such court.

(d) The practice and procedure for the trial of cases before officers serving under this chapter, and for the taking and hearing of appeals to the district courts, shall conform to rules promulgated by the Supreme Court pursuant to section 3402 of title 18, United States Code.

(e) In a proceeding before a magistrate, any of the following acts or conduct shall constitute a contempt of the district court for the district wherein the magistrate is sitting: (1) disobedience or resistance to any lawful order, process, or writ; (2) misbehavior at a hearing or other proceeding, or so near the place thereof as to obstruct the same; (3) failure to produce, after having been ordered to do so, any pertinent document; (4) refusal to appear after having been subpenaed or, upon appearing, refusal to take the oath or affirmation as a witness, or, having taken the oath or affirmation, refusal to be examined according to law; or (5) any other act or conduct which if committed before a judge of the district court would constitute contempt of such court. Upon the commission of any such act or conduct, the magistrate shall forthwith certify the facts to a judge of the district court and may serve or cause to be served upon any person whose behavior is brought into question under this section an order requiring such person to appear before a judge of that court upon a day certain to show cause why he should not be adjudged in contempt by reason of the facts so certified. A judge of the district court shall thereupon, in a summary manner, hear the evidence as to the act or conduct complained of and, if it is such as to warrant punishment, punish such person in the same manner and to the same extent as for a contempt committed before a judge of the court, or commit such person upon the conditions applicable in the case of defiance of the process of the district court or misconduct in the presence of a judge of that court.

(f) In an emergency and upon the concurrence of the chief judges of the districts involved, a United States magistrate may be temporarily assigned to perform any of the duties specified in subsection (a) or (b) of this section in a judicial district other than the judicial district for which he has been appointed. No magistrate shall perform any of such duties in a district to which he has been temporarily assigned until an order has been issued by the chief judge of such district specifying (1) the emergency by reason of which he has been transferred, (2) the duration of his assignment, and (3) the duties which he is authorized to perform. A magistrate so assigned shall not be entitled to additional compensation but shall be reimbursed for actual and necessary expenses incurred in the performance of his duties in accordance with section 635.

(g) A United States magistrate may perform the verification function required by section 4107 of title 18, United States Code. A magistrate may be assigned by a judge of any United States district court to perform the verification required by section 4108 and the appointment of counsel authorized by section 4109 of title 18, United States Code, and may perform such functions beyond the territorial limits of the United States. A magistrate assigned such functions shall have no authority to perform any other function within the territory of a foreign country.

§ 637. Training

The Federal Judicial Center shall conduct periodic training programs and seminars for both full-time and part-time United States magistrates, including an introductory training program for new magistrates, to be held within one year after initial appointment.

§ 638. Dockets and forms; United States Code; seals

(a) The Director shall furnish to United States magistrates adequate docket books and forms prescribed by the Director. The Director shall also furnish to each such officer a copy of the current edition of the United States Code.

(b) All property furnished to any such officer shall remain the property of the United States and, upon the termination of his term of office, shall be transmitted to his successor in office or otherwise disposed of as the Director orders.

(c) The Director shall furnish to each United States magistrate appointed under this chapter an official impression seal in a form prescribed by the conference. Each such officer shall affix his seal to every jurat or certificate of his official acts without fee.

§ 639. Definitions

As used in this chapter—

(1) "Conference" shall mean the Judicial Conference of the United States;

(2) "Council" shall mean the Judicial Council of the Circuit;

(3) "Director" shall mean the Director of the Administrative Office of the United States Courts;

(4) "Full-time magistrate" shall mean a full-time United States magistrate;

(5) "Part-time magistrate" shall mean a part-time United States magistrate; and

(6) "United States magistrate" and "magistrate" shall mean both full-time and part-time United States magistrates.

CHAPTER 45—SUPREME COURT

§ 671. Clerk

(a) The Supreme Court may appoint and fix the compensation of a clerk and one or more deputy clerks. The clerk shall be subject to removal by the Court. Deputy clerks shall be subject to removal by the clerk with the approval of the Court or the Chief Justice of the United States.

[(b) Repealed.]

(c) The clerk may appoint and fix the compensation of necessary assistants and messengers with the approval of the Chief Justice of the United States.

(d) The clerk shall pay into the Treasury all fees, costs, and other moneys collected by him. He shall make annual returns thereof to the Court under regulations prescribed by it.

§ 672. Marshal

(a) The Supreme Court may appoint a marshal, who shall be subject to removal by the Court, and may fix his compensation.

(b) The marshal may, with the approval of the Chief Justice of the United States, appoint and fix the compensation of necessary assistants and other employees to attend the Court, and necessary custodial employees.

(c) The marshal shall:

(1) Attend the Court at its sessions;

(2) Serve and execute all process and orders issued by the Court or a member thereof;

(3) Take charge of all property of the United States used by the Court or its members;

(4) Disburse funds appropriated for work upon the Supreme Court building and grounds under the jurisdiction of the Architect of the Capitol upon certified vouchers submitted by the Architect;

(5) Disburse funds appropriated for the purchase of books, pamphlets, periodicals and other publications, and for their repair, binding, and rebinding, upon vouchers certified by the librarian of the Court;

(6) Pay the salaries of the Chief Justice, associate justices, and all officers and employees of the Court and disburse other funds appropriated for disbursement, under the direction of the Chief Justice;

(7) Pay the expenses of printing briefs and travel expenses of attorneys in behalf of persons whose motions to appear in forma pauperis in the Supreme Court have been approved and when counsel have been appointed by the Supreme Court, upon vouchers certified by the clerk of the Court;

(8) Oversee the Supreme Court Police.

§ 673. Reporter

(a) The Supreme Court may appoint and fix the compensation of a reporter of its decisions who shall be subject to removal by the Court.

(b) The reporter may appoint and fix the compensation of necessary professional and clerical assistants and other employees, with the approval of the Court or the Chief Justice of the United States.

(c) The reporter shall, under the direction of the Court or the Chief Justice, prepare the decisions of the Court for publication in bound volumes and advance copies in pamphlet installments.

The reporter shall determine the quality and size of the paper, type, format, proofs and binding subject to the approval of the Court or the Chief Justice.

§ 674. Librarian

(a) The Supreme Court may appoint a librarian, whose salary it shall fix, and who shall be subject to removal by the Court.

(b) The librarian shall, with the approval of the Chief Justice, appoint necessary assistants and fix their compensation and make rules governing the use of the library.

(c) He shall select and acquire by purchase, gift, bequest, or exchange, such books, pamphlets, periodicals, microfilm and other processed copy as may be required by the Court for its official use and for the reasonable needs of its bar.

(d) The librarian shall certify to the marshal for payment vouchers covering expenditures for the purchase of such books and other material, and for binding, rebinding and repairing the same.

§ 675. Law clerks and secretaries

The Chief Justice of the United States, and the associate justices of the Supreme Court may appoint law clerks and secretaries whose salaries shall be fixed by the Court.

§ 676. Printing and binding

(a) The printing and binding for the Supreme Court, including the printing and binding of individual copies, advance pamphlet installments, and bound volumes, of its decisions, whether requisitioned or ordered by the Court or any of its officers or by any other office or agency, and whether paid for by, or charged to the appropriation for, the Court or any other office or agency, shall be done by the printer or printers whom the Court or the Chief Justice of the United States may select, unless it shall otherwise order.

(b) Whenever advance pamphlet installments and bound volumes of the Court's decisions are printed by a private printer, an adequate number of copies for distribution in accordance with the requirements of section 411 of this title and for sale to the public shall be provided and made available for these purposes in such manner and at such prices as may be determined from time to time by the Supreme Court or the Chief Justice of the United States, in lieu of compliance by the Public Printer and the Superintendent of Documents with the requirements of sections 411 and 412 of this title with respect to such copies. Pending distribution or sale, such copies shall be the property of the United States and shall be held in the custody of the marshal or such other person, organization, or agency, as the Supreme Court or the Chief Justice of the United States may designate.

§ 677. Administrative Assistant to the Chief Justice

(a) The Chief Justice of the United States may appoint an Administrative Assistant who shall serve at the pleasure of the Chief Justice and shall perform such duties as may be assigned to him by the Chief Justice. The salary payable to the Administrative Assistant shall be fixed by the Chief Justice at a rate which shall not exceed the salary payable to the Director of the Administrative Office of the United States Courts. The Administrative Assistant may elect to bring himself within the same retirement program available to the Director of the Administrative Office of the United States Courts, as provided by section 611 of this title, by filing a written election with the Chief Justice within the time and in the manner prescribed by section 611.

(b) The Administrative Assistant, with the approval of the Chief Justice, may appoint and fix the compensation of necessary employees. The Administrative Assistant and his employees shall be deemed employees of the Supreme Court.

CHAPTER 47—COURTS OF APPEALS

§ 711. Clerks and employees

(a) Each court of appeals may appoint a clerk who shall be subject to removal by the court.

(b) The clerk, with the approval of the court, may appoint necessary deputies, clerical assistants and employees in such number as may be approved by the Director of the Administrative Office of the United States Courts. Such deputies, clerical assistants and employees shall be subject to removal by the clerk with the approval of the court.

(c) The clerk shall pay into the Treasury all fees, costs and other moneys collected by him and make returns thereof to the Director of the Administrative Office of the United States Courts under regulations prescribed by him.

§ 712. Law clerks and secretaries

Circuit judges may appoint necessary law clerks and secretaries.

§ 713. Librarians

(a) Each court of appeals may appoint a librarian who shall be subject to removal by the court.

(b) The librarian, with the approval of the court, may appoint necessary library assistants in such numbers as the Director of the Administrative Office of the United States Courts may approve. The librarian may remove such library assistants with the approval of the court.

§ 714. Criers and messengers

(a) Each court of appeals may appoint a crier who shall be subject to removal by the court.

(b) The crier, with the approval of the court, may appoint necessary messengers in such number as the Director of the Administrative Office of the United States Courts may approve. The crier may remove such messengers with the approval of the court. The crier shall also perform the duties of bailiff and messenger.

§ 715. Staff attorneys and technical assistants

(a) The chief judge of each court of appeals, with the approval of the court, may appoint a senior staff attorney, who shall be subject to removal by the chief judge with the approval of the court.

(b) The senior staff attorney, with the approval of the chief judge, may appoint necessary staff attorneys and secretarial and clerical employees in such numbers as the Director of the Administrative Office of the United States Courts may approve, but in no event may the number of staff attorneys exceed the number of positions expressly authorized in an annual appropriation Act. The senior staff attorney may remove such staff attorneys and secretarial and clerical employees with the approval of the chief judge.

(c) The chief judge of the Court of Appeals for the Federal Circuit, with the approval of the court, may appoint a senior technical assistant who shall be subject to removal by the chief judge with the approval of the court.

(d) The senior technical assistant, with the approval of the court, may appoint necessary technical assistants in such number as the Director of the Administrative Office of the United States Courts may approve, but in no event may the number of technical assistants in the Court of Appeals for the Federal Circuit exceed the number of circuit judges in regular active service within such circuit. The senior technical assistant may remove such technical assistants with the approval of the court.

CHAPTER 49—DISTRICT COURTS

Sec.

§ 751. Clerks

(a) Each district court may appoint a clerk who shall be subject to removal by the court.

(b) The clerk may appoint, with the approval of the court, necessary deputies, clerical assistants and employees in such number as may be approved by the Director of the Administrative Office of the United States Courts. Such deputies, clerical assistants and employees shall be subject to removal by the clerk with the approval of the court.

(c) The clerk of each district court shall reside in the district for which he is appointed, except that the clerk of the district court for the District of Columbia and the Southern District of New York may reside within twenty miles thereof. The district court may designate places within the district for the offices of the clerk and his deputies, and their official stations.

(d) A clerk of a district court or his deputy or assistant shall not receive any compensation or emoluments through any office or position to which he is appointed by the court, other than that received as such clerk, deputy or assistant, whether from the United States or from private litigants.

This subsection shall not apply to clerks or deputy clerks appointed as United States commissioners pursuant to section 631 of this title.

(e) The clerk of each district court shall pay into the Treasury all fees, costs and other moneys collected by him, except naturalization fees listed in section 742 of Title 8 and uncollected fees not required by Act of Congress to be prepaid.

He shall make returns thereof to the Director of the Administrative Office of the United States Courts under regulations prescribed by him.

(f) When the Court of International Trade is sitting in a judicial district, other than the Southern District or Eastern District of New York, the clerk of the district court of such judicial district or an authorized deputy clerk, upon the request of the chief judge of the Court of International Trade and with the approval of such district court, shall act in the district as clerk of the Court of International Trade, as prescribed by the rules and orders of the Court of International Trade for all purposes relating to the civil action then pending before such court.

§ 752. Law clerks and secretaries

District judges may appoint necessary law clerks and secretaries subject to any limitation on the aggregate salaries of such employees which may be imposed by law.

§ 753. Reporters

(a) Each district court of the United States, the United States District Court for the District of the Canal Zone, the District Court of Guam, and the District Court of the Virgin Islands shall appoint one or more court reporters.

The number of reporters shall be determined by the Judicial Conference of the United States.

The qualifications of such reporters shall be determined by standards formulated by the Judicial Conference. Each reporter shall take an oath faithfully to perform the duties of his office.

Each such court, with the approval of the Director of the Administrative Office of the United States Courts, may appoint additional reporters for temporary service not exceeding three months, when there is more reporting work in the district than can be performed promptly by the authorized number of reporters and the urgency is so great as to render it impracticable to obtain the approval of the Judicial Conference.

If any such court and the Judicial Conference are of the opinion that it is in the public interest that the duties of reporter should be combined with those of any other employee of the court, the Judicial Conference may authorize such a combination and fix the salary for the performance of the duties combined.

(b) Each session of the court and every other proceeding designated by rule or order of the court or by one of the judges shall be recorded verbatim by shorthand, mechanical means, electronic sound recording, or any other method, subject to regulations promulgated by the Judicial Conference and subject to the discretion and approval of the judge. The regulations promulgated pursuant to the preceding sentence shall prescribe the types of electronic sound recording or other means which may be used. Proceedings to be recorded under this section include (1) all proceedings in criminal cases had in open court; (2) all proceedings in other cases had in open court unless the parties with the approval of the judge shall agree specifically to the contrary; and (3) such other proceedings as a judge of the court may direct or as may be required by rule or order of court as may be requested by any party to the proceeding.

The reporter or other individual designated to produce the record shall attach his official certificate to the original shorthand notes or other original records so taken and promptly file them with the clerk who shall preserve them in the public records of the court for not less than ten years.

The reporter or other individual designated to produce the record shall transcribe and certify such parts of the record of proceedings as may be required by any rule or order of court, including all arraignments, pleas, and proceedings in connection with the imposition of sentence in criminal cases unless they have been recorded by electronic sound recording as provided in this subsection and the original records so taken have been certified by him and filed with the clerk as provided in this subsection. He shall also transcribe and certify such other parts of the record of proceedings as may be required by rule or order of court. Upon the request of any party to any proceeding which has been so recorded who has agreed to pay the fee therefor, or of a judge of the court, the reporter or other individual designated to produce the record shall promptly transcribe the original records of the requested parts of the proceedings and attach to the transcript his official certificate, and deliver the same to the party or judge making the request.

The reporter or other designated individual shall promptly deliver to the clerk for the records of the court a certified copy of any transcript so made.

The transcript in any case certified by the reporter or other individual designated to produce the record shall be deemed prima facie a correct statement of the testimony taken and proceedings had. No transcripts of the proceedings of the court shall be considered as official except those made from the records certified by the reporter or other individual designated to produce the record.

The original notes or other original records and the copy of the transcript in the office of the clerk shall be open during office hours to inspection by any person without charge.

(c) The reporters shall be subject to the supervision of the appointing court and the Judicial Conference in the performance of their duties, including dealings with parties requesting transcripts.

(d) The Judicial Conference shall prescribe records which shall be maintained and reports which shall be filed by the reporters. Such records shall be inspected and audited in the same manner as the records and accounts of clerks of the district courts, and may include records showing:

(1) the quantity of transcripts prepared;

(2) the fees charged and the fees collected for transcripts;

(3) any expenses incurred by the reporters in connection with transcripts;

(4) the amount of time the reporters are in attendance upon the courts for the purpose of recording proceedings; and

(5) such other information as the Judicial Conference may require.

(e) Each reporter shall receive an annual salary to be fixed from time to time by the Judicial Conference of the United States. All supplies shall be furnished by the reporter at his own expense.

(f) Each reporter may charge and collect fees for transcripts requested by the parties, including the United States, at rates prescribed by the court subject to the approval of the Judicial Conference. He shall not charge a fee for any copy of a transcript delivered to the clerk for the records of court. Fees for transcripts furnished in criminal proceedings to persons proceeding under the Criminal Justice Act (18 U.S.C. § 3006A), or in habeas corpus proceedings to persons allowed to sue, defend, or appeal in forma pauperis, shall be paid by the United States out of moneys appropriated for those purposes. Fees for transcripts furnished in proceedings brought under section 2255 of this title to persons permitted to sue or appeal in forma pauperis shall be paid by the United States out of money appropriated for that purpose if the trial judge or a circuit judge certifies that the suit or appeal is not frivolous and that the transcript is needed to decide the issue presented by the suit or appeal. Fees for transcripts furnished in other proceedings to persons permitted to appeal in forma pauperis shall also be paid by the United States if the trial judge or a circuit judge certifies that the appeal is not frivolous (but presents a substantial question). The reporter may require any party requesting a transcript to prepay the estimated fee in advance except as to transcripts that are to be paid for by the United States.

(g) If, upon the advice of the chief judge of any district court within the circuit, the judicial council of any circuit determines that the number of court reporters provided such district court pursuant to subsection (a) of this section is insufficient to meet temporary demands and needs and that the services of additional court reporters for such district court should be provided the judges of such district court (including the senior judges thereof when such senior judges are performing substantial judicial services for such court) on a contract basis, rather than by appointment of court reporters as otherwise provided in this section, and such judicial council notifies the Director of the Administrative Office, in writing, of such determination, the Director of the Administrative Office is authorized to and shall contract, without regard to section 3709 of the Revised Statutes of the United States, as amended (41 U.S.C. § 5), with any suitable person, firm, association, or corporation for the providing of court reporters to serve such district court under such terms and conditions as the Director of the Administrative Office finds, after consultation with the chief judge of the district court, will best serve the needs of such district court.

§ 754. Receivers of property in different districts

A receiver appointed in any civil action or proceeding involving property, real, personal or mixed, situated in different districts shall, upon giving bond as required by the court, be vested with complete jurisdiction and control of all such property with the right to take possession thereof.

He shall have capacity to sue in any district without ancillary appointment, and may be sued with respect thereto as provided in section 959 of this title.

Such receiver shall, within ten days after the entry of his order of appointment, file copies of the complaint and such order of appointment in the district court for each district in which property is located. The failure to file such copies in any district shall divest the receiver of jurisdiction and control over all such property in that district.

§ 755. Criers and bailiffs

Each district judge may appoint a crier for the court in which he presides who shall perform also the duties of bailiff and messenger. A crier may perform also the duties of law clerk if he is qualified to do so and the district judge who appointed him designates him to serve as a crier-law clerk. A crier designated to serve as a crier-law clerk shall receive the compensation of a law clerk, but only so much of that compensation as is in excess of the compensation to which he would be entitled as a crier shall be deemed the compensation of a law clerk for the purposes of any limitation imposed by law upon the aggregate salaries of law clerks and secretaries appointed by a district judge.

Each United States marshal may employ, with the approval of the judge, not exceeding four bailiffs as the district judge may determine, to attend the court, maintain order, wait upon the grand and petit juries, and perform such other necessary duties as the judge or marshal may direct.

Each bailiff shall be allowed for his services $6 a day to be paid only for actual attendance on days when the court is in session or the judge or jury is present.

If the position of crier or bailiff is to be filled by the appointment of a person who has not previously served as either crier or bailiff, preference in the appointment shall be given to a person who has served in the military or naval forces of the United States in time of war and who has been honorably discharged therefrom, if in the opinion of the appointing officer such person is as well qualified as any other available person to perform to the satisfaction of the appointing officer all the duties of the position.

§ 756. Power to appoint

Whenever a majority of the district judges of any district court cannot agree upon the appointment of any officer of such court, the chief judge shall make such appointment.

CHAPTER 50—BANKRUPTCY COURTS

See editorial note to Chapter 6, *supra*, p. 15.

CHAPTER 51—UNITED STATES CLAIMS COURT

§ 791. Clerk

(a) The United States Claims Court may appoint a clerk, who shall be subject to removal by the court. The clerk, with the approval of the court, may appoint necessary deputies and employees in such numbers as may be approved by the Director of the Administrative Office of the United States Courts. Such deputies and employees shall be subject to removal by the clerk with the approval of the court.

(b) The clerk shall pay into the Treasury all fees, costs and other moneys collected by him. He shall make returns thereof to the Director of the Administrative Office of the United States Courts under regulations prescribed by him.

(c) On the first day of every regular session of Congress, the clerk shall transmit to Congress a full and complete statement of all the judgments rendered by the court during the previous year, showing the dates and amounts thereof and the parties in whose favor they were rendered, together with a brief synopsis of the nature of the claims upon which they were rendered, and a statement of the costs taxed in each case.

[§ 792. Repealed.]

[§ 793. Repealed.]

§ 794. Law clerks and secretaries

The judges of the United States Claims Court may appoint necessary law clerks and secretaries, in such numbers as the Judicial Conference of the United States may approve, subject to any limitation of the aggregate salaries of such employees which may be imposed by law.

§ 795. Bailiffs and messengers

The chief judge of United States Claims Court, with the approval of the court, may appoint necessary bailiffs and messengers, in such numbers as the Director of the Administrative Office of the United States Courts may approve, each of whom shall be subject to removal by the chief judge, with the approval of the court.

§ 796. Reporting of court proceedings

Subject to the approval of the United States Claims Court, the Director of the Administrative Office of the United States Courts is authorized to contract for the reporting of all proceedings had in open court, and in such contract to fix the terms and conditions under which such reporting services shall be performed, including the terms and conditions under which transcripts shall be supplied by the contractor to the court and to other persons, departments, and agencies.

§ 797. Recall of retired judges

(a) Any judge of the United States Claims Court who has retired from regular active service under subchapter III of chapter 83 of title 5 shall be known and designated as a senior judge and may perform duties as a judge when recalled pursuant to subsection (b) of this section.

(b) The chief judge of the Claims Court may, whenever he deems it advisable, recall any senior judge, with such judge's consent, to perform such duties as a judge and for such period of time as the chief judge may specify.

(c) Any senior judge performing duties pursuant to this section shall not be counted as a judge for purposes of the number of judgeships authorized by section 171 of this title.

(d) Any senior judge, while performing duties pursuant to this section, shall be paid the same allowances for travel and other expenses as a judge in active service. Such senior judge shall also receive from the Claims Court supplemental pay in an amount sufficient, when added to his civil service retirement annuity, to equal the salary of a judge in active service for the same period or periods of time. Such supplemental pay shall be paid in the same manner as the salary of a judge.

CHAPTER 55—COURT OF INTERNATIONAL TRADE

§ 871. Clerk, chief deputy clerk, assistant clerk, deputies, assistants, and other employees

The Court of International Trade may appoint a clerk, a chief deputy clerk, an assistant clerk, deputy clerks, and such deputies, assistants, and other employees as may be necessary for the effective dispatch of the business of the court, who shall be subject to removal by the court.

§ 872. Marshal and deputy marshals

The Court of International Trade may appoint a marshal and deputy marshals, who shall be subject to removal by the court.

The marshal and his deputies shall attend court at its sessions, serve and execute all process and orders issued by it, and exercise the powers and perform the duties concerning all matters within such court's jurisdiction assigned to them by the court.

Under regulations prescribed by the Director of the Administrative Office of the United States Courts, the marshal shall pay the salaries, office expenses, and travel and subsistence allowances of the judges, officers, and employees of the court, and shall disburse funds appropriated for all expenses of the court.

On all disbursements made by the marshal of the Court of International Trade for official salaries or expenses, the certificate of the payee shall be sufficient without verification on oath.

§ 873. Criers, bailiffs, and messengers

The Court of International Trade may appoint such criers as it may require for said court, which criers shall also perform the duties of bailiffs and messengers and such other duties as the court directs and shall be subject to removal by the court.

CHAPTER 57—GENERAL PROVISIONS APPLICABLE TO COURT OFFICERS AND EMPLOYEES

§ 951. Oath of office of clerks and deputies

Each clerk of court and his deputies shall take the following oath or affirmation before entering upon their duties: "I, ——— ———, having been appointed ———, do solemnly swear (or affirm) that I will truly and faithfully enter and record all orders, decrees, judgments and proceedings of such court, and will faithfully and impartially discharge all other duties of my office according to the best of my abilities and understanding. So help me God."

[§ 952. Repealed.]

§ 953. Administration of oaths and acknowledgments

Each clerk of court and his deputies may administer oaths and affirmations and take acknowledgments.

§ 954. Death of clerk; duties of deputies

Upon the death of any clerk of court, his deputy or deputies shall execute the duties of the deceased clerk in his name until his successor is appointed and qualifies.

The compensation of a deceased clerk of the Supreme Court may be paid to his personal representatives until his successor is appointed and qualifies.

§ 955. Practice of law restricted

The clerk of each court and his deputies and assistants shall not practice law in any court of the United States.

§ 956. Powers and duties of clerks and deputies

The clerk of each court and his deputies and assistants shall exercise the powers and perform the duties assigned to them by the court.

§ 957. Clerks ineligible for certain offices

A clerk of a district court or any of his deputies shall not be appointed a commissioner, master, referee or receiver in any case, unless there are special reasons requiring such appointment which are recited in the order of appointment.

§ 958. Persons ineligible as receivers

A person holding any civil or military office or employment under the United States or employed by any justice or judge of the United States shall not at the same time be appointed a receiver in any case in any court of the United States.

§ 959. Trustees and receivers suable; management; State laws

(a) Trustees, receivers or managers of any property, including debtors in possession, may be sued, without leave of the court appointing them, with respect to any of their acts or transactions in carrying on business connected with such property. Such actions shall be subject to the general equity power of such court so far as the same may be necessary to the ends of justice, but this shall not deprive a litigant of his right to trial by jury.

(b) Except as provided in section 1166 of title 11, a trustee, receiver or manager appointed in any cause pending in any court of the United States, including a debtor in possession, shall manage and operate the property in his possession as such trustee, receiver or manager according to the requirements of the valid laws of the State in which such property is situated, in the same manner that the owner or possessor thereof would be bound to do if in possession thereof.

§ 960. Tax liability

Any officers and agents conducting any business under authority of a United States court shall be subject to all Federal, State and local taxes applicable to such business to the same extent as if it were conducted by an individual or corporation.

§ 961. Office expenses of clerks

Each clerk of court shall be allowed his necessary office expenses when authorized by the Director of the Administrative Office of the United States Courts.

[§ 962. Repealed.]

§ 963. Courts defined

As used in this chapter, unless the context indicates otherwise, the words "court" and "courts" include the Supreme Court of the United States and the courts enumerated in section 610 of this title.

PART IV—JURISDICTION AND VENUE

CHAPTER 81—SUPREME COURT

§ 1251. Original jurisdiction

(a) The Supreme Court shall have original and exclusive jurisdiction of all controversies between two or more States.

(b) The Supreme Court shall have original but not exclusive jurisdiction of:

(1) All actions or proceedings to which ambassadors, other public ministers, consuls, or vice consuls of foreign states are parties;

(2) All controversies between the United States and a State;

(3) All actions or proceedings by a State against the citizens of another State or against aliens.

§ 1252. Direct appeals from decisions invalidating Acts of Congress

Any party may appeal to the Supreme Court from an interlocutory or final judgment, decree or order of any court of the United States, the United States District Court for the District of the Canal Zone, the District Court of Guam and the District Court of the Virgin Islands and any court of record of Puerto Rico, holding an Act of Congress unconstitutional in any civil action, suit, or proceeding to which the United States or any of its agencies, or any officer or employee thereof, as such officer or employee, is a party.

A party who has received notice of appeal under this section shall take any subsequent appeal or cross appeal to the Supreme Court.

All appeals or cross appeals taken to other courts prior to such notice shall be treated as taken directly to the Supreme Court.

§ 1253. Direct appeals from decisions of three-judge courts

Except as otherwise provided by law, any party may appeal to the Supreme Court from an order granting or denying, after notice and hearing, an interlocutory or permanent injunction in any civil action, suit or proceeding required by any Act of Congress to be heard and determined by a district court of three judges.

§ 1254. Courts of appeals; certiorari; appeal; certified questions

Cases in the courts of appeals may be reviewed by the Supreme Court by the following methods:

(1) By writ of certiorari granted upon the petition of any party to any civil or criminal case, before or after rendition of judgment or decree;

(2) By appeal by a party relying on a State statute held by a court of appeals to be invalid as repugnant to the Constitution, treaties or laws of the United States, but such appeal shall preclude review by writ of certiorari at the instance of such appellant, and the review on appeal shall be restricted to the Federal questions presented;

(3) By certification at any time by a court of appeals of any question of law in any civil or criminal case as to which instructions are desired, and upon such certification the Supreme Court may give binding instructions or require the entire record to be sent up for decision of the entire matter in controversy.

[§ 1255. Repealed.]

[§ 1256. Repealed.]

§ 1257. State courts; appeal; certiorari

Final judgments or decrees rendered by the highest court of a State in which a decision could be had, may be reviewed by the Supreme Court as follows:

(1) By appeal, where is drawn in question the validity of a treaty or statute of the United States and the decision is against its validity.

(2) By appeal, where is drawn in question the validity of a statute of any state on the ground of its being repugnant to the Constitution, treaties or laws of the United States, and the decision is in favor of its validity.

(3) By writ of certiorari, where the validity of a treaty or statute of the United States is drawn in question or where the validity of a State statute is drawn in question on the ground of its being repugnant to the Constitution, treaties or laws of the United States, or where any title, right, privilege or immunity is specially set up or claimed under the Constitution, treaties or statutes of, or commission held or authority exercised under, the United States.

For the purposes of this section, the term "highest court of a State" includes the District of Columbia Court of Appeals.

§ 1258. Supreme Court of Puerto Rico; appeal; certiorari

Final judgments or decrees rendered by the Supreme Court of the Commonwealth of Puerto Rico may be reviewed by the Supreme Court as follows:

(1) By appeal, where is drawn in question the validity of a treaty or statute of the United States and the decision is against its validity.

(2) By appeal, where is drawn in question the validity of a statute of the Commonwealth of Puerto Rico on the ground of its being repugnant to the Constitution, treaties, or laws of the United States, and the decision is in favor of its validity.

(3) By writ of certiorari, where the validity of a treaty or statute of the United States is drawn in question or where the validity of a statute of the Commonwealth of Puerto Rico is drawn in question on the ground of its being repugnant to the Constitution, treaties, or laws of the United States, or where any title, right, privilege, or immunity is specially set up or claimed under the Constitution, treaties, or statutes of, or commission held or authority exercised under, the United States.

CHAPTER 83—COURTS OF APPEALS

§ 1291. Final decisions of district courts

The courts of appeals (other than the United States Court of Appeal for the Federal Circuit) shall have jurisdiction of appeals from all final decisions of the district courts of the United States, the United States District Court for the District of the Canal Zone, the District Court of Guam, and the District Court of the Virgin Islands, except where a direct review may be had in the Supreme Court. The jurisdiction of the United States Court of Appeals for the Federal Circuit shall be limited to the jurisdiction described in sections 1292 (c) and (d) and 1295 of this title.

§ 1292. Interlocutory decisions

(a) Except as provided in subsections (c) and (d) of this section, the courts of appeals shall have jurisdiction of appeals from:

(1) Interlocutory orders of the district courts of the United States, the United States District Court for the District of the

Canal Zone, the District Court of Guam, and the District Court of the Virgin Islands, or of the judges thereof, granting, continuing, modifying, refusing or dissolving injunctions, or refusing to dissolve or modify injunctions, except where a direct review may be had in the Supreme Court;

(2) Interlocutory orders appointing receivers, or refusing orders to wind up receiverships or to take steps to accomplish the purposes thereof, such as directing sales or other disposals of property;

(3) Interlocutory decrees of such district courts on the judges thereof determining the rights and liabilities of the parties to admiralty cases in which appeals from final decrees are allowed.

(b) When a district judge, in making in a civil action an order not otherwise appealable under this section, shall be of the opinion that such order involves a controlling question of law as to which there is substantial ground for difference of opinion and that an immediate appeal from the order may materially advance the ultimate termination of the litigation, he shall so state in writing in such order. The Court of Appeals may thereupon, in its discretion, permit an appeal to be taken from such order, if application is made to it within ten days after the entry of the order: *Provided, however,* That application for an appeal hereunder shall not stay proceedings in the district court unless the district judge or the Court of Appeals or a judge thereof shall so order.

(c) The United States Court of Appeals for the Federal Circuit shall have exclusive jurisdiction—

(1) of an appeal from an interlocutory order or decree described in subsection (a) of this section in any case over which the court would have jurisdiction of an appeal under section 1295 of this title; and

(2) of an appeal from a judgment in a civil action for patent infringement which would otherwise be appealable to the United States Court of Appeals for the Federal Circuit and is final except for an accounting.

(d)(1) When the chief judge of the Court of International Trade issues an order under the provisions of section 256(b) of this title, or when any judge of the Court of International Trade, in issuing any other interlocutory order, includes in the order a statement that a controlling question of law is involved with respect to which there is a substantial ground for difference of opinion and that an immediate appeal from that order may materially advance the ultimate termination of the litigation, the United States Court of Appeals for the Federal Circuit may, in its discretion, permit an appeal to be taken from such order, if application is made to that Court within ten days after the entry of such order.

(2) When any judge of the United States Claims Court, in issuing an interlocutory order, includes in the order a statement that a

controlling question of law is involved with respect to which there is a substantial ground for difference of opinion and that an immediate appeal from that order may materially advance the ultimate termination of the litigation, the United States Court of Appeals for the Federal Circuit may, in its discretion, permit an appeal to be taken from such order, if application is made to that Court within ten days after the entry of such order.

(3) Neither the application for nor the granting of an appeal under this subsection shall stay proceedings in the Court of International Trade or in the Claims Court, as the case may be, unless a stay is ordered by a judge of the Court of International Trade or of the Claims Court or by the United States Court of Appeals for the Federal Circuit or a judge of that court.

[§ 1293. Repealed.]

§ 1294. Circuits in which decisions reviewable

Except as provided in sections 1292(c), 1292(d), and 1295 of this title, appeals from reviewable decisions of the district and territorial courts shall be taken to the courts of appeals as follows:

(1) From a district court of the United States to the court of appeals for the circuit embracing the district;

(2) From the United States District Court for the District of the Canal Zone, to the Court of Appeals for the Fifth Circuit;

(3) From the District Court of the Virgin Islands, to the Court of Appeals for the Third Circuit;

(4) From the District Court of Guam, to the Court of Appeals for the Ninth Circuit.

§ 1295. Jurisdiction of the United States Court of Appeals for the Federal Circuit

(a) The United States Court of Appeals for the Federal Circuit shall have exclusive jurisdiction—

(1) of an appeal from a final decision of a district court of the United States, the United States District Court for the District of the Canal Zone, the District Court of Guam, the District Court of the Virgin Islands, or the District Court for the Northern Mariana Islands, if the jurisdiction of that court was based, in whole or in part, on section 1338 of this title, except that a case involving a claim arising under any Act of Congress relating to copyrights or trademarks and no other claims under section 1338(a) shall be governed by sections 1291, 1292, and 1294 of this title;

(2) of an appeal from a final decision of a district court of the United States, the United States District Court for the District of the Canal Zone, the District Court of Guam, the District Court of the Virgin Islands, or the District Court for the Northern Mariana Islands, if the jurisdiction of that court was

based, in whole or in part, on section 1346 of this title, except that jurisdiction of an appeal in a case brought in a district court under section 1346(a)(1), 1346(b), 1346(e), or 1346(f) of this title or under section 1346(a)(2) when the claim is founded upon an Act of Congress or a regulation of an executive department providing for internal revenue shall be governed by sections 1291, 1292, and 1294 of this title;

(3) of an appeal from a final decision of the United States Claims Court;

(4) of an appeal from a decision of—

(A) the Board of Appeals or the Board of Patent Interferences of the Patent and Trademark Office with respect to patent applications and interferences, at the instance of an applicant for a patent or any party to a patent interference, and any such appeal shall waive the right of such applicant or party to proceed under section 145 or 146 of title 35;

(B) the Commissioner of Patents and Trademarks or the Trademark Trial and Appeal Board with respect to applications for registration of marks and other proceedings as provided in section 21 of the Trademark Act of 1946 (15 U.S.C. 1071); or

(C) a district court to which a case was directed pursuant to section 145 or 146 of title 35;

(5) of an appeal from a final decision of the United States Court of International Trade;

(6) to review the final determinations of the United States International Trade Commission relating to unfair practices in import trade, made under section 337 of the Tariff Act of 1930 (19 U.S.C. 1337);

(7) to review, by appeal on questions of law only, findings of the Secretary of Commerce under headnote 6 to schedule 8, part 4, of the Tariff Schedules of the United States (relating to importation of instruments or apparatus);

(8) of an appeal under section 71 of the Plant Variety Protection Act (7 U.S.C. 2461);

(9) of an appeal from a final order or final decision of the Merit Systems Protection Board, pursuant to sections 7703(b)(1) and 7703(d) of title 5; and

(10) of an appeal from a final decision of an agency board of contract appeals pursuant to section 8(g)(1) of the Contract Disputes Act of 1978 (41 U.S.C. 607(g)(1)).

(b) The head of any executive department or agency may, with the approval of the Attorney General, refer to the Court of Appeals for the Federal Circuit for judicial review of any final decision rendered by a board of contract appeals pursuant to the terms of any contract with the United States awarded by that department or agency which the head of such department or agency has concluded is not entitled to finality pursuant to the review standards specified in section 10(b) of the Contract Disputes Act of 1978 (41 U.S.C. 609(b)). The head of each executive department or agency shall make any referral under this section within one hundred and twenty days after the receipt of a copy of the final appeal decision.

(c) The Court of Appeals for the Federal Circuit shall review the matter referred in accordance with the standards specified in section 10(b) of the Contract Disputes Act of 1978. The court shall proceed with judicial review on the administrative record made before the board of contract appeals on matters so referred as in other cases pending in such court, shall determine the issue of finality of the appeal decision, and shall, if appropriate, render judgment thereon, or remand the matter to any administrative or executive body or official with such direction as it may deem proper and just.

§ 1296. Precedence of cases in the United States Court of Appeals for the Federal Circuit

Civil actions in the United States Court of Appeals for the Federal Circuit shall be given precedence, in accordance with the law applicable to such actions, in such order as the court may by rule establish.

CHAPTER 85—DISTRICT COURTS; JURISDICTION

Sec.

§ 1330. Actions against foreign states

(a) The district courts shall have original jurisdiction without regard to amount in controversy of any nonjury civil action against a foreign state as defined in section 1603(a) of this title as to any claim for relief in personam with respect to which the foreign state is not entitled to immunity either under sections 1605–1607 of this title or under any applicable international agreement.

(b) Personal jurisdiction over a foreign state shall exist as to every claim for relief over which the district courts have jurisdiction under subsection (a) where service has been made under section 1608 of this title.

(c) For purposes of subsection (b), an appearance by a foreign state does not confer personal jurisdiction with respect to any claim for relief not arising out of any transaction or occurrence enumerated in sections 1605–1607 of this title.

§ 1331. Federal question; amount in controversy; costs

The district courts shall have original jurisdiction of all civil actions arising under the Constitution, laws, or treaties of the United States.

* [Ed.] The triplicate designations seem to represent a drafting error that has not yet been corrected.

§ 1332. Diversity of citizenship; amount in controversy; costs

(a) The district courts shall have original jurisdiction of all civil actions where the matter in controversy exceeds the sum or value of $10,000, exclusive of interest and costs, and is between—

(1) citizens of different States;

(2) citizens of a State and citizens or subjects of a foreign state;

(3) citizens of different States and in which citizens or subjects of a foreign state are additional parties; and

(4) a foreign state, defined in section 1603(a) of this title, as plaintiff and citizens of a State or of different States.

(b) Except when express provision therefor is otherwise made in a statute of the United States, where the plaintiff who files the case originally in the Federal courts is finally adjudged to be entitled to recover less than the sum or value of $10,000, computed without regard to any setoff or counterclaim to which the defendant may be adjudged to be entitled, and exclusive of interest and costs, the district court may deny costs to the plaintiff and, in addition, may impose costs on the plaintiff.

(c) For the purposes of this section and section 1441 of this title, a corporation shall be deemed a citizen of any State by which it has been incorporated and of the State where it has its principal place of business: *Provided further*, That in any direct action against the insurer of a policy or contract of liability insurance, whether incorporated or unincorporated, to which action the insured is not joined as a party-defendant, such insurer shall be deemed a citizen of the State of which the insured is a citizen, as well as of any State by which the insurer has been incorporated and of the State where it has its principal place of business.

(d) The word "States", as used in this section, includes the Territories, the District of Columbia, and the Commonwealth of Puerto Rico.

§ 1333. Admiralty, maritime and prize cases

The district courts shall have original jurisdiction, exclusive of the courts of the States, of:

(1) Any civil case of admiralty or maritime jurisdiction, saving to suitors in all cases all other remedies to which they are otherwise entitled.

(2) Any prize brought into the United States and all proceedings for the condemnation of property taken as prize. As amended May 24, 1949, 63 Stat. 101.

§ 1334. Bankruptcy matters and proceedings

The district courts shall have original jurisdiction, exclusive of the courts of the States, of all matters and proceedings in bankruptcy.

§ 1335. Interpleader

(a) The district courts shall have original jurisdiction of any civil action of interpleader or in the nature of interpleader filed by any person, firm, or corporation, association, or society having in his or its custody or possession money or property of the value of $500 or more, or having issued a note, bond, certificate, policy of insurance, or other instrument of value or amount of $500 or more, or providing for the delivery or payment or the loan of money or property of such amount or value, or being under any obligation written or unwritten to the amount of $500 or more, if

(1) Two or more adverse claimants, of diverse citizenship as defined in section 1332 of this title, are claiming or may claim to be entitled to such money or property, or to any one or more of the benefits arising by virtue of any note, bond, certificate, policy or other instrument, or arising by virtue of any such obligation; and if (2) the plaintiff has deposited such money or property or has paid the amount of or the loan or other value of such instrument or the amount due under such obligation into the registry of the court, there to abide the judgment of the court, or has given bond payable to the clerk of the court in such amount and with such surety as the court or judge may deem proper, conditioned upon the compliance by the plaintiff with the future order or judgment of the court with respect to the subject matter of the controversy.

(b) Such an action may be entertained although the titles or claims of the conflicting claimants do not have a common origin, or are not identical, but are adverse to and independent of one another.

§ 1336. Interstate Commerce Commission's orders

(a) Except as otherwise provided by Act of Congress, the district courts shall have jurisdiction of any civil action to enforce, in whole or in part, any order of the Interstate Commerce Commission, and to enjoin or suspend, in whole or in part, any order of the Interstate Commerce Commission for the payment of money or the collection of fines, penalties, and forfeitures.

(b) When a district court or the United States Claims Court refers a question or issue to the Interstate Commerce Commission for determination, the court which referred the question or issue shall have exclusive jurisdiction of a civil action to enforce, enjoin, set aside, annul, or suspend, in whole or in part, any order of the Interstate Commerce Commission arising out of such referral.

(c) Any action brought under subsection (b) of this section shall be filed within 90 days from the date that the order of the Interstate Commerce Commission becomes final.

§ 1337. Commerce and antitrust regulations; amount in controversy, costs

(a) The district courts shall have original jurisdiction of any civil action or proceeding arising under any Act of Congress regulating commerce or protecting trade and commerce against restraints and monopolies: *Provided, however,* That the district courts shall have original jurisdiction of an action brought under section 11707 of title 49, only if the matter in controversy for each receipt or bill of lading exceeds $10,000, exclusive of interest and costs.

(b) Except when express provision therefor is otherwise made in a statute of the United States, where a plainiff who files the case under section 11707 of title 49 originally in the Federal courts is finally adjudged to be entitled to recover less than the sum or value of $10,000, computed without regard to any setoff or counterclaim to which the defendant may be adjudged to be entitled, and exclusive of any interest and costs, the district court may deny costs to the plaintiff and, in addition, may impose costs on the plaintiff.

(c) The district courts shall not have jurisdiction under this section of any matter within the exclusive jurisdiction of the Court of International Trade under chapter 95 of this title.

§ 1338. Patents, plant variety protection, copyrights, trade-marks and unfair competition

(a) The district courts shall have original jurisdiction of any civil action arising under any Act of Congress relating to patents, plant variety protection, copyrights and trade-marks. Such jurisdiction shall be exclusive of the courts of the states in patent, plant variety protection and copyright cases.

(b) The district courts shall have original jurisdiction of any civil action asserting a claim of unfair competition when joined with a substantial and related claim under the copyright, patent, plant variety protection, or trade-mark laws.

§ 1339. Postal matters

The district courts shall have original jurisdiction of any civil action arising under any Act of Congress relating to the postal service.

§ 1340. Internal revenue; customs duties

The district courts shall have original jurisdiction of any civil action arising under any Act of Congress providing for internal revenue, or revenue from imports or tonnage except matters within the jurisdiction of the Court of International Trade.

§ 1341. Taxes by States

The district courts shall not enjoin, suspend or restrain the assessment, levy or collection of any tax under State law where a plain, speedy and efficient remedy may be had in the courts of such State.

§ 1342. Rate orders of State agencies

The district courts shall not enjoin, suspend or restrain the operation of, or compliance with, any order affecting rates chargeable by a public utility and made by a State administrative agency or a rate-making body of a State political subdivision, where:

(1) Jurisdiction is based solely on diversity of citizenship or repugnance of the order to the Federal Constitution; and,

(2) The order does not interfere with interstate commerce; and,

(3) The order has been made after reasonable notice and hearing; and,

(4) A plain, speedy and efficient remedy may be had in the courts of such State.

§ 1343. Civil rights and elective franchise

(a) The district courts shall have original jurisdiction of any civil action authorized by law to be commenced by any person:

(1) To recover damages for injury to his person or property, or because of the deprivation of any right or privilege of a citizen of the United States, by any act done in furtherance of any conspiracy mentioned in section 1985 of Title 42;

(2) To recover damages from any person who fails to prevent or to aid in preventing any wrongs mentioned in section 1985 of Title 42 which he had knowledge were about to occur and power to prevent;

(3) To redress the deprivation, under color of any State law, statute, ordinance, regulation, custom or usage, of any right, privilege or immunity secured by the Constitution of the United States or by any Act of Congress providing for equal rights of citizens or of all persons within the jurisdiction of the United States;

(4) To recover damages or to secure equitable or other relief under any Act of Congress providing for the protection of civil rights, including the right to vote.

(b) For purposes of this section—

(1) the District of Columbia shall be considered to be a State; and

(2) any Act of Congress applicable exclusively to the District of Columbia shall be considered to be a statute of the District of Columbia.

§ 1344. Election disputes

The district courts shall have original jurisdiction of any civil action to recover possession of any office, except that of elector of President or Vice President, United States Senator, Representative in or delegate to Congress, or member of a state legislature, authorized by law to be commenced, wherein it appears that the sole question touching the title to office arises out of denial of the right to vote, to any citizen offering to vote, on account of race, color or previous condition of servitude.

The jurisdiction under this section shall extend only so far as to determine the rights of the parties to office by reason of the denial of the right, guaranteed by the Constitution of the United States and secured by any law, to enforce the right of citizens of the United States to vote in all the States.

§ 1345. United States as plaintiff

Except as otherwise provided by Act of Congress, the district courts shall have original jurisdiction of all civil actions, suits or proceedings commenced by the United States, or by any agency or officer thereof expressly authorized to sue by Act of Congress.

§ 1346. United States as defendant

(a) The district courts shall have original jurisdiction, concurrent with the United States Claims Court, of:

(1) Any civil action against the United States for the recovery of any internal-revenue tax alleged to have been erroneously or illegally assessed or collected, or any penalty claimed to have been collected without authority or any sum alleged to have been excessive or in any manner wrongfully collected under the internal-revenue laws;

(2) Any other civil action or claim against the United States, not exceeding $10,000 in amount, founded either upon the Constitution, or any Act of Congress, or any regulation of an executive department, or upon any express or implied contract with the United States, or for liquidated or unliquidated damages in cases not sounding in tort, except that the district courts shall not have jurisdiction of any civil action or claim against the United States founded upon any express or implied contract with the United States or for liquidated or unliquidated damages in cases not sounding in tort which are subject to sections 8(g)(1) and 10(a)(1) of the Contract Disputes Act of 1978. For the purpose of this paragraph, an express or implied contract with the Army and Air Force Exchange Service, Navy Exchanges, Marine Corps Exchanges, Coast Guard Exchanges, or Exchange Councils of the National Aeronautics and Space Administration shall be considered an express or implied contract with the United States.

(b) Subject to the provisions of chapter 171 of this title, the district courts, together with the United States District Court for the District of the Canal Zone and the District Court of the Virgin Islands, shall have exclusive jurisdiction of civil actions on claims against the United States, for money damages, accruing on and after January 1, 1945, for injury or loss of property, or personal injury or death caused by the negligent or wrongful act or omission of any employee of the Government while acting within the scope of his office or employment, under circumstances where the United States, if a private person, would be liable to the claimant in accordance with the law of the place where the act or omission occurred.

(c) The jurisdiction conferred by this section includes jurisdiction of any set-off, counterclaim, or other claim or demand whatever on the part of the United States against any plaintiff commencing an action under this section.

(d) The district courts shall not have jurisdiction under this section of any civil action or claim for a pension.

(e) The district courts shall have original jurisdiction of any civil action against the United States provided in section 6226, 6228(a), 7426, or 7428 (in the case of the United States district court for the District of Columbia) of the Internal Revenue Code of 1954.

(f) The district courts shall have exclusive original jurisdiction of civil actions under section 2409a to quiet title to an estate or interest in real property in which an interest is claimed by the United States.

§ 1347. Partition action where United States is joint tenant

The district courts shall have original jurisdiction of any civil action commenced by any tenant in common or joint tenant for the partition of lands where the United States is one of the tenants in common or joint tenants.

§ 1348. Banking association as party

The district courts shall have original jurisdiction of any civil action commenced by the United States, or by direction of any officer thereof, against any national banking association, any civil action to wind up the affairs of any such association, and any action by a banking association established in the district for which the court is held, under chapter 2 of Title 12, to enjoin the Comptroller of the Currency, or any receiver acting under his direction, as provided by such chapter.

All national banking associations shall, for the purposes of all other actions by or against them, be deemed citizens of the States in which they are respectively located.

§ 1349. Corporation organized under federal law as party

The district courts shall not have jurisdiction of any civil action by or against any corporation upon the ground that it was incorporated by or under an Act of Congress, unless the United States is the owner of more than one-half of its capital stock.

§ 1350. Alien's action for tort

The district courts shall have original jurisdiction of any civil action by an alien for a tort only, committed in violation of the law of nations or a treaty of the United States.

§ 1351. Consuls, vice consuls, and members of a diplomatic mission as defendant

The district courts shall have original jurisdiction, exclusive of the courts of the States, of all civil actions and proceedings against—

(1) consuls or vice consuls of foreign states; or

(2) members of a mission or members of their families (as such terms are defined in section 2 of the Diplomatic Relations Act).

§ 1352. Bonds executed under federal law

The district courts shall have original jurisdiction, concurrent with State courts, of any action on a bond executed under any law of the United States, except matters within the jurisdiction of the Court of International Trade under section 1582 of this title.

§ 1353. Indian allotments

The district courts shall have original jurisdiction of any civil action involving the right of any person, in whole or in part of Indian blood or descent, to any allotment of land under any Act of Congress or treaty.

The judgment in favor of any claimant to an allotment of land shall have the same effect, when properly certified to the Secretary of the Interior, as if such allotment had been allowed and approved by him; but this provision shall not apply to any lands held on or before December 21, 1911, by either of the Five Civilized Tribes, the Osage Nation of Indians, nor to any of the lands within the Quapaw Indian Agency.

§ 1354. Land grants from different states

The district courts shall have original jurisdiction of actions between citizens of the same state claiming lands under grants from different states.

§ 1355. Fine, penalty or forfeiture

The district courts shall have original jurisdiction, exclusive of the courts of the States, of any action or proceeding for the recovery or enforcement of any fine, penalty, or forfeiture, pecuniary or otherwise, incurred under any Act of Congress, except matters within the jurisdiction of the Court of International Trade under section 1582 of this title.

§ 1356. Seizures not within admiralty and maritime jurisdiction

The district courts shall have original jurisdiction, exclusive of the courts of the States, of any seizure under any law of the United States on land or upon waters not within admiralty and maritime jurisdiction, except matters within the jurisdiction of the Court of International Trade under section 1582 of this title.

§ 1357. Injuries under Federal laws

The district courts shall have original jurisdiction of any civil action commenced by any person to recover damages for any injury to his person or property on account of any act done by him, under any Act of Congress, for the protection or collection of any of the revenues, or to enforce the right of citizens of the United States to vote in any State.

§ 1358. Eminent domain

The district courts shall have original jurisdiction of all proceedings to condemn real estate for the use of the United States or its departments or agencies.

§ 1359. Parties collusively joined or made

A district court shall not have jurisdiction of a civil action in which any party, by assignment or otherwise, has been improperly or collusively made or joined to invoke the jurisdiction of such court.

§ 1360. State civil jurisdiction in actions to which Indians are parties

(a) Each of the States or Territories listed in the following table shall have jurisdiction over civil causes of action between Indians or to which Indians are parties which arise in the areas of Indian country listed opposite the name of the State or Territory to the same extent that such State or Territory has jurisdiction over other civil causes of action, and those civil laws of such State or Territory that are of general application to private persons or private property shall have the same force and effect within such Indian country as they have elsewhere within the State or Territory:

State or Territory of	Indian country affected
Alaska	All Indian country within the Territory [*sic.*]*
California	All Indian country within the State
Minnesota	All Indian country within the State, except the Red Lake Reservation
Nebraska	All Indian country within the State
Oregon	All Indian country within the State, except the Warm Springs Reservation
Wisconsin	All Indian country within the State

(b) Nothing in this section shall authorize the alienation, encumbrance, or taxation of any real or personal property, including water rights, belonging to any Indian or any Indian tribe, band, or community that is held in trust by the United States or is subject to a restriction against alienation imposed by the United States; or shall authorize regulation of the use of such property in a manner inconsistent with any Federal treaty, agreement, or statute or with any regulation made pursuant thereto; or shall confer jurisdiction upon the State to adjudicate, in probate proceedings or otherwise, the ownership or right to possession of such property or any interest therein.

(c) Any tribal ordinance or custom heretofore or hereafter adopted by an Indian tribe, band, or community in the exercise of any authority which it may possess shall, if not inconsistent with any applicable civil law of the State, be given full force and effect in the determination of civil causes of action pursuant to this section.

§ 1361. Action to compel an officer of the United States to perform his duty

The district courts shall have original jurisdiction of any action in the nature of mandamus to compel an officer or employee of the

* An amendment effective April 1, 1984 strikes out "Territory" and substitutes "State."

United States or any agency thereof to perform a duty owed to the plaintiff.

§ 1362. Indian tribes

The district courts shall have original jurisdiction of all civil actions, brought by any Indian tribe or band with a governing body duly recognized by the Secretary of the Interior, wherein the matter in controversy arises under the Constitution, laws, or treaties of the United States.

§ 1363. Jurors' employment rights

The district courts shall have original jurisdiction of any civil action brought for the protection of jurors' employment under section 1875 of this title.

§ 1364.* Construction of references to laws of the United States or Acts of Congress

For the purposes of this chapter, references to laws of the United States or Acts of Congress do not include laws applicable exclusively to the District of Columbia.

§ 1364.* Direct actions against insurers of members of diplomatic missions and their families

(a) The district courts shall have original and exclusive jurisdiction, without regard to the amount in controversy, of any civil action commenced by any person against an insurer who by contract has insured an individual, who is a member of a mission (within the meaning of section 2(3)) of the Diplomatic Relations Act (22 U.S.C. 254a(3)) or a member of the family of such a member of a mission, or an individual described in section 19 of the Convention on Privileges and Immunities of the United Nations of February 13, 1946, against liability for personal injury, death, or damage to property.

(b) Any direct action brought against an insurer under subsection (a) shall be tried without a jury, but shall not be subject to the defense that the insured is immune from suit, that the insured is an indispensable party, or in the absence of fraud or collusion, that the insured has violated a term of the contract, unless the contract was cancelled before the claim arose.

§ 1364.* Senate actions

(a) The United States District Court for the District of Columbia shall have original jurisdiction, without regard to the amount in controversy, over any civil action brought by the Senate or any authorized committee or subcommittee of the Senate to enforce, to secure a declaratory judgment concerning the validity of, or to prevent a threatened refusal or failure to comply with, any subpena or order issued by the Senate or committee or subcommittee of the Senate to any entity acting or purporting to act under color or authority of State law or to any natural person to secure the production

* As noted above, the triplicate designations seem to represent a drafting error that apparently has not yet been corrected.

of documents or other materials of any kind or the answering of any deposition or interrogatory or to secure testimony or any combination thereof. This section shall not apply to an action to enforce, to secure a declaratory judgment concerning the validity of, or to prevent a threatened refusal to comply with, any subpena or order issued to an officer or employee of the Federal Government acting within his official capacity.

(b) Upon application by the Senate or any authorized committee or subcommittee of the Senate, the district court shall issue an order to an entity or person refusing, or failing to comply with, or threatening to refuse or not to comply with, a subpena or order of the Senate or committee or subcommittee of the Senate requiring such entity or person to comply forthwith. Any refusal or failure to obey a lawful order of the district court issued pursuant to this section may be held by such court to be a contempt thereof. A contempt proceeding shall be commenced by an order to show cause before the court why the entity or person refusing or failing to obey the court order should not be held in contempt of court. Such contempt proceeding shall be tried by the court and shall be summary in manner. The purpose of sanctions imposed as a result of such contempt proceeding shall be to compel obedience to the order of the court. Process in any such action or contempt proceeding may be served in any judicial district wherein the entity or party refusing, or failing to comply, or threatening to refuse or not to comply, resides, transacts business, or may be found, and subpenas for witnesses who are required to attend such proceeding may run into any other district. Nothing in this section shall confer upon such court jurisdiction to affect by injunction or otherwise the issuance or effect of any subpena or order of the Senate or any committee or subcommittee of the Senate or to review, modify, suspend, terminate, or set aside any such subpena or order. An action, contempt proceeding, or sanction brought or imposed pursuant to this section shall not abate upon adjournment sine die by the Senate at the end of a Congress if the Senate or the committee or subcommittee of the Senate which issued the subpena or order certifies to the court that it maintains its interest in securing the documents, answers, or testimony during such adjournment.

(c) In any civil action or contempt proceeding brought pursuant to this section, the court shall assign the action or proceeding for hearing at the earliest practicable date and cause the action or proceeding in every way to be expedited. Any appeal or petition for review from any order or judgment in such action or proceeding shall be expedited in the same manner.

(d) The Senate or any committee or subcommittee of the Senate commencing and prosecuting a civil action or contempt proceeding under this section may be represented in such action by such attorneys as the Senate may designate.

(e) A civil action commenced or prosecuted under this section, may not be authorized pursuant to the Standing Order of the Senate "authorizing suits by Senate Committees" (S.Jour. 572, May 28, 1928).

(f) For the purposes of this section the term "committee" includes standing, select, or special committees of the Senate established by law or resolution.

CHAPTER 87—DISTRICT COURTS; VENUE

§ 1391. Venue generally

(a) A civil action wherein jurisdiction is founded only on diversity of citizenship may, except as otherwise provided by law, be brought only in the judicial district where all plaintiffs or all defendants reside, or in which the claim arose.

(b) A civil action wherein jurisdiction is not founded solely on diversity of citizenship may be brought only in the judicial district where all defendants reside, or in which the claim arose, except as otherwise provided by law.

(c) A corporation may be sued in any judicial district in which it is incorporated or licensed to do business or is doing business, and such judicial district shall be regarded as the residence of such corporation for venue purposes.

(d) An alien may be sued in any district.

(e) A civil action in which a defendant is an officer or employee of the United States or any agency thereof acting in his official capacity or under color of legal authority, or an agency of the United States, or the United States, may, except as otherwise provided by law, be brought in any judicial district in which (1) a defendant in the action resides, or (2) the cause of action arose, or (3) any real property involved in the action is situated, or (4) the plaintiff resides if no real property is involved in the action. Additional persons may be joined as parties to any such action in accordance with the Federal Rules of Civil Procedure and with such other venue requirements as would be applicable if the United States or one of its officers, employees, or agencies were not a party.

The summons and complaint in such an action shall be served as provided by the Federal Rules of Civil Procedure except that the delivery of the summons and complaint to the officer or agency as required by the rules may be made by certified mail beyond the territorial limits of the district in which the action is brought.

(f) A civil action against a foreign state as defined in section 1603 (a) of this title may be brought—

(1) in any judicial district in which a substantial part of the events or omissions giving rise to the claim occurred, or a substantial part of property that is the subject of the action is situated;

(2) in any judicial district in which the vessel or cargo of a foreign state is situated, if the claim is asserted under section 1605(b) of this title;

(3) in any judicial district in which the agency or instrumentality is licensed to do business or is doing business, if the action is brought against an agency or instrumentality of a foreign state as defined in section 1603(b) of this title; or

(4) in the United States District Court for the District of Columbia if the action is brought against a foreign state or political subdivision thereof.

§ 1392. Defendants or property in different districts in same State

(a) Any civil action, not of a local nature, against defendants residing in different districts in the same State, may be brought in any of such districts.

(b) Any civil action, of a local nature, involving property located in different districts in the same State, may be brought in any of such districts.

§ 1393. Divisions; single defendant; defendants in different divisions

(a) Except as otherwise provided, any civil action, not of a local nature, against a single defendant in a district containing more than one division must be brought in the division where he resides.

(b) Any such action, against defendants residing in different divisions of the same district or different districts in the same State, may be brought in any of such divisions.

§ 1394. Banking association's action against Comptroller of Currency

Any civil action by a national banking association to enjoin the Comptroller of the Currency, under the provisions of any Act of Congress relating to such associations, may be prosecuted in the judicial district where such association is located.

§ 1395. Fine, penalty or forfeiture

(a) A civil proceeding for the recovery of a pecuniary fine, penalty or forfeiture may be prosecuted in the district where it accrues or the defendant is found.

(b) A civil proceeding for the forfeiture of property may be prosecuted in any district where such property is found.

(c) A civil proceeding for the forfeiture of property seized outside any judicial district may be prosecuted in any district into which the property is brought.

(d) A proceeding in admiralty for the enforcement of fines, penalties and forfeitures against a vessel may be brought in any district in which the vessel is arrested.

(e) Any proceeding for the forfeiture of a vessel or cargo entering a port of entry closed by the President in pursuance of law, or of goods and chattels coming from a State or section declared by proclamation of the President to be in insurrection, or of any vessel or vehicle conveying persons or property to or from such State or section or belonging in whole or in part to a resident thereof, may be prosecuted in any district into which the property is taken and in which the proceeding is instituted.

§ 1396. Internal revenue taxes

Any civil action for the collection of internal revenue taxes may be brought in the district where the liability for such tax accrues, in the district of the taxpayer's residence, or in the district where the return was filed.

§ 1397. Interpleader

Any civil action of interpleader or in the nature of interpleader under section 1335 of this title may be brought in the judicial district in which one or more of the claimants reside.

§ 1398. Interstate Commerce Commission's orders

(a) Except as otherwise provided by law, a civil action brought under section 1336(a) of this title shall be brought only in a judicial district in which any of the parties bringing the action resides or has its principal office.

(b) A civil action to enforce, enjoin, set aside, annul, or suspend, in whole or in part, an order of the Interstate Commerce Commission made pursuant to the referral of a question or issue by a district court or by the United States Claims Court, shall be brought only in the court which referred the question or issue.

§ 1399. Partition action involving United States

Any civil action by any tenant in common or joint tenant for the partition of lands, where the United States is one of the tenants in common or joint tenants, may be brought only in the judicial district where such lands are located or, if located in different districts in the same State, in any of such districts.

§ 1400. Patents and copyrights

(a) Civil actions, suits, or proceedings arising under any Act of Congress relating to copyrights may be instituted in the district in which the defendant or his agent resides or may be found.

(b) Any civil action for patent infringement may be brought in the judicial district where the defendant resides, or where the defendant has committed acts of infringement and has a regular and established place of business.

§ 1401. Stockholder's derivative action

Any civil action by a stockholder on behalf of his corporation may be prosecuted in any judicial district where the corporation might have sued the same defendants.

§ 1402. United States as defendant

(a) Any civil action in a district court against the United States under subsection (a) of section 1346 of this title may be prosecuted only:

(1) Except as provided in paragraph (2), in the judicial district where the plaintiff resides;

(2) In the case of a civil action by a corporation under paragraph (1) of subsection (a) of section 1346, in the judicial district in which is located the principal place of business or principal office or agency of the corporation; or if it has no principal place of business or principal office or agency in any judicial district (A) in the judicial district in which is located the office to which was made the return of the tax in respect of which the claim is made, or (B) if no return was made, in the judicial district in which lies the District of Columbia. Notwithstanding the foregoing provisions of this paragraph a district court, for the convenience of the parties and witnesses, in the interest of justice, may transfer any such action to any other district or division.

(b) Any civil action on a tort claim against the United States under subsection (b) of section 1346 of this title may be prosecuted only in the judicial district where the plaintiff resides or wherein the act or omission complained of occurred.

(c) Any civil action against the United States under subsection (e) of section 1346 of this title may be prosecuted only in the judicial district where the property is situated at the time of levy, or if no levy is made, in the judicial district in which the event occurred which gave rise to the cause of action.

(d) Any civil action under section 2409a to quiet title to an estate or interest in real property in which an interest is claimed by the United States shall be brought in the district court of the district where the property is located or, if located in different districts, in any of such districts.

§ 1403. Eminent domain

Proceedings to condemn real estate for the use of the United States or its departments or agencies shall be brought in the district court of the district where the land is located or, if located in different districts in the same State, in any of such districts.

§ 1404. Change of venue

(a) For the convenience of parties and witnesses, in the interest of justice, a district court may transfer any civil action to any other district or division where it might have been brought.

(b) Upon motion, consent or stipulation of all parties, any action, suit or proceeding of a civil nature or any motion or hearing thereof, may be transferred, in the discretion of the court, from the division in which pending to any other division in the same district. Transfer of proceedings in rem brought by or on behalf of the United States may be transferred under this section without the consent of the United States where all other parties request transfer.

(c) A district court may order any civil action to be tried at any place within the division in which it is pending.

(d) As used in this section, "district court" includes the United States District Court for the District of the Canal Zone; and "district" includes the territorial jurisdiction of that court.

§ 1405. Creation or alteration of district or division

Actions or proceedings pending at the time of the creation of a new district or division or transfer of a county or territory from one division or district to another may be tried in the district or division as it existed at the institution of the action or proceeding, or in the district or division so created or to which the county or territory is so transferred as the parties shall agree or the court direct.

§ 1406. Cure or waiver of defects

(a) The district court of a district in which is filed a case laying venue in the wrong division or district shall dismiss, or if it be in the interest of justice, transfer such case to any district or division in which it could have been brought.

(b) Nothing in this chapter shall impair the jurisdiction of a district court of any matter involving a party who does not interpose timely and sufficient objection to the venue.

(c) As used in this section, "district court" includes the United States District Court for the District of the Canal Zone; and "district" includes the territorial jurisdiction of that court.

§ 1407. Multidistrict litigation

(a) When civil actions involving one or more common questions of fact are pending in different districts, such actions may be transferred to any district for coordinated or consolidated pretrial proceedings. Such transfers shall be made by the judicial panel on multidistrict litigation authorized by this section upon its determination that transfers for such proceedings will be for the convenience of parties and witnesses and will promote the just and efficient conduct of such actions. Each action so transferred shall be remanded by the panel at or before the conclusion of such pretrial proceedings to the district from which it was transferred unless it shall have been previously terminated: *Provided, however,* That the panel may separate any claim, cross-claim, counter-claim, or third-party claim and remand any of such claims before the remainder of the action is remanded.

(b) Such coordinated or consolidated pretrial proceedings shall be conducted by a judge or judges to whom such actions are assigned by the judicial panel on multidistrict litigation. For this purpose, upon request of the panel, a circuit judge or a district judge may be designated and assigned temporarily for service in the transferee district by the Chief Justice of the United States or the chief judge of the circuit, as may be required, in accordance with the provisions of chapter 13 of this title. With the consent of the transferee district court, such actions may be assigned by the panel to a judge or judges of such district. The judge or judges to whom such actions are assigned, the members of the judicial panel on multidistrict litigation, and other circuit and district judges designated when needed by the panel may exercise the powers of a district judge in any district for the purpose of conducting pretrial depositions in such coordinated or consolidated pretrial proceedings.

(c) Proceedings for the transfer of an action under this section may be initiated by—

(i) the judicial panel on multidistrict litigation upon its own initiative, or

(ii) motion filed with the panel by a party in any action in which transfer for coordinated or consolidated pretrial proceedings under this section may be appropriate. A copy of such motion shall be filed in the district court in which the moving party's action is pending.

The panel shall give notice to the parties in all actions in which transfers for coordinated or consolidated pretrial proceedings are contemplated, and such notice shall specify the time and place of any hearing to determine whether such transfer shall be made. Orders of the panel to set a hearing and other orders of the panel issued prior to the order either directing or denying transfer shall be filed in the office of the clerk of the district court in which a transfer hearing is to be or has been held. The panel's order of transfer shall be based upon a record of such hearing at which material evidence may be offered by any party to an action pending in any district that would be affected by the proceedings under this section, and shall be supported by findings of fact and conclusions of law based upon such record. Orders of transfer and such other orders as the panel may make thereafter shall be filed in the office of the clerk of the district court of the transferee district and shall be effective when thus filed. The clerk of the transferee district court shall forthwith transmit a certified copy of the panel's order to transfer to the clerk of the district court from which the action is being transferred. An order denying transfer shall be filed in each district wherein there is a case pending in which the motion for transfer has been made.

(d) The judicial panel on multidistrict litigation shall consist of seven circuit and district judges designated from time to time by the Chief Justice of the United States, no two of whom shall be from the same circuit. The concurrence of four members shall be necessary to any action by the panel.

(e) No proceedings for review of any order of the panel may be permitted except by extraordinary writ pursuant to the provisions of title 28, section 1651, United States Code. Petitions for an extraordinary writ to review an order of the panel to set a transfer hearing and other orders of the panel issued prior to the order either directing or denying transfer shall be filed only in the court of appeals having jurisdiction over the district in which a hearing is to be or has been held. Petitions for an extraordinary writ to review an order to transfer or orders subsequent to transfer shall be filed only in the court of appeals having jurisdiction over the transferee district. There shall be no appeal or review of an order of the panel denying a motion to transfer for consolidated or coordinated proceedings.

(f) The panel may prescribe rules for the conduct of its business not inconsistent with Acts of Congress and the Federal Rules of Civil Procedure.

(g) Nothing in this section shall apply to any action in which the United States is a complainant arising under the antitrust laws. "Anti-trust laws" as used herein include those acts referred to in the Act of October 15, 1914, as amended (38 Stat. 730; 15 U.S.C. § 12), and also include the Act of June 19, 1936 (49 Stat. 1526; 15 U.S.C. §§ 13, 13a, and 13b) and the Act of September 26, 1914, as added March 21, 1938 (52 Stat. 116, 117; 15 U.S.C. § 56); but shall not include section 4A of the Act of October 15, 1914 as added July 7, 1955 (69 Stat. 282; 15 U.S.C. § 15a).

(h) Notwithstanding the provisions of section 1404 or subsection (f) of this section, the judicial panel on multidistrict litigation may consolidate and transfer with or without the consent of the parties, for both pretrial purposes and for trial, any action brought under section 4C of the Clayton Act.

CHAPTER 89—DISTRICT COURTS; REMOVAL OF CASES FROM STATE COURTS

§ 1441. Actions removable generally

(a) Except as otherwise expressly provided by Act of Congress, any civil action brought in a State court of which the district courts of the United States have original jurisdiction, may be removed by the defendant or the defendants, to the district court of the United States for the district and division embracing the place where such action is pending.

(b) Any civil action of which the district courts have original jurisdiction founded on a claim or right arising under the Constitution, treaties or laws of the United States shall be removable without regard to the citizenship or residence of the parties. Any other such action shall be removable only if none of the parties in interest properly joined and served as defendants is a citizen of the State in which such action is brought.

(c) Whenever a separate and independent claim or cause of action, which would be removable if sued upon alone, is joined with one or more otherwise non-removable claims or causes of action, the entire case may be removed and the district court may determine all issues therein, or, in its discretion, may remand all matters not otherwise within its original jurisdiction.

(d) Any civil action brought in a State court against a foreign state as defined in section 1603(a) of this title may be removed by the foreign state to the district court of the United States for the district and division embracing the place where such action is pending. Upon removal the action shall be tried by the court without jury. Where removal is based upon this subsection, the time limitations of section 1446(b) of this chapter may be enlarged at any time for cause shown.

§ 1442. Federal officers sued or prosecuted

(a) A civil action or criminal prosecution commenced in a State court against any of the following persons may be removed by them to the district court of the United States for the district and division embracing the place wherein it is pending:

(1) Any officer of the United States or any agency thereof, or person acting under him, for any act under color of such office or on account of any right, title or authority claimed under any Act of Congress for the apprehension or punishment of criminals or the collection of the revenue.

(2) A property holder whose title is derived from any such officer, where such action or prosecution affects the validity of any law of the United States.

(3) Any officer of the courts of the United States, for any Act under color of office or in the performance of his duties;

(4) Any officer of either House of Congress, for any act in the discharge of his official duty under an order of such House.

(b) A personal action commenced in any State court by an alien against any citizen of a State who is, or at the time the alleged action accrued was, a civil officer of the United States and is a nonresident of such State, wherein jurisdiction is obtained by the State court by personal service of process, may be removed by the defendant to the district court of the United States for the district and division in which the defendant was served with process.

§ 1442a. Members of armed forces sued or prosecuted

A civil or criminal prosecution in a court of a State of the United States against a member of the armed forces of the United States on account of an act done under color of his office or status, or in respect to which he claims any right, title, or authority under a law of the United States respecting the armed forces thereof, or under the law of war, may at any time before the trial or final hearing thereof be removed for trial into the district court of the United States for the district where it is pending in the manner prescribed by law, and it shall thereupon be entered on the docket of the district court, which shall proceed as if the cause had been originally commenced therein and shall have full power to hear and determine the cause.

§ 1443. Civil rights cases

Any of the following civil actions or criminal prosecutions, commenced in a State court may be removed by the defendant to the district court of the United States for the district and division embracing the place wherein it is pending:

(1) Against any person who is denied or cannot enforce in the courts of such State a right under any law providing for the equal civil rights of citizens of the United States, or of all persons within the jurisdiction thereof;

(2) For any act under color of authority derived from any law providing for equal rights, or for refusing to do any act on the ground that it would be inconsistent with such law.

§ 1444. Foreclosure action against United States

Any action brought under section 2410 of this title against the United States in any State court may be removed by the United States to the district court of the United States for the district and division in which the action is pending.

§ 1445. Nonremovable actions

(a) A civil action in any State court against a railroad or its receivers or trustees, arising under sections 51–60 of Title 45, may not be removed to any district court of the United States.

(b) A civil action in any State court against a common carrier or its receivers or trustees to recover damages for delay, loss, or injury of shipments, arising under section 11707 of title 49, may not be removed to any district court of the United States unless the matter in controversy exceeds $10,000, exclusive of interest and costs.

(c) A civil action in any State court arising under the workmen's compensation laws of such State may not be removed to any district court of the United States.

§ 1446. Procedure for removal

(a) A defendant or defendants desiring to remove any civil action or criminal prosecution from a State court shall file in the district court of the United States for the district and division within which such action is pending a verified petition containing a short and plain statement of the facts which entitle him or them to removal together with a copy of all process, pleadings and orders served upon him or them in such action.

(b) The petition for removal of a civil action or proceeding shall be filed within thirty days after the receipt by the defendant, through service or otherwise, of a copy of the initial pleading setting forth the claim for relief upon which such action or proceeding is based, or within thirty days after the service of summons upon the defendant if such initial pleading has then been filed in court and is not required to be served on the defendant, whichever period is shorter.

If the case stated by the initial pleading is not removable, a petition for removal may be filed within thirty days after receipt by the defendant, through service or otherwise, of a copy of an amended pleading, motion, order or other paper from which it may first be ascertained that the case is one which is or has become removable.

(c)(1) A petition for removal of a criminal prosecution shall be filed not later than thirty days after the arraignment in the State court, or at any time before trial, whichever is earlier, except that for good cause shown the United States district court may enter an order granting the petitioner leave to file the petition at a later time.

(2) A petition for removal of a criminal prosecution shall include all grounds for such removal. A failure to state grounds which exist at the time of the filing of the petition shall constitute a waiver of such grounds, and a second petition may be filed only on grounds not existing at the time of the original petition. For good cause shown, the United States district court may grant relief from the limitations of this paragraph.

(3) The filing of a petition for removal of a criminal prosecution shall not prevent the State court in which such prosecution is pending from proceeding further, except that a judgment of conviction shall not be entered unless the petition is first denied.

(4) The United States district court to which such petition is directed shall examine the petition promptly. If it clearly appears on the face of the petition and any exhibits annexed thereto that the petition for removal should not be granted, the court shall make an order for its summary dismissal.

(5) If the United States district court does not order the summary dismissal of such petition, it shall order an evidentiary hearing to be held promptly and after such hearing shall make such disposition of the petition as justice shall require. If the United States district court determines that such petition shall be granted, it shall so notify the State court in which prosecution is pending, which shall proceed no further.

(d) Each petition for removal of a civil action or proceeding, except a petition in behalf of the United States, shall be accompanied by a bond with good and sufficient surety conditioned that the defendant or defendants will pay all costs and disbursements incurred by reason of the removal proceedings should it be determined that the case was not removable or was improperly removed.

(e) Promptly after the filing of such petition for the removal of a civil action and bond the defendant or defendants shall give written notice thereof to all adverse parties and shall file a copy of the petition with the clerk of such State court, which shall effect the removal and the State court shall proceed no further unless and until the case is remanded.

(f) If the defendant or defendants are in actual custody on process issued by the State court, the district court shall issue its writ of habeas corpus, and the marshal shall thereupon take such defendant or defendants into his custody and deliver a copy of the writ to the clerk of such State court.

§ 1447. Procedure after removal generally

(a) In any case removed from a State court, the district court may issue all necessary orders and process to bring before it all proper parties whether served by process issued by the State court or otherwise.

(b) It may require the petitioner to file with its clerk copies of all records and proceedings in such State court or may cause the same to be brought before it by writ of certiorari issued to such State court.

(c) If at any time before final judgment it appears that the case was removed improvidently and without jurisdiction, the district court shall remand the case, and may order the payment of just costs. A certified copy of the order of remand shall be mailed by its clerk to the clerk of the State court. The State court may thereupon proceed with such case.

(d) An order remanding a case to the State court from which it was removed is not reviewable on appeal or otherwise, except that an order remanding a case to the State court from which it was removed pursuant to section 1443 of this title shall be reviewable by appeal or otherwise.

§ 1448. Process after removal

In all cases removed from any State court to any district court of the United States in which any one or more of the defendants has not been served with process or in which the service has not been perfected prior to removal, or in which process served proves to be defective, such process or service may be completed or new process issued in the same manner as in cases originally filed in such district court.

This section shall not deprive any defendant upon whom process is served after removal of his right to move to remand the case.

§ 1449. State court record supplied

Where a party is entitled to copies of the records and proceedings in any suit or prosecution in a State court, to be used in any district court of the United States, and the clerk of such State court, upon demand, and the payment or tender of the legal fees, fails to deliver certified copies, the district court may, on affidavit reciting such facts, direct such record to be supplied by affidavit or otherwise. Thereupon such proceedings, trial, and judgment may be had in such district court, and all such process awarded, as if certified copies had been filed in the district court.

§ 1450. Attachment or sequestration; securities

Whenever any action is removed from a State court to a district court of the United States, any attachment or sequestration of the goods or estate of the defendant in such action in the State court shall hold the goods or estate to answer the final judgment or decree in the same manner as they would have been held to answer final judgment or decree had it been rendered by the State court.

All bonds, undertakings, or security given by either party in such action prior to its removal shall remain valid and effectual notwithstanding such removal.

All injunctions, orders, and other proceedings had in such action prior to its removal shall remain in full force and effect until dissolved or modified by the district court.

§ 1451. Definitions

For purposes of this chapter—

(1) The term "State court" includes the Superior Court of the District of Columbia.

(2) The term "State" includes the District of Columbia.

CHAPTER 90—BANKRUPTCY COURTS

See editorial note to Chapter 6, *supra*, p. 15.

CHAPTER 91—UNITED STATES CLAIMS COURT

§ 1491. Claims against United States generally; actions involving Tennessee Valley Authority

(a)(1) The United States Claims Court shall have jurisdiction to render judgment upon any claim against the United States founded either upon the Constitution, or any Act of Congress or any regulation of an executive department, or upon any express or implied contract with the United States, or for liquidated or unliquidated damages in cases not sounding in tort. For the purpose of this paragraph, an express or implied contract with the Army and Air Force Exchange Service, Navy Exchanges, Marine Corps Exchanges, Coast Guard Exchanges, or Exchange Councils of the National Aeronautics and Space Administration shall be considered an express or implied contract with the United States.

(2) To provide an entire remedy and to complete the relief afforded by the judgment, the court may, as an incident of and collateral to any such judgment, issue orders directing restoration to office or position, placement in appropriate duty or retirement status, and correction of applicable records, and such orders may be issued to any appropriate official of the United States. In any case within its jurisdiction, the court shall have the power to remand appropriate matters to any administrative or executive body or official with such direction as it may deem proper and just. The Claims Court shall have jurisdiction to render judgment upon any claim by or against, or dispute with, a contractor arising under section 10(a)(1) of the Contract Disputes Act of 1978.

(3) To afford complete relief on any contract claim brought before the contract is awarded, the court shall have exclusive jurisdiction to grant declaratory judgments and such equitable and extraordinary relief as it deems proper, including but not limited to injunctive relief. In exercising this jurisdiction, the court shall give due regard to the interests of national defense and national security.

(b) Nothing herein shall be construed to give the United States Claims Court jurisdiction of any civil action within the exclusive jurisdiction of the Court of International Trade, or of any action against, or founded on conduct of, the Tennessee Valley Authority, or to amend or modify the provisions of the Tennessee Valley Authority Act of 1933 with respect to actions by or against the Authority.

§ 1492. Congressional reference cases

Any bill, except a bill for a pension, may be referred by either House of Congress to the chief judge of the United States Claims Court for a report in conformity with section 2509 of this title.

[§ 1493. Repealed.]

§ 1494. Accounts of officers, agents or contractors

The United States Claims Court shall have jurisdiction to determine the amount, if any, due to or from the United States by reason of any unsettled account of any officer or agent of, or contractor with, the United States, or a guarantor, surety or personal representative of any such officer, agent or contractor, and to render judgment thereon, where—

(1) claimant or the person he represents has applied to the proper department of the Government for settlement of the account;

(2) three years have elapsed from the date of such application without settlement; and

(3) no suit upon the same has been brought by the United States.

§ 1495. Damages for unjust conviction and imprisonment; claim against United States

The United States Claims Court shall have jurisdiction to render judgment upon any claim for damages by any person unjustly convicted of an offense against the United States and imprisoned.

§ 1496. Disbursing officers' claims

The United States Claims Court shall have jurisdiction to render judgment upon any claim by a disbursing officer of the United States or by his administrator or executor for relief from responsibility for loss, in line of duty, of Government funds, vouchers, records or other papers in his charge.

§ 1497. Oyster growers' damages from dredging operations

The United States Claims Court shall have jurisdiction to render judgment upon any claim for damages to oyster growers on private or leased lands or bottoms arising from dredging operations or use of other machinery and equipment in making river and harbor improvements authorized by Act of Congress.

§ 1498. Patent and copyright cases

(a) Whenever an invention described in and covered by a patent of the United States is used or manufactured by or for the United States without license of the owner thereof or lawful right to use or manufacture the same the owner's remedy shall be by action against the United States in the United States Claims Court for the recovery of his reasonable and entire compensation for such use and manufacture.

For the purposes of this section, the use or manufacture of an invention described in and covered by a patent of the United States by a contractor, a subcontractor, or any person, firm, or corporation for the Government and with the authorization or consent of the Government, shall be construed as use or manufacture for the United States.

The court shall not award compensation under this section if the claim is based on the use or manufacture by or for the United States of any article owned, leased, used by, or in the possession of the United States prior to July 1, 1918.

A Government employee shall have the right to bring suit against the Government under this section except where he was in a position to order, influence, or induce use of the invention by the Government. This section shall not confer a right of action on any patentee or any assignee of such patentee with respect to any invention discovered or invented by a person while in the employment or service of the United States, where the invention was related to the official functions of the employee, in cases in which such functions included research and development, or in the making of which Government time, materials or facilities were used.

(b) Hereafter, whenever the copyright in any work protected under the copyright laws of the United States shall be infringed by the United States, by a corporation owned or controlled by the United States, or by a contractor, subcontractor, or any person, firm, or corporation acting for the Government and with the authorization or consent of the Government, the exclusive remedy of the owner of such copyright shall be by action against the United States in the Claims Court for the recovery of his reasonable and entire compensation as damages for such infringement, including the minimum statutory damages as set forth in section 504(c) of title 17, United States Code: *Provided*, That a Government employee shall have a right of action against the Government under this subsection except where he was in a position to order, influence, or induce use of the copyrighted work by the Government: *Provided, however*, That this subsection shall not confer a right of action on any copyright owner or any assignee of such owner with respect to any copyrighted work prepared by a person while in the employment or service of the United States, where the copyrighted work was prepared as a part of the official functions of the employee, or in the preparation of which Government time, material, or facilities were used: *And provided further,* That before such action against the United States has been instituted the appropriate corporation owned or controlled by the United States or the head of the appropriate department or agency of the Government, as the case may be, is authorized to enter into an agreement with the copyright owner in full settlement and compromise for the damages accruing to him by reason of such infringement and to settle the claim administratively out of available appropriations.

Except as otherwise provided by law, no recovery shall be had for any infringement of a copyright covered by this subsection committed more than three years prior to the filing of the complaint or counterclaim for infringement in the action, except that the period between the date of receipt of a written claim for compensation by the Department or agency of the Government or corporation owned or controlled by the United States, as the case may be, having authority to settle such claim and the date of mailing by the Government of a notice to the claimant that his claim has been denied shall not be counted as a part of the three years, unless suit is brought before the last-mentioned date.

(c) The provisions of this section shall not apply to any claim arising in a foreign country.

(d) Hereafter, whenever a plant variety protected by a certificate of plant variety protection under the laws of the United States shall be infringed by the United States, by a corporation owned or controlled by the United States, or by a contractor, subcontractor, or any person, firm, or corporation acting for the Government and with the authorization and consent of the Government, the exclusive remedy of the owner of such certificate shall be by action against the United States in the Claims Court for the recovery of his reasonable and entire compensation as damages for such infringement: *Provided,* That a Government employee shall have a right of action against the Government under this subsection except where he was in a position to order, influence, or induce use of the protected plant variety by the Government: *Provided, however,* That this subsection shall not confer a right of action on any certificate owner or any assignee of such owner with respect to any protected plant variety made by a person while in the employment or service of the United States, where such variety was prepared as a part of the official functions of the employee, or in the preparation of which Government time, material, or facilities were used: *And provided further,* That before such action against the United States has been instituted, the appropriate corporation owned or controlled by the United States or the head of the appropriate agency of the Government, as the case may be, is authorized to enter into an agreement with the certificate owner in full settlement and compromise, for the damages accrued to him by reason of such infringement and to settle the claim administratively out of available appropriations.

§ 1499. Liquidated damages withheld from contractors under Contract Work Hours and Safety Standards Act

The United States Claims Court shall have jurisdiction to render judgment upon any claim for liquidated damages withheld from a contractor or subcontractor under section 104 of the Contract Work Hours Standards Act.

§ 1500. Pendency of claims in other courts

The United States Claims Court shall not have jurisdiction of any claim for or in respect to which the plaintiff or his assignee has pending in any other court any suit or process against the United States or any person who, at the time when the cause of action alleged in such suit or process arose, was, in respect thereto, acting or professing to act, directly or indirectly under the authority of the United States.

§ 1501. Pensions

The United States Claims Court shall not have jurisdiction of any claim for a pension.

§ 1502. Treaty cases

Except as otherwise provided by Act of Congress, the United States Claims Court shall not have jurisdiction of any claim against the United States growing out of or dependent upon any treaty entered into with foreign nations.

§ 1503. Set-offs

The United States Claims Court shall have jurisdiction to render judgment upon any set-off or demand by the United States against any plaintiff in such court.

[§ 1504. Repealed.]

§ 1505. Indian claims

The United States Claims Court shall have jurisdiction of any claim against the United States accruing after August 13, 1946, in favor of any tribe, band, or other identifiable group of American Indians residing within the territorial limits of the United States or Alaska whenever such claim is one arising under the Constitution, laws or treaties of the United States, or Executive orders of the President, or is one which otherwise would be cognizable in the Claims Court if the claimant were not an Indian tribe, band or group.

[§ 1506. Repealed.]

§ 1507. Jurisdiction for certain declaratory judgments

The United States Claims Court shall have jurisdiction to hear any suit for and issue a declaratory judgment under section 7428 of the Internal Revenue Code of 1954.

§ 1508. Jurisdiction for certain partnership proceedings

The Claims Court shall have jurisdiction to hear and to render judgment upon any petition under section 6226 or 6228(a) of the Internal Revenue Code of 1954.

CHAPTER 95—COURT OF INTERNATIONAL TRADE

§ 1581. Civil actions against the United States and agencies and officers thereof

(a) The Court of International Trade shall have exclusive jurisdiction of any civil action commenced to contest the denial of a protest, in whole or in part, under section 515 of the Tariff Act of 1930.

(b) The Court of International Trade shall have exclusive jurisdiction of any civil action commenced under section 516 of the Tariff Act of 1930.

(c) The Court of International Trade shall have exclusive jurisdiction of any civil action commenced under section 516A of the Tariff Act of 1930.

(d) The Court of International Trade shall have exclusive jurisdiction of any civil action commenced to review—

(1) any final determination of the Secretary of Labor under section 223 of the Trade Act of 1974 with respect to the eligibility of workers for adjustment assistance under such Act;

(2) any final determination of the Secretary of Commerce under section 251 of the Trade Act of 1974 with respect to the eligibility of a firm for adjustment assistance under such Act; and

(3) any final determination of the Secretary of Commerce under section 271 of the Trade Act of 1974 with respect to the eligibility of a community for adjustment assistance under such Act.

(e) The Court of International Trade shall have exclusive jurisdiction of any civil action commenced to review any final determination of the Secretary of the Treasury under section 305(b)(1) of the Trade Agreements Act of 1979.

(f) The Court of International Trade shall have exclusive jurisdiction of any civil action involving an application for an order directing the administering authority or the International Trade Commission to make confidential information available under section 777(c)(2) of the Tariff Act of 1930.

(g) The Court of International Trade shall have exclusive jurisdiction of any civil action commenced to review—

(1) any decision of the Secretary of the Treasury to deny or revoke a customhouse broker's license under section 641(a) of the Tariff Act of 1930; and

(2) any order of the Secretary of the Treasury to revoke or suspend a customhouse broker's license under section 641(b) of the Tariff Act of 1930.

(h) The Court of International Trade shall have exclusive jurisdiction of any civil action commenced to review, prior to the importation of the goods involved, a ruling issued by the Secretary of the Treasury, or a refusal to issue or change such a ruling, relating to classification, valuation, rate of duty, marking, restricted merchandise, entry requirements, drawbacks, vessel repairs, or similar matters, but only if the party commencing the civil action demonstrates to the court that he would be irreparably harmed unless given an opportunity to obtain judicial review prior to such importation.

(i) In addition to the jurisdiction conferred upon the Court of International Trade by subsections (a)–(h) of this section and subject to the exception set forth in subsection (j) of this section, the Court of International Trade shall have exclusive jurisdiction of any civil action commenced against the United States, its agencies, or its officers, that arises out of any law of the United States providing for—

(1) revenue from imports or tonnage;

(2) tariffs, duties, fees, or other taxes on the importation of merchandise for reasons other than the raising of revenue;

(3) embargoes or other quantitative restrictions on the importation of merchandise for reasons other than the protection of the public health or safety; or

(4) administration and enforcement with respect to the matters referred to in paragraphs (1)–(3) of this subsection and subsections (a)–(h) of this section.

(j) The Court of International Trade shall not have jurisdiction of any civil action arising under section 305 of the Tariff Act of 1930.

§ 1582. Civil actions commenced by the United States

The Court of International Trade shall have exclusive jurisdiction of any civil action which arises out of an import transaction and which is commenced by the United States—

(1) to recover a civil penalty under section 592, 704(i)(2), or 734(i)(2) of the Tariff Act of 1930;

(2) to recover upon a bond relating to the importation of merchandise required by the laws of the United States or by the Secretary of the Treasury; or

(3) to recover customs duties.

§ 1583. Counterclaims, cross-claims, and third-party actions

In any civil action in the Court of International Trade, the court shall have exclusive jurisdiction to render judgment upon any counterclaim, cross-claim, or third-party action of any party, if (1) such claim or action involves the imported merchandise that is the subject matter of such civil action, or (2) such claim or action is to recover upon a bond or customs duties relating to such merchandise.

[§ 1584. Repealed.]

§ 1585. Powers in law and equity

The Court of International Trade shall possess all the powers in law and equity of, or as conferred by statute upon, a district court of the United States.

CHAPTER 97—JURISDICTIONAL IMMUNITIES OF FOREIGN STATES

§ 1602. Findings and declaration of purpose

The Congress finds that the determination by United States courts of the claims of foreign states to immunity from the jurisdiction of such courts would serve the interests of justice and would protect the rights of both foreign states and litigants in United States courts. Under international law, states are not immune from the jurisdiction of foreign courts insofar as their commercial activities are concerned, and their commercial property may be levied upon for the satisfaction of judgments rendered against them in connection with their commercial activities. Claims of foreign states to immunity should henceforth be decided by courts of the United States and of the States in conformity with the principles set forth in this chapter.

§ 1603. Definitions

For purposes of this chapter—

(a) A "foreign state", except as used in section 1608 of this title, includes a political subdivision of a foreign state or an agency or instrumentality of a foreign state as defined in subsection (b).

(b) An "agency or instrumentality of a foreign state" means any entity—

(1) which is a separate legal person, corporate or otherwise, and

(2) which is an organ of a foreign state or political subdivision thereof, or a majority of whose shares or other ownership

interest is owned by a foreign state or political subdivision thereof, and

(3) which is neither a citizen of a State of the United States as defined in section 1332(c) and (d) of this title, nor created under the laws of any third country.

(c) The "United States" includes all territory and waters, continental or insular, subject to the jurisdiction of the United States.

(d) A "commercial activity" means either a regular course of commercial conduct or a particular commercial transaction or act. The commercial character of an activity shall be determined by reference to the nature of the course of conduct or particular transaction or act, rather than by reference to its purpose.

(e) A "commercial activity carried on in the United States by a foreign state" means commercial activity carried on by such state and having substantial contact with the United States.

§ 1604. Immunity of a foreign state from jurisdiction

Subject to existing international agreements to which the United States is a party at the time of enactment of this Act a foreign state shall be immune from the jurisdiction of the courts of the United States and of the States except as provided in sections 1605 to 1607 of this chapter.

§ 1605. General exceptions to the jurisdictional immunity of a foreign state

(a) A foreign state shall not be immune from the jurisdiction of courts of the United States or of the States in any case—

(1) in which the foreign state has waived its immunity either explicitly or by implication, notwithstanding any withdrawal of the waiver which the foreign state may purport to effect except in accordance with the terms of the waiver;

(2) in which the action is based upon a commercial activity carried on in the United States by the foreign state; or upon an act performed in the United States in connection with a commercial activity of the foreign state elsewhere; or upon an act outside the territory of the United States in connection with a commercial activity of the foreign state elsewhere and that act causes a direct effect in the United States;

(3) in which rights in property taken in violation of international law are in issue and that property or any property exchanged for such property is present in the United States in connection with a commercial activity carried on in the United States by the foreign state; or that property or any property, exchanged for such property is owned or operated by an agency or instrumentality of the foreign state and that agency or instrumentality is engaged in a commercial activity in the United States;

(4) in which rights in property in the United States acquired by succession or gift or rights in immovable property situated in the United States are in issue; or

(5) not otherwise encompassed in paragraph (2) above, in which money damages are sought against a foreign state for personal injury or death, or damage to or loss of property, occurring in the United States and caused by the tortious act or omission of that foreign state or of any official or employee of that foreign state while acting within the scope of his office or employment; except this paragraph shall not apply to—

(A) any claim based upon the exercise or performance or the failure to exercise or perform a discretionary function regardless of whether the discretion be abused, or

(B) any claim arising out of malicious prosecution, abuse of process, libel, slander, misrepresentation, deceit, or interference with contract rights.

(b) A foreign state shall not be immune from the jurisdiction of the courts of the United States in any case in which a suit in admiralty is brought to enforce a maritime lien against a vessel or cargo of the foreign state, which maritime lien is based upon a commercial activity of the foreign state: *Provided,* That—

(1) notice of the suit is given by delivery of a copy of the summons and of the complaint to the person, or his agent, having possession of the vessel or cargo against which the maritime lien is asserted; but such notice shall not be deemed to have been delivered, nor may it thereafter be delivered, if the vessel or cargo is arrested pursuant to process obtained on behalf of the party bringing the suit—unless the party was unaware that the vessel or cargo of a foreign state was involved, in which event the service of process of arrest shall be deemed to constitute valid delivery of such notice; and

(2) notice to the foreign state of the commencement of suit as provided in section 1608 of this title is initiated within ten days either of the delivery of notice as provided in subsection (b)(1) of this section or, in the case of a party who was unaware that the vessel or cargo of a foreign state was involved, of the date such party determined the existence of the foreign state's interest.

Whenever notice is delivered under subsection (b)(1) of this section, the maritime lien shall thereafter be deemed to be an in personam claim against the foreign state which at that time owns the vessel or cargo involved. *Provided,* That a court may not award judgment against the foreign state in an amount greater than the value of the vessel or cargo upon which the maritime lien arose, such value to be determined as of the time notice is served under subsection (b)(1) of this section.

§ 1606. Extent of liability

As to any claim for relief with respect to which a foreign state is not entitled to immunity under section 1605 or 1607 of this chapter, the foreign state shall be liable in the same manner and to the same extent as a private individual under like circumstances; but a foreign state except for an agency or instrumentality thereof shall not be liable for punitive damages; if, however, in any case wherein death was caused, the law of the place where the action or omission occurred provides, or has been construed to provide, for damages only punitive in nature, the foreign state shall be liable for actual or compensatory damages measured by the pecuniary injuries resulting from such death which were incurred by the persons for whose benefit the action was brought.

§ 1607. Counterclaims

In any action brought by a foreign state, or in which a foreign state intervenes, in a court of the United States or of a State, the foreign state shall not be accorded immunity with respect to any counterclaim—

(a) for which a foreign state would not be entitled to immunity under section 1605 of this chapter had such claim been brought in a separate action against the foreign state; or

(b) arising out of the transaction or occurrence that is the subject matter of the claim of the foreign state; or

(c) to the extent that the counterclaim does not seek relief exceeding in amount or differing in kind from that sought by the foreign state.

§ 1608. Service; time to answer; default

(a) Service in the courts of the United States and of the States shall be made upon a foreign state or political subdivision of a foreign state:

(1) by delivery of a copy of the summons and complaint in accordance with any special arrangement for service between the plaintiff and the foreign state or political subdivision; or

(2) if no special arrangement exists, by delivery of a copy of the summons and complaint in accordance with an applicable international convention on service of judicial documents; or

(3) if service cannot be made under paragraphs (1) or (2), by sending a copy of the summons and complaint and a notice of suit, together with a translation of each into the official language of the foreign state, by any form of mail requiring a signed receipt, to be addressed and dispatched by the clerk of the court to the head of the ministry of foreign affairs of the foreign state concerned, or

(4) if service cannot be made within 30 days under paragraph (3), by sending two copies of the summons and complaint and a notice of suit, together with a translation of each into the

official language of the foreign state, by any form of mail requiring a signed receipt, to be addressed and dispatched by the clerk of the court to the Secretary of State in Washington, District of Columbia, to the attention of the Director of Special Consular Services—and the Secretary shall transmit one copy of the papers through diplomatic channels to the foreign state and shall send to the clerk of the court a certified copy of the diplomatic note indicating when the papers were transmitted.

As used in this subsection, a "notice of suit" shall mean a notice addressed to a foreign state and in a form prescribed by the Secretary of State by regulation.

(b) Service in the courts of the United States and of the States shall be made upon an agency or instrumentality of a foreign state:

(1) by delivery of a copy of the summons and complaint in accordance with any special arrangement for service between the plaintiff and the agency or instrumentality; or

(2) if no special arrangement exists, by delivery of a copy of the summons and complaint either to an officer, a managing or general agent, or to any other agent authorized by appointment or by law to receive service of process in the United States; or in accordance with an applicable international convention on service of judicial documents; or

(3) if service cannot be made under paragraphs (1) or (2), and if reasonably calculated to give actual notice, by delivery of a copy of the summons and complaint, together with a translation of each into the official language of the foreign state—

(A) as directed by an authority of the foreign state or political subdivision in response to a letter rogatory or request or

(B) by any form of mail requiring a signed receipt, to be addressed and dispatched by the clerk of the court to the agency or instrumentality to be served, or

(C) as directed by order of the court consistent with the law of the place where service is to be made.

(c) Service shall be deemed to have been made—

(1) in the case of service under subsection (a)(4), as of the date of transmittal indicated in the certified copy of the diplomatic note; and

(2) in any other case under this section, as of the date of receipt indicated in the certification, signed and returned postal receipt, or other proof of service applicable to the method of service employed.

(d) In any action brought in a court of the United States or of a State, a foreign state, a political subdivision thereof, or an agency or instrumentality of a foreign state shall serve an answer or other responsive pleading to the complaint within sixty days after service has been made under this section.

(c) No judgment by default shall be entered by a court of the United States or of a State against a foreign state, a political subdivision thereof, or an agency or instrumentality of a foreign state, unless the claimant establishes his claim or right to relief by evidence satisfactory to the court. A copy of any such default judgment shall be sent to the foreign state or political subdivision in the manner prescribed for service in this section.

§ 1609. Immunity from attachment and execution of property of a foreign state

Subject to existing international agreements to which the United States is a party at the time of enactment of this Act the property in the United States of a foreign state shall be immune from attachment arrest and execution except as provided in sections 1610 and 1611 of this chapter.

§ 1610. Exceptions to the immunity from attachment or execution

(a) The property in the United States of a foreign state, as defined in section 1603(a) of this chapter, used for a commercial activity in the United States, shall not be immune from attachment in aid of execution, or from execution, upon a judgment entered by a court of the United States or of a State after the effective date of this Act, if—

(1) the foreign state has waived its immunity from attachment in aid of execution or from execution either explicitly or by implication, notwithstanding any withdrawal of the waiver the foreign state may purport to effect except in accordance with the terms of the waiver, or

(2) the property is or was used for the commercial activity upon which the claim is based, or

(3) the execution relates to a judgment establishing rights in property which has been taken in violation of international law or which has been exchanged for property taken in violation of international law, or

(4) the execution relates to a judgment establishing rights in property—

(A) which is acquired by succession or gift, or

(B) which is immovable and situated in the United States: *Provided,* That such property is not used for purposes of maintaining a diplomatic or consular mission or the residence of the Chief of such mission, or

(5) the property consists of any contractual obligation or any proceeds from such a contractual obligation to indemnify or hold harmless the foreign state or its employees under a policy of automobile or other liability or casualty insurance covering the claim which merged into the judgment.

(b) In addition to subsection (a), any property in the United States of an agency or instrumentality of a foreign state engaged in commercial activity in the United States shall not be immune from attachment in aid of execution, or from execution, upon a judgment entered by a court of the United States or of a State after the effective date of this Act, if—

(1) the agency or instrumentality has waived its immunity from attachment in aid of execution or from execution either explicitly or implicitly, notwithstanding any withdrawal of the waiver the agency or instrumentality may purport to effect except in accordance with the terms of the waiver, or

(2) the judgment relates to a claim for which the agency or instrumentality is not immune by virtue of section 1605(a)(2), (3), or (5), or 1605(b) of this chapter, regardless of whether the property is or was used for the activity upon which the claim is based.

(c) No attachment or execution referred to in subsections (a) and (b) of this section shall be permitted until the court has ordered such attachment and execution after having determined that a reasonable period of time has elapsed following the entry of judgment and the giving of any notice required under section 1608(e) of this chapter.

(d) The property of a foreign state, as defined in section 1603(a) of this chapter, used for a commercial activity in the United States, shall not be immune from attachment prior to the entry of judgment in any action brought in a court of the United States or of a State, or prior to the elapse of the period of time provided in subsection (c) of this section, if—

(1) the foreign state has explicitly waived its immunity from attachment prior to judgment, notwithstanding any withdrawal of the waiver the foreign state may purport to effect except in accordance with the terms of the waiver, and

(2) the purpose of the attachment is to secure satisfaction of a judgment that has been or may ultimately be entered against the foreign state, and not to obtain jurisdiction.

§ 1611. Certain types of property immune from execution

(a) Notwithstanding the provisions of section 1610 of this chapter, the property of those organizations designated by the President as being entitled to enjoy the privileges, exemptions, and immunities provided by the International Organizations Immunities Act shall not be subject to attachment or any other judicial process impeding the disbursement of funds to, or on the order of, a foreign state as the result of an action brought in the courts of the United States or of the States.

(b) Notwithstanding the provisions of section 1610 of this chapter, the property of a foreign state shall be immune from attachment and from execution, if—

(1) the property is that of a foreign central bank or monetary authority held for its own account, unless such bank or authority, or its parent foreign government, has explicitly waived its immunity from attachment in aid of execution, or from execution, notwithstanding any withdrawal of the waiver which the bank, authority or government may purport to effect except in accordance with the terms of the waiver; or

(2) the property is, or is intended to be, used in connection with a military activity and

(A) is of a military character, or

(B) is under the control of a military authority or defense agency.

CHAPTER 99—GENERAL PROVISIONS

§ 1631. Transfer to cure want of jurisdiction

Whenever a civil action is filed in a court as defined in section 610 of this title or an appeal, including a petition for review of administrative action, is noticed for or filed with such a court and that court finds that there is a want of jurisdiction, the court shall, if it is in the interest of justice, transfer such action or appeal to any other such court in which the action or appeal could have been brought at the time it was filed or noticed, and the action or appeal shall proceed as if it had been filed in or noticed for the court to which it is transferred on the date upon which it was actually filed in or noticed for the court from which it is transferred.

PART V—PROCEDURE

CHAPTER 111—GENERAL PROVISIONS

§ 1651. Writs ("all Writs statute")

(a) The Supreme Court and all courts established by Act of Congress may issue all writs necessary or appropriate in aid of their respective jurisdictions and agreeable to the usages and principles of law.

(b) An alternative writ or rule nisi may be issued by a justice or judge of a court which has jurisdiction.

§ 1652. State laws as rules of decision

The laws of the several states, except where the Constitution or treaties of the United States or Acts of Congress otherwise require or provide, shall be regarded as rules of decision in civil actions in the courts of the United States, in cases where they apply.

§ 1653. Amendment of pleadings to show jurisdiction

Defective allegations of jurisdiction may be amended, upon terms, in the trial or appellate courts.

§ 1654. Appearance personally or by counsel

In all courts of the United States the parties may plead and conduct their own cases personally or by counsel, as, by the rules of such courts, respectively, are permitted to manage and conduct causes therein.

§ 1655. Lien enforcement; absent defendants

In an action in a district court to enforce any lien upon or claim to, or to remove any incumbrance or lien or cloud upon the title to, real or personal property within the district, where any defendant cannot be served within the State, or does not voluntarily appear, the court may order the absent defendant to appear or plead by a day certain.

Such order shall be served on the absent defendant personally if practicable, wherever found, and also upon the person or persons in possession or charge of such property, if any. Where personal service is not practicable, the order shall be published as the court may direct, not less than once a week for six consecutive weeks.

If an absent defendant does not appear or plead within the time allowed, the court may proceed as if the absent defendant had been served with process within the State, but any adjudication shall, as regards the absent defendant without appearance, affect only the property which is the subject of the action. When a part of the property is within another district, but within the same state, such action may be brought in either district.

Any defendant not so personally notified may, at any time within one year after final judgment, enter his appearance, and thereupon the court shall set aside the judgment and permit such defendant to plead on payment of such costs as the court deems just.

§ 1656. Creation of new district or division or transfer of territory; lien enforcement

The creation of a new district or division or the transfer of any territory to another district or division shall not affect or divest any lien theretofore acquired in a district court upon property within such district, division or territory.

To enforce such lien, the clerk of the court in which the same is acquired, upon the request and at the cost of the party desiring the same, shall make a certified copy of the record thereof, which, when filed in the proper court of the district or division in which such property is situated after such creation or transfer shall be evidence in all courts and places equally with the original thereof; and, thereafter like proceedings shall be had thereon, and with the same effect, as though the case or proceeding had been originally instituted in such court.

CHAPTER 113—PROCESS

§ 1691. Seal and teste of process

All writs and process issuing from a court of the United States shall be under the seal of the court and signed by the clerk thereof.

§ 1692. Process and orders affecting property in different districts

In proceedings in a district court where a receiver is appointed for property, real, personal, or mixed, situated in different districts, process may issue and be executed in any such district as if the property lay wholly within one district, but orders affecting the property shall be entered of record in each of such districts.

§ 1693. Place of arrest in civil action

Except as otherwise provided by Act of Congress, no person shall be arrested in one district for trial in another in any civil action in a district court.

§ 1694. Patent infringement action

In a patent infringement action commenced in a district where the defendant is not a resident but has a regular and established place of business, service of process, summons or subpoena upon such defendant may be made upon his agent or agents conducting such business.

§ 1695. Stockholder's derivative action

Process in a stockholder's action in behalf of his corporation may be served upon such corporation in any district where it is organized or licensed to do business or is doing business.

§ 1696. Service in foreign and international litigation

(a) The district court of the district in which a person resides or is found may order service upon him of any document issued in connection with a proceeding in a foreign or international tribunal. The order may be made pursuant to a letter rogatory issued, or request made, by a foreign or international tribunal or upon application of any interested person and shall direct the manner of service. Service pursuant to this subsection does not, of itself, require the recognition or enforcement in the United States of a judgment, decree, or order rendered by a foreign or international tribunal.

(b) This section does not preclude service of such a document without an order of court.

CHAPTER 115—EVIDENCE; DOCUMENTARY

§ 1731. Handwriting

The admitted or proved handwriting of any person shall be admissible, for purposes of comparison, to determine genuineness of other handwriting attributed to such person.

§ 1732. Record made in regular course of business; photographic copies

If any business, institution, member of a profession or calling, or any department or agency of government, in the regular course of business or activity has kept or recorded any memorandum, writing, entry, print, representation or combination thereof, of any act, transaction, occurrence, or event, and in the regular course of business has caused any or all of the same to be recorded, copied, or reproduced by any photographic, photostatic, microfilm, micro-card, miniature photographic, or other process which accurately reproduces or forms a durable medium for so reproducing the original, the original may be destroyed in the regular course of business unless its preservation is required by law. Such reproduction, when satisfactorily identified, is as admissible in evidence as the original itself in any judicial or administrative proceeding whether the original is in existence or not and an enlargement or facsimile of such reproduction is likewise admissible in evidence if the original reproduction is in existence and available for inspection under direction of court. The introduction of a reproduced record, enlargement, or facsimile does not preclude admission of the original. This subsection shall not be construed to exclude from evidence any document or copy thereof which is otherwise admissible under the rules of evidence.

§ 1733. Government records and papers; copies

(a) Books or records of account or minutes of proceedings of any department or agency of the United States shall be admissible to prove the act, transaction or occurrence as a memorandum of which the same were made or kept.

(b) Properly authenticated copies or transcripts of any books, records, papers or documents of any department or agency of the United States shall be admitted in evidence equally with the originals thereof.

(c) This section does not apply to cases, actions, and proceedings which the Federal Rules of Evidence apply.

§ 1734. Court record lost or destroyed, generally

(a) A lost or destroyed record of any proceeding in any court of the United States may be supplied on application of any interested party not at fault, by substituting a copy certified by the clerk of any court in which an authentic copy is lodged.

(b) Where a certified copy is not available, any interested person not at fault may file in such court a verified application for an order establishing the lost or destroyed record.

Every other interested person shall be served personally with a copy of the application and with notice of hearing on a day stated, not less than sixty days after service. Service may be made on any nonresident of the district anywhere within the jurisdiction of the United States or in any foreign country.

Proof of service in a foreign country shall be certified by a minister or consul of the United States in such country, under his official seal.

If, after the hearing, the court is satisfied that the statements contained in the application are true, it shall enter an order reciting the substance and effect of the lost or destroyed record. Such order, subject to intervening rights of third persons, shall have the same effect as the original record.

§ 1735. Court record lost or destroyed where United States interested

(a) When the record of any case or matter in any court of the United States to which the United States is a party, is lost or destroyed, a certified copy of any official paper of a United States attorney, United States marshal or clerk or other certifying or recording officer of any such court, made pursuant to law, on file in any department or agency of the United States and relating to such case or matter, shall, on being filed in the court to which it relates, have the same effect as an original paper filed in such court. If the copy so filed discloses the date and amount of a judgment or decree and the names of the parties thereto, the court may enforce the judgment or decree as though the original record had not been lost or destroyed.

(b) Whenever the United States is interested in any lost or destroyed records or files of a court of the United States, the clerk of such court and the United States attorney for the district shall take the steps necessary to restore such records or files, under the direction of the judges of such court.

§ 1736. Congressional Journals

Extracts from the Journals of the Senate and the House of Representatives, and from the Executive Journal of the Senate when the injunction of secrecy is removed, certified by the Secretary of the Senate or the Clerk of the House of Representatives shall be received in evidence with the same effect as the originals would have.

§ 1737. Copy of officer's bond

Any person to whose custody the bond of any officer of the United States has been committed shall, on proper request and payment of the fee allowed by any Act of Congress, furnish certified copies thereof, which shall be prima facie evidence in any court of the execution, filing and contents of the bond.

§ 1738. State and Territorial statutes and judicial proceedings; full faith and credit

The Acts of the legislature of any State, Territory, or Possession of the United States, or copies thereof, shall be authenticated by affixing the seal of such State, Territory or Possession thereto.

The records and judicial proceedings of any court of any such State, Territory or Possession, or copies thereof, shall be proved or admitted in other courts within the United States and its Territories and Possessions by the attestation of the clerk and seal of the court annexed, if a seal exists, together with a certificate of a judge of the court that the said attestation is in proper form.

Such Acts, records and judicial proceedings or copies thereof, so authenticated, shall have the same full faith and credit in every court within the United States and its Territories and Possessions as they have by law or usage in the courts of such State, Territory or Possession from which they are taken.

§ 1738A. Full faith and credit given to child custody determinations

(a) The appropriate authorities of every State shall enforce according to its terms, and shall not modify except as provided in subsection (f) of this section, any child custody determination made consistently with the provisions of this section by a court of another State.

(b) As used in this section, the term—

(1) "child" means a person under the age of eighteen;

(2) "contestant" means a person, including a parent, who claims a right to custody or visitation of a child;

(3) "custody determination" means a judgment, decree, or other order of a court providing for the custody or visitation of a child, and includes permanent and temporary orders, and initial orders and modifications;

(4) "home State" means the State in which, immediately preceding the time involved, the child lived with his parents, a parent, or a person acting as parent, for at least six consecutive months, and in the case of a child less than six months old, the State in which the child lived from birth with any of such persons. Periods of temporary absence of any of such persons are counted as part of the six-month or other period;

(5) "modification" and "modify" refer to a custody determination which modifies, replaces, supersedes, or otherwise is made subsequent to, a prior custody determination concerning the same child, whether made by the same court or not;

(6) "person acting as a parent" means a person, other than a parent, who has physical custody of a child and who has either been awarded custody by a court or claims a right to custody;

(7) "physical custody" means actual possession and control of a child; and

(8) "State" means a State of the United States, the District of Columbia, the Commonwealth of Puerto Rico, or a territory or possession of the United States.

(c) A child custody determination made by a court of a State is consistent with the provisions of this section only if—

(1) such court has jurisdiction under the law of such State; and

(2) one of the following conditions is met:

(A) such State (i) is the home State of the child on the date of the commencement of the proceeding, or (ii) had been the child's home State within six months before the date of the commencement of the proceeding and the child is absent from such State because of his removal or retention by a contestant or for other reasons, and a contestant continues to live in such State;

(B)(i) it appears that no other State would have jurisdiction under subparagraph (A), and (ii) it is in the best interest of the child that a court of such State assume jurisdiction because (I) the child and his parents, or the child and at least one contestant, have a significant connection with such State other than mere physical presence in such State, and (II) there is available in such State substantial evidence concerning the child's present or future care, protection, training, and personal relationships;

(C) the child is physically present in such State and (i) the child has been abandoned, or (ii) it is necessary in an emergency to protect the child because he has been subjected to or threatened with mistreatment or abuse;

(D)(i) it appears that no other State would have jurisdiction under subparagraph (A), (B), (C), or (E), or another State has declined to exercise jurisdiction on the ground that the State whose jurisdiction is in issue is the more appropriate forum to determine the custody of the child, and (ii) it is in the best interest of the child that such court assume jurisdiction; or

(E) the court has continuing jurisdiction pursuant to subsection (d) of this section.

(d) The jurisdiction of a court of a State which has made a child custody determination consistently with the provisions of this section continues as long as the requirement of subsection (c)(1) of this section continues to be met and such State remains the residence of the child or of any contestant.

(e) Before a child custody determination is made, reasonable notice and opportunity to be heard shall be given to the contestants, any parent whose parental rights have not been previously terminated and any person who has physical custody of a child.

(f) A court of a State may modify a determination of the custody of the same child made by a court of another State, if—

(1) it has jurisdiction to make such a child custody determination; and

(2) the court of the other State no longer has jurisdiction, or it has declined to exercise such jurisdiction to modify such determination.

(g) A court of a State shall not exercise jurisdiction in any proceeding for a custody determination commenced during the pendency of a proceeding in a court of another State where such court of that other State is exercising jurisdiction consistently with the provisions of this section to make a custody determination.

§ 1739. State and Territorial nonjudicial records; full faith and credit

All nonjudicial records or books kept in any public office of any State, Territory, or Possession of the United States, or copies thereof, shall be proved or admitted in any court or office in any other State, Territory, or Possession by the attestation of the custodian of such records or books, and the seal of his office annexed, if there be a seal, together with a certificate of a judge of a court of record of the county, parish, or district in which such office may be kept, or of the Governor, or secretary of state, the chancellor or keeper of the great seal, of the State, Territory, or Possession that the said attestation is in due form and by the proper officers.

If the certificate is given by a judge, it shall be further authenticated by the clerk or prothonotary of the court, who shall certify, under his hand and the seal of his office, that such judge is duly commissioned and qualified; or, if given by such Governor, secretary, chancellor, or keeper of the great seal, it shall be under the great seal of the State, Territory, or Possession in which it is made.

Such records or books, or copies thereof, so authenticated, shall have the same full faith and credit in every court and office within the United States and its Territories and Possessions as they have by law or usage in the courts or offices of the State, Territory, or Possession from which they are taken.

§ 1740. Copies of consular papers

Copies of all official documents and papers in the office of any consul or vice consul of the United States, and of all official entries in the books or records of any such office, authenticated by the consul or vice consul, shall be admissible equally with the originals.

§ 1741. Foreign official documents

An official record or document of a foreign country may be evidenced by a copy, summary, or excerpt authenticated as provided in the Federal Rules of Civil Procedure.

[§ 1742. Repealed.]

§ 1743. Demand on postmaster

The certificate of the Postmaster General or the General Accounting Office of the mailing to a postmaster of a statement of his account and that payment of the balance stated has not been received shall be sufficient evidence of a demand notwithstanding any allowances or credits subsequently made. A copy of such statement shall be attached to the certificate.

§ 1744. Copies of Patent Office documents, generally

Copies of letters patent or of any records, books, papers, or drawings belonging to the Patent Office and relating to patents, authenticated under the seal of the Patent Office and certified by the Commissioner of Patents, or by another officer of the Patent Office authorized to do so by the Commissioner, shall be admissible in evidence with the same effect as the originals.

Any person making application and paying the required fee may obtain such certified copies.

§ 1745. Copies of foreign patent documents

Copies of the specifications and drawings of foreign letters patent, or applications for foreign letters patent, and copies of excerpts of the official journals and other official publications of foreign patent offices belonging to the United States Patent Office, certified in the manner provided by section 1744 of this title are prima facie evidence of their contents and of the dates indicated on their face.

§ 1746. Unsworn declarations under penalty of perjury

Wherever, under any law of the United States or under any rule, regulation, order, or requirement made pursuant to law, any matter is required or permitted to be supported, evidenced, established, or proved by the sworn declaration, verification, certificate, statement, oath, or affidavit, in writing of the person making the same (other than a deposition, or an oath of office, or an oath required to be taken before a specified official other than a notary public), such matter may, with like force and effect, be supported, evidenced, established, or proved by the unsworn declaration, certificate, verification, or statement, in writing of such person which is subscribed by him, as true under penalty of perjury, and dated, in substantially the following form:

(1) If executed without the United States: "I declare (or certify, verify, or state) under penalty of perjury under the laws of the United States of America that the foregoing is true and correct. Executed on (date).

(Signature)."

(2) If executed within the United States, its territories, possessions, or commonwealths: "I declare (or certify, verify, or state) under penalty of perjury that the foregoing is true and correct. Executed on (date).

(Signature)."

CHAPTER 117—EVIDENCE; DEPOSITIONS

Sec.

§ 1781. Transmittal of letter rogatory or request

(a) The Department of State has power, directly, or through suitable channels—

(1) to receive a letter rogatory issued, or request made, by a foreign or international tribunal, to transmit it to the tribunal, officer, or agency in the United States to whom it is addressed, and to receive and return it after execution; and

(2) to receive a letter rogatory issued, or request made, by a tribunal in the United States, to transmit it to the foreign or international tribunal, officer, or agency to whom it is addressed, and to receive and return it after execution.

(b) This section does not preclude—

(1) the transmittal of a letter rogatory or request directly from a foreign or international tribunal to the tribunal, officer, or agency in the United States to whom it is addressed and its return in the same manner; or

(2) the transmittal of a letter rogatory or request directly from a tribunal in the United States to the foreign or international tribunal, officer, or agency to whom it is addressed and its return in the same manner.

§ 1782. Assistance to foreign and international tribunals and to litigants before such tribunals

(a) The district court of the district in which a person resides or is found may order him to give his testimony or statement or to produce a document or other thing for use in a proceeding in a foreign or international tribunal. The order may be made pursuant to a letter rogatory issued, or request made, by a foreign or international tribunal or upon the application of any interested person and may direct that the testimony or statement be given, or the document or other thing be produced, before a person appointed by the court. By virtue of his appointment, the person appointed has power to administer any necessary oath and take the testimony or statement. The order may prescribe the practice and procedure, which may be in whole or part the practice and procedure of the foreign country or the international tribunal, for taking the testimony or statement or producing the document or other thing. To the extent that the order does not prescribe otherwise, the testimony or statement shall be taken, and the document or other thing produced, in accordance with the Federal Rules of Civil Procedure.

A person may not be compelled to give his testimony or statement or to produce a document or other thing in violation of any legally applicable privilege.

(b) This chapter does not preclude a person within the United States from voluntarily giving his testimony or statement, or producing a document or other thing, for use in a proceeding in a foreign or international tribunal before any person and in any manner acceptable to him.

§ 1783. Subpoena of person in foreign country

(a) A court of the United States may order the issuance of a subpoena requiring the appearance as a witness before it, or before a person or body designated by it, of a national or resident of the United States who is in a foreign country, or requiring the production of a specified document or other thing by him, if the court finds that particular testimony or the production of the document or other thing by him is necessary in the interest of justice, and, in other than a criminal action or proceeding, if the court finds, in addition, that it is not possible to obtain his testimony in admissible form wthout his personal appearance or to obtain the production of the document or other thing in any other manner.

(b) The subpoena shall designate the time and place for the appearance or for the production of the document or other thing. Service of the subpoena and any order to show cause, rule, judgment, or decree authorized by this section or by section 1784 of this title shall be effected in accordance with the provisions of the Federal Rules of Civil Procedure relating to service of process on a person in a foreign country. The person serving the subpoena shall tender to the person to whom the subpoena is addressed his estimated necessary travel and attendance expenses, the amount of which shall be determined by the court and stated in the order directing the issuance of the subpoena.

§ 1784. Contempt

(a) The court of the United States which has issued a subpoena served in a foreign country may order the person who has failed to appear or who has failed to produce a document or other thing as directed therein to show cause before it at a designated time why he should not be punished for contempt.

(b) The court, in the order to show cause, may direct that any of the person's property within the United States be levied upon or seized, in the manner provided by law or court rules governing levy or seizure under execution, and held to satisfy any judgment that may be rendered against him pursuant to subsection (d) of this section if adequate security, in such amount as the court may direct in the order, be given for any damage that he might suffer should he not be found in contempt. Security under this subsection may not be required of the United States.

(c) A copy of the order to show cause shall be served on the person in accordance with section 1783(b) of this title.

(d) On the return day of the order to show cause or any later day to which the hearing may be continued, proof shall be taken. If the person is found in contempt, the court, notwithstanding any limitation upon its power generally to punish for contempt, may fine him not more than $100,000 and direct that the fine and costs of the proceedings be satisfied by a sale of the property levied upon or seized, conducted upon the notice required and in the manner provided for sales upon execution.

[§ 1785. Repealed.]

CHAPTER 119—EVIDENCE; WITNESSES

Sec.

§ 1821. Per diem and mileage generally; subsistence

(a)(1) Except as otherwise provided by law, a witness in attendance at any court of the United States, or before a United States Magistrate, or before any person authorized to take his deposition pursuant to any rule or order of a court of the United States, shall be paid the fees and allowances provided by this section.

(2) As used in this section, the term "court of the United States" includes, in addition to the courts listed in section 451 of this title, any court created by Act of Congress in a territory which is invested with any jurisdiction of a district court of the United States.

(b) A witness shall be paid an attendance fee of $30 per day for each day's attendance. A witness shall also be paid the attendance fee for the time necessarily occupied in going to and returning from the place of attendance at the beginning and end of such attendance or at any time during such attendance.

(c)(1) A witness who travels by common carrier shall be paid for the actual expenses of travel on the basis of the means of transportation reasonably utilized and the distance necessarily traveled to and from such witness's residence by the shortest practical route in going to and returning from the place of attendance. Such a witness shall utilize a common carrier at the most economical rate reasonably available. A receipt or other evidence of actual cost shall be furnished.

(2) A travel allowance equal to the mileage allowance which the Administrator of General Services has prescribed, pursuant to section 5704 of title 5, for official travel of employees of the Federal Government shall be paid to each witness who travels by privately owned vehicle. Computation of mileage under this paragraph shall be made on the basis of a uniformed table of distances adopted by the Administrator of General Services.

(3) Toll charges for toll roads, bridges, tunnels, and ferries, taxicab fares between places of lodging and carrier terminals, and parking fees (upon presentation of a valid parking receipt), shall be paid in full to a witness incurring such expenses.

(4) All normal travel expenses within and outside the judicial district shall be taxable as costs pursuant to section 1920 of this title.

(d)(1) A subsistence allowance shall be paid to a witness (other than a witness who is incarcerated) when an overnight stay is required at the place of attendance because such place is so far removed from the residence of such witness as to prohibit return thereto from day to day.

(2) A subsistence allowance for a witness shall be paid in an amount not to exceed the maximum per diem allowance prescribed by the Administrator of General Services, pursuant to section 5702(a) of title 5, for official travel in the area of attendance by employees of the Federal Government.

(3) A subsistence allowance for a witness attending in an area designated by the Administrator of General Services as a high-cost area shall be paid in an amount not to exceed the maximum actual subsistence allowance prescribed by the Administrator, pursuant to section 5702(c)(B) of title 5, for official travel in such area by employees of the Federal Government.

(4) When a witness is detained pursuant to section 3149 of title 18 for want of security for his appearance, he shall be entitled for each day of detention when not in attendance at court, in addition to his subsistence, to the daily attendance fee provided by subsection (b) of this section.

(e) An alien who has been paroled into the United States for prosecution, pursuant to section 212(d)(5) of the Immigration and Nationality Act (8 U.S.C. 1182(d)(5), or an alien who either has admitted belonging to a class of aliens who are deportable or has been determined pursuant to section 242(b) of such Act (8 U.S.C. 1252(b)) to be deportable, shall be ineligible to receive the fees or allowances provided by this section.

§ 1822. Competency of interested persons; share of penalties payable

Any person interested in a share of any fine, penalty or forfeiture incurred under any Act of Congress, may be examined as a witness in any proceeding for the recovery of such fine, penalty or forfeiture by any party thereto. Such examination shall not deprive the witness of his share.

[§ 1823. Repealed.]

§ 1824. Mileage fees under summons as both witness and juror

No constructive or double mileage fees shall be allowed by reason of any person being summoned both as a witness and a juror.

§ 1825. Payment of fees

In any case wherein the United States or an officer or agency thereof, is a party, the United States marshal for the district shall pay all fees of witnesses on the certificate of the United States Attorney or Assistant United States Attorney, and in the proceedings before a United States Commissioner, on the certificate of such commissioner.

In all proceedings, in forma pauperis, for a writ of habeas corpus or in proceedings under section 2255 of this title, the United States marshal for the district shall pay all fees of witnesses for the party authorized to proceed in forma pauperis, on the certificate of the district judge.

Fees and mileage need not be tendered to the witness upon service of a subpena issued in behalf of the United States or an officer or agency thereof, or upon service of a subpena issued on behalf of a party, authorized to proceed in forma pauperis, where the payment thereof is to be made by the United States marshal as authorized in this section.

§ 1826. Recalcitrant witnesses

(a) Whenever a witness in any proceeding before or ancillary to any court or grand jury of the United States refuses without just cause shown to comply with an order of the court to testify or provide other information, including any book, paper, document, record, recording or other material, the court, upon such refusal, or when such refusal is duly brought to its attention, may summarily order his confinement at a suitable place until such time as the witness is willing to give such testimony or provide such information. No period of such confinement shall exceed the life of—

(1) the court proceeding, or

(2) the term of the grand jury, including extensions,

before which such refusal to comply with the court order occurred, but in no event shall such confinement exceed eighteen months.

(b) No person confined pursuant to subsection (a) of this section shall be admitted to bail pending the determination of an appeal taken by him from the order for his confinement if it appears that the appeal is frivolous or taken for delay. Any appeal from an order of confinement under this section shall be disposed of as soon as practicable, but not later than thirty days from the filing of such appeal.

§ 1827. Interpreters in courts of the United States

(a) The Director of the Administrative Office of the United States Courts shall establish a program to facilitate the use of interpreters in courts of the United States.

(b) The Director shall prescribe, determine, and certify the qualifications of persons who may serve as certified interpreters in courts of the United States in bilingual proceedings and proceedings involving the hearing impaired (whether or not also speech impaired), and in so doing, the Director shall consider the education, training, and experience of those persons. The Director shall maintain a current master list of all interpreters certified by the Director and shall report annually on the frequency of requests for, and the use and effectiveness of, interpreters. The Director shall prescribe a schedule of fees for services rendered by interpreters.

(c) Each United States district court shall maintain on file in the office of the clerk of court a list of all persons who have been certified as interpreters, including bilingual interpreters and oral or manual interpreters for the hearing impaired (whether or not also speech impaired), by the Director of the Administrative Office of the United States Courts in accordance with the certification program established pursuant to subsection (b) of this section.

(d) The presiding judicial officer, with the assistance of the Director of the Administrative Office of the United States Courts, shall utilize the services of the most available certified interpreter, or when no certified interpreter is reasonably available, as determined by the presiding judicial officer, the services of an otherwise competent interpreter, in any criminal or civil action initiated by the United States in a United States district court (including a petition for a writ of habeas corpus initiated in the name of the United States by a relator), if the presiding judicial officer determines on such officer's own motion or on the motion of a party that such party (including a defendant in a criminal case), or a witness who may present testimony in such action—

(1) speaks only or primarily a language other than the English language; or

(2) suffers from a hearing impairment (whether or not suffering also from a speech impairment)

so as to inhibit such party's comprehension of the proceedings or communication with counsel or the presiding judicial officer, or so as to inhibit such witness' comprehension of questions and the presentation of such testimony.

(e)(1) If any interpreter is unable to communicate effectively with the presiding judicial officer, the United States attorney, a party (including a defendant in a criminal case), or a witness, the presiding judicial officer shall dismiss such interpreter and obtain the services of another interpreter in accordance with this section.

(2) In any criminal or civil action in a United States district court, if the presiding judicial officer does not appoint an interpreter under subsection (d) of this section, an individual requiring the services of an interpreter may seek assistance of the clerk of court or the Director of the Administrative Office of the United States Courts in obtaining the assistance of a certified interpreter.

(f)(1) Any individual other than a witness who is entitled to interpretation under subsection (d) of this section may waive such interpretation in whole or in part. Such a waiver shall be effective only if approved by the presiding judicial officer and made expressly by such individual on the record after opportunity to consult with counsel and after the presiding judicial officer has explained to such individual, utilizing the services of the most available certified interpreter, or when no certified interpreter is reasonably available, as determined by the presiding judicial officer, the services of an otherwise competent interpreter, the nature and effect of the waiver.

(2) An individual who waives under paragraph (1) of this subsection the right to an interpreter may utilize the services of a non-

certified interpreter of such individual's choice whose fees, expenses, and costs shall be paid in the manner provided for the payment of such fees, expenses, and costs of an interpreter appointed under subsection (d) of this section.

(g)(1) Except as otherwise provided in this subsection or section 1828 of this title, the salaries, fees, expenses, and costs incident to providing the services of interpreters under subsection (d) of this section shall be paid by the Director of the Administrative Office of the United States Courts from sums appropriated to the Federal judiciary.

(2) Such salaries, fees, expenses, and costs that are incurred with respect to Government witnesses shall, unless direction is made under paragraph (3) of this subsection, be paid by the Attorney General from sums appropriated to the Department of Justice.

(3) The presiding judicial officer may in such officer's discretion direct that all or part of such salaries, fees, expenses, and costs shall be apportioned between or among the parties or shall be taxed as costs in a civil action.

(4) Any moneys collected under this subsection may be used to reimburse the appropriations obligated and disbursed in payment for such services.

(h) In any action in a court of the United States where the presiding judicial officer establishes, fixes, or approves the compensation and expenses payable to an interpreter from funds appropriated to the Federal judiciary, the presiding judicial officer shall not establish, fix, or approve compensation and expenses in excess of the maximum allowable under the schedule of fees for services prescribed pursuant to subsection (b) of this section.

(i) The term "presiding judicial officer" as used in this section and section 1828 of this title includes a judge of a United States district court, a United States magistrate, and a referee in bankruptcy.

(j) The term "United States district court" as used in this section and section 1828 of this title includes any court created by Act of Congress in a territory which is invested with any jurisdiction of a district court of the United States established by section 132 of this title.

(k) The interpretation provided by certified interpreters pursuant to this section shall be in the consecutive mode except that the presiding judicial officer, with the approval of all interested parties, may authorize a simultaneous or summary interpretation when such officer determines that such interpretation will aid in the efficient administration of justice. The presiding judicial officer on such officer's motion or on the motion of a party may order that special interpretation services as authorized in section 1828 of this title be provided if such officer determines that the provision of such services will aid in the efficient administration of justice.

§ 1828. Special interpretation services

(a) The Director of the Administrative Office of the United States Courts shall establish a program for the provision of special interpretation services in criminal actions and in civil actions initiated by the United States (including petitions for writs of habeas corpus initiated in the name of the United States by relators) in a United States district court. The program shall provide a capacity for simultaneous interpretation services in multidefendant criminal actions and multidefendant civil actions.

(b) Upon the request of any person in any action for which special interpretation services established pursuant to subsection (a) are not otherwise provided, the Director, with the approval of the presiding judicial officer, may make such services available to the person requesting the services on a reimbursable basis at rates established in conformity with section 9701 of title 31, but the Director may require the prepayment of the estimated expenses of providing the services by the person requesting them.

(c) Except as otherwise provided in this subsection, the expenses incident to providing services under subsection (a) of this section shall be paid by the Director from sums appropriated to the Federal judiciary. A presiding judicial officer, in such officer's discretion, may order that all or part of the expenses shall be apportioned between or among the parties or shall be taxed as costs in a civil action, and any moneys collected as a result of such order may be used to reimburse the appropriations obligated and disbursed in payment for such services.

(d) Appropriations available to the Director shall be available to provide services in accordance with subsection (b) of this section, and moneys collected by the Director under that subsection may be used to reimburse the appropriations charged for such services. A presiding judicial officer, in such officer's discretion, may order that all or part of the expenses shall be apportioned between or among the parties or shall be taxed as costs in the action.

CHAPTER 121—JURIES; TRIAL BY JURY

Sec.

§ 1861. Declaration of policy

It is the policy of the United States that all litigants in Federal courts entitled to trial by jury shall have the right to grand and petit juries selected at random from a fair cross section of the community in the district or division wherein the court convenes. It is further the policy of the United States that all citizens shall have the opportunity to be considered for service on grand and petit juries in the district courts of the United States, and shall have an obligation to serve as jurors when summoned for that purpose.

§ 1862. Discrimination prohibited

No citizen shall be excluded from service as a grand or petit juror **in the district courts of the United States or in the Court of International Trade on account of race, color, religion, sex, national origin, or economic status.**

§ 1863. Plan for random jury selection

(a) Each United States district court shall devise and place into operation a written plan for random selection of grand and petit jurors that shall be designed to achieve the objectives of sections 1861 and 1862 of this title, and that shall otherwise comply with the provisions of this title. The plan shall be placed into operation after approval by a reviewing panel consisting of the members of the judicial council of the circuit and either the chief judge of the district whose plan is being reviewed or such other active district judge of that district as the chief judge of the district may designate. The panel shall examine the plan to ascertain that it complies with the provisions of this title. If the reviewing panel finds that the plan does not comply, the panel shall state the particulars in which the plan fails to comply and direct the district court to present within a reasonable time an alternative plan remedying the defect or defects. Separate plans may be adopted for each division or combination of divisions within a judicial district. The district court may modify a plan at any time and it shall modify the plan when so directed by the reviewing panel. The district court shall promptly notify the panel, the Administrative Office of the United States Courts, and the Attorney General of the United States, of the initial adoption and future modifications of the plan by filing copies therewith. Modifications of the plan made at the instance of the district court shall become effective after approval by the panel. Each district court shall submit a report on the jury selection process within its jurisdiction to the Administrative Office of the United States Courts in such form and at such times as the Judicial Conference of the United States may specify. The Judicial Conference of the United States may, from time to time, adopt rules and regulations governing the provisions and the operation of the plans formulated under this title.

(b) Among other things, such plan shall—

(1) either establish a jury commission, or authorize the clerk of the court, to manage the jury selection process. If the plan establishes a jury commission, the district court shall appoint one citizen to serve with the clerk of the court as the jury commission: *Provided, however,* That the plan for the District of Columbia may establish a jury commission consisting of three citizens. The citizen jury commissioner shall not belong to the same political party as the clerk serving with him. The clerk or the jury commission, as the case may be, shall act under the supervision and control of the chief judge of the district court or such other judge of the district court as the plan may provide. Each jury commissioner shall, during his tenure in office, reside in the judicial district or division for which he is appointed. Each citizen jury commissioner shall receive compensation to be fixed by the district court plan at a rate not to exceed $50 per day for each day necessarily employed in the performance of his duties, plus reimbursement for travel, subsistence, and other necessary expenses incurred by him in the performance of such duties. The Judicial Conference of the United States may establish standards for allowance of travel, subsistence, and other necessary expenses incurred by jury commissioners.

(2) specify whether the names of prospective jurors shall be selected from the voter registration lists or the lists of actual voters of the political subdivisions within the district or division. The plan shall prescribe some other source or sources of names in addition to voter lists where necessary to foster the policy and protect the rights secured by sections 1861 and 1862 of this title. The plan for the District of Columbia may require the names of prospective jurors to be selected from the city directory rather than from voter lists. The plans for the districts of Puerto Rico and the Canal Zone may prescribe some other source or sources of names of prospective jurors in lieu of voter lists, the use of which shall be consistent with the policies declared and rights secured by sections 1861 and 1862 of this title.

(3) specify detailed procedures to be followed by the jury commission or clerk in selecting names from the sources specified in paragraph (2) of this subsection. These procedures shall be designed to ensure the random selection of a fair cross section of the persons residing in the community in the district or division wherein the court convenes. They shall ensure that names of persons residing in each of the counties, parishes, or similar political subdivisions within the judicial district or division are placed in a master jury wheel; and shall ensure that each coun-

ty, parish, or similar political subdivision within the district or division is substantially proportionally represented in the master jury wheel for that judicial district, division, or combination of divisions. For the purposes of determining proportional representation in the master jury wheel, either the number of actual voters at the last general election in each county, parish, or similar political subdivision, or the number of registered voters if registration of voters is uniformly required throughout the district or division, may be used.

(4) provide for a master jury wheel (or a device similar in purpose and function) into which the names of those randomly selected shall be placed. The plan shall fix a minimum number of names to be placed initially in the master jury wheel, which shall be at least one-half of 1 per centum of the total number of persons on the lists used as a source of names for the district or division; but if this number of names is believed to be cumbersome and unnecessary, the plan may fix a smaller number of names to be placed in the master wheel, but in no event less than one thousand. The chief judge of the district court, or such other district court judge as the plan may provide, may order additional names to be placed in the master jury wheel from time to time as necessary. The plan shall provide for periodic emptying and refilling of the master jury wheel at specified times, the interval for which shall not exceed four years.

(5) specify those groups of persons or occupational classes whose members shall, on individual request therefor, be excused from jury service. Such groups or classes shall be excused only if the district court finds, and the plan states, that jury service by such class or group would entail undue hardship or extreme inconvenience to the members thereof, and excuse of members thereof would not be inconsistent with sections 1861 and 1862 of this title.

(6) specify those groups of persons or occupational classes whose members shall be barred from jury service on the ground that they are exempt. Such groups or classes shall be exempt only if the district court finds, and the plan states, that their exemption is in the public interest and would not be inconsistent with sections 1861 and 1862 of this title. The plan shall provide for exemption of the following persons: (i) members in active service in the Armed Forces of the United States; (ii) members of the fire or police departments of any State, district, territory, possession, or subdivision thereof; (iii) public officers in the executive, legislative, or judicial branches of the Government of the United States, or any State, district, territory, or possession or subdivision thereof, who are actively engaged in the performance of official duties.

(7) fix the time when the names drawn from the qualified jury wheel shall be disclosed to parties and to the public. If the

plan permits these names to be made public, it may nevertheless permit the chief judge of the district court, or such other district court judge as the plan may provide, to keep these names confidential in any case where the interests of justice so require.

(8) **specify the procedures to be followed by the clerk or jury** commission in assigning persons whose names have been drawn from the qualified jury wheel to grand and petit jury panels.

(c) The initial plan shall be devised by each district court and transmitted to the reviewing panel specified in subsection (a) of this section within one hundred and twenty days of the date of enactment of the Jury Selection and Service Act of 1968. The panel shall approve or direct the modification of each plan so submitted within sixty days thereafter. Each plan or modification made at the direction of the panel shall become effective after approval at such time thereafter as the panel directs, in no event to exceed ninety days from the date of approval. Modifications made at the instance of the district court under subsection (a) of this section shall be effective at such time thereafter as the panel directs, in no event to exceed ninety days from the date of modification.

(d) State, local, and Federal officials having custody, possession, or control of voter registration lists, lists of actual voters, or other appropriate records shall make such lists and records available to the jury commission or clerks for inspection, reproduction, and copying at all reasonable times as the commission or clerk may deem necessary and proper for the performance of duties under this title. The district courts shall have jurisdiction upon application by the Attorney General of the United States to compel compliance with this subsection by appropriate process.

§ 1864. Drawing of names from the master jury wheel; completion of juror qualification form

(a) From time to time as directed by the district court, the clerk or a district judge shall publicly draw at random from the master jury wheel the names of as many persons as may be required for jury service. The clerk or jury commission shall prepare an alphabetical list of the names drawn, which list shall not be disclosed to any person except pursuant to the district court plan and to sections 1867 and 1868 of this title. The clerk or jury commission shall mail to every person whose name is drawn from the master wheel a juror qualification form accompanied by instructions to fill out and return the form, duly signed and sworn, to the clerk or jury commission by mail within ten days. If the person is unable to fill out the form, another shall do it for him, and shall indicate that he has done so and the reason therefor. In any case in which it appears that there is an omission, ambiguity, or error in a form, the clerk or jury commission shall return the form with instructions to the person to make such additions or corrections as may be necessary and to return the form to the clerk or jury commission within ten days. Any person who fails to return a completed juror qualification form as instructed may be summoned by the clerk or jury commission forthwith to appear before the clerk or jury commission to fill out a juror qualification form. A person summoned to appear because of failure to return a juror qualification form as instructed who personally appears and executes a juror qualification form before the clerk or jury commission may, at the discretion of the district court, except where his prior failure to execute and mail such form was willful, be entitled to receive for such appearance the same fees and travel allowances paid to jurors under section 1871 of this title. At the time of his appearance for jury service, any person may be required to fill out another juror qualification form in the presence of the jury commission or the clerk or the court, at which time, in such cases as it appears warranted, the person may be questioned, but only with regard to his responses to questions contained on the form. Any information thus acquired by the clerk or jury commission may be noted on the juror qualification form and transmitted to the chief judge or such district court judge as the plan may provide.

(b) Any person summoned pursuant to subsection (a) of this section who fails to appear as directed shall be ordered by the district court forthwith to appear and show cause for his failure to comply with the summons. Any person who fails to appear pursuant to such order or who fails to show good cause for noncompliance with the summons may be fined not more than $100 or imprisoned not more than three days, or both. Any person who willfully misrepresents a material fact on a juror qualification form for the purpose of avoiding or securing service as a juror may be fined not more than $100 or imprisoned not more than three days, or both.

§ 1865. Qualifications for jury service

(a) The chief judge of the district court, or such other district court judge as the plan may provide, on his initiative or upon recommendation of the clerk or jury commission, shall determine solely on the basis of information provided on the juror qualification form and other competent evidence whether a person is unqualified for, or exempt, or to be excused from jury service. The clerk shall enter such determination in the space provided on the juror qualification form and the alphabetical list of names drawn from the master jury wheel. If a person did not appear in response to a summons, such fact shall be noted on said list.

(b) In making such determination the chief judge of the district court, or such other district court judge as the plan may provide, shall deem any person qualified to serve on grand and petit juries in the district court unless he—

(1) is not a citizen of the United States eighteen years old who has resided for a period of one year within the judicial district;

(2) is unable to read, write, and understand the English language with a degree of proficiency sufficient to fill out satisfactorily the juror qualification form;

(3) is unable to speak the English language;

(4) is incapable, by reason of mental or physical infirmity, to render satisfactory jury service; or

(5) has a charge pending against him for the commission of, or has been convicted in a State or Federal court of record of, a crime punishable by imprisonment for more than one year and his civil rights have not been restored.

§ 1866. Selection and summoning of jury panels

(a) The jury commission, or in the absence thereof the clerk, shall maintain a qualified jury wheel and shall place in such wheel names of all persons drawn from the master jury wheel who are determined to be qualified as jurors and not exempt or excused pursuant to the district court plan. From time to time, the jury commission or the clerk shall publicly draw at random from the qualified jury wheel such number of names of persons as may be required for assignment to grand and petit jury panels. The jury commission or the clerk shall prepare a separate list of names of persons assigned to each grand and petit jury panel.

(b) When the court orders a grand or petit jury to be drawn, the clerk or jury commission or their duly designated deputies shall issue summonses for the required number of jurors.

Each person drawn for jury service may be served personally, or by registered, certified, or first-class mail addressed to such person at his usual residence or business address.

If such service is made personally, the summons shall be delivered by the clerk or the jury commission or their duly designated deputies to the marshal who shall make such service.

If such service is made by mail, the summons may be served by the marshal or by the clerk, the jury commission or their duly designated deputies, who shall make affidavit of service and shall attach thereto any receipt from the addressee for a registered or certified summons.

(c) Except as provided in section 1865 of this title or in any jury selection plan provision adopted pursuant to paragraph (5) or (6), of section 1863(b) of this title, no person or class of persons shall be disqualified, excluded, excused, or exempt from service as jurors: *Provided,* That any person summoned for jury service may be (1) excused by the court, upon a showing of undue hardship or extreme inconvenience, for such period as the court deems necessary, at the conclusion of which such person shall be summoned again for jury service under subsections (b) and (c) of this section, or (2) excluded by the court on the ground that such person may be unable to render impartial jury service or that his service as a juror would be likely to disrupt the proceedings, or (3) excluded upon peremptory challenge as provided by law, or (4) excluded pursuant to the procedure specified by law upon a challenge by any party for good cause shown, or (5) excluded upon determination by the court that his service as a juror would be likely to threaten the secrecy of the proceedings, or otherwise adversely affect the integrity of jury deliberations. No person shall be excluded under clause (5) of this subsection unless the judge, in open court, determines that such is warranted and that exclusion of the person will not be inconsistent with sections 1861 and 1862 of this title. The number of persons excluded under clause (5) of this subsection shall not exceed one per centum of the number of persons who return executed jury qualification forms during the period, specified in the plan, between two consecutive fillings of the master jury wheel. The names of persons excluded under clause (5) of this subsection, together with detailed explanations for the exclusions, shall be forwarded immediately to the judicial council of the circuit, which shall have the power to make any appropriate order, prospective or retroactive, to redress any misapplication of clause (5) of this subsection, but otherwise exclusions effectuated under such clause shall not be subject to challenge under the provisions of this title. Any person excluded from a particular jury under clause (2), (3), or (4) of this subsection shall be eligible to sit on another jury if the basis for his initial exclusion would not be relevant to his ability to serve on such other jury.

(d) Whenever a person is disqualified, excused, exempt, or excluded from jury service, the jury commission or clerk shall note in the space provided on his juror qualification form or on the juror's card drawn from the qualified jury wheel the specific reason therefor.

(e) In any two-year period, no person shall be required to (1) serve or attend court for prospective service as a petit juror for a total of more than thirty days, except when necessary to complete service in a particular case, or (2) serve on more than one grand jury, or (3) serve as both a grand and petit juror.

(f) When there is an unanticipated shortage of available petit jurors drawn from the qualified jury wheel, the court may require the marshal to summon a sufficient number of petit jurors selected at random from the voter registration lists, lists of actual voters, or other lists specified in the plan, in a manner ordered by the court consistent with sections 1861 and 1862 of this title.

(g) Any person summoned for jury service who fails to appear as directed shall be ordered by the district court to appear forthwith and show cause for his failure to comply with the summons. Any person who fails to show good cause for noncompliance with a summons may be fined not more than $100 or imprisoned not more than three days, or both.

§ 1867. Challenging compliance with selection procedures

(a) In criminal cases, before the voir dire examination begins, or within seven days after the defendant discovered or could have discovered, by the exercise of diligence, the grounds therefor, whichever is earlier, the defendant may move to dismiss the indictment or stay the proceedings against him on the ground of substantial failure to comply with the provisions of this title in selecting the grand or petit jury.

(b) In criminal cases, before the voir dire examination begins, or within seven days after the Attorney General of the United States discovered or could have discovered, by the exercise of diligence, the grounds therefor, whichever is earlier, the Attorney General may move to dismiss the indictment or stay the proceedings on the ground of substantial failure to comply with the provisions of this title in selecting the grand or petit jury.

(c) In civil cases, before the voir dire examination begins, or within seven days after the party discovered or could have discovered, by the exercise of diligence, the grounds therefor, whichever is earlier, any party may move to stay the proceedings on the ground of substantial failure to comply with the provisions of this title in selecting the petit jury.

(d) Upon motion filed under subsection (a), (b), or (c) of this section, containing a sworn statement of facts which, if true, would constitute a substantial failure to comply with the provisions of this title, the moving party shall be entitled to present in support of such motion the testimony of the jury commission or clerk, if available, any relevant records and papers not public or otherwise available used by the jury commissioner or clerk, and any other relevant evidence. If the court determines that there has been a substantial failure to comply with the provisions of this title in selecting the grand jury, the court shall stay the proceedings pending the selection of a grand jury in conformity with this title or dismiss the indictment, whichever is appropriate. If the court determines that there has been a substantial failure to comply with the provisions of this title in selecting the petit jury, the court shall stay the proceedings pending the selection of a petit jury in conformity with this title.

(e) The procedures prescribed by this section shall be the exclusive means by which a person accused of a Federal crime, the Attorney General of the United States or a party in a civil case may challenge any jury on the ground that such jury was not selected in conformity with the provisions of this title. Nothing in this section shall preclude any person or the United States from pursuing any other remedy, civil or criminal, which may be available for the vindication or enforcement of any law prohibiting discrimination on account of race, color, religion, sex, national origin or economic status in the selection of persons for service on grand or petit juries.

(f) The contents of records or papers used by the jury commission or clerk in connection with the jury selection process shall not be disclosed, except pursuant to the district court plan or as may be necessary in the preparation or presentation of a motion under subsection (a), (b), or (c) of this section, until after the master jury wheel has been emptied and refilled pursuant to section 1863(b) (4) of this title and all persons selected to serve as jurors before the master wheel was emptied have completed such service. The parties in a case shall be allowed to inspect, reproduce, and copy such records or papers at all reasonable times during the preparation and pendency of such a motion. Any person who discloses the contents of any record or paper in violation of this subsection may be fined not more than $1,000 or imprisoned not more than one year, or both.

§ 1868. Maintenance and inspection of records

After the master jury wheel is emptied and refilled pursuant to section 1863(b) (4) of this title, and after all persons selected to serve as jurors before the master wheel was emptied have completed such service, all records and papers compiled and maintained by the jury commission or clerk before the master wheel was emptied shall be preserved in the custody of the clerk for four years or for such longer period as may be ordered by a court, and shall be available for public inspection for the purpose of determining the validity of the selection of any jury.

§ 1869. Definitions

For purposes of this chapter—

(a) "clerk" and "clerk of the court" shall mean the clerk of the district court of the United States or any authorized deputy clerk;

(b) "chief judge" shall mean the chief judge of any district court of the United States;

(c) "voter registration lists" shall mean the official records maintained by State or local election officials of persons registered to vote in either the most recent State or the most recent Federal general election, or, in the case of a State or political subdivision thereof that does not require registration as a prerequisite to voting, other official lists of persons qualified to vote in such election. The term shall also include the list of eligible voters maintained by any Federal examiner pursuant to the Voting Rights Act of 1965 where the names on such list have not been included on the official registration lists or other official lists maintained by the appropriate State or local officials. With respect to the districts of Guam and the Virgin Islands, "voter registration lists" shall mean the official records maintained by territorial election officials of persons registered to vote in the most recent territorial general election;

(d) "lists of actual voters" shall mean the official lists of persons actually voting in either the most recent State or the most recent Federal general election;

(e) "division" shall mean: (1) one or more statutory divisions of a judicial district; or (2) in statutory divisions that contain more than one place of holding court, or in judicial districts where there are no statutory divisions, such counties, parishes, or similar political subdivisions surrounding the places where court is held as the district court plan shall determine: *Provided,* That each county, parish, or similar political subdivision shall be included in some such division;

(f) "district court of the United States," "district court," and "court" shall mean courts constituted under chapter 5 of title 28, United States Code, section 22 of the Organic Act of Guam, as amended (64 Stat. 389; 48 U.S.C. § 1424), section 21 of the Revised Organic Act of the Virgin Islands (68 Stat. 506; 48 U.S.C. § 1611), and section 1 of title 3, Canal Zone Code; except that for purposes of sections 1861, 1862, 1866(c), 1866(d), and 1867 of this chapter such terms shall include the Superior Court of the District of Columbia;

(g) "jury wheel" shall include any device or system similar in purpose or function, such as a properly programed electronic data processing system or device;

(h) "juror qualification form" shall mean a form prescribed by the Administrative Office of the United States Courts and approved by the Judicial Conference of the United States, which shall elicit the name, address, age, race, occupation, education, length of residence within the judicial district, distance from residence to place of holding court, prior jury service, and citizenship of a potential juror, and whether he should be excused or exempted from jury service, has any physical or mental infirmity impairing his capacity to serve as juror, is able to read, write, speak, and understand the English language, has pending against him any charge for the commission of a State or Federal criminal offense punishable by imprisonment for more than one year, or has been convicted in any State or Federal court of record of a crime punishable by imprisonment for more than one year and has not had his civil rights restored. The form shall request, but not require, any other information not inconsistent with the provisions of this title and required by the district court plan in the interests of the sound administration of justice. The form shall also elicit the sworn statement that his responses are true to the best of his knowledge. Notarization shall not be required. The form shall contain words clearly informing the person that the furnishing of any information with respect to his religion, national origin, or economic status is not a prerequisite to his qualification for jury service, that such information need not be furnished if the person finds it objectionable to do so, and that information concerning race is required solely to enforce nondiscrimination in jury selection and has no bearing on an individual's qualification for jury service.

(i) "public officer" shall mean a person who is either elected to public office or who is directly appointed by a person elected to public office.

(j) "undue hardship or extreme inconvenience", as a basis for excuse from immediate jury service under section 1866(c)(1) of this chapter, shall mean great distance, either in miles or travel-time, from the place of holding court, grave illness in the family or any other emergency which outweighs in immediacy and urgency the obligation to serve as a juror when summoned, or any other factor which the court determines to constitute an undue hardship or to create an extreme inconvenience to the juror; and in addition, in situations where it is anticipated that a trial or grand jury proceeding may require more than thirty days of service, the court may consider, as a further basis for temporary excuse, severe economic hardship to an employer which would result from the absence of a key employee during the period of such service;

(k) "publicly draw", as referred to in sections 1864 and 1866 of this chapter, shall mean a drawing which is conducted within the district after reasonable public notice and which is open to the public at large under the supervision of the clerk or jury commission, except that when a drawing is made by means of electronic data processing, "publicly draw" shall mean a drawing which is conducted at a data processing center located in or out of the district, after reasonable public notice given in the district for which juror names are being drawn, and which is open to the public at large under such supervision of the clerk or jury commission as the Judicial Conference of the United States shall by regulation require; and

(*l*) "jury summons" shall mean a summons issued by a clerk of court, jury commission, or their duly designated deputies, containing either a preprinted or stamped seal of court, and containing the name of the issuing clerk imprinted in preprinted, type, or facsimile manner on the summons or the envelopes transmitting the summons.

§ 1870. Challenges

In civil cases, each party shall be entitled to three peremptory challenges. Several defendants or several plaintiffs may be considered as a single party for the purposes of making challenges, or the court may allow additional peremptory challenges and permit them to be exercised separately or jointly.

All challenges for cause or favor, whether to the array or panel or to individual jurors, shall be determined by the court.

§ 1871. Fees

(a) Grand and petit jurors in district courts appearing pursuant to this chapter shall be paid the fees and allowances provided by this section. The requisite fees and allowances shall be disbursed on the certificate of the clerk of court in accordance with the procedure established by the Director of the Administrative Office of the United States Courts. Attendance fees for extended service under subsection (b) of this section shall be certified by the clerk only upon the order of a district judge.

(b)(1) A juror shall be paid an attendance fee of $30 per day for actual attendance at the place of trial or hearing. A juror shall also be paid the attendance fee for the time necessarily occupied in going to and returning from such place at the beginning and end of such service or at any time during such service.

(2) A petit juror required to attend more than thirty days in hearing one case may be paid, in the discretion of the trial judge, an additional fee, not exceeding $5 more than the attendance fee, for each day in excess of thirty days on which he is required to hear such case.

(3) A grand juror required to attend more than forty-five days of actual service may be paid, in the discretion of the district judge in charge of the particular grand jury, an additional fee, not exceeding $5 more than the attendance fee, for each day in excess of forty-five days of actual service.

(4) A grand or petit juror required to attend more than ten days of actual service may be paid, in the discretion of the judge, the appropriate fees at the end of the first ten days and at the end of every ten days of service thereafter.

(5) Certification of additional attendance fees may be ordered by the judge to be made effective commencing on the first day of extended service, without reference to the date of such certification.

(c)(1) A travel allowance not to exceed the maximum rate per mile that the Director of the Administrative Office of the United States Courts has prescribed pursuant to section 604(a)(7) of this title for payment to supporting court personnel in travel status using privately owned automobiles shall be paid to each juror, regardless of the mode of transportation actually employed. The prescribed rate shall be paid for the distance necessarily traveled to and from a juror's residence by the shortest practical route in going to and returning from the place of service. Actual mileage in full at the prescribed rate is payable at the beginning and at the end of a juror's term of service.

(2) The Director shall promulgate rules regulating interim travel allowances to jurors. Distances traveled to and from court should coincide with the shortest practical route.

(3) Toll charges for toll roads, bridges, tunnels, and ferries shall be paid in full to the juror incurring such charges. In the discretion of the court, reasonable parking fees may be paid to the juror incurring such fees upon presentation of a valid parking receipt. Parking fees shall not be included in any tabulation of mileage cost allowances.

(4) Any juror who travels to district court pursuant to summons in an area outside of the contiguous forty-eight States of the United States shall be paid the travel expenses provided under this section, or actual reasonable transportation expenses subject to the discretion of the district judge or clerk of court as circumstances indicate, exercising due regard for the mode of transportation, the availability of

alternative modes, and the shortest practical route between residence and court.

(d)(1) A subsistence allowance covering meals and lodging of jurors shall be established from time to time by the Director of the Administrative Office of the United States Courts pursuant to section 604(a)(7) of this title, except that such allowance shall not exceed the allowance for supporting court personnel in travel status in the same geographical area. Claims for such allowance shall not require itemization.

(2) A subsistence allowance shall be paid to a juror when an overnight stay is required at the place of holding court, and for the time necessarily spent in traveling to and from the place of attendance if an overnight stay is required.

(3) A subsistence allowance for jurors serving in district courts outside of the contiguous forty-eight States of the United States shall be allowed at a rate not to exceed that per diem allowance which is paid to supporting court personnel in travel status in those areas where the Director of the Administrative Office of the United States Courts has prescribed an increased per diem fee pursuant to section 604(a)(7) of this title.

(e) During any period in which a jury is ordered to be kept together and not to separate, the actual cost of subsistence shall be paid upon the order of the court in lieu of the subsistence allowances payable under subsection (d) of this section. Such allowance for the jurors ordered to be kept separate or sequestered shall include the cost of meals, lodging, and other expenditures ordered in the discretion of the court for their convenience and comfort.

(f) A juror who must necessarily use public transportation in traveling to and from court, the full cost of which is not met by the transportation expenses allowable under subsection (c) of this section on account of the short distance traveled in miles, may be paid, in the discretion of the court, the actual reasonable expense of such public transportation, pursuant to the methods of payment provided by this section. Jurors who are required to remain at the court beyond the normal business closing hour for deliberation or for any other reason may be transported to their homes, or to temporary lodgings where such lodgings are ordered by the court, in a manner directed by the clerk and paid from funds authorized under this section.

(g) The Director of the Administrative Office of the United States Courts shall promulgate such regulations as may be necessary to carry out his authority under this section.

§ 1872. Issues of fact in Supreme Court

In all original actions at law in the Supreme Court against citizens of the United States, issues of fact shall be tried by a jury.

§ 1873. Admiralty and maritime cases

In any case of admiralty and maritime jurisdiction relating to any matter of contract or tort arising upon or concerning any vessel of twenty tons or upward, enrolled and licensed for the coasting trade, and employed in the business of commerce and navigation between places in different states upon the lakes and navigable waters connecting said lakes, the trial of all issues of fact shall be by jury if either party demands it.

§ 1874. Actions on bonds and specialties

In all actions to recover the forfeiture annexed to any articles of agreement, covenant, bond, or other specialty, wherein the forfeiture, breach, or nonperformance appears by default or confession of the defendant, the court shall render judgment for the plaintiff for such amount as is due. If the sum is uncertain, it shall, upon request of either party, be assessed by a jury.

§ 1875. Protection of jurors' employment

(a) No employer shall discharge, threaten to discharge, intimidate, or coerce any permanent employee by reason of such employee's jury service, or the attendance or scheduled attendance in connection with such service, in any court of the United States.

(b) Any employer who violates the provisions of this section—

(1) shall be liable for damages for any loss of wages or other benefits suffered by an employee by reason of such violation;

(2) may be enjoined from further violations of this section and ordered to provide other appropriate relief, including but not limited to the reinstatement of any employee discharged by reason of his jury service; and

(3) shall be subject to a civil penalty of not more than $1,000 for each violation as to each employee.

(c) Any individual who is reinstated to a position of employment in accordance with the provisions of this section shall be considered as having been on furlough or leave of absence during his period of jury service, shall be reinstated to his position of employment without loss of seniority, and shall be entitled to participate in insurance or other benefits offered by the employer pursuant to established rules and practices relating to employees on furlough or leave of absence in effect with the employer at the time such individual entered upon jury service.

(d)(1) An individual claiming that his employer has violated the provisions of this section may make application to the district court for the district in which such employer maintains a place of business and the court shall, upon finding probable merit in such claim, appoint counsel to represent such individual in any action in the district court necessary to the resolution of such claim. Such counsel shall be compensated and necessary expenses repaid to the extent provided by section 3006A of title 18, United States Code.

(2) In any action or proceeding under this section, the court may award a prevailing employee who brings such action by retained counsel a reasonable attorney's fee as part of the costs. The court may tax a defendant employer, as costs payable to the court, the attorney fees and expenses incurred on behalf of a prevailing employee, where such costs were expended by the court pursuant to paragraph (1) of this subsection. The court may award a prevailing employer a reasonable attorney's fee as part of the costs only if the court finds that the action is frivolous, vexatious, or brought in bad faith.

§ 1876. Trial by jury in the Court of International Trade

(a) In any civil action in the Court of International Trade which is to be tried before a jury, the jury shall be selected in accordance with the provisions of this chapter and under the procedures set forth in the jury selection plan of the district court for the judicial district in which the case is to be tried.

(b) Whenever the Court of International Trade conducts a jury trial—

(1) the clerk of the district court for the judicial district in which the Court of International Trade is sitting, or an authorized deputy clerk, shall act as clerk of the Court of International Trade for the purposes of selecting and summoning the jury;

(2) the qualifications for jurors shall be the same as those established by section 1865(b) of this title for jurors in the district courts of the United States;

(3) each party shall be entitled to challenge jurors in accordance with section 1870 of this title; and

(4) jurors shall be compensated in accordance with section 1871 of this title.

§ 1877. Protection of jurors

(a) Subject to the provisions of this section and title 5 of the United States Code, subchapter 1 of chapter 81, title 5, United States Code, applies to a Federal grand or petit juror, except that entitlement to disability compensation payments does not commence until the day after the date of termination of service as a juror.

(b) In administering this section with respect to a juror covered by this section—

(1) a juror is deemed to receive monthly pay at the minimum rate for grade GS–2 of the General Schedule unless his actual pay as a Government employee while serving on court leave is higher, in which case monthly pay is determined in accordance with section 8114 of title 5, United States Code, and

(2) performance of duty as a juror includes that time when a juror is (A) in attendance at court pursuant to a summons, (B) in deliberation, (C) sequestered by order of a judge, or (D) at a site, by order of the court, for the taking of a view.

CHAPTER 123—FEES AND COSTS

§ 1911. Supreme Court

The Supreme Court may fix the fees to be charged by its clerk.

The fees of the clerk, cost of serving process, and other necessary disbursements incidental to any case before the court, may be taxed against the litigants as the court directs.

§ 1912. Damages and costs on affirmance

Where a judgment is affirmed by the Supreme Court or a court of appeals, the court in its discretion may adjudge to the prevailing party just damages for his delay, and single or double costs.

§ 1913. Courts of appeals

The fees and costs to be charged and collected in each court of appeals shall be prescribed from time to time by the Judicial Conference of the United States. Such fees and costs shall be reasonable and uniform in all the circuits.

§ 1914. District court; filing and miscellaneous fees; rules of court

(a) The clerk of each district court shall require the parties instituting any civil action, suit or proceeding in such court, whether by original process, removal or otherwise, to pay a filing fee of $60, except that on application for a writ of habeas corpus the filing fee shall be $5.

(b) The clerk shall collect from the parties such additional fees only as are prescribed by the Judicial Conference of the United States.

(c) Each district court by rule or standing order may require advance payment of fees.

(d) This section shall not apply to the District of Columbia.

§ 1915. Proceedings in forma pauperis

(a) Any court of the United States may authorize the commencement, prosecution or defense of any suit, action or proceeding, civil or criminal, or appeal therein, without prepayment of fees and costs or security therefor, by a person who makes affidavit that he is unable to pay such costs or give security therefor. Such affidavit shall state the nature of the action, defense or appeal and affiant's belief that he is entitled to redress.

An appeal may not be taken in forma pauperis if the trial court certifies in writing that it is not taken in good faith.

(b) Upon the filing of an affidavit in accordance with subsection (a) of this section, the court may direct payment by the United States of the expenses of (1) printing the record on appeal in any civil or criminal case, if such printing is required by the appellate court; (2) preparing a transcript of proceedings before a United States magistrate in any civil or criminal case, if such transcript is required by the district court, in the case of proceedings conducted under section 636(b) of this title or under section 3401(b) of title 18, United States Code; and (3) printing the record on appeal if such printing is required by the appellate court, in the case of proceedings conducted pursuant to section 636(c) of this title. Such expenses shall be paid when authorized by the Director of the Administrative Office of the United States Courts.

(c) The officers of the court shall issue and serve all process, and perform all duties in such cases. Witnesses shall attend as in other cases, and the same remedies shall be available as are provided for by law in other cases.

(d) The court may request an attorney to represent any such person unable to employ counsel and may dismiss the case if the allegation of poverty is untrue, or if satisfied that the action is frivolous or malicious.

(e) Judgment may be rendered for costs at the conclusion of the suit or action as in other cases, but the United States shall not be liable for any of the costs thus incurred. If the United States has paid the cost of a stenographic transcript or printed record for the prevailing party, the same shall be taxed in favor of the United States.

§ 1916. Seamen's suits

In all courts of the United States, seamen may institute and prosecute suits and appeals in their own names and for their own benefit for wages or salvage or the enforcement of laws enacted for their health or safety without prepaying fees or costs or furnishing security therefor.

§ 1917. District courts; fee on filing notice of or petition for appeal

Upon the filing of any separate or joint notice of appeal or application for appeal or upon the receipt of any order allowing, or notice of the allowance of, an appeal or of a writ of certiorari $5 shall be paid to the clerk of the district court, by the appellant or petitioner.

§ 1918. District courts; fines, forfeitures and criminal proceedings

(a) Costs shall be included in any judgment, order, or decree rendered against any person for the violation of an Act of Congress in which a civil fine or forfeiture of property is provided for.

(b) Whenever any conviction for any offense not capital is obtained in a district court, the court may order that the defendant pay the costs of prosecution.

§ 1919. District courts; dismissal for lack of jurisdiction

Whenever any action or suit is dismissed in any district court or the Court of International Trade for want of jurisdiction, such court may order the payment of just costs.

§ 1920. Taxation of costs

A judge or clerk of any court of the United States may tax as costs the following:

(1) Fees of the clerk and marshal;

(2) Fees of the court reporter for all or any part of the stenographic transcript necessarily obtained for use in the case;

(3) Fees and disbursements for printing and witnesses;

(4) Fees for exemplification and copies of papers necessarily obtained for use in the case;

(5) Docket fees under section 1923 of this title.

(6) Compensation of court appointed experts, compensation of interpreters, and salaries, fees, expenses, and costs of special interpretation services under section 1828 of this title.

A bill of costs shall be filed in the case and, upon allowance, included in the judgment or decree.

§ 1921. United States marshal's fees

Only the following fees of United States marshals shall be collected and taxed as costs, except as otherwise provided:

For serving a writ of possession, partition, execution, attachment in rem, or libel in admiralty, warrant, attachment, summons, capias, or any other writ, order, or process in any case or proceeding, except as otherwise provided, $3;

For serving a subpena or summons for a witness or appraiser, $2;

For forwarding any writ, order, or process to another judicial district for service, in addition to the prescribed fee, $1;

For the preparation of any notice of sale, proclamation in admiralty, or other public notice or bill of sale, $3;

For seizing or levying on property (including seizures in admiralty), disposing of the same by sale, setoff, or otherwise and receiving and paying over money, commissions of 3 per centum on the first $1,000 of the amounts collected and 1½ per centum on the excess of any sum over $1,000. If not disposed of by marshal's sale, the commission shall be in such amount as may be allowed by the court. In all cases in which the vessel or other property is sold by a public auctioneer, or by some party other than the marshal or his deputy, the commission herein authorized to be paid to the marshal shall be reduced by the amount paid to said auctioneer or other party;

For the keeping of property attached (including boats, vessels, or other property attached or libeled) actual expenses incurred, such as storage, moving, boat hire, or other special transportation, watchmen's or keepers' fees, insurance, and $3 per hour for each deputy marshal required for special services, such as guarding, inventorying, moving, and so forth. The marshals shall collect, in advance, a deposit to cover the initial expenses for such services and periodically thereafter such amounts as may be necessary to pay such expenses until the litigation is concluded;

For copies of writs or other papers furnished at the request of any party, 30 cents per folio of one hundred words or fraction thereof;

For all services in a criminal case except for the summoning of witnesses, a sum to be fixed by the court not exceeding $25 where conviction is for a misdemeanor and not exceeding $100 where conviction is for a felony;

For necessary travel in serving or endeavoring to serve any process, writ, or order, 12 cents per mile, or fraction thereof, to be computed from the place where service is returnable to the place of service or endeavor; or, where two or more services or endeavors, or where an endeavor and a service, are made in behalf of the same party in the same case on the same trip, mileage shall be computed to the place of service or endeavor which is most remote from the place where service is returnable, adding thereto any additional mileage traveled in serving or endeavoring to serve in behalf of that party. When two or more writs of any kind, required to be served in behalf of the same party, on the same person, in the same case or proceeding, may be served at the same time, mileage on only one such writ shall be collected;

No mileage fees shall be collected for services or endeavors to serve in the District of Columbia;

The marshal may require a deposit to cover all fees and expenses herein prescribed.

§ 1922. Witness fees before United States commissioners *

The fees of more than four witnesses shall not be taxed against the United States, in the examination of any criminal case before a United States commissioner, unless their materiality and importance are first approved and certified to by the United States attorney for the district in which the examination is had.

§ 1923. Docket fees and costs of briefs

(a) Attorney's and proctor's docket fees in courts of the United States may be taxed as costs as follows:

$20 on trial or final hearing (including a default judgment whether entered by the court or by the clerk) in civil, criminal, or admiralty cases, except that in cases of admiralty and maritime jurisdiction where the libellant recovers less than $50 the proctor's docket fee shall be $10;

$20 in admiralty appeals involving not over $1,000;

$50 in admiralty appeals involving not over $5,000;

$100 in admiralty appeals involving more than $5,000;

$5 on discontinuance of a civil action;

$5 on motion for judgment and other proceedings on recognizances;

$2.50 for each deposition admitted in evidence.

(b) The docket fees of United States attorneys and United States trustees shall be paid to the clerk of court and by him paid into the Treasury.

(c) In admiralty appeals the court may allow as costs for printing the briefs of the successful party not more than:

$25 where the amount involved is not over $1,000;

$50 where the amount involved is not over $5,000;

$75 where the amount involved is over $5,000.

§ 1924. Verification of bill of costs

Before any bill of costs is taxed, the party claiming any item of cost or disbursement shall attach thereto an affidavit, made by himself or by his duly authorized attorney or agent having knowledge of the facts, that such item is correct and has been necessarily incurred in the case and that the services for which fees have been charged were actually and necessarily performed.

§ 1925. Admiralty and maritime cases

Except as otherwise provided by Act of Congress, the allowance and taxation of costs in admiralty and maritime cases shall be prescribed by rules promulgated by the Supreme Court.

* Probably should now be "Magistrate." Since October 17, 1968, any reference to a United States Commissioner in any previously promulgated rule of any court of the United States has been deemed a reference to a United States Magistrate duly appointed under 28 U.S.C. § 631. Pub.L. 90–578, 82 Stat. 1118.

§ 1926. Claims Court

(a) The Judicial Conference of the United States shall prescribe from time to time the fees and costs to be charged and collected in the United States Claims Court.

(b) The court and its officers shall collect only such fees and costs as the Judicial Conference prescribes. The court may require advance payment of fees by rule.

§ 1927. Counsel's liability for excessive costs

Any attorney or other person admitted to conduct cases in any court of the United States or any Territory thereof who so multiplies the proceedings in any case unreasonably and vexatiously may be required by the court to satisfy personally the excess costs, expenses, and attorneys' fees reasonably incurred because of such conduct.

§ 1928. Patent infringement action; disclaimer not filed

Whenever a judgment is rendered for the plaintiff in any patent infringement action involving a part of a patent and it appears that the patentee, in his specifications, claimed to be, but was not, the original and first inventor or discoverer of any material or substantial part of the thing patented, no costs shall be included in such judgment, unless the proper disclaimer has been filed in the Patent Office prior to the commencement of the action.

§ 1929. Extraordinary expenses not expressly authorized

Where the ministerial officers of the United States incur extraordinary expense in executing Acts of Congress, the payment of which is not specifically provided for, the Attorney General may allow the payment thereof.

§ 1930. Bankruptcy courts

(a) Notwithstanding section 1915 of this title, the parties commencing a case under title 11 shall pay to the clerk of the bankruptcy court the following filing fees:

(1) For a case commenced under chapter 7 or 13 of title 11, $60.

(2) For a case commenced under chapter 9 of title 11, $300.

(3) For a case commenced under chapter 11 of title 11 that does not concern a railroad, as defined in section 101 of title 11, $200.

(4) For a case commenced under chapter 11 of title 11 concerning a railroad, as so defined, $500.

An individual commencing a voluntary case or a joint case under title 11 may pay such fee in installments.

(b) The Judicial Conference of the United States may prescribe additional fees in cases under title 11 of the same kind as the Judicial Conference prescribes under section 1914(b) of this title.

(c) Upon the filing of any separate or joint notice of appeal or application for appeal or upon the receipt of any order allowing, or notice of the allowance of, an appeal or a writ of certiorari $5 shall be paid to the clerk of the bankruptcy court, by the appellant or petitioner.

(d) Whenever any case or proceeding is dismissed in any bankruptcy court for want of jurisdiction, such court may order the payment of just costs.

(e) The clerk of the bankruptcy court may collect only the fees prescribed under this section.

CHAPTER 125—PENDING ACTIONS AND JUDGMENTS

§ 1961. Interest

(a) Interest shall be allowed on any money judgment in a civil case recovered in a district court. Execution therefor may be levied by the marshal, in any case where, by the law of the State in which such court is held, execution may be levied for interest on judgments recovered in the courts of the State. Such interest shall be calculated from the date of the entry of the judgment, at a rate equal to the coupon issue yield equivalent (as determined by the Secretary of the Treasury) of the average accepted auction price for the last auction of fifty-two week United States Treasury bills settled immediately prior to the date of the judgment. The Director of the Administrative Office of the United States Courts shall distribute notice of that rate and any changes in it to all Federal judges.

(b) Interest shall be computed daily to the date of payment except as provided in section 2516(b) of this title and section 1304(b)(1) of title 31, and shall be compounded annually.

(c)(1) This section shall not apply in any judgment of any court with respect to any internal revenue tax case. Interest shall be allowed in such cases at a rate established under section 6621 of the Internal Revenue Code of 1954.

(2) Except as otherwise provided in paragraph (1) of this subsection, interest shall be allowed on all final judgments against the United States in the United States Court of Appeals for the Federal circuit, at the rate provided in subsection (a) and as provided in subsection (b).

(3) Interest shall be allowed, computed, and paid on judgments of the United States Claims Court only as provided in paragraph (1) of this subsection or in any other provision of law.

(4) This section shall not be construed to affect the interest on any judgment of any court not specified in this section.

§ 1962. Lien

Every judgment rendered by a district court within a State shall be a lien on the property located in such State in the same manner, to the same extent and under the same conditions as a judgment of a court of general jurisdiction in such State, and shall cease to be a lien in the same manner and time. Whenever the law of any State requires a judgment of a State court to be registered, recorded, docketed or indexed, or any other act to be done, in a particular manner, or in a certain office or county or parish before such lien attaches, such requirements shall apply only if the law of such State authorizes the judgment of a court of the United States to be registered, recorded, docketed, indexed or otherwise conformed to rules and requirements relating to judgments of the courts of the State.

§ 1963. Registration in other districts

A judgment in an action for the recovery of money or property now or hereafter entered in any district court which has become final by appeal or expiration of time for appeal may be registered in any other district by filing therein a certified copy of such judgment. A judgment so registered shall have the same effect as a judgment of the district court of the district where registered and may be enforced in like manner.

A certified copy of the satisfaction of any judgment in whole or in part may be registered in like manner in any district in which the judgment is a lien.

§ 1963A. Registration of judgments of the Court of International Trade

(a) A judgment in any civil action for the recovery of money or property entered by the Court of International Trade which has become final by appeal or expiration of time for appeal may be registered in any judicial district by filing a certified copy of such judgment. A judgment so registered shall have the same effect as a judgment of the district court of the district where registered and may be enforced in like manner.

(b) A certified copy of the satisfaction of any judgment in whole or in part may be registered in like manner in any district in which the judgment is a lien.

§ 1964. Constructive notice of pending actions

Where the law of a State requires a notice of an action concerning real property pending in a court of the State to be registered, recorded, docketed, or indexed in a particular manner, or in a certain office or county or parish in order to give constructive notice of the action as it relates to the real property, and such law authorizes a notice of an action concerning real property pending in a United States district court to be registered, recorded, docketed, or indexed in the same manner, or in the same place, those requirements of the State law must be complied with in order to give constructive notice of such an action pending in a United States district court as it relates to real property in such State.

CHAPTER 127—EXECUTIONS AND JUDICIAL SALES

§ 2001. Sale of realty generally

(a) Any realty or interest therein sold under any order or decree of any court of the United States shall be sold as a whole or in separate parcels at public sale at the courthouse of the county, parish, or city in which the greater part of the property is located, or upon the premises or some parcel thereof located therein, as the court directs. Such sale shall be upon such terms and conditions as the court directs.

Property in the possession of a receiver or receivers appointed by one or more district courts shall be sold at public sale in the district wherein any such receiver was first appointed, at the courthouse of the county, parish, or city situated therein in which the greater part of the property in such district is located, or on the premises or some parcel thereof located in such county, parish, or city, as such court directs, unless the court orders the sale of the property or one or more parcels thereof in one or more ancillary districts.

(b) After a hearing, of which notice to all interested parties shall be given by publication or otherwise as the court directs, the court may order the sale of such realty or interest or any part thereof at private sale for cash or other consideration and upon such terms and conditions as the court approves, if it finds that the best interests of the estate will be conserved thereby. Before confirmation of any private sale, the court shall appoint three disinterested persons to appraise such property or different groups of three appraisers each to appraise properties of different classes or situated in different localities. No private sale shall be confirmed at a price less than two-thirds of the appraised value. Before confirmation of any private sale, the terms thereof shall be published in such newspaper or newspapers of general circulation as the court directs at least ten days before confirmation. The private sale shall not be confirmed if a bona fide offer is made, under conditions prescribed by the court, which guarantees at least a 10 per centum increase over the price offered in the private sale.

(c) This section shall not apply to sales and proceedings under Title 11 or by receivers or conservators of banks appointed by the Comptroller of the Currency.

§ 2002. Notice of sale of realty

A public sale of realty or interest therein under any order, judgment or decree of any court of the United States shall not be made without notice published once a week for at least four weeks prior to the sale in at least one newspaper regularly issued and of general circulation in the county, state, or judicial district of the United States wherein the realty is situated.

If such realty is situated in more than one county, state, district or circuit, such notice shall be published in one or more of the counties, states, or districts wherein it is situated, as the court directs. The notice shall be substantially in such form and contain such description of the property by reference or otherwise as the court approves. The court may direct that the publication be made in other newspapers.

This section shall not apply to sales and proceedings under Title 11 or by receivers or conservators of banks appointed by the Comptroller of the Currency.

§ 2003. Marshal's incapacity after levy on or sale of realty

Whenever a United States marshal dies, is removed from office, or the term of his commission expires, after levying on realty or any interest therein under a writ of execution issued by a court of the United States, and before sale or other final disposition thereof, like process shall issue to the succeeding marshal and the same proceedings shall be had as if such contingency had not occurred.

Whenever any such contingency arises after a marshal has sold any realty or interest therein and before a deed is executed, the court may, on application by the purchaser, or the plaintiff in whose action the sale was made, setting forth the facts of the case and the reason why the title was not perfected by such marshal, order the succeeding marshal to perfect the title and execute a deed to the purchaser, upon payment of the purchase money and unpaid costs.

§ 2004. Sale of personalty generally

Any personalty sold under any order or decree of any court of the United States shall be sold in accordance with section 2001 of this title, unless the court orders otherwise.

This section shall not apply to sales and proceedings under Title 11 or by receivers or conservators of banks appointed by the Comptroller of the Currency.

§ 2005. Appraisal of goods taken on execution

Whenever State law requires that goods taken on execution be appraised before sale, goods taken under execution issued from a court of the United States shall be appraised in like manner.

The United States marshal shall summon the appraisers in the same manner as the sheriff is required to summon appraisers under State law.

If the appraisers failed to attend and perform their required duties, the marshal may sell the goods without an appraisal. Appraisers attending and performing their duties, shall receive the fees allowed for appraisals under State law.

§ 2006. Execution against revenue officer

Execution shall not issue against a collector or other revenue officer on a final judgment in any proceeding against him for any of his acts, or for the recovery of any money exacted by or paid to him and subsequently paid into the Treasury, in performing his official duties, if the court certifies that:

(1) probable cause existed; or

(2) the officer acted under the directions of the Secretary of the Treasury or other proper Government officer.

When such certificate has been issued, the amount of the judgment shall be paid out of the proper appropriation by the Treasury.

§ 2007. Imprisonment for debt

(a) A person shall not be imprisoned for debt on a writ of execution or other process issued from a court of the United States in any State wherein imprisonment for debt has been abolished. All modifications, conditions, and restrictions upon such imprisonment provided by State law shall apply to any writ of execution or process issued from a court of the United States in accordance with the procedure applicable in such State.

(b) Any person arrested or imprisoned in any State on a writ of execution or other process issued from any court of the United States in a civil action shall have the same jail privileges and be governed by the same regulations as persons confined in like cases on process issued from the courts of such State. The same requirements governing discharge as are applicable in such State shall apply. Any proceedings for discharge shall be conducted before a United States commissioner * for the judicial district wherein the defendant is held.

CHAPTER 129—MONEYS PAID INTO COURT

Sec.

* See footnote to § 1922, *supra*, p. 189.

§ 2041. Deposit of moneys in pending or adjudicated cases

All moneys paid into any court of the United States, or received by the officers thereof, in any case pending or adjudicated in such court, shall be forthwith deposited with the Treasurer of the United States or a designated depositary, in the name and to the credit of such court.

This section shall not prevent the delivery of any such money to the rightful owners upon security, according to agreement of parties, under the direction of the court.

§ 2042. Withdrawal

No money deposited under section 2041 of this title shall be withdrawn except by order of court.

In every case in which the right to withdraw money deposited in court under section 2041 has been adjudicated or is not in dispute and such money has remained so deposited for at least five years unclaimed by the person entitled thereto, such court shall cause such money to be deposited in the Treasury in the name and to the credit of the United States. Any claimant entitled to any such money may, on petition to the court and upon notice to the United States attorney and full proof of the right thereto, obtain an order directing payment to him.

§ 2043. Deposit of other moneys

Except for public moneys deposited under section 2041 of this title, each clerk of the United States courts shall deposit public moneys that the clerk collects into a checking account in the Treasury, subject to disbursement by the clerk. At the end of each accounting period, the earned part of public moneys accruing to the United States shall be deposited in the Treasury to the credit of the appropriate receipt accounts.

CHAPTER 131—RULES OF COURTS

Sec.

§ 2071. Rule-making power generally

The Supreme Court and all courts established by Act of Congress may from time to time prescribe rules for the conduct of their business. Such rules shall be consistent with Acts of Congress and rules of practice and procedure prescribed by the Supreme Court.

§ 2072. Rules of civil procedure

The Supreme Court shall have the power to prescribe by general rules, the forms of process, writs, pleadings, and motions, and the practice and procedure of the district courts and courts of appeals of the United States in civil actions, including admiralty and maritime cases, and appeals therein, and the practice and procedure in proceedings for the review by the courts of appeals of decisions of the Tax Court of the United States and for the judicial review or enforcement of orders of administrative agencies, boards, commissions, and officers.

Such rules shall not abridge, enlarge or modify any substantive right and shall preserve the right of trial by jury as at common law and as declared by the Seventh Amendment to the Constitution.

Such rules shall not take effect until they have been reported to Congress by the Chief Justice at or after the beginning of a regular session thereof but not later than the first day of May, and until the expiration of ninety days after they have been thus reported.

All laws in conflict with such rules shall be of no further force or effect after such rules have taken effect. Nothing in this title, anything therein to the contrary notwithstanding, shall in any way limit, supersede, or repeal any such rules heretofore prescribed by the Supreme Court.

[§ 2073. Repealed.]

[§ 2074. Repealed.]

§ 2075. Bankruptcy rules

The Supreme Court shall have the power to prescribe by general rules, the forms of process, writs, pleadings, and motions, and the practice and procedure in cases under title 11.

Such rules shall not abridge, enlarge, or modify any substantive right.

Such rules shall not take effect until they have been reported to Congress by the Chief Justice at or after the beginning of a regular session thereof but not later than the first day of May and until the expiration of ninety days after they have been thus reported.

§ 2076. Rules of evidence

The Supreme Court of the United States shall have the power to prescribe amendments to the Federal Rules of Evidence. Such amendments shall not take effect until they have been reported to Congress by the Chief Justice at or after the beginning of a regular session of Congress but not later than the first day of May, and until the expiration of one hundred and eighty days after they have been so reported; but if either House of Congress within that time shall by resolution disapprove any amendment so reported it shall not take effect. The effective date of any amendment so reported may be deferred by either House of Congress to a later date or until approved by Act of Congress. Any rule whether proposed or in force may be amended by Act of Congress. Any provision of law in force at the expiration of such time and in conflict with any such amendment not disapproved shall be of no further force or effect after such amendment has taken effect. Any such amendment creating, abolishing, or modifying a privilege shall have no force or effect unless it shall be approved by Act of Congress.

§ 2077. Publication of rules; advisory committees

(a) The rules for the conduct of the business of each court of appeals, including the operating procedures of such court, shall be published. Each court of appeals shall print or cause to be printed necessary copies of the rules. The Judicial Conference shall prescribe the fees for sales of copies under section 1913 of this title, but the Judicial Conference may provide for free distribution of copies to members of the bar of each court and to other interested persons.

(b) Each court of appeals shall appoint an advisory committee for the study of the rules of practice and internal operating procedures of the court of appeals. The advisory committee shall make recommendations to the court concerning such rules and procedures. Members of the committee shall serve without compensation, but the Director may pay travel and transportation expenses in accordance with section 5703 of title 5.

CHAPTER 133—REVIEW—MISCELLANEOUS PROVISIONS

Sec.

§ 2101. Supreme Court; time for appeal or certiorari; docketing; stay

(a) A direct appeal to the Supreme Court from any decision under sections 1252, 1253 and 2282 of this title, holding unconstitutional in whole or in part, any Act of Congress, shall be taken within thirty days after the entry of the interlocutory or final order, judgment or decree. The record shall be made up and the case docketed within sixty days from the time such appeal is taken under rules prescribed by the Supreme Court.

(b) Any other direct appeal to the Supreme Court which is authorized by law, from a decision of a district court in any civil action, suit or proceeding, shall be taken within thirty days from the judgment, order or decree, appealed from, if interlocutory, and within sixty days if final.

(c) Any other appeal or any writ of certiorari intended to bring any judgment or decree in a civil action, suit or proceeding before the Supreme Court for review shall be taken or applied for within ninety days after the entry of such judgment or decree. A justice of the Supreme Court, for good cause shown, may extend the time for applying for a writ of certiorari for a period not exceeding sixty days.

(d) The time for appeal or application for a writ of certiorari to review the judgment of a State court in a criminal case shall be as prescribed by rules of the Supreme Court.

(e) An application to the Supreme Court for a writ of certiorari to review a case before judgment has been rendered in the court of appeals may be made at any time before judgment.

(f) In any case in which the final judgment or decree of any court is subject to review by the Supreme Court on writ of certiorari, the execution and enforcement of such judgment or decree may be stayed for a reasonable time to enable the party aggrieved to obtain a writ of certiorari from the Supreme Court. The stay may be granted by a judge of the court rendering the judgment or decree or by a justice of the Supreme Court, and may be conditioned on the giving of security, approved by such judge or justice, that if the aggrieved party fails to make application for such writ within the period allotted therefor, or fails to obtain an order granting his application, or fails to make his plea good in the Supreme Court, he shall answer for all damages and costs which the other party may sustain by reason of the stay.

§ 2102. Priority of criminal case on appeal from State court

Criminal cases on review from State courts shall have priority, on the docket of the Supreme Court, over all cases except cases to which the United States is a party and such other cases as the court may decide to be of public importance.

§ 2103. Appeal from State court or from a United States court of appeals improvidently taken regarded as petition for writ of certiorari

If an appeal to the Supreme Court is improvidently taken from the decision of the highest court of a State, or of a United States court of appeals, in a case where the proper mode of a review is by petition for certiorari, this alone shall not be ground for dismissal; but the papers whereon the appeal was taken shall be regarded and acted on as a petition for writ of certiorari and as if duly presented to the Supreme Court at the time the appeal was taken. Where in such a case there appears to be no reasonable ground for granting a petition for writ of certiorari it shall be competent for the Supreme Court to adjudge to the respondent reasonable damages for his delay, and single or double costs.

§ 2104. Appeals from State courts

An appeal to the Supreme Court from a State court shall be taken in the same manner and under the same regulations, and shall have the same effect, as if the judgment or decree appealed from had been rendered in a court of the United States.

§ 2105. Scope of review; abatement

There shall be no reversal in the Supreme Court or a court of appeals for error in ruling upon matters in abatement which do not involve jurisdiction.

§ 2106. Determination

The Supreme Court or any other court of appellate jurisdiction may affirm, modify, vacate, set aside or reverse any judgment, decree, or order of a court lawfully brought before it for review, and may remand the cause and direct the entry of such appropriate judgment, decree, or order, or require such further proceedings to be had as may be just under the circumstances.

§ 2107. Time for appeal to court of appeals

Except as otherwise provided in this section, no appeal shall bring any judgment, order or decree in an action, suit or proceeding of a civil nature before a court of appeals for review unless notice of appeal is filed, within thirty days after the entry of such judgment, order or decree.

In any such action, suit or proceeding in which the United States or an officer or agency thereof is a party, the time as to all parties shall be sixty days from such entry.

In any action, suit or proceeding in admiralty, the notice of appeal shall be filed within ninety days after the entry of the order, judgment or decree appealed from, if it is a final decision, and within fifteen days after its entry if it is an interlocutory decree.

The district court may extend the time for appeal not exceeding thirty days from the expiration of the original time herein prescribed, upon a showing of excusable neglect based on failure of a party to learn of the entry of the judgment, order or decree.

This section shall not apply to bankruptcy matters or other proceedings under Title 11.

§ 2108. Proof of amount in controversy

Where the power of any court of appeals to review a case depends upon the amount or value in controversy, such amount or value, if not otherwise satisfactorily disclosed upon the record, may be shown and ascertained by the oath of a party to the case or by other competent evidence.

§ 2109. Quorum of Supreme Court justices absent

If a case brought to the Supreme Court by direct appeal from a district court cannot be heard and determined because of the absence of a quorum of qualified justices, the Chief Justice of the United States may order it remitted to the court of appeals for the circuit including the district in which the case arose, to be heard and determined by that court either sitting in banc or specially constituted and composed of the three circuit judges senior in commission who are able to sit, as such order may direct. The decision of such court shall be final and conclusive. In the event of the disqualification or disability of one or more of such circuit judges, such court shall be filled as provided in chapter 15 of this title.

In any other case brought to the Supreme Court for review, which cannot be heard and determined because of the absence of a quorum of qualified justices, if a majority of the qualified justices shall be of opinion that the case cannot be heard and determined at the next ensuing term, the court shall enter its order affirming the judgment of the court from which the case was brought for review with the same effect as upon affirmance by an equally divided court.

[§ 2110. Repealed]

§ 2111. Harmless error

On the hearing of any appeal or writ of certiorari in any case, the court shall give judgment after an examination of the record without regard to errors or defects which do not affect the substantial rights of the parties.

§ 2112. Record on review and enforcement of agency orders

(a) The rules prescribed under the authority of section 2072 of this title may provide for the time and manner of filing and the contents of the record in all proceedings instituted in the courts of appeals to enjoin, set aside, suspend, modify, or otherwise review or enforce orders of administrative agencies, boards, commissions, and officers. Such rules may authorize the agency, board, commission, or officer to file in the court a certified list of the materials comprising the record and retain and hold for the court all such materials and transmit the same or any part thereof to the court, when and as required by it, at any time prior to the final determination of the proceeding, and such filing of such certified list of the materials comprising the record and such subsequent transmittal of any such materials when and as required shall be deemed full compliance with any provision of law requiring the filing of the record in the court. The record in such proceedings shall be certified and filed in or held for and transmitted to the court of appeals by the agency, board, commission, or officer concerned within the time and in the manner prescribed by such rules. If proceedings have been instituted in two or more courts of appeals with respect to the same order the agency, board, commission, or officer concerned shall file the record in that one of such courts in which a proceeding with respect to such order was first instituted. The other courts in which such proceedings are pending shall thereupon transfer them to the court of appeals in which the record has been filed. For the convenience of the parties in the interest of justice such court may thereafter transfer all the proceedings with respect to such order to any other court of appeals.

(b) The record to be filed in the court of appeals in such a proceeding shall consist of the order sought to be reviewed or enforced, the findings or report upon which it is based, and the pleadings, evidence, and proceedings before the agency, board, commission, or officer concerned, or such portions thereof (1) as the rules prescribed under the authority of section 2072 of this title may require to be included therein, or (2) as the agency, board, commission, or officer concerned, the petitioner for review or respondent in enforcement, as the case may be, and any intervenor in the court proceeding by written stipulation filed with the agency, board, commission, or officer concerned or in the court in any such proceeding may consistently with the rules prescribed under the authority of section 2072 of this title designate to be included therein, or (3) as the court upon motion of a party or, after a prehearing conference, upon its own motion may by order in any such proceeding designate to be included therein. Such a stipulation or order may provide in an appropriate case that no record need be filed in the court of appeals. If, however, the correctness of a finding of fact by the agency, board, commission, or officer is in question all of the evidence before the agency, board, commission, or officer shall be included in the record except such as the agency, board, commission, or officer concerned, the petitioner for review or respondent in enforcement, as the case may be, and any intervenor in the court proceeding by written stipulation filed with the agency, board, commission, or officer concerned or in the court agree to omit as wholly immaterial to the questioned finding. If there is omitted from the record any portion of the proceedings before the agency, board, commission, or officer which the court subsequently determines to be proper for it to consider to enable it to review or enforce the order in question the court may direct that such additional portion of the proceedings be filed as a supplement to the record. The agency, board, commission, or officer concerned may, at its option and without regard to the foregoing provisions of this subsection, and if so requested by the petitioner for review or respondent in enforcement shall, file in the court the entire record of the proceedings before it without abbreviation.

(c) The agency, board, commission, or officer concerned may transmit to the court of appeals the original papers comprising the whole or any part of the record or any supplemental record, otherwise true copies of such papers certified by an authorized officer or deputy of the agency, board, commission, or officer concerned shall be transmitted. Any original papers thus transmitted to the court of appeals shall be returned to the agency, board, commission, or officer concerned upon the final determination of the review or enforcement proceeding. Pending such final determination any such papers may be returned by the court temporarily to the custody of the agency, board, commission, or officer concerned if needed for the transaction of the public business. Certified copies of any papers included in the record or any supplemental record may also be returned to the agency, board, commission, or officer concerned upon the final determination of review or enforcement proceedings.

(d) The provisions of this section are not applicable to proceedings to review decisions of the Tax Court of the United States or to proceedings to review or enforce those orders of administrative agencies, boards, commissions, or officers which are by law reviewable or enforceable by the district courts.

§ 2113. Definition

For purposes of this chapter, the terms "State court", "State courts", and "highest court of a State" include the District of Columbia Court of Appeals.

PART VI—PARTICULAR PROCEEDINGS

CHAPTER 151—DECLARATORY JUDGMENTS

§ 2201. Creation of remedy

In a case of actual controversy within its jurisdiction, except with respect to Federal taxes other than actions brought under section 7428 of the Internal Revenue Code of 1954 or a proceeding under section 505 or 1146 of title 11, any court of the United States, upon the filing of an appropriate pleading, may declare the rights and other legal relations of any interested party seeking such declaration, whether or not further relief is or could be sought. Any such declaration shall have the force and effect of a final judgment or decree and shall be reviewable as such.

§ 2202. Further relief

Further necessary or proper relief based on a declaratory judgment or decree may be granted, after reasonable notice and hearing, against any adverse party whose rights have been determined by such judgment.

CHAPTER 153—HABEAS CORPUS

§ 2241. Power to grant writ

(a) Writs of habeas corpus may be granted by the Supreme Court, any justice thereof, the district courts and any circuit judge within their respective jurisdictions. The order of a circuit judge shall be entered in the records of the district court of the district wherein the restraint complained of is had.

(b) The Supreme Court, any justice thereof, and any circuit judge may decline to entertain an application for a writ of habeas corpus and may transfer the application for hearing and determination to the district court having jurisdiction to entertain it.

(c) The writ of habeas corpus shall not extend to a prisoner unless—

(1) He is in custody under or by color of the authority of the United States or is committed for trial before some court thereof; or

(2) He is in custody for an act done or omitted in pursuance of an Act of Congress, or an order, process, judgment or decree of a court or judge of the United States; or

(3) He is in custody in violation of the Constitution or laws or treaties of the United States; or

(4) He, being a citizen of a foreign state and domiciled therein is in custody for an act done or omitted under any alleged right, title, authority, privilege, protection, or exemption claimed under the commission, order or sanction of any foreign state, or under color thereof, the validity and effect of which depend upon the law of nations; or

(5) It is necessary to bring him into court to testify or for trial.

(d) Where an application for a writ of habeas corpus is made by a person in custody under the judgment and sentence of a State court of a State which contains two or more Federal judicial districts, the application may be filed in the district court for the district wherein such person is in custody or in the district court for the district within which the State court was held which convicted and sentenced him and each of such district courts shall have concurrent jurisdiction to entertain the application. The district court for the district wherein such an application is filed in the exercise of its discretion and in furtherance of justice may transfer the application to the other district court for hearing and determination.

§ 2242. Application

Application for a writ of habeas corpus shall be in writing signed and verified by the person for whose relief it is intended or by someone acting in his behalf.

It shall allege the facts concerning the applicant's commitment or detention, the name of the person who has custody over him and by virtue of what claim or authority, if known.

It may be amended or supplemented as provided in the rules of procedure applicable to civil actions.

If addressed to the Supreme Court, a justice thereof or a circuit judge it shall state the reasons for not making application to the district court of the district in which the applicant is held.

§ 2243. Issuance of writ; return; hearing; decision

A court, justice or judge entertaining an application for a writ of habeas corpus shall forthwith award the writ or issue an order directing the respondent to show cause why the writ should not be granted, unless it appears from the application that the applicant or person detained is not entitled thereto.

The writ, or order to show cause shall be directed to the person having custody of the person detained. It shall be returned within three days unless for good cause additional time, not exceeding twenty days, is allowed.

The person to whom the writ or order is directed shall make a return certifying the true cause of the detention.

When the writ or order is returned a day shall be set for hearing, not more than five days after the return unless for good cause additional time is allowed.

Unless the application for the writ and the return present only issues of law the person to whom the writ is directed shall be required to produce at the hearing the body of the person detained.

The applicant or the person detained may, under oath, deny any of the facts set forth in the return or allege any other material facts.

The return and all suggestions made against it may be amended, by leave of court, before or after being filed.

The court shall summarily hear and determine the facts, and dispose of the matter as law and justice require.

§ 2244. Finality of determination

(a) No circuit or district judge shall be required to entertain an application for a writ of habeas corpus to inquire into the detention of a person pursuant to a judgment of a court of the United States if it appears that the legality of such detention has been determined by a judge or court of the United States on a prior application for a writ of habeas corpus and the petition presents no new ground not theretofore presented and determined, and the judge or court is satisfied that the ends of justice will not be served by such inquiry.

(b) When after an evidentiary hearing on the merits of a material factual issue, or after a hearing on the merits of an issue of law, a person in custody pursuant to the judgment of a State court has been denied by a court of the United States or a justice or judge of the United States release from custody or other remedy on an application for a writ of habeas corpus, a subsequent application for a writ of habeas corpus in behalf of such person need not be entertained by a court of the United States or a justice or judge of the United States unless the application alleges and is predicated on a factual or other ground not adjudicated on the hearing of the earlier application for the writ, and unless the court, justice, or judge is satisfied that the applicant has not on the earlier application deliberately withheld the newly asserted ground or otherwise abused the writ.

(c) In a habeas corpus proceeding brought in behalf of a person in custody pursuant to the judgment of a State court, a prior judgment of the Supreme Court of the United States on an appeal or review by a writ of certiorari at the instance of the prisoner of the decision of such State court, shall be conclusive as to all issues of fact or law with respect to an asserted denial of a Federal right which constitutes ground for discharge in a habeas corpus proceeding, actually adjudicated by the Supreme Court therein, unless the applicant for the writ of habeas corpus shall plead and the court shall find the existence of a material and controlling fact which did not appear in the record of the proceeding in the Supreme Court and the court shall further find that the applicant for the writ of habeas corpus could not have caused such fact to appear in such record by the exercise of reasonable diligence.

§ 2245. Certificate of trial judge admissible in evidence

On the hearing of an application for a writ of habeas corpus to inquire into the legality of the detention of a person pursuant to a judgment the certificate of the judge who presided at the trial resulting in the judgment, setting forth the facts occurring at the trial, shall be admissible in evidence. Copies of the certificate shall be filed with the court in which the application is pending and in the court in which the trial took place.

§ 2246. Evidence; depositions; affidavits

On application for a writ of habeas corpus, evidence may be taken orally or by deposition, or, in the discretion of the judge, by affidavit.

If affidavits are admitted any party shall have the right to propound written interrogatories to the affiants, or to file answering affidavits.

§ 2247. Documentary evidence

On application for a writ of habeas corpus documentary evidence, transcripts of proceedings upon arraignment, plea and sentence and a transcript of the oral testimony introduced on any previous similar application by or in behalf of the same petitioner, shall be admissible in evidence.

§ 2248. Return or answer; conclusiveness

The allegations of a return to the writ of habeas corpus or of an answer to an order to show cause in a habeas corpus proceeding, if not traversed, shall be accepted as true except to the extent that the judge finds from the evidence that they are not true.

§ 2249. Certified copies of indictment, plea and judgment; duty of respondent

On application for a writ of habeas corpus to inquire into the detention of any person pursuant to a judgment of a court of the United States, the respondent shall promptly file with the court certified copies of the indictment, plea of petitioner and the judgment, or such of them as may be material to the questions raised, if the petitioner fails to attach them to his petition, and same shall be attached to the return to the writ, or to the answer to the order to show cause.

§ 2250. Indigent petitioner entitled to documents without cost

If on any application for a writ of habeas corpus an order has been made permitting the petitioner to prosecute the application in forma pauperis, the clerk of any court of the United States shall furnish to the petitioner without cost certified copies of such documents or parts of the record on file in his office as may be required by order of the judge before whom the application is pending.

§ 2251. Stay of State court proceedings

A justice or judge of the United States before whom a habeas corpus proceeding is pending, may, before final judgment or after final judgment of discharge, or pending appeal, stay any proceeding against the person detained in any State court or by or under the authority of any State for any matter involved in the habeas corpus proceeding.

After the granting of such a stay, any such proceeding in any State court or by or under the authority of any State shall be void. If no stay is granted, any such proceeding shall be as valid as if no habeas corpus proceedings or appeal were pending.

§ 2252. Notice

Prior to the hearing of a habeas corpus proceeding in behalf of a person in custody of State officers or by virtue of State laws notice shall be served on the attorney general or other appropriate officer of such State as the justice or judge at the time of issuing the writ shall direct.

§ 2253. Appeal

In a habeas corpus proceeding before a circuit or district judge, the final order shall be subject to review, on appeal, by the court of appeals for the circuit where the proceeding is had.

There shall be no right of appeal from such an order in a proceeding to test the validity of a warrant to remove, to another district or place for commitment or trial, a person charged with a criminal offense against the United States, or to test the validity of his detention pending removal proceedings.

An appeal may not be taken to the court of appeals from the final order in a habeas corpus proceeding where the detention complained of arises out of process issued by a State court, unless the justice or judge who rendered the order or a circuit justice or judge issues a certificate of probable cause.

§ 2254. State custody; remedies in Federal courts

(a) The Supreme Court, a Justice thereof, a circuit judge, or a district court shall entertain an application for a writ of habeas corpus in behalf of a person in custody pursuant to the judgment of a State court only on the ground that he is in custody in violation of the Constitution or laws or treaties of the United States.

(b) An application for a writ of habeas corpus in behalf of a person in custody pursuant to the judgment of a State court shall not be granted unless it appears that the applicant has exhausted the remedies available in the courts of the State, or that there is either an absence of available State corrective process or the existence of circumstances rendering such process ineffective to protect the rights of the prisoner.

(c) An applicant shall not be deemed to have exhausted the remedies available in the courts of the State, within the meaning of this section, if he has the right under the law of the State to raise, by any available procedure, the question presented.

(d) In any proceeding instituted in a Federal court by an application for a writ of habeas corpus by a person in custody pursuant to the judgment of a State court, a determination after a hearing on the merits of a factual issue, made by a State court of competent jurisdiction in a proceeding to which the applicant for the writ and the State or an officer or agent thereof were parties, evidenced by a written finding, written opinion, or other reliable and adequate written indicia, shall be presumed to be correct, unless the applicant shall establish or it shall otherwise appear, or the respondent shall admit—

(1) that the merits of the factual dispute were not resolved in the State court hearing;

(2) that the factfinding procedure employed by the State court was not adequate to afford a full and fair hearing;

(3) that the material facts were not adequately developed at the State court hearing;

(4) that the State court lacked jurisdiction of the subject matter or over the person of the applicant in the State court proceeding;

(5) that the applicant was an indigent and the State court, in deprivation of his constitutional right, failed to appoint counsel to represent him in the State court proceeding;

(6) that the applicant did not receive a full, fair, and adequate hearing in the State court proceeding; or

(7) that the applicant was otherwise denied due process of law in the State court proceeding;

(8) or unless that part of the record of the State court proceeding in which the determination of such factual issue was made, pertinent to a determination of the sufficiency of the evidence to support such factual determination, is produced as provided for hereinafter, and the Federal court on a consideration of such part of the record as a whole concludes that such factual determination is not fairly supported by the record:

And in an evidentiary hearing in the proceeding in the Federal court, when due proof of such factual determination has been made, unless the existence of one or more of the circumstances respectively set forth in paragraphs numbered (1) to (7), inclusive, is shown by the applicant, otherwise appears, or is admitted by the respondent, or unless the court concludes pursuant to the provisions of paragraph numbered (8) that the record in the State court proceeding, considered as a whole, does not fairly support such factual determination, the burden shall rest upon the applicant to establish by convincing evidence that the factual determination by the State court was erroneous.

(e) If the applicant challenges the sufficiency of the evidence adduced in such State court proceeding to support the State court's determination of a factual issue made therein, the applicant, if able, shall produce that part of the record pertinent to a determination of the sufficiency of the evidence to support such determination. If the applicant, because of indigency or other reason is unable to produce such part of the record, then the State shall produce such part of the record and the Federal court shall direct the State to do so by order directed to an appropriate State official. If the State cannot provide such pertinent part of the record, then the court shall determine under the existing facts and circumstances what weight shall be given to the State court's factual determination.

(f) A copy of the official records of the State court, duly certified by the clerk of such court to be a true and correct copy of a finding, judicial opinion, or other reliable written indicia showing such a factual determination by the State court shall be admissible in the Federal court proceeding.

§ 2255. Federal custody; remedies on motion attacking sentence

A prisoner in custody under sentence of a court established by Act of Congress claiming the right to be released upon the ground that the sentence was imposed in violation of the Constitution or laws of the United States, or that the court was without jurisdiction to impose such sentence, or that the sentence was in excess of the maximum authorized by law, or is otherwise subject to collateral attack, may move the court which imposed the sentence to vacate, set aside or correct the sentence.

A motion for such relief may be made at any time.

Unless the motion and the files and records of the case conclusively show that the prisoner is entitled to no relief, the court shall cause notice thereof to be served upon the United States attorney, grant a prompt hearing thereon, determine the issues and make findings of fact and conclusions of law with respect thereto. If the court finds that the judgment was rendered without jurisdiction, or that the sentence imposed was not authorized by law or otherwise open to collateral attack, or that there has been such a denial or infringement of the constitutional rights of the prisoner as to render the judgment vulnerable to collateral attack, the court shall vacate and set the judgment aside and shall discharge the prisoner or resentence him or grant a new trial or correct the sentence as may appear appropriate.

A court may entertain and determine such motion without requiring the production of the prisoner at the hearing.

The sentencing court shall not be required to entertain a second or successive motion for similar relief on behalf of the same prisoner.

An appeal may be taken to the court of appeals from the order entered on the motion as from a final judgment on application for a writ of habeas corpus.

An application for a writ of habeas corpus in behalf of a prisoner who is authorized to apply for relief by motion pursuant to this section, shall not be entertained if it appears that the applicant has failed to apply for relief, by motion, to the court which sentenced him, or that such court has denied him relief, unless it also appears that the remedy by motion is inadequate or ineffective to test the legality of his detention.

CHAPTER 155—INJUNCTIONS; THREE-JUDGE COURTS

Sec.

§ 2283. Stay of State court proceedings

A court of the United States may not grant an injunction to stay proceedings in a State court except as expressly authorized by Act

—previously attached

of Congress, or where necessary in aid of its jurisdiction, or to protect or effectuate its judgments.

§ 2284. Three-judge court; when required; composition; procedure

(a) A district court of three judges shall be convened when otherwise required by Act of Congress, or when an action is filed challenging the constitutionality of the apportionment of congressional districts or the apportionment of any statewide legislative body.

(b) In any action required to be heard and determined by a district court of three judges under subsection (a) of this section, the composition and procedure of the court shall be as follows:

(1) Upon the filing of a request for three judges, the judge to whom the request is presented shall, unless he determines that three judges are not required, immediately notify the chief judge of the circuit, who shall designate two other judges, at least one of whom shall be a circuit judge. The judges so designated, and the judge to whom the request was presented, shall serve as members of the court to hear and determine the action or proceeding.

(2) If the action is against a State, or officer or agency thereof, at least five days' notice of hearing of the action shall be given by registered or certified mail to the Governor and attorney general of the State. The hearing shall be given precedence and held at the earliest practicable day.

(3) A single judge may conduct all proceedings except the trial, and enter all orders permitted by the rules of civil procedure except as provided in this subsection. He may grant a temporary restraining order on a specific finding, based on evidence submitted, that specified irreparable damage will result if the order is not granted, which order, unless previously revoked by the district judge, shall remain in force only until the hearing and determination by the district court of three judges of an application for a preliminary injunction. A single judge shall not appoint a master, or order a reference, or hear and determine any application for a preliminary or permanent injunction or motion to vacate such an injunction, or enter judgment on the merits. Any action of a single judge may be reviewed by the full court at any time before final judgment.

CHAPTER 157.—INTERSTATE COMMERCE COMMISSION ORDERS; ENFORCEMENT AND REVIEW

Sec.

§ 2321. Judicial review of Commission's orders and decisions; procedure generally; process

(a) Except as otherwise provided by an Act of Congress, a proceeding to enjoin or suspend, in whole or in part, a rule, regulation, or order of the Interstate Commerce Commission shall be brought in the court of appeals as provided by and in the manner prescribed in chapter 158 of this title.

(b) The procedure in the district courts in actions to enforce, in whole or in part, any order of the Interstate Commerce Commission other than for payment of money or the collection of fines, penalties, and forfeitures, shall be as provided in this chapter.

(c) The orders, writs, and process of the district courts may, in the cases specified in subsection (b) and in enforcement actions and actions to collect civil penalties under subtitle IV of title 49, run, be served and be returnable anywhere in the United States.

§ 2322. United States as party

All actions specified in section 2321 of this title shall be brought by or against the United States.

§ 2323. Duties of Attorney General; intervenors

The Attorney General shall represent the Government in the actions specified in section 2321 of this title and in enforcement actions and actions to collect civil penalties under subtitle IV of title 49.

The Interstate Commerce Commission and any party or parties in interest to the proceeding before the Commission, in which an order or requirement is made, may appear as parties of their own motion and as of right, and be represented by their counsel, in any action involving the validity of such order or requirement or any part thereof, and the interest of such party.

Communities, associations, corporations, firms, and individuals interested in the controversy or question before the Commission, or in any action commenced under the aforesaid sections may intervene in said action at any time after commencement thereof.

The Attorney General shall not dispose of or discontinue said action or proceeding over the objection of such party or intervenor, who may prosecute, defend, or continue said action or proceeding unaffected by the action or nonaction of the Attorney General therein.

CHAPTER 158—ORDERS OF FEDERAL AGENCIES; REVIEW

§ 2341. Definitions

As used in this chapter—

(1) "clerk" means the clerk of the court in which the petition for the review of an order, reviewable under this chapter, is filed;

(2) "petitioner" means the party or parties by whom a petition to review an order, reviewable under this chapter, is filed; and

(3) "agency" means—

(A) the Commission, when the order sought to be reviewed was entered by the Federal Communications Commission, the Federal Maritime Commission, the Interstate Commerce Commission, or the Atomic Energy Commission, as the case may be;

(B) the Secretary, when the order was entered by the Secretary of Agriculture; and

(C) the Administration, when the order was entered by the Maritime Administration.

§ 2342. Jurisdiction of court of appeals

The court of appeals (other than the United States Court of Appeals for the Federal Circuit) has exclusive jurisdiction to enjoin, set aside, suspend (in whole or in part), or to determine the validity of—

(1) all final orders of the Federal Communications Commission made reviewable by section 402(a) of title 47;

(2) all final orders of the Secretary of Agriculture made under chapters 9 and 20A of title 7, except orders issued under sections 210(e), 217a, and 499g(a) of title 7;

(3) such final orders of the Federal Maritime Commission or the Maritime Administration entered under chapters 23 and 23A of title 46 as are subject to judicial review under section 830 of title 46;

(4) all final orders of the Atomic Energy Commission made reviewable by section 2239 of title 42; and

(5) all rules, regulations, or final orders of the Interstate Commerce Commission made reviewable by section 2321 of this

title and all final orders of such Commission made reviewable under section 11901(i)(2) of title 49, United States Code.

Jurisdiction is invoked by filing a petition as provided by section 2344 of this title.

§ 2343. Venue

The venue of a proceeding under this chapter is in the judicial circuit in which the petitioner resides or has its principal office, or in the United States Court of Appeals for the District of Columbia Circuit.

§ 2344. Review of orders; time; notice; contents of petition; service

On the entry of a final order reviewable under this chapter, the agency shall promptly give notice thereof by service or publication in accordance with its rules. Any party aggrieved by the final order may, within 60 days after its entry, file a petition to review the order in the court of appeals wherein venue lies. The action shall be against the United States. The petition shall contain a concise statement of—

(1) the nature of the proceedings as to which review is sought;

(2) the facts on which venue is based;

(3) the grounds on which relief is sought; and

(4) the relief prayed.

The petitioner shall attach to the petition, as exhibits, copies of the order, report, or decision of the agency. The clerk shall serve a true copy of the petition on the agency and on the Attorney General by registered mail, with request for a return receipt.

§ 2345. Prehearing conference

The court of appeals may hold a prehearing conference or direct a judge of the court to hold a prehearing conference.

§ 2346. Certification of record on review

Unless the proceeding has been terminated on a motion to dismiss the petition, the agency shall file in the office of the clerk the record on review as provided by section 2112 of this title.

§ 2347. Petitions to review; proceedings

(a) Unless determined on a motion to dismiss, petitions to review orders reviewable under this chapter are heard in the court of appeals on the record of the pleadings, evidence adduced, and proceedings before the agency, when the agency has held a hearing whether or not required to do so by law.

(b) When the agency has not held a hearing before taking the action of which review is sought by the petition, the court of appeals shall determine whether a hearing is required by law. After that determination, the court shall—

(1) remand the proceedings to the agency to hold a hearing, when a hearing is required by law;

(2) pass on the issues presented, when a hearing is not required by law and it appears from the pleadings and affidavits filed by the parties that no genuine issue of material fact is presented; or

(3) transfer the proceedings to a district court for the district in which the petitioner resides or has its principal office for a hearing and determination as if the proceedings were originally initiated in the district court, when a hearing is not required by law and a genuine issue of material fact is presented. The procedure in these cases in the district court is governed by the Federal Rules of Civil Procedure.

(c) If a party to a proceeding to review applies to the court of appeals in which the proceeding is pending for leave to adduce additional evidence and shows to the satisfaction of the court that—

(1) the additional evidence is material; and

(2) there were reasonable grounds for failure to adduce the evidence before the agency;

the court may order the additional evidence and any counterevidence the opposite party desires to offer to be taken by the agency. The agency may modify its findings of fact, or make new findings, by reason of the additional evidence so taken, and may modify or set aside its order, and shall file in the court the additional evidence, the modified findings or new findings, and the modified order or the order setting aside the original order.

§ 2348. Representation in proceeding; intervention

The Attorney General is responsible for and has control of the interests of the Government in all court proceedings under this chapter. The agency, and any party in interest in the proceeding before the agency whose interests will be affected if an order of the agency is or is not enjoined, set aside, or suspended, may appear as parties thereto of their own motion and as of right, and be represented by counsel in any proceeding to review the order. Communities, associations, corporations, firms, and individuals, whose interests are affected by the order of the agency, may intervene in any proceeding to review the order. The Attorney General may not dispose of or discontinue the proceeding to review over the objection of any party or intervenor, but any intervenor may prosecute, defend, or continue the proceeding unaffected by the action or inaction of the Attorney General.

§ 2349. Jurisdiction of the proceeding

(a) The court of appeals has jurisdiction of the proceeding on the filing and service of a petition to review. The court of appeals in which the record on review is filed, on the filing, has jurisdiction to vacate stay orders or interlocutory injunctions previously granted by any court, and has exclusive jurisdiction to make and enter, on the petition, evidence, and proceedings set forth in the record on review, a judgment determining the validity of, and enjoining, setting aside, or suspending, in whole or in part, the order of the agency.

(b) The filing of the petition to review does not of itself stay or suspend the operation of the order of the agency, but the court of appeals in its discretion may restrain or suspend, in whole or in part, the operation of the order pending the final hearing and determination of the petition. When the petitioner makes application for an interlocutory injunction restraining or suspending the enforcement, operation, or execution of, or setting aside, in whole or in part, any order reviewable under this chapter, at least 5 days' notice of the hearing thereon shall be given to the agency and to the Attorney General. In a case in which irreparable damage would otherwise result to the petitioner, the court of appeals may, on hearing, after reasonable notice to the agency and to the Attorney General, order a temporary stay or suspension, in whole or in part, of the operation of the order of the agency for not more than 60 days from the date of the order pending the hearing on the application for the interlocutory injunction, in which case the order of the court of appeals shall contain a specific finding, based on evidence submitted to the court of appeals, and identified by reference thereto, that irreparable damage would result to the petitioner and specifying the nature of the damage. The court of appeals, at the time of hearing the application for an interlocutory injunction, on a like finding, may continue the temporary stay or suspension, in whole or in part, until decision on the application. The hearing on an application for an interlocutory injunction shall be given preference and expedited and shall be heard at the earliest practicable date after the expiration of the notice of hearing on the application. On the final hearing of any proceeding to review any order under this chapter, the same requirements as to precedence and expedition apply.

§ 2350. Review in Supreme Court on certiorari or certification

(a) An order granting or denying an interlocutory injunction under section 2349(b) of this title and a final judgment of the court of appeals in a proceeding to review under this chapter are subject to review by the Supreme Court on a writ of certiorari as provided by section 1254(1) of this title. Application for the writ shall be made within 45 days after entry of the order and within 90 days after entry of the judgment, as the case may be. The United States, the agency, or an aggrieved party may file a petition for a writ of certiorari.

(b) The provisions of section 1254(3) of this title, regarding certification, and of section 2101(f) of this title, regarding stays, also apply to proceedings under this chapter.

§ 2351. Enforcement of orders by district courts

The several district courts have jurisdiction specifically to enforce, and to enjoin and restrain any person from violating any order issued under section 193 of title 7.

CHAPTER 159—INTERPLEADER

§ 2361. Process and procedure

In any civil action of interpleader or in the nature of interpleader under section 1335 of this title, a district court may issue its process for all claimants and enter its order restraining them from instituting or prosecuting any proceeding in any State or United States court affecting the property, instrument or obligation involved in the interpleader action until further order of the court. Such process and order shall be returnable at such time as the court or judge thereof directs, and shall be addressed to and served by the United States marshals for the respective districts where the claimants reside or may be found.

Such district court shall hear and determine the case, and may discharge the plaintiff from further liability, make the injunction permanent, and make all appropriate orders to enforce its judgment.

CHAPTER 161—UNITED STATES AS PARTY GENERALLY

§ 2401. Time for commencing action against United States

(a) Except as provided by the Contract Disputes Act of 1978, every civil action commenced against the United States shall be barred unless the complaint is filed within six years after the right of action first accrues. The action of any person under legal disability or beyond the seas at the time the claim accrues may be commenced within three years after the disability ceases.

(b) A tort claim against the United States shall be forever barred unless it is presented in writing to the appropriate Federal agency within two years after such claim accrues or unless action is begun within six months after the date of mailing, by certified or registered mail, of notice of final denial of the claim by the agency to which it was presented.

§ 2402. Jury trial in actions against United States

Any action against the United States under section 1346 shall be tried by the court without a jury, except that any action against the United States under section 1346(a) (1) shall, at the request of either party to such action, be tried by the court with a jury.

§ 2403. Intervention by United States or a State; constitutional question

(a) In any action, suit or proceeding in a court of the United States to which the United States or any agency, officer or employee thereof is not a party, wherein the constitutionality of any Act of Congress affecting the public interest is drawn in question, the court shall certify such fact to the Attorney General, and shall permit the United States to intervene for presentation of evidence, if evidence is otherwise admissible in the case, and for argument on the question of constitutionality. The United States shall, subject to the applicable provisions of law, have all the rights of a party and be subject to all liabilities of a party as to court costs to the extent necessary for a proper presentation of the facts and law relating to the question of constitutionality.

(b) In any action, suit, or proceeding in a court of the United States to which a State or any agency, officer, or employee thereof is not a party, wherein the constitutionality of any statute of that State affecting the public interest is drawn in question, the court shall certify such fact to the attorney general of the State, and shall permit the State to intervene for presentation of evidence, if evidence is otherwise admissible in the case, and for argument on the question of constitutionality. The State shall, subject to the applicable provisions of law, have all the rights of a party and be subject to all liabilities of a party as to court costs to the extent necessary for a proper presentation of the facts and law relating to the question of constitutionality.

§ 2404. Death of defendant in damage action

A civil action for damages commenced by or on behalf of the United States or in which it is interested shall not abate on the death of a defendant but shall survive and be enforceable against his estate as well as against surviving defendants.

§ 2405. Garnishment

In any action or suit commenced by the United States against a corporation for the recovery of money upon a bill, note, or other security, the debtors of the corporation may be summoned as garnishees. Any person so summoned shall appear in open court and depose in writing to the amount of his indebtedness to the corporation at the time of the service of the summons and at the time of making the deposition, and judgment may be entered in favor of the United States for the sum admitted by the garnishee to be due the corporation as if it had been due the United States. A judgment shall not be entered against any garnishee until after judgment has been rendered against the corporation, nor until the sum in which the garnishee is indebted is actually due.

When any garnishee deposes in open court that he is not and was not at the time of the service of the summons indebted to the corporation, an issue may be tendered by the United States upon such deposition. If, upon the trial of that issue, a verdict is rendered against the garnishee, judgment shall be entered in favor of the United States, pursuant to such verdict, with costs.

Any garnishee who fails to appear at the term to which he is summoned shall be subject to attachment for contempt.

§ 2406. Credits in actions by United States; prior disallowance

In an action by the United States against an individual, evidence supporting the defendant's claim for a credit shall not be admitted unless he first proves that such claim has been disallowed, in whole or in part, by the General Accounting Office, or that he has, at the time of the trial, obtained possession of vouchers not previously procurable and has been prevented from presenting such claim to the General Accounting Office by absence from the United States or unavoidable accident.

§ 2407. Delinquents for public money; judgment at return term; continuance

In an action by the United States against any person accountable for public money who fails to pay into the Treasury the sum reported due the United States, upon the adjustment of his account the court shall grant judgment upon motion unless a continuance is granted as specified in this section.

A continuance may be granted if the defendant, in open court and in the presence of the United States attorney, states under oath that he is equitably entitled to credits which have been disallowed by the General Accounting Office prior to the commencement of the action, specifying each particular claim so rejected, and stating that he cannot safely come to trial.

A continuance may also be granted if such an action is commenced on a bond or other sealed instrument and the court requires the original instrument to be produced.

§ 2408. Security not required of United States

Security for damages or costs shall not be required of the United States, any department or agency thereof or any party acting under the direction of any such department or agency on the issuance of process or the institution or prosecution of any proceeding.

Costs taxable, under other Acts of Congress, against the United States or any such department, agency or party shall be paid out of the contingent fund of the department or agency which directed the proceedings to be instituted.

§ 2409. Partition actions involving United States

Any civil action by any tenant in common or joint tenant owning an undivided interest in lands, where the United States is one of such tenants in common or joint tenants, against the United States alone or against the United States and any other of such owners, shall proceed, and be determined, in the same manner as would a similar action between private persons.

Whenever in such action the court orders a sale of the property or any part thereof the Attorney General may bid for the same in behalf of the United States. If the United States is the purchaser, the amount of the purchase money shall be paid from the Treasury upon a warrant drawn by the Secretary of the Treasury on the requisition of the Attorney General.

§ 2409a. Real property quiet title actions

(a) The United States may be named as a party defendant in a civil action under this section to adjudicate a disputed title to real property in which the United States claims an interest, other than a security interest or water rights. This section does not apply to trust or restricted Indian lands, nor does it apply to or affect actions which may be or could have been brought under sections 1346, 1347, 1491, or 2410 of this title, sections 7424, 7425, or 7426 of the Internal Revenue Code of 1954, as amended (26 U.S.C. §§ 7424, 7425, and 7426), or section 208 of the Act of July 10, 1952 (43 U.S.C. § 666).

(b) The United States shall not be disturbed in possession or control of any real property involved in any action under this section pending a final judgment or decree, the conclusion of any appeal therefrom, and sixty days; and if the final determination shall be adverse to the United States, the United States nevertheless may retain such possession or control of the real property or of any part thereof as it may elect, upon payment to the person determined to be entitled thereto of an amount which upon such election the district court in the same action shall determine to be just compensation for such possession or control.

(c) The complaint shall set forth with particularity the nature of the right, title, or interest which the plaintiff claims in the real property, the circumstances under which it was acquired, and the right, title, or interest claimed by the United States.

(d) If the United States disclaims all interest in the real property or interest therein adverse to the plaintiff at any time prior to the actual commencement of the trial, which disclaimer is confirmed by order of the court, the jurisdiction of the district court shall cease unless it has jurisdiction of the civil action or suit on ground other than and independent of the authority conferred by section 1346(f) of this title.

(e) A civil action against the United States under this section shall be tried by the court without a jury.

(f) Any civil action under this section shall be barred unless it is commenced within twelve years of the date upon which it accrued. Such action shall be deemed to have accrued on the date the plaintiff or his predecessor in interest knew or should have known of the claim of the United States.

(g) Nothing in this section shall be construed to permit suits against the United States based upon adverse possession.

§ 2410. Actions affecting property on which United States has lien

(a) Under the conditions prescribed in this section and section 1444 of this title for the protection of the United States, the United States may be named a party in any civil action or suit in any district court, or in any State court having jurisdiction of the subject matter—

(1) to quiet title to,

(2) to foreclose a mortgage or other lien upon,

(3) to partition,

(4) to condemn, or

(5) of interpleader or in the nature of interpleader with respect to,

real or personal property on which the United States has or claims a mortgage or other lien.

(b) The complaint or pleading shall set forth with particularity the nature of the interest or lien of the United States. In actions or suits involving liens arising under the internal revenue laws, the complaint or pleading shall include the name and address of the taxpayer whose liability created the lien and, if a notice of the tax lien was filed, the identity of the internal revenue office which filed the notice, and the date and place such notice of lien was filed. In actions in the State courts service upon the United States shall be made by serving the process of the court with a copy of the complaint upon the United States attorney for the district in which the action is brought or upon an assistant United States attorney or clerical employee designated by the United States attorney in writing filed with the clerk of the court in which the action is brought and by sending copies of the process and complaint, by registered mail, or by certified mail, to the Attorney General of the United States at Washington, District of Columbia. In such actions the United States may appear and answer, plead or demur within sixty days after such service or such further time as the court may allow.

(c) A judgment or decree in such action or suit shall have the same effect respecting the discharge of the property from the mortgage or other lien held by the United States as may be provided with respect to such matters by the local law of the place where the court is situated. However, an action to foreclose a mortgage or other lien, naming the United States as a party under this section, must seek judicial sale. A sale to satisfy a lien inferior to one of the United States shall be made subject to and without disturbing the lien of the United States, unless the United States consents that the property may be sold free of its lien and the proceeds divided as the parties may be entitled. Where a sale of real estate is made to satisfy a lien prior to that of the United States, the United States shall have one year from the date of sale within which to redeem, except that with respect to a lien arising under the internal revenue laws the period shall be 120 days or the period allowable for redemption under State law, whichever is longer, and in any case in which, under the provisions of section 505 of the Housing Act of 1950, as amended (12 U.S.C. § 1701k), and subsection (d) of section 1820 of title 38 of the United States Code, the right to redeem does not arise, there shall be no right of redemption. In any case where the debt owing the United States is due, the United States may ask, by way of affirmative relief, for the foreclosure of its own lien and where property is sold to satisfy a first lien held by the United States, the United States may bid at the sale such sum, not exceeding the amount of its claim with expenses of sale, as may be directed by the head (or his delegate) of the department or agency of the United States which has charge of the administration of the laws in respect to which the claim of the United States arises.

(d) In any case in which the United States redeems real property under this section or section 7425 of the Internal Revenue Code of 1954, the amount to be paid for such property shall be the sum of—

(1) the actual amount paid by the purchaser at such sale (which, in the case of a purchaser who is the holder of the lien being foreclosed, shall include the amount of the obligation secured by such lien to the extent satisfied by reason of such sale),

(2) interest on the amount paid (as determined under paragraph (1)) at 6 percent per annum from the date of such sale, and

(3) the amount (if any) equal to the excess of (A) the expenses necessarily incurred in connection with such property, over (B) the income from such property plus (to the extent such property is used, by the purchaser) a reasonable rental value of such property.

(e) Whenever any person has a lien upon any real or personal property, duly recorded in the jurisdiction in which the property is located, and a junior lien, other than a tax lien, in favor of the United States attaches to such property, such person may make a written request to the officer charged with the administration of the laws in respect of which the lien of the United States arises, to have the same extinguished. If after appropriate investigation, it appears to such officer that the proceeds from the sale of the property would be insufficient to wholly or partly satisfy the lien of the United States, or that the claim of the United States has been satisfied or by lapse of time or otherwise has become unenforceable, such officer shall so report to the Comptroller General who may issue a certificate releasing the property from such lien.

§ 2411. Interest

In any judgment of any court rendered (whether against the United States, a collector or deputy collector of internal revenue, a former collector or deputy collector, or the personal representative in case of death) for any overpayment in respect of any internal revenue tax, interest shall be allowed at the rate of 9 per centum per annum upon the amount of the overpayment, from the date of the payment or collection thereof to a date preceding the date of the refund check by not more than thirty days, such date to be determined by the Commissioner of Internal Revenue. The Commissioner is authorized to tender by check payment of any such judgment, with interest as herein provided, at any time after such judgment becomes final, whether or not a claim for such payment has been duly filed, and such tender shall stop the running of interest, whether or not such refund check is accepted by the judgment creditor.

§ 2412. Costs and fees

(a) Except ase otherwise specifically provided by statute, a judgment for costs, as enumerated in section 1920 of this title, but not including the fees and expenses of attorneys, may be awarded to the prevailing party in any civil action brought by or against the United States or any agency and any official of the United States acting in his or her official capacity in any court having jurisdiction of such action. A judgment for costs when taxed against the United States shall, in an amount established by statute, court rule, or order, be limited to reimbursing in whole or in part the prevailing party for the costs incurred by such party in the litigation.

(b) Unless expressly prohibited by statute, a court may award reasonable fees and expenses of attorneys, in addition to the costs which may be awarded pursuant to subsection (a), to the prevailing party in any civil action brought by or against the United States or any agency and any official of the United States acting in his or her official capacity in any court having jurisdiction of such action. The United States shall be liable for such fees and expenses to the same extent that any other party would be liable under the common law or under the terms of any statute which specifically provides for such an award.

(c)(1) Any judgment against the United States or any agency and any official of the United States acting in his or her official capacity for costs pursuant to subsection (a) shall be paid as provided in sections 2414 and 2517 of this title and shall be in addition to any relief provided in the judgment.

(2) Any judgment against the United States or any agency and any official of the United States acting in his or her official capacity for fees and expenses of attorneys pursuant to subsection (b) shall be paid as provided in sections 2414 and 2517 of this title, except that if the basis for the award is a finding that the United States acted in bad faith, then the award shall be paid by any agency found to have acted in bad faith and shall be in addition to any relief provided in the judgment.

(d)(1)(A) Except as otherwise specifically provided by statute, a court shall award to a prevailing party other than the United States fees and other expenses, in addition to any costs awarded pursuant to subsection (a), incurred by that party in any civil action (other than cases sounding in tort) brought by or against the United States in any court having jurisdiction of that action, unless the court finds that the position of the United States was substantially justified or that special circumstances make an award unjust.

(B) A party seeking an award of fees and other expenses shall, within thirty days of final judgment in the action, submit to the court an application for fees and other expenses which shows that the party is a prevailing party and is eligible to receive an award under this subsection, and the amount sought, including an itemized statement from any attorney or expert witness representing or appearing in behalf of the party stating the actual time expended and the rate at which fees and other expenses were computed. The party shall also allege that the position of the United States was not substantially justified.

(C) The court, in its discretion, may reduce the amount to be awarded pursuant to this subsection, or deny an award, to the extent that the prevailing party during the course of the proceedings engaged in conduct which unduly and unreasonably protracted the final resolution of the matter in controversy.

(2) For the purposes of this subsection—

(A) "fees and other expenses" includes the reasonable expenses of expert witnesses, the reasonable cost of any study, analysis, engineering report, test, or project which is found by the court to be necessary for the preparation of the party's case, and reasonable attorney fees. (The amount of fees awarded under this subsection shall be based upon prevailing market rates for the kind and quality of the services furnished, except that (i) no expert witness shall be compensated at a rate in excess of the highest rate of compensation for expert witnesses paid by the United States; and (ii) attorney fees shall not be awarded in excess of $75 per hour unless the court determines that an increase in the cost of living or a special factor, such as the limited availability of qualified attorneys for the proceedings involved, justifies a higher fee.);

(B) "party" means (i) an individual whose net worth did not exceed $1,000,000 at the time the civil action was filed, (ii) a sole owner of an unincorporated business, or a partnership, corporation, association, or organization whose net worth did not exceed $5,000,000 at the time the civil action was filed, except that an organization described in section 501(c)(3) of the Internal Revenue Code of 1954 (26 U.S.C. 501(c)(3)) exempt from taxation under section 501(a) of the Code and a cooperative association as defined in section 15(a) of the Agricultural Marketing Act (12 U.S.C. 1141j(a)), may be a party regardless of the net worth of such organization or cooperative association, or (iii) a sole owner of an unincorporated business, or a partnership, corporation, association, or organization, having not more than 500 employees at the time the civil action was filed; and

(C) "United States" includes any agency and any official of the United States acting in his or her official capacity.

(3) In awarding fees and other expenses under this subsection to a prevailing party in any action for judicial review of an adversary adjudication, as defined in subsection (b)(1)(C) of section 504 of title 5, United States Code, or an adversary adjudication subject to the Contract Disputes Act of 1978, the court shall include in that award fees and other expenses to the same extent authorized in subsection (a) of such section, unless the court finds that during such adversary adjudication the position of the United States was substantially justified, or that special circumstances make an award unjust.

(4)(A) Fees and other expenses awarded under this subsection may be paid by any agency over which the party prevails from any funds made available to the agency, by appropriation or otherwise, for such purpose. If not paid by any agency, the fees and other expenses shall be paid in the same manner as the payment of final judgments is made in accordance with sections 2414 and 2517 of this title.

(B) There is authorized to be appropriated to each agency for each of the fiscal years 1982, 1983, and 1984, such sums as may be necessary to pay fees and other expenses awarded pursuant to this subsection in such fiscal years.

(5) The Director of the Administrative Office of the United States Courts shall include in the annual report prepared pursuant to section 604 of this title, the amount of fees and other expenses awarded during the preceding fiscal year pursuant to this subsection. The report shall describe the number, nature, and amount of the awards, the claims involved in the controversy, and any other relevant information which may aid the Congress in evaluating the scope and impact of such awards.

(e) The provisions of this section shall not apply to any costs, fees, and other expenses in connection with any proceeding to which section 7430 of the Internal Revenue Code of 1954 applies (determined without regard to subsections (b) and (f) of such section). Nothing in the preceding sentence shall prevent the awarding under subsection (a) of section 2412 of title 28, United States Code, of costs enumerated in section 1920 of such title (as in effect on October 1, 1981).

§ 2413. Executions in favor of United States

A writ of execution on a judgment obtained for the use of the United States in any court thereof shall be issued from and made returnable to the court which rendered the judgment, but may be executed in any other State, in any Territory, or in the District of Columbia.

§ 2414. Payment of judgments and compromise settlements

Except as provided by the Contract Disputes Act of 1978, payment of final judgments rendered by a district court or the Court of International Trade against the United States shall be made on settlements by the General Accounting Office. Payment of final judgments rendered by a State or foreign court or tribunal against the United States, or against its agencies or officials upon obligations or liabilities of the United States, shall be made on settlements by the General Accounting Office after certification by the Attorney General that it is in the interest of the United States to pay the same.

Whenever the Attorney General determines that no appeal shall be taken from a judgment or that no further review will be sought from a decision affirming the same, he shall so certify and the judgment shall be deemed final.

Except as otherwise provided by law, compromise settlements of claims referred to the Attorney General for defense of imminent litigation or suits against the United States, or against its agencies or officials upon obligations or liabilities of the United States, made by the Attorney General or any person authorized by him, shall be settled and paid in a manner similar to judgments in like causes and appropriations or funds available for the payment of such judgments are hereby made available for the payment of such compromise settlements.

§ 2415. Time for commencing actions brought by the United States

(a) Subject to the provisions of section 2416 of this title, and except as otherwise provided by Congress, every action for money damages brought by the United States or an officer or agency thereof which is founded upon any contract express or implied in law or fact, shall be barred unless the complaint is filed within six years after the right of action accrues or within one year after final decisions have been rendered in applicable administrative proceedings required by contract or by law, whichever is later: *Provided*, That in the event of later partial payment or written acknowledgment of debt, the right of action shall be deemed to accrue again at the time of each such payment or acknowledgment: *Provided further*, That an action for money damages brought by the United States for or on behalf of a recognized tribe, band or group of American Indians shall not be barred unless the complaint is filed more than six years and ninety days after the right of action accrued: *Provided further*, That an action for money damages which accrued on the date of enactment of this Act in accordance with subsection (g) brought by the United States for or on behalf of a recognized tribe, band, or group of American Indians, or on behalf of an individual Indian whose land is held in trust or restricted status, shall not be barred unless the complaint is filed sixty days after the date of publication of the list required by section 4(c) of the Indian Claims Act of 1982: *Provided*, That, for those claims that are on either of the two lists published pursuant to the Indian Claims Act of 1982, any right of action shall be barred unless the complaint is filed within (1) one year after the Secretary of the Interior has published in the Federal Register a notice rejecting such claim or (2) three years after the date the Secretary of the Interior has submitted legislation or legislative report to Congress to resolve such claim or more than two years after a final decision has been rendered in applicable administrative proceedings required by contract or by law, whichever is later.

(b) Subject to the provisions of section 2416 of this title, and except as otherwise provided by Congress, every action for money damages brought by the United States or an officer or agency thereof which is founded upon a tort shall be barred unless the complaint is filed within three years after the right of action first accrues: *Provided,* That an action to recover damages resulting from a trespass on lands of the United States; an action to recover damages resulting from fire to such lands; an action to recover for diversion of money paid under a grant program; and an action for conversion of property of the United States may be brought within six years after the right of action accrues, except that such actions for or on behalf of a recognized tribe, band or group of American Indians, including actions relating to allotted trust or restricted Indian lands, may be brought within six years and ninety days after the right of action accrues, except that such actions for or on behalf of a recognized tribe, band, or group of American Indians, including actions relating to allotted trust or restricted Indian lands, or on behalf of an individual Indian whose land is held in trust or restricted status which accrued on the date of enactment of this Act in accordance with subsection (g) may be brought on or before sixty days after the date of the publication of the list required by section 4(c) of the Indian Claims Act of 1982: *Provided,* That, for those claims that are on either of the two lists published pursuant to the Indian Claims Act of 1982, any right of action shall be barred unless the complaint is filed within (1) one year after the Secretary of the Interior has published in the Federal Register a notice rejecting such claim or (2) three years after the Secretary of the Interior has submitted legislation or legislative report to Congress to resolve such claim.

(c) Nothing herein shall be deemed to limit the time for bringing an action to establish the title to, or right of possession of, real or personal property.

(d) Subject to the provisions of section 2416 of this title and except as otherwise provided by Congress, every action for the recovery of money erroneously paid to or on behalf of any civilian employee of any agency of the United States or to or on behalf of any member or dependent of any member of the uniformed services of the United States, incident to the employment or services of such employee or member, shall be barred unless the complaint is filed within six years after the right of action accrues:

Provided, That in the event of later partial payment or written acknowledgment of debt, the right of action shall be deemed to accrue again at the time of each such payment or acknowledgment.

(e) In the event that any action to which this section applies is timely brought and is thereafter dismissed without prejudice, the action may be recommenced within one year after such dismissal, regardless of whether the action would otherwise then be barred by this section. In any action so recommenced the defendant shall not be barred from interposing any claim which would not have been barred in the original action.

(f) The provisions of this section shall not prevent the assertion, in an action against the United States or an officer or agency thereof, of any claim of the United States or an officer or agency thereof against an opposing party, a co-party, or a third party that arises out of the transaction or occurrence that is the subject matter of the opposing party's claim. A claim of the United States or an officer or agency thereof that does not arise out of the transaction or occurrence that is the subject matter of the opposing party's claim may, if time-barred, be asserted only by way of offset and may be allowed in an amount not to exceed the amount of the opposing party's recovery.

(g) Any right of action subject to the provisions of this section which accrued prior to the date of enactment of this Act shall, for purposes of this section, be deemed to have accrued on the date of enactment of this Act.

(h) Nothing in this Act shall apply to actions brought under the Internal Revenue Code or incidental to the collection of taxes imposed by the United States.

(i) The provisions of this section shall not prevent the United States or an officer or agency thereof from collecting any claim of the United States by means of administrative offset, in accordance with section 5 of the Federal Claims Collection Act of 1966.

§ 2416. Time for commencing actions brought by the United States —Exclusions

For the purpose of computing the limitations periods established in section 2415, there shall be excluded all periods during which—

(a) the defendant or the res is outside the United States, its territories and possessions, the District of Columbia, or the Commonwealth of Puerto Rico; or

(b) the defendant is exempt from legal process because of infancy, mental incompetence, diplomatic immunity, or for any other reason; or

(c) facts material to the right of action are not known and reasonably could not be known by an official of the United States charged with the responsibility to act in the circumstances; or

(d) the United States is in a state of war declared pursuant to article I, section 8, of the Constitution of the United States.

CHAPTER 163—FINES, PENALTIES, AND FORFEITURES

§ 2461. Mode of recovery

(a) Whenever a civil fine, penalty or pecuniary forfeiture is prescribed for the violation of an Act of Congress without specifying the mode of recovery or enforcement thereof, it may be recovered in a civil action.

(b) Unless otherwise provided by Act of Congress, whenever a forfeiture of property is prescribed as a penalty for violation of an Act of Congress and the seizure takes place on the high seas or on navigable waters within the admiralty and maritime jurisdiction of the United States, such forfeiture may be enforced by libel in admiralty but in cases of seizures on land the forfeiture may be enforced by a proceeding by libel which shall conform as near as may be to proceedings in admiralty.

§ 2462. Time for commencing proceedings

Except as otherwise provided by Act of Congress, an action, suit or proceeding for the enforcement of any civil fine, penalty, or forfeiture, pecuniary or otherwise, shall not be entertained unless commenced within five years from the date when the claim first accrued if, within the same period, the offender or the property is found within the United States in order that proper service may be made thereon.

§ 2463. Property taken under revenue law not repleviable

All property taken or detained under any revenue law of the United States shall not be repleviable, but shall be deemed to be in the custody of the law and subject only to the orders and decrees of the courts of the United States having jurisdiction thereof.

§ 2464. Security; special bond

(a) Except in cases of seizures for forfeiture under any law of the United States, whenever a warrant of arrest or other process in rem is issued in any admiralty case, the United States marshal shall stay the execution of such process, or discharge the property arrested if the process has been levied, on receiving from the respondent or claimant of the property a bond or stipulation in double the amount claimed by the libellant, with sufficient surety, to be approved by the judge of the district court where the case is pending, or, in his absence, by the collector of the port, conditioned to answer the decree of the court in such case. Such bond or stipulation shall be returned to the court, and judgment or decree thereon, against both the principal and sureties, may be secured at the time of rendering the decree in the original case. The owner of any vessel may deliver to the marshal a bond or stipulation, with sufficient surety, to be approved by the judge of the district court, conditioned to answer the decree of such court in all or any cases that are brought thereafter in such court against the vessel. Thereupon the execution of all such process against such vessel shall be stayed so long as the amount secured by such bond or stipulation is at least double the aggregate amount claimed by libellants in such suits which are begun and pending against such vessel. Similar judgments or decrees and remedies may be had on such bond or stipulation as if a special bond or stipulation had been filed in each of such suits.

(b) The court may make necessary orders to carry this section into effect, particularly in giving proper notice of any such suit. Such bond or stipulation shall be indorsed by the clerk with a minute of the suits wherein process is so stayed. Further security may be required by the court at any time.

(c) If a special bond or stipulation in the particular case is given under this section, the liability as to said case on the general bond or stipulation shall cease. The parties may stipulate the amount of the bond or stipulation for the release of a vessel or other property to be not more than the amount claimed in the libel, with interest, plus an allowance for libellant's costs. In the event of the inability or refusal of the parties to so stipulate, the court shall fix the amount, but if not so fixed then a bond shall be required in the amount prescribed in this section.

§ 2465. Return of property to claimant; certificate of reasonable cause; liability for wrongful seizure

Upon the entry of judgment for the claimant in any proceeding to condemn or forfeit property seized under any Act of Congress, such property shall be returned forthwith to the claimant or his agent; but if it appears that there was reasonable cause for the seizure, the court shall cause a proper certificate thereof to be entered and the claimant shall not, in such case, be entitled to costs, nor shall the person who made the seizure, nor the prosecutor, be liable to suit or judgment on account of such suit or prosecution.

CHAPTER 165—UNITED STATES CLAIMS COURT PROCEDURE

Sec.

§ 2501. Time for filing suit

Every claim of which the United States Claims Court has jurisdiction shall be barred unless the petition thereon is filed, within six years after such claim first accrues.

Every claim under section 1497 of this title shall be barred unless the petition thereon is filed within two years after the termination of the river and harbor improvements operations on which the claim is based.

A petition on the claim of a person under legal disability or beyond the seas at the time the claim accrues may be filed within three years after the disability ceases.

A suit for the fees of an officer of the United States shall not be filed until his account for such fees has been finally acted upon, unless the General Accounting Office fails to act within six months after receiving the account.

§ 2502. Aliens' privilege to sue

(a) Citizens or subjects of any foreign government which accords to citizens of the United States the right to prosecute claims against their government in its courts may sue the United States in the United States Claims Court if the subject matter of the suit is otherwise within such court's jurisdiction.

(b) See section 7422(f) of the Internal Revenue Code of 1954 for exception with respect to suits involving internal revenue taxes.

§ 2503. Proceedings generally

(a) Parties to any suit in the United States Claims Court may appear before a judge of that court in person or by attorney, produce evidence, and examine witnesses.

(b) The proceedings of the Claims Court shall be in accordance with such rules of practice and procedure (other than the rules of evidence) as the Claims Court may prescribe and in accordance with the Federal Rules of Evidence.

(c) The judges of the Claims Court shall fix times for trials, administer oaths or affirmations, examine witnesses, receive evidence, and enter dispositive judgments. Hearings shall, if convenient, be held in the counties where the witnesses reside.

§ 2504. Plaintiff's testimony

The United States Claims Court may, at the instance of the Attorney General, order any plaintiff to appear, upon reasonable notice, before any judge of the court and be examined on oath as to all matters pertaining to his claim. Such examination shall be reduced to writing by the judge, and shall be returned to and filed in the court, and may, at the discretion of the attorneys for the United States, be read and used as evidence on the trial. If any plaintiff, after such order is made and due and reasonable notice thereof is given to him, fails to appear, or refuses to testify or answer fully as to all material matters within his knowledge, the court may order that the case shall not be tried until he fully complies with such order.

§ 2505. Trial before judges

Any judge of the United States Claims Court may sit at any place within the United States to take evidence and enter judgment.

§ 2506. Interest of witness

A witness in a suit in the United States Claims Court shall not be exempt or disqualified because he is a party to or interested in such suit.

§ 2507. Calls and discovery

(a) The United States Claims Court may call upon any department or agency of the United States or upon any party for any information or papers, not privileged, for purposes of discovery or for use as evidence. The head of any department or agency may refuse to comply with a call issued pursuant to this subsection when, in his opinion, compliance will be injurious to the public interest.

(b) Without limitation on account of anything contained in subsection (a) of this section, the court may, in accordance with its rules, provide additional means for the discovery of any relevant facts, books, papers, documents or tangible things, not privileged.

(c) The Claims Court may use all recorded and printed reports made by the committees of the Senate or House of Representatives.

§ 2508. Counterclaim or set-off; registration of judgment

Upon the trial of any suit in the United States Claims Court in which any set-off, counterclaim, claim for damages, or other demand is set up on the part of the United States against any plaintiff making claim against the United States in said court, the court shall hear and determine such claim or demand both for and against the United States and plaintiff.

If upon the whole case it finds that the plaintiff is indebted to the United States it shall render judgment to that effect, and such judgment shall be final and reviewable.

The transcript of such judgment, filed in the clerk's office of any district court, shall be entered upon the records and shall be enforceable as other judgments.

§ 2509. Congressional reference cases

(a) Whenever a bill, except a bill for a pension, is referred by either House of Congress to the chief judge of the United States Claims Court pursuant to section 1492 of this title, the chief judge shall designate a judge as hearing officer for the case and a panel of three judges of the court to serve as a reviewing body. One member of the review panel shall be designated as presiding officer of the panel.

(b) Proceedings in a congressional reference case shall be under rules and regulations prescribed for the purpose by the chief judge who is hereby authorized and directed to require the application of the pertinent rules of practice of the Claims Court insofar as feasible. Each hearing officer and each review panel shall have authority to do and perform any acts which may be necessary or proper for the efficient performance of their duties, including the power of subpena and the power to administer oaths and affirmations. None of the rules, rulings, findings, or conclusions authorized by this section shall be subject to judicial review.

(c) The hearing officer to whom a congressional reference case is assigned by the chief judge shall proceed in accordance with the applicable rules to determine the facts, including facts relating to delay or laches, facts bearing upon the question whether the bar of any statute of limitation should be removed, or facts claimed to excuse the claimant for not having resorted to any established legal remedy. He shall append to his findings of fact conclusions sufficient to inform Congress whether the demand is a legal or equitable claim or a gratuity, and the amount, if any, legally or equitably due from the United States to the claimant.

(d) The findings and conclusions of the hearing officer shall be submitted by him, together with the record in the case, to the review panel for review by it pursuant to such rules as may be provided for the purpose, which shall include provision for submitting the report of the hearing officer to the parties for consideration, exception, and argument before the panel. The panel, by majority vote, shall adopt or modify the findings or the conclusions of the hearing officer.

(e) The panel shall submit its report to the chief judge for transmission to the appropriate House of Congress.

(f) Any act or failure to act or other conduct by a party, a witness, or an attorney which would call for the imposition of sanctions under the rules of practice of the Claims Court shall be noted by the panel or the hearing officer at the time of occurrence thereof and upon failure of the delinquent or offending party, witness, or attorney to make prompt compliance with the order of the panel or the hearing officer a full statement of the circumstances shall be incorporated in the report of the panel.

(g) The Claims Court is hereby authorized and directed, under such regulations as it may prescribe, to provide the facilities and services of the office of the clerk of the court for the filing, processing, hearing, and dispatch of congressional reference cases and to include within its annual appropriations the costs thereof and other costs of administration, including (but without limitation to the items herein listed) the salaries and traveling expenses of the judges serving as hearing officers and panel members, mailing and service of process, necessary physical facilities, equipment, and supplies, and personnel (including secretaries and law clerks).

§ 2510. Referral of cases by Comptroller General

(a) The Comptroller General may transmit to the United States Claims Court for trial and adjudication any claim or matter of which the Claims Court might take jurisdiction on the voluntary action of the claimant, together with all vouchers, papers, documents, and proofs pertaining thereto.

(b) The Claims Court shall proceed with the claims or matters so referred as in other cases pending in such Court and shall render judgment thereon.

§ 2511. Accounts of officers, agents or contractors

Notice of suit under section 1494 of this title shall be given to the Attorney General, to the Comptroller General, and to the head of the department requested to settle the account in question.

The judgment of the United States Claims Court in such suit shall be conclusive upon the parties, and payment of the amount found due shall discharge the obligation.

The transcript of such judgment, filed in the clerk's office of any district court, shall be entered upon the records, and shall be enforceable as other judgments.

§ 2512. Disbursing officers; relief

Whenever the United States Claims Court finds that any loss by a disbursing officer of the United States was without his fault or negligence, it shall render a judgment setting for the amount thereof, and the General Accounting Office shall allow the officer such amount as a credit in the settlement of his accounts.

§ 2513. Unjust conviction and imprisonment

(a) Any person suing under section 1495 of this title must allege and prove that:

(1) His conviction has been reversed or set aside on the ground that he is not guilty of the offense of which he was convicted, or on new trial or rehearing he was found not guilty of

such offense, as appears from the record or certificate of the court setting aside or reversing such conviction, or that he has been pardoned upon the stated ground of innocence and unjust conviction and

(2) He did not commit any of the acts charged or his acts, deeds, or omissions in connection with such charge constituted no offense against the United States, or any State, Territory or the District of Columbia, and he did not by misconduct or neglect cause or bring about his own prosecution.

(b) Proof of the requisite facts shall be by a certificate of the court or pardon wherein such facts are alleged to appear, and other evidence thereof shall not be received.

(c) No pardon or certified copy of a pardon shall be considered by the United States Claims Court unless it contains recitals that the pardon was granted after applicant had exhausted all recourse to the courts and that the time for any court to exercise its jurisdiction had expired.

(d) The Court may permit the plaintiff to prosecute such action in forma pauperis.

(e) The amount of damages awarded shall not exceed the sum of $5,000.

§ 2514. Forfeiture of fraudulent claims

A claim against the United States shall be forfeited to the United States by any person who corruptly practices or attempts to practice any fraud against the United States in the proof, statement, establishment, or allowance thereof.

In such cases the United States Claims Court shall specifically find such fraud or attempt and render judgment of forfeiture.

§ 2515. New trial; stay of judgment

(a) The United States Claims Court may grant a plaintiff a new trial on any ground established by rules of common law or equity applicable as between private parties.

(b) Such court, at any time while any suit is pending before it, or after proceedings for review have been instituted, or within two years after the final disposition of the suit, may grant the United States a new trial and stay the payment of any judgment upon satisfactory evidence, cumulative or otherwise, that any fraud, wrong, or injustice has been done the United States.

§ 2516. Interest on claims and judgments

(a) Interest on a claim against the United States shall be allowed in a judgment of the United States Claims Court only under a contract or Act of Congress expressly providing for payment thereof.

(b) Interest on a judgment against the United States affirmed by the Supreme Court after review on petition of the United States is paid at a rate equal to the coupon issue yield equivalent (as determined by the Secretary of the Treasury) of the average accepted auction price for the last auction of fifty-two week United States Treasury bills settled immediately before the date of the judgment.

§ 2517. Payment of judgments

(a) Except as provided by the Contracts Disputes Act of 1978, every final judgment rendered by the United States Claims Court against the United States shall be paid out of any general appropriation therefor, on presentation to the General Accounting Office of a certification of the judgment by the clerk and chief judge of the court.

(b) Payment of any such judgment and of interest thereon shall be a full discharge to the United States of all claims and demands arising out of the matters involved in the case or controversy, unless the judgment is designated a partial judgment, in which event only the matters described therein shall be discharged.

[§ 2518. Repealed.]

§ 2519. Conclusiveness of judgment

A final judgment of the United States Claims Court against any plaintiff shall forever bar any further claim, suit, or demand against the United States arising out of the matters involved in the case or controversy.

§ 2520. Fees

The United States Claims Court shall by rules impose a fee not exceeding $60, for the filing of any petition.

§ 2521. Subpoenas

Subpoenas requiring the attendance of parties or witnesses and subpoenas requiring the production of books, papers, documents or tangible things by any party or witness having custody or control thereof, may be issued for purposes of discovery or for use of the things produced as evidence in accordance with the rules and orders of the court. Such subpoenas shall be issued and served and compliance therewith shall be compelled as provided in the rules and orders of the court.

§ 2522. Notice of appeal

Review of a decision of the United States Claims Court shall be obtained by filing a notice of appeal with the clerk of the Claims Court within the time and in the manner prescribed for appeals to United States courts of appeals from the United States district courts.

CHAPTER 169—COURT OF INTERNATIONAL TRADE PROCEDURE

§ 2631. Persons entitled to commence a civil action

(a) A civil action contesting the denial of a protest, in whole or in part, under section 515 of the Tariff Act of 1930 may be commenced in the Court of International Trade by the person who filed the protest pursuant to section 514 of such Act, or by a surety on the transaction which is the subject of the protest.

(b) A civil action contesting the denial of a petition under section 516 of the Tariff Act of 1930 may be commenced in the Court of International Trade by the person who filed such petition.

(c) A civil action contesting a determination listed in section 516A of the Tariff Act of 1930 may be commenced in the Court of International Trade by any interested party who was a party to the proceeding in connection with which the matter arose.

(d)(1) A civil action to review any final determination of the Secretary of Labor under section 223 of the Trade Act of 1974 with respect to the eligibility of workers for adjustment assistance under such Act may be commenced in the Court of International Trade by a worker, group of workers, certified or recognized union, or authorized representative of such worker or group that applies for assistance under such Act and is aggrieved by such final determination.

(2) A civil action to review any final determination of the Secretary of Commerce under section 251 of the Trade Act of 1974 with respect to the eligibility of a firm for adjustment assistance under such Act may be commenced in the Court of International Trade by a firm or its representative that applies for assistance under such

Act and is aggrieved by such final determination, or by any other interested domestic party that is aggrieved by such final determination.

(3) A civil action to review any final determination of the Secretary of Commerce under section 271 of the Trade Act of 1974 with respect to the eligibility of a community for adjustment assistance under such Act may be commenced in the Court of International Trade by a community that applies for assistance under such Act and is aggrieved by such final determination, or by any other interested domestic party that is aggrieved by such final determination.

(e) A civil action to review a final determination made under section 305(b)(1) of the Trade Agreements Act of 1979 may be commenced in the Court of International Trade by any person who was a party-at-interest with respect to such determination.

(f) A civil action involving an application for the issuance of an order directing the administering authority or the International Trade Commission to make confidential information available under section 777(c)(2) of the Tariff Act of 1930 may be commenced in the Court of International Trade by any interested party whose application for disclosure of such confidential information was denied under section 777(c)(1) of such Act.

(g)(1) A civil action to review any decision of the Secretary of the Treasury to deny or revoke a customhouse broker's license under section 641(a) of the Tariff Act of 1930 may be commenced in the Court of International Trade by the person whose license was denied or revoked.

(2) A civil action to review any order of the Secretary of the Treasury to revoke or suspend a customhouse broker's license under section 641(b) of the Tariff Act of 1930 may be commenced in the Court of International Trade by the person whose license was revoked or suspended.

(h) A civil action described in section 1581(h) of this title may be commenced in the Court of International Trade by the person who would have standing to bring a civil action under section 1581(a) of this title if he imported the goods involved and filed a protest which was denied, in whole or in part, under section 515 of the Tariff Act of 1930.

(i) Any civil action of which the Court of International Trade has jurisdiction, other than an action specified in subsections (a)–(h) of this section, may be commenced in the court by any person adversely affected or aggrieved by agency action within the meaning of section 702 of title 5.

(j)(1) Any person who would be adversely affected or aggrieved by a decision in a civil action pending in the Court of International Trade may, by leave of court, intervene in such action, except that—

(A) no person may intervene in a civil action under section 515 or 516 of the Tariff Act of 1930;

(B) in a civil action under section 516A of the Tariff Act of 1930, only an interested party who was a party to the proceeding in connection with which the matter arose may intervene, and such person may intervene as a matter of right; and

(C) in a civil action under section 777(c)(2) of the Tariff Act of 1930, only a person who was a party to the investigation may intervene, and such person may intervene as a matter of right.

(2) In those civil actions in which intervention is by leave of court, the Court of International Trade shall consider whether the intervention will unduly delay or prejudice the adjudication of the rights of the original parties.

(k) In this section—

(1) "interested party" has the meaning given such term in section 771(9) of the Tariff Act of 1930; and

(2) "party-at-interest" means—

(A) a foreign manufacturer, producer, or exporter, or a United States importer, of merchandise which is the subject of a final determination under section 305(b)(1) of the Trade Agreements Act of 1979;

(B) a manufacturer, producer, or wholesaler in the United States of a like product;

(C) United States members of a labor organization or other association of workers whose members are employed in the manufacture, production, or wholesale in the United States of a like product; and

(D) a trade or business association a majority of whose members manufacture, produce, or wholesale a like product in the United States.

§ 2632. Commencement of a civil action

(a) Except for civil actions specified in subsections (b) and (c) of this section, a civil action in the Court of International Trade shall be commenced by filing concurrently with the clerk of the court a summons and complaint, with the content and in the form, manner, and style prescribed by the rules of the court.

(b) A civil action in the Court of International Trade under section 515 or section 516 of the Tariff Act of 1930 shall be commenced by filing with the clerk of the court a summons, with the content and in the form, manner, and style prescribed by the rules of the court.

(c) A civil action in the Court of International Trade under section 516A of the Tariff Act of 1930 shall be commenced by filing with the clerk of the court a summons or a summons and a complaint, as prescribed in such section, with the content and in the form, manner, and style prescribed by the rules of the court.

(d) The Court of International Trade may prescribe by rule that any summons, pleading, or other paper mailed by registered or certified mail properly addressed to the clerk of the court with the proper postage affixed and return receipt requested shall be deemed filed as of the date of mailing.

§ 2633. Procedure and fees

(a) A filing fee shall be payable to the clerk of the Court of International Trade upon the commencement of a civil action in such court. The amount of the fee shall be prescribed by the rules of the court, but shall be not less than $5 nor more than the filing fee for commencing a civil action in a district court of the United States. The court may fix all other fees to be charged by the clerk of the court.

(b) The Court of International Trade shall prescribe rules governing the summons, pleadings, and other papers, for their amendment, service, and filing, for consolidations, severances, suspensions of cases, and for other procedural matters.

(c) All summons, pleadings, and other papers filed in the Court of International Trade shall be served on all parties in accordance with rules prescribed by the court. When the United States, its agencies, or its officers are adverse parties, service of the summons shall be made upon the Attorney General and the head of the Government agency whose action is being contested. When injunctive relief is sought, the summons, pleadings, and other papers shall also be served upon the named officials sought to be enjoined.

§ 2634. Notice

Reasonable notice of the time and place of trial or hearing before the Court of International Trade shall be given to all parties to any civil action, as prescribed by the rules of the court.

§ 2635. Filing of official documents

(a)(1) Upon service of the summons on the Secretary of the Treasury in any civil action contesting the denial of a protest under section 515 of the Tariff Act of 1930 or the denial of a petition under section 516 of such Act, the appropriate customs officer shall forthwith transmit to the clerk of the Court of International Trade, as prescribed by is rules, and as a part of the official record—

(A) the consumption or other entry and the entry summary;

(B) the commercial invoice;

(C) the special customs invoice;

(D) a copy of the protest or petition;

(E) a copy of the denial, in whole or in part, of the protest or petition;

(F) the importer's exhibits;

(G) the official and other representative samples;

(H) any official laboratory reports; and

(I) a copy of any bond relating to the entry.

(2) If any of the items listed in paragraph (1) of this subsection do not exist in a particular civil action, an affirmative statement to that effect shall be transmitted to the clerk of the court.

(b)(1) In any civil action commenced in the Court of International Trade under section 516A of the Tariff Act of 1930, within forty days or within such other period of time as the court may specify, after the date of service of a complaint on the administering authority established to administer title VII of the Tariff Act of 1930 or the United States International Trade Commission, the administering authority or the Commission shall transmit to the clerk of the court the record of such action, as prescribed by the rules of the court. The record shall, unless otherwise stipulated by the parties, consist of—

(A) a copy of all information presented to or obtained by the administering authority or the Commission during the course of the administrative proceedings, including all governmental memoranda pertaining to the case and the record of ex parte meetings required to be maintained by section 777(a)(3) of the Tariff Act of 1930; and

(B)(i) a copy of the determination and the facts and conclusions of law upon which such determination was based, (ii) all transcripts or records of conferences or hearings, and (iii) all notices published in the Federal Register.

(2) The administering authority or the Commission shall identify and transmit under seal to the clerk of the court any document, comment, or information that is accorded confidential or privileged status by the Government agency whose action is being contested and that is required to be transmitted to the clerk under paragraph (1) of this subsection. Any such document, comment, or information shall be accompanied by a nonconfidential description of the nature of the material being transmitted. The confidential or privileged status of such material shall be preserved in the civil action, but the court may examine the confidential or privileged material in camera and may make such material available under such terms and conditions as the court may order.

(c) Within fifteen days, or within such other period of time as the Court of International Trade may specify, after service of a summons and complaint in a civil action involving an application for an order directing the administering authority or the International Trade Commission to make confidential information available under section 777(c)(2) of the Tariff Act of 1930, the administering authority or the Commission shall transmit under seal to the clerk of the Court of International Trade, as prescribed by its rules, the confidential information involved, together with pertinent parts of the record. Such information shall be accompanied by a nonconfidential description of the nature of the information being transmitted. The confidential status of such information shall be preserved in the civil action, but the court may examine the confidential information in camera and may make such information available under a protective order consistent with section 777(c)(2) of the Tariff Act of 1930.

(d)(1) In any other civil action in the Court of International Trade in which judicial review is to proceed upon the basis of the record made before an agency, the agency shall, within forty days or within such other period of time as the court may specify, after the date of service of the summons and complaint upon the agency, transmit to the clerk of the court, as prescribed by its rules—

(A) a copy of the contested determination and the findings or report upon which such determination was based;

(B) a copy of any reported hearings or conferences conducted by the agency; and

(C) any documents, comments, or other papers filed by the public, interested parties, or governments with respect to the agency's action.

(2) The agency shall identify and transmit under seal to the clerk of the court any document, comment, or other information that was obtained on a confidential basis and that is required to be transmitted to the clerk under paragraph (1) of this subsection. Any such document, comment, or information shall include a nonconfidential description of the nature of the material being transmitted. The confidential or privileged status of such material shall be preserved in the civil action, but the court may examine such material in camera and may make such material available under such terms and conditions as the court may order.

(3) The parties may stipulate that fewer documents, comments, or other information than those specified in paragraph (1) of this subsection shall be transmitted to the clerk of the court.

§ 2636. Time for commencement of action

(a) A civil action contesting the denial, in whole or in part, of a protest under section 515 of the Tariff Act of 1930 is barred unless commenced in accordance with the rules of the Court of International Trade—

(1) within one hundred and eighty days after the date of mailing of notice of denial of a protest under section 515(a) of such Act; or

(2) within one hundred and eighty days after the date of denial of a protest by operation of law under the provisions of section 515(b) of such Act.

(b) A civil action contesting the denial of a petition under section 516 of the Tariff Act of 1930 is barred unless commenced in accordance with the rules of the Court of International Trade within thirty days after the date of mailing of a notice pursuant to section 516 (c) of such Act.

(c) A civil action contesting a reviewable determination listed in section 516A of the Tariff Act of 1930, other than a determination under section 703(b), 703(c), 733(b), or 733(c) of such Act, is barred unless commenced in accordance with the rules of the Court of International Trade within thirty days after the date of the publication of such determination in the Federal Register.

(d)(1) A civil action contesting a determination by the administering authority under section 703(c) or 733(c) of the Tariff Act of 1930 that a case is extraordinarily complicated is barred unless commenced in accordance with the rules of the Court of International Trade within ten days after the date of the publication of such determination in the Federal Register.

(2) A civil action contesting a negative determination by the administering authority under section 703(b) or 733(b) of the Tariff Act of 1930 is barred unless commenced in accordance with the rules of the Court of International Trade within ten days after the date of the publication of such determination in the Federal Register.

(e) A civil action contesting a final determination of the Secretary of Labor under section 223 of the Trade Act of 1974 or a final determination of the Secretary of Commerce under section 251 or section 271 of such Act is barred unless commenced in accordance with the rules of the Court of International Trade within sixty days after the date of notice of such determination.

(f) A civil action contesting a final determination made under section 305(b)(1) of the Trade Agreements Act of 1979 is barred unless commenced in accordance with the rules of the Court of International Trade within thirty days after the date of the publication of such determination in the Federal Register.

(g) A civil action involving an application for the issuance of an order making confidential information available under section 777(c) (2) of the Tariff Act of 1930 is barred unless commenced in accordance with the rules of the Court of International Trade within ten days after the date of the denial of the request for such confidential information.

(h) A civil action contesting the denial or revocation by the Secretary of the Treasury of a customhouse broker's license under section 641(a) of the Tariff Act of 1930 or the revocation or suspension by such Secretary of a customhouse broker's license under section 641(b) of such Act is barred unless commenced in accordance with the rules of the Court of International Trade within sixty days after the date of the entry of the decision or order of such Secretary.

(i) A civil action of which the Court of International Trade has jurisdiction under section 1581 of this title, other than an action specified in subsections (a)–(h) of this section, is barred unless commenced in accordance with the rules of the court within two years after the cause of action first accrues.

§ 2637. Exhaustion of administrative remedies

(a) A civil action contesting the denial of a protest under section 515 of the Tariff Act of 1930 may be commenced in the Court of International Trade only if all liquidated duties, charges, or exactions have been paid at the time the action is commenced, except that a surety's obligation to pay such liquidated duties, charges, or exactions is limited to the sum of any bond related to each entry included in the denied protest.

(b) A civil action contesting the denial of a petition under section 516 of the Tariff Act of 1930 may be commenced in the Court of International Trade only by a person who has first exhausted the procedures set forth in such section.

(c) A civil action described in section 1581(h) of this title may be commenced in the Court of International Trade prior to the exhaustion of administrative remedies if the person commencing the action makes the demonstration required by such section.

(d) In any civil action not specified in this section, the Court of International Trade shall, where appropriate, require the exhaustion of administrative remedies.

§ 2638. New grounds in support of a civil action

In any civil action under section 515 of the Tariff Act of 1930 in which the denial, in whole or in part, of a protest is a precondition to the commencement of a civil action in the Court of International Trade, the court, by rule, may consider any new ground in support of the civil action if such new ground—

(1) applies to the same merchandise that was the subject of the protest; and

(2) is related to the same administrative decision listed in section 514 of the Tariff Act of 1930 that was contested in the protest.

§ 2639. Burden of proof; evidence of value

(a)(1) Except as provided in paragraph (2) of this subsection, in any civil action commenced in the Court of International Trade under section 515, 516, or 516A of the Tariff Act of 1930, the decision of the Secretary of the Treasury, the administering authority, or the International Trade Commission is presumed to be correct. The burden of proving otherwise shall rest upon the party challenging such decision.

(2) The provisions of paragraph (1) of this subsection shall not apply to any civil action commenced in the Court of International Trade under section 1582 of this title.

(b) In any civil action described in section 1581(h) of this title, the person commencing the action shall have the burden of making the demonstration required by such section by clear and convincing evidence.

(c) Where the value of merchandise or any of its components is in issue in any civil action in the Court of International Trade—

(1) reports or depositions of consuls, customs officers, and other officers of the United States, and depositions and affidavits of other persons whose attendance cannot reasonably be had, may be admitted into evidence when served upon the opposing party as prescribed by the rules of the court; and

(2) price lists and catalogs may be admitted in evidence when duly authenticated, relevant, and material.

§ 2640. Scope and standard of review

(a) The Court of International Trade shall make its determinations upon the basis of the record made before the court in the following categories of civil actions:

(1) Civil actions contesting the denial of a protest under section 515 of the Tariff Act of 1930.

(2) Civil actions commenced under section 516 of the Tariff Act of 1930.

(3) Civil actions commenced to review a final determination made under section 305(b)(1) of the Trade Agreements Act of 1979.

(4) Civil actions commenced under section 777(c)(2) of the Tariff Act of 1930.

(5) Civil actions commenced to review any decision of the Secretary of the Treasury to deny or revoke a customhouse broker's license under section 641(a) of the Tariff Act of 1930.

(6) Civil actions commenced under section 1582 of this title.

(b) In any civil action commenced in the Court of International Trade under section 516A of the Tariff Act of 1930, the court shall review the matter as specified in subsection (b) of such section.

(c) In any civil action commenced in the Court of International Trade to review any final determination of the Secretary of Labor under section 223 of the Trade Act of 1974 or any final determination of the Secretary of Commerce under section 251 or section 271 of such Act, the court shall review the matter as specified in section 284 of such Act.

(d) In any civil action not specified in this section, the Court of International Trade shall review the matter as provided in section 706 of title 5.

§ 2641. Witnesses; inspection of documents

(a) Except as otherwise provided by law, in any civil action in the Court of International Trade, each party and its counsel shall have an opportunity to introduce evidence, to hear and cross-examine the witnesses of the other party, and to inspect all samples and papers admitted or offered as evidence, as prescribed by the rules of the court. Except as provided in section 2639 of this title, subsection

(b) of this section, or the rules of the court, the Federal Rules of Evidence shall apply to all civil actions in the Court of International Trade.

(b) The Court of International Trade may order that trade secrets and commercial or financial information which is privileged and confidential, or any information provided to the United States by any foreign government or foreign person, may be disclosed to a party, its counsel, or any other person under such terms and conditions as the court may order.

§ 2642. Analysis of imported merchandise

The Court of International Trade may order an analysis of imported merchandise and reports thereon by laboratories or agencies of the United States.

§ 2643. Relief

(a) The Court of International Trade may enter a money judgment—

(1) for or against the United States in any civil action commenced under section 1581 or 1582 of this title; and

(2) for or against the United States or any other party in any counterclaim, cross-claim, or third-party action under section 1583 of this title.

(b) If the Court of International Trade is unable to determine the correct decision on the basis of the evidence presented in any civil action, the court may order a retrial or rehearing for all purposes, or may order such further administrative or adjudicative procedures as the court considers necessary to enable it to reach the correct decision.

(c)(1) Except as provided in paragraphs (2), (3), and (4) of this subsection, the Court of International Trade may, in addition to the orders specified in subsections (a) and (b) of this section, order any other form of relief that is appropriate in a civil action, including, but not limited to, declaratory judgments, orders of remand, injunctions, and writs of mandamus and prohibition.

(2) The Court of International Trade may not grant an injunction or issue a writ of mandamus in any civil action commenced to review any final determination of the Secretary of Labor under section 223 of the Trade Act of 1974, or any final determination of the Secretary of Commerce under section 251 or section 271 of such Act.

(3) In any civil action involving an application for the issuance of an order directing the administering authority or the International Trade Commission to make confidential information available under section 777(c)(2) of the Tariff Act of 1930, the Court of International Trade may issue an order of disclosure only with respect to the information specified in such section.

(4) In any civil action described in section 1581(h) of this title, the Court of International Trade may only order the appropriate declaratory relief.

(d) If a surety commences a civil action in the Court of International Trade, such surety shall recover only the amount of the liquidated duties, charges, or exactions paid on the entries included in such action. The excess amount of any recovery shall be paid to the importer of record.

§ 2644. Interest

If, in a civil action in the Court of International Trade under section 515 of the Tariff Act of 1930, the plaintiff obtains monetary relief by a judgment or under a stipulation agreement, interest shall be allowed at an annual rate established under section 6621 of the Internal Revenue Code of 1954. Such interest shall be calculated from the date of the filing of the summons in such action to the date of the refund.

§ 2645. Decisions

(a) A final decision of the Court of International Trade in a contested civil action or a decision granting or refusing a preliminary injunction shall be supported by—

(1) a statement of findings of fact and conclusions of law; or

(2) an opinion stating the reasons and facts upon which the decision is based.

(b) After the Court of International Trade has rendered a judgment, the court may, upon the motion of a party or upon its own motion, amend its findings or make additional findings and may amend the decision and judgment accordingly. A motion of a party or the court shall be made not later than thirty days after the date of entry of the judgment.

(c) A decision of the Court of International Trade is final and conclusive, unless a retrial or rehearing is granted pursuant to section 2646 of this title or an appeal is taken to the Court of Appeals for the Federal Circuit by filing a notice of appeal with the clerk of the Court of International Trade within the time and in the manner prescribed for appeals to United States courts of appeals from the United States district courts.

§ 2646. Retrial or rehearing

After the Court of International Trade has rendered a judgment or order, the court may, upon the motion of a party or upon its own motion, grant a retrial or rehearing, as the case may be. A motion of a party or the court shall be made not later than thirty days after the date of entry of the judgment or order.

§ 2647. Precedence of cases

The following civil actions in the Court of International Trade shall be given precedence, in the following order, over other civil actions pending before the court, and shall be assigned for hearing at the earliest practicable date and expedited in every way:

(1) First, a civil action involving the exclusion of perishable merchandise or the redelivery of such merchandise.

(2) Second, a civil action for the review of a determination under section 516A(a)(1)(B)(i) or (ii) of the Tariff Act of 1930.

(3) Third, a civil action commenced under section 515 of the Tariff Act of 1930 involving the exclusion or redelivery of merchandise.

(4) Fourth, a civil action commenced under section 516 or 516A of the Tariff Act of 1930, other than a civil action described in paragraph (2) of this section.

CHAPTER 171—TORT CLAIMS PROCEDURE

Sec.

§ 2671. Definitions

As used in this chapter and sections 1346(b) and 2401(b) of this title, the term—

"Federal agency" includes the executive departments, the military departments, independent establishments of the United States, and corporations primarily acting as instrumentalities or agencies of the United States, but does not include any contractor with the United States.

"Employee of the government" includes officers or employees of any federal agency, members of the military or naval forces of the United States, members of the National Guard while engaged in training or duty under section 316, 502, 503, 504, or 505 of title 32, and persons acting on behalf of a federal agency in an official capacity, temporarily or permanently in the service of the United States, whether with or without compensation.

"Acting within the scope of his office or employment", in the case of a member of the military or naval forces of the United States or a member of the National Guard as defined in section 101(3) of title 32, means acting in line of duty.

§ 2672. Administrative adjustment of claims

The head of each Federal agency or his designee, in accordance with regulations prescribed by the Attorney General, may consider, ascertain, adjust, determine, compromise, and settle any claim for money damages against the United States for injury or loss of property or personal injury or death caused by the negligent or wrongful act or omission of any employee of the agency while acting within the scope of his office or employment, under circumstances where the United States, if a private person, would be liable to the claimant in accordance with the law of the place where the act or omission occurred: *Provided,* That any award, compromise, or settlement in excess of $25,000 shall be effected only with the prior written approval of the Attorney General or his designee.

Subject to the provisions of this title relating to civil actions on tort claims against the United States, any such award, compromise, settlement, or determination shall be final and conclusive on all officers of the Government, except when procured by means of fraud.

Any award, compromise, or settlement in an amount of $2,500 or less made pursuant to this section shall be paid by the head of the Federal agency concerned out of appropriations available to that agency. Payment of any award, compromise, or settlement in an amount in excess of $2,500 made pursuant to this section or made by the Attorney General in any amount pursuant to section 2677 of this title shall be paid in a manner similar to judgments and compromises in like causes and appropriations or funds available for the payment of such judgments and compromises are hereby made available for the payment of awards, compromises, or settlements under this chapter.

§ 2673. Reports to Congress

The head of each federal agency shall report annually to Congress all claims paid by it under section 2672 of this title, stating the name of each claimant, the amount claimed, the amount awarded, and a brief description of the claim.

§ 2674. Liability of United States

The United States shall be liable, respecting the provisions of this title relating to tort claims, in the same manner and to the same extent as a private individual under like circumstances, but shall not be liable for interest prior to judgment or for punitive damages.

If, however, in any case wherein death was caused, the law of the place where the act or omission complained of occurred provides, or has been construed to provide, for damages only punitive in nature, the United States shall be liable for actual or compensatory damages, measured by the pecuniary injuries resulting from such death to the persons respectively, for whose benefit the action was brought, in lieu thereof.

§ 2675. Disposition by federal agency as prerequisite; evidence

(a) An action shall not be instituted upon a claim against the United States for money damages for injury or loss of property or personal injury or death caused by the negligent or wrongful act or omission of any employee of the Government while acting within the scope of his office or employment, unless the claimant shall have first presented the claim to the appropriate Federal agency and his claim shall have been finally denied by the agency in writing and sent by certified or registered mail. The failure of an agency to make final disposition of a claim within six months after it is filed shall, at the option of the claimant any time thereafter, be deemed a final denial of the claim for purposes of this section. The provisions of this subsection shall not apply to such claims as may be asserted under the Federal Rules of Civil Procedure by third party complaint, cross-claim, or counterclaim.

(b) Action under this section shall not be instituted for any sum in excess of the amount of the claim presented to the federal agency, except where the increased amount is based upon newly discovered evidence not reasonably discoverable at the time of presenting the claim to the federal agency, or upon allegation and proof of intervening facts, relating to the amount of the claim.

(c) Disposition of any claim by the Attorney General or other head of a federal agency shall not be competent evidence of liability or amount of damages.

§ 2676. Judgment as bar

The judgment in an action under section 1346(b) of this title shall constitute a complete bar to any action by the claimant, by reason of the same subject matter, against the employee of the government whose act or omission gave rise to the claim.

§ 2677. Compromise

The Attorney General or his designee may arbitrate, compromise, or settle any claim cognizable under section 1346(b) of this title, after the commencement of an action thereon.

§ 2678. Attorney fees; penalty

No attorney shall charge, demand, receive, or collect for services rendered, fees in excess of 25 per centum of any judgment rendered pursuant to section 1346(b) of this title or any settlement made pursuant to section 2677 of this title, or in excess of 20 per centum of any award, compromise, or settlement made pursuant to section 2672 of this title.

Any attorney who charges, demands, receives, or collects for services rendered in connection with such claim any amount in excess of that allowed under this section, if recovery be had, shall be fined not more than $2,000 or imprisoned not more than one year, or both.

§ 2679. Exclusiveness of remedy

(a) The authority of any federal agency to sue and be sued in its own name shall not be construed to authorize suits against such federal agency on claims which are cognizable under section 1346(b) of this title, and the remedies provided by this title in such cases shall be exclusive.

(b) The remedy against the United States provided by sections 1346(b) and 2672 of this title for injury or loss of property or personal injury or death, resulting from the operation by any employee of the Government of any motor vehicle while acting within the scope of his office or employment, shall hereafter be exclusive of any other civil action or proceeding by reason of the same subject matter against the employee or his estate whose act or omission gave rise to the claim.

(c) The Attorney General shall defend any civil action or proceeding brought in any court against any employee of the Government or his estate for any such damage or injury. The employee against whom such civil action or proceeding is brought shall deliver within such time after date of service or knowledge of service as determined by the Attorney General, all process served upon him or an attested true copy thereof to his immediate superior or to whomever was designated by the head of his department to receive such papers and such person shall promptly furnish copies of the pleadings and process therein to the United States attorney for the district embracing the place wherein the proceeding is brought, to the Attorney General, and to the head of his employing Federal agency.

(d) Upon a certification by the Attorney General that the defendant employee was acting within the scope of his employment at the time of the incident out of which the suit arose, any such civil action or proceeding commenced in a State court shall be removed without bond at any time before trial by the Attorney General to the district court of the United States for the district and division embracing the place wherein it is pending and the proceedings deemed a tort action brought against the United States under the provisions of this title and all references thereto. Should a United States district court determine on a hearing on a motion to remand held before a trial on the merits that the case so removed is one in which a remedy by suit within the meaning of subsection (b) of this section is not available against the United States, the case shall be remanded to the State court.

(e) The Attorney General may compromise or settle any claim asserted in such civil action or proceeding in the manner provided in section 2677, and with the same effect.

§ 2680. Exceptions

The provisions of this chapter and section 1346(b) of this title shall not apply to—

(a) Any claim based upon an act or omission of an employee of the Government, exercising due care, in the execution of a statute or regulation, whether or not such statute or regulation be valid, or based upon the exercise or performance or the failure to exercise or perform a discretionary function or duty on the part of a federal agency or an employee of the Government, whether or not the discretion involved be abused.

(b) Any claim arising out of the loss, miscarriage, or negligent transmission of letters or postal matter.

(c) Any claim arising in respect of the assessment or collection of any tax or customs duty, or the detention of any goods or merchandise by any officer of customs or excise or any other law-enforcement officer.

(d) Any claim for which a remedy is provided by sections 741–752, 781–790 of Title 46, relating to claims or suits in admiralty against the United States.

(e) Any claim arising out of an act or omission of any employee of the Government in administering the provisions of sections 1–31 of Title 50, Appendix.

(f) Any claim for damages caused by the imposition or establishment of a quarantine by the United States.

[(g) Repealed.]

(h) Any claim arising out of assault, battery, false imprisonment, false arrest, malicious prosecution, abuse of process, libel, slander, misrepresentation, deceit, or interference with contract rights: *Provided*, That, with regard to acts or omissions of investigative or law enforcement officers of the United States Government, the provisions of this chapter and section 1346(b) of this title shall apply to any claim arising, on or after the date of the enactment of this proviso, out of assault, battery, false imprisonment, false arrest, abuse of process, or malicious prosecution. For the purpose of this subsection, "investigative law or enforcement officer" means any officer of the United States who is empowered by law to execute searches, to seize evidence, or to make arrests for violations of Federal law.

(i) Any claim for damages caused by the fiscal operations of the Treasury or by the regulation of the monetary system.

(j) Any claim arising out of the combatant activities of the military or naval forces, or the Coast Guard, during time of war.

(k) Any claim arising in a foreign country.

(*l*) Any claim arising from the activities of the Tennessee Valley Authority.

(m) Any claim arising from the activities of the Panama Canal Company.

(n) Any claim arising from the activities of a Federal land bank, a Federal intermediate credit bank, or a bank for cooperatives.

CHAPTER 173—ATTACHMENT IN POSTAL SUITS

§ 2710. Right of attachment

(a) Where debts are due from a defaulting or delinquent postmaster, contractor, or other officer, agent or employee of the Post Office Department, a warrant of attachment may issue against all property and legal and equitable rights belonging to him, and his sureties, or either of them, where he—

(1) is a nonresident of the district where he was appointed, or has departed from that district for the purpose of permanently residing outside thereof, or of avoiding the service of civil process; and

(2) has conveyed away, or is about to convey away any of his property, or has removed or is about to remove the same from the district wherein it is situated, with intent to defraud the United States.

(b) When the property has been removed, the marshal of the district into which it has been removed, upon receipt of certified copies of the warrant, may seize the property and convey it to a convenient place within the jurisdiction of the court which issued the warrant. Alias warrants may be issued upon due application. The warrant first issued remains valid until the return day thereof.

§ 2711. Application for warrant

A United States attorney or assistant United States attorney or a person authorized by the Attorney General—

(1) upon his own affidavit or that of another credible person, stating the existence of either of the grounds of attachments enumerated in section 2710 of this title and

(2) upon production of legal evidence of the debt

may apply for a warrant of attachment to a judge, or, in his absence, to the clerk of any court of the United States having original jurisdiction of the cause of action.

§ 2712. Issue of warrant

Upon an order of a judge of a court, or, in his absence and upon the clerk's own initiative, the clerk shall issue a warrant for the attachment of the property belonging to the person specified in the affidavit. The marshal shall execute the warrant forthwith and take the property attached, if personal, in his custody, subject to the interlocutory or final orders of the court.

§ 2713. Trial of ownership of property

Not later than twenty days before the return day of a warrant issued under section 2712 of this title, the party whose property is attached, on notice to the United States Attorney, may file a plea in abatement, denying the allegations of the affidavit, or denying ownership in the defendant of the property attached. The court, upon application of either party, shall order a trial by jury of the issues. Where the parties, by consent, waive a trial by jury, the court shall decide the issues. A party claiming ownership of the property attached and seeking its return is limited to the remedy afforded by this section, but his right to an action of trespass, or other action for damages, is not impaired.

§ 2714. Investment of proceeds of attached property

When the property attached is sold on an interlocutory order or is producing revenue, the money arising from the sale or revenue shall be invested, under the order of the court, in securities of the United States. The accretions therefrom are subject to the order of the court.

§ 2715. Publication

The marshal shall cause publication of an executed warrant of attachment—

(1) for two months in case of an absconding debtor, and

(2) for four months in case of a nonresident debtor

in a newspaper published in the district where the property is situated pursuant to the details of the order under which the warrant is issued.

§ 2716. Personal notice

After the first publication of the notice of attachment, a person indebted to, or having possession of property of a defendant and having knowledge of the notice, shall answer for the amount of his debt or the value of the property. Any disposal or attempted disposal of the property, to the injury of the United States, is unlawful. When the person indebted to, or having possession of the property of a defendant, is known to the United States attorney or marshal, the officer shall cause a personal notice of the attachment to be served upon him, but the lack of the notice does not invalidate the attachment.

§ 2717. Discharge

The court, or a judge thereof, upon—

(1) application of the party when property has been attached and

(2) execution to the United States of a penal bond, approved by a judge, in double the value of the property attached and conditioned upon the return of the property or the payment of any judgment rendered by the court

may discharge the warrant of attachment as to the property of the applicant.

§ 2718. Interest on balances due department

In suits for balances due the Post Office Department may recover interest at the rate of 6 per centum per year from the time of default.

CHAPTER 175—CIVIL COMMITMENT AND REHABILITATION OF NARCOTIC ADDICTS

Sec.

§ 2901. Definitions

As used in this chapter—

(a) "Addict" means any individual who habitually uses any narcotic drug as defined by section 102(16) of the Controlled Substances Act, so as to endanger the public morals, health, safety, or welfare, or who is so far addicted to the use of such narcotic drugs as to have lost the power of self-control with reference to his addiction.

(b) "Surgeon General" means the Surgeon General of the Public Health Service.

(c) "Crime of violence" includes voluntary manslaughter, murder, rape, mayhem, kidnaping, robbery, burglary or housebreaking in the nighttime, extortion accompanied by threats of violence, assault with a dangerous weapon or assault with intent to commit any offense punishable by imprisonment for more than one year, arson punishable as a felony, or an attempt or conspiracy to commit any of the foregoing offenses.

(d) "Treatment" includes confinement and treatment in an institution and under supervised aftercare in the community and includes, but is not limited to, medical, educational, social, psychological, and vocational services, corrective and preventive guidance and training, and other rehabilitative services designed to protect the public and benefit the addict by eliminating his dependence on addicting drugs, or by controlling his dependence, and his susceptibility to addiction.

(e) "Felony" includes any offense in violation of a law of the United States classified as a felony under section 1 of title 18 of the United States Code, and further includes any offense in violation of a law of any State, any possession or territory of the United States, the District of Columbia, the Canal Zone, or the Commonwealth of Puerto Rico, which at the time of the offense was classified as a felony by the law of the place where that offense was committed.

(f) "Conviction" and "convicted" mean the final judgment on a verdict or finding of guilty, a plea of guilty, or a plea of nolo contendere, but do not include a final judgment which has been expunged by pardon, reversed, set aside or otherwise rendered nugatory.

(g) "Eligible individual" means any individual who is charged with an offense against the United States, but does not include—

(1) an individual charged with a crime of violence.

(2) an individual charged with unlawfully importing, selling, or conspiring to import or sell, a narcotic drug.

(3) an individual against whom there is pending a prior charge of a felony which has not been finally determined or who is on probation or whose sentence following conviction on such a charge, including any time on parole or mandatory release, has not been fully served: *Provided,* That an individual on probation, parole, or mandatory release shall be included if the authority authorized to require his return to custody consents to his commitment.

(4) an individual who has been convicted of a felony on two or more occasions.

(5) an individual who has been civilly committed under this Act, under the District of Columbia Code, or any State proceeding because of narcotic addiction on three or more occasions.

§ 2902. Discretionary authority of court; examination, report, and determination by court; termination of civil commitment

(a) If the United States district court believes that an eligible individual is an addict, the court may advise him at his first appearance or thereafter at the sole discretion of the court that the prosecution of the criminal charge will be held in abeyance if he elects to submit to an immediate examination to determine whether he is an addict and is likely to be rehabilitated through treatment. In offering an individual an election, the court shall advise him that if he elects to be examined, he will be confined during the examination for a period not to exceed sixty days; that if he is determined to be an addict who is likely to be rehabilitated, he will be civilly committed to the Surgeon General for treatment; that he may not voluntarily withdraw from the examination or any treatment which may follow; that the treatment may last for thirty-six months; that during treatment, he will be confined in an institution and, at the discretion of the Surgeon General, he may be conditionally released for supervised aftercare treatment in the community; and that if he successfully completes treatment the charge will be dismissed, but if he does not, prosecution on the charge will be resumed. An individual upon being advised that he may elect to submit to an examination shall be permitted a maximum of five days within which to make his election. Except on a showing that a timely election could not have been made, an individual shall be barred from an election after the prescribed period. An individual who elects civil commitment shall be placed in the custody of the Attorney General or the Surgeon General, as the court directs, for an examination by the Surgeon General during a period not to exceed thirty days. This period may, upon notice to the court and the appropriate United States attorney, be extended by the Surgeon General for an additional thirty days.

(b) The Surgeon General shall report to the court the results of the examination and recommend whether the individual should be civilly committed. A copy of the report shall be made available to the individual and the United States attorney. If the court, acting on the report and other information coming to its attention, determines that the individual is not an addict or is an addict not likely to be rehabilitated through treatment, the individual shall be held to answer the abeyant charge. If the court determines that the individual is an addict and is likely to be rehabilitated through treatment, the court shall commit him to the custody of the Surgeon General for treatment, except that no individual shall be committed under this chapter if the Surgeon General certifies that adequate facilities or personnel for treatment are unavailable.

(c) Whenever an individual is committed to the custody of the Surgeon General for treatment under this chapter the criminal charge against him shall be continued without final disposition and shall be dismissed if the Surgeon General certifies to the court that the individual has successfully completed the treatment program. On receipt of such certification, the court shall discharge the individual from custody and dismiss the charge against him. If prior to such certification the Surgeon General determines that the individual cannot be further treated as a medical problem, he shall advise the court. The court shall thereupon terminate the commitment, and the pending criminal proceeding shall be resumed.

(d) An individual committed for examination or treatment shall not be released on bail or on his own recognizance.

(e) Whoever escapes or attempts to escape while committed to institutional custody for examination or treatment, or whoever rescues or attempts to rescue or instigates, aids, or assists the escape or attempt to escape of such a person, shall be subject to the penalties provided in sections 751 and 752 of title 18, United States Code.

§ 2903. Authority and responsibilities of the Surgeon General; institutional custody; aftercare; maximum period of civil commitment; credit toward sentence

(a) An individual who is committed to the custody of the Surgeon General for treatment under this chapter shall not be conditionally released from institutional custody until the Surgeon General determines that he has made sufficient progress to warrant release to a supervisory aftercare authority. If the Surgeon General is unable to make such a determination at the expiration of twenty-four months after the commencement of institutional custody, he shall advise the court and the appropriate United States attorney whether treatment should be continued. The court may affirm the commitment or terminate it and resume the pending criminal proceeding.

(b) An individual who is conditionally released from institutional custody shall, while on release, remain in the legal custody of the Surgeon General and shall report for such supervised aftercare treatment as the Surgeon General directs. He shall be subject to home visits and to such physical examination and reasonable regulation of his conduct as the supervisory aftercare authority establishes, subject to the approval of the Surgeon General. The Surgeon General may, at any time, order a conditionally released individual to return for institutional treatment. The Surgeon General's order shall be a sufficient warrant for the supervisory aftercare authority, a probation officer, or any Federal officer authorized to serve criminal process within the United States to apprehend and return the individual to institutional custody as directed. If it is determined that an individual has returned to the use of narcotics, the Surgeon General shall inform the court of the conditions under which the return occurred and make a recommendation as to whether treatment should be continued. The court may affirm the commitment or terminate it and resume the pending criminal proceeding.

(c) The total period of treatment for any individual committed to the custody of the Surgeon General shall not exceed thirty-six months. If, at the expiration of such maximum period, the Surgeon General is unable to certify that the individual has successfully completed his treatment program the pending criminal proceeding shall be resumed.

(d) Whenever a pending criminal proceeding against an individual is resumed under this chapter, he shall receive full-credit toward the service of any sentence which may be imposed for any time spent in the institutional custody of the Surgeon General or the Attorney General or any other time spent in institutional custody in connection with the matter for which sentence is imposed.

§ 2904. Civil commitment not a conviction; use of test results

The determination of narcotic addiction and the subsequent civil commitment under this chapter shall not be deemed a criminal conviction. The results of any tests or procedures conducted by the Surgeon General or the supervisory aftercare authority to determine narcotic addiction may only be used in a further proceeding under this chapter. They shall not be used against the examined individual in any criminal proceeding except that the fact that he is a narcotic addict may be elicited on his cross-examination as bearing on his credibility as a witness.

§ 2905. Delegation of functions by Surgeon General; use of Federal, State, and private facilities

(a) The Surgeon General may from time to time make such provision as he deems appropriate authorizing the performance of any of his functions under this chapter by any other officer or employee of the Public Health Service, or with the consent of the head of the Department or Agency concerned, by any Federal or other public or private agency or officer or employee thereof.

(b) The Surgeon General is authorized to enter into arrangements with any public or private agency or any person under which appropriate facilities or services of such agency or person will be made available, on a reimbursable basis or otherwise, for the examination or treatment of individuals who elect civil commitment under this chapter.

§ 2906. Absence of offer by the court to a defendant of an election under section 2902(a) or any determination as to civil commitment, not reviewable on appeal or otherwise

The failure of a court to offer a defendant an election under section 2902(a) of this chapter, or a determination relative to civil commitment under this chapter shall not be reviewable on appeal or otherwise.

TITLE 18, UNITED STATES CODE

CRIMES AND CRIMINAL PROCEDURE

(As enacted in Public Law 772, 80th Congress, Second Session, and as amended to August 1, 1983)

Editorial Note: The introductory note, p. 1, *supra*, to Title 28 of the Code describes the earlier codifications of the criminal laws of the United States. The present revision was approved June 25, 1948, and became effective September 1, 1948. It was amended to correct minor errors by Public Law 72, 81st Congress, First Session, and further amendments have been made since then.

The revision was originally in four parts, entitled Crimes, Criminal Procedure, Prisons and Prisoners, and Correction of Youthful Offenders. A fifth part, entitled Immunity of Witnesses, was added in 1970. This reprint includes only Chapter 119 of Part I, Part II with some omissions, and Part V.

A complete revision of Title 18 in the form of a Federal Criminal Code has been the subject of congressional consideration for more than a decade. The latest versions of the Code are S. 1437, 95th Cong., 1st Sess., approved by the Senate with amendments on January 30, 1978; S.1722, 96th Cong., 1st Sess., approved by the Senate Judiciary Committee with amendments on December 4, 1979; H.R. 6233, 96th Cong., 2d Sess., approved by a subcommittee of the House Judiciary Committee on March 11, 1980; H.R. 6915, 96th Cong., 2d Sess., approved with amendments by the House Judiciary Committee on September 25, 1980; and S. 1630, 97th Cong., 2d Sess., approved by Senate Judiciary Committee on January 25, 1982. The enactment of the Code would, of course, supersede the portions of Title 18 reproduced here.

PART I—CRIMES

CHAPTER 119. WIRE INTERCEPTION AND INTERCEPTION OF ORAL COMMUNICATIONS *

---

* In connection with the enactment of Chapter 119, section 605 of the Communications Act of 1934 (47 U.S.C. § 605) was amended to bring it into conformity therewith. Oct. 15, 1970, 84 Stat. 961.

§ 2510. Definitions

As used in this chapter—

(1) "wire communication" means any communication made in whole or in part through the use of facilities for the transmission of communications by the aid of wire, cable, or other like connection between the point of origin and the point of reception furnished or operated by any person engaged as a common carrier in providing or operating such facilities for the transmission of interstate or foreign communications;

(2) "oral communication" means any oral communication uttered by a person exhibiting an expectation that such communication is not subject to interception under circumstances justifying such expectation;

(3) "State" means any State of the United States, the District of Columbia, the Commonwealth of Puerto Rico, and any territory or possession of the United States;

(4) "intercept" means the aural acquisition of the contents of any wire or oral communication through the use of any electronic, mechanical, or other device.

(5) "electronic, mechanical, or other device" means any device or apparatus which can be used to intercept a wire or oral communication other than—

(a) any telephone or telegraph instrument, equipment or facility, or any component thereof, (i) furnished to the subscriber or user by a communications common carrier in the ordinary course of its business and being used by the subscriber or user in the ordinary course of its business; or (ii) being used by a communications common carrier in the ordinary course of its business, or by an investigative or law enforcement officer in the ordinary course of his duties;

(b) a hearing aid or similar device being used to correct subnormal hearing to not better than normal;

(6) "person" means any employee, or agent of the United States or any State or political subdivision thereof, and any individual, partnership, association, joint stock company, trust, or corporation;

(7) "Investigative or law enforcement officer" means any officer of the United States or of a State or political subdivision thereof, who is empowered by law to conduct investigations of or to make arrests for offenses enumerated in this chapter, and any attorney authorized by law to prosecute or participate in the prosecution of such offenses;

(8) "contents," when used with respect to any wire or oral communication, includes any information concerning the identity of the parties to such communication or the existence, substance, purport, or meaning of that communication;

(9) "Judge of competent jurisdiction" means—

(a) a judge of a United States district court or a United States court of appeals; and

(b) a judge of any court of general criminal jurisdiction of a State who is authorized by a statute of that State to enter orders authorizing interceptions of wire or oral communications;

(10) "communication common carrier" shall have the same meaning which is given the term "common carrier" by section 153(h) of title 47 of the United States Code; and

(11) "aggrieved person" means a person who was a party to any intercepted wire or oral communication or a person against whom the interception was directed.

§ 2511. Interception and disclosure of wire or oral communications prohibited

(1) Except as otherwise specifically provided in this chapter any person who—

(a) willfully intercepts, endeavors to intercept, or procures any other person to intercept or endeavor to intercept, any wire or oral communication;

(b) willfully uses, endeavors to use, or procures any other person to use or endeavor to use any electronic, mechanical, or other device to intercept any oral communication when—

(i) such device is affixed to, or otherwise transmits a signal through, a wire, cable, or other like connection used in wire communication; or

(ii) such device transmits communications by radio, or interferes with the transmission of such communication; or

(iii) such person knows, or has reason to know, that such device or any component thereof has been sent through the mail or transported in interstate or foreign commerce; or

(iv) such use or endeavor to use (A) takes place on the premises of any business or other commercial establishment the operations of which affect interstate or foreign commerce; or (B) obtains or is for the purpose of obtaining information relating to the operations of any business or other commercial establishment the operations of which affect interstate or foreign commerce; or

(v) such person acts in the District of Columbia, the Commonwealth of Puerto Rico, or any territory or possession of the United States;

(c) willfully discloses, or endeavors to disclose, to any other person the contents of any wire or oral communication, knowing or having reason to know that the information was obtained through the interception of a wire or oral communication in violation of this subsection; or

(d) willfully uses, or endeavors to use, the contents of any wire or oral communication, knowing or having reason to know that the information was obtained through the interception of a wire or oral communication in violation of this subsection;

shall be fined not more than $10,000 or imprisoned not more than five years, or both.

(2) (a)(i) It shall not be unlawful under this chapter for an operator of a switchboard, or an officer, employee, or agent of any communication common carrier, whose facilities are used in the transmission of a wire communication, to intercept, disclose, or use that communication in the normal course of his employment while engaged in any activity which is a necessary incident to the rendition of his service or to the protection of the rights or property of the carrier of such communication: *Provided,* That said communication common carriers shall not utilize service observing or random monitoring except for mechanical or service quality control checks.

(ii) Notwithstanding any other law, communication common carriers, their officers, employees, and agents, landlords, custodians, or other persons, are authorized to provide information, facilities, or technical assistance to persons authorized by law to intercept wire or oral communications or to conduct electronic surveillance, as defined in section 101 of the Foreign Intelligence Surveillance Act of 1978, if the common carrier, its officers, employees, or agents, landlord, custodian, or other specified person, has been provided with—

(A) a court order directing such assistance signed by the authorizing judge, or

(B) a certification in writing by a person specified in section 2518(7) of this title or the Attorney General of the United States that no warrant or court order is required by law, that all statutory requirements have been met, and that the specified assistance is required,

setting forth the period of time during which the provision of the information, facilities, or technical assistance is authorized and specifying the information, facilities, or technical assistance required. No communication common carrier, officer, employee, or agent thereof, or landlord, custodian, or other specified person shall disclose the existence of any interception or surveillance or the device used to accomplish the interception or surveillance with respect to which the person has been furnished an order or certification under this subparagraph, except as may otherwise be required by legal process and then only after prior notification to the Attorney General or to the principal prosecuting attorney of a State or any political subdivision of a State, as may be appropriate. Any violation of this subparagraph by a communication common carrier or an officer, employee, or agent thereof, shall render the carrier liable for the civil damages provided for in section 2520. No cause of action shall lie in any court against any communication common carrier, its officers, employees, or agents, landlord, custodian, or other specified person for providing information, facilities, or assistance in accordance with the terms of an order or certification under this subparagraph.

(b) It shall not be unlawful under this chapter for an officer, employee, or agent of the Federal Communications Commission, in the normal course of his employment and in discharge of the monitoring responsibilities exercised by the Commission in the enforcement of chapter 5 of title 47 of the United States Code, to intercept a wire communication, or oral communication transmitted by radio, or to disclose or use the information thereby obtained.

(c) It shall not be unlawful under this chapter for a person acting under color of law to intercept a wire or oral communication, where such person is a party to the communication or one of the parties to the communication has given prior consent to such interception.

(d) It shall not be unlawful under this chapter for a person not acting under color of law to intercept a wire or oral communication where such person is a party to the communication or where one of the parties to the communication has given prior consent to such interception unless such communication is intercepted for the purpose of committing any criminal or tortious act in violation of the Constitution or laws of the United States or of any State or for the purpose of committing any other injurious act.

(e) Notwithstanding any other provision of this title or section 605 or 606 of the Communications Act of 1934, it shall not be unlawful for an officer, employee, or agent of the United States in the normal course of his official duty to conduct electronic surveillance, as defined in section 101 of the Foreign Intelligence Surveillance Act of 1978, as authorized by that Act.

(f) Nothing contained in this chapter, or section 605 of the Communications Act of 1934, shall be deemed to affect the acquisition by the United States Government of foreign intelligence information from international or foreign communications by a means other than electronic surveillance as defined in section 101 of the Foreign Intelligence Surveillance Act of 1978, and procedures in this chapter and the Foreign Intelligence Surveillance Act of 1978 shall be the exclusive means by which electronic surveillance, as defined in section 101 of such Act, and the interception of domestic wire and oral communications may be conducted.

§ 2512. Manufacture, distribution, possession, and advertising of wire or oral communication intercepting devices prohibited

(1) Except as otherwise specifically provided in this chapter, any person who willfully—

(a) sends through the mail, or sends or carries in interstate or foreign commerce, any electronic, mechanical, or other device, knowing or having reason to know that the design of such device renders it primarily useful for the purpose of the surreptitious interception of wire or oral communications;

(b) manufactures, assembles, possesses, or sells any electronic, mechanical, or other device, knowing or having reason to know that the design of such device renders it primarily useful for the purpose of the surreptitious interception of wire or oral communications, and that such device or any component thereof has been or will be sent through the mail or transported in interstate or foreign commerce; or

(c) places in any newspaper, magazine, handbill, or other publication any advertisement of—

(i) any electronic, mechanical, or other device knowing or having reason to know that the design of such device renders it primarily useful for the purpose of the surreptitious interception of wire or oral communications; or

(ii) any other electronic, mechanical, or other device, where such advertisement promotes the use of such device for the purpose of the surreptitious interception of wire or oral communications,

knowing or having reason to know that such advertisement will be sent through the mail or transported in interstate or foreign commerce,

shall be fined not more than $10,000 or imprisoned not more than five years, or both.

(2) It shall not be unlawful under this section for—

(a) a communications common carrier or an officer, agent, or employee of, or a person under contract with, a communications common carrier, in the normal course of the communications common carrier's business, or

(b) an officer, agent, or employee of, or a person under contract with, the United States, a State, or a political subdivision thereof, in the normal course of the activities of the United States, a State, or a political subdivision thereof, to send through the mail, send or carry in interstate or foreign commerce, or manufacture, assemble, possess, or sell any electronic, mechanical, or other device knowing or having reason to know that the design of such device renders it primarily useful for the purpose of the surreptitious interception of wire or oral communications.

§ 2513. Confiscation of wire or oral communication intercepting devices

Any electronic, mechanical, or other device used, sent, carried, manufactured, assembled, possessed, sold, or advertised in violation of section 2511 or section 2512 of this chapter may be seized and forfeited to the United States. All provisions of law relating to (1) the seizure, summary and judicial forfeiture, and condemnation of vessels, vehicles, merchandise, and baggage for violations of the customs laws contained in title 19 of the United States Code, (2) the disposition of such vessels, vehicles, merchandise, and baggage or the proceeds from the sale thereof, (3) the remission or mitigation of such forfeiture, (4) the compromise of claims, and (5) the award of compensation to informers in respect of such forfeitures, shall apply to seizures and forfeitures incurred, or alleged to have been incurred, under the provisions of this section, insofar as applicable and not inconsistent with the provisions of this section; except that such duties as are imposed upon the collector of customs or any other person with respect to the seizure and forfeiture of vessels, vehicles, merchandise, and baggage under the provisions of the customs laws contained in title 19 of the United States Code shall be performed with respect to seizure and forfeiture of electronic, mechanical, or other intercepting devices under this section by such officers, agents, or other persons as may be authorized or designated for that purpose by the Attorney General.

[§ 2514. Repealed.]

§ 2515. Prohibition of use as evidence of intercepted wire or oral communications

Whenever any wire or oral communication has been intercepted, no part of the contents of such communication and no evidence derived therefrom may be received in evidence in any trial, hearing, or other proceeding in or before any court, grand jury, department, officer, agency, regulatory body, legislative committee, or other authority of the United States, a State, or a political subdivision thereof if the disclosure of that information would be in violation of this chapter.

§ 2516. Authorization for interception of wire or oral communications

(1) The Attorney General, or any Assistant Attorney General specially designated by the Attorney General, may authorize an application to a Federal judge of competent jurisdiction for, and such judge may grant in conformity with section 2518 of this chapter an order authorizing or approving the interception of wire or oral communications by the Federal Bureau of Investigation, or a Federal agency having responsibility for the investigation of the offense as to which the application is made, when such interception may provide or has provided evidence of—

(a) any offense punishable by death or by imprisonment for more than one year under sections 2274 through 2277 of title 42 of the United States Code (relating to the enforcement of the Atomic Energy Act of 1954), or under the following chapters of this title: chapter 37 (relating to espionage), chapter 105 (relating to sabotage), chapter 115 (relating to treason), or chapter 102 (relating to riots);

(b) a violation of section 186 or section 501(c) of title 29, United States Code (dealing with restrictions on payments and loans to labor organizations), or any offense which involves murder, kidnapping, robbery, or extortion, and which is punishable under this title;

(c) any offense which is punishable under the following sections of this title: section 201 (bribery of public officials and witnesses), section 224 (bribery in sporting contests), subsection (d), (e), (f), (g), (h) or (i) of section 844 (unlawful use of explosives), section 1084 (transmission of wagering information), section 1503 (influencing or injuring an officer, juror, or witness, generally), section 1510 (obstruction of criminal investigations), section 1511 (obstruction of State or local law enforcement), section 1751 (Presidential and Presidential staff assassinations, kidnapping, and assault), section 1951 (interference with commerce by threats or violence), section 1952 (interstate and foreign travel or transportation in aid of racketeering enterprises), section 1954 (offer, acceptance, or solicitation to influence operations of employee benefit plan), section 1955 (prohibition of business enterprises of gambling), section 659 (theft from interstate shipment), section 664 (embezzlement from pension and welfare funds), sections 2314 and 2315 (interstate transportation of stolen property), section 1963 (violations with respect to racketeer influenced and corrupt organizations) or section 351 (violations with respect to congressional, Cabinet, or Supreme Court assassinations, kidnapping, and assault);

(d) any offense involving counterfeiting punishable under section 471, 472, or 473 of this title;

(e) any offense involving fraud connected with a case under title 11 or the manufacture, importation, receiving, concealment, buying, selling, or otherwise dealing in narcotic drugs, marihuana, or other dangerous drugs, punishable under any law of the United States;

(f) any offense including extortionate credit transactions under sections 892, 893, or 894 of this title; or

(g) any conspiracy to commit any of the foregoing offenses.

(2) The principal prosecuting attorney of any State, or the principal prosecuting attorney of any political subdivision thereof, if such attorney is authorized by a statute of that State to make application to a State court judge of competent jurisdiction for an order authorizing or approving the interception of wire or oral communications, may apply to such judge for, and such judge may grant in conformity

with section 2518 of this chapter and with the applicable State statute an order authorizing, or approving the interception of wire or oral communications by investigative or law enforcement officers having responsibility for the investigation of the offense as to which the application is made, when such interception may provide or has provided evidence of the commission of the offense of murder, kidnapping, gambling, robbery, bribery, extortion, or dealing in narcotic drugs, marihuana or other dangerous drugs, or other crime dangerous to life, limb, or property, and punishable by imprisonment for more than one year, designated in any applicable State statute authorizing such interception, or any conspiracy to commit any of the foregoing offenses.

§ 2517. Authorization for disclosure and use of intercepted wire or oral communications

(1) Any investigative or law enforcement officer who, by any means authorized by this chapter, has obtained knowledge of the contents of any wire or oral communication, or evidence derived therefrom, may disclose such contents to another investigative or law enforcement officer to the extent that such disclosure is appropriate to the proper performance of the official duties of the officer making or receiving the disclosure.

(2) Any investigative or law enforcement officer who, by any means authorized by this chapter, has obtained knowledge of the contents of any wire or oral communication or evidence derived therefrom may use such contents to the extent such use is appropriate to the proper performance of his official duties.

(3) Any person who has received, by any means authorized by this chapter, any information concerning a wire or oral communication, or evidence derived therefrom intercepted in accordance with the provisions of this chapter may disclose the contents of that communication or such derivative evidence while giving testimony under oath or affirmation in any proceeding held under the authority of the United States or of any State or political subdivision thereof.

(4) No otherwise privileged wire or oral communication intercepted in accordance with, or in violation of, the provisions of this chapter shall lose its privileged character.

(5) When an investigative or law enforcement officer, while engaged in intercepting wire or oral communications in the manner authorized herein, intercepts wire or oral communications relating to offenses other than those specified in the order of authorization or approval, the contents thereof, and evidence derived therefrom, may be disclosed or used as provided in subsections (1) and (2) of this section. Such contents and any evidence derived therefrom may be used under subsection (3) of this section when authorized or approved by a judge of competent jurisdiction where such judge finds on subsequent application that the contents were otherwise intercepted in accordance with the provisions of this chapter. Such application shall be made as soon as practicable.

§ 2518. Procedure for interception of wire or oral communications

(1) Each application for an order authorizing or approving the interception of a wire or oral communication under this chapter shall be made in writing upon oath or affirmation to a judge of competent jurisdiction and shall state the applicant's authority to make such application. Each application shall include the following information:

(a) the identity of the investigative or law enforcement officer making the application, and the officer authorizing the application;

(b) a full and complete statement of the facts and circumstances relied upon by the applicant, to justify his belief that an order should be issued, including (i) details as to the particular offense that has been, is being, or is about to be committed, (ii) a particular description of the nature and location of the facilities from which or the place where the communication is to be intercepted, (iii) a particular description of the type of communications sought to be intercepted, (iv) the identity of the person, if known, committing the offense and whose communications are to be intercepted;

(c) a full and complete statement as to whether or not other investigative procedures have been tried and failed or why they reasonably appear to be unlikely to succeed if tried or to be too dangerous;

(d) a statement of the period of time for which the interception is required to be maintained. If the nature of the investigation is such that the authorization for interception should not automatically terminate when the described type of communication has been first obtained, a particular description of facts establishing probable cause to believe that additional communications of the same type will occur thereafter;

(e) a full and complete statement of the facts concerning all previous applications known to the individual authorizing and making the application, made to any judge for authorization to intercept, or for approval of interceptions of, wire or oral communications involving any of the same persons, facilities or places specified in the application, and the action taken by the judge on each such application; and

(f) where the application is for the extension of an order, a statement setting forth the results thus far obtained from the interception, or a reasonable explanation of the failure to obtain such results.

(2) The judge may require the applicant to furnish additional testimony or documentary evidence in support of the application.

(3) Upon such application the judge may enter an ex parte order, as requested or as modified, authorizing or approving interception of wire or oral communications within the territorial jurisdiction of the

court in which the judge is sitting, if the judge determines on the basis of the facts submitted by the applicant that—

(a) there is probable cause for belief that an individual is committing, has committed, or is about to commit a particular offense enumerated in section 2516 of this chapter;

(b) there is probable cause for belief that particular communications concerning that offense will be obtained through such interception;

(c) normal investigative procedures have been tried and have failed or reasonably appear to be unlikely to succeed if tried or to be too dangerous;

(d) there is probable cause for belief that the facilities from which, or the place where, the wire or oral communications are to be intercepted are being used, or are about to be used, in connection with the commission of such offense, or are leased to, listed in the name of, or commonly used by such person.

(4) Each order authorizing or approving the interception of any wire or oral communication under this chapter shall specify—

(a) the identity of the person, if known, whose communications are to be intercepted;

(b) the nature and location of the communications facilities as to which, or the place where, authority to intercept is granted;

(c) a particular description of the type of communication sought to be intercepted, and a statement of the particular offense to which it relates;

(d) the identity of the agency authorized to intercept the communications, and of the person authorizing the application; and

(e) the period of time during which such interception is authorized, including a statement as to whether or not the interception shall automatically terminate when the described communication has been first obtained.

An order authorizing the interception of a wire or oral communication under this chapter shall, upon request of the applicant, direct that a communication common carrier, landlord, custodian or other person shall furnish the applicant forthwith all information, facilities, and technical assistance necessary to accomplish the interception unobtrusively and with a minimum of interference with the services that such carrier, landlord, custodian, or person is according the person whose communications are to be intercepted. Any communication common carrier, landlord, custodian or other person furnishing such facilities or technical assistance shall be compensated therefor by the applicant at the prevailing rates.

(5) No order entered under this section may authorize or approve the interception of any wire or oral communication for any period longer than is necessary to achieve the objective of the authorization, nor in any event longer than thirty days. Extensions of an order may

be granted, but only upon application for an extension made in accordance with subsection (1) of this section and the court making the findings required by subsection (3) of this section. The period of extension shall be no longer than the authorizing judge deems necessary to achieve the purposes for which it was granted and in no event for longer than thirty days. Every order and extension thereof shall contain a provision that the authorization to intercept shall be executed as soon as practicable, shall be conducted in such a way as to minimize the interception of communications not otherwise subject to interception under this chapter, and must terminate upon attainment of the authorized objective, or in any event in thirty days.

(6) Whenever an order authorizing interception is entered pursuant to this chapter, the order may require reports to be made to the judge who issued the order showing what progress has been made toward achievement of the authorized objective and the need for continued interception. Such reports shall be made at such intervals as the judge may require.

(7) Notwithstanding any other provision of this chapter, any investigative or law enforcement officer, specially designated by the Attorney General or by the principal prosecuting attorney of any State or subdivision thereof acting pursuant to a statute of that State, who reasonably determines that—

(a) an emergency situation exists with respect to conspiratorial activities threatening the national security interest or to conspiratorial activities characteristic of organized crime that requires a wire or oral communication to be intercepted before an order authorizing such interception can with due diligence be obtained, and

(b) there are grounds upon which an order could be entered under this chapter to authorize such interception,

may intercept such wire or oral communication if an application for an order approving the interception is made in accordance with this section within forty-eight hours after the interception has occurred, or begins to occur. In the absence of an order, such interception shall immediately terminate when the communication sought is obtained or when the application for the order is denied, whichever is earlier. In the event such application for approval is denied, or in any other case where the interception is terminated without an order having been issued, the contents of any wire or oral communication intercepted shall be treated as having been obtained in violation of this chapter, and an inventory shall be served as provided for in subsection (d) of this section on the person named in the application.

(8) (a) The contents of any wire or oral communication intercepted by any means authorized by this chapter shall, if possible, be recorded on tape or wire or other comparable device. The recording of the contents of any wire or oral communication under this subsection shall be done in such way as will protect the recording from editing or other alterations. Immediately upon the expiration of

the period of the order, or extensions thereof, such recordings shall be made available to the judge issuing such order and sealed under his directions. Custody of the recordings shall be wherever the judge orders. They shall not be destroyed except upon an order of the issuing or denying judge and in any event shall be kept for ten years. Duplicate recordings may be made for use or disclosure pursuant to the provisions of subsections (1) and (2) of section 2517 of this chapter for investigations. The presence of the seal provided for by this subsection, or a satisfactory explanation for the absence thereof, shall be a prerequisite for the use or disclosure of the contents of any wire or oral communication or evidence derived therefrom under subsection (3) of section 2517.

(b) Applications made and orders granted under this chapter shall be sealed by the judge. Custody of the applications and orders shall be wherever the judge directs. Such applications and orders shall be disclosed only upon a showing of good cause before a judge of competent jurisdiction and shall not be destroyed except on order of the issuing or denying judge, and in any event shall be kept for ten years.

(c) Any violation of the provisions of this subsection may be punished as contempt of the issuing or denying judge.

(d) Within a reasonable time but not later than ninety days after the filing of an application for an order of approval under section 2518(7) (b) which is denied or the termination of the period of an order or extensions thereof, the issuing or denying judge shall cause to be served, on the persons named in the order or the application, and such other parties to intercepted communications as the judge may determine in his discretion that is in the interest of justice, an inventory which shall include notice of—

(1) the fact of the entry of the order or the application;

(2) the date of the entry and the period of authorized, approved or disapproved interception, or the denial of the application; and

(3) the fact that during the period wire or oral communications were or were not intercepted.

The judge, upon the filing of a motion, may in his discretion make available to such person or his counsel for inspection such portions of the intercepted communications, applications and orders as the judge determines to be in the interest of justice. On an ex parte showing of good cause to a judge of competent jurisdiction the serving of the inventory required by this subsection may be postponed.

(9) The contents of any wire or oral communication intercepted pursuant to this chapter or evidence derived therefrom shall not be received in evidence or otherwise disclosed in any trial, hearing, or other proceeding in a Federal or State court unless each party, not less than ten days before the trial, hearing, or proceeding, has been furnished with a copy of the court order, and accompanying application, under which the interception was authorized or approv-

ed. This ten-day period may be waived by the judge if he finds that it was not possible to furnish the party with the above information ten days before the trial, hearing, or proceeding and that the party will not be prejudiced by the delay in receiving such information.

(10) (a) Any aggrieved person in any trial, hearing, or proceeding in or before any court, department, officer, agency, regulatory body, or other authority of the United States, a State, or a political subdivision thereof, may move to suppress the contents of any wire or oral communication intercepted pursuant to this chapter, or evidence derived therefrom, on the grounds that—

(i) the communication was unlawfully intercepted;

(ii) the order of authorization or approval under which it was intercepted is insufficient on its face; or

(iii) the interception was not made in conformity with the order of authorization or approval.

Such motion shall be made before the trial, hearing, or proceeding unless there was no opportunity to make such motion or the person was not aware of the grounds of the motion. If the motion is granted, the contents of the intercepted wire or oral communication, or evidence derived therefrom, shall be treated as having been obtained in violation of this chapter. The judge, upon the filing of such motion by the aggrieved person, may in his discretion make available to the aggrieved person or his counsel for inspection such portions of the intercepted communication or evidence derived therefrom as the judge determines to be in the interests of justice.

(b) In addition to any other right to appeal, the United States shall have the right to appeal from an order granting a motion to suppress made under paragraph (a) of this subsection, or the denial of an application for an order of approval, if the United States attorney shall certify to the judge or other official granting such motion or denying such application that the appeal is not taken for purposes of delay. Such appeal shall be taken within thirty days after the date the order was entered and shall be diligently prosecuted.

§ 2519. Reports concerning intercepted wire or oral communications

(1) Within thirty days after the expiration of an order (or each extension thereof) entered under section 2518, or the denial of an order approving an interception, the issuing or denying judge shall report to the Administrative Office of the United States Courts—

(a) the fact that an order or extension was applied for;

(b) the kind of order or extension applied for;

(c) the fact that the order or extension was granted as applied for, was modified, or was denied;

(d) the period of interceptions authorized by the order, and the number and duration of any extensions of the order;

(e) the offense specified in the order or application, or extension of an order;

(f) the identity of the applying investigative or law enforcement officer and agency making the application and the person authorizing the application; and

(g) the nature of the facilities from which or the place where communications were to be intercepted.

(2) In January of each year the Attorney General, an Assistant Attorney General specially designated by the Attorney General, or the principal prosecuting attorney of a State, or the principal prosecuting attorney for any political subdivision of a State, shall report to the Administrative Office of the United States Courts—

(a) the information required by paragraphs (a) through (g) of subsection (1) of this section with respect to each application for an order or extension made during the preceding calendar year;

(b) a general description of the interceptions made under such order or extension, including (i) the approximate nature and frequency of incriminating communications intercepted, (ii) the approximate nature and frequency of other communications intercepted, (iii) the approximate number of persons whose communications were intercepted, and (iv) the approximate nature, amount, and cost of the manpower and other resources used in the interceptions;

(c) the number of arrests resulting from interceptions made under such order or extension, and the offenses for which arrests were made;

(d) the number of trials resulting from such interceptions;

(e) the number of motions to suppress made with respect to such interceptions, and the number granted or denied;

(f) the number of convictions resulting from such interceptions and the offenses for which the convictions were obtained and a general assessment of the importance of the interceptions; and

(g) the information required by paragraphs (b) through (f) of this subsection with respect to orders or extensions obtained in a preceding calendar year.

(3) In April of each year the Director of the Administrative Office of the United States Courts shall transmit to the Congress a full and complete report concerning the number of applications for orders authorizing or approving the interception of wire or oral communications pursuant to this chapter and the number of orders and extensions granted or denied during the preceding calendar year. Such report shall include a summary and analysis of the data required to be filed with the Administrative Office by subsections (1) and (2) of this section. The Director of the Administrative Office of the United States Courts is authorized to issue binding regulations dealing with

the content and form of the reports required to be filed by subsections (1) and (2) of this section.

§ 2520. Recovery of civil damages authorized

Any person whose wire or oral communication is intercepted, disclosed, or used in violation of this chapter shall (1) have a civil cause of action against any person who intercepts, discloses, or uses, or procures any other person to intercept, disclose, or use such communications, and (2) be entitled to recover from any such person—

(a) actual damages but not less than liquidated damages computed at the rate of $100 a day for each day of violation or $1,000, whichever is higher;

(b) punitive damages; and

(c) a reasonable attorney's fee and other litigation costs reasonably incurred.

A good faith reliance on a court order or legislative authorization shall constitute a complete defense to any civil or criminal action brought under this chapter or under any other law.

PART II—CRIMINAL PROCEDURE

* Omitted from this compilation.

CHAPTER 201—GENERAL PROVISIONS

§ 3001. Procedure governed by rules; scope, purpose and effect; definition of terms; local rules; forms—(Rule)

SEE FEDERAL RULES OF CRIMINAL PROCEDURE

Scope, Rule 1.
Purpose and construction, Rule 2.
Proceedings to which rules apply, Rules 54 and 59.
Definitions, Rule 54(c).
Rules of District Courts, Rule 57.
Forms, Rule 58.
Effective date, Rule 59.
Citation of rule, Rule 60.

§ 3002. Courts always open—(Rule)

SEE FEDERAL RULES OF CRIMINAL PROCEDURE

Business hours, Rule 56.

§ 3003. Calendars—(Rule)

SEE FEDERAL RULES OF CRIMINAL PROCEDURE

Preference to criminal cases, Rule 50.

§ 3004. Decorum in court room—(Rule)

SEE FEDERAL RULES OF CRIMINAL PROCEDURE

Photographing or radio broadcasting prohibited, Rule 53.

§ 3005. Counsel and witnesses in capital cases

Whoever is indicted for treason or other capital crime shall be allowed to make his full defense by counsel learned in the law; and the court before which he is tried, or some judge thereof, shall immediately, upon his request, assign to him such counsel, not exceeding two, as he may desire, who shall have free access to him at all reasonable hours. He shall be allowed, in his defense to make any proof that he can produce by lawful witnesses, and shall have the like process of the court to compel his witnesses to appear at his trial, as is usually granted to compel witnesses to appear on behalf of the prosecution.

§ 3006. Assignment of counsel—(Rule)

SEE FEDERAL RULES OF CRIMINAL PROCEDURE

Appointment by court, Rule 44.
Accused to be informed of right to counsel, Rules 5 and 44.

§ 3006A. Adequate representation of defendants

(a) Choice of plan.—Each United States district court, with the approval of the judicial council of the circuit, shall place in operation throughout the district a plan for furnishing representation for any person financially unable to obtain adequate representation (1) who is charged with a felony or misdemeanor (other than a petty offense as defined in section 1 of this title) or with juvenile delinquency by the commission of an act which, if committed by an adult, would be such a felony or misdemeanor or with a violation of probation, (2) who is under arrest, when such representation is required by law, (3) who is subject to revocation of parole, in custody as a material witness, or seeking collateral relief, as provided in subsection (g), or, (4) for whom the Sixth Amendment to the Constitution requires the appointment of counsel or for whom, in a case in which he faces loss of liberty, any Federal law requires the appointment of counsel. Representation under each plan shall include counsel and investigative, expert, and other services necessary for an adequate defense. Each plan shall include a provision for private attorneys. The plan may include, in addition to a provision for private attorneys in a substantial proportion of cases, either of the following or both:

(1) attorneys furnished by a bar association or a legal aid agency; or

(2) attorneys furnished by a defender organization established in accordance with the provisions of subsection (h).

Prior to approving the plan for a district, the judicial council of the circuit shall supplement the plan with provisions for representation on appeal. The district court may modify the plan at any time with the approval of the judicial council of the circuit. It shall modify the plan when directed by the judicial council of the circuit. The district court shall notify the Administrative Office of the United States Courts of any modification of its plan.

(b) Appointment of counsel.—Counsel furnishing representation under the plan shall be selected from a panel of attorneys designated or approved by the court, or from a bar association, legal aid agency, or defender organization furnishing representation pursuant to the plan. In every criminal case in which the defendant is charged with a felony or a misdemeanor (other than a petty offense as defined in section 1 of this title) or with juvenile delinquency by the commission of an act which, if committed by an adult, would be such a felony or misdemeanor or with a violation of probation and appears without counsel, the United States magistrate or the court shall advise the defendant that he has the right to be represented by counsel and that counsel will be appointed to represent him if he is financially unable to obtain counsel. Unless the defendant waives representation by counsel, the United States magistrate or the court, if satisfied after appropriate inquiry that the defendant is financially unable to obtain counsel, shall appoint counsel to represent him. Such appointment may be made retroactive to include any representation furnished pursuant to the plan prior to appointment. The United States magistrate or the court shall appoint separate counsel for defendants having interests that cannot properly be represented by the same counsel, or when other good cause is shown.

(c) Duration and substitution of appointments.—A person for whom counsel is appointed shall be represented at every stage of the proceedings from his initial appearance before the United States magistrate or the court through appeal, including ancillary matters appropriate to the proceedings. If at any time after the appointment of counsel the United States magistrate or the court finds that the person is financially able to obtain counsel or to make partial payment for the representation, it may terminate the appointment of counsel or authorize payment as provided in subsection (f), as the interests of justice may dictate. If at any stage of the proceedings, including an appeal, the United States magistrate or the court finds that the person is financially unable to pay counsel whom he had retained, it may appoint counsel as provided in subsection (b) and authorize payment as provided in subsection (d), as the interests of justice may dictate. The United States magistrate or the court may, in the interests of justice, substitute one appointed counsel for another at any stage of the proceedings.

(d) Payment for representation.—

(1) Hourly rate.—Any attorney appointed pursuant to this section or a bar association or legal aid agency or community defender organization which has provided the appointed attorney shall, at the conclusion of the representation or any segment thereof, be compensated at a rate not exceeding $30 per hour for time expended in court or before a United States magistrate and $20 per hour for time reasonably expended out of court, or such other hourly rate, fixed by the Judicial Council of the Circuit, not to exceed the minimum hourly scale established by a bar association for similar services rendered in the district. Such attorney shall be reimbursed for expenses reasonably incurred, including the costs of transcripts authorized by the United States magistrate or the court.

(2) Maximum amounts.—For representation of a defendant before the United States magistrate or the district court, or both, the compensation to be paid to an attorney or to a bar association or legal aid agency or community defender organization shall not exceed $1,000 for each attorney in a case in which one or more felonies are charged, and $400 for each attorney in a case in which only misdemeanors are charged. For representation of a defendant in an appellate court, the compensation to be paid to an attorney or to a bar association or legal aid agency or community defender organization shall not exceed $1,000 for each attorney in each court. For representation in connection with a post-trial motion made after the entry of judgment or in a probation revocation proceeding or for representation provided under subsection (g) the compensation shall not exceed $250 for each attorney in each proceeding in each court.

(3) Waiving maximum amounts.—Payment in excess of any maximum amount provided in paragraph (2) of this subsection may be made for extended or complex representation whenever the court in which the representation was rendered, or the United States magistrate if the representation was furnished exclusively before him, certifies that the amount of the excess payment is necessary to provide fair compensation and the payment is approved by the chief judge of the circuit.

(4) Filing claims.—A separate claim for compensation and reimbursement shall be made to the district court for representation before the United States magistrate and the court, and to each appellate court before which the attorney represented the defendant. Each claim shall be supported by a sworn written statement specifying the time expended, services rendered, and expenses incurred while the case was pending before the United States magistrate and the court, and the compensation and reimbursement applied for or received in the same case from any other source. The court shall fix the compensation and reimbursement to be paid to the attorney or to the bar association or legal aid agency or community defender organization which provided the appointed attorney. In cases where representation is furnished exclusively before a United States magistrate, the claim shall be submitted to him and he shall fix the compensation and reimbursement to be paid. In cases where representation is furnished other than before the United States magistrate, the district court, or an appellate court, claims shall be submitted to the district court which shall fix the compensation and reimbursement to be paid.

(5) New trials.—For purposes of compensation and other payments authorized by this section, an order by a court granting a new trial shall be deemed to initiate a new case.

(6) Proceedings before appellate courts.—If a person for whom counsel is appointed under this section appeals to an appellate court or petitions for a writ of certiorari, he may do so without prepayment of fees and costs or security therefor and without filing the affidavit required by section 1915(a) of title 28.

(e) Services other than counsel.—

(1) Upon request.—Counsel for a person who is financially unable to obtain investigative, expert, or other services necessary for an adequate defense may request them in an ex parte application. Upon finding, after appropriate inquiry in an ex parte proceeding, that the services are necessary and that the person is financially unable to obtain them, the court, or the United States magistrate if the services are required in connection with a matter over which he has jurisdiction, shall authorize counsel to obtain the services.

(2) Without prior request.—Counsel appointed under this section may obtain, subject to later review, investigative, expert, or other services without prior authorization if necessary for an adequate defense. The total cost of services obtained without prior authorization may not exceed $150 and expenses reasonably incurred.

(3) Maximum amounts.—Compensation to be paid to a person for services rendered by him to a person under this subsection, or to be paid to an organization for services rendered by an employee thereof, shall not exceed $300, exclusive of reimbursement for expenses reasonably incurred, unless payment in excess of that limit is certified by the court, or by the United States magistrate if the services were rendered in connection with a case disposed of entirely before him, as necessary to provide fair compensation for services of an unusual character or duration, and the amount of the excess payment is approved by the chief judge of the circuit.

(f) Receipt of other payments.—Whenever the United States magistrate or the court finds that funds are available for payment from or on behalf of a person furnished representation, it may authorize or direct that such funds be paid to the appointed attorney, to the bar association or legal aid agency or community defender organization which provided the appointed attorney, to any person or organization authorized pursuant to subsection (e) to render investigative, expert, or other services, or to the court for deposit in the Treasury as a reimbursement to the appropriation, current at the time of payment, to carry out the provisions of this section. Except as so authorized or directed, no such person or organization may request or accept any payment or promise of payment for representing a defendant.

(g) Discretionary appointments.—Any person subject to revocation of parole, in custody as a material witness, or seeking relief under section 2241, 2254, or 2255 of title 28 or section 4245 of title 18 may be furnished representation pursuant to the plan whenever the United States magistrate or the court determines that the interests of justice so require and such person is financially unable to obtain representation. Payment for such representation may be as provided in subsections (d) and (e).

(h) Defender organization.—

(1) Qualifications.—A district or a part of a district in which at least two hundred persons annually require the appointment of counsel may establish a defender organization as provided for either under subparagraphs (A) or (B) of paragraph (2) of this subsection or both. Two adjacent districts or parts of districts may aggregate the number of persons required to be represented to establish eligibility for a defender organization to serve both areas. In the event that adjacent districts or parts of districts are located in different circuits, the plan for furnishing representation shall be approved by the judicial council of each circuit.

(2) Types of defender organizations.—

(A) Federal Public Defender Organization.—A Federal Public Defender Organization shall consist of one or more full-time salaried attorneys. An organization for a district or part of a district or two adjacent districts or parts of districts shall be supervised by a Federal Public Defender appointed by the court of appeals of the circuit, without regard to the provisions of title 5 governing appointments in the competitive service, after considering recommendations from the district court or courts to be served. Nothing contained herein shall be deemed to authorize more than one Federal Public Defender within a single judicial district. The Federal Public Defender shall be appointed for a term of four years, unless sooner removed by the court of appeals of the circuit for incompetency, misconduct in office, or neglect of duty. The compensation of the Federal Public Defender shall be fixed by the court of appeals of the circuit at a rate not to exceed the compensation received by the United States attorney for the district where representation is furnished or, if two districts or parts of districts are involved, the compensation of the higher paid United States attorney of the districts. The Federal Public Defender may appoint, without regard to the provisions of title 5 governing appointments in the competitive service, full-time attorneys in such number as may be approved by the court of appeals of the circuit and other personnel in such number as may be approved by the Director of the Administrative Office of the United States Courts. Compensation paid to such attorneys and other personnel of the organization shall be fixed by the Federal Public Defender at a rate not to exceed that paid to attorneys and other personnel of similar qualifications and experience in the Office of the United States attorney in the district where representation is furnished or, if two districts or parts of districts are involved, the higher compensation paid to persons of similar qualifications and experience in the districts. Neither the Federal Public Defender nor any attorney so appointed by him may engage in the private practice of law. Each organization shall submit to the Director of the Administrative Office of the United States Courts, at the time and in the form prescribed by him, reports of its activities and financial position and its proposed budget. The Director of the Administrative Office shall submit, similarly as under title 28, United States Code, section 605, and subject to the conditions of that section, a budget for each organization for each fiscal year and shall out of the appropriations therefor make payments to and on behalf of each organization. Payments under this subparagraph to an organization shall be in lieu of payments under subsection (d) or (e).

(B) Community Defender Organization.—A Community Defender Organization shall be a nonprofit defense counsel service established and administered by any group authorized by the plan to provide representation. The organization shall be eligible to furnish attorneys and receive payments under this section if its bylaws are set forth in the plan of the district or districts in which it will serve. Each organization shall submit to the Judicial Conference of the United States an annual report setting forth its activities and financial position and the anticipated caseload and expenses for the coming year. Upon application an organization may, to the extent approved by the Judicial Conference of the United States:

(i) receive an initial grant for expenses necessary to establish the organization; and

(ii) in lieu of payments under subsection (d) or (e), receive periodic sustaining grants to provide representation and other expenses pursuant to this section.

(i) Rules and reports.—Each district court and court of appeals of a circuit shall submit a report on the appointment of counsel within its jurisdiction to the Administrative Office of the United States Courts in such form and at such times as the Judicial Conference of the United States may specify. The Judicial Conference of the United States may, from time to time, issue rules and regulations governing the operation of plans formulated under this section.

(j) Appropriations.—There are authorized to be appropriated to the United States courts, out of any money in the Treasury not otherwise appropriated, sums necessary to carry out the provisions of this section. When so specified in appropriation acts, such appropriations shall remain available until expended. Payments from such appropriations shall be made under the supervision of the Director of the Administrative Office of the United States Courts.

(k) Districts included.—The term "district court" as used in this section includes the District Court of the Virgin Islands, the District Court of Guam, and the district courts of the United States created by chapter 5 of title 28, United States Code.

(*l*) Applicability in the District of Columbia.—The provisions of this Act, other than subsection (h) of section 1, shall apply in the United States District Court for the District of Columbia and the United States Court of Appeals for the District of Columbia Circuit. The provisions of this Act shall not apply to the Superior Court of the District of Columbia and the District of Columbia Court of Appeals.

§ 3007. Motions—(Rule)

SEE FEDERAL RULES OF CRIMINAL PROCEDURE

Motions substituted for pleas in abatement and special pleas in bar, Rule 12. Form and contents, Rule 47.

§ 3008. Service and filing of papers—(Rule)

SEE FEDERAL RULES OF CRIMINAL PROCEDURE

Requirement and manner of service; notice of orders; filing papers, Rule 49.

§ 3009. Records—(Rule)

SEE FEDERAL RULES OF CRIMINAL PROCEDURE

Keeping of records by district court clerks and magistrates, Rule 55. As amended Oct. 17, 1968, 82 Stat. 1115.

§ 3010. Exceptions unnecessary—(Rule)

SEE FEDERAL RULES OF CRIMINAL PROCEDURE

Objections substituted for exceptions, Rule 51.

§ 3011. Computation of time—(Rule)

SEE FEDERAL RULES OF CRIMINAL PROCEDURE

Computation; enlargement; expiration of term; motions and affidavits; service by mail, Rule 45.

§ 3012. Orders respecting persons in custody

Prisoners or persons in custody shall be brought into court or returned on order of the Court or of the United States Attorney, for which no fee shall be charged and no writ required.

CHAPTER 203—ARREST AND COMMITMENT

§ 3041. Powers of courts and magistrates

For any offense against the United States, the offender may, by any justice or judge of the United States, or by any United States magistrate, or by any chancellor, judge of a supreme or superior court, chief or first judge of common pleas, mayor of a city, justice of the peace, or other magistrate, of any state where the offender may be found, and at the expense of the United States, be arrested and imprisoned, or released as provided in chapter 207 of this title, as the case may be, for trial before such court of the United States as by law has cognizance of the offense. Copies of the process shall be returned as speedily as may be into the office of the clerk of such court, together with the recognizances of the witnesses for their appearances to testify in the case.

A United States judge or commissioner * shall proceed under this section according to rules promulgated by the Supreme Court of the United States. Any state judge or magistrate acting hereunder may proceed according to the usual mode of procedure of his state but his acts and orders shall have no effect beyond determining to hold the prisoner for trial or to discharge him from arrest.

§ 3042. Extraterritorial jurisdiction

Section 3041 of this title shall apply in any country where the United States exercises extraterritorial jurisdiction for the arrest and removal therefrom to the United States of any citizen or national of the United States who is a fugitive from justice charged with or convicted of the commission of any offense against the United States, and shall also apply throughout the United States for the arrest and removal therefrom to the jurisdiction of any officer or representative of the United States vested with judicial authority in any country in which the United States exercises extraterritorial jurisdiction, of any citizen or national of the United States who is a fugitive from justice charged with or convicted of the commission of any offense against the United States in any country where it exercises extraterritorial jurisdiction.

Such fugitive first mentioned may, by any officer or representative of the United States vested with judicial authority in any country in which the United States exercises extraterritorial jurisdiction and agreeably to the usual mode of process against offenders subject to such jurisdiction, be arrested and imprisoned or admitted to bail, as the case may be, pending the issuance of a warrant for his removal, which warrant the principal officer or representative of the United States vested with judicial authority in the country where the fugitive shall be found shall seasonably issue, and the United States marshal or corresponding officer shall execute.

Such marshal or other officer, or the deputies of such marshal or officer, when engaged in executing such warrant without the jurisdic-

---

*** Probably should now be "Magistrate." Since October 17, 1968, any reference to a United States Commissioner in any previously promulgated rule of any court of the United States has been deemed a reference to a United States Magistrate duly appointed under 28 U.S.C. § 631. Pub.L. 90–578, 82 Stat. 1118.**

tion of the court to which they are attached, shall have all the powers of a marshal of the United States so far as such powers are requisite for the prisoner's safekeeping and the execution of the warrant.

§ 3043. Security of the peace and good behavior

The justices or judges of the United States, the United States magistrates, and the judges and other magistrates of the several States, who are or may be authorized by law to make arrests for offenses against the United States, shall have the like authority to hold to security of the peace and for good behavior, in cases arising under the Constitution and laws of the United States, as may be lawfully exercised by any judge or justice of the peace of the respective States, in cases cognizable before them.

§ 3044. Complaint—(Rule)

SEE FEDERAL RULES OF CRIMINAL PROCEDURE

Contents of complaint; oath, Rule 3.

§ 3045. Internal revenue violations

Warrants of arrest for violations of internal revenue laws may be issued by United States magistrates upon the complaint of a United States attorney, assistant United States attorney, collector, or deputy collector of internal revenue or revenue agent, or private citizen; but no such warrant of arrest shall be issued upon the complaint of a private citizen unless first approved in writing by a United States attorney.

§ 3046. Warrant or summons—(Rule)

SEE FEDERAL RULES OF CRIMINAL PROCEDURE

Issuance upon complaint, Rule 4.
Issuance upon indictment, Rule 9.
Summons on request of government; form; contents; service; return, Rules 4, 9.

§ 3047. Multiple warrants unnecessary

When two or more charges are made, or two or more indictments are found against any person, only one writ or warrant shall be necessary to commit him for trial. It shall be sufficient to state in the writ the name or general character of the offenses, or to refer to them only in general terms.

§ 3048. Commitment to another district; removal—(Rule)

SEE FEDERAL RULES OF CRIMINAL PROCEDURE

Arrest in nearby or distant districts; informative statement by judge or magistrate; hearing and removal; warrant; Rule 40. As amended Oct. 17, 1968, 82 Stat. 1115.

§ 3049. Warrant for removal

Only one writ or warrant is necessary to remove a prisoner from one district to another. One copy thereof may be delivered to the sheriff or jailer from whose custody the prisoner is taken, and another to the sheriff or jailer to whose custody he is committed, and the original writ, with the marshal's return thereon, shall be returned to the clerk of the district to which he is removed.

§ 3050. Bureau of Prisons employees' powers

An officer or employee of the Bureau of Prisons of the Department of Justice may make arrests without warrant for violations of any of the provisions of sections 751, 752, 1791, or 1792 of this title, if he has reasonable grounds to believe that the arrested person is guilty of such offense, and if there is likelihood of his escaping before a warrant can be obtained for his arrest. If the arrested person is a fugitive from custody, he shall be returned to custody. Officers and employees of the said Bureau of Prisons may carry firearms under such rules and regulations as the Attorney General may prescribe.

[§ 3051. Repealed.]

§ 3052. Powers of Federal Bureau of Investigation

The Director, Associate Director, Assistant to the Director, Assistant Directors, inspectors, and agents of the Federal Bureau of Investigation of the Department of Justice may carry firearms, serve warrants and subpoenas issued under the authority of the United States and make arrests without warrant for any offense against the United States committed in their presence, or for any felony cognizable under the laws of the United States if they have reasonable grounds to believe that the person to be arrested has committed or is committing such felony.

§ 3053. Powers of marshals and deputies

United States marshals and their deputies may carry firearms and may make arrests without warrant for any offense against the United States committed in their presence, or for any felony cognizable under the laws of the United States if they have reasonable grounds to believe that the person to be arrested has committed or is committing such felony.

[§ 3054. Repealed.]

§ 3055. Officers' powers to suppress Indian liquor traffic

The chief special officer for the suppression of the liquor traffic among Indians and duly authorized officers working under his supervision whose appointments are made or affirmed by the Commissioner of Indian Affairs or the Secretary of the Interior may execute all warrants of arrest and other lawful precepts issued under the authority of the United States and in the execution of his duty he may command all necessary assistance.

§ 3056. Secret service powers

(a) Subject to the direction of the Secretary of the Treasury, the United States Secret Service, Treasury Department, is authorized to protect the person of the President of the United States, the members of his immediate family, the President-elect, the Vice President or other officer next in the order of succession to the Office of President, and the Vice President-elect, and the members of their immediate families unless the members decline such protection; protect the person of a former President and his wife during his lifetime, the person of a widow of a former President until her death or remarriage, and minor children of a former President until they reach sixteen years of age, unless such protection is declined; protect the person of a visiting head of a foreign state or foreign government and, at the direction of the President, other distinguished foreign visitors to the United States and official representatives of the United States performing special missions abroad; detect and arrest any person committing any offense against the laws of the United States relating to coins, obligations, and securities of the United States and of foreign governments; detect and arrest any person violating any of the provisions of sections 508, 509, 871, and 879 of this title and, insofar as the Federal Deposit Insurance Corporation, Federal land banks and Federal land bank associations are concerned, of sections 213, 216, 433, 493, 657, 709, 1006, 1007, 1011, 1013, 1014, 1907, and 1909 of this title; execute warrants issued under the authority of the United States; carry firearms; offer and pay rewards for services or information looking toward the apprehension of criminals; pay expenses for unforeseen emergencies of a confidential nature under the direction of the Secretary of the Treasury and accounted for solely on his certificate; and perform such other functions and duties as are authorized by law. In the performance of their duties under this section, the Director, Deputy Director, Assistant Directors, Assistants to the Director, inspectors, and agents of the Secret Service are authorized to make arrests without warrant for any offense against the United States committed in their presence, or for any felony cognizable under the laws of the United States if they have reasonable grounds to believe that the person to be arrested has committed or is committing such felony. Moneys expended from Secret Service appropriations for the purchase of counterfeits and subsequently recovered shall be reimbursed to the appropriation current at the time of deposit.

(b) Whoever knowingly and willfully obstructs, resists, or interferes with an agent of the United States Secret Service or other Federal law enforcement agent engaged in the performance of the protective functions authorized by this section, by the Act of June 6, 1968 (82 Stat. 170) or by section 1752 of Title 18, United States Code, shall be fined not more than $1,000 or imprisoned not more than one year or both.

§ 3057. Bankruptcy investigations

(a) Any referee, receiver, or trustee having reasonable grounds for believing that any violations of the bankruptcy laws or other laws of the United States relating to insolvent debtors, receiverships or reorganization plans has been committed, or that an investigation should be had in connection therewith, shall report to the appropriate United States attorney all the facts and circumstances of the case, the names of the witnesses and the offense or offenses believed to have been committed. Where one of such officers has made such report, the others need not do so.

(b) The United States attorney thereupon shall inquire into the facts and report thereon to the referee, and if it appears probable that any such offense has been committed, shall without delay, present the matter to the grand jury, unless upon inquiry and examination he decides that the ends of public justice do not require investigation or prosecution, in which case he shall report the facts to the Attorney General for his direction.

§ 3058. Interned belligerent nationals

Whoever, belonging to the armed land or naval forces of a belligerent nation or belligerent faction and being interned in the United States, in accordance with the law of nations, leaves or attempts to leave said jurisdiction, or leaves or attempts to leave the limits of internment without permission from the proper official of the United States in charge, or willfully overstays a leave of absence granted by such official, shall be subject to arrest by any marshal or deputy marshal of the United States, or by the military or naval authorities thereof, and shall be returned to the place of internment and there confined and safely kept for such period of time as the official of the United States in charge shall direct.

§ 3059. Rewards and appropriations therefor

(a)(1) There is authorized to be appropriated, out of any money in the Treasury not otherwise appropriated, the sum of $25,000 as a reward or rewards for the capture of anyone who is charged with violation of criminal laws of the United States or any State or of the District of Columbia, and an equal amount as a reward or rewards for information leading to the arrest of any such person, to be apportioned and expended in the discretion of, and upon such conditions as may be imposed by, the Attorney General of the United States. Not more than $25,000 shall be expended for information or capture of any one person.

(2) If any of the said persons shall be killed in resisting lawful arrest, the Attorney General may pay any part of the reward money in his discretion to the person or persons whom he shall adjudge to be entitled thereto but no reward money shall be paid to any official or employee of the Department of Justice of the United States.

(b) The Attorney General each year may spend not more than $10,000 for services or information looking toward the apprehension of narcotic law violators who are fugitives from justice.

§ 3060. Preliminary examination

(a) Except as otherwise provided by this section, a preliminary examination shall be held within the time set by the judge or magistrate pursuant to subsection (b) of this section, to determine whether there is probable cause to believe that an offense has been committed and that the arrested person has committed it.

(b) The date for the preliminary examination shall be fixed by the judge or magistrate at the initial appearance of the arrested person. Except as provided by subsection (c) of this section, or unless the arrested person waives the preliminary examination, such examination shall be held within a reasonable time following initial appearance, but in any event not later than—

(1) the tenth day following the date of the initial appearance of the arrested person before such officer if the arrested person is held in custody without any provision for release, or is held in custody for failure to meet the conditions of release imposed, or is released from custody only during specified hours of the day; or

(2) the twentieth day following the date of the initial appearance if the arrested person is released from custody under any condition other than a condition described in paragraph (1) of this subsection.

(c) With the consent of the arrested person, the date fixed by the judge or magistrate for the preliminary examination may be a date later than that prescribed by subsection (b), or may be continued one or more times to a date subsequent to the date initially fixed therefor. In the absence of such consent of the accused, the date fixed for the preliminary hearing may be a date later than that prescribed by subsection (b), or may be continued to a date subsequent to the date initially fixed therefor, only upon the order of a judge of the appropriate United States district court after a finding that extraordinary circumstances exist, and that the delay of the preliminary hearing is indispensable to the interests of justice.

(d) Except as provided by subsection (e) of this section, an arrested person who has not been accorded the preliminary examination required by subsection (a) within the period of time fixed by the judge or magistrate in compliance with subsections (b) and (c), shall be discharged from custody or from the requirement of bail or any other condition of release, without prejudice, however, to the institution of further criminal proceedings against him upon the charge upon which he was arrested.

(e) No preliminary examination in compliance with subsection (a) of this section shall be required to be accorded an arrested person, nor shall such arrested person be discharged from custody or from the requirement of bail or any other condition of release pursuant to subsection (d), if at any time subsequent to the initial appearance of such person before a judge or magistrate and prior to the date fixed for the preliminary examination pursuant to subsections (b) and (c) an indictment is returned or, in appropriate cases, an information is filed against such person in a court of the United States.

(f) Proceedings before United States magistrates under this section shall be taken down by a court reporter or recorded by suitable sound recording equipment. A copy of the record of such proceeding shall be made available at the expense of the United States to a person who makes affidavit that he is unable to pay or give security therefor, and the expense of such copy shall be paid by the Director of the Administrative Office of the United States Courts.

§ 3061. Powers of postal personnel

(a) Subject to subsection (b) of this section, officers and employees of the Postal Service performing duties related to the inspection of postal matters may, to the extent authorized by the Board of Governors—

(1) serve warrants and subpenas issued under the authority of the United States;

(2) make arrests without warrant for offenses against the United States committed in their presence; and

(3) make arrests without warrant for felonies cognizable under the laws of the United States if they have reasonable grounds to believe that the person to be arrested has committed or is committing such a felony.

(b) The powers granted by subsection (a) of this section shall be exercised only in the enforcement of laws regarding property of the United States in the custody of the Postal Service, including property of the Postal Service, the use of the mails, and other postal offenses.

CHAPTER 205—SEARCHES AND SEIZURES

Sec.

§ 3101. Effect of rules of court—(rule)

SEE FEDERAL RULES OF CRIMINAL PROCEDURE

Rules generally applicable throughout United States, Rule 54.
Acts of Congress superseded, Rule 41(g).

§ 3102. Authority to issue search warrant—(rule)

SEE FEDERAL RULES OF CRIMINAL PROCEDURE

Federal, State or Territorial Judges, or U. S. Magistrates authorized to issue search warrants, Rule 41(a). As amended Oct. 17, 1968, 82 Stat. 1115.

§ 3103. Grounds for issuing search warrant—(rule)

SEE FEDERAL RULES OF CRIMINAL PROCEDURE

Grounds prescribed for issuance of search warrant, Rule 41(b).

§ 3103a. Additional grounds for issuing warrant

In addition to the grounds for issuing a warrant in section 3103 of this title, a warrant may be issued to search for and seize any property that constitutes evidence of a criminal offense in violation of the laws of the United States.

§ 3104. Issuance of search warrant; contents—(rule)

SEE FEDERAL RULES OF CRIMINAL PROCEDURE

Issuance of search warrant on affidavit; contents to identify persons or place; command to search forthwith, Rule 41(c).

§ 3105. Persons authorized to serve search warrant

A search warrant may in all cases be served by any of the officers mentioned in its direction or by an officer authorized by law to serve such warrant, but by no other person, except in aid of the officer on his requiring it, he being present and acting in its execution.

§ 3106. Officer authorized to serve search warrant—(rule)

SEE FEDERAL RULES OF CRIMINAL PROCEDURE

Officer to whom search warrant shall be directed, Rule 41(c).

§ 3107. Service of warrants and seizures by Federal Bureau of Investigation

The Director, Associate Director, Assistant to the Director, Assistant Directors, agents, and inspectors of the Federal Bureau of Investigation of the Department of Justice are empowered to make seizures under warrant for violation of the laws of the United States.

§ 3108. Execution, service, and return—(rule)

SEE FEDERAL RULES OF CRIMINAL PROCEDURE

Method and time for execution, service and return of search warrant, Rule 41 (c), (d).

§ 3109. Breaking doors or windows for entry or exit

The officer may break open any outer or inner door or window of a house, or any part of a house, or anything therein, to execute a search warrant, if, after notice of his authority and purpose, he is refused admittance or when necessary to liberate himself or a person aiding him in the execution of the warrant.

§ 3110. Property defined—(rule)

SEE FEDERAL RULES OF CRIMINAL PROCEDURE

Term "property" as used in Rule 41 includes documents, books, papers and any other tangible objects, Rule 41(g).

§ 3111. Property seizable on search warrant—(rule)

SEE FEDERAL RULES OF CRIMINAL PROCEDURE

Specified property seizable on search warrant, Rule 41(b).

[§ 3112. Repealed.]

§ 3113. Liquor violations in Indian country

If any superintendent of Indian affairs, or commanding officer of a military post, or special agent of the Office of Indian Affairs for the suppression of liquor traffic among Indians and in the Indian country and any authorized deputies under his supervision has probable cause to believe that any person is about to introduce or has introduced any spirituous liquor, beer, wine or other intoxicating liquors named in sections 1154 and 1156 of this title into the Indian country in violation of law, he may cause the places, conveyances, and packages of such person to be searched. If any such intoxicating liquor is found therein, the same, together with such conveyances and packages of such person, shall be seized and delivered to the proper officer, and shall be proceeded against by libel in the proper court, and forfeited, one-half to the informer and one-half to the use of the United States. If such person be a trader, his license shall be revoked and his bond put in suit.

Any person in the service of the United States authorized by this section to make searches and seizures, or any Indian may take and destroy any ardent spirits or wine found in the Indian country, except such as are kept or used for scientific, sacramental, medicinal, or mechanical purposes or such as may be introduced therein by the Department of the Army.

In all cases arising under this section and sections 1154 and 1156 of this title, Indians shall be competent witnesses.

§ 3114. Return of seized property and suppression of evidence; motion—(rule)

SEE FEDERAL RULES OF CRIMINAL PROCEDURE

Return of property and suppression of evidence upon motion, Rule 41(e).

§ 3115. Inventory upon execution and return of search warrant—(rule)

SEE FEDERAL RULES OF CRIMINAL PROCEDURE

Inventory of property seized under search warrant, and copies to persons affected, Rule 41(d).

§ 3116. Records of examining magistrate; return to clerk of court —(rule)

SEE FEDERAL RULES OF CRIMINAL PROCEDURE

Magistrates and clerks of court to keep records as prescribed by Director of the Administrative Office of the United States Courts, Rule 55.

Return or filing of records with clerk, Rule 41(f).

CHAPTER 207—RELEASE

Sec.

§ 3141. Power of courts and magistrates

Bail may be taken by any court, judge or magistrate authorized to arrest and commit offenders but only a court of the United States having original jurisdiction in criminal cases, or a justice or judge thereof, may admit to bail or otherwise release a person charged with an offense punishable by death.

§ 3142. Surrender by bail

Any party charged with a criminal offense who is released on the execution of an appearance bail bond with one or more sureties, may in vacation, be arrested by his surety, and delivered to the marshal or his deputy, and brought before any judge or other officer having power to commit for such offense; and at the request of such surety, the judge or other officer shall recommit the party so arrested to the custody of the marshal, and indorse on the recognizance, or certified copy thereof, the discharge and exoneratur [*sic.*], of such surety; and the person so committed shall be held in custody until discharged by due course of law.

§ 3143. Additional bail

When proof is made to any judge of the United States, or other magistrate authorized to commit on criminal charges, that a person previously released on the execution of an appearance bail bond with one or more sureties on any such charge is about to abscond, and that his bail is insufficient, the judge or magistrate shall require such person to give better security, or, for default thereof, cause him to be committed; and an order for his arrest may be indorsed on the former commitment, or a new warrant therefor may be issued, by such judge or magistrate, setting forth the cause thereof.

§ 3144. Cases removed from State courts

Whenever the judgment of a State Court in any criminal proceeding is brought to the Supreme Court of the United States for review, the defendant shall not be released from custody until a final judgment upon such review, or, if the offense be bailable, until a bond, with sufficient sureties, in a reasonable sum, is given.

§ 3145. Parties and witnesses—(rule)

SEE FEDERAL RULES OF CRIMINAL PROCEDURE

On Preliminary Examination, Rule 5(c).
Before conviction; amount; sureties; forfeiture; exoneration, Rule 46.
Pending sentence, Rule 32(a).
Pending appeal or certiorari, Rule 39(a), 46(a, 2).
Witness, Rule 46(b).

§ 3146. Release in noncapital cases prior to trial

(a) Any person charged with an offense, other than an offense punishable by death, shall, at his appearance before a judicial officer, be ordered released pending trial on his personal recognizance or upon the execution of an unsecured appearance bond in an amount specified by the judicial officer, subject to the condition that such person not commit an offense under section 1503, 1512, or 1513 of this title, unless the officer determines, in the exercise of his discretion, that such a release will not reasonably assure the appearance of the person as required. When such a determination is made, the judicial officer shall, either in lieu of or in addition to the above methods of release, impose a condition of release that such person not commit an offense under section 1503, 1512, or 1513 of this title and impose the first of the following conditions of release which will reasonably assure the appearance of the person for trial or, if no single condition gives that assurance, any combination of the following conditions:

(1) place the person in the custody of a designated person or organization agreeing to supervise him;

(2) place restrictions on the travel, association, or place of abode of the person during the period of release;

(3) require the execution of an appearance bond in a specified amount and the deposit in the registry of the court, in cash or other security as directed, of a sum not to exceed 10 per centum of the amount of the bond, such deposit to be returned upon the performance of the conditions of release;

(4) require the execution of a bail bond with sufficient solvent sureties, or the deposit of cash in lieu thereof; or

(5) impose any other condition deemed reasonably necessary to assure appearance as required, including a condition requiring that the person return to custody after specified hours.

(b) In determining which conditions of release will reasonably assure appearance, the judicial officer shall, on the basis of available information, take into account the nature and circumstances of the offense charged, the weight of the evidence against the accused, the accused's family ties, employment, financial resources, character and mental condition, the length of his residence in the community, his record of convictions, and his record of appearance at court proceedings or of flight to avoid prosecution or failure to appear at court proceedings.

(c) A judicial officer authorizing the release of a person under this section shall issue an appropriate order containing a statement of the conditions imposed, if any, shall inform such person of the penalties applicable to violations of the conditions of his release and shall advise him that a warrant for his arrest will be issued immediately upon any such violation.

(d) A person for whom conditions of release are imposed and who after twenty-four hours from the time of the release hearing continues to be detained as a result of his inability to meet the conditions of release, shall, upon application, be entitled to have the conditions reviewed by the judicial officer who imposed them. Unless the conditions of release are amended and the person is thereupon released, the judicial officer shall set forth in writing the reasons for requiring the conditions imposed. A person who is ordered released on a condition which requires that he return to custody after specified hours shall, upon application, be entitled to a review by the judicial officer who imposed the condition. Unless the requirement is removed and the person is thereupon released on another condition, the judicial officer shall set forth in writing the reasons for continuing the requirement. In the event that the judicial officer who imposed conditions of release is not available, any other judicial officer in the district may review such conditions.

(e) A judicial officer ordering the release of a person on any condition specified in this section may at any time amend his order to impose additional or different conditions of release: *Provided,* That, if the imposition of such additional or different conditions results in the detention of the person as a result of his inability to meet such conditions or in the release of the person on a condition requiring him to return to custody after specified hours, the provisions of subsection (d) shall apply.

(f) Information stated in, or offered in connection with, any order entered pursuant to this section need not conform to the rules pertaining to the admissibility of evidence in a court of law.

(g) Nothing contained in this section shall be construed to prevent the disposition of any case or class of cases by forfeiture of collateral security where such disposition is authorized by the court.

§ 3147. Appeal from conditions of release

(a) A person who is detained, or whose release on a condition requiring him to return to custody after specified hours is continued, after review of his application pursuant to section 3146(d) or section 3146(e) by a judicial officer, other than a judge of the court having original jurisdiction over the offense with which he is charged or a judge of a United States court of appeals or a Justice of the Supreme Court, may move the court having original jurisdiction over the offense with which he is charged to amend the order. Said motion shall be determined promptly.

(b) In any case in which a person is detained after (1) a court denies a motion under subsection (a) to amend an order imposing conditions of release, or (2) conditions of release have been imposed or amended by a judge of the court having original jurisdiction over the offense charged, an appeal may be taken to the court having appellate jurisdiction over such court. Any order so appealed shall be affirmed if it is supported by the proceedings below. If the order is not so supported, the court may remand the case for a further hearing, or may, with or without additional evidence, order the person released pursuant to section 3146(a). The appeal shall be determined promptly.

§ 3148. Release in capital cases or after conviction

A person (1) who is charged with an offense punishable by death, or (2) who has been convicted of an offense and is either awaiting sentence or sentence review under section 3576 of this title or has filed an appeal or a petition for a writ of certiorari, shall be treated in accordance with the provisions of section 3146 unless the court or judge has reason to believe that no one or more conditions of release will reasonably assure that the person will not flee or pose a danger to any other person or to the community. If such a risk of flight or danger is believed to exist, or if it appears that an appeal is frivolous or taken for delay, the person may be ordered detained. The provisions of section 3147 shall not apply to persons described in this section: *Provided,* That other rights to judicial review of conditions of release or orders of detention shall not be affected.

§ 3149. Release of material witnesses

If it appears by affidavit that the testimony of a person is material in any criminal proceeding, and if it is shown that it may become impracticable to secure his presence by subpena, a judicial officer shall impose conditions of release pursuant to section 3146. No material witness shall be detained because of inability to comply with any condition of release if the testimony of such witness can adequately be secured by deposition, and further detention is not necessary to prevent a failure of justice. Release may be delayed for a reasonable period of time until the deposition of the witness can be taken pursuant to the Federal Rules of Criminal Procedure.

§ 3150. Penalties for failure to appear

Whoever, having been released pursuant to this chapter, willfully fails to appear before any court or judicial officer as required, shall, subject to the provisions of the Federal Rules of Criminal Procedure, incur a forfeiture of any security which was given or pledged for his release, and, in addition, shall, (1) if he was released in connection with a charge of felony, or while awaiting sentence or pending appeal or certiorari after conviction of any offense, be fined not more than $5,000 or imprisoned not more than five years, or both, or (2) if he was released in connection with a charge of misdemeanor, be fined not more than the maximum provided for such misdemeanor or imprisoned for not more than one year, or both, or (3) if he was released for appearance as a material witness, shall be fined not more than $1,000 or imprisoned for not more than one year, or both.

§ 3150a. Refund of forfeited bail

Appropriations available to refund money erroneously received and deposited in the Treasury are available to refund any part of forfeited bail deposited into the general fund of the Treasury and ordered remitted under the Federal Rules of Criminal Procedure.

§ 3151. Contempt

Nothing in this chapter shall interfere with or prevent the exercise by any court of the United States of its power to punish for contempt.

§ 3152. Establishment of pretrial services

(a) On and after the date of the enactment of the Pretrial Services Act of 1982, the Director of the Administrative Office of the United States Courts (hereinafter in this chapter referred to as the 'Director') shall, under the supervision and direction of the Judicial Conference of the United States, provide directly, or by contract or otherwise (to such extent and in such amounts as are provided in appropriation Acts), for the establishment of pretrial services in each judicial district (other than the District of Columbia). Pretrial services established under this section shall be supervised by a chief probation officer appointed under section 3654 of this title or by a chief pretrial services officer selected under subsection (c) of this section.

(b) Beginning eighteen months after the date of the enactment of the Pretrial Services Act of 1982, if an appropriate United States district court and the circuit judicial council jointly recommend the establishment under this subsection of pretrial services in a particular district, pretrial services shall be established under the general authority of the Administrative Office of the United States Courts.

(c) The pretrial services established under subsection (b) of this section shall be supervised by a chief pretrial services officer selected by a panel consisting of the chief judge of the circuit, the chief judge of the district, and a magistrate of the district or their designees. The chief pretrial services officer appointed under this subsection shall be an individual other than one serving under authority of section 3654 of this title.

§ 3153. Organization and administration of pretrial services

(a)(1) With the approval of the district court, the chief pretrial services officer in districts in which pretrial services are established under section 3152(b) of this title shall appoint such other personnel as may be required. The position requirements and rate of compensation of the chief pretrial services officer and such other personnel shall be established by the Director with the approval of the Judicial Conference of the United States, except that no such rate of compensation shall exceed the rate of basic pay in effect and then payable for grade GS–16 of the General Schedule under section 5332 of title 5, United States Code.

(2) The chief pretrial services officer in districts in which pretrial services are established under section 3152(b) of this title is authorized, subject to the general policy established by the Director and the approval of the district court, to procure temporary and intermittent services to the extent authorized by section 3109 of title 5, United States Code. The staff, other than clerical staff, may be drawn from law school students, graduate students, or such other available personnel.

(b) The chief probation officer in all districts in which pretrial services are established under section 3152(a) of this title shall designate personnel appointed under chapter 231 of this title to perform pretrial services under this chapter.

(c)(1) Except as provided in paragraph (2) of this subsection, information obtained in the course of performing pretrial services functions in relation to a particular accused shall be used only for the purposes of a bail determination and shall otherwise be confidential. Each pretrial services report shall be made available to the attorney for the accused and the attorney for the Government.

(2) The Director shall issue regulations establishing the policy for release of information made confidential by paragraph (1) of this subsection. Such regulations shall provide exceptions to the confidentiality requirements under paragraph (1) of this subsection to allow access to such information—

(A) by qualified persons for purposes of research related to the administration of criminal justice;

(B) by persons under contract under section 3154(4) of this title;

(C) by probation officers for the purpose of compiling presentence reports;

(D) insofar as such information is a pretrial diversion report, to the attorney for the accused and the attorney for the Government; and

(E) in certain limited cases, to law enforcement agencies for law enforcement purpose.

(3) Information made confidential under paragraph (1) of this subsection is not admissible on the issue of guilt in a criminal judicial proceeding unless such proceeding is a prosecution for a crime committed in the course of obtaining pretrial release or a prosecution for failure to appear for the criminal judicial proceeding with respect to which pretrial services were provided.

§ 3154. Functions and powers relating to pretrial services

Pretrial services functions shall include the following:

(1) Collect, verify, and report to the judicial officer, prior to the pretrial release hearing, information pertaining to the pretrial release of each individual charged with an offense, including information relating to any danger that the release of such person may pose to any other person or the community, and recommend appropriate release conditions for such individual.

(2) Review and modify the reports and recommendations specified in paragraph (1) of this section for persons seeking release pursuant to section 3146(e) or section 3147 of this chapter.

(3) Supervise persons released into its custody under this chapter.

(4) Operate or contract for the operation of appropriate facilities for the custody or care of persons released under this chapter including residential halfway houses, addict and alcoholic treatment centers, and counseling services.

(5) Inform the court and the United States attorney of all apparent violations of pretrial release conditions, arrests of persons released to the custody of providers of pretrial services or under the supervision of providers of pretrial services, and any danger that any such person may come to pose to any other person or the community, and recommend appropriate modifications of release conditions.

(6) Serve as coordinator for other local agencies which serve or are eligible to serve as custodians under this chapter and advise the court as to the eligibility, availability, and capacity of such agencies.

(7) Assist persons released under this chapter in securing any necessary employment, medical, legal, or social services.

(8) Prepare, in cooperation with the United States marshal and the United States attorney such pretrial detention reports as are required by the provisions of the Federal Rules of Criminal Procedure relating to the supervision of detention pending trial.

(9) Develop and implement a system to monitor and evaluate bail activities, provide information to judicial officers on the results of bail decisions, and prepare periodic reports to assist in the improvement of the bail process.

(10) To the extent provided for in an agreement between a chief pretrial services officer in districts in which pretrial services are established under section 3152(b) of this title, or the chief probation officer in all other districts, and the United States attorney, collect, verify, and prepare reports for the United States attorney's office of information pertaining to the pretrial diversion of any individual who is or may be charged with an offense, and perform such other duties as may be required under any such agreement.

(11) Make contracts, to such extent and in such amounts as are provided in appropriation Acts, for the carrying out of any pretrial services functions.

(12) Perform such other functions as specified under this chapter.

§ 3155. Annual reports

Each chief pretrial services officer in districts in which pretrial services are established under section 3152(b) of this title, and each chief probation officer in all other districts, shall prepare an annual report to the chief judge of the district court and the Director concerning the administration and operation of pretrial services. The Director shall be required to include in the Director's annual report to the Judicial Conference under section 604 of title 28 a report on the administration and operation of the pretrial services for the previous year.

§ 3156. Definitions

(a) As used in sections 3146–3150 of this chapter—

(1) The term "judicial officer" means, unless otherwise indicated, any person or court authorized pursuant to section 3041 of this title, or the Federal Rules of Criminal Procedure, to bail or otherwise release a person before trial or sentencing or pending appeal in a court of the United States, and any judge of the Superior Court of the District of Columbia; and

(2) The term "offense" means any criminal offense, other than an offense triable by court-martial, military commission, provost court, or other military tribunal, which is in violation of an Act of Congress and is triable in any court established by Act of Congress.

(b) As used in sections 3152–3155 of this chapter—

(1) the term "judicial officer" means, unless otherwise indicated, any person or court authorized pursuant to section 3041 of this title, or the Federal Rules of Criminal Procedure, to bail or otherwise release a person before trial or sentencing or pending appeal in a court of the United States, and

(2) the term "offense" means any Federal criminal offense which is in violation of any Act of Congress and is triable by any court established by Act of Congress (other than a petty offense as defined in section 1(3) of this title, or an offense triable by court-martial, military commission, provost court, or other military tribunal).

CHAPTER 208—SPEEDY TRIAL

§ 3161. Time limits and exclusions

(a) In any case involving a defendant charged with an offense, the appropriate judicial officer, at the earliest practicable time, shall, after consultation with the counsel for the defendant and the attorney for the Government, set the case for trial on a day certain, or list it for trial on a weekly or other short-term trial calendar at a place within the judicial district, so as to assure a speedy trial.

(b) Any information or indictment charging an individual with the commission of an offense shall be filed within thirty days from the date on which such individual was arrested or served with a summons in connection with such charges. If an individual has been charged with a felony in a district in which no grand jury has been in session during such thirty-day period, the period of time for filing of the indictment shall be extended an additional thirty days.

(c)(1) In any case in which a plea of not guilty is entered, the trial of a defendant charged in an information or indictment with the commission of an offense shall commence within seventy days from the filing date (and making public) of the information or indictment, or from the date the defendant has appeared before a judicial officer of the court in which such charge is pending, whichever date last occurs. If a defendant consents in writing to be tried before a magistrate on a complaint, the trial shall commence within seventy days from the date of such consent.

(2) Unless the defendant consents in writing to the contrary, the trial shall not commence less than thirty days from the date on which the defendant first appears through counsel or expressly waives counsel and elects to proceed pro se.

(d)(1) If any indictment or information is dismissed upon motion of the defendant, or any charge contained in a complaint filed against an individual is dismissed or otherwise dropped, and thereafter a complaint is filed against such defendant or individual charging him with the same offense or an offense based on the same conduct or arising from the same criminal episode, or an information or indictment is filed charging such defendant with the same offense or an offense based on the same conduct or arising from the same criminal episode, the provisions of subsections (b) and (c) of this section shall be applicable with respect to such subsequent complaint, indictment, or information, as the case may be.

(2) If the defendant is to be tried upon an indictment or information dismissed by a trial court and reinstated following an appeal, the trial shall commence within seventy days from the date the action occasioning the trial becomes final, except that the court retrying the case may extend the period for trial not to exceed one hundred and eighty days from the date the action occasioning the trial becomes final if the unavailability of witnesses or other factors resulting from the passage of time shall make trial within seventy days impractical. The periods of delay enumerated in section 3161(h) are excluded in computing the time limitations specified in this section. The sanctions of section 3162 apply to this subsection.

(e) If the defendant is to be tried again following a declaration by the trial judge of a mistrial or following an order of such judge for a new trial, the trial shall commence within seventy days from the date the action occasioning the retrial becomes final. If the defendant is to be tried again following an appeal or a collateral attack, the trial shall commence within seventy days from the date the action occasioning the retrial becomes final, except that the court retrying the case may extend the period for retrial not to exceed one hundred and eighty days from the date the action occasioning the retrial becomes final if unavailability of witnesses or other factors resulting from passage of time shall make trial within seventy days impractical. The periods of delay enumerated in section 3161(h) are excluded in computing the time limitations specified in this section. The sanctions of section 3162 apply to this subsection.

(f) Notwithstanding the provisions of subsection (b) of this section, for the first twelve-calendar-month period following the effective date of this section as set forth in section 3163(a) of this chapter the time limit imposed with respect to the period between arrest and indictment by subsection (b) of this section shall be sixty days, for the second such twelve-month period such time limit shall be forty-five days and for the third such period such time limit shall be thirty-five days.

(g) Notwithstanding the provisions of subsection (c) of this section, for the first twelve-calendar-month period following the effective date of this section as set forth in section 3163(b) of this chapter, the time limit with respect to the period between arraignment and trial imposed by subsection (c) of this section shall be one hundred and eighty days, for the second such twelve-month period such time limit shall be one hundred and twenty days, and for the third such period such time limit with respect to the period between arraignment and trial shall be eighty days.

(h) The following periods of delay shall be excluded in computing the time within which an information or an indictment must be filed, or in computing the time within which the trial of any such offense must commence:

(1) Any period of delay resulting from other proceedings concerning the defendant, including but not limited to—

(A) delay resulting from any proceeding, including any examinations, to determine the mental competency or physical capacity of the defendant;

(B) delay resulting from any proceeding, including any examination of the defendant, pursuant to section 2902 of title 28, United States Code;

(C) delay resulting from deferral of prosecution pursuant to section 2902 of title 28, United States Code;

(D) delay resulting from trial with respect to other charges against the defendant;

(E) delay resulting from any interlocutory appeal;

(F) delay resulting from any pretrial motion, from the filing of the motion through the conclusion of the hearing on, or other prompt disposition of, such motion;

(G) delay resulting from any proceeding relating to the transfer of a case or the removal of any defendant from another district under the Federal Rules of Criminal Procedure;

(H) delay resulting from transportation of any defendant from another district, or to and from places of examination or hospitalization, except that any time consumed in excess of ten days from the date an order of removal or an order directing such transportation, and the defendant's arrival at the destination shall be presumed to be unreasonable;

(I) delay resulting from consideration by the court of a proposed plea agreement to be entered into by the defendant and the attorney for the Government; and

(J) delay reasonably attributable to any period, not to exceed thirty days, during which any proceeding concerning the defendant is actually under advisement by the court.

(2) Any period of delay during which prosecution is deferred by the attorney for the Government pursuant to written agreement with the defendant, with the approval of the court, for the purpose of allowing the defendant to demonstrate his good conduct.

(3)(A) Any period of delay resulting from the absence or unavailability of the defendant or an essential witness.

(B) For purposes of subparagraph (A) of this paragraph, a defendant or an essential witness shall be considered absent when his whereabouts are unknown and, in addition, he is attempting to avoid apprehension or prosecution or his whereabouts cannot be determined by due diligence. For purposes of such subparagraph, a defendant or an essential witness shall be considered unavailable whenever his whereabouts are known but his presence for trial cannot be obtained by due diligence or he resists appearing at or being returned for trial.

(4) Any period of delay resulting from the fact that the defendant is mentally incompetent or physically unable to stand trial.

(5) Any period of delay resulting from the treatment of the defendant pursuant to section 2902 of title 28, United States Code.

(6) If the information or indictment is dismissed upon motion of the attorney for the Government and thereafter a charge is filed against the defendant for the same offense, or any offense required to be joined with that offense, any period of delay from the date the charge was dismissed to the date the time limitation would commence to run as to the subsequent charge had there been no previous charge.

(7) A reasonable period of delay when the defendant is joined for trial with a codefendant as to whom the time for trial has not run and no motion for severance has been granted.

(8)(A) Any period of delay resulting from a continuance granted by any judge on his own motion or at the request of the defendant or his counsel or at the request of the attorney for the Government, if the judge granted such continuance on the basis of his findings that the ends of justice served by taking such action outweigh the best interest of the public and the defendant in a speedy trial. No such period of delay resulting from a continuance granted by the court in accordance with this paragraph shall be excludable under this subsection unless the court sets forth, in the record of the case, either orally or in writing, its reasons for finding that the ends of justice served by the granting of such continuance outweigh the best interests of the public and the defendant in a speedy trial.

(B) The factors, among others, which a judge shall consider in determining whether to grant a continuance under subparagraph (A) of this paragraph in any case are as follows:

(i) Whether the failure to grant such a continuance in the proceeding would be likely to make a continuation of such proceeding impossible, or result in a miscarriage of justice.

(ii) Whether the case is so unusual or so complex, due to the number of defendants, the nature of the prosecution, or the existence of novel questions of fact or law, that it is unreasonable to expect adequate preparation for pretrial proceedings or for the trial itself within the time limits established by this section.

(iii) Whether, in a case in which arrest precedes indictment, delay in the filing of the indictment is caused because the arrest occurs at a time such that it is unreasonable to expect return and filing of the indictment within the period specified in section 3161(b), or because the facts upon which the grand jury must base its determination are unusual or complex.

(iv) Whether the failure to grant such a continuance in a case which, taken as a whole, is not so unusual or so complex as to fall within clause (ii), would deny the defendant reasonable time to obtain counsel, would unreasonably deny the defendant or the Government continuity of counsel, or would deny counsel for the defendant or the attorney for the Government the reasonable time necessary for effective preparation, taking into account the exercise of due diligence.

(C) No continuance under paragraph (8)(A) of this subsection shall be granted because of general congestion of the court's calendar, or lack of diligent preparation or failure to obtain available witnesses on the part of the attorney for the Government.

(i) If trial did not commence within the time limitation specified in section 3161 because the defendant had entered a plea of guilty or nolo contendere subsequently withdrawn to any or all charges in an indictment or information, the defendant shall be deemed indicted with respect to all charges therein contained within the meaning of section 3161, on the day the order permitting withdrawal of the plea becomes final.

(j)(1) If the attorney for the Government knows that a person charged with an offense is serving a term of imprisonment in any penal institution, he shall promptly—

(A) undertake to obtain the presence of the prisoner for trial; or

(B) cause a detainer to be filed with the person having custody of the prisoner and request him to so advise the prisoner and to advise the prisoner of his right to demand trial.

(2) If the person having custody of such prisoner receives a detainer, he shall promptly advise the prisoner of the charge and of the prisoner's right to demand trial. If at any time thereafter the prisoner informs the person having custody that he does demand trial, such person shall cause notice to that effect to be sent promptly to the attorney for the Government who caused the detainer to be filed.

(3) Upon receipt of such notice, the attorney for the Government shall promptly seek to obtain the presence of the prisoner for trial.

(4) When the person having custody of the prisoner receives from the attorney for the Government a properly supported request for temporary custody of such prisoner for trial, the prisoner shall be made available to that attorney for the Government (subject, in cases of interjurisdictional transfer, to any right of the prisoner to contest the legality of his delivery).

§ 3162. Sanctions

(a)(1) If, in the case of any individual against whom a complaint is filed charging such individual with an offense, no indictment or information is filed within the time limit required by section 3161(b) as extended by section 3161(h) of this chapter, such charge against that individual contained in such complaint shall be dismissed or otherwise dropped. In determining whether to dismiss the case with or without prejudice, the court shall consider, among others, each of the following factors: the seriousness of the offense; the facts and circumstances of the case which led to the dismissal; and the impact of a reprosecution on the administration of this chapter and on the administration of justice.

(2) If a defendant is not brought to trial within the time limit required by section 3161(c) as extended by section 3161(h), the information or indictment shall be dismissed on motion of the defendant. The defendant shall have the burden of proof of supporting such motion but the Government shall have the burden of going forward with the evidence in connection with any exclusion of time under subparagraph 3161(h)(3). In determining whether to dismiss the case with or without prejudice, the court shall consider, among others, each of the following factors: the seriousness of the offense; the facts and circumstances of the case which led to the dismissal; and the impact of a reprosecution on the administration of this chapter and on the administration of justice. Failure of the defendant to move for dismissal prior to trial or entry of a plea of guilty or nolo contendere shall constitute a waiver of the right to dismissal under this section.

(b) In any case in which counsel for the defendant or the attorney for the Government (1) knowingly allows the case to be set for trial without disclosing the fact that a necessary witness would be unavailable for trial; (2) files a motion solely for the purpose of delay which he knows is totally frivolous and without merit; (3) makes a statement for the purpose of obtaining a continuance which he knows to be false and which is material to the granting of a continuance; or (4) otherwise willfully fails to proceed to trial without justification consistent with section 3161 of this chapter, the court may punish any such counsel or attorney, as follows:

(A) in the case of an appointed defense counsel, by reducing the amount of compensation that otherwise would have been paid to such counsel pursuant to section 3006A of this title in an amount not to exceed 25 per centum thereof;

(B) in the case of a counsel retained in connection with the defense of a defendant, by imposing on such counsel a fine of not to exceed 25 per centum of the compensation to which he is entitled in connection with his defense of such defendant;

(C) by imposing on any attorney for the Government a fine of not to exceed $250;

(D) by denying any such counsel or attorney for the Government the right to practice before the court considering such case for a period of not to exceed ninety days; or

(E) by filing a report with an appropriate disciplinary committee.

The authority to punish provided for by this subsection shall be in addition to any other authority or power available to such court.

(c) The court shall follow procedures established in the Federal Rules of Criminal Procedure in punishing any counsel or attorney for the Government pursuant to this section.

§ 3163. Effective dates

(a) The time limitation in section 3161(b) of this chapter—

(1) shall apply to all individuals who are arrested or served with a summons on or after the date of expiration of the twelve-calendar-month period following July 1, 1975; and

(2) shall commence to run on such date of expiration to all individuals who are arrested or served with a summons prior to the date of expiration of such twelve-calendar-month period, in connection with the commission of an offense, and with respect to which offense no information or indictment has been filed prior to such date of expiration.

(b) The time limitation in section 3161(c) of this chapter—

(1) shall apply to all offenses charged in informations or indictments filed on or after the date of expiration of the twelve-calendar-month period following July 1, 1975; and

(2) shall commence to run on such date of expiration as to all offenses charged in informations or indictments filed prior to that date.

(c) Subject to the provisions of section 3174(c), section 3162 of this chapter shall become effective and apply to all cases commenced by arrest or summons, and all informations or indictments filed, on or after July 1, 1980.

§ 3164. Persons detained or designated as being of high risk

(a) The trial or other disposition of cases involving—

(1) a detained person who is being held in detention solely because he is awaiting trial, and

(2) a released person who is awaiting trial and has been designated by the attorney for the Government as being of high risk, shall be accorded priority.

(b) The trial of any person described in subsection (a)(1) or (a)(2) of this section shall commence not later than ninety days following the beginning of such continuous detention or designation of high risk by the attorney for the Government. The periods of delay enumerated in section 3161(h) are excluded in computing the time limitation specified in this section.

(c) Failure to commence trial of a detainee as specified in subsection (b), through no fault of the accused or his counsel, or failure to commence trial of a designated releasee as specified in subsection (b), through no fault of the attorney for the Government, shall result in the automatic review by the court of the conditions of release. No detainee, as defined in subsection (a), shall be held in custody pending trial after the expiration of such ninety-day period required for the commencement of his trial. A designated releasee, as defined in subsection (a), who is found by the court to have intentionally delayed the trial of his case shall be subject to an order of the court modifying his nonfinancial conditions of release under this title to insure that he shall appear at trial as required.

§ 3165. District plans—generally

(a) Each district court shall conduct a continuing study of the administration of criminal justice in the district court and before United States magistrates of the district and shall prepare plans for the disposition of criminal cases in accordance with this chapter. Each such plan shall be formulated after consultation with, and after considering the recommendations of, the Federal Judicial Center and the planning group established for that district pursuant to section 3168. The plans shall be prepared in accordance with the schedule set forth in subsection (e) of this section.

(b) The planning and implementation process shall seek to accelerate the disposition of criminal cases in the district consistent with the time standards of this chapter and the objectives of effective law enforcement, fairness to accused persons, efficient judicial administration, and increased knowledge concerning the proper functioning of the criminal law. The process shall seek to avoid underenforcement, overenforcement and discriminatory enforcement of the law, prejudice to the prompt disposition of civil litigation, and undue pressure as well as undue delay in the trial of criminal cases.

(c) The plans prepared by each district court shall be submitted for approval to a reviewing panel consisting of the members of the judicial council of the circuit and either the chief judge of the district court whose plan is being reviewed or such other active judge of that court as the chief judge of that district court may designate. If approved by the reviewing panel, the plan shall be forwarded to the Administrative Office of the United States Courts, which office shall report annually on the operation of such plans to the Judicial Conference of the United States.

(d) The district court may modify the plan at any time with the approval of the reviewing panel. It shall modify the plan when directed to do so by the reviewing panel or the Judicial Conference of the United States. Modifications shall be reported to the Administrative Office of the United States Courts.

(e)(1) Prior to the expiration of the twelve-calendar-month period following July 1, 1975, each United States district court shall prepare and submit a plan in accordance with subsections (a) through (d) above to govern the trial or other disposition of offenses within the jurisdiction of such court during the second and third twelve-calendar-month periods following the effective date of subsection 3161(b) and subsection 3161(c).

(2) Prior to the expiration of the thirty-sixth calendar-month period following July 1, 1975, each United States district court shall prepare and submit a plan in accordance with subsections (a) through (d) above to govern the trial or other disposition of offenses within the jurisdiction of such court during the fourth and fifth twelve-calendar-month periods following the effective date of subsection 3161(b) and subsection 3161(c).

(3) Not later than June 30, 1980, each United States district court with respect to which implementation has not been ordered under section 3174(c) shall prepare and submit a plan in accordance with subsections (a) through (d) to govern the trial or other disposition of offenses within the jurisdiction of such court during the sixth and subsequent twelve-calendar-month periods following the effective date of subsection 3161(b) and subsection 3161(c) in effect prior to the date of enactment of this paragraph.

(f) Plans adopted pursuant to this section shall, upon adoption, and recommendations of the district planning group shall, upon completion, become public documents.

§ 3166. District plans—contents

(a) Each plan shall include a description of the time limits, procedural techniques, innovations, systems and other methods, including the development of reliable methods for gathering and monitoring information and statistics, by which the district court, the United States attorney, the Federal public defender, if any, and private attorneys experienced in the defense of criminal cases, have expedited or intend to expedite the trial or other disposition of criminal cases, consistent with the time limits and other objectives of this chapter.

(b) Each plan shall include information concerning the implementation of the time limits and other objectives of this chapter, including:

(1) the incidence of and reasons for, requests or allowances of extensions of time beyond statutory or district standards;

(2) the incidence of, and reasons for, periods of delay under section 3161(h) of this title;

(3) the incidence of, and reasons for, the invocation of sanctions for noncompliance with time standards, or the failure to invoke such sanctions, and the nature of the sanction, if any invoked for noncompliance;

(4) the new timetable set, or requested to be set, for an extension;

(5) the effect on criminal justice administration of the prevailing time limits and sanctions, including the effects on the prosecution, the defense, the courts, the correctional process, costs, transfers and appeals;

(6) the incidence and length of, reasons for, and remedies for detention prior to trial, and information required by the provisions of the Federal Rules of Criminal Procedure relating to the supervision of detention pending trial;

(7) the identity of cases which, because of their special characteristics, deserve separate or different time limits as a matter of statutory classifications;

(8) the incidence of, and reasons for each thirty-day extension under section 3161(b) with respect to an indictment in that district; and

(9) the impact of compliance with the time limits of subsections (b) and (c) of section 3161 upon the civil case calendar in the district.

(c) Each district plan required by section 3165 shall include information and statistics concerning the administration of criminal justice within the district, including, but not limited to:

(1) the time span between arrest and indictment, indictment and trial, and conviction and sentencing;

(2) the number of matters presented to the United States Attorney for prosecution, and the numbers of such matters prosecuted and not prosecuted;

(3) the number of matters transferred to other districts or to States for prosecution;

(4) the number of cases disposed of by trial and by plea;

(5) the rates of nolle prosequi, dismissal, acquittal, conviction, diversion, or other disposition;

(6) the extent of preadjudication detention and release, by numbers of defendants and days in custody or at liberty prior to disposition; and

(7)(A) the number of new civil cases filed in the twelve-calendar-month period preceding the submission of the plan;

(B) the number of civil cases pending at the close of such period; and

(C) the increase or decrease in the number of civil cases pending at the close of such period, compared to the number pending at the close of the previous twelve-calendar-month period, and the length of time each such case has been pending.

(d) Each plan shall further specify the rule changes, statutory amendments, and appropriations needed to effectuate further improvements in the administration of justice in the district which cannot be accomplished without such amendments or funds.

(e) Each plan shall include recommendations to the Administrative Office of the United States Courts for reporting forms, procedures, and time requirements. The Director of the Administrative Office of the United States Courts, with the approval of the Judicial Conference of the United States, shall prescribe such forms and procedures and time requirements consistent with section 3170 after consideration of the recommendations contained in the district plan and the need to reflect both unique local conditions and uniform national reporting standards.

(f) Each plan may be accompanied by guidelines promulgated by the judicial council of the circuit for use by all district courts within that circuit to implement and secure compliance with this chapter.

§ 3167. Reports to Congress

(a) The Administrative Office of the United States Courts, with the approval of the Judicial Conference, shall submit periodic reports to Congress detailing the plans submitted pursuant to section 3165. The reports shall be submitted within three months following the final dates for the submission of plans under section 3165(e) of this title.

(b) Such reports shall include recommendations for legislative changes or additional appropriations to achieve the time limits and objectives of this chapter. The report shall also contain pertinent information such as the state of the criminal docket at the time of the adoption of the plan; the extent of pretrial detention and release; and a description of the time limits, procedural techniques, innovations, systems, and other methods by which the trial or other disposition of criminal cases have been expedited or may be expedited in the districts. Such reports shall also include the following:

(1) The reasons why, in those cases not in compliance with the time limits of subsections (b) and (c) of section 3161, the provisions of section 3161(h) have not been adequate to accommodate reasonable periods of delay.

(2) The category of offenses, the number of defendants, and the number of counts involved in those cases which are not meeting the time limits specified in subsections (b) and (c) of section 3161.

(3) The additional judicial resources which would be necessary in order to achieve compliance with the time limits specified in subsections (b) and (c) of section 3161.

(4) The nature of the remedial measures which have been employed to improve conditions and practices in those districts with low compliance experience under this chapter or to promote the adoption of practices and procedures which have been successful in those districts with high compliance experience under this chapter.

(5) If a district has experienced difficulty in complying with this chapter, but an application for relief under section 3174 has not been made, the reason why such application has not been made.

(6) The impact of compliance with the time limits of subsections (b) and (c) of section 3161 upon the civil case calendar in

each district as demonstrated by the information assembled and statistics compiled and submitted under sections 3166 and 3170.

(c) Not later than December 31, 1979, the Department of Justice shall prepare and submit to the Congress a report which sets forth the impact of the implementation of this chapter upon the office of the United States Attorney in each district and which shall also include—

(1) the reasons why, in those cases not in compliance, the provisions of section 3161(h) have not been adequate to accommodate reasonable periods of delay;

(2) the nature of the remedial measures which have been employed to improve conditions and practices in the offices of the United States Attorneys in those districts with low compliance experience under this chapter or to promote the adoption of practices and procedures which have been successful in those districts with high compliance experience under this chapter;

(3) the additional resources for the offices of the United States Attorneys which would be necessary to achieve compliance with the time limits of subsections (b) and (c) of section 3161;

(4) suggested changes in the guidelines or other rules implementing this chapter or statutory amendments which the Department of Justice deems necessary to further improve the administration of justice and meet the objectives of this chapter; and

(5) the impact of compliance with the time limits of subsections (b) and (c) of section 3161 upon the litigation of civil cases by the offices of the United States Attorneys and the rule changes, statutory amendments, and resources necessary to assure that such litigation is not prejudiced by full compliance with this chapter.

§ 3168. Planning process

(a) Within sixty days after July 1, 1975, each United States district court shall convene a planning group consisting at minimum of the Chief Judge, a United States magistrate, if any designated by the Chief Judge, the United States Attorney, the Clerk of the district court, the Federal Public Defender, if any, two private attorneys, one with substantial experience in the defense of criminal cases in the district and one with substantial experience in civil litigation in the district, the Chief United States Probation Officer for the district, and a person skilled in criminal justice research who shall act as reporter for the group. The group shall advise the district court with respect to the formulation of all district plans and shall submit its recommendations to the district court for each of the district plans required by section 3165. The group shall be responsible for the initial formulation of all district plans and of the reports required by this chapter and in aid thereof, it shall be entitled to the planning funds specified in section 3171.

(b) The planning group shall address itself to the need for reforms in the criminal justice system, including but not limited to changes in the grand jury system, the finality of criminal judgments, habeas corpus and collateral attacks, pretrial diversion, pretrial detention, excessive reach of Federal criminal law, simplification and improvement of pretrial and sentencing procedures, and appellate delay.

(c) Members of the planning group with the exception of the reporter shall receive no additional compensation for their services, but shall be reimbursed for travel, subsistence and other necessary expenses incurred by them in carrying out the duties of the advisory group in accordance with the provisions of title 5, United States Code, chapter 57. The reporter shall be compensated in accordance with section 3109 of title 5, United States Code, and notwithstanding other provisions of law he may be employed for any period of time during which his services are needed.

§ 3169. Federal Judicial Center

The Federal Judicial Center shall advise and consult with the planning groups and the district courts in connection with their duties under this chapter.

§ 3170. Speedy trial data

(a) To facilitate the planning process, the implementation of the time limits, and continuous and permanent compliance with the objectives of this chapter, the clerk of each district court shall assemble the information and compile the statistics described in sections 3166(b) and (c) of this title. The clerk of each district court shall assemble such information and compile such statistics on such forms and under such regulations as the Administrative Office of the United States Courts shall prescribe with the approval of the Judicial Conference and after consultation with the Attorney General.

(b) The clerk of each district court is authorized to obtain the information required by sections 3166(b) and (c) from all relevant sources including the United States Attorney, Federal Public Defender, private defense counsel appearing in criminal cases in the district, United States district court judges, and the chief Federal Probation Officer for the district. This subsection shall not be construed to require the release of any confidential or privileged information.

(c) The information and statistics compiled by the clerk pursuant to this section shall be made available to the district court, the planning group, the circuit council, and the Administrative Office of the United States Courts.

§ 3171. Planning appropriations

(a) There is authorized to be appropriated for the fiscal year ending June 30, 1975, to the Federal judiciary the sum of $2,500,000 to be allocated by the Administrative Office of the United States Courts to Federal judicial districts to carry out the initial phases of planning and implementation of speedy trial plans under this chapter. The funds so appropriated shall remain available until expended.

(b) No funds appropriated under this section may be expended in any district except by two-thirds vote of the planning group. Funds to the extent available may be expended for personnel, facilities, and any other purpose permitted by law.

§ 3172. Definitions

As used in this chapter—

(1) the terms "judge" or "judicial officer" mean, unless otherwise indicated, any United States magistrate, Federal district judge, and

(2) the term "offense" means any Federal criminal offense which is in violation of any Act of Congress and is triable by any court established by Act of Congress (other than a petty offense as defined in section 1(3) of this title, or an offense triable by court-martial, military commission, provost court, or other military tribunal).

§ 3173. Sixth amendment rights

No provision of this chapter shall be interpreted as a bar to any claim of denial of speedy trial as required by amendment VI of the Constitution.

§ 3174. Judicial emergency and implementation

(a) In the event that any district court is unable to comply with the time limits set forth in section 3161(c) due to the status of its court calendars, the chief judge, where the existing resources are being efficiently utilized, may, after seeking the recommendations of the planning group, apply to the judicial council of the circuit for a suspension of such time limits as provided in subsection (b). The judicial council of the circuit shall evaluate the capabilities of the district, the availability of visiting judges from within and without the circuit, and make any recommendations it deems appropriate to alleviate calendar congestion resulting from the lack of resources.

(b) If the judicial council of the circuit finds that no remedy for such congestion is reasonably available, such council may, upon application by the chief judge of a district, grant a suspension of the time limits in section 3161(c) in such district for a period of time not to exceed one year for the trial of cases for which indictments or informations are filed during such one-year period. During such period of suspension, the time limits from arrest to indictment, set forth in section 3161(b), shall not be reduced, nor shall the sanctions set forth in section 3162 be suspended; but such time limits from indictment to trial shall not be increased to exceed one hundred and eighty days. The time limits for the trial of cases of detained persons who are being detained solely because they are awaiting trial shall not be affected by the provisions of this section.

(c)(1) If, prior to July 1, 1980, the chief judge of any district concludes, with the concurrence of the planning group convened in the district, that the district is prepared to implement the provisions of section 3162 in their entirety, he may apply to the judicial council of the circuit in which the district is located to implement such provisions. Such application shall show the degree of compliance in the district with the time limits set forth in subsections (b) and (c) of section 3161 during the twelve-calendar-month period preceding the date of such application and shall contain a proposed order and schedule for such implementation, which includes the date on which the provisions of section 3162 are to become effective in the district, the effect such implementation will have upon such district's practices and procedures, and provision for adequate notice to all interested parties.

(2) After review of any such application, the judicial council of the circuit shall enter an order implementing the provisions of section 3162 in their entirety in the district making application, or shall return such application to the chief judge of such district, together with an explanation setting forth such council's reasons for refusing to enter such order.

(d)(1) The approval of any application made pursuant to subsection (a) or (c) by a judicial council of a circuit shall be reported within ten days to the Director of the Administrative Office of the United States Courts, together with a copy of the application, a written report setting forth in sufficient detail the reasons for granting such application, and, in the case of an application made pursuant to subsection (a), a proposal for alleviating congestion in the district.

(2) The Director of the Administrative Office of the United States Courts shall not later than ten days after receipt transmit such report to the Congress and to the Judicial Conference of the United States. The judicial council of the circuit shall not grant a suspension to any district within six months following the expiration of a prior suspension without the consent of the Congress by Act of Congress. The limitation on granting a suspension made by this paragraph shall not apply with respect to any judicial district in which the prior suspension is in effect on the date of the enactment of the Speedy Trial Act Amendments Act of 1979.

(e) If the chief judge of the district court concludes that the need for suspension of time limits in such district under this section is of great urgency, he may order the limits suspended for a period not to exceed thirty days. Within ten days of entry of such order, the chief judge shall apply to the judicial council of the circuit for a suspension pursuant to subsection (a).

CHAPTER 209—EXTRADITION

§ 3181. Scope and limitation of chapter

The provisions of this chapter relating to the surrender of persons who have committed crimes in foreign countries shall continue in force only during the existence of any treaty of extradition with such foreign government.

§ 3182. Fugitives from State or Territory to State, District or Territory

Whenever the executive authority of any State or Territory demands any person as a fugitive from justice, of the executive authority of any State, District or Territory to which such person has fled, and produces a copy of an indictment found or an affidavit made before a magistrate of any State or Territory, charging the person demanded with having committed treason, felony, or other crime, certified as authentic by the governor or chief magistrate of the State or Territory from whence the person so charged has fled, the executive authority of the State, District or Territory to which such person has fled shall cause him to be arrested and secured, and notify the executive authority making such demand, or the agent of such authority appointed to receive the fugitive, and shall cause the fugitive to be delivered to such agent when he shall appear. If no such agent appears within thirty days from the time of the arrest, the prisoner may be discharged.

§ 3183. Fugitives from State, Territory, or Possession into extraterritorial jurisdiction of United States

Whenever the executive authority of any State, Territory, District, or possession of the United States or the Panama Canal Zone, demands any American citizen or national as a fugitive from justice who has fled to a country in which the United States exercises extraterritorial jurisdiction, and produces a copy of an indictment found or an affidavit made before a magistrate of the demanding jurisdiction, charging the fugitive so demanded with having committed treason, felony, or other offense, certified as authentic by the Governor or chief magistrate of such demanding jurisdiction, or other person authorized to act, the officer or representative of the United States vested with judicial authority to whom the demand has been made shall cause such fugitive to be arrested and secured, and notify the executive authorities making such demand, or the agent of such authority appointed to receive the fugitive, and shall cause the fugitive to be delivered to such agent when he shall appear.

If no such agent shall appear within three months from the time of the arrest, the prisoner may be discharged.

The agent who receives the fugitive into his custody shall be empowered to transport him to the jurisdiction from which he has fled.

§ 3184. Fugitives from foreign country to United States

Whenever there is a treaty or convention for extradition between the United States and any foreign government, any justice or judge of the United States, or any magistrate authorized so to do by a court of the United States, or any judge of a court of record of general jurisdiction of any State, may, upon complaint made under oath, charging any person found within his jurisdiction, with having committed within the jurisdiction of any such foreign government any of the crimes provided for by such treaty or convention, issue his warrant for the apprehension of the person so charged, that he may be brought before such justice, judge, or magistrate, to the end that the evidence of criminality may be heard and considered. If, on such hearing, he deems the evidence sufficient to sustain the charge under the provisions of the proper treaty or convention, he shall certify the same, together with a copy of all the testimony taken before him, to the Secretary of State, that a warrant may issue upon the requisition of the proper authorities of such foreign government, for the surrender of such person, according to the stipulations of the treaty or convention; and he shall issue his warrant for the commitment of the person so charged to the proper jail, there to remain until such surrender shall be made.

§ 3185. Fugitives from country under control of United States into the United States

Whenever any foreign country or territory, or any part thereof, is occupied by or under the control of the United States, any person who, having violated the criminal laws in force therein by the commission of any of the offenses enumerated below, departs or flees from justice therein to the United States, shall, when found therein, be liable to arrest and detention by the authorities of the United States, and on the written request or requisition of the military governor or other chief executive officer in control of such foreign country or territory shall be returned and surrendered as hereinafter provided to such authorities for trial under the laws in force in the place where such offense was committed.

(1) Murder and assault with intent to commit murder;

(2) Counterfeiting or altering money, or uttering or bringing into circulation counterfeit or altered money;

(3) Counterfeiting certificates or coupons of public indebtedness, bank notes, or other instruments of public credit, and the utterance or circulation of the same;

(4) Forgery or altering and uttering what is forged or altered;

(5) Embezzlement or criminal malversation of the public funds, committed by public officers, employees, or depositaries;

(6) Larceny or embezzlement of an amount not less than $100 in value;

(7) Robbery;

(8) Burglary, defined to be the breaking and entering by nighttime into the house of another person with intent to commit a felony therein;

(9) Breaking and entering the house or building of another, whether in the day or nighttime, with the intent to commit a felony therein;

(10) Entering, or breaking and entering the offices of the Government and public authorities, or the offices of banks, banking houses, savings banks, trust companies, insurance or other companies, with the intent to commit a felony therein;

(11) Perjury or the subornation of perjury;

(12) Rape;

(13) Arson;

(14) Piracy by the law of nations;

(15) Murder, assault with intent to kill, and manslaughter, committed on the high seas, on board a ship owned by or in control of citizens or residents of such foreign country or territory and not under the flag of the United States, or of some other government;

(16) Malicious destruction of or attempt to destroy railways, trams, vessels, bridges, dwellings, public edifices, or other buildings, when the act endangers human life.

This chapter, so far as applicable, shall govern proceedings authorized by this section. Such proceedings shall be had before a judge of the courts of the United States only, who shall hold such person on evidence establishing probable cause that he is guilty of the offense charged.

No return or surrender shall be made of any person charged with the commission of any offense of a political nature.

If so held, such person shall be returned and surrendered to the authorities in control of such foreign country or territory on the order of the Secretary of State of the United States, and such authorities shall secure to such a person a fair and impartial trial.

§ 3186. Secretary of State to surrender fugitive

The Secretary of State may order the person committed under sections 3184 or 3185 of this title to be delivered to any authorized agent of such foreign government, to be tried for the offense of which charged.

Such agent may hold such person in custody, and take him to the territory of such foreign government, pursuant to such treaty.

A person so accused who escapes may be retaken in the same manner as any person accused of any offense.

§ 3187. Provisional arrest and detention within extraterritorial jurisdiction

The provisional arrest and detention of a fugitive, under sections 3042 and 3183 of this title, in advance of the presentation of formal proofs, may be obtained by telegraph upon the request of the authority competent to request the surrender of such fugitive addressed to the authority competent to grant such surrender. Such request shall be accompanied by an express statement that a warrant for the fugitive's arrest has been issued within the jurisdiction of the authority making such request charging the fugitive with the commission of the crime for which his extradition is sought to be obtained.

No person shall be held in custody under telegraphic request by virtue of this section for more than ninety days.

§ 3188. Time of commitment pending extradition

Whenever any person who is committed for rendition to a foreign government to remain until delivered up in pursuance of a requisition is not so delivered up and conveyed out of the United States within two calendar months after such commitment, over and above the time actually required to convey the prisoner from the jail to which he was committed, by the readiest way, out of the United States, any judge of the United States, or of any State, upon application made to him by or on behalf of the person so committed, and upon proof made to him that reasonable notice of the intention to make such application has been given to the Secretary of State, may order the person so committed to be discharged out of custody, unless sufficient cause is shown to such judge why such discharge ought not to be ordered.

§ 3189. Place and character of hearing

Hearings in cases of extradition under treaty stipulation or convention shall be held on land, publicly, and in a room or office easily accessible to the public.

§ 3190. Evidence on hearing

Depositions, warrants, or other papers or copies thereof offered in evidence upon the hearing of any extradition case shall be received and admitted as evidence on such hearing for all the purposes of such hearing if they shall be properly and legally authenticated so as to entitle them to be received for similar purposes by the tribunals of the foreign country from which the accused party shall have escaped, and the certificate of the principal diplomatic or consular officer of the United States resident in such foreign country shall be proof that the same, so offered, are authenticated in the manner required.

§ 3191. Witnesses for indigent fugitives

On the hearing of any case under a claim of extradition by a foreign government, upon affidavit being filed by the person charged setting forth that there are witnesses whose evidence is material to his defense, that he cannot safely go to trial without them, what he expects to prove by each of them, and that he is not possessed of sufficient means, and is actually unable to pay the fees of such witnesses, the judge or magistrate hearing the matter may order that such witnesses be subpenaed; and the costs incurred by the process, and the fees of witnesses, shall be paid in the same manner as in the case of witnesses subpenaed in behalf of the United States.

§ 3192. Protection of accused

Whenever any person is delivered by any foreign government to an agent of the United States, for the purpose of being brought within the United States and tried for any offense of which he is duly accused, the President shall have power to take all necessary measures for the transportation and safekeeping of such accused person, and for his security against lawless violence, until the final conclusion of his trial for the offenses specified in the warrant of extradition, and until his final discharge from custody or imprisonment for or on account of such offenses, and for a reasonable time thereafter, and may employ such portion of the land or naval forces of the United States, or of the militia thereof, as may be necessary for the safekeeping and protection of the accused.

§ 3193. Receiving agent's authority over offenders

A duly appointed agent to receive, in behalf of the United States, the delivery, by a foreign government, of any person accused of crime committed within the United States, and to convey him to the place of his trial, shall have all the powers of a marshal of the United States, in the several districts through which it may be necessary for him to pass with such prisoner, so far as such power is requisite for the prisoner's safe-keeping.

§ 3194. Transportation of fugitive by receiving agent

Any agent appointed as provided in section 3182 of this title who receives the fugitive into his custody is empowered to transport him to the State or Territory from which he has fled.

§ 3195. Payment of fees and costs

All costs or expenses incurred in any extradition proceeding in apprehending, securing, and transmitting a fugitive shall be paid by the demanding authority.

All witness fees and costs of every nature in cases of international extradition, including the fees of the magistrate, shall be certified by the judge or magistrate before whom the hearing shall take place to the Secretary of State of the United States, and the same shall be paid out of appropriations to defray the expenses of the judiciary or the Department of Justice as the case may be.

The Attorney General shall certify to the Secretary of State the amounts to be paid to the United States on account of said fees and costs in extradition cases by the foreign government requesting the extradition, and the Secretary of State shall cause said amounts to be collected and transmitted to the Attorney General for deposit in the Treasury of the United States.

CHAPTER 211—JURISDICTION AND VENUE

Sec.

§ 3231. District courts

The district courts of the United States shall have original jurisdiction, exclusive of the courts of the States, of all offenses against the laws of the United States.

Nothing in this title shall be held to take away or impair the jurisdiction of the courts of the several States under the laws thereof.

§ 3232. District of offense—(rule)

SEE FEDERAL RULES OF CRIMINAL PROCEDURE

Proceedings to be in district and division in which offense committed, Rule 18.

§ 3233. Transfer within district—(rule)

SEE FEDERAL RULES OF CRIMINAL PROCEDURE

Arraignment, plea, trial, sentence in district of more than one division, Rule 19.

§ 3234. Change of venue to another district—(rule)

SEE FEDERAL RULES OF CRIMINAL PROCEDURE

Plea or disposal of case in district other than that in which defendant was arrested, Rule 20.

§ 3235. Venue in capital cases

The trial of offenses punishable with death shall be had in the county where the offense was committed, where that can be done without great inconvenience.

§ 3236. Murder or manslaughter

In all cases of murder or manslaughter, the offense shall be deemed to have been committed at the place where the injury was inflicted, or the poison administered or other means employed which caused the death, without regard to the place where the death occurs.

§ 3237. Offenses begun in one district and completed in another

(a) Except as otherwise expressly provided by enactment of Congress, any offense against the United States begun in one district and completed in another, or committed in more than one district, may be inquired of and prosecuted in any district in which such offense was begun, continued, or completed.

Any offense involving the use of the mails, or transportation in interstate or foreign commerce, is a continuing offense and, except as otherwise expressly provided by enactment of Congress, may be inquired of and prosecuted in any district from, through, or into which such commerce or mail matter moves.

(b) Notwithstanding subsection (a), where an offense is described in section 7203 of the Internal Revenue Code of 1954, or where an offense involves use of the mails and is an offense described in section 7201 or 7206(1), (2), or (5) of such Code (whether or not the offense is also described in another provision of law), and prosecution is begun in a judicial district other than the judicial district in which the defendant resides, he may upon motion filed in the district in which the prosecution is begun, elect to be tried in the district in which he was residing at the time the alleged offense was committed: *Provided,* That the motion is filed within twenty days after arraignment of the defendant upon indictment or information.

§ 3238. Offenses not committed in any district

The trial of all offenses begun or committed upon the high seas, or elsewhere out of the jurisdiction of any particular State or district, shall be in the district in which the offender, or any one of two or more joint offenders, is arrested or is first brought; but if such offender or offenders are not so arrested or brought into any district, an indictment or information may be filed in the district of the last known residence of the offender or of any one of two or more joint offenders, or if no such residence is known the indictment or information may be filed in the District of Columbia.

§ 3239. Threatening communications

Any defendant indicted under sections 875, 876 or 877 of this title, with respect to communications originating in the United States, shall, upon motion duly made, be entitled as of right to be tried in the district in which the matter mailed or otherwise transmitted was first set in motion, in the mails or in commerce between the States.

§ 3240. Creation of new district or division

Whenever any new district or division is established, or any county or territory is transferred from one district or division to another district or division, prosecutions for offenses committed within such district, division, county, or territory prior to such transfer, shall be commenced and proceeded with the same as if such new district or division had not been created, or such county or territory had not been transferred, unless the court, upon the application of the defendant, shall order the case to be removed to the new district or division for trial.

§ 3241. Jurisdiction of offenses under certain sections

The United States District Court for the Canal Zone and the District Court of the Virgin Islands shall have jurisdiction of offenses under the laws of the United States, not locally inapplicable, committed within the territorial jurisdiction of such courts, and jurisdiction, concurrently with the district courts of the United States, of offenses against the laws of the United States committed upon the high seas.

§ 3242. Indians committing certain offenses; acts on reservations

All Indians committing any of the following offenses; namely, murder, manslaughter, rape, carnal knowledge of any female, not his wife, who has not attained the age of sixteen years, assault with intent to commit rape, incest, assault with intent to kill, assault with a dangerous weapon, arson, burglary, robbery, and larceny on and within the Indian country shall be tried in the same courts, and in the same manner, as are all other persons committing any of the above crimes within the exclusive jurisdiction of the United States.

§ 3243. Jurisdiction of State of Kansas over offenses committed by or against Indians on Indian reservations

Jurisdiction is conferred on the State of Kansas over offenses committed by or against Indians on Indian reservations, including trust or restricted allotments, within the State of Kansas, to the same extent as its courts have jurisdiction over offenses committed elsewhere within the State in accordance with the laws of the State.

This section shall not deprive the courts of the United States of jurisdiction over offenses defined by the laws of the United States committed by or against Indians on Indian reservations.

§ 3244. Jurisdiction of proceedings relating to transferred offenders

When a treaty is in effect between the United States and a foreign country providing for the transfer of convicted offenders—

(1) the country in which the offender was convicted shall have exclusive jurisdiction and competence over proceedings seeking to challenge, modify, or set aside convictions or sentences handed down by a court of such country;

(2) all proceedings instituted by or on behalf of an offender transferred from the United States to a foreign country seeking to challenge, modify, or set aside the conviction or sentence upon which the transfer was based shall be brought in the court which would have jurisdiction and competence if the offender had not been transferred;

(3) all proceedings instituted by or on behalf of an offender transferred to the United States pertaining to the manner of execution in the United States of the sentence imposed by a foreign court shall be brought in the United States district court for the district in which the offender is confined or in which supervision is exercised and shall name the Attorney General and the official having immediate custody or exercising immediate supervision of the offender as respondents. The Attorney General shall defend against such proceedings;

(4) all proceedings instituted by or on behalf of an offender seeking to challenge the validity or legality of the offender's transfer from the United States shall be brought in the United States district court of the district in which the proceedings to determine the validity of the offender's consent where held and shall name the Attorney General as respondent; and

(5) all proceedings instituted by or on behalf of an offender seeking to challenge the validity or legality of the offender's transfer to the United States shall be brought in the United States district court of the district in which the offender is confined or of the district in which supervision is exercised and shall name the Attorney General and the official having immediate custody or exercising immediate supervision of the offender as respondents. The Attorney General shall defend against such proceedings.

CHAPTER 215—GRAND JURY

§ 3321. Number of grand jurors; summoning additional jurors

Every grand jury impaneled before any district court shall consist of not less than sixteen nor more than twenty-three persons. If less than sixteen of the persons summoned attend, they shall be placed on the grand jury, and the court shall order the marshal to summon, either immediately or for a day fixed, from the body of the district, and not from the bystanders, a sufficient number of persons to complete the grand jury. Whenever a challenge to a grand juror is allowed, and there are not in attendance other jurors sufficient to complete the grand jury, the court shall make a like order to the marshal to summon a sufficient number of persons for that purpose.

§ 3322. Number; summoning—(rule)

SEE FEDERAL RULES OF CRIMINAL PROCEDURE

Summoning grand jury; number of grand jurors, Rule 6(a).

§ 3323. Objections and motions—(rule)

SEE FEDERAL RULES OF CRIMINAL PROCEDURE

Challenging array of grand jurors or individual grand jurors; motions to dismiss, Rule 6(b).

§ 3324. Foreman and deputies; powers and duties; records—(rule)

SEE FEDERAL RULES OF CRIMINAL PROCEDURE

Appointment of grand jury foreman and deputy foreman; oaths, affirmations and indictments; records of jurors concurring, Rule 6(c).

§ 3325. Persons present at proceedings—(rule)

SEE FEDERAL RULES OF CRIMINAL PROCEDURE

Persons who may be present while grand jury is in session; exclusion while jury is deliberating or voting, Rule 6(d).

§ 3326. Secrecy of proceedings and disclosure—(rule)

SEE FEDERAL RULES OF CRIMINAL PROCEDURE

Disclosure of proceedings to government attorneys; disclosure by direction of court or permission of defendant; secrecy of indictment, Rule 6(e).

---

* So in original. Catchline reads "deputies".

§ 3327. Indictment; finding and return—(rule)

SEE FEDERAL RULES OF CRIMINAL PROCEDURE

Concurrence of twelve or more jurors in indictment; return of indictment to judge in open court, Rule 6(f).

§ 3328. Discharging jury and excusing juror—(rule)

SEE FEDERAL RULES OF CRIMINAL PROCEDURE

Discharge of grand jury by court; limitation of service; excusing juror for cause, Rule 6(g).

CHAPTER 216—SPECIAL GRAND JURY

§ 3331. Summoning and term

(a) In addition to such other grand juries as shall be called from time to time, each district court which is located in a judicial district containing more than four million inhabitants or in which the Attorney General, the Deputy Attorney General, or any designated Assistant Attorney General, certifies in writing to the chief judge of the district that in his judgment a special grand jury is necessary because of criminal activity in the district shall order a special grand jury to be summoned at least once in each period of eighteen months unless another special grand jury is then serving. The grand jury shall serve for a term of eighteen months unless an order for its discharge is entered earlier by the court upon a determination of the grand jury by majority vote that its business has been completed. If, at the end of such term or any extension thereof, the district court determines the business of the grand jury has not been completed, the court may enter an order extending such term for an additional period of six months. No special grand jury term so extended shall exceed thirty-six months, except as provided in subsection (e) of section 3333 of this chapter.

(b) If a district court within any judicial circuit fails to extend the term of a special grand jury or enters an order for the discharge of such grand jury before such grand jury determines that it has completed its business, the grand jury, upon the affirmative vote of a majority of its members, may apply to the chief judge of the circuit for an order for the continuance of the term of the grand jury. Upon the making of such an application by the grand jury, the term thereof shall continue until the entry upon such application by the chief judge of the circuit of an appropriate order. No special grand jury term so extended shall exceed thirty-six months, except as provided in subsection (e) of section 3333 of this chapter.

§ 3332. Powers and duties

(a) It shall be the duty of each such grand jury impaneled within any judicial district to inquire into offenses against the criminal laws of the United States alleged to have been committed within that district. Such alleged offenses may be brought to the attention of the grand jury by the court or by any attorney appearing on behalf of the United States for the presentation of evidence. Any such attorney receiving information concerning such an alleged offense from any other person shall, if requested by such other person, inform the grand jury of such alleged offense, the identity of such other person, and such attorney's action or recommendation.

(b) Whenever the district court determines that the volume of business of the special grand jury exceeds the capacity of the grand jury to discharge its obligations, the district court may order an additional special grand jury for that district to be impaneled.

§ 3333. Reports

(a) A special grand jury impaneled by any district court, with the concurrence of a majority of its members, may, upon completion of its original term, or each extension thereof, submit to the court a report—

(1) concerning noncriminal misconduct, malfeasance, or misfeasance in office involving organized criminal activity by an appointed public officer or employee as the basis for a recommendation of removal or disciplinary action; or

(2) regarding organized crime conditions in the district.

(b) The court to which such report is submitted shall examine it and the minutes of the special grand jury and, except as otherwise provided in subsections (c) and (d) of this section, shall make an order accepting and filing such report as a public record only if the court is satisfied that it complies with the provisions of subsection (a) of this section and that—

(1) the report is based upon facts revealed in the course of an investigation authorized by subsection (a) of section 3332 and is supported by the preponderance of the evidence; and

(2) when the report is submitted pursuant to paragraph (1) of subsection (a) of this section, each person named therein and any reasonable number of witnesses in his behalf as designated by him to the foreman of the grand jury were afforded an opportunity to testify before the grand jury prior to the filing of such report, and when the report is submitted pursuant to paragraph (2) of subsection (a) of this section, it is not critical of an identified person.

(c) (1) An order accepting a report pursuant to paragraph (1) of subsection (a) of this section and the report shall be sealed by the court and shall not be filed as a public record or be subject to subpena or otherwise made public (i) until at least thirty-one days after a copy of the order and report are served upon each public officer or employee named therein and an answer has been filed or the time for filing an answer has expired, or (ii) if an appeal is taken, until all rights of review of the public officer or employee named therein have expired or terminated in an order accepting the report. No order accepting a report pursuant to paragraph (1) of subsection (a) of this section shall be entered until thirty days after the delivery of such report to the public officer or body pursuant to paragraph (3) of subsection (c) of this section. The court may issue such orders as it shall deem appropriate to prevent unauthorized publication of a report. Unauthorized publication may be punished as contempt of the court.

(2) Such public officer or employee may file with the clerk a verified answer to such a report not later than twenty days after service of the order and report upon him. Upon a showing of good cause, the court may grant such public officer or employee an extension of time within which to file such answer and may authorize such limited publication of the report as may be necessary to prepare such answer. Such an answer shall plainly and concisely state the facts and law constituting the defense of the public officer or employee to the charges in said report, and, except for those parts thereof which the court determines to have been inserted scandalously, prejudiciously, or unnecessarily, such answer shall become an appendix to the report.

(3) Upon the expiration of the time set forth in paragraph (1) of subsection (c) of this section, the United States attorney shall deliver a true copy of such report, and the appendix, if any, for appropriate action to each public officer or body having jurisdiction, responsibility, or authority over each public officer or employee named in the report.

(d) Upon the submission of a report pursuant to subsection (a) of this section, if the court finds that the filing of such report as a public record may prejudice fair consideration of a pending criminal matter, it shall order such report sealed and such report shall not be subject to subpena or public inspection during the pendency of such criminal matter, except upon order of the court.

(e) Whenever the court to which a report is submitted pursuant to paragraph (1) of subsection (a) of this section is not satisfied that the report complies with the provisions of subsection (b) of this section, it may direct that additional testimony be taken before the same grand jury, or it shall make an order sealing such report, and it shall not be filed as a public record or be subject to subpena or otherwise made public until the provisions of subsection (b) of this section are met. A special grand jury term may be extended by the district court beyond thirty-six months in order that such additional testimony may be taken or the provisions of subsection (b) of this section may be met.

(f) As used in this section, "public officer or employee" means any officer or employee of the United States, any State, the District of Columbia, the Commonwealth of Puerto Rico, any territory or possession of the United States, or any political subdivision, or any department, agency, or instrumentality thereof.

§ 3334. General provisions

The provisions of chapter 215, title 18, United States Code, and the Federal Rules of Criminal Procedure applicable to regular grand juries shall apply to special grand juries to the extent not inconsistent with sections 3331, 3332, or 3333 of this chapter.

CHAPTER 217—INDICTMENT AND INFORMATION

§ 3361. Form and contents—(rule)

SEE FEDERAL RULES OF CRIMINAL PROCEDURE

Contents and form; striking surplusage, Rule 7(a), (c), (d).

§ 3362. Waiver of indictment and prosecution on information—(rule)

SEE FEDERAL RULES OF CRIMINAL PROCEDURE

Waiver of indictment for offenses not punishable by death, Rule 7(b).

§ 3363. Joinder of offenses—(rule)

SEE FEDERAL RULES OF CRIMINAL PROCEDURE

Joinder of two or more offenses in same indictment, Rule 8(a).
Trial together of indictments or informations, Rule 13.

§ 3364. Joinder of defendants—(rule)

SEE FEDERAL RULES OF CRIMINAL PROCEDURE

Joinder of two or more defendants charged in same indictment, Rule 8(b).
Relief from prejudicial joinder, Rule 14.

§ 3365. Amendment of information—(rule)

SEE FEDERAL RULES OF CRIMINAL PROCEDURE

Amendment of information, time and conditions, Rule 7(e).

§ 3366. Bill of particulars—(rule)

SEE FEDERAL RULES OF CRIMINAL PROCEDURE

Bill of particulars for cause; motion after arraignment; time; amendment, Rule 7(f).

§ 3367. Dismissal—(rule)

SEE FEDERAL RULES OF CRIMINAL PROCEDURE

Dismissal filed by Attorney General or United States Attorney, Rule 48.

Dismissal on objection to array of grand jury or lack of legal qualification of individual grand juror, Rule 6(b) (2).

CHAPTER 219—TRIAL BY UNITED STATES MAGISTRATES

§ 3401. Misdemeanors; application of probation laws

(a) When specially designated to exercise such jurisdiction by the district court or courts he serves, any United States magistrate shall have jurisdiction to try persons accused of, and sentence persons convicted of, misdemeanors committed within that judicial district.

(b) Any person charged with a misdemeanor may elect, however, to be tried before a judge of the district court for the district in which the offense was committed. The magistrate shall carefully explain to the defendant that he has a right to trial, judgment, and sentencing by a judge of the district court and that he may have a right to trial by jury before a district judge or magistrate. The magistrate shall not proceed to try the case unless the defendant, after such explanation, files a written consent to be tried before the magistrate that specifically waives trial, judgment, and sentencing by a judge of the district court.

(c) A magistrate who exercises trial jurisdiction under this section, and before whom a person is convicted or pleads either guilty or nolo contendere, may, with the approval of a judge of the district court, direct the probation service of the court to conduct a presentence investigation on that person and render a report to the magistrate prior to the imposition of sentence.

(d) The probation laws shall be applicable to persons tried by a magistrate under this section, and such officer shall have power to grant probation and to revoke or reinstate the probation of any person granted probation by him.

(e) Proceedings before United States magistrates under this section shall be taken down by a court reporter or recorded by suitable sound recording equipment. For purposes of appeal a copy of the record of such proceedings shall be made available at the expense of the United States to a person who makes affidavit that he is unable to pay or give security therefor, and the expense of such copy shall be paid by the Director of the Administrative Office of the United States Courts.

(f) The district court may order that proceedings in any misdemeanor case be conducted before a district judge rather than a United States magistrate upon the court's own motion or, for good cause shown, upon petition by the attorney for the Government. Such petition should note the novelty, importance, or complexity of the case, or other pertinent factors, and be filed in accordance with regulations promulgated by the Attorney General.

(g) The magistrate may, in a case involving a youth offender in which consent to trial before a magistrate has been filed under subsection (b) of this section, impose sentence and exercise the other powers granted to the district court under chapter 402 and section 4216 of this title, except that—

(1) the magistrate may not sentence the youth offender to the custody of the Attorney General pursuant to such chapter for a period in excess of 1 year for conviction of a misdemeanor or 6 months for conviction of a petty offense;

(2) such youth offender shall be released conditionally under supervision no later than 3 months before the expiration of the term imposed by the magistrate, and shall be discharged unconditionally on or before the expiration of the maximum sentence imposed; and

(3) the magistrate may not suspend the imposition of sentence and place the youth offender on probation for a period in excess of 1 year for conviction of a misdemeanor or 6 months for conviction of a petty offense.

(h) The magistrate may, in a petty offense case involving a juvenile in which consent to trial before a magistrate has been filed under subsection (b) of this section, exercise all powers granted to the district court under chapter 403 of this title. For purposes of this subsection, proceedings under chapter 403 of this title may be instituted against a juvenile by a violation notice or complaint, except that no such case may proceed unless the certification referred to in section 5032 of this title has been filed in open court at the arraignment. No term of imprisonment shall be imposed by the magistrate in any such case.

§ 3402. Rules of procedure; practice and appeal

In all cases of conviction by a United States magistrate an appeal of right shall lie from the judgment of the magistrate to a judge of the district court of the district in which the offense was committed.

The Supreme Court shall prescribe rules of procedure and practice for the trial of cases before magistrates and for taking and hearing of appeals to the judges of the district courts of the United States.

CHAPTER 221—ARRAIGNMENT, PLEAS AND TRIAL

§ 3431. Term of court; power of court unaffected by expiration—(rule)

SEE FEDERAL RULES OF CRIMINAL PROCEDURE

Expiration of term without significance in criminal cases, Rule 45(c).

§ 3432. Indictment and list of jurors and witnesses for prisoner in capital cases

A person charged with treason or other capital offense shall at least three entire days before commencement of trial be furnished with a copy of the indictment and a list of the veniremen, and of the witnesses to be produced on the trial for proving the indictment, stating the place of abode of each venireman and witness.

§ 3433. Arraignment—(rule)

SEE FEDERAL RULES OF CRIMINAL PROCEDURE

Reading and furnishing copy of indictment to accused, Rule 10.

§ 3434. Presence of defendant—(rule)

SEE FEDERAL RULES OF CRIMINAL PROCEDURE

Right of defendant to be present generally; corporation; waiver, Rule 43.

§ 3435. Receiver of stolen property triable before or after principal

A person charged with receiving or concealing stolen property may be tried either before or after the trial of the principal offender.

§ 3436. Consolidation of indictments or informations—(rule)

SEE FEDERAL RULES OF CRIMINAL PROCEDURE

Two or more indictments or informations triable together, Rule 13.

§ 3437. Severance—(rule)

SEE FEDERAL RULES OF CRIMINAL PROCEDURE

Relief from prejudicial joinder of defendants or offenses, Rule 14.

§ 3438. Pleas—(rule)

SEE FEDERAL RULES OF CRIMINAL PROCEDURE

Plea of guilty, not guilty, or nolo contendere; acceptance by court; refusal to plead; corporation failing to appear, Rule 11.

Withdrawal of plea of guilty, Rule 32(d).

§ 3439. Demurrers and special pleas in bar or abatement abolished; relief on motion—(rule)

SEE FEDERAL RULES OF CRIMINAL PROCEDURE

Motion to dismiss or for appropriate relief substituted for demurrer or dilatory plea or motion to quash, Rule 12.

§ 3440. Defenses and objections determined on motion—(rule)

SEE FEDERAL RULES OF CRIMINAL PROCEDURE

Defenses or objections which may or must be raised before trial; time; hearing; effect of determination; limitations by law unaffected, Rule 12(b).

§ 3441. Jury; number of jurors; waiver—(rule)

SEE FEDERAL RULES OF CRIMINAL PROCEDURE

Jury trial, waiver, twelve jurors or less by written stipulation, trial by court on general or special findings, Rule 23.

§ 3442. Jurors, examination, peremptory challenges; alternates—(rule)

SEE FEDERAL RULES OF CRIMINAL PROCEDURE

Examination and peremptory challenges of trial jurors; alternate jurors, Rule 24.

§ 3443. Instructions to jury—(rule)

SEE FEDERAL RULES OF CRIMINAL PROCEDURE

Court's instructions to jury, written requests and copies, objections, Rule 30.

§ 3444. Disability of judge—(rule)

SEE FEDERAL RULES OF CRIMINAL PROCEDURE

Disability of judge after verdict or finding of guilt, Rule 25(b).

§ 3445. Motion for judgment of acquittal—(rule)

SEE FEDERAL RULES OF CRIMINAL PROCEDURE

Motions for directed verdict abolished, Rule 29(a).

Motions for judgment of acquittal adopted; court may reserve decision; renewal, Rule 29.

§ 3446. New trial—(rule)

SEE FEDERAL RULES OF CRIMINAL PROCEDURE

Granting of new trial, grounds, and motion, Rule 33.

CHAPTER 223—WITNESSES AND EVIDENCE

Sec.

§ 3481. Competency of accused

In trial of all persons charged with the commission of offenses against the United States and in all proceedings in courts martial and courts of inquiry in any State, District, Possession or Territory, the person charged shall, at his own request, be a competent witness. His failure to make such request shall not create any presumption against him.

§ 3482. Evidence and witnesses—(rule)

SEE FEDERAL RULES OF CRIMINAL PROCEDURE

Competency and privileges of witnesses and admissibility of evidence governed by principles of common law, Rule 26.

§ 3483. Indigent defendants, process to produce evidence—(rule)

SEE FEDERAL RULES OF CRIMINAL PROCEDURE

Subpoena for indigent defendants, motion, affidavit, costs, Rule 17(b).

§ 3484. Subpoenas—(rule)

SEE FEDERAL RULES OF CRIMINAL PROCEDURE

Form, contents and issuance of subpoena, Rule 17(a).
Service in United States, Rule 17(d), (e, 1).
Service in foreign country, Rule 17(d), (e, 2).
Indigent defendants, Rule 17(b).
On taking depositions, Rule 17(f).

Papers and documents, Rule 17(c).
Disobedience of subpoena as contempt of court, Rule 17(g).

§ 3485. Expert witnesses—(rule)

SEE FEDERAL RULES OF CRIMINAL PROCEDURE

Selection and appointment of expert witnesses by court or parties; compensation, Rule 28.

[§ 3486. Repealed.]

§ 3487. Refusal to pay as evidence of embezzlement

The refusal of any person, whether in or out of office, charged with the safe-keeping, transfer, or disbursement of the public money to pay any draft, order, or warrant, drawn upon him by the General Accounting Office, for any public money in his hands belonging to the United States, no matter in what capacity the same may have been received, or may be held, or to transfer or disburse any such money, promptly, upon the legal requirement of any authorized officer, shall be deemed, upon the trial of any indictment against such person for embezzlement, prima facie evidence of such embezzlement.

§ 3488. Intoxicating liquor in Indian country as evidence of unlawful introduction

The possession by a person of intoxicating liquors in Indian country where the introduction is prohibited by treaty or Federal statute shall be prima facie evidence of unlawful introduction.

§ 3489. Discovery and inspection—(rule)

SEE FEDERAL RULES OF CRIMINAL PROCEDURE

Inspection of documents and papers taken from defendant, Rule 16.

§ 3490. Official record or entry—(rule)

SEE FEDERAL RULES OF CRIMINAL PROCEDURE

Proof of official record or entry as in civil actions, Rule 27.

§ 3491. Foreign documents

Any book, paper, statement, record, account, writing, or other document, or any portion thereof, of whatever character and in whatever form, as well as any copy thereof equally with the original, which is not in the United States shall, when duly certified as provided in section 3494 of this title, be admissible in evidence in any criminal action or proceeding in any court of the United States if the court shall find, from all the testimony taken with respect to such foreign document pursuant to a commission executed under section 3492 of this title, that such document (or the original thereof in case such document is a copy) satisfies the authentication requirements of the Federal Rules of Evidence, unless in the event that the genuineness of such document is denied, any party to such criminal action or proceeding making such denial shall establish to the satisfaction of the court that such document is not genuine. Nothing contained herein shall be deemed to require authentication under the provisions of section 3494 of this title of any such foreign documents which may otherwise be properly authenticated by law.

§ 3492. Commission to consular officers to authenticate foreign documents

(a) The testimony of any witness in a foreign country may be taken either on oral or written interrogatories, or on interrogatories partly oral and partly written, pursuant to a commission issued, as hereinafter provided, for the purpose of determining whether any foreign documents sought to be used in any criminal action or proceeding in any court of the United States are genuine, and whether the authentication requirements of the Federal Rules of Evidence are satisfied with respect to any such document (or the original thereof in case such document is a copy). Application for the issuance of a commission for such purpose may be made to the court in which such action or proceeding is pending by the United States or any other party thereto, after five days' notice in writing by the applicant party, or his attorney, to the opposite party, or his attorney of record, which notice shall state the names and addresses of witnesses whose testimony is to be taken and the time when it is desired to take such testimony. In granting such application the court shall issue a commission for the purpose of taking the testimony sought by the applicant addressed to any consular officer of the United States conveniently located for the purpose. In cases of testimony taken on oral or partly oral interrogatories, the court shall make provisions in the commission for the selection as hereinafter provided of foreign counsel to represent each party (except the United States) to the criminal action or proceeding in which the foreign documents in question are to be used, unless such party has, prior to the issuance of the commission, notified the court that he does not desire the selection of foreign counsel to represent him at the time of taking of such testimony. In cases of testimony taken on written interrogatories, such provision shall be made only upon the request of any such party prior to the issuance of such commission. Selection of foreign counsel shall be made by the party whom such foreign counsel is to represent within ten days prior to the taking of testimony or by the court from which the commission issued, upon the request of such party made within such time.

(b) Any consular officer to whom a commission is addressed to take testimony, who is interested in the outcome of the criminal action or proceeding in which the foreign documents in question are to be used or has participated in the prosecution of such action or proceeding, whether by investigations, preparation of evidence, or otherwise, may be disqualified on his own motion or on that of the United States or any other party to such criminal action or proceeding made to the court from which the commission issued at any time prior to the execution thereof. If after notice and hearing, the court grants the motion, it shall instruct the consular officer thus disqualified to send the commission to any other consular officer of the

United States named by the court, and such other officer shall execute the commission according to its terms and shall for all purposes be deemed the officer to whom the commission is addressed.

(c) The provisions of this section and sections 3493–3496 of this title applicable to consular officers shall be applicable to diplomatic officers pursuant to such regulations as may be prescribed by the President.

§ 3493. Deposition to authenticate foreign documents

The consular officer to whom any commission authorized under section 3492 of this title is addressed shall take testimony in accordance with its terms. Every person whose testimony is taken shall be cautioned and sworn to testify the whole truth and carefully examined. His testimony shall be reduced to writing or typewriting by the consular officer taking the testimony, or by some person under his personal supervision, or by the witness himself, in the presence of the consular officer and by no other person, and shall, after it has been reduced to writing or typewriting, be subscribed by the witness. Every foreign document, with respect to which testimony is taken, shall be annexed to such testimony and subscribed by each witness who appears for the purpose of establishing the genuineness of such document. When counsel for all the parties attend the examination of any witness whose testimony is to be taken on written interrogatories, they may consent that oral interrogatories in addition to those accompanying the commission may be put to the witness. The consular officer taking any testimony shall require an interpreter to be present when his services are needed or are requested by any party or his attorney

§ 3494. Certification of genuineness of foreign document

If the consular officer executing any commission authorized under section 3492 of this title shall be satisfied, upon all the testimony taken, that a foreign document is genuine, he shall certify such document to be genuine under the seal of his office. Such certification shall include a statement that he is not subject to disqualification under the provisions of section 3492 of this title. He shall thereupon transmit, by mail, such foreign documents, together with the record of all testimony taken and the commission which has been executed, to the clerk of the court from which such commission issued, in the manner in which his official dispatches are transmitted to the Government. The clerk receiving any executed commission shall open it and shall make any foreign documents and record of testimony, transmitted with such commission, available for inspection by the parties to the criminal action or proceeding in which such documents are to be used, and said parties shall be furnished copies of such documents free of charge.

§ 3495. Fees and expenses of consuls, counsel, interpreters and witnesses

(a) The consular fees prescribed under section 1201 of Title 22, for official services in connection with the taking of testimony under sections 3492–3494 of this title, and the fees of any witness whose testimony is taken shall be paid by the party who applied for the commission pursuant to which such testimony was taken. Every witness under section 3493 of this title shall be entitled to receive, for each day's attendance, fees prescribed under section 3496 of this title. Every foreign counsel selected pursuant to a commission issued on application of the United States, and every interpreter whose services are required by a consular officer under section 3493 of this title, shall be paid by the United States, such compensation, together with such personal and incidental expense upon verified statements filed with the consular officer, as he may allow. Compensation and expenses of foreign counsel selected pursuant to a commission issued on application of any party other than the United States shall be paid by the party whom such counsel represents and shall be allowed in the same manner.

(b) Whenever any party makes affidavit, prior to the issuance of a commission for the purpose of taking testimony, that he is not possessed of sufficient means and is actually unable to pay any fees and costs incurred under this section, such fees and costs shall, upon order of the court, be paid in the same manner as fees and costs are paid which are chargeable to the United States.

(c) Any appropriation available for the payment of fees and costs in the case of witnesses subpenaed in behalf of the United States in criminal cases shall be available for any fees or costs which the United States is required to pay under this section.

§ 3496. Regulations by President as to commissions, fees of witnesses, counsel and interpreters

The President is authorized to prescribe regulations governing the manner of executing and returning commissions by consular officers under the provisions of sections 3492–3494 of this title and schedules of fees allowable to witnesses, foreign counsel, and interpreters under section 3495 of this title.

§ 3497. Account as evidence of embezzlement

Upon the trial of any indictment against any person for embezzling public money it shall be sufficient evidence, prima facie, for the purpose of showing a balance against such person, to produce a transcript from the books and proceedings of the General Accounting Office.

§ 3498. Depositions—(rule)

SEE FEDERAL RULES OF CRIMINAL PROCEDURE

Time, manner and conditions of taking depositions; costs; notice; use; objections; written interrogatories, Rule 15.

Subpoenas on taking depositions, Rule 17(f).

§ 3499. Contempt of court by witness—(rule)

SEE FEDERAL RULES OF CRIMINAL PROCEDURE

Disobedience of subpoena without excuse as contempt, Rule 17(g).

§ 3500. Demands for production of statements and reports of witnesses

(a) In any criminal prosecution brought by the United States, no statement or report in the possession of the United States which was made by a Government witness or prospective Government witness (other than the defendant) shall be the subject of subpena, discovery, or inspection until said witness has testified on direct examination in the trial of the case.

(b) After a witness called by the United States has testified on direct examination, the court shall, on motion of the defendant, order the United States to produce any statement (as hereinafter defined) of the witness in the possession of the United States which relates to the subject matter as to which the witness has testified. If the entire contents of any such statement relate to the subject matter of the testimony of the witness, the court shall order it to be delivered directly to the defendant for his examination and use.

(c) If the United States claims that any statement ordered to be produced under this section contains matter which does not relate to the subject matter of the testimony of the witness, the court shall order the United States to deliver such statement for the inspection of the court in camera. Upon such delivery the court shall excise the portions of such statement which do not relate to the subject matter of the testimony of the witness. With such material excised, the court shall then direct delivery of such statement to the defendant for his use. If, pursuant to such procedure, any portion of such statement is withheld from the defendant and the defendant objects to such withholding, and the trial is continued to an adjudication of the guilt of the defendant, the entire text of such statement shall be preserved by the United States and, in the event the defendant appeals, shall be made available to the appellate court for the purpose of determining the correctness of the ruling of the trial judge. Whenever any statement is delivered to a defendant pursuant to this section, the court in its discretion, upon application of said defendant, may recess proceedings in the trial for such time as it may determine to be reasonably required for the examination of such statement by said defendant and his preparation for its use in the trial.

(d) If the United States elects not to comply with an order of the court under subsection (b) or (c) hereof to deliver to the defendant any such statement, or such portion thereof as the court may direct, the court shall strike from the record the testimony of the witness, and the trial shall proceed unless the court in its discretion shall determine that the interests of justice require that a mistrial be declared.

(e) The term "statement", as used in subsections (b), (c), and (d) of this section in relation to any witness called by the United States, means—

(1) a written statement made by said witness and signed or otherwise adopted or approved by him;

(2) a stenographic, mechanical, electrical, or other recording, or a transcription thereof, which is a substantially verbatim recital of an oral statement made by said witness and recorded contemporaneously with the making of such oral statement; or

(3) a statement, however taken or recorded, or a transcription thereof, if any, made by said witness to a grand jury.

§ 3501. Admissibility of confessions

(a) In any criminal prosecution brought by the United States or by the District of Columbia, a confession, as defined in subsection (e) hereof, shall be admissible in evidence if it is voluntarily given. Before such confession is received in evidence, the trial judge shall, out of the presence of the jury, determine any issue as to voluntariness. If the trial judge determines that the confession was voluntarily made it shall be admitted in evidence and the trial judge shall permit the jury to hear relevant evidence on the issue of voluntariness and shall instruct the jury to give such weight to the confession as the jury feels it deserves under all the circumstances.

(b) The trial judge in determining the issue of voluntariness shall take into consideration all the circumstances surrounding the giving of the confession, including (1) the time elapsing between arrest and arraignment of the defendant making the confession, if it was made after arrest and before arraignment, (2) whether such defendant knew the nature of the offense with which he was charged or of which he was suspected at the time of making the confession, (3) whether or not such defendant was advised or knew that he was not required to make any statement and that any such statement could be used against him, (4) whether or not such defendant had been advised prior to questioning of his right to the assistance of counsel; and (5) whether or not such defendant was without the assistance of counsel when questioned and when giving such confession.

The presence or absence of any of the above-mentioned factors to be taken into consideration by the judge need not be conclusive on the issue of voluntariness of the confession.

(c) In any criminal prosecution by the United States or by the District of Columbia, a confession made or given by a person who is a defendant therein, while such person was under arrest or other detention in the custody of any law-enforcement officer or law-enforcement agency, shall not be inadmissible solely because of delay in bringing such person before a magistrate or other officer empowered to commit persons charged with offenses against the laws of the United States or of the District of Columbia if such confession is found by the trial judge to have been made voluntarily and if the weight to be given the confession is left to the jury and if such confession was made or given by such person within six hours immediately following his arrest or other detention: *Provided,* That the time limitation contained in this subsection shall not apply in any case in which the delay in bringing such person before such magistrate or other officer beyond such six-hour period is found by the trial judge to be reasonable considering the means of transportation and the distance to be traveled to the nearest available such magistrate or other officer.

(d) Nothing contained in this section shall bar the admission in evidence of any confession made or given voluntarily by any person to any other person without interrogation by anyone, or at any time at which the person who made or gave such confession was not under arrest or other detention.

(e) As used in this section, the term "confession" means any confession of guilt of any criminal offense or any self-incriminating statement made or given orally or in writing.

§ 3502. Admissibility in evidence of eye witness testimony

The testimony of a witness that he saw the accused commit or participate in the commission of the crime for which the accused is being tried shall be admissible in evidence in a criminal prosecution in any trial court ordained and established under article III of the Constitution of the United States.

§ 3503. Depositions to preserve testimony

(a) Whenever due to exceptional circumstances it is in the interest of justice that the testimony of a prospective witness of a party be taken and preserved, the court at any time after the filing of an indictment or information may upon motion of such party and notice to the parties order that the testimony of such witness be taken by deposition and that any designated book, paper, document, record, recording, or other material not privileged be produced at the same time and place. If a witness is committed for failure to give bail to appear to testify at a trial or hearing, the court on written motion of the witness and upon notice to the parties may direct that his deposition be taken. After the deposition has been subscribed the court may discharge the witness. A motion by the Government to obtain an order under this section shall contain certification by the Attorney General or his designee that the legal proceeding is against a person who is believed to have participated in an organized criminal activity.

(b) The party at whose instance a deposition is to be taken shall give to every party reasonable written notice of the time and place for taking the deposition. The notice shall state the name and address of each person to be examined. On motion of a party upon whom the notice is served, the court for cause shown may extend or shorten the time or change the place for taking the deposition. The officer having custody of a defendant shall be notified of the time and place set for the examination, and shall produce him at the examination and keep him in the presence of the witness during the examination. A defendant not in custody shall have the right to be present at the examination, but his failure, absent good cause shown, to appear after notice and tender of expenses shall constitute a waiver of that right and of any objection to the taking and use of the deposition based upon that right.

(c) If a defendant is without counsel, the court shall advise him of his rights and assign counsel to represent him unless the defendant elects to proceed without counsel or is able to obtain counsel of his own choice. Whenever a deposition is taken at the instance of the Government, or whenever a deposition is taken at the instance of a defendant who appears to be unable to bear the expense of taking of the deposition, the court may direct that the expenses of travel and subsistence of the defendant and his attorney for attendance at the examination shall be paid by the Government. In such event the marshal shall make payment accordingly.

(d) A deposition shall be taken and filed in the manner provided in civil actions, provided that (1) in no event shall a deposition be taken of a party defendant without his consent, and (2) the scope of examination and cross-examination shall be such as would be allowed in the trial itself. On request or waiver by the defendant the court may direct that a deposition be taken on written interrogatories in the manner provided in civil actions. Such request shall constitute a waiver of any objection to the taking and use of the deposition based upon its being so taken.

(e) The Government shall make available to the defendant for his examination and use at the taking of the deposition any statement of the witness being deposed which is in the possession of the Government and which the Government would be required to make available to the defendant if the witness were testifying at the trial.

(f) At the trial or upon any hearing, a part or all of a deposition, so far as otherwise admissible under the rules of evidence, may be used if it appears: That the witness is dead; or that the witness is out of the United States, unless it appears that the absence of the witness was procured by the party offering the deposition; or that the witness is unable to attend or testify because of sickness or infirmity; or that the witness refuses in the trial or hearing to testify concerning the subject of the deposition or part offered; or that the party offering the deposition has been unable to procure the attendance of the witness by subpena. Any deposition may also be used by any party for the purpose of contradicting or impeaching the testimony of the deponent as a witness. If only a part of a deposition is offered in evidence by a party, an adverse party may require him to offer all of it which is relevant to the part offered and any party may offer other parts.

(g) Objections to receiving in evidence a deposition or part thereof may be made as provided in civil actions.

§ 3504. Litigation concerning sources of evidence

(a) In any trial, hearing, or other proceeding in or before any court, grand jury, department, officer, agency, regulatory body, or other authority of the United States—

(1) upon a claim by a party aggrieved that evidence is inadmissible because it is the primary product of an unlawful act or because it was obtained by the exploitation of an unlawful act,

the opponent of the claim shall affirm or deny the occurrence of the alleged unlawful act;

(2) disclosure of information for a determination if evidence is inadmissible because it is the primary product of an unlawful act occurring prior to June 19, 1968, or because it was obtained by the exploitation of an unlawful act occurring prior to June 19, 1968, shall not be required unless such information may be relevant to a pending claim of such inadmissibility; and

(3) no claim shall be considered that evidence of an event is inadmissible on the ground that such evidence was obtained by the exploitation of an unlawful act occurring prior to June 19, 1968, if such event occurred more than five years after such allegedly unlawful act.

(b) As used in this section "unlawful act" means any act the use of any electronic, mechanical, or other device (as defined in section 2510(5) of this title) in violation of the Constitution or laws of the United States or any regulation or standard promulgated pursuant thereto.

CHAPTER 225—VERDICT

§ 3531. Return; several defendants; conviction of less offense; poll of jury—(rule)

SEE FEDERAL RULES OF CRIMINAL PROCEDURE

Verdict to be unanimous; return; several defendants; disagreement; conviction of less offense; poll of jury, Rule 31.

§ 3532. Setting aside verdict of guilty; judgment notwithstanding verdict—(rule)

SEE FEDERAL RULES OF CRIMINAL PROCEDURE

Setting aside verdict of guilty on motion for judgment of acquittal, entering of such judgment, or ordering new trial; absence of verdict, Rule 29(b).

CHAPTER 227—SENTENCE, JUDGMENT, AND EXECUTION

§ 3561. Judgment form and entry—(rule)

SEE FEDERAL RULES OF CRIMINAL PROCEDURE

Judgment to be signed by judge and entered by clerk, Rule 32(b).

§ 3562. Sentence—(rule)

SEE FEDERAL RULES OF CRIMINAL PROCEDURE

Imposition of sentence; commitment; bail; presentence investigation and report, Rule 32(a, c).

§ 3563. Corruption of blood or forfeiture of estate

No conviction or judgment shall work corruption of blood or any forfeiture of estate.

§ 3564. Pillory and whipping

The punishment of whipping and of standing in the pillory shall not be inflicted.

§ 3565. Collection and payment of fines and penalties

In all criminal cases in which judgment or sentence is rendered, imposing the payment of a fine or penalty, whether alone or with any other kind of punishment, such judgment, so far as the fine or penalty is concerned, may be enforced by execution against the property of the defendant in like manner as judgments in civil cases. Where the judgment directs imprisonment until the fine or penalty imposed is paid, the issue of execution on the judgment shall not discharge the defendant from imprisonment until the amount of the judgment is paid.

§ 3566. Execution of death sentence

The manner of inflicting the punishment of death shall be that prescribed by the laws of the place within which the sentence is imposed. The United States marshal charged with the execution of the sentence may use available local facilities and the services of an appropriate local official or employ some other person for such purpose, and pay the cost thereof in an amount approved by the Attorney General. If the laws of the place within which sentence is imposed make no provision for the infliction of the penalty of death, then the court shall designate some other place in which such sentence shall be executed in the manner prescribed by the laws thereof.

§ 3567. Death sentence may prescribe dissection

The court before which any person is convicted of murder in the first degree, or rape, may, in its discretion, add to the judgment of death, that the body of the offender be delivered to a surgeon for dissection; and the marshal who executes such judgment shall deliver the body, after execution, to such surgeon as the court may direct; and such surgeon, or some person appointed by him, shall receive and take away the body at the time of execution.

§ 3568. Effective date of sentence

The sentence of imprisonment of any person convicted of an offense shall commence to run from the date on which such person is received at the penitentiary, reformatory, or jail for service of such sentence. The Attorney General shall give any such person credit toward service of his sentence for any days spent in custody in connection with the offense or acts for which sentence was imposed. As used in this section, the term "offense" means any criminal offense, other than an offense triable by court-martial, military commission, provost court, or other military tribunal, which is in violation of an Act of Congress and is triable in any court established by Act of Congress.

If any such person shall be committed to a jail or other place of detention to await transportation to the place at which his sentence is to be served, his sentence shall commence to run from the date on which he is received at such jail or other place of detention.

No sentence shall prescribe any other method of computing the term.

§ 3569. Discharge of indigent prisoner

(a) When a poor convict, sentenced for violation of any law of the United States by any court established by enactment of Congress, to be imprisoned and pay a fine, or fine and costs, or to pay a fine, or fine and costs, has been confined in prison thirty days, solely for the nonpayment of such fine, or fine and costs, such convict may make application in writing to the nearest United States magistrate in the district where he is imprisoned setting forth his inability to pay such fine, or fine and costs, and after notice to the district attorney of the United States, who may appear, offer evidence, and be heard, the commissioner shall proceed to hear and determine the matter.

If on examination it shall appear to him that such convict is unable to pay such fine, or fine and costs, and that he has not any property exceeding $20 in value, except such as is by law exempt from being taken on execution for debt, the magistrate shall administer to him the following oath: "I do solemnly swear that I have not any property, real or personal, exceeding $20, except such as is by law exempt from being taken on civil process for debt; and that I have no property in any way conveyed or concealed, or in any way disposed of, for my future use or benefit. So help me God." Upon taking such oath such convict shall be discharged; and the magistrate shall file with the institution in which the convict is confined, a certificate setting forth the facts. In case the convict is found by the magistrate to possess property valued at an amount in excess of said exemption, nevertheless, if the Attorney General finds that the retention by such convict of all of such property is reasonably necessary for his support or that of his family, such convict shall be released without further imprisonment solely for the nonpayment of such fine, or fine and costs; or if he finds that the retention by such convict of any part of such property is reasonably necessary for his support or that of his family, such convict shall be released without further imprisonment solely for nonpayment of such fine or fine and costs upon payment on account of his fine and costs, of that portion of his property in excess of the amount found to be reasonably necessary for his support or that of his family.

(b) Any such indigent prisoner in a Federal institution may, in the first instance, make his application to the warden of such institution, who shall have all the powers of a United States magistrate in such matters, and upon proper showing in support of the application shall administer the oath required by subsection (a) of this section, discharge the prisoner, and file his certificate to that effect in the records of the institution.

Any such indigent prisoner, to whom the warden shall fail or refuse to administer the oath may apply to the nearest magistrate for the relief authorized by this section and the magistrate shall proceed de novo to hear and determine the matter.

§ 3570. Presidential remission as affecting unremitted part

Whenever, by the judgment of any court or judicial officer of the United States, in any criminal proceeding, any person is sentenced to two kinds of punishment, the one pecuniary and the other corporal, the President's remission in whole or in part of either kind shall not impair the legal validity of the other kind, or of any portion of either kind, not remitted.

§ 3571. Clerical mistakes—(rule)

SEE FEDERAL RULES OF CRIMINAL PROCEDURE

Court empowered to correct clerical mistakes in judgments, orders, or record, Rule 36.

§ 3572. Correction or reduction of sentence—(rule)

SEE FEDERAL RULES OF CRIMINAL PROCEDURE

Court empowered to correct or reduce sentence; time; Rule 35.

§ 3573. Arrest or setting aside of judgment—(rule)

SEE FEDERAL RULES OF CRIMINAL PROCEDURE

Arrest of judgment, grounds and motion, time, Rule 34.
Setting aside judgment and permitting withdrawal of plea of guilty, Rule 32(d).

§ 3574. Stay of execution; supersedeas—(rule)

SEE FEDERAL RULES OF CRIMINAL PROCEDURE

Death or imprisonment sentence, fines stayed on appeal; conditions and power of court, Rule 38(a).

§ 3575. Increased sentence for dangerous special offenders

(a) Whenever an attorney charged with the prosecution of a defendant in a court of the United States for an alleged felony committed when the defendant was over the age of twenty-one years has reason to believe that the defendant is a dangerous special offender such attorney, a reasonable time before trial or acceptance by the court of a plea of guilty or nolo contendere, may sign and file with the court, and may amend, a notice (1) specifying that the defendant is a dangerous special offender who upon conviction for such felony is subject to the imposition of a sentence under subsection (b) of this section, and (2) setting out with particularity the reasons why such attorney believes the defendant to be a dangerous special offender. In no case shall the fact that the defendant is alleged to be a dangerous special offender be an issue upon the trial of such felony, be disclosed to the jury, or be disclosed before any plea of guilty or nolo contendere or verdict or finding of guilty to the presiding judge without the consent of the parties. If the court finds that the filing of the notice as a public record may prejudice fair consideration of a pending criminal matter, it may order the notice sealed and the notice shall not be subject to subpena or public inspection during the pendency of such criminal matter, except on order of the court, but shall be subject to inspection by the defendant alleged to be a dangerous special offender and his counsel.

(b) Upon any plea of guilty or nolo contendere or verdict or finding of guilty of the defendant of such felony, a hearing shall be held, before sentence is imposed, by the court sitting without a jury. The court shall fix a time for the hearing, and notice thereof shall be given to the defendant and the United States at least ten days prior thereto. The court shall permit the United States and counsel for the defendant, or the defendant if he is not represented by counsel, to inspect the presentence report sufficiently prior to the hearing as to afford a reasonable opportunity for verification. In extraordinary cases, the court may withhold material not relevant to a proper sentence, diagnostic opinion which might seriously disrupt a program of rehabilitation, any source of information obtained on a promise of confidentiality, and material previously disclosed in open court. A court withholding all or part of a presentence report shall inform the parties of its action and place in the record the reasons therefor. The court may require parties inspecting all or part of a presentence report to give notice of any part thereof intended to be controverted. In connection with the hearing, the defendant and the United States shall be entitled to assistance of counsel, compulsory process, and cross-examination of such witnesses as appear at the hearing. A duly authenticated copy of a former judgment or commitment shall be prima facie evidence of such former judgment or commitment. If it appears by a preponderance of the information, including information submitted during the trial of such felony and the sentencing hearing and so much of the presentence report as the court relies upon, that the defendant is a dangerous special offender, the court shall sentence the defendant to imprisonment for an appropriate term not to exceed twenty-five years and not disproportionate in severity to the maximum term otherwise authorized by law for such felony. Otherwise it shall sentence the defendant in accordance with the law prescribing penalties for such felony. The court shall place in the record its findings, including an identification of the information relied upon in making such findings, and its reasons for the sentence imposed.

(c) This section shall not prevent the imposition and execution of a sentence of death or of imprisonment for life or for a term exceeding twenty-five years upon any person convicted of an offense so punishable.

(d) Notwithstanding any other provision of this section, the court shall not sentence a dangerous special offender to less than any mandatory minimum penalty prescribed by law for such felony. This section shall not be construed as creating any mandatory minimum penalty.

(e) A defendant is a special offender for purposes of this section if—

(1) the defendant has previously been convicted in courts of the United States, a State, the District of Columbia, the Commonwealth of Puerto Rico, a territory or possession of the United States, any political subdivision, or any department, agency, or instrumentality thereof for two or more offenses committed on occasions different from one another and from such felony and punishable in such courts by death or imprisonment in excess of one year, for one or more of such convictions the defendant has been imprisoned prior to the commission of such felony, and less than five years have elapsed between the commission of such felony and either the defendant's release, on parole or otherwise, from imprisonment for one such conviction or his commission of the last such previous offense or another offense punishable by death or imprisonment in excess of one year under applicable laws of the United States, a State, the District of Columbia, the Commonwealth of Puerto Rico, a territory or possession of the United States, any political subdivision, or any department, agency or instrumentality thereof; or

(2) the defendant committed such felony as part of a pattern of conduct which was criminal under applicable laws of any jurisdiction, which constituted a substantial source of his income, and in which he manifested special skill or expertise; or

(3) such felony was, or the defendant committed such felony in furtherance of, a conspiracy with three or more other persons to engage in a pattern of conduct criminal under applicable laws of any jurisdiction, and the defendant did, or agreed that he would, initiate, organize, plan, finance, direct, manage, or supervise all or part of such conspiracy or conduct, or give or receive a bribe or use force as all or part of such conduct.

A conviction shown on direct or collateral review or at the hearing to be invalid or for which the defendant has been pardoned on the ground of innocence shall be disregarded for purposes of paragraph (1) of this subsection. In support of findings under paragraph (2) of this subsection, it may be shown that the defendant has had in his own name or under his control income or property not explained as derived from a source other than such conduct. For purposes of paragraph (2) of this subsection, a substantial source of income means a source of income which for any period of one year or more exceeds the minimum wage, determined on the basis of a forty-hour week and a fifty-week year, without reference to exceptions, under section 6(a) (1) of the Fair Labor Standards Act of 1938 (52 Stat. 1602, as amended 80 Stat. 838), and as hereafter amended, for an employee engaged in commerce or in the production of goods for commerce, and which for the same period exceeds fifty percent of the defendant's declared adjusted gross income under section 62 of the Internal Revenue Act of 1954 (68A Stat. 17, as amended 83 Stat. 655), and as hereafter amended. For purposes of paragraph (2) of this subsection, special skill or expertise in criminal conduct includes unusual knowledge, judgment or ability, including manual dexterity, facilitating the initiation, organizing, planning, financing, direction, management, supervision, execution or concealment of criminal conduct, the enlistment of accomplices in such conduct, the escape from detection or apprehension for such conduct, or the disposition of the fruits or proceeds of such conduct. For purposes of paragraphs (2) and (3) of this subsection, criminal conduct forms a pattern if it embraces criminal acts that have the same or similar purposes, results, participants, victims, or methods of commission, or otherwise are interrelated by distinguishing characteristics and are not isolated events.

(f) A defendant is dangerous for purposes of this section if a period of confinement longer than that provided for such felony is required for the protection of the public from further criminal conduct by the defendant.

(g) The time for taking an appeal from a conviction for which sentence is imposed after proceedings under this section shall be measured from imposition of the original sentence.

§ 3576. Review of sentence

With respect to the imposition, correction, or reduction of a sentence after proceedings under section 3575 of this chapter, a review of the sentence on the record of the sentencing court may be taken by the defendant or the United States to a court of appeals. Any review of the sentence taken by the United States shall be taken at least five days before expiration of the time for taking a review of the sentence or appeal of the conviction by the defendant and shall be diligently prosecuted. The sentencing court may, with or without motion and notice, extend the time for taking a review of the sentence for a period not to exceed thirty days from the expiration of the time otherwise prescribed by law. The court shall not extend the time for taking a review of the sentence by the United States after the time has expired. A court extended the time for taking a review of the sentence by the United States shall extend the time for taking a review of the sentence or appeal of the conviction by the defendant for the same period. The taking of a review of the sentence by the United States shall be deemed the taking of a review of the sentence and an appeal of the conviction by the defendant. Review of the sentence shall include review of whether the procedure employed was lawful, the findings made were clearly erroneous, or the sentencing court's discretion was abused. The court of appeals on review of the sentence may, after considering the record, including the entire presentence report, information submitted during the trial of such felony and the sentencing hearing, and the findings and reasons of the sentencing court, affirm the sentence, impose or direct the imposition of any sentence which the sentencing court could originally have imposed, or remand for further sentencing proceedings and imposition of sentence, except that a sentence may be made more severe only on review of the sentence taken by the United States and after hearing. Failure of the United States to take a review of the imposition of the sentence shall, upon review taken by the United States of the correction or reduction of the sentence, foreclose imposition of a sentence more severe than that previously imposed. Any withdrawal or dismissal of review of the sentence taken by the United States shall foreclose imposition of a sentence more severe than that reviewed but shall not otherwise foreclose the review of the sentence or the appeal of the conviction. The court of appeals shall state in writing the reasons for its disposition of the review of the sentence. Any review of the sentence taken by the United States may be dismissed on a showing of abuse of the right of the United States to take such review.

§ 3577. Use of information for sentencing

No limitation shall be placed on the information concerning the background, character, and conduct of a person convicted of an offense which a court of the United States may receive and consider for the purpose of imposing an appropriate sentence.

§ 3578. Conviction records

(a) The Attorney General of the United States is authorized to establish in the Department of Justice a repository for records of convictions and determinations of the validity of such convictions.

(b) Upon the conviction thereafter of a defendant in a court of the United States, the District of Columbia, the Commonwealth of Puerto Rico, a territory or possession of the United States, any political subdivision, or any department, agency, or instrumentality thereof for an offense punishable in such court by death or imprisonment in excess of one year, or a judicial determination of the validity of such conviction on collateral review, the court shall cause a certified record of the conviction or determination to be made to the repository in such form and containing such information as the Attorney General of the United States shall by regulation prescribe.

(c) Records maintained in the repository shall not be public records. Certified copies thereof—

(1) may be furnished for law enforcement purposes on request of a court or law enforcement or corrections officer of the United States, the District of Columbia, the Commonwealth of Puerto Rico, a territory or possession of the United States, any political subdivision, or any department, agency, or instrumentality thereof;

(2) may be furnished for law enforcement purposes on request of a court or law enforcement or corrections officer of a State, any political subdivision, or any department, agency, or instrumentality thereof, if a statute of such State requires that, upon the conviction of a defendant in a court of the State or any political subdivision thereof for an offense punishable in such court by death or imprisonment in excess of one year, or a judicial determination of the validity of such conviction on collateral review, the court cause a certified record of the conviction or determination to be made to the repository in such form and containing such information as the Attorney General of the United States shall by regulation prescribe; and

(3) shall be prima facie evidence in any court of the United States, the District of Columbia, the Commonwealth of Puerto Rico, a territory or possession of the United States, any political subdivision, or any department, agency, or instrumentality thereof, that the convictions occurred and whether they have been judicially determined to be invalid on collateral review.

(d) The Attorney General of the United States shall give reasonable public notice, and afford to interested parties opportunity for hearing, prior to prescribing regulations under this section.

§ 3579. Order of restitution

(a)(1) The court, when sentencing a defendant convicted of an offense under this title or under subsection (h), (i), (j), or (n) of section 902 of the Federal Aviation Act of 1958 (49 U.S.C. 1472), may order, in addition to or in lieu of any other penalty authorized by law, that the defendant make restitution to any victim of the offense.

(2) If the court does not order restitution, or orders only partial restitution, under this section, the court shall state on the record the reasons therefor.

(b) The order may require that such defendant—

(1) in the case of an offense resulting in damage to or loss or destruction of property of a victim of the offense—

(A) return the property to the owner of the property or someone designated by the owner; or

(B) if return of the property under subparagraph (A) is impossible, impractical, or inadequate, pay an amount equal to the greater of—

(i) the value of the property on the date of the damage, loss, or destruction, or

(ii) the value of the property on the date of sentencing,

less the value (as of the date the property is returned) of any part of the property that is returned;

(2) in the case of an offense resulting in bodily injury to a victim—

(A) pay an amount equal to the cost of necessary medical and related professional services and devices relating to physical, psychiatric, and psychological care, including nonmedical care and treatment rendered in accordance with a method of healing recognized by the law of the place of treatment;

(B) pay an amount equal to the cost of necessary physical and occupational therapy and rehabilitation; and

(C) reimburse the victim for income lost by such victim as a result of such offense;

(3) in the case of an offense resulting in bodily injury also results in the death of a victim, pay an amount equal to the cost of necessary funeral and related services; and

(4) in any case, if the victim (or if the victim is deceased, the victim's estate) consents, make restitution in services in lieu of money, or make restitution to a person or organization designated by the victim or the estate.

(c) If the Court decides to order restitution under this section, the court shall, if the victim is deceased, order that the restitution be made to the victim's estate.

(d) The court shall impose an order of restitution to the extent that such order is as fair as possible to the victim and the imposition of such order will not unduly complicate or prolong the sentencing process.

(e)(1) The court shall not impose restitution with respect to a loss for which the victim has received or is to receive compensation, except that the court may, in the interest of justice, order restitution to any person who has compensated the victim for such loss to the extent that such person paid the compensation. An order of restitution shall require that all restitution to victims under such order be made before any restitution to any other person under such order is made.

(2) Any amount paid to a victim under an order of restitution shall be set off against any amount later recovered as compensatory damages by such victim in—

(A) any Federal civil proceeding; and

(B) any State civil proceeding, to the extent provided by the law of that State.

(f)(1) The court may require that such defendant make restitution under this section within a specified period or in specified installments.

(2) The end of such period or the last such installment shall not be later than—

(A) the end of the period of probation, if probation is ordered;

(B) five years after the end of the term of imprisonment imposed, if the court does not order probation; and

(C) five years after the date of sentencing in any other case.

(3) If not otherwise provided by the court under this subsection, restitution shall be made immediately.

(g) If such defendant is placed on probation or paroled under this title, any restitution ordered under this section shall be a condition of such probation or parole. The court may revoke probation and the Parole Commission may revoke parole if the defendant fails to comply with such order. In determining whether to revoke probation or parole, the court or Parole Commission shall consider the defendant's employment status, earning ability, financial resources, the willfulness of the defendant's failure to pay, and any other special circumstances that may have a bearing on the defendant's ability to pay.

(h) An order of restitution may be enforced by the United States or a victim named in the order to receive the restitution in the same manner as a judgment in a civil action.

§ 3580. Procedure for isusing order of restitution

(a) The court, in determining whether to order restitution under section 3579 of this title and the amount of such restitution, shall consider the amount of the loss sustained by any victim as a result of the offense, the financial resources of the defendant, the financial needs and earning ability of the defendant and the defendant's dependents, and such other factors as the court deems appropriate.

(b) The court may order the probation service of the court to obtain information pertaining to the factors set forth in subsection (a) of this section. The probation service of the court shall include the information collected in the report of presentence investigation or in a separate report, as the court directs.

(c) The court shall disclose to both the defendant and the attorney for the Government all portions of the presentence or other report pertaining to the matters described in subsection (a) of this section.

(d) Any dispute as to the proper amount or type of restitution shall be resolved by the court by the preponderance of the evidence. The burden of demonstrating the amount of the loss sustained by a victim as a result of the offense shall be on the attorney for the Government. The burden of demonstrating the financial resources of the defendant and the financial needs of the defendant and such defendant's dependents shall be on the defendant. The burden of demonstrating such other matters as the court deems appropriate shall be upon the party designated by the court as justice requires.

(e) A conviction of a defendant for an offense involving the act giving rise to restitution under this section shall estop the defendant from denying the essential allegations of that offense in any subsequent Federal civil proceeding or State civil proceeding, to the extent consistent with State law, brought by the victim.

CHAPTER 231—PROBATION

Sec.

§ 3651. Suspension of sentence and probation

Upon entering a judgment of conviction of any offense not punishable by death or life imprisonment, any court having jurisdiction to try offenses against the United States when satisfied that the ends of justice and the best interest of the public as well as the defendant will be served thereby, may suspend the imposition or execution of sentence and place the defendant on probation for such period and upon such terms and conditions as the court deems best.

Upon entering a judgment of conviction of any offense not punishable by death or life imprisonment, if the maximum punishment provided for such offense is more than six months, any court having jurisdiction to try offenses against the United States, when satisfied that the ends of justice and the best interest of the public as well as the defendant will be served thereby, may impose a sentence in excess of six months and provide that the defendant be confined in a jail-type institution or a treatment institution for a period not exceeding six months and that the execution of the remainder of the sentence be suspended and the defendant placed on probation for such period and upon such terms and conditions as the court deems best.

Probation may be granted whether the offense is punishable by fine or imprisonment or both. If an offense is punishable by both fine and imprisonment, the court may impose a fine and place the defendant on probation as to imprisonment. Probation may be limited to one or more counts or indictments, but, in the absence of express limitation, shall extend to the entire sentence and judgment.

The court may revoke or modify any condition of probation, or may change the period of probation.

The period of probation, together with any extension thereof, shall not exceed five years.

While on probation and among the conditions thereof, the defendant—

May be required to pay a fine in one or several sums; and

May be required to make restitution or reparation to aggrieved parties for actual damages or loss caused by the offense for which conviction was had; and

May be required to provide for the support of any persons, for whose support he is legally responsible.

The court may require a person as conditions of probation to reside in or participate in the program of a residential community treatment center, or both, for all or part of the period of probation: *Provided,* That the Attorney General certifies that adequate treatment facilities, personnel, and programs are available. If the Attorney General determines that the person's residence in the center or participation in its program, or both, should be terminated, because the person can derive no further significant benefits from such residence or participation, or both, or because his such residence or participation adversely affects the rehabilitation of other residents or participants, he shall so notify the court, which shall thereupon, by order, make such other provision with respect to the person on probation as it deems appropriate.

A person residing in a residential community treatment center may be required to pay such costs incident to residence as the Attorney General deems appropriate.

The court may require a person who is an addict within the meaning of section 4251(a) of this title, or a drug dependent person within the meaning of section 2(q) of the Public Health Service Act, as amended (42 U.S.C. § 201), as a condition of probation, to participate in the community supervision programs authorized by section 4255 of this title for all or part of the period of probation.

The defendant's liability for any fine or other punishment imposed as to which probation is granted, shall be fully discharged by the fulfillment of the terms and conditions of probation.

§ 3652. Probation—(rule)

SEE FEDERAL RULES OF CRIMINAL PROCEDURE

Probation as provided by law, Rule 32(e).
Presentence investigation, Rule 32(c).

§ 3653. Report of probation officer and arrest of probationer

When directed by the court, the probation officer shall report to the court, with a statement of the conduct of the probationer while on probation. The court may thereupon discharge the probationer from further supervision and may terminate the proceedings against him, or may extend the probation, as shall seem advisable.

Whenever during the period of his probation, a probationer heretofore or hereafter placed on probation, goes from the district in which he is being supervised to another district, jurisdiction over him may be transferred, in the discretion of the court, from the court for the district from which he goes to the court for the other district, with the concurrence of the latter court. Thereupon the court for the district to which jurisdiction is transferred shall have all power with respect to the probationer that was previously possessed by the court for the district from which the transfer is made, except that the period of probation shall not be changed without the consent of the sentencing court. This process under the same conditions may be repeated whenever during the period of his probation the probationer goes from the district in which he is being supervised to another district.

At any time within the probation period, the probation officer may for cause arrest the probationer wherever found, without a warrant. At any time within the probation period, or within the maximum probation period permitted by section 3651 of this title, the court for the district in which the probationer is being supervised or if he is no longer under supervision, the court for the district in which he was last under supervision, may issue a warrant for his arrest for violation of probation occurring during the probation period. Such warrant may be executed in any district by the probation officer or the United States marshal of the district in which the warrant was issued or of any district in which the probationer is found. If the probationer shall be arrested in any district other than that in which he was last supervised, he shall be returned to the district in which the warrant was issued, unless jurisdiction over him is transferred as above provided to the district in which he is found, and in that case he shall be detained pending further proceedings in such district.

As speedily as possible after arrest the probationer shall be taken before the court for the district having jurisdiction over him. Thereupon the court may revoke the probation and require him to serve the sentence imposed, or any lesser sentence, and, if imposition of sentence was suspended, may impose any sentence which might originally have been imposed.

§ 3654. Appointment and removal of probation officers

Any court having original jurisdiction to try offenses against the United States may appoint one or more suitable persons to serve as probation officers within the jurisdiction and under the direction of the court making such appointment.

All such probation officers shall serve without compensation except that in case it shall appear to the court that the needs of the service require that there should be salaried probation officers, such court may appoint such officers.

Such court may in its discretion remove a probation officer serving in such court.

The appointment of a probation officer shall be in writing and shall be entered on the records of the court, and a copy of the order of appointment shall be delivered to the officer so appointed and a copy sent to the Director of the Administrative Office of the United States Courts.

Whenever such court shall have appointed more than one probation officer, one may be designated chief probation officer and shall direct the work of all probation officers serving in such court.

§ 3655. Duties of probation officers

The probation officer shall furnish to each probationer under his supervision a written statement of the conditions of probation and shall instruct him regarding the same.

He shall keep informed concerning the conduct and condition of each probationer under his supervision and shall report thereon to the court placing such person on probation.

He shall use all suitable methods, not inconsistent with the conditions imposed by the court, to aid probationers and to bring about improvements in their conduct and condition.

He shall keep records of his work; shall keep accurate and complete accounts of all moneys collected from persons under his supervision; shall give receipts therefor, and shall make at least monthly returns thereof; shall make such reports to the Director of the Administrative Office of the United States Courts as he may at any time require; and shall perform such other duties as the court may direct.

Each probation officer shall perform such duties with respect to persons on parole as the United States Parole Commission shall request.

§ 3656. Duties of Director of Administrative Office of the United States Courts

The Director of the Administrative Office of the United States Courts, or his authorized agent, shall investigate the work of the probation officers and make recommendations concerning the same to the respective judges and shall have access to the records of all probation officers.

He shall collect for publication statistical and other information concerning the work of the probation officers.

He shall prescribe record forms and statistics to be kept by the probation officers and shall formulate general rules for the proper conduct of the probation work.

He shall endeavor by all suitable means to promote the efficient administration of the probation system and the enforcement of the probation laws in all United States courts.

He shall, under the supervision and direction of the Judicial Conference of the United States, fix the salaries of probation officers and shall provide for their necessary expenses including clerical service and travel expenses.

He shall incorporate in his annual report a statement concerning the operation of the probation system in such courts.

CHAPTER 233—CONTEMPTS

§ 3691. Jury trial of criminal contempts

Whenever a contempt charged shall consist in willful disobedience of any lawful writ, process, order, rule, decree, or command of any district court of the United States by doing or omitting any act or thing in violation thereof, and the act or thing done or omitted also constitutes a criminal offense under any Act of Congress, or under the laws of any state in which it was done or omitted, the accused, upon demand therefor, shall be entitled to trial by a jury, which shall conform as near as may be to the practice in other criminal cases.

This section shall not apply to contempts committed in the presence of the court, or so near thereto as to obstruct the administration of justice, nor to contempts committed in disobedience of any lawful writ, process, order, rule, decree, or command entered in any suit or action brought or prosecuted in the name of, or on behalf of, the United States.

§ 3692. Jury trial for contempt in labor dispute cases

In all cases of contempt arising under the laws of the United States governing the issuance of injunctions or restraining orders in any case involving or growing out of a labor dispute, the accused shall enjoy the right to a speedy and public trial by an impartial jury of the State and district wherein the contempt shall have been committed.

This section shall not apply to contempts committed in the presence of the court or so near thereto as to interfere directly with the administration of justice nor to the misbehavior, misconduct, or disobedience of any officer of the court in respect to the writs, orders or process of the court.

§ 3693. Summary disposition or jury trial; notice—(rule)

SEE FEDERAL RULES OF CRIMINAL PROCEDURE

Summary punishment; certificate of judge; order; notice; jury trial; bail; disqualification of judge, Rule 42.

CHAPTER 235—APPEAL

§ 3731. Appeal by United States

In a criminal case an appeal by the United States shall lie to a court of appeals from a decision, judgment, or order of a district court dismissing an indictment or information as to any one or more counts, except that no appeal shall lie where the double jeopardy clause of the United States Constitution prohibits further prosecution.

An appeal by the United States shall lie to a court of appeals from a decision or order of a district court suppressing or excluding evidence or requiring the return of seized property in a criminal proceeding, not made after the defendant has been put in jeopardy and before the verdict or finding on an indictment or information, if the United States attorney certifies to the district court that the appeal is not taken for purpose of delay and that the evidence is a substantial proof of a fact material in the proceeding.

The appeal in all such cases shall be taken within thirty days after the decision, judgment or order has been rendered and shall be diligently prosecuted.

Pending the prosecution and determination of the appeal in the foregoing instances, the defendant shall be released in accordance with chapter 207 of this title.

The provisions of this section shall be liberally construed to effectuate its purposes.

§ 3732. Taking of appeal; notice; time—(rule)*

§ 3733. Assignment of errors—(rule)*

* In connection with §§ 3732-3740, see FEDERAL RULES OF APPELLATE PROCEDURE.

§ 3734. Bill of exceptions abolished—(rule)*

§ 3735. Bail on appeal or certiorari—(rule)*

§ 3736. Certiorari—(rule)*

§ 3737. Record—(rule)*

§ 3738. Docketing appeal and record—(rule)*

§ 3739. Supervision—(rule)*

§ 3740. Argument—(rule)*

§ 3741. Harmless error and plain error—(rule)

SEE FEDERAL RULES OF CRIMINAL PROCEDURE

Error or defect as affecting substantial rights, Rule 52.
Defects in indictment, Rule 7.
Waiver of error, Rules 12(b) (2) and 30.

CHAPTER 237—RULES OF CRIMINAL PROCEDURE

§ 3771. Procedure to and including verdict

The Supreme Court of the United States shall have the power to prescribe, from time to time, rules of pleading, practice, and procedure with respect to any or all proceedings prior to and including verdict, or finding of guilty or not guilty by the court if a jury has been waived, or plea of guilty, in criminal cases and proceedings to punish for criminal contempt of court in the United States district courts, in the district courts for the district of the Canal Zone and the Virgin Islands, in the Supreme Court of Puerto Rico, and in proceedings before United States commissioners. Such rules shall not take effect until they have been reported to Congress by the Chief Justice at or after the beginning of a regular session thereof but not later than the first day of May, and until the expiration of ninety days after they have been thus reported. All laws in conflict with such rules shall be of no further force or effect after such rules have taken effect.

Nothing in this title, anything therein in the contrary notwithstanding, shall in any way limit, supersede, or repeal any such rules heretofore prescribed by the Supreme Court.

§ 3772. Procedure after verdict

The Supreme Court of the United States shall have the power to prescribe, from time to time, rules of practice and procedure with respect to any or all proceedings after verdict, or finding of guilt by

* In connection with §§ 3732–3740, see FEDERAL RULES OF APPELLATE PROCEDURE.

the court if a jury has been waived, or plea of guilty, in criminal cases and proceedings to punish for criminal contempt in the United States district courts, in the district courts for the District of the Canal Zone and the Virgin Islands, in the Supreme Court of Puerto Rico, in the United States courts of appeals, and in the Supreme Court of the United States. This section shall not give the Supreme Court power to abridge the right of the accused to apply for withdrawal of a plea of guilty, if such application be made within ten days after entry of such plea, and before sentence is imposed.

The right of appeal shall continue in those cases in which appeals are authorized by law, but the rules made as herein authorized may prescribe the times for and manner of taking appeals and applying for writs of certiorari and preparing records and bills of exceptions and the conditions on which supersedeas or bail may be allowed.

The Supreme Court may fix the dates when such rules shall take effect and the extent to which they shall apply to proceedings then pending, and after they become effective all laws in conflict therewith shall be of no further force.

Nothing in this title, anything therein to the contrary notwithstanding, shall in any way limit, supersede, or repeal any such rules heretofore prescribed by the Supreme Court.

PART V—IMMUNITY OF WITNESSES

Sec.

§ 6001. Definitions

As used in this part—

(1) "agency of the United States" means any executive department as defined in section 101 of title 5, United States Code, a military department as defined in section 102 of title 5, United States Code, the Atomic Energy Commission, the China Trade Act registrar appointed under 53 Stat. 1432 (15 U.S.C. § 143), the Civil Aeronautics Board, the Commodity Futures Trading Commission, the Federal Communications Commission, the Federal Deposit Insurance Corporation, the Federal Maritime Commission the Federal Power Commission, the Federal Trade Commission, the Interstate Commerce Commission, the National Labor Relations Board, the National Transportation Safety Board, the Railroad Retirement Board, an arbitration board established under 48 Stat. 1193 (45 U.S.C. § 157), the Securities and Exchange Commission, the Subversive Activities Control Board, or a board established under 49 Stat. 31 (15 U.S.C. § 715d);

(2) "other information" includes any book, paper, document, record, recording, or other material;

(3) "proceeding before an agency of the United States" means any proceeding before such an agency with respect to which it is authorized to issue subpenas and to take testimony or receive other information from witnesses under oath; and

(4) "court of the United States" means any of the following courts: the Supreme Court of the United States, a United States court of appeals, a United States district court established under chapter 5, title 28, United States Code, a United States bankruptcy court established under chapter 6, title 28, United States Code, the District of Columbia Court of Appeals, the Superior Court of the District of Columbia, the District Court of Guam, the District Court of the Virgin Islands, the United States Claims Court, the Tax Court of the United States, the Court of International Trade and the Court of Military Appeals.

§ 6002. Immunity generally

Whenever a witness refuses, on the basis of his privilege against self-incrimination, to testify or provide other information in a proceeding before or ancillary to—

(1) a court or grand jury of the United States,

(2) an agency of the United States, or

(3) either House of Congress, a joint committee of the two Houses, or a committee or a subcommittee of either House,

and the person presiding over the proceeding communicates to the witness an order issued under this part, the witness may not refuse to comply with the order on the basis of his privilege against self-incrimination; but no testimony or other information compelled under the order (or any information directly or indirectly derived from such testimony or other information) may be used against the witness in any criminal case, except a prosecution for perjury, giving a false statement, or otherwise failing to comply with the order.

§ 6003. Court and grand jury proceedings

(a) In the case of any individual who has been or may be called to testify or provide other information at any proceeding before or ancillary to a court of the United States or a grand jury of the United States, the United States district court for the judicial district in which the proceeding is or may be held shall issue, in accordance with subsection (b) of this section, upon the request of the United States attorney for such district, an order requiring such individual to give testimony or provide other information which he refuses to give or provide on the basis of his privilege against self-incrimination, such order to become effective as provided in section 6002 of this part.

(b) A United States attorney may, with the approval of the Attorney General, the Deputy Attorney General, or any designated Assistant Attorney General, request an order under subsection (a) of this section when in his judgment—

(1) the testimony or other information from such individual may be necessary to the public interest; and

(2) such individual has refused or is likely to refuse to testify or provide other information on the basis of his privilege against self-incrimination.

§ 6004. Certain administrative proceedings

(a) In the case of any individual who has been or who may be called to testify or provide other information at any proceeding before an agency of the United States, the agency may, with the approval of the Attorney General, issue, in accordance with subsection (b) of this section, an order requiring the individual to give testimony or provide other information which he refuses to give or provide on the basis of his privilege against self-incrimination, such order to become effective as provided in section 6002 of this part.

(b) An agency of the United States may issue an order under subsection (a) of this section only if in its judgment—

(1) the testimony or other information from such individual may be necessary to the public interest; and

(2) such individual has refused or is likely to refuse to testify or provide other information on the basis of his privilege against self-incrimination.

§ 6005. Congressional proceedings

(a) In the case of any individual who has been or may be called to testify or provide other information at any proceeding before either House of Congress, or any committee, or any subcommittee of either House, or any joint committee of the two Houses, a United States district court shall issue, in accordance with subsection (b) of this section, upon the request of a duly authorized representative of the House of Congress or the committee concerned, an order requiring such individual to give testimony or provide other information which he refuses to give or provide on the basis of his privilege against self-incrimination, such order to become effective as provided in section 6002 of this part.

(b) Before issuing an order under subsection (a) of this section, a United States district court shall find that—

(1) in the case of a proceeding before either House of Congress, the request for such an order has been approved by an affirmative vote of a majority of the Members present of that House;

(2) in the case of a proceeding before a committee or a subcommittee of either House of Congress or a joint committee of both Houses, the request for such an order has been approved by an affirmative vote of two-thirds of the members of the full committee; and

(3) ten days or more prior to the day on which the request for such an order was made, the Attorney General was served with notice of an intention to request the order

(c) Upon application of the Attorney General, the United States district court shall defer the issuance of any order under subsection (a) of this section for such period, not longer than twenty days from the date of the request for such order, as the Attorney General may specify.

FEDERAL
RULES OF CIVIL PROCEDURE
FOR THE
UNITED STATES DISTRICT COURTS

WITH AMENDMENTS TO AUGUST 1, 1983

Editorial Note: By the Act of June 19, 1934, 48 Stat. 1064, Congress authorized the Supreme Court to prescribe uniform rules of civil procedure for the federal district courts. The Act provided:

"* * * That the Supreme Court of the United States shall have the power to prescribe, by general rules, for the district courts of the United States and for the courts of the District of Columbia, the forms of process, writs, pleadings, and motions, and the practice and procedure in civil actions at law. Said rules shall neither abridge, enlarge, nor modify the substantive rights of any litigant. They shall take effect six months after their promulgation, and thereafter all laws in conflict therewith shall be of no further force or effect.

"Sec. 2. The court may at any time unite the general rules prescribed by it for cases in equity with those in actions at law so as to secure one form of civil action and procedure for both: *Provided, however,* That in such union of rules the right of trial by jury as at common law and declared by the seventh amendment to the Constitution shall be preserved to the parties inviolate. Such united rules shall not take effect until they shall have been reported to Congress by the Attorney General at the beginning of a regular session thereof and until after the close of such session. [Act of June 19, 1943, c. 651, Secs. 1, 2, 48 Stat. 1064.]"

In 1935, the Court appointed an advisory committee of lawyers, judges and law teachers to assist it in preparing rules pursuant to this authority. After extensive consultation with the bar and long consideration by both committee and Court, a set of 84 rules was approved by the Court, and became effective on September 16, 1938, in accordance with the Act. (308 U.S. 645).

The Rules remained in force for more than eight years without change, save for an amendment extending their application to proceedings under the Longshoremen's and Harbor Workers' Compensation Act. In 1942, however, the advisory committee undertook a thorough examination of the operation of the Rules, which culminated in the adoption by the Court of numerous amendments, effective March 19, 1948. (329 U.S. 839). On December 29, 1948, the Court adopted a further series of amendments, largely formal, to conform with the revision of Title 28 of the United States Code. These amendments were transmitted by the Attorney General to the Eighty-first Congress at the beginning of its first regular session, in accordance with Title 28, U.S.C. § 2072, and took effect at the close of that session. (335 U.S. 919). Thereafter, the Rules were amended by the addition of Rule 71A on condemnation procedure, with accompanying forms, effective August 1, 1951. (341 U.S. 959). On October 1, 1956, the Advisory Committee was discharged and the Court's order of January 5, 1942, making the Committee a continuing body, was revoked. (352 U.S. 803.)

A new dispensation began with the enactment by Congress of the Act of July 11, 1958, amending 28 U.S.C. § 331, p. 21, *supra*. The amendment directed the Judicial Conference of the United States to "carry on a continuous study of the operation and effect of the general rules of practice and procedure now or hereafter in use as prescribed by the Supreme Court for the other courts of the United States pursuant to law," and from time to time to recommend desirable changes in the rules "to the Supreme Court for its consideration and adoption, modification or rejection, in accordance with law." Thereafter, Chief Justice Warren, as Chairman of the Judicial Conference, announced the appointment of a Standing Committee on Rules of Practice and Procedure, and of a series of Advisory Committees on Civil Rules, Criminal Rules, Admiralty Rules, General Orders in Bankruptcy, and Appellate Rules, respectively together with a Special Committee on Evidence. Each of the committees was composed of judges, lawyers, and law teachers. The various Advisory Committees and the Special Committee, for each of which a reporter was appointed, were directed to conduct basic studies and to develop reports and recommendations for the Standing Committee which in turn would transmit its own recommendations to the Conference for further proceedings in accordance with the statute. Three substantive amendments to the Rules of Civil Procedure, effective July 19, 1961, were the first product of this new procedure (368 U.S. 1009). Additional amendments became effective on July 1, 1963 (374 U.S. 861), July 1, 1966 (383 U.S. 1029), July 1, 1968 (389 U.S. 1121), July 1, 1970 (398 U.S. 977), and July 1, 1971 (401 U.S. 1021).

Former Chapter 14, entitled Appeals, was abrogated by the Supreme Court, effective July 1, 1968, the subject being covered by the new Federal Rules of Appellate Procedure.

RULES OF CIVIL PROCEDURE

In the orders of November 20, 1972, and December 18, 1972, undertaking to prescribe Federal Rules of Evidence, the Supreme Court also prescribed amendments of Rules 30(c), 43 and 44.1 of the Federal Rules of Civil Procedure and abrogated Rule 32(c). The controversy about the Rules of Evidence led to the enactment of Pub.L. 93–12 of March 30, 1973, postponing the effective date of the rules and amendments until Congress should "expressly approve" them. By the Act of January 2, 1975, Pub. L. 93–595, 88 Stat. 1926, rules of evidence were enacted in statutory form. The Act also provided that "Congress expressly approves the amendments to the Federal Rules of Civil Procedure . . . embraced by" the Supreme Court orders and fixed their effective date in 180 days. See 419 U.S. 1133.

Additional amendments transmitted to Congress by the Court in accordance with 28 U.S.C. § 2072 on April 29, 1980, and April 28, 1983, took effect on August 1, 1980, and August 1, 1983, respectively; and Congress itself enacted an amendment to Rule 4 on January 12, 1983. Pub.L. 97–462, 96 Stat. 2527. All these amendments are incorporated in the rules as they appear below.

TABLE OF RULES

VIII. Provisional and Final Remedies and Special Proceedings—Continued

TABLE OF RULES

SUPPLEMENTAL RULES FOR CERTAIN ADMIRALTY AND MARITIME CLAIMS

TABLE OF RULES

FEDERAL
RULES OF CIVIL PROCEDURE
FOR THE
UNITED STATES DISTRICT COURTS

I. SCOPE OF RULES—ONE FORM OF ACTION

Rule 1.
SCOPE OF RULES

These rules govern the procedure in the United States district courts in all suits of a civil nature whether cognizable as cases at law or in equity or in admiralty, with the exceptions stated in Rule 81. They shall be construed to secure the just, speedy, and inexpensive determination of every action.

Rule 2.
ONE FORM OF ACTION

There shall be one form of action to be known as "civil action"

II. COMMENCEMENT OF ACTION; SERVICE OF PROCESS, PLEADINGS, MOTIONS AND ORDERS

Rule 3.
COMMENCEMENT OF ACTION

A civil action is commenced by filing a complaint with the court.

Rule 4.
PROCESS

(a) Summons: Issuance. Upon the filing of the complaint the clerk shall forthwith issue a summons and deliver the summons to the plaintiff or the plaintiff's attorney, who shall be responsible for prompt service of the summons and a copy of the complaint. Upon request of the plaintiff separate or additional summons shall issue against any defendants.

(b) Same: Form. The summons shall be signed by the clerk, be under the seal of the court, contain the name of the court and the names of the parties, be directed to the defendant, state the name and address of the plaintiff's attorney, if any, otherwise the plaintiff's address, and the time within which these rules require the defendant to appear and defend, and shall notify him that in case of his failure to do so judgment by default will be rendered against him for the relief demanded in the complaint. When, under Rule 4(e), service is made pursuant to a statute or rule of court of a state, the summons, or notice, or order in lieu of summons shall correspond as nearly as may be to that required by the statute or rule.

(c) Service

(1) Process, other than a subpoena or a summons and complaint, shall be served by a United States marshal or deputy United States marshal, or by a person specially appointed for that purpose.

(2)(A) A summons and complaint shall, except as provided in subparagraphs (B) and (C) of this paragraph, be served by any person who is not a party and is not less than 18 years of age.

(B) A summons and complaint shall, at the request of the party seeking service or such party's attorney, be served by a United States marshal or deputy United States marshal, or by a person specially appointed by the court for that purpose, only—

(i) on behalf of a party authorized to proceed in forma pauperis pursuant to Title 28, U.S.C. § 1915, or of a seaman authorized to proceed under Title 28, U.S.C. § 1916,

(ii) on behalf of the United States or an officer or agency of the United States, or

(iii) pursuant to an order issued by the court stating that a United States marshal or deputy United States marshal, or a person specially appointed for that purpose, is required to serve the summons and complaint in order that service be properly effected in that particular action.

(C) A summons and complaint may be served upon a defendant of any class referred to in paragraph (1) or (3) of subdivision (d) of this rule—

(i) pursuant to the law of the State in which the district court is held for the service of summons or other like process upon such defendant in an action brought in the courts of general jurisdiction of that State, or

(ii) by mailing a copy of the summons and of the complaint (by first-class mail, postage prepaid) to the person to be served, together with two copies of a notice and acknowledgment conforming substantially to form 18–A and a return envelope, postage prepaid, addressed to the sender. If no acknowledgment of service under this subdivision of this rule is received by the sender within 20 days after the date of mailing, service of such summons and complaint shall be made under subparagraph (A) or (B) of this paragraph in the manner prescribed by subdivision (d)(1) or (d)(3).

(D) Unless good cause is shown for not doing so the court shall order the payment of the costs of personal service by the person served if such person does not complete and return within 20 days after mailing, the notice and acknowledgment of receipt of summons.

(E) The notice and acknowledgment of receipt of summons and complaint shall be executed under oath or affirmation.

(3) The court shall freely make special appointments to serve summonses and complaints under paragraph (2)(B) of this subdivision of this rule and all other process under paragraph (1) of this subdivision of this rule.

(d) Summons and Complaint: Person to be Served. The summons and complaint shall be served together. The plaintiff shall furnish the person making service with such copies as are necessary. Service shall be made as follows:

(1) Upon an individual other than an infant or an incompetent person, by delivering a copy of the summons and of the complaint to him personally or by leaving copies thereof at his dwelling house or usual place of abode with some person of suitable age and discretion then residing therein or by delivering a copy of the summons and of the complaint to an agent authorized by appointment or by law to receive service of process.

(2) Upon an infant or an incompetent person, by serving the summons and complaint in the manner prescribed by the law of the state in which the service is made for the service of summons or other like process upon any such defendant in an action brought in the courts of general jurisdiction of that state.

(3) Upon a domestic or foreign corporation or upon a partnership or other unincorporated association which is subject to suit under a common name, by delivering a copy of the summons and

of the complaint to an officer, a managing or general agent, or to any other agent authorized by appointment or by law to receive service of process and, if the agent is one authorized by statute to receive service and the statute so requires, by also mailing a copy to the defendant.

(4) Upon the United States, by delivering a copy of the summons and of the complaint to the United States attorney for the district in which the action is brought or to an assistant United States attorney or clerical employee designated by the United States attorney in a writing filed with the clerk of the court and by sending a copy of the summons and of the complaint by registered or certified mail to the Attorney General of the United States at Washington, District of Columbia, and in any action attacking the validity of an order of an officer or agency of the United States not made a party, by also sending a copy of the summons and of the complaint by registered or certified mail to such officer or agency.

(5) Upon an officer or agency of the United States, by serving the United States and by sending a copy of the summons and of the complaint by registered or certified mail to such officer or agency. If the agency is a corporation the copy shall be delivered as provided in paragraph (3) of this subdivision of this rule.

(6) Upon a state or municipal corporation or other governmental organization thereof subject to suit, by delivering a copy of the summons and of the complaint to the chief executive officer thereof or by serving the summons and complaint in the manner prescribed by the law of that state for the service of summons or other like process upon any such defendant.

(e) Summons: Service Upon Party Not Inhabitant of or Found Within State. Whenever a statute of the United States or an order of court thereunder provides for service of a summons, or of a notice, or of an order in lieu of summons upon a party not an inhabitant of or found within the state in which the district court is held, service may be made under the circumstances and in the manner prescribed by the statute or order, or, if there is no provision therein prescribing the manner of service, in a manner stated in this rule. Whenever a statute or rule of court of the state in which the district court is held provides (1) for service of a summons, or of a notice, or of an order in lieu of summons upon a party not an inhabitant of or found within the state, or (2) for service upon or notice to him to appear and respond or defend in an action by reason of the attachment or garnishment or similar seizure of his property located within the state, service may in either case be made under the circumstances and in the manner prescribed in the statute or rule.

(f) Territorial Limits of Effective Service. All process other than a subpoena may be served anywhere within the territorial limits of the state in which the district court is held, and, when authorized by a statute of the United States or by these rules, beyond the territorial limits of that state. In addition, persons who are brought in as parties pursuant to Rule 14, or as additional parties to a pending action or a counterclaim or cross-claim therein pursuant to Rule 19, may be served in the manner stated in paragraphs (1)–(6) of subdivision (d) of this rule at all places outside the state but within the United States that are not more than 100 miles from the place in which the action is commenced, or to which it is assigned or transferred for trial; and persons required to respond to an order of commitment for civil contempt may be served at the same places. A subpoena may be served within the territorial limits provided in Rule 45.

(g) Return. The person serving the process shall make proof of service thereof to the court promptly and in any event within the time during which the person served must respond to the process. If service is made by a person other than a United States marshal or deputy United States marshal, such person shall make affidavit thereof. If service is made under subdivision (c)(2)(C)(ii) of this rule, return shall be made by the sender's filing with the court the acknowledgment received pursuant to such subdivision. Failure to make proof of service does not affect the validity of the service.

(h) Amendment. At any time in its discretion and upon such terms as it deems just, the court may allow any process or proof of service thereof to be amended, unless it clearly appears that material prejudice would result to the substantial rights of the party against whom the process issued.

(i) Alternative Provisions for Service in a Foreign Country.

(1) Manner. When the federal or state law referred to in subdivision (e) of this rule authorizes service upon a party not an inhabitant of or found within the state in which the district court is held, and service is to be effected upon the party in a foreign country, it is also sufficient if service of the summons and complaint is made: (A) in the manner prescribed by the law of the foreign country for service in that country in an action in any of its courts of general jurisdiction; or (B) as directed by

the foreign authority in response to a letter rogatory, when service in either case is reasonably calculated to give actual notice; or (C) upon an individual, by delivery to him personally, and upon a corporation or partnership or association, by delivery to an officer, a managing or general agent; or (D) by any form of mail, requiring a signed receipt, to be addressed and dispatched by the clerk of the court to the party to be served; or (E) as directed by order of the court. Service under (C) or (E) above may be made by any person who is not a party and is not less than 18 years of age or who is designated by order of the district court or by the foreign court. On request, the clerk shall deliver the summons to the plaintiff for transmission to the person or the foreign court or officer who will make the service.

(2) Return. Proof of service may be made as prescribed by subdivision (g) of this rule, or by the law of the foreign country, or by order of the court. When service is made pursuant to subparagraph (1) (D) of this subdivision, proof of service shall include a receipt signed by the addressee or other evidence of delivery to the addressee satisfactory to the court.

(j) Summons: Time Limit for Service. If a service of the summons and complaint is not made upon a defendant within 120 days after the filing of the complaint and the party on whose behalf such service was required cannot show good cause why such service was not made within that period, the action shall be dismissed as to that defendant without prejudice upon the court's own initiative with notice to such party or upon motion. This subdivision shall not apply to service in a foreign country pursuant to subdivision (i) of this rule.

Rule 5.

SERVICE AND FILING OF PLEADINGS AND OTHER PAPERS

(a) Service: When Required. Except as otherwise provided in these rules, every order required by its terms to be served, every pleading subsequent to the original complaint unless the court otherwise orders because of numerous defendants, every paper relating to discovery required to be served upon a party unless the court otherwise orders, every written motion other than one which may be heard ex parte, and every written notice, appearance, demand, offer of judgment, designation of record on appeal, and similar paper shall be served upon each of the parties. No service need be made on parties in default for failure to appear except that pleadings asserting new or additional claims for relief against them shall be served upon them in the manner provided for service of summons in Rule 4.

In an action begun by seizure of property, in which no person need be or is named as defendant, any service required to be made prior to the filing of an answer, claim, or appearance shall be made upon the person having custody or possession of the property at the time of its seizure.

(b) Same: How Made. Whenever under these rules service is required or permitted to be made upon a party represented by an attorney the service shall be made upon the attorney unless service upon the party himself is ordered by the court. Service upon the attorney or upon a party shall be made by delivering a copy to him or by mailing it to him at his last known address or, if no address is known, by leaving it with the clerk of the court. Delivery of a copy within this rule means: handing it to the attorney or to the party; or leaving it at his office with his clerk or other person in charge thereof; or, if there is no one in charge, leaving it in a conspicuous place therein; or, if the office is closed or the person to be served has no office, leaving it at his dwelling house or usual place of abode with some person of suitable age and discretion then residing therein. Service by mail is complete upon mailing.

(c) Same: Numerous Defendants. In any action in which there are unusually large numbers of defendants, the court, upon motion or of its own initiative, may order that service of the pleadings of the defendants and replies thereto need not be made as between the defendants and that any cross-claim, counterclaim, or matter constituting an avoidance or affirmative defense contained therein shall be deemed to be denied or avoided by all other parties and that the filing of any such pleading and service thereof upon the plaintiff constitutes due notice of it to the parties. A copy of every such order shall be served upon the parties in such manner and form as the court directs.

(d) Filing. All papers after the complaint required to be served upon a party shall be filed with the court either before service or within a reasonable time thereafter, but the court may on motion of a party or on its own initiative order that depositions upon oral examination and interrogatories, requests for documents, requests for admission, and answers and responses thereto not be filed unless on order of the court or for use in the proceeding.

(e) Filing With the Court Defined. The filing of pleadings and other papers with the court as required by these rules shall be made by filing them with the clerk of the court, except that the judge may permit the papers to be filed with him, in which event he shall note thereon the filing date and forthwith transmit them to the office of the clerk.

Rule 6.

TIME

(a) Computation. In computing any period of time prescribed or allowed by these rules, by the local rules of any district court, by order of court, or by any applicable statute, the day of the act, event, or default from which the designated period of time begins to run shall not be included. The last day of the period so computed shall be included, unless it is a Saturday, a Sunday, or a legal holiday, in which event the period runs until the end of the next day which is not a Saturday, a Sunday, or a legal holiday. When the period of time prescribed or allowed is less than 7 days, intermediate Saturdays, Sundays, and legal holidays shall be excluded in the computation. As used in this rule and in Rule 77(c), "legal holiday" includes New Year's Day, Washington's Birthday, Memorial Day, Independence Day, Labor Day, Columbus Day, Veterans Day, Thanksgiving Day, Christmas Day, and any other day appointed as a holiday by the President or the Congress of the United States, or by the state in which the district court is held.

(b) Enlargement. When by these rules or by a notice given thereunder or by order of court an act is required or allowed to be done at or within a specified time, the court for cause shown may at any time in its discretion (1) with or without motion or notice order the period enlarged if request therefor is made before the expiration of the period originally prescribed or as extended by a previous order, or (2) upon motion made after the expiration of the specified period permit the act to be done where the failure to act was the result of excusable neglect; but it may not extend the time for taking any action under Rules 50(b) and (c)(2), 52(b), 59(b), (d) and (e), 60(b), and 74(a), except to the extent and under the conditions stated in them.

[(c) **Rescinded.**]

(d) For Motions—Affidavits. A written motion, other than one which may be heard ex parte, and notice of the hearing thereof shall be served not later than 5 days before the time specified for the hearing, unless a different period is fixed by these rules or by order of the court. Such an order may for cause shown be made on ex parte application. When a motion is supported by affidavit, the affidavit shall be served with the motion; and, except as otherwise provided in Rule 59(c), opposing affidavits may be served not later than 1 day before the hearing, unless the court permits them to be served at some other time.

(e) Additional Time After Service by Mail. Whenever a party has the right or is required to do some act or take some proceedings within a prescribed period after the service of a notice or other paper upon him and the notice or paper is served upon him by mail, 3 days shall be added to the prescribed period.

III. PLEADINGS AND MOTIONS

Rule 7.

PLEADINGS ALLOWED; FORM OF MOTIONS

(a) Pleadings. There shall be a complaint and an answer; a reply to a counterclaim denominated as such; an answer to a cross-claim, if the answer contains a cross-claim; a third-party complaint, if a person who was not an original party is summoned under the provisions of Rule 14; and a third-party answer, if a third-party complaint is served. No other pleading shall be allowed, except that the court may order a reply to an answer or a third-party answer.

(b) Motions and Other Papers.

(1) An application to the court for an order shall be by motion which, unless made during a hearing or trial, shall be made in writing, shall state with particularity the grounds therefor, and shall set forth the relief or order sought. The requirement of writing is fulfilled if the motion is stated in a written notice of the hearing of the motion.

(2) The rules applicable to captions and other matters of form of pleadings apply to all motions and other papers provided for by these rules.

(3) All motions shall be signed in accordance with Rule 11.

(c) Demurrers, Pleas, Etc., Abolished. Demurrers, pleas, and exceptions for insufficiency of a pleading shall not be used.

Rule 8.

GENERAL RULES OF PLEADING

(a) Claims for Relief. A pleading which sets forth a claim for relief, whether an original claim, counterclaim, cross-claim, or third-party claim, shall contain (1) a short and plain statement of the grounds upon which the court's jurisdiction depends, unless the court already has jurisdiction and the claim needs no new grounds of jurisdiction to support it, (2) a short and plain statement of the claim showing that the pleader is entitled to relief, and (3) a demand for judgment for the relief to which he deems himself entitled. Relief in the alternative or of several different types may be demanded.

(b) Defenses; Form of Denials. A party shall state in short and plain terms his defenses to each claim asserted and shall admit or deny the averments upon which the adverse party relies. If he is without knowledge or information sufficient to form a belief as to the truth or an averment, he shall so state and this has the effect of a denial. Denials shall fairly meet the substance of the averments denied. When a pleader intends in good faith to deny only a part or a qualification of an averment, he shall specify so much of it as is true and material and shall deny only the remainder. Unless the pleader intends in good faith to controvert all the averments of the preceding pleading, he may make his denials as specific denials of designated averments or paragraphs, or he may generally deny all the averments except such designated averments or paragraphs as he expressly admits; but, when he does so intend to controvert all its averments, including averments of the grounds upon which the court's jurisdiction depends, he may do so by general denial subject to the obligations set forth in Rule 11.

(c) Affirmative Defenses. In pleading to a preceding pleading, a party shall set forth affirmatively accord and satisfaction, arbitration and award, assumption of risk, contributory negligence, discharge in bankruptcy, duress, estoppel, failure of consideration, fraud, illegality, injury by fellow servant, laches, license, payment, release, res judicata, statute of frauds, statute of limitations, waiver, and any other matter constituting an avoidance or affirmative defense. When a party has mistakenly designated a defense as a counterclaim or a counterclaim as a defense, the court on terms, if justice so requires, shall treat the pleading as if there had been a proper designation.

(d) Effect of Failure to Deny. Averments in a pleading to which a responsive pleading is required, other than those as to the amount of damage, are admitted when not denied in the responsive pleading. Averments in a pleading to which no responsive pleading is required or permitted shall be taken as denied or avoided.

(e) Pleading to be Concise and Direct; Consistency.

(1) Each averment of a pleading shall be simple, concise, and direct. No technical forms of pleading or motions are required.

(2) A party may set forth two or more statements of a claim or defense alternately or hypothetically, either in one count or defense or in separate counts or defenses. When two or more statements are made in the alternative and one of them if made independently would be sufficient, the pleading is not made insufficient by the insufficiency of one or more of the alternative statements. A party may also state as many separate claims or defenses as he has regardless of consistency and whether based on legal, equitable, or maritime grounds. All statements shall be made subject to the obligations set forth in Rule 11.

(f) Construction of Pleadings. All pleadings shall be so construed as to do substantial justice.

Rule 9.

PLEADING SPECIAL MATTERS

(a) Capacity. It is not necessary to aver the capacity of a party to sue or be sued or the authority of a party to sue or be sued in a representative capacity or the legal existence of an organized association of persons that is made a party, except to the extent required to show the jurisdiction of the court. When a party desires to raise an issue as to the legal existence of any party or the capacity of any party to sue or be sued or the authority of a party to sue or be sued in a representative capacity, he shall do so by specific negative averment, which shall include such supporting particulars as are peculiarly within the pleader's knowledge.

(b) Fraud, Mistake, Condition of the Mind. In all averments of fraud or mistake, the circumstances constituting fraud or mistake shall be stated with particularity. Malice, intent, knowledge, and other condition of mind of a person may be averred generally.

(c) Conditions Precedent. In pleading the performance or occurrence of conditions precedent, it is sufficient to aver generally that all conditions precedent have been performed or have occurred. A denial of performance or occurrence shall be made specifically and with particularity.

(d) Official Document or Act. In pleading an official document or official act it is sufficient to aver that the document was issued or the act done in compliance with law.

(e) Judgment. In pleading a judgment or decision of a domestic or foreign court, judicial or quasi-judicial tribunal, or of a board or officer, it is sufficient to aver the judgment or decision without setting forth matter showing jurisdiction to render it.

(f) Time and Place. For the purpose of testing the sufficiency of a pleading, averments of time and place are material and shall be considered like all other averments of material matter.

(g) Special Damage. When items of special damage are claimed, they shall be specifically stated.

(h) Admiralty and Maritime Claims. A pleading or count setting forth a claim for relief within the admiralty and maritime jurisdiction that is also within the jurisdiction of the district court on some other ground may contain a statement identifying the claim as an admiralty or maritime claim for the purposes of Rules 14(c), 38(e), 82, and the Supplemental Rules for Certain Admiralty and Maritime Claims. If the claim is cognizable only in admiralty, it is an admiralty or maritime claim for those purposes whether so identified or not. The amendment of a pleading to add or withdraw an identifying statement is governed by the principles of Rule 15. The reference in Title 28, U.S.C., § 1292(a) (3), to admiralty cases shall be construed to mean admiralty and maritime claims within the meaning of this subdivision (h).

Rule 10.

FORM OF PLEADINGS

(a) Caption; Names of Parties. Every pleading shall contain a caption setting forth the name of the court, the title of the action, the file number, and a designation as in Rule 7(a). In the complaint the title of the action shall include the names of all the parties, but in other pleadings it is sufficient to state the name of the first party on each side with an appropriate indication of other parties.

(b) Paragraphs; Separate Statements. All averments of claim or defense shall be made in numbered paragraphs, the contents of each of which shall be limited as far as practicable to a statement of a single set of circumstances; and a paragraph may be referred to by number in all succeeding pleadings. Each claim founded upon a separate transaction or occurrence and each defense other than denials shall be stated in a separate count or defense whenever a separation facilitates the clear presentation of the matters set forth.

(c) Adoption by Reference; Exhibits. Statements in a pleading may be adopted by reference in a different part of the same pleading or in another pleading or in any motion. A copy of any written instrument which is an exhibit to a pleading is a part thereof for all purposes.

Rule 11.

SIGNING OF PLEADINGS, MOTIONS, AND OTHER PAPERS; SANCTIONS

Every pleading, motion, and other paper of a party represented by an attorney shall be signed by at least one attorney of record in his individual name, whose address shall be stated. A party who is not represented by an attorney shall sign his pleading, motion, or other paper and state his address. Except when otherwise specifically provided by rule or statute, pleadings need not be verified or accompanied by affidavit. The rule in equity that the averments of an answer under oath must be overcome by the testimony of two witnesses or of one witness sustained by corroborating circumstances is abolished. The signature of an attorney or party constitutes a certificate by him that he has read the pleading, motion, or other paper; that to the best of his knowledge, information, and belief formed after reasonable inquiry it is well grounded in fact and is warranted by existing law or a good faith argument for the extension, modification, or reversal of existing law, and that it is not interposed for any improper purpose, such as to harass or to cause unnecessary delay or needless increase in the cost of litigation. If a pleading, motion, or other paper is not signed, it shall be stricken unless it is signed promptly after the omission is called to the attention of the pleader or movant. If a pleading, motion, or other paper is signed in violation of this rule, the court, upon motion or upon its own initiative, shall impose upon the person who signed it, a represented party, or both, an appropriate sanction, which may include an order to pay to the other party or parties the amount of the reasonable expenses incurred because of the filing of the pleading, motion, or other paper, including a reasonable attorney's fee.

Rule 12.

DEFENSES AND OBJECTIONS—WHEN AND HOW PRESENTED—BY PLEADING OR MOTION—MOTION FOR JUDGMENT ON THE PLEADINGS

(a) When Presented. A defendant shall serve his answer within 20 days after the service of the summons and complaint upon him, except when service is made under Rule 4(e) and a different time is prescribed in the order of court under the statute of the United States or in the statute or rule of court of the state. A party served with a pleading stating a cross-claim against him shall serve an answer thereto within 20 days after the service upon him. The plaintiff shall serve his reply to a counterclaim in the answer within 20 days after service of the answer or, if a reply is ordered by the court, within 20 days after service of the order, unless the order otherwise directs. The United States or an officer or agency thereof shall serve an answer to the complaint or to a cross-claim, or a reply to a counterclaim, within 60 days after the service upon the United States attorney of the pleading in which the claim is asserted. The service of a motion permitted under this rule alters these periods to time as follows, unless a different time is fixed by order of the court: (1) if the court denies the motion or postpones its disposition until the trial on the merits, the responsive pleading shall be served within 10 days after notice of the court's action; (2) if the court grants a motion for a more definite statement the responsive pleading shall be served within 10 days after the service of the more definite statement.

(b) How Presented. Every defense, in law or fact, to a claim for relief in any pleading, whether a claim, counterclaim, cross-claim, or third-party claim, shall be asserted in the responsive pleading thereto if one is required, except that the following defenses may at the option of the pleader be made by motion: (1) lack of jurisdiction over the subject matter, (2) lack of jurisdiction over the person, (3) improper venue, (4) insufficiency of process, (5) insufficiency of service of process, (6) failure to state a claim upon which relief can be granted, (7) failure to join a party under Rule 19. A motion making any of these defenses shall be made before pleading if a further pleading is permitted. No defense or objection is waived by being joined with one or more other defenses or objections in a responsive pleading or motion. If a pleading sets forth a claim for relief to which the adverse party is not required to serve a responsive pleading, he may assert at the trial any defense in law or fact to that claim for relief. If, on a motion asserting the defense numbered (6) to dismiss for failure of the pleading to state a claim upon which relief can be granted, matters outside the pleading are presented to and not excluded by the court, the motion shall be treated as one for summary judgment and disposed of as provided in Rule 56, and all parties shall be given reasonable opportunity to present all material made pertinent to such a motion by Rule 56.

(c) Motion for Judgment on the Pleadings. After the pleadings are closed but within such time as not to delay the trial, any party may move for judgment on the pleadings. If, on a motion for judgment on the pleadings, matters outside the pleadings are presented to and not excluded by the court, the motion shall be treated as one for summary judgment and disposed of as provided in Rule 56, and all parties shall be given reasonable opportunity to present all material made pertinent to such a motion by Rule 56.

(d) Preliminary Hearings. The defenses specifically enumerated (1)—(7) in subdivision (b) of this rule, whether made in a pleading or by motion, and the motion for judgment mentioned in subdivision (c) of this rule shall be heard and determined before trial on application of any party, unless the court orders that the hearing and determination thereof be deferred until the trial.

(e) Motion for More Definite Statement. If a pleading to which a responsive pleading is permitted is so vague or ambiguous that a party cannot reasonably be required to frame a responsive pleading, he may move for a more definite statement before interposing his responsive pleading. The motion shall point out the defects complained of and the details desired. If the motion is granted and the order of the court is not obeyed within 10 days after notice of the order or within such other time as the court may fix, the court may strike the pleading to which the motion was directed or make such order as it deems just.

(f) Motion to Strike. Upon motion made by a party before responding to a pleading or, if no responsive pleading is permitted by these rules, upon motion made by a party within 20 days after the service of the pleading upon him or upon the court's own initiative at any time, the court may order stricken from any pleading any insufficient defense or any redundant, immaterial, impertinent, or scandalous matter.

(g) Consolidation of Defenses in Motion. A party who makes a motion under this rule may join with it any other motions herein provided for and then available to him. If a party makes a motion under this rule but omits therefrom any defense or objection then available to him which this rule permits to be raised by motion, he shall not thereafter make a motion based on the defense or objection so omitted, except a motion as provided in subdivision (h) (2) hereof on any of the grounds there stated.

(h) Waiver or Preservation of Certain Defenses. (1) A defense of lack of jurisdiction over the person, improper venue, insufficiency of process, or insufficiency of service of process is waived (A) if omitted from a motion in the circumstances described in subdivision (g), or (B) if it is neither made by motion under this rule nor included in a responsive pleading or an amendment thereof permitted by Rule 15(a) to be made as a matter of course.

(2) A defense of failure to state a claim upon which relief can be granted, a defense of failure to join a party indispensable under Rule 19, and an objection of failure to state a legal defense to a claim may be made in any pleading permitted or ordered under Rule 7(a), or by motion for judgment on the pleadings, or at the trial on the merits.

(3) Whenever it appears by suggestion of the parties or otherwise that the court lacks jurisdiction of the subject matter, the court shall dismiss the action.

Rule 13.

COUNTERCLAIM AND CROSS-CLAIM

(a) Compulsory Counterclaims. A pleading shall state as a counterclaim any claim which at the time of serving the pleading the pleader has against any opposing party, if it arises out of the transaction or occurrence that is the subject matter of the opposing party's claim and does not require for its adjudication the presence of third parties of whom the court cannot acquire jurisdiction. But the pleader need not state the claim if (1) at the time the action was commenced the claim was the subject of another pending action, or (2) the opposing party brought suit upon his claim by attachment or other process by which the court did not acquire jurisdiction to render a personal judgment on that claim, and the pleader is not stating any counterclaim under this Rule 13.

(b) Permissive Counterclaims. A pleading may state as a counterclaim any claim against an opposing party not arising out of the transaction or occurrence that is the subject matter of the opposing party's claim.

(c) Counterclaim Exceeding Opposing Claim. A counterclaim may or may not diminish or defeat the recovery sought by the opposing party. It may claim relief exceeding in amount or different in kind from that sought in the pleading of the opposing party.

(d) Counterclaim Against the United States. These rules shall not be construed to enlarge beyond the limits now fixed by law the right to assert counterclaims or to claim credits against the United States or an officer or agency thereof.

(e) Counterclaim Maturing or Acquired After Pleading. A claim which either matured or was acquired by the pleader after serving his pleading may, with the permission of the court, be presented as a counterclaim by supplemental pleading.

(f) Omitted Counterclaim. When a pleader fails to set up a counterclaim through oversight, inadvertence, or excusable neglect, or when justice requires, he may by leave of court set up the counterclaim by amendment.

(g) Cross-Claim Against Co-Party. A pleading may state as a cross-claim any claim by one party against a co-party arising out of the transaction or occurrence that is the subject matter either of the original action or of a counterclaim therein or relating to any property that is the subject matter of the original action. Such cross-claim may include a claim that the party against whom it is asserted is or may be liable to the cross-claimant for all or part of a claim asserted in the action against the cross-claimant.

(h) Joinder of Additional Parties. Persons other than those made parties to the original action may be made parties to a counterclaim or cross-claim in accordance with the provisions of Rules 19 and 20.

(i) Separate Trials; Separate Judgments. If the court orders separate trials as provided in Rule 42(b), judgment on a counterclaim or cross-claim may be rendered in accordance with the terms of Rule 54(b) when the court has jurisdiction so to do, even if the claims of the opposing party have been dismissed or otherwise disposed of.

Rule 14.

THIRD-PARTY PRACTICE

(a) When Defendant May Bring in Third Party. At any time after commencement of the action a defending party, as a third-party plaintiff, may cause a summons and complaint to be served upon a person not a party to the action who is or may be liable to him for all or part of the plaintiff's claim against him. The third-party plaintiff need not obtain leave to make the service if he files the third-party complaint not later than 10 days after he serves his original answer. Otherwise he must obtain leave on motion upon notice to all parties to the action. The person served with the summons and third-party complaint, hereinafter called the third-party defendant, shall make his defenses to the third-party plaintiff's claim as provided in Rule 12 and his counterclaims against the third-party plaintiff and cross-claims against other third-party defendants as provided in Rule 13. The third-party defendant may assert against the plaintiff any defenses which the third-party plaintiff has to the plaintiff's claim. The third-party defendant may also assert any claim against the plaintiff arising out of the transaction or occurrence that is the subject matter of the plaintiff's claim against the third-party plaintiff. The plaintiff may assert any claim against the third-party defendant arising out of the transaction or occurrence that is the subject matter of the plaintiff's claim against the third-party plaintiff, and the third-party defendant thereupon shall assert his defenses as provided in Rule 12 and his counterclaims and cross-claims as provided in Rule 13. Any party may move to strike the third-party claim, or for its severance or separate trial. A third-party defendant may proceed under this rule against any person not a party to the action who is or may be liable to him for all or part of the claim made in the action against the third-party defendant. The third-party complaint, if within the admiralty and maritime jurisdiction, may be in rem against a vessel, cargo, or other property subject to admiralty or maritime process in rem, in which case references in this rule to the summons include the warrant of arrest, and references to the third-party plaintiff or defendant include, where appropriate, the claimant of the property arrested.

(b) When Plaintiff May Bring in Third Party. When a counterclaim is asserted against a plaintiff, he may cause a third party to be brought in under circumstances which under this rule would entitle a defendant to do so.

(c) Admiralty and Maritime Claims. When a plaintiff asserts an admiralty or maritime claim within the meaning of Rule 9(h), the defendant or claimant, as a third-party plaintiff, may bring in a third-party defendant who may be wholly or partly liable, either to the plaintiff or to the third-party plaintiff, by way of remedy over, contribution, or otherwise on account of the same transaction, occurrence, or series of transactions or occurrences. In such a case the third-party plaintiff may also demand judgment against the third-party defendant in favor of the plaintiff, in which event the third-party defendant shall make his defenses to the claim of the plaintiff as well as to that of the third-party plaintiff in the manner provided in Rule 12 and the action shall proceed as if the plaintiff had commenced it against the third-party defendant as well as the third-party plaintiff.

Rule 15.

AMENDED AND SUPPLEMENTAL PLEADINGS

(a) Amendments. A party may amend his pleading once as a matter of course at any time before a responsive pleading is served or, if the pleading is one to which no responsive pleading is permitted and the action has not been placed upon the trial calendar, he may so amend it at any time within 20 days after it is served. Otherwise a party may amend his pleading only by leave of court or by written consent of the adverse party; and leave shall be freely given when justice so requires. A party shall plead in response to an amended pleading within the time remaining for response to the original pleading or within 10 days after service of the amended pleading, whichever period may be the longer, unless the court otherwise orders.

(b) Amendments to Conform to the Evidence. When issues not raised by the pleadings are tried by express or implied consent of the parties, they shall be treated in all respects as if they had been raised in the pleadings. Such amendment of the pleadings as may be necessary to cause them to conform to the evidence and to raise these issues may be made upon motion of any party at any time, even after judgment; but failure so to amend does not affect the result of the trial of these issues. If evidence is objected to at the trial on the ground that it is not within the issues made by the pleadings, the court may allow the pleadings to be amended and shall do so freely when the presentation of the merits of the action will be subserved thereby and the objecting party fails to satisfy the court that the admission of such evidence would prejudice him in maintaining his action or defense upon the merits. The court may grant a continuance to enable the objecting party to meet such evidence.

(c) Relation Back of Amendments. Whenever the claim or defense asserted in the amended pleading arose out of the conduct, transaction, or occurrence set forth or attempted to be set forth in the original pleading, the amendment relates back to the date of the original pleading. An amendment changing the party against whom a claim is asserted relates back if the foregoing provision is satisfied and, within the period provided by law for commencing the action against him, the party to be brought in by amendment (1) has received such notice of the institution of the action that he will not be prejudiced in maintaining his defense on the merits, and (2) knew or should have known that, but for a mistake concerning the identity of the proper party, the action would have been brought against him.

The delivery or mailing of process to the United States Attorney, or his designee, or the Attorney General of the United States, or an agency or officer who would have been a proper defendant if named, satisfies the requirement of clauses (1) and (2) hereof with respect to the United States or any agency or officer thereof to be brought into the action as a defendant.

(d) Supplemental Pleadings. Upon motion of a party the court may, upon reasonable notice and upon such terms as are just, permit him to serve a supplemental pleading setting forth transactions or occurrences or events which have happened since the date of the pleading sought to be supplemented. Permission may be granted even though the original pleading is defective in its statement of a claim for relief or defense. If the court deems it advisable that the adverse party plead to the supplemental pleading, it shall so order, specifying the time therefor.

Rule 16.

PRETRIAL CONFERENCES; SCHEDULING; MANAGEMENT

(a) Pretrial Conferences; Objectives. In any action, the court may in its discretion direct the attorneys for the parties and any unrepresented parties to appear before it for a conference or conferences before trial for such purposes as

(1) expediting the disposition of the action;

(2) establishing early and continuing control so that the case will not be protracted because of lack of management;

(3) discouraging wasteful pretrial activities;

(4) improving the quality of the trial through more thorough preparation, and

(5) facilitating the settlement of the case.

(b) Scheduling and Planning. Except in categories of actions exempted by district court rule as inappropriate, the judge, or a magistrate when authorized by district court rule, shall, after consulting with the attorneys for the parties and any unrepresented parties, by a scheduling conference, telephone, mail, or other suitable means, enter a scheduling order that limits the time

(1) to join other parties and to amend the pleadings;

(2) to file and hear motions; and

(3) to complete discovery.

The scheduling order also may include

(4) the date or dates for conferences before trial, a final pretrial conference, and trial; and

(5) any other matters appropriate in the circumstances of the case.

The order shall issue as soon as practicable but in no event more than 120 days after filing of the complaint. A schedule shall not be modified except by leave of the judge or a magistrate when authorized by district court rule upon a showing of good cause.

(c) Subjects to be Discussed at Pretrial Conferences. The participants at any conference under this rule may consider and take action with respect to

(1) the formulation and simplification of the issues, including the elimination of frivolous claims or defenses;

(2) the necessity or desirability of amendments to the pleadings;

(3) the possibility of obtaining admissions of fact and of documents which will avoid unnecessary proof, stipulations regarding the authenticity of documents, and advance rulings from the court on the admissibility of evidence;

(4) the avoidance of unnecessary proof and of cumulative evidence;

(5) the identification of witnesses and documents, the need and schedule for filing and exchanging pretrial briefs, and the date or dates for further conferences and for trial;

(6) the advisability of referring matters to a magistrate or master;

(7) the possibility of settlement or the use of extrajudicial procedures to resolve the dispute;

(8) the form and substance of the pretrial order;

(9) the disposition of pending motions;

(10) the need for adopting special procedures for managing potentially difficult or protracted actions that may involve complex issues, multiple parties, difficult legal questions, or unusual proof problems; and

(11) such other matters as may aid in the disposiiton of the action.

At least one of the attorneys for each party participating in any conference before trial shall have authority to enter into stipulations and to make admissions regarding all matters that the participants may reasonably anticipate may be discussed.

(d) Final Pretrial Conference. Any final pretrial conference shall be held as close to the time of trial as reasonable under the circumstances. The participants at any such conference shall formulate a plan for trial, including a program for facilitating the admission of evidence. The conference shall be attended by at least one of the attorneys who will conduct the trial for each of the parties and by any unrepresented parties.

(e) Pretrial Orders. After any conference held pursuant to this rule, an order shall be entered reciting the action taken. This order shall control the subsequent course of the action unless modified by a subsequent order. The order following a final pretrial conference shall be modified only to prevent manifest injustice.

(f) Sanctions. If a party or party's attorney fails to obey a scheduling or pretrial order, or if no appearance is made on behalf of a party at a scheduling or pretrial conference, or if a party or party's attorney is substantially unprepared to participate in the conference, or if a party or party's attorney fails to participate in good faith, the judge, upon motion or his own initiative, may make such orders with regard thereto as are just, and among others any of the orders provided in Rule 37(b)(2)(B), (C), (D). In lieu of or in addition to any other sanction, the judge shall require the party or the attorney representing him or both to pay the reasonable expenses incurred because of any noncompliance with this rule, including attorney's fees, unless the judge finds that the noncompliance was substantially justified or that other circumstances make an award of expenses unjust.

IV. PARTIES

Rule 17.

PARTIES PLAINTIFF AND DEFENDANT; CAPACITY

(a) Real Party in Interest. Every action shall be prosecuted in the name of the real party in interest. An executor, administrator, guardian, bailee, trustee of an express trust, a party with whom or in whose name a contract has been made for the benefit of another, or a party authorized by statute may sue in his own name without joining with him the party for whose benefit the action is brought; and when a statute of the United States so provides, an action for the use or benefit of another shall be brought in the name of the United States. No action shall be dismissed on the ground that it is not prosecuted in the name of the real party in interest until a reasonable time has been allowed after objection for ratification of commencement of the action by, or joinder or substitution of, the real party in interest; and such ratification, joinder, or substitution shall have the same effect as if the action had been commenced in the name of the real party in interest.

(b) Capacity to Sue or Be Sued. The capacity of an individual, other than one acting in a representative capacity, to sue or be sued shall be determined by the law of his domicile. The capacity of a corporation to sue or be sued shall be determined by the law under which it was organized. In all other cases capacity to sue or be sued shall be determined by the law of the state in which the district court is held, except (1) that a partnership or other unincorporated association, which has no such capacity by the law of such state, may sue or be sued in its common name for the purpose of enforcing for or against it a substantive right existing under the Constitution or laws of the United States, and (2) that the capacity of a receiver appointed by a court of the United States to sue or be sued in a court of the United States is governed by Title 28, U.S.C., §§ 754 and 959(a).

(c) Infants or Incompetent Persons. Whenever an infant or incompetent person has a representative, such as a general guardian, committee, conservator, or other like fiduciary, the representative may sue or defend on behalf of the infant or incompetent person. If an infant or incompetent person does not have a duly appointed representative he may sue by his next friend or by a guardian ad litem. The court shall appoint a guardian ad litem for an infant or incompetent person not otherwise represented in an action or shall make such other order as it deems proper for the protection of the infant or incompetent person.

Rule 18.

JOINDER OF CLAIMS AND REMEDIES

(a) Joinder of Claims. A party asserting a claim to relief as an original claim, counterclaim, cross-claim, or third-party claim, may join, either as independent or as alternate claims, as many claims, legal, equitable, or maritime, as he has against an opposing party.

(b) Joinder of Remedies; Fraudulent Conveyances. Whenever a claim is one heretofore cognizable only after another claim has been prosecuted to a conclusion, the two claims may be joined in a single action; but the court shall grant relief in that action only in accordance with the relative substantive rights of the parties. In particular, a plaintiff may state a claim for money and a claim to have set aside a conveyance fraudulent as to him, without first having obtained a judgment establishing the claim for money.

Rule 19.

JOINDER OF PERSONS NEEDED FOR JUST ADJUDICATION

(a) Persons to Be Joined if Feasible. A person who is subject to service of process and whose joinder will not deprive the court of jurisdiction over the subject matter of the action shall be joined as a party in the action if (1) in his absence complete relief cannot be accorded among those already parties, or (2) he claims an interest relating to the subject of the action and is so situated that the disposition of the action in his absence may (i) as a practical matter impair or impede his ability to protect that interest or (ii) leave any of the persons already parties subject to a substantial risk of incurring double, multiple, or otherwise inconsistent obligations by reason of his claimed interest. If he has not been so joined, the court shall order that he be made a party. If he should join as a plaintiff but refuses to do so, he may be made a defendant, or, in a proper case, an involuntary plaintiff. If the joined party objects to venue and his joinder would render the venue of the action improper, he shall be dismissed from the action.

(b) Determination by Court Whenever Joinder Not Feasible. If a person as described in subdivision (a) (1)–(2) hereof cannot be made a party, the court shall determine whether in equity and good conscience the action should proceed among the parties before it, or should be dismissed, the absent person being thus regarded as indispensable. The factors to be considered by the court include: first, to what extent a judgment rendered in the person's absence might be prejudicial to him or those already parties; second, the extent to which, by protective provisions in the judgment, by the shaping of relief, or other measures, the prejudice can be lessened or avoided; third, whether a judgment rendered in the person's absence will be adequate; fourth, whether the plaintiff will have an adequate remedy if the action is dismissed for nonjoinder.

(c) Pleading Reasons for Nonjoinder. A pleading asserting a claim for relief shall state the names, if known to the pleader, of any persons as described in subdivision (a) (1)–(2) hereof who are not joined, and the reasons why they are not joined.

(d) Exception of Class Actions. This rule is subject to the provisions of Rule 23.

Rule 20.

PERMISSIVE JOINDER OF PARTIES

(a) Permissive Joinder. All persons may join in one action as plaintiffs if they assert any right to relief jointly, severally, or in the alternative in respect of or arising out of the same transaction, occurrence, or series of transactions or occurrences and if any question of law or fact common to all these persons will arise in the action. All persons (and any vessel, cargo or other property subject to admiralty process in rem) may be joined in one action as defendants if there is asserted against them jointly, severally, or in the alternative, any right to relief in respect of or arising out of the same transaction, occurrence, or series of transactions or occurrences and if any question of law or fact common to all defendants will arise in the action. A plaintiff or defendant need not be interested in obtaining or defending against all the relief demanded. Judgment may be given for one or more of the plaintiffs according to their respective rights to relief, and against one or more defendants according to their respective liabilities.

(b) Separate Trials. The court may make such orders as will prevent a party from being embarrassed, delayed, or put to expense by the inclusion of a party against whom he asserts no claim and who asserts no claim against him, and may order separate trials or make other orders to prevent delay or prejudice.

Rule 21.

MISJOINDER AND NON-JOINDER OF PARTIES

Misjoinder of parties is not ground for dismissal of an action. Parties may be dropped or added by order of the court on motion of any party or of its own initiative at any stage of the action and on such terms as are just. Any claim against a party may be severed and proceeded with separately.

Rule 22.

INTERPLEADER

(1) Persons having claims against the plaintiff may be joined as defendants and required to interplead when their claims are such that the plaintiff is or may be exposed to double or multi-

ple liability. It is not ground for objection to the joinder that the claims of the several claimants or the titles on which their claims depend do not have a common origin or are not identical but are adverse to and independent of one another, or that the plaintiff avers that he is not liable in whole or in part to any or all of the claimants. A defendant exposed to similar liability may obtain such interpleader by way of cross-claim or counterclaim. The provisions of this rule supplement and do not in any way limit the joinder of parties permitted in Rule 20.

(2) The remedy herein provided is in addition to and in no way supersedes or limits the remedy provided by Title 28, U.S.C., §§ 1335, 1397, and 2361. Actions under those provisions shall be conducted in accordance with these rules.

Rule 23.

CLASS ACTIONS

(a) Prerequisites to a Class Action. One or more members of a class may sue or be sued as representative parties on behalf of all only if (1) the class is so numerous that joinder of all members is impracticable, (2) there are questions of law or fact common to the class, (3) the claims or defenses of the representative parties are typical of the claims or defenses of the class, and (4) the representative parties will fairly and adequately protect the interests of the class.

(b) Class Actions Maintainable. An action may be maintained as a class action if the prerequisites of subdivision (a) are satisfied, and in addition:

(1) the prosecution of separate actions by or against individual members of the class would create a risk of

(A) inconsistent or varying adjudications with respect to individual members of the class which would establish incompatible standards of conduct for the party opposing the class, or

(B) adjudications with respect to individual members of the class which would as a practical matter be dispositive of the interests of the other members not parties to the adjudications or substantially impair or impede their ability to protect their interests; or

(2) the party opposing the class has acted or refused to act on grounds generally applicable to the class, thereby making

appropriate final injunctive relief or corresponding declaratory relief with respect to the class as a whole; or

(3) the court finds that the questions of law or fact common to the members of the class predominate over any questions affecting only individual members, and that a class action is superior to other available methods for the fair and efficient adjudication of the controversy. The matters pertinent to the findings include: (A) the interest of members of the class in individually controlling the prosecution or defense of separate actions; (B) the extent and nature of any litigation concerning the controversy already commenced by or against members of the class; (C) the desirability or undesirability of concentrating the litigation of the claims in the particular forum; (D) the difficulties likely to be encountered in the management of a class action.

(c) Determination by Order Whether Class Action to be Maintained; Notice; Judgment; Actions Conducted Partially as Class Actions.

(1) As soon as practicable after the commencement of an action brought as a class action, the court shall determine by order whether it is to be so maintained. An order under this subdivision may be conditional, and may be altered or amended before the decision on the merits.

(2) In any class action maintained under subdivision (b) (3), the court shall direct to the members of the class the best notice practicable under the circumstances, including individual notice to all members who can be identified through reasonable effort. The notice shall advise each member that (A) the court will exclude him from the class if he so requests by a specified date; (B) the judgment, whether favorable or not, will include all members who do not request exclusion; and (C) any member who does not request exclusion may, if he desires, enter an appearance through his counsel.

(3) The judgment in an action maintained as a class action under subdivision (b) (1) or (b) (2), whether or not favorable to the class, shall include and describe those whom the court finds to be members of the class. The judgment in an action maintained as a class action under subdivision (b) (3), whether or not favorable to the class, shall include and specify or describe those to whom the notice provided in subdivision (c) (2) was directed, and who have not requested exclusion, and whom the court finds to be members of the class.

(4) When appropriate (A) an action may be brought or maintained as a class action with respect to particular issues, or (B) a class may be divided into subclasses and each subclass treated as a class, and the provisions of this rule shall then be construed and applied accordingly.

(d) Orders in Conduct of Actions. In the conduct of actions to which this rule applies, the court may make appropriate orders: (1) determining the course of proceedings or prescribing measures to prevent undue repetition or complication in the presentation of evidence or argument; (2) requiring, for the protection of the members of the class or otherwise for the fair conduct of the action, that notice be given in such manner as the court may direct to some or all of the members of any step in the action, or of the proposed extent of the judgment, or of the opportunity of members to signify whether they consider the representation fair and adequate, to intervene and present claims or defenses, or otherwise to come into the action; (3) imposing conditions on the representative parties or on intervenors; (4) requiring that the pleadings be amended to eliminate therefrom allegations as to representation of absent persons, and that the action proceed accordingly; (5) dealing with similar procedural matters. The orders may be combined with an order under Rule 16, and may be altered or amended as may be desirable from time to time.

(e) Dismissal or Compromise. A class action shall not be dismissed or compromised without the approval of the court, and notice of the proposed dismissal or compromise shall be given to all members of the class in such manner as the court directs.

Rule 23.1.

DERIVATIVE ACTIONS BY SHAREHOLDERS

In a derivative action brought by one or more shareholders or members to enforce a right of a corporation or of an unincorporated association, the corporation or association having failed to enforce a right which may properly be asserted by it, the complaint shall be verified and shall allege (1) that the plaintiff was a shareholder or member at the time of the transaction of which he complains or that his share or membership thereafter devolved on him by operation of law, and (2) that the action is not a collusive one to confer jurisdiction on a court of the United States which it would not otherwise have. The complaint shall also allege with particularity the efforts, if any, made by the plaintiff to obtain the action he desires from the directors or comparable authority and, if necessary, from the shareholders or members, and the reasons for his failure to obtain the action or for not making the effort. The derivative action may not be maintained if it appears that the plaintiff does not fairly and adequately represent the interests of the shareholders or members similarly situated in enforcing the right of the corporation or association. The action shall not be dismissed or compromised without the approval of the court, and notice of the proposed dismissal or compromise shall be given to shareholders or members in such manner as the court directs.

Rule 23.2.

ACTIONS RELATING TO UNINCORPORATED ASSOCIATIONS

An action brought by or against the members of an unincorporated association as a class by naming certain members as representative parties may be maintained only if it appears that the representative parties will fairly and adequately protect the interests of the association and its members. In the conduct of the action the court may make appropriate orders corresponding with those described in Rule 23(d), and the procedure for dismissal or compromise of the action shall correspond with that provided in Rule 23(e).

Rule 24.

INTERVENTION

(a) Intervention of Right. Upon timely application anyone shall be permitted to intervene in an action: (1) when a statute of the United States confers an unconditional right to intervene; or (2) when the applicant claims an interest relating to the property or transaction which is the subject of the action and he is so situated that the disposition of the action may as a practical matter impair or impede his ability to protect that interest, unless the applicant's interest is adequately represented by existing parties.

(b) Permissive Intervention. Upon timely application anyone may be permitted to intervene in an action: (1) when a statute of the United States confers a conditional right to intervene; or (2) when an applicant's claim or defense and the main action have a question of law or fact in common. When a party to an action relies for ground of claim or defense upon any statute or executive order administered by a federal or state governmental officer or agency or upon any regulation, order, requirement or agreement issued or made pursuant to the statute or executive order, the officer or agency upon timely application may be permitted to intervene in the action. In exercising its discretion the court shall consider whether the intervention will unduly delay or prejudice the adjudication of the rights of the original parties.

(c) Procedure. A person desiring to intervene shall serve a motion to intervene upon the parties as provided in Rule 5. The motion shall state the grounds therefor and shall be accompanied by a pleading setting forth the claim or defense for which intervention is sought. The same procedure shall be followed when a statute of the United States gives a right to intervene. When the constitutionality of an act of Congress affecting the public interest is drawn in question in any action to which the United States or an officer, agency, or employee thereof is not a party, the court shall notify the Attorney General of the United States as provided in Title 28, U.S.C., § 2403.

Rule 25.
SUBSTITUTION OF PARTIES

(a) Death.

(1) If a party dies and the claim is not thereby extinguished, the court may order substitution of the proper parties. The motion for substitution may be made by any party or by the successors or representatives of the deceased party and, together with the notice of hearing, shall be served on the parties as provided in Rule 5 and upon persons not parties in the manner provided in Rule 4 for the service of a summons, and may be served in any judicial district. Unless the motion for substitution is made not later than 90 days after the death is suggested upon the record by service of a statement of the fact of the death as provided herein for the service of the motion, the action shall be dismissed as to the deceased party.

(2) In the event of the death of one or more of the plaintiffs or of one or more of the defendants in an action in which the right sought to be enforced survives only to the surviving plaintiffs or only against the surviving defendants, the action does not abate. The death shall be suggested upon the record and the action shall proceed in favor of or against the surviving parties.

(b) Incompetency. If a party becomes incompetent, the court upon motion served as provided in subdivision (a) of this rule may allow the action to be continued by or against his representative.

(c) Transfer of Interest. In case of any transfer of interest, the action may be continued by or against the original party, unless the court upon motion directs the person to whom the interest is transferred to be substituted in the action or joined with the original party. Service of the motion shall be made as provided in subdivision (a) of this rule.

(d) Public Officers; Death or Separation from Office.

(1) When a public officer is a party to an action in his official capacity and during its pendency dies, resigns, or otherwise ceases to hold office, the action does not abate and his successor is automatically substituted as a party. Proceedings following the substitution shall be in the name of the substituted party, but any misnomer not affecting the substantial rights of the parties shall be disregarded. An order of substitution may be entered at any time, but the omission to enter such an order shall not affect the substitution.

(2) When a public officer sues or is sued in his official capacity, he may be described as a party by his official title rather than by name; but the court may require his name to be added.

V. DEPOSITIONS AND DISCOVERY

Rule 26.

GENERAL PROVISIONS GOVERNING DISCOVERY

(a) Discovery Methods. Parties may obtain discovery by one or more of the following methods: depositions upon oral examination or written questions; written interrogatories; production of documents or things or permission to enter upon land or other property, for inspection and other purposes; physical and mental examinations; and requests for admission.

(b) Discovery Scope and Limits. Unless otherwise limited by order of the court in accordance with these rules, the scope of discovery is as follows:

(1) *In General.*—Parties may obtain discovery regarding any matter, not privileged, which is relevant to the subject matter involved in the pending action, whether it relates to the claim or defense of the party seeking discovery or to the claim or defense of any other party, including the existence, description, nature, custody, condition and location of any books, documents, or other tangible things and the identity and location of persons having knowledge of any discoverable matter. It is not ground for objection that the information sought will be inadmissible at the trial if the information sought appears rea-

sonably calculated to lead tc the discovery of admissible evidence.

The frequency or extent of use of the discovery methods set forth in subdivision (a) shall be limited by the court if it determines that: (i) the discovery sought is unreasonably cumulative or duplicative, or is obtainable from some other source that is more convenient, less burdensome, or less expensive; (ii) the party seeking discovery has had ample opportunity by discovery in the action to obtain the information sought; or (iii) the discovery is unduly burdensome or expensive, taking into account the needs of the case, the amount in controversy, limitations on the parties' resources, and the importance of the issues at stake in the litigation. The court may act upon its own initiative after reasonable notice or pursuant to a motion under subdivision (c).

(2) *Insurance Agreements.*—A party may obtain discovery of the existence and contents of any insurance agreement under which any person carrying on an insurance business may be liable to satisfy part or all of a judgment which may be entered in the action or to indemnify or reimburse for payments made to satisfy the judgment. Information concerning the insurance agreement is not by reason of disclosure admissible in evidence at trial. For purposes of this paragraph, an application for insurance shall not be treated as part of an insurance agreement.

(3) *Trial Preparation: Materials.*—Subject to the provisions of subdivision (b) (4) of this rule, a party may obtain discovery of documents and tangible things otherwise discoverable under subdivision (b) (1) of this rule and prepared in anticipation of litigation or for trial by or for another party or by or for that other party's representative (including his attorney, consultant, surety, indemnitor, insurer, or agent) only upon a showing that the party seeking discovery has substantial need of the materials in the preparation of his case and that he is unable without undue hardship to obtain the substantial equivalent of the materials by other means. In ordering discovery of such materials when the required showing has been made, the court shall protect against disclosure of the mental impressions, conclusions, opinions, or legal theories of an attorney or other representative of a party concerning the litigation.

A party may obtain without the required showing a statement concerning the action or its subject matter previously made by that party. Upon request, a person not a party may obtain without the required showing a statement concerning the action or its subject matter previously made by that person. If the request is refused, the person may move for a court order. The provisions of Rule 37(a) (4) apply to the award of expenses incurred in relation to the motion. For purposes of this paragraph, a statement previously made is (A) a written statement signed or otherwise adopted or approved by the person making it, or (B) a stenographic, mechanical, electrical, or other recording, or a transcription thereof, which is a substantially verbatim recital of an oral statement by the person making it and contemporaneously recorded.

(4) *Trial Preparation: Experts.*—Discovery of facts known and opinions held by experts, otherwise discoverable under the provisions of subdivision (b) (1) of this rule and acquired or developed in anticipation of litigation or for trial, may be obtained only as follows:

(A) (i) A party may through interrogatories require any other party to identify each person whom the other party expects to call as an expert witness at trial, to state the subject matter on which the expert is expected to testify, and to state the substance of the facts and opinions to which the expert is expected to testify and a summary of the grounds for each opinion. (ii) Upon motion, the court may order further discovery by other means, subject to such restrictions as to scope and such provisions, pursuant to subdivision (b) (4) (C) of this rule, concerning fees and expenses as the court may deem appropriate.

(B) A party may discover facts known or opinions held by an expert who has been retained or specially employed by another party in anticipation of litigation or preparation for trial and who is not expected to be called as a witness at trial, only as provided in Rule 35(b) or upon a showing of exceptional circumstances under which it is impracticable for the party seeking discovery to obtain facts or opinions on the same subject by other means.

(C) Unless manifest injustice would result, (i) the court shall require that the party seeking discovery pay the expert a reasonable fee for time spent in responding to discovery under subdivisions (b) (4) (A) (ii) and (b) (4) (B) of this rule; and (ii) with respect to discovery obtained under subdivision (b) (4) (A) (ii) of this rule the court may require, and with respect to discovery obtained under subdivision (b) (4) (B) of this rule the court shall require, the party seeking discovery to pay the other party a fair portion of the fees and expenses reasonably incurred by the latter party in obtaining facts and opinions from the expert.

(c) Protective Orders. Upon motion by a party or by the person from whom discovery is sought, and for good cause shown, the court in which the action is pending or alternatively, on matters relating to a deposition, the court in the district where the deposition is to be taken may make any order which justice requires to protect a party or person from annoyance, embarrassment, oppression, or undue burden or expense, including one or more of the following: (1) that the discovery not be had; (2) that the discovery may be had only on specified terms and conditions, including a designation of the time or place; (3) that the discovery may be had only by a method of discovery other than that selected by the party seeking discovery; (4) that certain matters not be inquired into, or that the scope of the discovery be limited to certain matters; (5) that discovery be conducted with no one present except persons designated by the court; (6) that a deposition after being sealed be opened only by order of the court; (7) that a trade secret or other confidential research, development, or commercial information not be disclosed or be disclosed only in a designated way; (8) that the parties simultaneously file specified documents or information enclosed in sealed envelopes to be opened as directed by the court.

If the motion for a protective order is denied in whole or in part, the court may, on such terms and conditions as are just, order that any party or person provide or permit discovery. The provisions of Rule 37(a) (4) apply to the award of expenses incurred in relation to the motion.

(d) Sequence and Timing of Discovery. Unless the court upon motion, for the convenience of parties and witnesses and in the interests of justice, orders otherwise, methods of discovery may be used in any sequence and the fact that a party is conducting discovery, whether by deposition or otherwise, shall not operate to delay any other party's discovery.

(e) Supplementation of Responses. A party who has responded to a request for discovery with a response that was complete when made is under no duty to supplement his response to include information thereafter acquired, except as follows:

(1) A party is under a duty seasonably to supplement his response with respect to any question directly addressed to (A) the identity and location of persons having knowledge of discoverable matters, and (B) the identity of each person expected to be called as an expert witness at trial, the subject matter on which he is expected to testify, and the substance of his testimony.

(2) A party is under a duty seasonably to amend a prior response if he obtains information upon the basis of which (A)

he knows that the response was incorrect when made, or (B) he knows that the response though correct when made is no longer true and the circumstances are such that a failure to amend the response is in substance a knowing concealment.

(3) A duty to supplement responses may be imposed by order of the court, agreement of the parties, or at any time prior to trial through new requests for supplementation of prior responses.

(f) Discovery Conference. At any time after commencement of an action the court may direct the attorneys for the parties to appear before it for a conference on the subject of discovery. The court shall do so upon motion by the attorney for any party if the motion includes:

(1) A statement of the issues as they then appear;

(2) A proposed plan and schedule of discovery;

(3) Any limitations proposed to be placed on discovery;

(4) Any other proposed orders with respect to discovery; and

(5) A statement showing that the attorney making the motion has made a reasonable effort to reach agreement with opposing attorneys on the matters set forth in the motion. Each party and his attorney are under a duty to participate in good faith in the framing of a discovery plan if a plan is proposed by the attorney for any party. Notice of the motion shall be served on all parties. Objections or additions to matters set forth in the motion shall be served not later than 10 days after service of the motion.

Following the discovery conference, the court shall enter an order tentatively identifying the issues for discovery purposes, establishing a plan and schedule for discovery, setting limitations on discovery, if any; and determining such other matters, including the allocation of expenses, as are necessary for the proper management of discovery in the action. An order may be altered or amended whenever justice so requires.

Subject to the right of a party who properly moves for a discovery conference to prompt convening of the conference, the court may combine the discovery conference with a pretrial conference authorized by Rule 16.

(g) Signing of Discovery Requests, Responses, and Objections. Every request for discovery or response or objection thereto made by a party represented by an attorney shall be signed by at least one attorney of record in his individual name, whose address shall be stated. A party who is not represented by an attorney shall sign the request, response, or objection and state his address. The signature of the attorney or party constitutes a certification that he has read the request, response, or objection, and that to the best of his knowledge, information, and belief formed after a reasonable inquiry it is: (1) consistent with these rules and warranted by existing law or a good faith argument for the extension, modification, or reversal of existing law; (2) not interposed for any improper purpose, such as to harass or to cause unnecessary delay or needless increase in the cost of litigation; and (3) not unreasonable or unduly burdensome or expensive, given the needs of the case, the discovery already had in the case, the amount in controversy, and the importance of the issues at stake in the litigation. If a request, response, or objection is not signed, it shall be stricken unless it is signed promptly after the omission is called to the attention of the party making the request, response or objection and a party shall not be obligated to take any action with respect to it until it is signed.

If a certification is made in violation of the rule, the court, upon motion or upon its own initiative, shall impose upon the person who made the certification, the party on whose behalf the request, response, or objection is made, or both, an appropriate sanction, which may include an order to pay the amount of the reasonable expenses incurred because of the violation, including a reasonable attorney's fee.

Rule 27.

DEPOSITIONS BEFORE ACTION OR PENDING APPEAL

(a) Before Action.

(1) *Petition.* A person who desires to perpetuate his own testimony or that of another person regarding any matter that may be cognizable in any court of the United States may file a verified petition in the United States district court in the district of the residence of any expected adverse party. The petition shall be entitled in the name of the petitioner and shall show: 1, that the petitioner expects to be a party to an action cognizable in a court of the United States but is presently unable to bring it or cause it to be brought, 2, the subject matter of the expected action and his interest therein, 3, the facts which he desires to establish by the proposed testimony and his reasons for desiring to perpetuate it, 4, the names or a description of the persons he expects will be adverse parties and their addresses so far as known, and 5, the names and addresses of the persons to be examined and the substance of the testimony which he expects to elicit from each, and shall ask for an order authorizing the petitioner to take the depositions of the persons to be examined named in the petition, for the purpose of perpetuating their testimony.

(2) *Notice and Service.* The petitioner shall thereafter serve a notice upon each person named in the petition as an expected adverse party, together with a copy of the petition, stating that the petitioner will apply to the court, at a time and place named therein, for the order described in the petition. At least 20 days before the date of hearing the notice shall be served either within or without the district or state in the manner provided in Rule 4(d) for service of summons; but if such service cannot with due diligence be made upon any expected adverse party named in the petition, the court may make such order as is just for service by publication or otherwise, and shall appoint, for persons not served in the manner provided in Rule 4(d), an attorney who shall represent them, and, in case they are not otherwise represented, shall cross-examine the deponent. If any expected adverse party is a minor or incompetent the provisions of Rule 17(c) apply.

(3) *Order and Examination.* If the court is satisfied that the perpetuation of the testimony may prevent a failure or delay of justice, it shall make an order designating or describing the persons whose depositions may be taken and specifying the subject matter of the examination and whether the depositions shall be taken upon oral examination or written interrogatories. The depositions may then be taken in accordance with these rules; and the court may make orders of the character provided for by Rules 34 and 35. For the purpose of applying these rules to depositions for perpetuating testimony, each reference therein to the court in which the action is pending shall be deemed to refer to the court in which the petition for such deposition was filed.

(4) *Use of Deposition.* If a deposition to perpetuate testimony is taken under these rules or if, although not so taken, it would be admissible in evidence in the courts of the state in which it is taken, it may be used in any action involving the same subject matter subsequently brought in a United States district court, in accordance with the provisions of Rule 32(a).

(b) Pending Appeal. If an appeal has been taken from a judgment of a district court or before the taking of an appeal if the time therefor has not expired, the district court in which the judgment was rendered may allow the taking of the depositions of witnesses to perpetuate their testimony for use in the event of further proceedings in the district court. In such case the party who desires to perpetuate the testimony may make a motion in the district court for leave to take the depositions, upon the same notice and service thereof as if the action was pending in the district court. The motion shall show (1) the names and addresses of persons to be examined and the substance of the testimony which he expects to elicit from each; (2) the reasons for perpetuating their testimony. If the court finds that the perpetuation of the testimony is proper to avoid a failure or delay of justice, it may make an order allowing the depositions to be taken and may make orders of the character provided for by Rules 34 and 35, and thereupon the depositions may be taken and used in the same manner and under the same conditions as are prescribed in these rules for depositions taken in actions pending in the district court.

(c) Perpetuation by Action. **This rule does not limit the power of a court to entertain an action to perpetuate testimony.**

Rule 28.

PERSONS BEFORE WHOM DEPOSITIONS MAY BE TAKEN

(a) Within the United States. Within the United States or within a territory or insular possession subject to the jurisdiction of the United States, depositions shall be taken before an officer authorized to administer oaths by the laws of the United States or of the place where the examination is held, or before a person appointed by the court in which the action is pending. A person so appointed has power to administer oaths and take testimony. The term officer as used in Rules 30, 31 and 32 includes a person appointed by the court or designated by the parties under Rule 29.

(b) In Foreign Countries. In a foreign country, depositions may be taken (1) on notice before a person authorized to administer oaths in the place in which the examination is held, either by the law thereof or by the law of the United States, or (2) before a person commissioned by the court, and a person so commissioned shall have the power by virtue of his commission to administer any necessary oath and take testimony, or (3) pursuant to a letter rogatory. A commission or a letter rogatory shall be issued on application and notice and on terms that are just and appropriate. It is not requisite to the issuance of a commission or a letter rogatory that the taking of the deposition in any other manner is impracticable or inconvenient; and both a commission and a letter rogatory may be issued in proper cases. A notice or commission may designate the person before whom the deposition is to be taken either by name or descriptive title. A letter rogatory may be addressed "To the Appropriate Authority in [here name the country]." Evidence obtained in response to a letter rogatory need not be excluded merely for the reason that it is not a verbatim transcript or that the testimony was not taken under oath or for any similar departure from the requirements for depositions taken within the United States under these rules.

(c) Disqualification for Interest. No deposition shall be taken before a person who is a relative or employee or attorney or counsel of any of the parties, or is a relative or employee of such attorney or counsel, or is financially interested in the action.

Rule 29.

STIPULATIONS REGARDING DISCOVERY PROCEDURE

Unless the court orders otherwise, the parties may by written stipulation (1) provide that depositions may be taken before any person, at any time or place, upon any notice, and in any manner and when so taken may be used like other depositions, and (2) modify the procedures provided by these rules for other methods of discovery, except that stipulations extending the time provided in Rules 33, 34, and 36 for responses to discovery may be made only with the approval of the court.

Rule 30.

DEPOSITIONS UPON ORAL EXAMINATION

(a) When Depositions May Be Taken. After commencement of the action, any party may take the testimony of any person, including a party, by deposition upon oral examination. Leave of court, granted with or without notice, must be obtained only if the plaintiff seeks to take a deposition prior to the expiration of 30 days after service of the summons and complaint upon any defendant or service made under Rule 4(e), except that leave is not required (1) if a defendant has served a notice of taking deposition or otherwise sought discovery, or (2) if special notice is given as provided in subdivision (b) (2) of this rule. The attendance of witnesses may be compelled by subpoena as provided in Rule 45. The deposition of a person confined in prison may be taken only by leave of court on such terms as the court prescribes.

(b) Notice of Examination: General Requirements; Special Notice; Non-Stenographic Recording; Production of Documents and Things; Deposition of Organization; Deposition by Telephone.

(1) A party desiring to take the deposition of any person upon oral examination shall give reasonable notice in writing to every other party to the action. The notice shall state the time and place for taking the deposition and the name and address of each person to be examined, if known, and, if the name is not known, a general description sufficient to identify him or the particular class or group to which he belongs. If a subpoena duces tecum is to be served on the person to be examined, the designation of the materials to be produced as set forth in the subpoena shall be attached to or included in the notice.

(2) Leave of court is not required for the taking of a deposition by plaintiff if the notice (A) states that the person to be examined is about to go out of the district where the action is pending and more than 100 miles from the place of trial, or is about to go out of the United States, or is bound on a voyage to sea, and will be unavailable for examination unless his deposition is taken before expiration of the 30-day period, and (B) sets forth facts to support the statement. The plaintiff's attorney shall sign the notice, and his signature constitutes a certification by him that to the best of his knowledge, information, and belief the statement and supporting facts are true. The sanctions provided by Rule 11 are applicable to the certification.

If a party shows that when he was served with notice under this subdivision (b) (2) he was unable through the exercise of diligence to obtain counsel to represent him at the taking of the deposition, the deposition may not be used against him.

(3) The court may for cause shown enlarge or shorten the time for taking the deposition.

(4) The parties may stipulate in writing or the court may upon motion order that the testimony at a deposition be recorded by other than stenographic means. The stipulation or

order shall designate the person before whom the deposition shall be taken, the manner of recording, preserving and filing the deposition, and may include other provisions to assure that the recorded testimony will be accurate and trustworthy. A party may arrange to have a stenographic transcription made at his own expense. Any objections under subdivision (c), any changes made by the witness, his signature identifying the deposition as his own or the statement of the officer that is required if the witness does not sign, as provided in subdivision (e), and the certification of the officer required by subdivision (f) shall be set forth in a writing to accompany a deposition recorded by non-stenographic means.

(5) The notice to a party deponent may be accompanied by a request made in compliance with Rule 34 for the production of documents and tangible things at the taking of the deposition. The procedure of Rule 34 shall apply to the request.

(6) A party may in his notice and in a subpoena name as the deponent a public or private corporation or a partnership or association or governmental agency and describe with reasonable particularity the matters on which examination is requested. In that event, the organization so named shall designate one or more officers, directors, or managing agents, or other persons who consent to testify on its behalf, and may set forth, for each person designated, the matters on which he will testify. A subpoena shall advise a non-party organization of its duty to make such a designation. The persons so designated shall testify as to matters known or reasonably available to the organization. This subdivision (b) (6) does not preclude taking a deposition by any other procedure authorized in these rules.

(7) The parties may stipulate in writing or the court may upon motion order that a deposition be taken by telephone. For the purposes of this rule and Rules 28(a), 37(a)(1), 37(b)(1) and 45(d), a deposition taken by telephone is taken in the district and at the place where the deponent is to answer questions propounded to him.

(c) Examination and Cross-Examination; Record of Examination; Oath; Objections. Examination and cross-examination of witnesses may proceed as permitted at the trial under the provisions of the Federal Rules of Evidence. The officer before whom the deposition is to be taken shall put the witness on oath and shall personally, or by someone acting under his direction and in his presence, record the testimony of the witness. The testimony shall be taken stenographically or recorded by any other means ordered in accordance with subdivision (b)(4) of this rule. If requested by one of the parties, the testimony shall be transcribed. All objections made at the time of the examination to the qualifications of the officer taking the deposition, or to the manner of taking it, or to the evidence presented, or to the conduct of any party, and any other objection to the proceedings, shall be noted by the officer upon the deposition. Evidence objected to shall be taken subject to the objections. In lieu of participating in the oral examination, parties may serve written questions in a sealed envelope on the party taking the deposition and he shall transmit them to the officer, who shall propound them to the witness and record the answers verbatim.

(d) Motion to Terminate or Limit Examination. At any time during the taking of the deposition, on motion of a party or of the deponent and upon a showing that the examination is being conducted in bad faith or in such manner as unreasonably to annoy, embarrass, or oppress the deponent or party, the court in which the action is pending or the court in the district where the deposition is being taken may order the officer conducting the examination to cease forthwith from taking the deposition, or may limit the scope and manner of the taking of the deposition as provided in Rule 26(c). If the order made terminates the examination, it shall be resumed thereafter only upon the order of the court in which the action is pending. Upon demand of the objecting party or deponent, the taking of the deposition shall be suspended for the time necessary to make a motion for an order. The provisions of Rule 37(a) (4) apply to the award of expenses incurred in relation to the motion.

(e) Submission to Witness; Changes; Signing. When the testimony is fully transcribed the deposition shall be submitted to the witness for examination and shall be read to or by him, unless such examination and reading are waived by the witness and by the parties. Any changes in form or substance which the witness desires to make shall be entered upon the deposition by the officer with a statement of the reasons given by the witness for making them. The deposition shall then be signed by the witness, unless the parties by stipulation waive the signing or the witness is ill or cannot be found or refuses to sign. If the deposition is not signed by the witness within 30 days of its submission to him, the officer shall sign it and state on the record the fact of the waiver or of the illness or absence of the witness or the fact of the refusal to sign together with the reason, if any, given therefor; and the deposition may then be used as fully as though signed unless on a motion to suppress under Rule 32(d) (4) the court holds that the reasons given for the refusal to sign require rejection of the deposition in whole or in part.

(f) Certification and Filing by Officer; Exhibits; Copies; Notice of Filing. (1) The officer shall certify on the deposition that the witness was duly sworn by him and that the deposition is a true record of the testimony given by the witness. Unless otherwise ordered by the court, he shall then securely seal the deposition in an envelope indorsed with the title of the action and marked "Deposition of [here insert name of witness]" and shall promptly file it with the court in which the action is pending or send it by registered or certified mail to the clerk thereof for filing.

Documents and things produced for inspection during the examination of the witness, shall, upon the request of a party, be marked for identification and annexed to the deposition and may be inspected and copied by any party, except that if the person producing the materials desires to retain them he may (A) offer copies to be marked for identification and annexed to the deposition and to serve thereafter as originals if he affords to all parties fair opportunity to verify the copies by comparison with the originals, or (B) offer the originals to be marked for identification, after giving to each party an opportunity to inspect and copy them, in which event the materials may then be used in the same manner as if annexed to the deposition. Any party may move for an order that the original be annexed to and returned with the deposition to the court, pending final disposition of the case.

(2) Upon payment of reasonable charges therefor, the officer shall furnish a copy of the deposition to any party or to the deponent.

(3) The party taking the deposition shall give prompt notice of its filing to all other parties.

(g) Failure to Attend or to Serve Subpoena; Expenses.

(1) If the party giving the notice of the taking of a deposition fails to attend and proceed therewith and another party attends in person or by attorney pursuant to the notice, the court may order the party giving the notice to pay to such other party the reasonable expenses incurred by him and his attorney in attending, including reasonable attorney's fees.

(2) If the party giving the notice of the taking of a deposition of a witness fails to serve a subpoena upon him and the witness because of such failure does not attend, and if another party attends in person or by attorney because he expects the

deposition of that witness to be taken, the court may order the party giving the notice to pay to such other party the reasonable expenses incurred by him and his attorney in attending, including reasonable attorney's fees.

Rule 31.

DEPOSITIONS UPON WRITTEN QUESTIONS

(a) Serving Questions; Notice. After commencement of the action, any party may take the testimony of any person, including a party, by deposition upon written questions. The attendance of witnesses may be compelled by the use of subpoena as provided in Rule 45. The deposition of a person confined in prison may be taken only by leave of court on such terms as the court prescribes.

A party desiring to take a deposition upon written questions shall serve them upon every other party with a notice stating (1) the name and address of the person who is to answer them, if known, and if the name is not known, a general description sufficient to identify him or the particular class or group to which he belongs, and (2) the name or descriptive title and address of the officer before whom the deposition is to be taken. A deposition upon written questions may be taken of a public or private corporation or a partnership or association or governmental agency in accordance with the provisions of Rule 30(b) (6).

Within 30 days after the notice and written questions are served, a party may serve cross questions upon all other parties. Within 10 days after being served with cross questions, a party may serve redirect questions upon all other parties. Within 10 days after being served with redirect questions, a party may serve recross questions upon all other parties. The court may for cause shown enlarge or shorten the time.

(b) Officer to Take Responses and Prepare Record. A copy of the notice and copies of all questions served shall be delivered by the party taking the deposition to the officer designated in the notice, who shall proceed promptly, in the manner provided by Rule 30(c), (e), and (f), to take the testimony of the witness in response to the questions and to prepare, certify, and file or mail the deposition, attaching thereto the copy of the notice and the questions received by him.

(c) Notice of Filing. When the deposition is filed the party taking it shall promptly give notice thereof to all other parties.

Rule 32.

USE OF DEPOSITIONS IN COURT PROCEEDINGS

(a) Use of Depositions. At the trial or upon the hearing of a motion or an interlocutory proceeding, any part or all of a deposition, so far as admissible under the rules of evidence applied as though the witness were then present and testifying, may be used against any party who was present or represented at the taking of the deposition or who had reasonable notice thereof, in accordance with any of the following provisions:

(1) Any deposition may be used by any party for the purpose of contradicting or impeaching the testimony of deponent as a witness, or for any other purpose permitted by the Federal Rules of Evidence.

(2) The deposition of a party or of anyone who at the time of taking the deposition was an officer, director, or managing agent, or a person designated under Rule 30(b) (6) or 31(a) to testify on behalf of a public or private corporation, partnership or association or governmental agency which is a party may be used by an adverse party for any purpose.

(3) The deposition of a witness, whether or not a party, may be used by any party for any purpose if the court finds: (A) that the witness is dead; or (B) that the witness is at a greater distance than 100 miles from the place of trial or hearing, or is out of the United States, unless it appears that the absence of the witness was procured by the party offering the deposition; or (C) that the witness is unable to attend or testify because of age, illness, infirmity, or imprisonment; or (D) that the party offering the deposition has been unable to procure the attendance of the witness by subpoena; or (E) upon application and notice, that such exceptional circumstances exist as to make it desirable, in the interest of justice and with due regard to the importance of presenting the testimony of witnesses orally in open court, to allow the deposition to be used.

(4) If only part of a deposition is offered in evidence by a party, an adverse party may require him to introduce any other part which ought in fairness to be considered with the part introduced, and any party may introduce any other parts.

Substitution of parties pursuant to Rule 25 does not affect the right to use depositions previously taken; and when an action has been brought in any court of the United States or of any State and another action involving the same subject matter is afterward brought between the same parties or their representatives or successors in interest, all depositions lawfully taken and duly filed in the former action may be used in the latter as if originaly taken therefor. A deposition previously taken may also be used as permitted by the Federal Rules of Evidence.

(b) Objections to Admissibility. Subject to the provisions of Rule 28(b) and subdivision (d) (3) of this rule, objection may be made at the trial or hearing to receiving in evidence any deposition or part thereof for any reason which would require the exclusion of the evidence if the witness were then present and testifying.

[c. Abrogated]

(d) Effect of Errors and Irregularities in Depositions.

(1) *As to Notice.*—All errors and irregularities in the notice for taking a deposition are waived unless written objection is promptly served upon the party giving the notice.

(2) *As to Disqualification of Officer.*—Objection to taking a deposition because of disqualification of the officer before whom it is to be taken is waived unless made before the taking of the deposition begins or as soon thereafter as the disqualification becomes known or could be discovered with reasonable diligence.

(3) *As to Taking of Deposition.*—

(A) Objections to the competency of a witness or to the competency, relevancy, or materiality of testimony are not waived by failure to make them before or during the taking of the deposition, unless the ground of the objection is one which might have been obviated or removed if presented at that time.

(B) Errors and irregularities occurring at the oral examination in the manner of taking the deposition, in the form of the questions or answers, in the oath or affirmation, or in the conduct of parties, and errors of any kind which might be obviated, removed, or cured if promptly presented, are waived unless seasonable objection thereto is made at the taking of the deposition.

(C) Objections to the form of written questions submitted under Rule 31 are waived unless served in writing upon the party propounding them within the time allowed for serving the succeeding cross or other questions and within 5 days after service of the last questions authorized.

(4) *As to Completion and Return of Deposition.*—Errors and irregularities in the manner in which the testimony is transcribed or the deposition is prepared, signed, certified, sealed,

indorsed, transmitted, filed, or otherwise dealt with by the officer under Rules 30 and 31 are waived unless a motion to suppress the deposition or some part thereof is made with reasonable promptness after such defect is, or with due diligence might have been, ascertained.

Rule 33.

INTERROGATORIES TO PARTIES

(a) Availability; Procedures for Use. Any party may serve upon any other party written interrogatories to be answered by the party served or, if the party served is a public or private corporation or a partnership or association or governmental agency, by any officer or agent, who shall furnish such information as is available to the party. Interrogatories may, without leave of court, be served upon the plaintiff after commencement of the action and upon any other party with or after service of the summons and complaint upon that party.

Each interrogatory shall be answered separately and fully in writing under oath, unless it is objected to, in which event the reasons for objection shall be stated in lieu of an answer. The answers are to be signed by the person making them, and the objections signed by the attorney making them. The party upon whom the interrogatories have been served shall serve a copy of the answers, and objections if any, within 30 days after the service of the interrogatories, except that a defendant may serve answers or objections within 45 days after service of the summons and complaint upon that defendant. The court may allow a shorter or longer time. The party submitting the interrogatories may move for an order under Rule 37(a) with respect to any objection to or other failure to answer an interrogatory.

(b) Scope; Use at Trial. Interrogatories may relate to any matters which can be inquired into under Rule 26(b), and the answers may be used to the extent permitted by the rules of evidence.

An interrogatory otherwise proper is not necessarily objectionable merely because an answer to the interrogatory involves an opinion or contention that relates to fact or the application of law to fact, but the court may order that such an interrogatory need not be answered until after designated discovery has been completed or until a pre-trial conference or other later time.

(c) Option to Produce Business Records. Where the answer to an interrogatory may be derived or ascertained from the business records of the party upon whom the interrogatory has been served or from an examination, audit or inspection of such business records, including a compilation, abstract or summary thereof, and the burden of deriving or ascertaining the answer is substantially the same for the party serving the interrogatory as for the party served, it is a sufficient answer to such interrogatory to specify the records from which the answer may be derived or ascertained and to afford to the party serving the interrogatory reasonable opportunity to examine, audit or inspect such records and to make copies, compilations, abstracts or summaries. A specification shall be in sufficient detail to permit the interrogating party to locate and to identify, as readily as can the party served, the records from which the answer may be ascertained.

Rule 34.

PRODUCTION OF DOCUMENTS AND THINGS AND ENTRY UPON LAND FOR INSPECTION AND OTHER PURPOSES

(a) Scope. Any party may serve on any other party a request (1) to produce and permit the party making the request, or someone acting on his behalf, to inspect and copy, any designated documents (including writings, drawings, graphs, charts, photographs, phono-records, and other data compilations from which information can be obtained, translated, if necessary, by the respondent through detection devices into reasonably usable form), or to inspect and copy, test, or sample any tangible things which constitute or contain matters within the scope of Rule 26(b) and which are in the possession, custody or control of the party upon whom the request is served; or (2) to permit entry upon designated land or other property in the possession or control of the party upon whom the request is served for the purpose of inspection and measuring, surveying, photographing, testing, or sampling the property or any designated object or operation thereon, within the scope of Rule 26(b).

(b) Procedure. The request may, without leave of court, be served upon the plaintiff after commencement of the action and upon any other party with or after service of the summons and complaint upon that party. The request shall set forth the items to be inspected either by individual item or by category, and decribe each item and category with reasonable particularity. The request shall specify a reasonable time, place, and manner of making the inspection and performing the related acts.

The party upon whom the request is served shall serve a written response within 30 days after the service of the request, except that a defendant may serve a response within 45 days after service of the summons and complaint upon that defendant. The court may allow a shorter or longer time. The response shall state, with respect to each item or category, that inspection and related activities will be permitted as requested, unless the request is objected to, in which event the reasons for objection shall be stated. If objection is made to part of an item or category, the part shall be specified. The party submitting the request may move for an order under Rule 37(a) with respect to any objection to or other failure to respond to the request or any part thereof, or any failure to permit inspection as requested.

A party who produces documents for inspection shall produce them as they are kept in the usual course of business or shall organize and label them to correspond with the categories in the request.

(c) Persons Not Parties. This rule does not preclude an independent action against a person not a party for production of documents and things and permission to enter upon land.

Rule 35.

PHYSICAL AND MENTAL EXAMINATION OF PERSONS

(a) Order for Examination. When the mental or physical condition (including the blood group) of a party, or of a person in the custody or under the legal control of a party, is in controversy, the court in which the action is pending may order the party to submit to a physical or mental examination by a physician or to produce for examination the person in his custody or legal control. The order may be made only on motion for good cause shown and upon notice to the person to be examined and to all parties and shall specify the time, place, manner, conditions, and scope of the examination and the person or persons by whom it is to be made.

(b) Report of Examining Physician.

(1) If requested by the party against whom an order is made under Rule 35(a) or the person examined, the party causing the examination to be made shall deliver to him a copy of a detailed written report of the examining physician setting out his findings, including results of all tests made, diagnoses and conclusions, together with like reports of all earlier examinations of the same condition. After delivery the party

causing the examination shall be entitled upon request to receive from the party against whom the order is made a like report of any examination, previously or thereafter made, of the same condition, unless, in the case of a report of examination of a person not a party, the party shows that he is unable to obtain it. The court on motion may make an order against a party requiring delivery of a report on such terms as are just, and if a physician fails or refuses to make a report the court may exclude his testimony if offered at the trial.

(2) By requesting and obtaining a report of the examination so ordered or by taking the deposition of the examiner, the party examined waives any privilege he may have in that action or any other involving the same controversy, regarding the testimony of every other person who has examined or may thereafter examine him in respect of the same mental or physical condition.

(3) This subdivision applies to examinations made by agreement of the parties, unless the agreement expressly provides otherwise. This subdivision does not preclude discovery of a report of an examining physician or the taking of a deposition of the physician in accordance with the provisions of any other rule.

Rule 36.

REQUESTS FOR ADMISSION

(a) Request for Admission. A party may serve upon any other party a written request for the admission, for purposes of the pending action only, of the truth of any matters within the scope of Rule 26(b) set forth in the request that relate to statements or opinions of fact or of the application of law to fact, including the genuineness of any documents described in the request. Copies of documents shall be served with the request unless they have been or are otherwise furnished or made available for inspection and copying. The request may, without leave of court, be served upon the plaintiff after commencement of the action and upon any other party with or after service of the summons and complaint upon that party.

Each matter of which an admission is requested shall be separately set forth. The matter is admitted unless, within 30 days after service of the request, or within such shorter or longer time as the court may allow, the party to whom the request is directed serves upon the party requesting the admission a written answer or objection addressed to the matter, signed by the party or by his attorney, but, unless the court shortens the time, a defendant shall not be required to serve answers or objections before the expiration of 45 days after service of the summons and complaint upon him. If objection is made, the reasons therefor shall be stated. The answer shall specifically deny the matter or set forth in detail the reasons why the answering party cannot truthfully admit or deny the matter. A denial shall fairly meet the substance of the requested admission, and when good faith requires that a party qualify his answer or deny only a part of the matter of which an admission is requested, he shall specify so much of it as is true and qualify or deny the remainder. An answering party may not give lack of information or knowledge as a reason for failure to admit or deny unless he states that he has made reasonable inquiry and that the information known or readily obtainable by him is insufficient to enable him to admit or deny. A party who considers that a matter of which an admission has been requested presents a genuine issue for trial may not, on that ground alone, object to the request; he may, subject to the provisions of Rule 37(c), deny the matter or set forth reasons why he cannot admit or deny it.

The party who has requested the admissions may move to determine the sufficiency of the answers or objections. Unless the court determines that an objection is justified, it shall order that an answer be served. If the court determines that an answer does not comply with the requirements of this rule, it may order either that the matter is admitted or that an amended answer be served. The court may, in lieu of these orders, determine that final disposition of the request be made at a pre-trial conference or at a designated time prior to trial. The provisions of Rule 37(a) (4) apply to the award of expenses incurred in relation to the motion.

(b) Effect of Admission. Any matter admitted under this rule is conclusively established unless the court on motion permits withdrawal or amendment of the admission. Subject to the provisions of Rule 16 governing amendment of a pre-trial order, the court may permit withdrawal or amendment when the presentation of the merits of the action will be subserved thereby and the party who obtained the admission fails to satisfy the court that withdrawal or amendment will prejudice him in maintaining his action or defense on the merits. Any admission made by a party under this rule is for the purpose of the pending action only and is not an admission by him for any other purpose nor may it be used against him in any other proceeding.

Rule 37.

FAILURE TO MAKE OR COOPERATE IN DISCOVERY: SANCTIONS

(a) Motion for Order Compelling Discovery. A party, upon reasonable notice to other parties and all persons affected thereby, may apply for an order compelling discovery as follows:

(1) *Appropriate Court.*—An application for an order to a party may be made to the court in which the action is pending, or, on matters relating to a deposition, to the court in the district where the deposition is being taken. An application for an order to a deponent who is not a party shall be made to the court in the district where the deposition is being taken.

(2) *Motion.*—If a deponent fails to answer a question propounded or submitted under Rule 30 or 31, or a corporation or other entity fails to make a designation under Rule 30(b)(6) or 31(a), or a party fails to answer an interrogatory submitted under Rule 33, or if a party, in response to a request for inspection submitted under Rule 34, fails to respond that inspection will be permitted as requested or fails to permit inspection as requested, the discovering party may move for an order compelling an answer, or a designation, or an order compelling inspection in accordance with the request. When taking a deposition on oral examination, the proponent of the question may complete or adjourn the examination before he applies for an order.

If the court denies the motion in whole or in part, it may make such protective order as it would have been empowered to make on a motion made pursuant to Rule 26(c).

(3) *Evasive or Incomplete Answer.*—For purposes of this subdivision an evasive or incomplete answer is to be treated as a failure to answer.

(4) *Award of Expenses of Motion.*—If the motion is granted, the court shall, after opportunity for hearing, require the party or deponent whose conduct necessitated the motion or the party or attorney advising such conduct or both of them to pay to the moving party the reasonable expenses incurred in obtaining the order, including attorney's fees, unless the court finds that the opposition to the motion was substantially justified or that other circumstances make an award of expenses unjust.

If the motion is denied, the court shall, after opportunity for hearing, require the moving party or the attorney advising the motion or both of them to pay to the party or deponent who opposed the motion the reasonable expenses incurred in opposing the motion, including attorney's fees, unless the court finds that the making of the motion was substantially justified or that other circumstances make an award of expenses unjust.

If the motion is granted in part and denied in part, the court may apportion the reasonable expenses incurred in relation to the motion among the parties and persons in a just manner.

(b) Failure to Comply with Order.

(1) *Sanctions by Court in District Where Deposition Is Taken.*—If a deponent fails to be sworn or to answer a question after being directed to do so by the court in the district in which the deposition is being taken, the failure may be considered a contempt of that court.

(2) *Sanctions by Court in Which Action Is Pending.*—If a party or an officer, director, or managing agent of a party or a person designated under Rule 30(b)(6) or 31(a) to testify on behalf of a party fails to obey an order to provide or permit discovery, including an order made under subdivision (a) of this rule or Rule 35, or if a party fails to obey an order entered under Rule 26(f), the court in which the action is pending may make such orders in regard to the failure as are just, and among others the following:

(A) An order that the matters regarding which the order was made or any other designated facts shall be taken to be established for the purposes of the action in accordance with the claim of the party obtaining the order;

(B) An order refusing to allow the disobedient party to support or oppose designated claims or defenses, or prohibiting him from introducing designated matters in evidence;

(C) An order striking out pleadings or parts thereof, or staying further proceedings until the order is obeyed, or dismissing the action or proceeding or any part thereof, or rendering a judgment by default against the disobedient party;

(D) In lieu of any of the foregoing orders or in addition thereto, an order treating as a contempt of court the failure to obey any orders except an order to submit to a physical or mental examination;

(E) Where a party has failed to comply with an order under Rule 35(a) requiring him to produce another for examination, such orders as are listed in paragraphs (A), (B), and (C) of this subdivision, unless the party failing to comply shows that he is unable to produce such person for examination.

In lieu of any of the foregoing orders or in addition thereto, the court shall require the party failing to obey the order or the attorney advising him or both to pay the reasonable expenses, including attorney's fees, caused by the failure, unless the court finds that the failure was substantially justified or that other circumstances make an award of expenses unjust.

(c) Expenses on Failure to Admit. If a party fails to admit the genuineness of any document or the truth of any matter as requested under Rule 36, and if the party requesting the admissions thereafter proves the genuineness of the document or the truth of the matter, he may apply to the court for an order requiring the other party to pay him the reasonable expenses incurred in making that proof, including reasonable attorney's fees. The court shall make the order unless it finds that (1) the request was held objectionable pursuant to Rule 36(a), or (2) the admission sought was of no substantial importance, or (3) the party failing to admit had reasonable ground to believe that he might prevail on the matter, or (4) there was other good reason for the failure to admit.

(d) Failure of Party to Attend at Own Deposition or Serve Answers to Interrogatories or Respond to Request for Inspection. If a party or an officer, director, or managing agent of a party or a person designated under Rule 30(b) (6) or 31(a) to testify on behalf of a party fails (1) to appear before the officer who is to take his deposition, after being served with a proper notice, or (2) to serve answers or objections to interrogatories submitted under Rule 33, after proper service of the interrogatories, or (3) to serve a written response to a request for inspection submitted under Rule 34, after proper service of the request, the court in which the action is pending on motion may make such orders in regard to the failure as are just, and among others it may take any action authorized under paragraphs (A), (B), and (C) of subdivision (b) (2) of this rule. In lieu of any order or in addition thereto, the court shall require the party failing to act or the attorney advising him or both to pay the reasonable expenses, including attorney's fees, caused by the failure, unless the court finds that the failure was substantially justified or that other circumstances make an award of expenses unjust.

The failure to act described in this subdivision may not be excused on the ground that the discovery sought is objectionable unless the party failing to act has applied for a protective order as provided by Rule 26(c).

[(e) Abrogated.]

[(f) Repealed.]

(g) Failure to Participate in the Framing of a Discovery Plan. If a party or his attorney fails to participate in good faith in the framing of a discovery plan by agreement as is required by Rule 26(f), the court may, after opportunity for hearing, require such party or his attorney to pay to any other party the reasonable expenses, including attorney's fees, caused by the failure.

VI. TRIALS

Rule 38.

JURY TRIAL OF RIGHT

(a) Right Preserved. The right of trial by jury as declared by the Seventh Amendment to the Constitution or as given by a statute of the United States shall be preserved to the parties inviolate.

(b) Demand. Any party may demand a trial by jury of any issue triable of right by a jury by serving upon the other parties a demand therefor in writing at any time after the commencement of the action and not later than 10 days after the service of the last pleading directed to such issue. Such demand may be indorsed upon a pleading of the party.

(c) Same: Specification of Issues. In his demand a party may specify the issues which he wishes so tried; otherwise he shall be deemed to have demanded trial by jury for all the issues so triable. If he has demanded trial by jury for only some of the issues, any other party within 10 days after service of the demand or such lesser time as the court may order, may serve a demand for trial by jury of any other or all of the issues of fact in the action.

(d) Waiver. The failure of a party to serve a demand as required by this rule and to file it as required by Rule 5(d) constitutes a waiver by him of trial by jury. A demand for trial by jury made as herein provided may not be withdrawn without the consent of the parties.

(e) Admiralty and Maritime Claims. These rules shall not be construed to create a right to trial by jury of the issues in an admiralty or maritime claim within the meaning of Rule 9(h).

Rule 39.

TRIAL BY JURY OR BY THE COURT

(a) By Jury. When trial by jury has been demanded as provided in Rule 38, the action shall be designated upon the docket as a jury action. The trial of all issues so demanded shall be by jury, unless (1) the parties or their attorneys of record, by written stipulation filed with the court or by an oral stipulation made in open court and entered in the record, consent to trial by the court sitting without a jury or (2) the court upon motion or of its own initiative finds that a right of trial by jury of some or all of those issues does not exist under the Constitution or statutes of the United States.

(b) By the Court. Issues not demanded for trial by jury as provided in Rule 38 shall be tried by the court; but, notwithstanding the failure of a party to demand a jury in an action in which such a demand might have been made of right, the court in its discretion upon motion may order a trial by a jury of any or all issues.

(c) Advisory Jury and Trial by Consent. In all actions not triable of right by a jury the court upon motion or of its own initiative may try any issue with an advisory jury or, except in actions against the United States when a statute of the United States provides for trial without a jury, the court, with the consent of both parties, may order a trial with a jury whose verdict has the same effect as if trial by jury had been a matter of right.

Rule 40.

ASSIGNMENT OF CASES FOR TRIAL

The district courts shall provide by rule for the placing of actions upon the trial calendar (1) without request of the parties or (2) upon request of a party and notice to the other parties or (3) in such other manner as the courts deem expedient. Precedence shall be given to actions entitled thereto by any statute of the United States.

Rule 41.

DISMISSAL OF ACTIONS

(a) Voluntary Dismissal: Effect Thereof.

(1) *By Plaintiff; by Stipulation.* Subject to the provisions of Rule 23(e), of Rule 66, and of any statute of the United States, an

action may be dismissed by the plaintiff without order of court (i) by filing a notice of dismissal at any time before service by the adverse party of an answer or of a motion for summary judgment, whichever first occurs, or (ii) by filing a stipulation of dismissal signed by all parties who have appeared in the action. Unless otherwise stated in the notice of dismissal or stipulation, the dismissal is without prejudice, except that a notice of dismissal operates as an adjudication upon the merits when filed by a plaintiff who has once dismissed in any court of the United States or of any state an action based on or including the same claim.

(2) *By Order of Court.* Except as provided in paragraph (1) of this subdivision of this rule, an action shall not be dismissed at the plaintiff's instance save upon order of the court and upon such terms and conditions as the court deems proper. If a counterclaim has been pleaded by a defendant prior to the service upon him of the plaintiff's motion to dismiss, the action shall not be dismissed against the defendant's objection unless the counterclaim can remain pending for independent adjudication by the court. Unless otherwise specified in the order, a dismissal under this paragraph is without prejudice.

(b) Involuntary Dismissal: Effect Thereof. For failure of the plaintiff to prosecute or to comply with these rules or any order of court, a defendant may move for dismissal of an action or of any claim against him. After the plaintiff, in an action tried by the court without a jury, has completed the presentation of his evidence, the defendant, without waiving his right to offer evidence in the event the motion is not granted, may move for a dismissal on the ground that upon the facts and the law the plaintiff has shown no right to relief. The court as trier of the facts may then determine them and render judgment against the plaintiff or may decline to render any judgment until the close of all the evidence. If the court renders judgment on the merits against the plaintiff, the court shall make findings as provided in Rule 52 (a). Unless the court in its order for dismissal otherwise specifies, a dismissal under this subdivision and any dismissal not provided for in this rule, other than a dismissal for lack of jurisdiction, for improper venue, or for failure to join a party under Rule 19, operates as an adjudication upon the merits.

(c) Dismissal of Counterclaim, Cross-Claim, or Third-Party Claim. The provisions of this rule apply to the dismissal of any counterclaim, cross-claim, or third-party claim. A voluntary dismissal by the claimant alone pursuant to paragraph (1) of subdivision (a) of this rule shall be made before a responsive pleading is served or, if there is none, before the introduction of evidence at the trial or hearing.

(d) Costs of Previously-Dismissed Action. If a plaintiff who has once dismissed an action in any court commences an action based upon or including the same claim against the same defendant, the court may make such order for the payment of costs of the action previously dismissed as it may deem proper and may stay the proceedings in the action until the plaintiff has complied with the order.

Rule 42.

CONSOLIDATION; SEPARATE TRIALS

(a) Consolidation. When actions involving a common question of law or fact are pending before the court, it may order a joint hearing or trial of any or all the matters in issue in the actions; it may order all the actions consolidated; and it may make such orders concerning proceedings therein as may tend to avoid unnecessary costs or delay.

(b) Separate Trials. The court, in furtherance of convenience or to avoid prejudice, or when separate trials will be conducive to expedition and economy, may order a separate trial of any claim, cross-claim, counterclaim, or third-party claim, or of any separate issue or of any number of claims, cross-claims, counterclaims, third-party claims, or issues, always preserving inviolate the right of trial by jury as declared by the Seventh Amendment to the Constitution or as given by a statute of the United States.

Rule 43.

TAKING OF TESTIMONY

(a) Form. In all trials the testimony of witnesses shall be taken orally in open court, unless otherwise provided by an Act of Congress or by these rules, the Federal Rules of Evidence, or other rules adopted by the Supreme Court.

[**(b) Scope of Examination and Cross-Examination.** Abrogated.]

[**(c) Record of Excluded Evidence.** Abrogated.]

(d) Affirmation in Lieu of Oath. Whenever under these rules an oath is required to be taken, a solemn affirmation may be accepted in lieu thereof.

(e) Evidence on Motions. When a motion is based on facts not appearing of record the court may hear the matter on affidavits presented by the respective parties, but the court may direct that the matter be heard wholly or partly on oral testimony or deposition.

(f) Interpreters. The court may appoint an interpreter of its own selection and may fix his reasonable compensation. The compensation shall be paid out of funds provided by law or by one or more of the parties as the court may direct, and may be taxed ultimately as costs, in the discretion of the court.

Rule 44.

PROOF OF OFFICIAL RECORD

(a) Authentication.

(1) *Domestic.* An official record kept within the United States, or any state, district, commonwealth, territory, or insular possession thereof, or within the Panama Canal Zone, the Trust Territory of the Pacific Islands, or the Ryukyu Islands, or an entry therein, when admissible for any purpose, may be evidenced by an official publication thereof or by a copy attested by the officer having the legal custody of the record, or by his deputy, and accompanied by a certificate that such officer has the custody. The certificate may be made by a judge of a court of record of the district or political subdivision in which the record is kept, authenticated by the seal of the court, or may be made by any public officer having a seal of office and having official duties in the district or political subdivision in which the record is kept, authenticated by the seal of his office.

(2) *Foreign.* A foreign official record, or an entry therein, when admissible for any purpose, may be evidenced by an official publication thereof; or a copy thereof, attested by a person authorized to make the attestation, and accompanied by a final certification as to the genuineness of the signature and official position (i) of the attesting person, or (ii) of any foreign official whose certificate of genuineness of signature and official position relates to the attestation or is in a chain of certificates of genuineness of signature and official position relating to the attestation. A final certification may be made by a secretary of embassy or legation, consul general, consul, vice consul, or consular agent of the United States, or a diplomatic or consular official of the foreign country assigned or accredited to the United States. If reasonable opportunity has been given to all parties to investigate the authenticity and accuracy of the documents, the court may, for good cause shown, (i) admit an attested copy without final certification or (ii) permit the foreign official record to be evidenced by an attested summary with or without a final certification.

(b) Lack of Record. A written statement that after diligent search no record or entry of a specified tenor is found to exist in the records designated by the statement, authenticated as provided in subdivision (a) (1) of this rule in the case of a domestic record, or complying with the requirements of subdivision (a) (2) of this rule for a summary in the case of a foreign record, is admissible as evidence that the records contain no such record or entry.

(c) Other Proof. This rule does not prevent the proof of official records or of entry or lack of entry therein by any other method authorized by law.

Rule 44.1.

DETERMINATION OF FOREIGN LAW

A party who intends to raise an issue concerning the law of a foreign country shall give notice in his pleadings or other reasonable written notice. The court, in determining foreign law, may consider any relevant material or source, including testimony, whether or not submitted by a party or admissible under the Federal Rules of Evidence. The court's determination shall be treated as a ruling on a question of law.

Rule 45.

SUBPOENA

(a) For Attendance of Witnesses; Form; Issuance. Every subpoena shall be issued by the clerk under the seal of the court, shall state the name of the court and the title of the action, and shall command each person to whom it is directed to attend and give testimony at a time and place therein specified. The clerk shall issue a subpoena, or a subpoena for the production of documentary evidence, signed and sealed but otherwise in blank, to a party requesting it, who shall fill it in before service.

(b) For Production of Documentary Evidence. A subpoena may also command the person to whom it is directed to produce the books, papers, documents, or tangible things designated therein; but the court, upon motion made promptly and in any event at or before the time specified in the subpoena for compliance therewith, may (1) quash or modify the subpoena if it is unreasonable and oppressive or (2) condition denial of the motion upon the advancement by the person in whose behalf the subpoena is issued of the reasonable cost of producing the books, papers, documents, or tangible things.

(c) Service. A subpoena may be served by the marshal, by his deputy, or by any other person who is not a party and is not less than 18 years of age. Service of a subpoena upon a person named therein shall be made by delivering a copy thereof to such person and by tendering to him the fees for one day's attendance and the mileage allowed by law. When the subpoena is issued on behalf of the United States or an officer or agency thereof, fees and mileage need not be tendered.

(d) Subpoena for Taking Depositions; Place of Examination.

(1) Proof of service of a notice to take a deposition as provided in Rules 30(b) and 31(a) constitutes a sufficient authorization for the issuance by the clerk of the district court for the district in which the deposition is to be taken of subpoenas for the persons named or described therein. Proof of service may be made by filing with the clerk of the district court for the district in which the deposition is to be taken a copy of the notice together with a statement of the date and manner of service and of the names of the persons served, certified by the person who made service. The subpoena may command the person to whom it is directed to produce and permit inspection and copying of designated books, papers, documents, or tangible things which constitute or contain matters within the scope of the examination permitted by Rule 26(b), but in that event the subpoena will be subject to the provisions of Rule 26(c) and subdivision (b) of this rule.

The person to whom the subpoena is directed may, within 10 days after the service thereof or on or before the time specified in the subpoena for compliance if such time is less than 10 days after service, serve upon the attorney designated in the subpoena written objection to inspection or copying of any or all of the designated materials. If objection is made, the party serving the subpoena shall not be entitled to inspect and copy the materials except pursuant to an order of the court from which the subpoena was issued. The party serving the subpoena may, if objection has been made, move upon notice to the deponent for an order at any time before or during the taking of the deposition.

(2) A resident of the district in which the deposition is to be taken may be required to attend an examination only in the county wherein he resides or is employed or transacts his business in person, or at such other convenient place as is fixed by an order of court. A nonresident of the district may be required to attend only in the county wherein he is served with a subpoena, or

within 40 miles from the place of service, or at such other convenient place as is fixed by an order of court.

(e) Subpoena for a Hearing or Trial.

(1) At the request of any party subpoenas for attendance at a hearing or trial shall be issued by the clerk of the district court for the district in which the hearing or trial is held. A subpoena requiring the attendance of a witness at a hearing or trial may be served at any place within the district, or at any place without the district that is within 100 miles of the place of the hearing or trial specified in the subpoena, or at a place within the state where a state statute or rule of court permits service of a subpoena issued by a state court of general jurisdiction sitting in the place where the district court is held. When a statute of the United States provides therefor, the court upon proper application and cause shown may authorize the service of a subpoena at any other place.

(2) A subpoena directed to a witness in a foreign country shall issue under the circumstances and in the manner and be served as provided in Title 28, U.S.C., § 1783.

(f) Contempt. Failure by any person without adequate excuse to obey a subpoena served upon him may be deemed a contempt of the court from which the subpoena issued.

Rule 46.

EXCEPTIONS UNNECESSARY

Formal exceptions to rulings or orders of the court are unnecessary; but for all purposes for which an exception has heretofore been necessary it is sufficient that a party, at the time the ruling or order of the court is made or sought, makes known to the court the action which he desires the court to take or his objection to the action of the court and his grounds therefor; and, if a party has no opportunity to object to a ruling or order at the time it is made, the absence of an objection does not thereafter prejudice him.

Rule 47.

JURORS

(a) Examination of Jurors. The court may permit the parties or their attorneys to conduct the examination of prospective jurors or may itself conduct the examination. In the latter event, the court shall permit the parties or their attorneys to supplement the examination by such further inquiry as it deems proper or shall itself submit to the prospective jurors such additional questions of the parties or their attorneys as it deems proper.

(b) Alternate Jurors. The court may direct that not more than six jurors in addition to the regular jury be called and impanelled to sit as alternate jurors. Alternate jurors in the order in which they are called shall replace jurors who, prior to the time the jury retires to consider its verdict, become unable or disqualified to perform their duties. Alternate jurors shall be drawn in the same manner, shall have the same qualifications, shall be subject to the same examination and challenges, shall take the same oath, and shall have the same functions, powers, facilities, and privileges as the regular jurors. An alternate juror who does not replace a regular juror shall be discharged after the jury retires to consider its verdict. Each side is entitled to 1 peremptory challenge in addition to those otherwise allowed by law if 1 or 2 alternate jurors are to be impanelled, 2 peremptory challenges if 3 or 4 alternate jurors are to be impanelled, and 3 peremptory challenges if 5 or 6 alternate jurors are to be impanelled. The additional peremptory challenges may be used against an alternate juror only, and the other peremptory challenges allowed by law shall not be used against an alternate juror.

Rule 48.

JURIES OF LESS THAN TWELVE—MAJORITY VERDICT

The parties may stipulate that the jury shall consist of any number less than twelve or that a verdict or a finding of a stated majority of the jurors shall be taken as the verdict or finding of the jury.

Rule 49.

SPECIAL VERDICTS AND INTERROGATORIES

(a) Special Verdicts. The court may require a jury to return only a special verdict in the form of a special written finding upon each issue of fact. In that event the court may submit to the jury written questions susceptible of categorical or other brief answer or may submit written forms of the several special findings which might properly be made under the pleadings and evidence; or it may use such other method of submitting the issues and requiring the written findings thereon as it deems most appropriate. The court shall give to the jury such explanation and instruction concerning the matter thus submitted as may be necessary to enable the jury to make its findings upon each issue. If in so doing the court omits any issue of fact raised by the pleadings or by the evidence, each party waives his right to a trial by jury of the issue so omitted unless before the jury retires he demands its submission to the jury. As to an issue omitted without such demand the court may make a finding; or, if it fails to do so, it shall be deemed to have made a finding in accord with the judgment on the special verdict.

(b) General Verdict Accompanied by Answer to Interrogatories. The court may submit to the jury, together with appropriate forms for a general verdict, written interrogatories upon one or more issues of fact the decision of which is necessary to a verdict. The court shall give such explanation or instruction as may be necessary to enable the jury both to make answers to the interrogatories and to render a general verdict, and the court shall direct the jury both to make written answers and to render a general verdict. When the general verdict and the answers are harmonious, the appropriate judgment upon the verdict and answers shall be entered pursuant to Rule 58. When the answers are consistent with each other but one or more is inconsistent with the general verdict, judgment may be entered pursuant to Rule 58 in accordance with the answers, notwithstanding the general verdict, or the court may return the jury for further consideration of its answers and verdict or may order a new trial. When the answers are inconsistent with each other and one or more is likewise inconsistent with the general verdict, judgment shall not be entered, but the court shall return the jury for further consideration of its answers and verdict or shall order a new trial.

Rule 50.

MOTION FOR A DIRECTED VERDICT AND FOR JUDGMENT NOTWITHSTANDING THE VERDICT

(a) Motion for Directed Verdict: When Made; Effect. A party who moves for a directed verdict at the close of the evidence offered by an opponent may offer evidence in the event that the motion is not granted, without having reserved the right so to do and to the same extent as if the motion had not been made. A motion for a directed verdict which is not granted is not a waiver of trial by jury even though all parties to the action have moved for directed verdicts. A motion for a directed verdict shall state the specific grounds therefor. The order of the court granting a motion for a directed verdict is effective without any assent of the jury.

(b) Motion for Judgment Notwithstanding the Verdict. Whenever a motion for a directed verdict made at the close of all the evidence is denied or for any reason is not granted, the court is deemed to have submitted the action to the jury subject to a later determination of the legal questions raised by the motion. Not later than 10 days after entry of judgment, a party who has moved for a directed verdict may move to have the verdict and any judgment entered thereon set aside and to have judgment entered in accordance with his motion for a directed verdict; or if a verdict was not returned such party, within 10 days after the jury has been discharged, may move for judgment in accordance with his motion for a directed verdict. A motion for a new trial may be joined with this motion, or a new trial may be prayed for in the alternative. If a verdict was returned the court may allow the judgment to stand or may reopen the judgment and either order a new trial or direct the entry of judgment as if the requested verdict had been directed. If no verdict was returned the court may direct the entry of judgment as if the requested verdict had been directed or may order a new trial.

(c) Same: Conditional Rulings on Grant of Motion.

(1) If the motion for judgment notwithstanding the verdict, provided for in subdivision (b) of this rule, is granted, the court shall also rule on the motion for a new trial, if any, by determining whether it should be granted if the judgment is thereafter vacated or reversed, and shall specify the grounds for granting or denying the motion for the new trial. If the motion for a new trial is thus conditionally granted, the order thereon does not affect the finality of the judgment. In case the motion for a new trial has been conditionally granted and the judgment is reversed on appeal, the new trial shall proceed unless the appellate court has otherwise ordered. In case the motion for a new trial has been conditionally denied, the appellee on appeal may assert error in that denial; and if the judgment is reversed on appeal, subsequent proceedings shall be in accordance with the order of the appellate court.

(2) The party whose verdict has been set aside on motion for judgment notwithstanding the verdict may serve a motion for a new trial pursuant to Rule 59 not later than 10 days after entry of the judgment notwithstanding the verdict.

(d) Same: Denial of Motion. If the motion for judgment notwithstanding the verdict is denied, the party who prevailed on that motion may, as appellee, assert grounds entitling him to a new trial in the event the appellate court concludes that the trial court erred in denying the motion for judgment notwithstanding the verdict. If the appellate court reverses the judgment, nothing in this rule precludes it from determining that the appellee is entitled to a new trial, or from directing the trial court to determine whether a new trial shall be granted.

Rule 51.

INSTRUCTIONS TO JURY: OBJECTION

At the close of the evidence or at such earlier time during the trial as the court reasonably directs, any party may file written requests that the court instruct the jury on the law as set forth in the requests. The court shall inform counsel of its proposed action upon the requests prior to their arguments to the jury, but the court shall instruct the jury after the arguments are completed. No party may assign as error the giving or the failure to give an instruction unless he objects thereto before the jury retires to consider its verdict, stating distinctly the matter to which he objects and the grounds of his objection. Opportunity shall be given to make the objection out of the hearing of the jury.

Rule 52.

FINDINGS BY THE COURT

(a) Effect. In all actions tried upon the facts without a jury or with an advisory jury, the court shall find the facts specially and state separately its conclusions of law thereon, and judgment shall be entered pursuant to Rule 58; and in granting or refusing interlocutory injunctions the court shall similarly set forth the findings of fact and conclusions of law which constitute the grounds of its action. Requests for findings are not necessary for purposes of review. Findings of fact shall not be set aside unless clearly erroneous, and due regard shall be given to the opportunity of the trial court to judge of the credibility of the witnesses. The findings of a master, to the extent that the court adopts them, shall be considered as the findings of the court. It will be sufficient if the findings of fact and conclusions of law are stated orally and recorded in open court following the close of the evidence or appear in an opinion or memorandum of decision filed by the court. Findings of fact and conclusions of law are unnecessary on decisions of motions under Rules 12 or 56 or any other motion except as provided in Rule 41(b).

(b) Amendment. Upon motion of a party made not later than 10 days after entry of judgment the court may amend its findings or make additional findings and may amend the judgment accordingly. The motion may be made with a motion for a new trial pursuant to Rule 59. When findings of fact are made in actions tried by the court without a jury, the question of the sufficiency of the evidence to support the findings may thereafter be raised whether or not the party raising the question has made in the district court an objection to such findings or has made a motion to amend them or a motion for judgment.

Rule 53.

MASTERS

(a) Appointment and Compensation. The court in which any action is pending may appoint a special master therein. As used in these rules the word "master" includes a referee, an auditor, an examiner, and an assessor. The compensation to be allowed to a master shall be fixed by the court, and shall be charged upon such of the parties or paid out of any fund or subject matter of the action, which is in the custody and control of the court as the court may direct; provided that this provision for compensation shall not apply when a United States magistrate is designated to serve as a master pursuant to Title 28, U.S.C. § 636(b)(2). The master shall not retain his report as security for his compensation; but when the party ordered to pay the compensation allowed by the court does not pay it after notice and within the time prescribed by the court, the master is entitled to a writ of execution against the delinquent party.

(b) Reference. A reference to a master shall be the exception and not the rule. In actions to be tried by a jury, a reference shall be made only when the issues are complicated; in actions to be tried without a jury, save in matters of account and of difficult computation of damages, a reference shall be made only upon a showing that some exceptional condition requires it. Upon the consent of the parties, a magistrate may be designated to serve as a special master without regard to the provisions of this subdivision.

(c) Powers. The order of reference to the master may specify or limit his powers and may direct him to report only upon particular issues or to do or perform particular acts or to receive and report evidence only and may fix the time and place for beginning and closing the hearings and for the filing of the master's report. Subject to the specifications and limitations stated in the order, the master has and shall exercise the power to regulate all proceedings in every hearing before him and to do all acts and take all measures necessary or proper for the efficient performance of his duties under the order. He may require the production before him of evidence upon all matters embraced in the reference, including the production of all books, papers, vouchers, documents, and writings applicable thereto. He may rule upon the admissibility of evidence unless otherwise directed by the order of reference and has the authority to put witnesses on oath and may himself examine them and may call the parties to the action and examine them upon oath. When a party so requests, the master shall make a record of the evidence offered and excluded in the same manner and subject to the same limitations as provided in the Federal Rules of Evidence for a court sitting without a jury.

(d) Proceedings.

(1) *Meetings.* When a reference is made, the clerk shall forthwith furnish the master with a copy of the order of reference. Upon receipt thereof unless the order of reference otherwise provides, the master shall forthwith set a time and place for the first meeting of the parties or their attorneys to be held within 20 days after the date of the order of reference and shall notify the parties or their attorneys. It is the duty of the master to proceed with all reasonable diligence. Either party, on notice to the parties and master, may apply to the court for an order requiring the master to speed the proceedings and to make his report. If a party fails to appear at the time and place appointed, the master may proceed ex parte or, in his discretion, adjourn the proceedings to a future day, giving notice to the absent party of the adjournment.

(2) *Witnesses.* The parties may procure the attendance of witnesses before the master by the issuance and service of subpoenas as provided in Rule 45. If without adequate excuse a witness fails to appear or give evidence, he may be punished as for a contempt and be subjected to the consequences, penalties, and remedies provided in Rules 37 and 45.

(3) *Statement of Accounts.* When matters of accounting are in issue before the master, he may prescribe the form in which the accounts shall be submitted and in any proper case may require or receive in evidence a statement by a certified public ac-

countant who is called as a witness. Upon objection of a party to any of the items thus submitted or upon a showing that the form of statement is insufficient, the master may require a different form of statement to be furnished, or the accounts or specific items thereof to be proved by oral examination of the accounting parties or upon written interrogatories or in such other manner as he directs.

(e) Report.

(1) *Contents and Filing.* The master shall prepare a report upon the matters submitted to him by the order of reference and, if required to make findings of fact and conclusions of law, he shall set them forth in the report. He shall file the report with the clerk of the court and in an action to be tried without a jury, unless otherwise directed by the order of reference, shall file with it a transcript of the proceedings and of the evidence and the original exhibits. The clerk shall forthwith mail to all parties notice of the filing.

(2) *In Non-Jury Actions.* In an action to be tried without a jury the court shall accept the master's findings of fact unless clearly erroneous. Within 10 days after being served with notice of the filing of the report any party may serve written objections thereto upon the other parties. Application to the court for action upon the report and upon objections thereto shall be by motion and upon notice as prescribed in Rule 6(d). The court after hearing may adopt the report or may modify it or may reject it in whole or in part or may receive further evidence or may recommit it with instructions.

(3) *In Jury Actions.* In an action to be tried by a jury the master shall not be directed to report the evidence. His findings upon the issues submitted to him are admissible as evidence of the matters found and may be read to the jury, subject to the ruling of the court upon any objections in point of law which may be made to the report.

(4) *Stipulation as to Findings.* The effect of a master's report is the same whether or not the parties have consented to the reference; but, when the parties stipulate that a master's findings of fact shall be final, only questions of law arising upon the report shall thereafter be considered.

(5) *Draft Report.* Before filing his report a master may submit a draft thereof to counsel for all parties for the purpose of receiving their suggestions.

(f) A magistrate is subject to this rule only when the order referring a matter to the magistrate expressly provides that the reference is made under this Rule.

VII. JUDGMENT

Rule 54.

JUDGMENTS; COSTS

(a) Definition; Form. "Judgment" as used in these rules includes a decree and any order from which an appeal lies. A judgment shall not contain a recital of pleadings, the report of a master, or the record of prior proceedings.

(b) Judgment Upon Multiple Claims or Involving Multiple Parties. When more than one claim for relief is presented in an action, whether as a claim, counterclaim, cross-claim, or third-party claim, or when multiple parties are involved, the court may direct the entry of a final judgment as to one or more but fewer than all of the claims or parties only upon an express determination that there is no just reason for delay and upon an express direction for the entry of judgment. In the absence of such determination and direction, any order or other form of decision, however designated, which adjudicates fewer than all the claims or the rights and liabilities of fewer than all the parties shall not terminate the action as to any of the claims or parties, and the order or other form of decision is subject to revision at any time before the entry of judgment adjudicating all the claims and the rights and liabilities of all the parties.

(c) Demand for Judgment. A judgment by default shall not be different in kind from or exceed in amount that prayed for in the demand for judgment. Except as to a party against whom a judgment is entered by default, every final judgment shall grant the relief to which the party in whose favor it is rendered is entitled, even if the party has not demanded such relief in his pleadings.

(d) Costs. Except when express provision therefor is made either in a statute of the United States or in these rules, costs shall be allowed as of course to the prevailing party unless the court otherwise directs; but costs against the United States, its officers, and agencies shall be imposed only to the extent permitted by law. Costs may be taxed by the clerk on one day's notice. On motion served within 5 days thereafter, the action of the clerk may be reviewed by the court.

Rule 55.

DEFAULT

(a) Entry. When a party against whom a judgment for affirmative relief is sought has failed to plead or otherwise defend as provided by these rules and that fact is made to appear by affidavit or otherwise, the clerk shall enter his default.

(b) Judgment. Judgment by default may be entered as follows:

(1) *By the Clerk.* When the plaintiff's claim against a defendant is for a sum certain or for a sum which can by computation be made certain, the clerk upon request of the plaintiff and upon affidavit of the amount due shall enter judgment for that amount and costs against the defendant, if he has been defaulted for failure to appear and if he is not an infant or incompetent person.

(2) *By the Court.* In all other cases the party entitled to a judgment by default shall apply to the court therefor; but no judgment by default shall be entered against an infant or incompetent person unless represented in the action by a general guardian, committee, conservator, or other such representative who has appeared therein. If the party against whom judgment by default is sought has appeared in the action, he (or, if appearing by representative, his representative) shall be served with written notice of the application for judgment at least 3 days prior to the hearing on such application. If, in order to enable the court to enter judgment or to carry it into effect, it is necessary to take an account or to determine the amount of damages or to establish the truth of any averment by evidence or to make an investigation of any other matter, the court may conduct such hearings or order such references as it deems necessary and proper and shall accord a right of trial by jury to the parties when and as required by any statute of the United States.

(c) Setting Aside Default. For good cause shown the court may set aside an entry of default and, if a judgment by default has been entered, may likewise set it aside in accordance with Rule 60(b).

(d) Plaintiffs, Counterclaimants, Cross-Claimants. The provisions of this rule apply whether the party entitled to the judgment by default is a plaintiff, a third-party plaintiff, or a party who has pleaded a cross-claim or counterclaim. In all cases a judgment by default is subject to the limitations of Rule 54(c).

(e) Judgment Against the United States. No judgment by default shall be entered against the United States or an officer or agency thereof unless the claimant establishes his claim or right to relief by evidence satisfactory to the court.

Rule 56.
SUMMARY JUDGMENT

(a) For Claimant. A party seeking to recover upon a claim, counterclaim, or cross-claim or to obtain a declaratory judgment may, at any time after the expiration of 20 days from the commencement of the action or after service of a motion for summary judgment by the adverse party, move with or without supporting affidavits for a summary judgment in his favor upon all or any part thereof.

(b) For Defending Party. A party against whom a claim, counterclaim, or cross-claim is asserted or a declaratory judgment is sought may, at any time, move with or without supporting affidavits for a summary judgment in his favor as to all or any part thereof.

(c) Motion and Proceedings Thereon. The motion shall be served at least 10 days before the time fixed for the hearing. The adverse party prior to the day of hearing may serve opposing affidavits. The judgment sought shall be rendered forthwith if the pleadings, depositions, answers to interrogatories, and admissions on file, together with the affidavits, if any, show that there is no genuine issue as to any material fact and that the moving party is entitled to a judgment as a matter of law. A summary judgment, interlocutory in character, may be rendered on the issue of liability alone although there is a genuine issue as to the amount of damages.

(d) Case Not Fully Adjudicated on Motion. If on motion under this rule judgment is not rendered upon the whole case or for all the relief asked and a trial is necessary, the court at the hearing of the motion, by examining the pleadings and the evidence before it and by interrogating counsel, shall if practicable ascertain what material facts exist without substantial controversy and what material facts are actually and in good faith controverted. It shall thereupon make an order specifying the facts that appear without substantial controversy, including the extent to which the amount of damages or other relief is not in controversy, and directing such further proceedings in the action as are just. Upon the trial of the action the facts so specified shall be deemed established, and the trial shall be conducted accordingly.

(e) Form of Affidavits; Further Testimony; Defense Required. Supporting and opposing affidavits shall be made on personal knowledge, shall set forth such facts as would be admissible in evidence, and shall show affirmatively that the affiant is competent to testify to the matters stated therein. Sworn or certified copies of all papers or parts thereof referred to in an affidavit shall be attached thereto or served therewith. The court may permit affidavits to be supplemented or opposed by depositions, answers to interrogatories, or further affidavits. When a motion for summary judgment is made and supported as provided in this rule, an adverse party may not rest upon the mere allegations or denials of his pleading, but his response, by affidavits or as otherwise provided in this rule, must set forth specific facts showing that there is a genuine issue for trial. If he does not so respond, summary judgment, if appropriate, shall be entered against him.

(f) When Affidavits Are Unavailable. Should it appear from the affidavits of a party opposing the motion that he cannot for reasons stated present by affidavit facts essential to justify his opposition, the court may refuse the application for judgment or may order a continuance to permit affidavits to be obtained or depositions to be taken or discovery to be had or may make such other order as is just.

(g) Affidavits Made in Bad Faith. Should it appear to the satisfaction of the court at any time that any of the affidavits presented pursuant to this rule are presented in bad faith or solely for the purpose of delay, the court shall forthwith order the party employing them to pay to the other party the amount of the reasonable expenses which the filing of the affidavits caused him to incur, including reasonable attorney's fees, and any offending party or attorney may be adjudged guilty of contempt.

Rule 57.

DECLARATORY JUDGMENTS

The procedure for obtaining a declaratory judgment pursuant to Title 28 U.S.C., § 2201, shall be in accordance with these rules, and the right to trial by jury may be demanded under the circumstances and in the manner provided in Rules 38 and 39. The existence of another adequate remedy does not preclude a judgment for declaratory relief in cases where it is appropriate. The court may order a speedy hearing of an action for a declaratory judgment and may advance it on the calendar.

Rule 58.

ENTRY OF JUDGMENT

Subject to the provisions of Rule 54(b): (1) upon a general verdict of a jury, or upon a decision by the court that a party shall recover only a sum certain or costs or that all relief shall be denied, the clerk, unless the court otherwise orders, shall forthwith prepare, sign, and enter the judgment without awaiting any direction by the court; (2) upon a decision by the court granting other relief, or upon a special verdict or a general verdict accompanied by answers to interrogatories, the court shall promptly approve the form of the judgment, and the clerk shall thereupon enter it. Every judgment shall be set forth on a separate document. A judgment is effective only when so set forth and when entered as provided in Rule 79(a). Entry of the judgment shall not be delayed for the taxing of costs. Attorneys shall not submit forms of judgment except upon direction of the court, and these directions shall not be given as a matter of course.

Rule 59.

NEW TRIALS; AMENDMENT OF JUDGMENTS

(a) Grounds. A new trial may be granted to all or any of the parties and on all or part of the issues (1) in an action in which there has been a trial by jury, for any of the reasons for which new trials have heretofore been granted in actions at law in the courts of the United States; and (2) in an action tried without a jury, for any of the reasons for which rehearings have heretofore been granted in suits in equity in the courts of the United States. On a motion for a new trial in an action tried without a jury, the court may open the judgment if one has been entered, take additional testimony, amend findings of fact and conclusions of law or make new findings and conclusions, and direct the entry of a new judgment.

(b) Time for Motion. A motion for a new trial shall be served not later than 10 days after the entry of the judgment.

(c) Time for Serving Affidavits. When a motion for new trial is based upon affidavits they shall be served with the motion. The opposing party has 10 days after such service within which to serve opposing affidavits, which period may be extended for an additional period not exceeding 20 days either by the court for good cause shown or by the parties by written stipulation. The court may permit reply affidavits.

(d) On Initiative of Court. Not later than 10 days after entry of judgment the court of its own initiative may order a new trial for any reason for which it might have granted a new trial on motion of a party. After giving the parties notice and an opportunity to be heard on the matter, the court may grant a motion for a new trial, timely served, for a reason not stated in the motion. In either case, the court shall specify in the order the grounds therefor.

(e) Motion to Alter or Amend a Judgment. A motion to alter or amend the judgment shall be served not later than 10 days after entry of the judgment.

Rule 60.

RELIEF FROM JUDGMENT OR ORDER

(a) Clerical Mistakes. Clerical mistakes in judgments, orders or other parts of the record and errors therein arising from oversight or omission may be corrected by the court at any time of its own initiative or on the motion of any party and after such notice, if any, as the court orders. During the pendency of an appeal, such mistakes may be so corrected before the appeal is docketed in the appellate court, and thereafter while the appeal is pending may be so corrected with leave of the appellate court.

(b) Mistakes; Inadvertence; Excusable Neglect; Newly Discovered Evidence; Fraud, etc. On motion and upon such terms as are just, the court may relieve a party or his legal representative from a final judgment, order, or proceeding for the following reasons: (1) mistake, inadvertence, surprise, or excusable neglect; (2) newly discovered evidence which by due diligence could not have been discovered in time to move for a new trial under Rule 59(b); (3) fraud (whether heretofore denominated intrinsic or extrinsic), misrepresentation, or other misconduct of an adverse party; (4) the judgment is void; (5) the judgment has been satisfied, released, or discharged, or a prior judgment upon which it is based has been reversed or otherwise vacated, or it is no longer equitable that the judgment should have prospective application; or (6) any other reason justifying relief from the operation of the judgment. The motion shall be made within a reasonable time, and for reasons (1), (2), and (3) not more than one year after the judgment, order, or proceeding was entered or taken. A motion under this subdivision (b) does not affect the finality of a judgment or suspend its operation. This rule does not limit the power of a court to entertain an independent action to relieve a party from a judgment, order, or proceeding, or to grant relief to a defendant not actually personally notified as provided in Title 28, U.S.C., § 1655, or to set aside a judgment for fraud upon the court. Writs of coram nobis, coram vobis, audita querela, and bills of review and bills in the nature of a bill of review, are abolished, and the procedure for obtaining any relief from a judgment shall be by motion as prescribed in these rules or by an independent action.

Rule 61.

HARMLESS ERROR

No error in either the admission or the exclusion of evidence and no error or defect in any ruling or order or in anything done or omitted by the court or by any of the parties is ground for granting a new trial or for setting aside a verdict or for vacating, modifying or otherwise disturbing a judgment or order, unless refusal to take such action appears to the court inconsistent with substantial justice. The court at every stage of the proceeding must disregard any error or defect in the proceeding which does not affect the substantial rights of the parties.

Rule 62.

STAY OF PROCEEDINGS TO ENFORCE A JUDGMENT

(a) Automatic Stay; Exceptions—Injunctions, Receiverships, and Patent Accountings. Except as stated herein, no execution shall issue upon a judgment nor shall proceedings be taken for its enforcement until the expiration of 10 days after its entry. Unless otherwise ordered by the court, an interlocutory or final judgment in an action for an injunction or in a receivership action, or a judgment or order directing an accounting in an action for infringement of letters patent, shall not be stayed during the period after its entry and until an appeal is taken or during the pendency of an appeal. The provisions of subdivision (c) of this rule govern the suspending, modifying, restoring, or granting of an injunction during the pendency of an appeal.

(b) Stay on Motion for New Trial or for Judgment. In its discretion and on such conditions for the security of the adverse party as are proper, the court may stay the execution of or any proceedings to enforce a judgment pending the disposition of a motion for a new trial or to alter or amend a judgment made pursuant to Rule 59, or of a motion for relief from a judgment or order made pursuant to Rule 60, or of a motion for judgment in accordance with a motion for a directed verdict made pursuant to Rule 50, or of a motion for amendment to the findings or for additional findings made pursuant to Rule 52(b).

(c) Injunction Pending Appeal. When an appeal is taken from an interlocutory or final judgment granting, dissolving, or denying an injunction, the court in its discretion may suspend, modify, restore, or grant an injunction during the pendency of the appeal upon such terms as to bond or otherwise as it considers proper for the security of the rights of the adverse party. If the judgment appealed from is rendered by a district court of three judges specially constituted pursuant to a statute of the United States, no such order shall be made except (1) by such court sitting in open court or (2) by the assent of all the judges of such court evidenced by their signatures to the order.

(d) Stay Upon Appeal. When an appeal is taken the appellant by giving a supersedeas bond may obtain a stay subject to the exceptions contained in subdivision (a) of this rule. The bond may be given at or after the time of filing the notice of appeal or of procuring the order allowing the appeal, as the case may be. The stay is effective when the supersedeas bond is approved by the court.

(e) Stay in Favor of the United States or Agency Thereof. When an appeal is taken by the United States or an officer or agency thereof or by direction of any department of the Government of the United States and the operation or enforcement of the judgment is stayed, no bond, obligation, or other security shall be required from the appellant.

(f) Stay According to State Law. In any state in which a judgment is a lien upon the property of the judgment debtor and in which the judgment debtor is entitled to a stay of execution, a judgment debtor is entitled, in the district court held therein, to such stay as would be accorded him had the action been maintained in the courts of that state.

(g) Power of Appellate Court Not Limited. The provisions in this rule do not limit any power of an appellate court or of a judge or justice thereof to stay proceedings during the pendency of an appeal or to suspend, modify, restore, or grant an injunction during the pendency of an appeal or to make any order appropriate to preserve the status quo or the effectiveness of the judgment subsequently to be entered.

(h) Stay of Judgment as to Multiple Claims or Multiple Parties. When a court has ordered a final judgment under the conditions stated in Rule 54(b), the court may stay enforcement of that judgment until the entering of a subsequent judgment or judgments and may prescribe such conditions as are necessary to secure the benefit thereof to the party in whose favor the judgment is entered.

Rule 63.

DISABILITY OF A JUDGE

If by reason of death, sickness, or other disability, a judge before whom an action has been tried is unable to perform the duties to be performed by the court under these rules after a verdict is returned or findings of fact and conclusions of law are filed, then any other judge regularly sitting in or assigned to the court in which the action was tried may perform those duties; but if such other judge is satisfied that he cannot perform those duties because he did not preside at the trial or for any other reason, he may in his discretion grant a new trial.

VIII. PROVISIONAL AND FINAL REMEDIES AND SPECIAL PROCEEDINGS

Rule 64.

SEIZURE OF PERSON OR PROPERTY

At the commencement of and during the course of an action, all remedies providing for seizure of person or property for the purpose of securing satisfaction of the judgment ultimately to be entered in the action are available under the circumstances and in the manner provided by the law of the state in which the district court is held, existing at the time the remedy is sought, subject to the following qualifications: (1) any existing statute of the United States governs to the extent to which it is applicable; (2) the action in which any of the foregoing remedies is used shall be commenced and prosecuted or, if removed from a state court, shall be prosecuted after removal, pursuant to these rules. The remedies thus available include arrest, attachment, garnishment, replevin, sequestration, and other corresponding or equivalent remedies, however designated and regardless of whether by state procedure the remedy is ancillary to an action or must be obtained by an independent action.

Rule 65.

INJUNCTIONS

(a) Preliminary Injunction.

(1) *Notice.* No preliminary injunction shall be issued without notice to the adverse party.

(2) *Consolidation of Hearing With Trial on Merits.* Before or after the commencement of the hearing of an application for a preliminary injunction, the court may order the trial of the action on the merits to be advanced and consolidated with the hearing of the application. Even when this consolidation is not ordered, any evidence received upon an application for a preliminary injunction which would be admissible upon the trial on the merits becomes part of the record on the trial and need not be repeated upon the trial. This subdivision (a) (2) shall be so construed and applied as to save to the parties any rights they may have to trial by jury.

(b) Temporary Restraining Order; Notice; Hearing; Duration. A temporary restraining order may be granted without written or oral notice to the adverse party or his attorney only if (1) it clearly appears from specific facts shown by affidavit or by the verified complaint that immediate and irreparable injury, loss, or damage will result to the applicant before the adverse party or his attorney can be heard in opposition, and (2) the applicant's attorney certifies to the court in writing the efforts, if any, which have been made to give the notice and the reasons supporting his claim that notice should not be required. Every temporary restraining order granted without notice shall be indorsed with the date and hour of issuance; shall be filed forthwith in the clerk's office and entered of record; shall define the injury and state why it is irreparable and why the order was granted without notice; and shall expire by its terms within such time after entry, not to exceed 10 days, as the court fixes, unless within the time so fixed the order, for good cause shown, is extended for a like period or unless the party against whom the order is directed consents that it may be extended for a longer period. The reasons for the extension shall be entered of record. In case a temporary restraining order is granted without notice, the motion for a preliminary injunction shall be set down for hearing at the earliest possible time and takes precedence of all matters except older matters of the same character; and when the motion comes on for hearing the party who obtained the temporary restraining order shall proceed with the application for a preliminary injunction and, if he does not do so, the court shall dissolve the temporary restraining order. On 2 days' notice to the party who obtained the temporary restraining order without notice or on such shorter notice to that party as the court may prescribe, the adverse party may appear and move its dissolution or modification and in that event the court shall proceed to hear and determine such motion as expeditiously as the ends of justice require.

(c) Security. No restraining order or preliminary injunction shall issue except upon the giving of security by the applicant, in such sum as the court deems proper, for the payment of such costs and damages as may be incurred or suffered by any party who is found to have been wrongfully enjoined or restrained. No such security shall be required of the United States or of an officer or agency thereof.

The provisions of Rule 65.1 apply to a surety upon a bond or undertaking under this rule.

(d) Form and Scope of Injunction or Restraining Order. Every order granting an injunction and every restraining order shall set forth the reasons for its issuance; shall be specific in terms; shall describe in reasonable detail, and not by reference to the complaint or other document, the act or acts sought to be restrained; and is binding only upon the parties to the action, their officers, agents, servants, employees, and attorneys, and upon those persons in active concert or participation with them who receive actual notice of the order by personal service or otherwise.

(e) Employer and Employee; Interpleader; Constitutional Cases. These rules do not modify any statute of the United States relating to temporary restraining orders and preliminary injunctions in actions affecting employer and employee; or the provisions of Title 28, U.S.C., § 2361, relating to preliminary injunctions in actions of interpleader or in the nature of interpleader; or Title 28, U.S.C., § 2284, relating to actions required by Act of Congress to be heard and determined by a district court of three judges.

Rule 65.1.

SECURITY: PROCEEDINGS AGAINST SURETIES

Whenever these rules, including the Supplemental Rules for Certain Admiralty and Maritime Claims, require or permit the giving of security by a party, and security is given in the form of a bond or stipulation or other undertaking with one or more sureties, each surety submits himself to the jurisdiction of the court and irrevocably appoints the clerk of the court as his agent upon whom any papers affecting his liability on the bond or undertaking may be served. His liability may be enforced on motion without the necessity of an independent action. The motion and such notice of the motion as the court prescribes may be served on the clerk of the court, who shall forthwith mail copies to the sureties if their addresses are known.

Rule 66.

RECEIVERS APPOINTED BY FEDERAL COURTS

An action wherein a receiver has been appointed shall not be dismissed except by order of the court. The practice in the administration of estates by receivers or by other similar officers appointed by the court shall be in accordance with the practice heretofore followed in the courts of the United States or as provided in rules promulgated by the district courts. In all other respects the action in which the appointment of a receiver is sought or which is brought by or against a receiver is governed by these rules.

Rule 67.

DEPOSIT IN COURT

In an action in which any part of the relief sought is a judgment for a sum of money or the disposition of a sum of money or the disposition of any other thing capable of delivery, a party, upon notice to every other party, and by leave of court, may deposit with the court all or any part of such sum or thing, whether or not that party claims all or any part of the sum or thing. The party making the deposit shall serve the order permitting deposit on the clerk of the court. Money paid into court under this rule shall be deposited and withdrawn in accordance with the provisions of Title 28, U.S.C., §§ 2041, and 2042; the Act of June 26, 1934, c. 756, § 23, as amended (48 Stat. 1236, 58 Stat. 845), U.S.C., Title 31, § 725v; or any like statute. The fund shall be deposited in an interest-bearing account or invested in an interest-bearing instrument approved by the court.

Rule 68.

OFFER OF JUDGMENT

At any time more than 10 days before the trial begins, a party defending against a claim may serve upon the adverse party an offer to allow judgment to be taken against him for the money or property or to the effect specified in his offer, with costs then accrued. If within 10 days after the service of the offer the adverse party serves written notice that the offer is accepted, either party may then file the offer and notice of acceptance together with proof of service thereof and thereupon the clerk shall enter judgment. An offer not accepted shall be deemed withdrawn and evidence thereof is not admissible except in a proceeding to determine costs. If the judgment finally obtained by the offeree is not more favorable than the offer, the offeree must pay the costs incurred after the making of the offer. The fact that an offer is made but not accepted does not preclude a subsequent offer. When the liability of one party to another has been determined by verdict or order or judgment, but the amount or extent of the liability remains to be determined by further proceedings, the party adjudged liable may make an offer of judgment, which shall have the same effect as an offer made before trial if it is served within a reasonable time not less than 10 days prior to the commencement of hearings to determine the amount or extent of liability.

Rule 69.

EXECUTION

(a) In General. Process to enforce a judgment for the payment of money shall be a writ of execution, unless the court directs otherwise. The procedure on execution, in proceedings supplementary to and in aid of a judgment, and in proceedings on and in aid of execution shall be in accordance with the practice and procedure of the state in which the district court is held, existing at the time the remedy is sought, except that any statute of the United States governs to the extent that it is applicable. In aid of the judgment or execution, the judgment creditor or his successor in interest when that interest appears of record, may obtain discovery from any person, including the judgment debtor, in the manner provided in these rules or in the manner provided by the practice of the state in which the district court is held.

(b) Against Certain Public Officers. When a judgment has been entered against a collector or other officer of revenue under the circumstances stated in Title 28, U.S.C., § 2006, or against an officer of Congress in an action mentioned in the Act of March 3, 1875, c. 130, § 8 (18 Stat. 401), U.S.C., Title 2, § 118, and when the court has given the certificate of probable cause for his act as provided in those statutes, execution shall not issue against the officer or his property but the final judgment shall be satisfied as provided in such statutes.

Rule 70.

JUDGMENT FOR SPECIFIC ACTS; VESTING TITLE

If a judgment directs a party to execute a conveyance of land or to deliver deeds or other documents or to perform any other specific act and the party fails to comply within the time specified, the court may direct the act to be done at the cost of the disobedient party by some other person appointed by the court and the act when so done has like effect as if done by the party. On application of the party entitled to performance, the clerk shall issue a writ of attachment or sequestration against the property of the disobedient party to compel obedience to the judgment. The court may also in proper cases adjudge the party in contempt. If real or personal property is within the district, the court in lieu of directing a conveyance thereof may enter a judgment divesting the title of any party and vesting it in others and such judgment has the effect of a conveyance executed in due form of law. When any order or judgment is for the delivery of possession, the party in whose favor it is entered is entitled to a writ of execution or assistance upon application to the clerk.

Rule 71.

PROCESS IN BEHALF OF AND AGAINST PERSONS NOT PARTIES

When an order is made in favor of a person who is not a party to the action, he may enforce obedience to the order by the same process as if he were a party; and, when obedience to an order may be lawfully enforced against a person who is not a party, he is liable to the same process for enforcing obedience to the order as if he were a party.

Rule 71A.

CONDEMNATION OF PROPERTY

(a) Applicability of Other Rules. The Rules of Civil Procedure for the United States District Courts govern the procedure for the condemnation of real and personal property under the power of eminent domain, except as otherwise provided in this rule.

(b) Joinder of Properties. The plaintiff may join in the same action one or more separate pieces of property, whether in the same or different ownership and whether or not sought for the same use.

(c) Complaint.

(1) *Caption.* The complaint shall contain a caption as provided in Rule 10(a), except that the plaintiff shall name as defendants the property, designated generally by kind, quantity, and location, and at least one of the owners of some part of or interest in the property.

(2) *Contents.* The complaint shall contain a short and plain statement of the authority for the taking, the use for which the property is to be taken, a description of the property sufficient for its identification, the interests to be acquired, and as to each separate piece of property a designation of the defendants who have been joined as owners thereof or of some interest therein. Upon the commencement of the action, the plaintiff need join as defendants only the persons having or claiming an interest in the property whose names are then known, but prior to any hearing involving the compensation to be paid for a piece of property, the plaintiff shall add as defendants all persons having or claiming an interest in that property whose names can be ascertained by a reasonably diligent search of the records, considering the character and value of the property involved and the interests to be acquired, and also those whose names have otherwise been learned. All others may be made defendants under the designation "Unknown Owners." Process shall be served as provided in subdivision (d) of this rule upon all defendants, whether named as defendants at the time of the commencement of the action or subsequently added, and a defendant may answer as provided in subdivision (e) of this rule. The court meanwhile may order such distribution of a deposit as the facts warrant.

(3) *Filing.* In addition to filing the complaint with the court, the plaintiff shall furnish to the clerk at least one copy thereof for the use of the defendants and additional copies at the request of the clerk or of a defendant.

(d) Process.

(1) *Notice; Delivery.* Upon the filing of the complaint the plaintiff shall forthwith deliver to the clerk joint or several notices directed to the defendants named or designated in the complaint. Additional notices directed to defendants subsequently added shall be so delivered. The delivery of the notice and its service have the same effect as the delivery and service of the summons under Rule 4.

(2) *Same; Form.* Each notice shall state the court, the title of the action, the name of the defendant to whom it is directed, that the action is to condemn property, a description of his property sufficient for its identification, the interest to be taken, the authority for the taking, the uses for which the property is to be taken, that the defendant may serve upon the plaintiff's attorney an answer within 20 days after service of the notice, and that the failure so to serve an answer constitutes a consent to the taking and to the authority of the court to proceed to hear the action and to fix the compensation. The notice shall conclude with the name of the plaintiff's attorney and an address within the district in which action is brought where he may be served. The notice need contain a description of no other property than that to be taken from the defendants to whom it is directed.

(3) *Service of Notice.*

(i) *Personal Service.* Personal service of the notice (but without copies of the complaint) shall be made in accordance with Rule 4(c) and (d) upon a defendant who resides within the United States or its territories or insular possessions and whose residence is known.

(ii) *Service by Publication.* Upon the filing of a certificate of the plaintiff's attorney stating that he believes a defendant cannot be personally served, because after diligent inquiry within the state in which the complaint is filed his place of residence cannot be ascertained by the plaintiff or, if ascertained, that it is beyond the territorial limits of personal service as provided in this rule, service of the notice shall be made on this defendant by publication in a newspaper published in the county where the property is located, or if there is no such newspaper, then in a newspaper having a general circulation where the property is located, once a week for not less than three successive weeks. Prior to the last publication, a copy of the notice shall also be mailed to a defendant who cannot be personally served as provided in this rule but whose place of residence is then known. Unknown owners may be served by publication in like manner by a notice addressed to "Unknown Owners."

Service by publication is complete upon the date of the last publication. Proof of publication and mailing shall be made by certificate of the plaintiff's attorney, to which shall be attached a printed copy of the published notice with the name and dates of the newspaper marked thereon.

(4) *Return; Amendment.* Proof of service of the notice shall be made and amendment of the notice or proof of its service al-

lowed in the manner provided for the return and amendment of the summons under Rule 4(g) and (h).

(e) Appearance or Answer. If a defendant has no objection or defense to the taking of his property, he may serve a notice of appearance designating the property in which he claims to be interested. Thereafter he shall receive notice of all proceedings affecting it. If a defendant has any objection or defense to the taking of his property, he shall serve his answer within 20 days after the service of notice upon him. The answer shall identify the property in which he claims to have an interest, state the nature and extent of the interest claimed, and state all his objections and defenses to the taking of his property. A defendant waives all defenses and objections not so presented, but at the trial of the issue of just compensation, whether or not he has previously appeared or answered, he may present evidence as to the amount of the compensation to be paid for his property, and he may share in the distribution of the award. No other pleading or motion asserting any additional defense or objection shall be allowed.

(f) Amendment of Pleadings. Without leave of court, the plaintiff may amend the complaint at any time before the trial of the issue of compensation and as many times as desired, but no amendment shall be made which will result in a dismissal forbidden by subdivision (i) of this rule. The plaintiff need not serve a copy of an amendment, but shall serve notice of the filing, as provided in Rule 5(b), upon any party affected thereby who has appeared and, in the manner provided in subdivision (d) of this rule, upon any party affected thereby who has not appeared. The plaintiff shall furnish to the clerk of the court for the use of the defendants at least one copy of each amendment, and he shall furnish additional copies on the request of the clerk or of a defendant. Within the time allowed by subdivision (e) of this rule a defendant may serve his answer to the amended pleading, in the form and manner and with the same effect as there provided.

(g) Substitution of Parties. If a defendant dies or becomes incompetent or transfers his interest after his joinder, the court may order substitution of the proper party upon motion and notice of hearing. If the motion and notice of hearing are to be served upon a person not already a party, service shall be made as provided in subdivision (d) (3) of this rule.

(h) Trial. If the action involves the exercise of the power of eminent domain under the law of the United States, any tribunal specially constituted by an Act of Congress governing the case for the trial of the issue of just compensation shall be the tribunal for the determination of that issue; but if there is no such specially constituted tribunal any party may have a trial by jury of the issue of just compensation by filing a demand therefor within the time allowed for answer or within such further time as the court may fix, unless the court in its discretion orders that, because of the character, location, or quantity of the property to be condemned, or for other reasons in the interest of justice, the issue of compensation shall be determined by a commission of three persons appointed by it. If a commission is appointed it shall have the powers of a master provided in subdivision (c) of Rule 53 and proceedings before it shall be governed by the provisions of paragraphs (1) and (2) of subdivision (d) of Rule 53. Its action and report shall be determined by a majority and its findings and report shall have the effect, and be dealt with by the court in accordance with the practice, prescribed in paragraph (2) of subdivision (e) of Rule 53. Trial of all issues shall otherwise be by the court.

(i) Dismissal of Action.

(1) *As of Right.* If no hearing has begun to determine the compensation to be paid for a piece of property and the plaintiff has not acquired the title or a lesser interest in or taken possession, the plaintiff may dismiss the action as to that property, without an order of the court, by filing a notice of dismissal setting forth a brief description of the property as to which the action is dismissed.

(2) *By Stipulation.* Before the entry of any judgment vesting the plaintiff with title or a lesser interest in or possession of property, the action may be dismissed in whole or in part, without an order of the court, as to any property by filing a stipulation of dismissal by the plaintiff and the defendant affected thereby; and, if the parties so stipulate, the court may vacate any judgment that has been entered.

(3) *By Order of the Court.* At any time before compensation for a piece of property has been determined and paid and after motion and hearing, the court may dismiss the action as to that property, except that it shall not dismiss the action as to any part of the property of which the plaintiff has taken possession or in which the plaintiff has taken title or a lesser interest, but shall award just compensation for the possession, title or lesser interest so taken. The court at any time may drop a defendant unnecessarily or improperly joined.

(4) *Effect.* Except as otherwise provided in the notice, or stipulation of dismissal, or order of the court, any dismissal is without prejudice.

(j) Deposit and Its Distribution. The plaintiff shall deposit with the court any money required by law as a condition to the exercise of the power of eminent domain; and, although not so required, may make a deposit when permitted by statute. In such cases the court and attorneys shall expedite the proceedings for the distribution of the money so deposited and for the ascertainment and payment of just compensation. If the compensation finally awarded to any defendant exceeds the amount which has been paid to him on distribution of the deposit, the court shall enter judgment against the plaintiff and in favor of that defendant for the deficiency. If the compensation finally awarded to any defendant is less than the amount which has been paid to him, the court shall enter judgment against him and in favor of the plaintiff for the overpayment.

(k) Condemnation Under a State's Power of Eminent Domain. The practice as herein prescribed governs in actions involving the exercise of the power of eminent domain under the law of a state, provided that if the state law makes provision for trial of any issue by jury, or for trial of the issue of compensation by jury or commission or both, that provision shall be followed.

(*l*) **Costs.** Costs are not subject to Rule 54(d).

Rule 72.

MAGISTRATES; PRETRIAL MATTERS

(a) Nondispositive Matters. A magistrate to whom a pretrial matter not dispositive of a claim or defense of a party is referred to hear and determine shall promptly conduct such proceedings as are required and when appropriate enter into the record a written order setting forth the disposition of the matter. The district judge to whom the case is assigned shall consider objections made by the parties, provided they are served and filed within 10 days after the entry of the order, and shall modify or set aside any portion of the magistrate's order found to be clearly erroneous or contrary to law.

(b) Dispositive Motions and Prisoner Petitions. A magistrate assigned without consent of the parties to hear a pretrial matter dispositive of a claim or defense of a party or a prisoner petition challenging the conditions of confinement shall promptly conduct such proceedings as are required. A record shall be made of all evidentiary proceedings before the magistrate, and a record may be made of such other proceedings as the magistrate deems necessary. The magistrate shall enter into the record a recommendation for disposition of the matter, including proposed findings of fact when appropriate. The clerk shall forthwith mail copies to all parties.

A party objecting to the recommended disposition of the matter shall promptly arrange for the transcription of the record, or portions of it as all parties may agree upon or the magistrate deems sufficient, unless the district judge otherwise directs. Within 10 days after being served with a copy of the recommended disposition, a party may serve and file specific, written objections to the proposed findings and recommendations. A party may respond to another party's objections within 10 days after being served with a copy thereof. The district judge to whom the case is assigned shall make a de novo determination upon the record, or after additional evidence, of any portion of the magistrate's disposition to which specific written objection has been made in accordance with this rule. The district judge may accept, reject, or modify the recommended decision, receive further evidence, or recommit the matter to the magistrate with instructions.

Rule 73.

MAGISTRATES; TRIAL BY CONSENT AND APPEAL OPTIONS

(a) Powers; Procedure. When specially designated to exercise such jurisdiction by local rule or order of the district court and when all parties consent thereto, a magistrate may exercise the authority provided by Title 28, U.S.C. § 636(c) and may conduct any or all proceedings, including a jury or nonjury trial, in a civil case. A record of the proceedings shall be made in accordance with the requirements of Title 28, U.S.C. § 636(c)(7).

(b) Consent. When a magistrate has been designated to exercise civil trial jurisdiction, the clerk shall give written notice to the parties of their opportunity to consent to the exercise by a magistrate of civil jurisdiction over the case, as authorized by Title 28, U.S.C. § 636(c). If, within the period specified by local rule, the parties agree to a magistrate's exercise of such authority, they shall execute and file a joint form of consent or separate forms of consent setting forth such election.

No district judge, magistrate, or other court official shall attempt to persuade or induce a party to consent to a reference of a civil matter to a magistrate under this rule, nor shall a district judge or magistrate be informed of a party's response to the clerk's notification, unless all parties have consented to the referral of the matter to a magistrate.

The district judge, for good cause shown on his own motion or under extraordinary circumstances shown by a party, may vacate a reference of a civil matter to a magistrate under this subdivision.

(c) Normal Appeal Route. In accordance with Title 28, U.S.C. § 636(c)(3), unless the parties otherwise agree to the optional appeal route provided for in subdivision (d) of this rule, appeal from a judgment entered upon direction of a magistrate in proceedings under this rule will lie to the court of appeals as it would from a judgment of the district court.

(d) Optional Appeal Route. In accordance with Title 28, U.S.C. § 636(c)(4), at the time of reference to a magistrate, the parties may consent to appeal on the record to a judge of the district court and thereafter, by petition only, to the court of appeals.

Rule 74.

METHOD OF APPEAL FROM MAGISTRATE TO DISTRICT JUDGE UNDER TITLE 28, U.S.C. § 636(c)(4) AND RULE 73(d)

(a) When Taken. When the parties have elected under Rule 73(d) to proceed by appeal to a district judge from an appealable decision made by a magistrate under the consent provisions of Title 28, U.S.C. § 636(c)(4), an appeal may be taken from the decision of a magistrate by filing with the clerk of the district court a notice of appeal within 30 days of the date of entry of the judgment appealed from; but if the United States or an officer or agency thereof is a party, the notice of appeal may be filed by any party within 60 days of such entry. If a timely notice of appeal is filed by a party, any other party may file a notice of appeal within 14 days thereafter, or within the time otherwise prescribed by this subdivision, whichever period last expires.

The running of the time for filing a notice of appeal is terminated as to all parties by the timely filing of any of the following motions with the magistrate by any party, and the full time for appeal from the judgment entered by the magistrate commences to run anew from entry of any of the following orders: (1) granting or denying a motion for judgment under Rule 50(b); (2) granting or denying a motion under Rule 52 (b) to amend or make additional findings of fact, whether or not an alteration of the judgment would be required if the motion is granted; (3) granting or denying a motion under Rule 59 to alter or amend the judgment; (4) denying a motion for a new trial under Rule 59.

An interlocutory decision or order by a magistrate which, if made by a judge of the district court, could be appealed under any provision of law, may be appealed to a judge of the district court by filing a notice of appeal within 15 days after entry of the decision or order, provided the parties have elected to appeal to a judge of the district court under Rule 73(d). An appeal of such interlocutory decision or order shall not stay the proceedings before the magistrate unless the magistrate or judge shall so order.

Upon a showing of excusable neglect, the magistrate may extend the time for filing a notice of appeal upon motion filed not later than 20 days after the expiration of the time otherwise prescribed by this rule.

(b) Notice of Appeal; Service. The notice of appeal shall specify the party or parties taking the appeal, designate the judgment, order or part thereof appealed from, and state that the appeal is to a judge of the district court. The clerk shall mail copies of the notice to all other parties and note the date of mailing in the civil docket.

(c) Stay Pending Appeal. Upon a showing that the magistrate has refused or otherwise failed to stay the judgment pending appeal to the district judge under Rule 73(d), the appellant may make application for a stay to the district judge with reasonable notice to all parties. The stay may be conditioned upon the filing in the district court of a bond or other appropriate security.

(d) Dismissal. For failure to comply with these rules or any local rule or order, the district judge may take such action as is deemed appropriate, including dismissal of the appeal. The district judge also may dismiss the appeal upon the filing of a stipulation signed by all parties, or upon motion and notice by the appellant.

Rule 75.

PROCEEDINGS ON APPEAL FROM MAGISTRATE TO DISTRICT JUDGE UNDER RULE 73(d)

(a) Applicability. In proceedings under Title 28, U.S.C. § 636(c), when the parties have previously elected under Rule 73(d) to appeal to a district judge rather than to the court of appeals, this rule shall govern the proceedings on appeal.

(b) Record on Appeal.

(1) *Composition.* The original papers and exhibits filed with the clerk of the district court, the transcript of the proceedings, if any, and the docket entries shall constitute the record on appeal. In lieu of this record the parties, within 10 days after the filing of the notice of appeal, may file a joint statement of the case showing how the issues presented by the appeal arose and were decided by the magistrate, and setting forth only so many of the facts averred and proved or sought to be proved as are essential to a decision of the issues presented.

(2) *Transcript.* Within 10 days after filing the notice of appeal the appellant shall make arrangements for the production of a transcript of such parts of the proceedings as he deems necessary. Unless the entire transcript is to be included, the appellant, within the time provided above, shall serve on the appellee and file with the court a description of the parts of the transcript which he intends to present on the appeal. If the appellee deems a transcript of other parts of the proceedings to be necessary, within 10 days after the service of the statement of the appellant, he shall serve on the appellant and file with the court a designation of additional parts to be included. The appellant shall promptly make arrangements for the inclusion of all such parts unless the magistrate, upon motion, exempts the appellant from providing certain parts, in which case the appellee may provide for their transcription.

(3) *Statement in Lieu of Transcript.* If no record of the proceedings is available for transcription, the parties shall, within ten days after the filing of the notice of appeal, file a statement of the evidence from the best available means to be submitted in lieu of the transcript. If the parties cannot agree they shall submit a statement of their differences to the magistrate for settlement.

(c) Time for Filing Briefs. Unless a local rule or court order otherwise provides, the following time limits for filing briefs shall apply.

(1) The appellant shall serve and file his brief within 20 days after the filing of the transcript, statement of the case, or statement of the evidence.

(2) The appellee shall serve and file his brief within 20 days after service of the brief of the appellant.

(3) The appellant may serve and file a reply brief within 10 days after service of the brief of the appellee.

(4) If the appellee has filed a cross-appeal, he may file a reply brief limited to the issues on the cross-appeal within 10 days after service of the reply brief of the appellant.

(d) Length and Form of Briefs. Briefs may be typewritten. The length and form of briefs shall be governed by local rule.

(e) Oral Argument. The opportunity for the parties to be heard on oral argument shall be governed by local rule.

Rule 76.

JUDGMENT OF THE DISTRICT JUDGE ON THE APPEAL UNDER RULE 73(d) AND COSTS

(a) Entry of Judgment. When the parties have elected under Rule 73(d) to appeal from a judgment of the magistrate to a district judge, the clerk shall prepare, sign, and enter judgment in accordance with the order or decision of the district judge following an appeal from a judgment of the magistrate, unless the district judge directs otherwise. The clerk shall mail to all parties a copy of the order or decision of the district judge.

(b) Stay of Judgments. The decision of the district judge shall be stayed for 10 days during which time a party may petition the district judge for rehearing, and a timely petition shall stay the decision of the district judge pending disposition of a petition for rehearing. Upon the motion of a party, the decision of the district judge may be stayed in order to allow a party to petition the court of appeals for leave to appeal.

(c) Costs. Except as otherwise provided by law or ordered by the district judge, costs shall be taxed against the losing party; if a judgment of the magistrate is affirmed in part or reversed in part, or is vacated, costs shall be allowed only as ordered by the district judge. The cost of the transcript, if necessary for the determination of the appeal, and the premiums paid for bonds to preserve rights pending appeal shall be taxed as costs by the clerk.

[IX. APPEALS] *

X. DISTRICT COURTS AND CLERKS

Rule 77.

DISTRICT COURTS AND CLERKS

(a) District Courts Always Open. The district courts shall be deemed always open for the purpose of filing any pleading or other proper paper, of issuing and returning mesne and final process, and of making and directing all interlocutory motions, orders, and rules.

(b) Trials and Hearings; Orders in Chambers. All trials upon the merits shall be conducted in open court and so far as convenient in a regular court room. All other acts or proceedings may be done or conducted by a judge in chambers, without the attendance of the clerk or other court officials and at any place either within or without the district; but no hearing, other than one ex parte, shall be conducted outside the district without the consent of all parties affected thereby.

(c) Clerk's Office and Orders by Clerk. The clerk's office with the clerk or a deputy in attendance shall be open during business hours on all days except Saturdays, Sundays, and legal holidays, but a district court may provide by local rule or order that its clerk's office shall be open for specified hours on Saturdays or particular legal holidays other than New Year's Day, Washington's Birthday, Memorial Day, Independence Day, Labor Day, Columbus Day, Veterans Day, Thanksgiving Day, and Christmas Day. All motions and applications in the clerk's office for issuing mesne process, for issuing final process to enforce and execute judgments, for entering defaults or judgments by default, and for other proceedings which do not require allowance or order of the court are grantable of course by the clerk; but his action may be suspended or altered or rescinded by the court upon cause shown.

(d) Notice of Orders or Judgments. Immediately upon the entry of an order or judgment the clerk shall serve a notice of the entry by mail in the manner provided for in Rule 5 upon each

* Former Title IX was abrogated in 1968, when the Federal Rules of Appellate Procedure supplanted original Rules 72 to 76. Present Rules 72 to 76 became effective August 1, 1983.

party who is not in default for failure to appear, and shall make a note in the docket of the mailing. Such mailing is sufficient notice for all purposes for which notice of the entry of an order is required by these rules; but any party may in addition serve a notice of such entry in the manner provided in Rule 5 for the service of papers. Lack of notice of the entry by the clerk does not affect the time to appeal or relieve or authorize the court to relieve a party for failure to appeal within the time allowed, except as permitted in Rule 4(a) of the Federal Rules of Appellate Procedure.

Rule 78.

MOTION DAY

Unless local conditions make it impracticable, each district court shall establish regular times and places, at intervals sufficiently frequent for the prompt dispatch of business, at which motions requiring notice and hearing may be heard and disposed of; but the judge at any time or place and on such notice, if any, as he considers reasonable may make orders for the advancement, conduct, and hearing of actions.

To expedite its business, the court may make provision by rule or order for the submission and determination of motions without oral hearing upon brief written statements of reasons in support and opposition.

Rule 79.

BOOKS AND RECORDS KEPT BY THE CLERK AND ENTRIES THEREIN

(a) Civil Docket. The clerk shall keep a book known as "civil docket" of such form and style as may be prescribed by the Director of the Administrative Office of the United States Courts with the approval of the Judicial Conference of the United States, and shall enter therein each civil action to which these rules are made applicable. Actions shall be assigned consecutive file numbers. The file number of each action shall be noted on the folio of the docket whereon the first entry of the action is made. All papers filed with the clerk, all process issued and returns made thereon, all appearances, orders, verdicts, and judgments shall be entered chronologically in the civil docket on the folio assigned to the action and shall be marked with its file number. These entries shall be brief but shall show the nature of each paper filed or writ issued and the substance of each order or judgment of the court and of the returns showing execution of process. The entry of an order or judgment shall show the date the entry is made. When in an action trial by jury has been properly demanded or ordered the clerk shall enter the word "jury" on the folio assigned to that action.

(b) Civil Judgments and Orders. The clerk shall keep, in such form and manner as the Director of the Administrative Office of the United States Courts with the approval of the Judicial Conference of the United States may prescribe, a correct copy of every final judgment or appealable order, or order affecting title to or lien upon real or personal property, and any other order which the court may direct to be kept.

(c) Indices; Calendars. Suitable indices of the civil docket and of every civil judgment and order referred to in subdivision (b) of this rule shall be kept by the clerk under the direction of the court. There shall be prepared under the direction of the court calendars of all actions ready for trial, which shall distinguish "jury actions" from "court actions."

(d) Other Books and Records of the Clerk. The clerk shall also keep such other books and records as may be required from time to time by the Director of the Administrative Office of the United States Courts with the approval of the Judicial Conference of the United States.

Rule 80.

STENOGRAPHER; STENOGRAPHIC REPORT OR TRANSCRIPT AS EVIDENCE

[**(a) Stenographer.** Abrogated.]

[**(b) Official Stenographer.** Abrogated.]

(c) Stenographic Report or Transcript as Evidence. Whenever the testimony of a witness at a trial or hearing which was stenographically reported is admissible in evidence at a later trial, it may be proved by the transcript thereof duly certified by the person who reported the testimony.

XI. GENERAL PROVISIONS

Rule 81.

APPLICABILITY IN GENERAL

(a) To What Proceedings Applicable.

(1) These rules do not apply to prize proceedings in admiralty governed by Title 10, U.S.C., §§ 7651–7681. They do not apply to proceedings in bankruptcy or proceedings in copyright under Title 17, U.S.C., except in so far as they may be made applicable thereto by rules promulgated by the Supreme Court of the United States. They do not apply to mental health proceedings in the United States District Court for the District of Columbia.

(2) These rules are applicable to proceedings for admission to citizenship, habeas corpus, and quo warranto, to the extent that the practice in such proceedings is not set forth in statutes of the United States and has heretofore conformed to the practice in civil actions. The writ of habeas corpus, or order to show cause, shall be directed to the person having custody of the person detained. It shall be returned within 3 days unless for good cause shown additional time is allowed which in cases brought under 28 U.S.C. § 2254 shall not exceed 40 days, and in all other cases shall not exceed 20 days.

(3) In proceedings under Title 9, U.S.C., relating to arbitration, or under the Act of May 20, 1926, ch. 347, § 9 (44 Stat. 585), U.S.C., Title 45, § 159, relating to boards of arbitration of railway labor disputes, these rules apply only to the extent that matters of procedure are not provided for in those statutes. These rules apply to proceedings to compel the giving of testimony or production of documents in accordance with a subpoena issued by an officer or agency of the United States under any statute of the United States except as otherwise provided by statute or by rules of the district court or by order of the court in the proceedings.

(4) These rules do not alter the method prescribed by the Act of February 18, 1922, c. 57, § 2 (42 Stat. 388), U.S.C., Title 7, § 292; or by the Act of June 10, 1930, c. 436, § 7 (46 Stat. 534), as amended, U.S.C., Title 7, § 499g(c), for instituting proceedings in the United States district courts to review orders of the Secretary of Agriculture; or prescribed by the Act of June 25, 1934, c. 742, § 2 (48 Stat. 1214), U.S.C., Title 15, § 522, for instituting proceedings to review orders of the Secretary of the Interior; or prescribed by the Act of February 22, 1935, c. 18, § 5 (49 Stat. 31), U.S.C., Title 15, § 715d(c), as extended,

for instituting proceedings to review orders of petroleum control boards; but the conduct of such proceedings in the district courts shall be made to conform to these rules as far as applicable.

(5) These rules do not alter the practice in the United States district courts prescribed in the Act of July 5, 1935, c. 372, §§ 9 and 10 (49 Stat. 453), as amended, U.S.C., Title 29, §§ 159 and 160, for beginning and conducting proceedings to enforce orders of the National Labor Relations Board; and in respects not covered by those statutes, the practice in the district courts shall conform to these rules so far as applicable.

(6) These rules apply to proceedings for enforcement or review of compensation orders under the Longshoremen's and Harbor Workers' Compensation Act, Act of March 4, 1927, c. 509, §§ 18, 21 (44 Stat. 1434, 1436), as amended, U.S.C., Title 33, §§ 918, 921, except to the extent that matters of procedure are provided for in that Act. The provisions for service by publication and for answer in proceedings to cancel certificates of citizenship under the Act of June 27, 1952, c. 477, Title III, c. 2, § 340 (66 Stat. 260), U.S.C., Title 8, § 1451, remain in effect.

(b) Scire Facias and Mandamus. The writs of scire facias and mandamus are abolished. Relief heretofore available by mandamus or scire facias may be obtained by appropriate action or by appropriate motion under the practice prescribed in these rules.

(c) Removed Actions. These rules apply to civil actions removed to the United States district courts from the state courts and govern procedure after removal. Repleading is not necessary unless the court so orders. In a removed action in which the defendant has not answered, he shall answer or present the other defenses or objections available to him under these rules within 20 days after the receipt through service or otherwise of a copy of the initial pleading setting forth the claim for relief upon which the action or proceeding is based, or within 20 days after the service of summons upon such initial pleading, then filed, or within 5 days after the filing of the petition for removal, whichever period is longest. If at the time of removal all necessary pleadings have been served, a party entitled to trial by jury under Rule 38 shall be accorded it, if his demand therefor is served within 10 days after the petition for removal is filed if he is the petitioner, or if he is not the petitioner within 10 days after service on him of the notice of filing the petition. A party who, prior to removal, has made an express demand for trial by jury in accordance with state law, need not make a demand after removal. If state law applicable in the court from which the case is removed does not require the parties to make express demands in order to claim trial by jury, they need not make demands after removal unless the court directs that they do so within a specified time if they desire to claim trial by jury. The court may make this direction on its own motion and shall do so as a matter of course at the request of any party. The failure of a party to make demand as directed constitutes a waiver by him of trial by jury.

[**(d) District of Columbia; Courts and Judges.** Abrogated.]

(e) Law Applicable. Whenever in these rules the law of the state in which the district court is held is made applicable, the law applied in the District of Columbia governs proceedings in the United States District Court for the District of Columbia. When the word "state" is used, it includes, if appropriate, the District of Columbia. When the term "statute of the United States" is used, it includes, so far as concerns proceedings in the United States District Court for the District of Columbia, any Act of Congress locally applicable to and in force in the District of Columbia. When the law of a state is referred to, the word "law" includes the statutes of that state and the state judicial decisions construing them.

(f) References to Officer of the United States. Under any rule in which reference is made to an officer or agency of the United States, the term "officer" includes a district director of internal revenue, a former district director or collector of internal revenue, or the personal representative of a deceased district director or collector of internal revenue.

Rule 82.
JURISDICTION AND VENUE UNAFFECTED

These rules shall not be construed to extend or limit the jurisdiction of the United States district courts or the venue of actions therein. An admiralty or maritime claim within the meaning of Rule 9(h) shall not be treated as a civil action for the purposes of Title 28, U.S.C., §§ 1391–93.

Rule 83.
RULES BY DISTRICT COURTS

Each district court by action of a majority of the judges thereof may from time to time make and amend rules governing its practice not inconsistent with these rules. Copies of rules and amendments so made by any district court shall upon their promulgation be furnished to the Supreme Court of the United States. In all cases not provided for by rule, the district courts may regulate their practice in any manner not inconsistent with these rules.

Rule 84.

FORMS

The forms contained in the Appendix of Forms are sufficient under the rules and are intended to indicate the simplicity and brevity of statement which the rules contemplate.

Rule 85.

TITLE

These rules may be known and cited as the Federal Rules of Civil Procedure.

Rule 86.

EFFECTIVE DATE

(a) [Effective date of original rules]. These rules will take effect on the day which is 3 months subsequent to the adjournment of the second regular session of the 75th Congress, but if that day is prior to September 1, 1938, then these rules will take effect on September 1, 1938. They govern all proceedings in actions brought after they take effect and also all further proceedings in actions then pending, except to the extent that in the opinion of the court their application in a particular action pending when the rules take effect would not be feasible or would work injustice, in which event the former procedure applies.

(b) Effective Date of Amendments. The amendments adopted by the Supreme Court on December 27, 1946, and transmitted to the Attorney General on January 2, 1947, shall take effect on the day which is three months subsequent to the adjournment of the first regular session of the 80th Congress, but, if that day is prior to September 1, 1947, then these amendments shall take effect on September 1, 1947. They govern all proceedings in actions brought after they take effect and also all further proceedings in actions then pending, except to the extent that in the opinion of the court their application in a particular action pending when the amendments take effect would not be feasible or would work injustice, in which event the former procedure applies.

(c) Effective Date of Amendments. The amendments adopted by the Supreme Court on December 29, 1948, and transmitted to the Attorney General on December 31, 1948, shall take effect on the day following the adjournment of the first regular session of the 81st Congress.

(d) Effective Date of Amendments. The amendments adopted by the Supreme Court on April 17, 1961, and transmitted to the Congress on April 18, 1961, shall take effect on July 19, 1961. They govern all proceedings in actions brought after they take effect and also all further proceedings in actions then pending, except to the extent that in the opinion of the court their application in a particular action pending when the amendments take effect would not be feasible or would work injustice in which event the former procedure applies.

(e) Effective Date of Amendments. The amendments adopted by the Supreme Court on January 21, 1963, and transmitted to the Congress on January 21, 1963 shall take effect on July 1, 1963. They govern all proceedings in actions brought after they take effect and also all further proceedings in actions then pending, except to the extent that in the opinion of the court their application in a particular action pending when the amendments take effect would not be feasible or would work injustice, in which event the former procedure applies.

NOTE: The amendments adopted by the Supreme Court on February 28, 1966, and transmitted to the Congress on that day became effective on July 1, 1966. The amendments adopted by the Supreme Court on December 4, 1967, transmitted to the Congress on that day and resubmitted on January 15, 1968, became effective July 1, 1968. Those adopted by the Supreme Court on March 30, 1970 and submitted to Congress on that day became effective July 1, 1970, and those adopted March 1, 1971, became effective July 1, 1971. The amendments proposed November 20 and December 18, 1972, became effective July 1, 1975. Further amendments were transmitted to Congress on April 29, 1980, and became effective August 1, 1980. The most recent amendments became effective on August 1, 1983. See Editorial Note, *supra*, p. 366.

APPENDIX OF FORMS

Editorial Note: The Introductory Statement, footnotes, "Notes" and "Explanatory Notes" are by the Court.

(See Rule 84)

Introductory Statement

1. The following forms are intended for illustration only. They are limited in number. No attempt is made to furnish a manual of forms. Each form assumes the action to be brought in the Southern District of New York. If the district in which an action is brought has divisions, the division should be indicated in the caption.

2. Except where otherwise indicated each pleading, motion, and other paper should have a caption similar to that of the summons, with the designation of the particular paper substituted for the word "Summons". In the caption of the summons and in the caption of the complaint all parties must be named but in other pleadings and papers, it is sufficient to state the name of the first party on either side, with an appropriate indication of other parties. See Rules 4(b), 7(b) (2), and 10(a).

3. In Form 3 and the forms following, the words, "Allegation of jurisdiction," are used to indicate the appropriate allegation in Form 2.

4. Each pleading, motion, and other paper is to be signed in his individual name by at least one attorney of record (Rule 11). The attorney's name is to be followed by his address as indicated in Form 3. In forms following Form 3 the signature and address are not indicated.

5. If a party is not represented by an attorney, the signature and address of the party are required in place of those of the attorney.

Form 1.

SUMMONS

UNITED STATES DISTRICT COURT FOR THE SOUTHERN DISTRICT OF NEW YORK

Civil Action, File Number ....

A. B., Plaintiff
v. } *Summons*
C. D., Defendant

To the above-named Defendant:

You are hereby summoned and required to serve upon ......, plaintiff's attorney, whose address is ...., an answer to the complaint which is herewith served upon you, within 20 [1] days after service of this summons upon you, exclusive of the day of service. If you fail to do so, judgment by default will be taken against you for the relief demanded in the complaint.

....................,
Clerk of Court.

[Seal of the U. S. District Court]
Dated ....

(This summons is issued pursuant to Rule 4 of the Federal Rules of Civil Procedure)

Form 2.

ALLEGATION OF JURISDICTION

(a) Jurisdiction founded on diversity of citizenship and amount.

Plaintiff is a [citizen of the State of Connecticut] [2] [corporation incorporated under the laws of the State of Connecticut having its principal place of business in the State of Connecticut] and defendant is a corporation incorporated under the laws of the State of New York having its principal place of business in a State other than the State of Connecticut. The matter in controversy exceeds, exclusive of interest and costs, the sum of ten thousand dollars.

---

1 If the United States or an officer or agency thereof is a defendant, the time to be inserted as to it is 60 days.

2 Form for natural person.

(b) Jurisdiction founded on the existence of a Federal question and amount in controversy.

The action arises under [the Constitution of the United States, Article ___, Section ___]; [the ___ Amendment to the Constitution of the United States, Section ___]; [the Act of ___, ___ Stat. ___; U.S.C., Title ___, § ___]; [the Treaty of the United States (here describe the treaty)],[3] as hereinafter more fully appears. The matter in controversy exceeds, exclusive of interest and costs, the sum of ten thousand dollars.

(c) Jurisdiction founded on the existence of a question arising under particular statutes.

The action arises under the Act of ___, ___ Stat. ___; U.S.C., Title ___, § ___, as hereinafter more fully appears. As amended Apr. 17, 1961, eff. July 19, 1961.

(d) Jurisdiction founded on the admiralty or maritime character of the claim.

This is a case of admiralty and maritime jurisdiction, as hereinafter more fully appears. [If the pleader wishes to invoke the distinctively maritime procedures referred to in Rule 9(h), add the following or its substantial equivalent: This is an admiralty or maritime claim within the meaning of Rule 9(h).]

Form 3.

COMPLAINT ON A PROMISSORY NOTE

1. Allegation of jurisdiction.

2. Defendant on or about June 1, 1935, executed and delivered to plaintiff a promissory note [in the following words and figures: (here set out the note verbatim)]; [a copy of which is hereto annexed as Exhibit A]; [whereby defendant promised to pay to plaintiff or order on June 1, 1936 the sum of ...... dollars with interest thereon at the rate of six percent per annum].

3. Defendant owes to plaintiff the amount of said note and interest.

[3] Use the appropriate phrase or phrases. The general allegation of the existence of a Federal question is ineffective unless the matters constituting the claim for relief as set forth in the complaint raise a Federal question.

Wherefore plaintiff demands judgment against defendant for the sum of ...... dollars, interest, and costs.

Signed: ....
Attorney for Plaintiff

Address: ....

Notes

1. The pleader may use the material in one of the three sets of brackets. His choice will depend upon whether he desires to plead the document verbatim, or by exhibit, or according to its legal effect.

2. Under the rules free joinder of claims is permitted. See Rules 8(e) and 18. Consequently the claims set forth in each and all of the following forms may be joined with this complaint or with each other. Ordinarily each claim should be stated in a separate division of the complaint, and the divisions should be designated as counts successively numbered. In particular the rules permit alternative and inconsistent pleading. See Form 10.

Form 4.

COMPLAINT ON AN ACCOUNT

1. Allegation of jurisdiction.

2. Defendant owes plaintiff ...... dollars according to the account hereto annexed as Exhibit A.

Wherefore (etc. as in Form 3).

Form 5.

COMPLAINT FOR GOODS SOLD AND DELIVERED

1. Allegation of jurisdiction.

2. Defendant owes plaintiff ...... dollars for goods sold and delivered by plaintiff to defendant between June 1, 1936 and December 1, 1936.

Wherefore (etc. as in Form 3).

Note

This form may be used where the action is for an agreed price or for the reasonable value of the goods.

Form 6.

COMPLAINT FOR MONEY LENT

1. Allegation of jurisdiction.

2. Defendant owes plaintiff ...... dollars for money lent by plaintiff to defendant on June 1, 1936.

Wherefore (etc. as in Form 3).

Form 7

COMPLAINT FOR MONEY PAID BY MISTAKE

1. Allegation of jurisdiction.

2. Defendant owes plaintiff ...... dollars for money paid by plaintiff to defendant by mistake on June 1, 1936, under the following circumstances: [here state the circumstances with particularity—see Rule 9 (b)].

Wherefore (etc. as in Form 3).

Form 8.

COMPLAINT FOR MONEY HAD AND RECEIVED

1. Allegation of jurisdiction.

2. Defendant owes plaintiff ...... dollars for money had and received from one G. H. on June 1, 1936, to be paid by defendant to plaintiff.

Wherefore (etc. as in Form 3).

Form 9.

COMPLAINT FOR NEGLIGENCE

1. Allegation of jurisdiction.

2. On June 1, 1936, in a public highway called Boylston Street in Boston, Massachusetts, defendant negligently drove a motor vehicle against plaintiff who was then crossing said highway.

3. As a result plaintiff was thrown down and had his leg broken and was otherwise injured, was prevented from transacting his business, suffered great pain of body and mind, and incurred expenses for medical attention and hospitalization in the sum of one thousand dollars.

Wherefore plaintiff demands judgment against defendant in the sum of ...... dollars and costs.

Note

Since contributory negligence is an affirmative defense, the complaint need contain no allegation of due care of plaintiff.

Form 10.

COMPLAINT FOR NEGLIGENCE WHERE PLAINTIFF IS UNABLE TO DETERMINE DEFINITELY WHETHER THE PERSON RESPONSIBLE IS C. D. OR E. F. OR WHETHER BOTH ARE RESPONSIBLE AND WHERE HIS EVIDENCE MAY JUSTIFY A FINDING OF WILFULNESS OR OF RECKLESSNESS OR OF NEGLIGENCE

A. B., Plaintiff
v.
C. D. and E. F., Defendants } *Complaint*

1. Allegation of jurisdiction.

2. On June 1, 1936, in a public highway called Boylston Street in Boston, Massachusetts, defendant C. D. or defendant E. F., or both defendants C. D. and E. F. wilfully or recklessly or negligently drove or caused to be driven a motor vehicle against plaintiff who was then crossing said highway.

3. As a result plaintiff was thrown down and had his leg broken and was otherwise injured, was prevented from transacting his business, suffered great pain of body and mind, and incurred expenses for medical attention and hospitalization in the sum of one thousand dollars.

Wherefore plaintiff demands judgment against C. D. or against E. F. or against both in the sum of ...... dollars and costs.

Form 11.

COMPLAINT FOR CONVERSION

1. Allegation of jurisdiction.

2. On or about December 1, 1936, defendant converted to his own use ten bonds of the .... Company (here insert brief identification as by number and issue) of the value of ...... dollars, the property of plaintiff.

Wherefore plaintiff demands judgment against defendant in the sum of ...... dollars, interest, and costs.

Form 12.

COMPLAINT FOR SPECIFIC PERFORMANCE OF CONTRACT TO CONVEY LAND

1. Allegation of jurisdiction.

2. On or about December 1, 1936, plaintiff and defendant entered into an agreement in writing a copy of which is hereto annexed as Exhibit A.

3. In accord with the provisions of said agreement plaintiff tendered to defendant the purchase price and requested a conveyance of the land, but defendant refused to accept the tender and refused to make the conveyance.

4. Plaintiff now offers to pay the purchase price.

Wherefore plaintiff demands (1) that defendant be required specifically to perform said agreement, (2) damages in the sum of one thousand dollars, and (3) that if specific performance is not granted plaintiff have judgment against defendant in the sum of . . . . . . dollars.

Note

Here, as in Form 3, plaintiff may set forth the contract verbatim in the complaint or plead it, as indicated, by exhibit, or plead it according to its legal effect. Furthermore, plaintiff may seek legal or equitable relief or both even though this was impossible under the system in operation before these rules.

Form 13.

COMPLAINT ON CLAIM FOR DEBT AND TO SET ASIDE FRAUDULENT CONVEYANCE UNDER RULE 18(b)

A. B., Plaintiff
v. } *Complaint*
C. D. and E. F., Defendants

1. Allegation of jurisdiction.

2. Defendant C. D. on or about . . . . executed and delivered to plaintiff a promissory note [in the following words and figures: (here set out the note verbatim)]; [a copy of which is hereto annexed as Exhibit A]; [whereby defendant C. D. promised to pay to plaintiff or order on . . . . the sum of five thousand dollars with interest thereon at the rate of . . . . percent. per annum].

3. Defendant C. D. owes to plaintiff the amount of said note and interest.

4. Defendant C. D. on or about .... conveyed all his property, real and personal [or specify and describe] to defendant E. F. for the purpose of defrauding plaintiff and hindering and delaying the collection of the indebtedness evidenced by the note above referred to.

Wherefore plaintiff demands:

(1) That plaintiff have judgment against defendant C. D. for ...... dollars and interest; (2) that the aforesaid conveyance to defendant E. F. be declared void and the judgment herein be declared a lien on said property; (3) that plaintiff have judgment against the defendants for costs.

Form 14.

COMPLAINT FOR NEGLIGENCE UNDER FEDERAL EMPLOYER'S LIABILITY ACT

1. Allegation of jurisdiction.

2. During all the times herein mentioned defendant owned and operated in interstate commerce a railroad which passed through a tunnel located at .... and known as Tunnel No. .....

3. On or about June 1, 1936, defendant was repairing and enlarging the tunnel in order to protect interstate trains and passengers and freight from injury and in order to make the tunnel more conveniently usable for interstate commerce.

4. In the course of thus repairing and enlarging the tunnel on said day defendant employed plaintiff as one of its workmen, and negligently put plaintiff to work in a portion of the tunnel which defendant had left unprotected and unsupported.

5. By reason of defendant's negligence in thus putting plaintiff to work in that portion of the tunnel, plaintiff was, while so working pursuant to defendant's orders, struck and crushed by a rock, which fell from the unsupported portion of the tunnel, and was (here describe plaintiff's injuries).

6. Prior to these injuries, plaintiff was a strong, able-bodied man, capable of earning and actually earning ...... dollars per day. By these injuries he has been made incapable of any gainful activity, has suffered great physical and mental pain, and has incurred expense in the amount of ...... dollars for medicine, medical attendance, and hospitalization.

Wherefore plaintiff demands judgment against defendant in the sum of ...... dollars and costs.

Form 15.

COMPLAINT FOR DAMAGES UNDER MERCHANT MARINE ACT

1. Allegation of jurisdiction. [If the pleader wishes to invoke the distinctively maritime procedures referred to in Rule 9(h), add the following or its substantial equivalent: This is an admiralty or maritime claim within the meaning of Rule 9(h).]

2. During all the times herein mentioned defendant was the owner of the steamship ______ and used it in the transportation of freight for hire by water in interstate and foreign commerce.

3. During the first part of (month and year) at ______ plaintiff entered the employ of defendant as an able seaman on said steamship under seamen's articles of customary form for a voyage from ______ ports to the Orient and return at a wage of ______ dollars per month and found, which is equal to a wage of ______ dollars per month as a shore worker.

4. On June 1, 1936, said steamship was about ______ days out of the port of ______ and was being navigated by the master and crew on the return voyage to ______ ports. (Here describe weather conditions and the condition of the ship and state as in an ordinary complaint for personal injuries the negligent conduct of defendant.)

5. By reason of defendant's negligence in thus (brief statement of defendant's negligent conduct) and the unseaworthiness of said steamship, plaintiff was (here describe plaintiff's injuries).

6. Prior to these injuries, plaintiff was a strong, able-bodied man, capable of earning and actually earning ______ dollars per day. By these injuries he has been made incapable of any gainful activity; has suffered great physical and mental pain, and has incurred expense in the amount of ______ dollars for medicine, medical attendance, and hospitalization.

Wherefore plaintiff demands judgment against defendant in the sum of ______ dollars and costs.

Form 16.

COMPLAINT FOR INFRINGEMENT OF PATENT

1. Allegation of jurisdiction.

2. On May 16, 1934, United States Letters Patent No. .... were duly and legally issued to plaintiff for an invention in an

electric motor; and since that date plaintiff has been and still is the owner of those Letters Patent.

3. Defendant has for a long time past been and still is infringing those Letters Patent by making, selling, and using electric motors embodying the patented invention, and will continue to do so unless enjoined by this court.

4. Plaintiff has placed the required statutory notice on all electric motors manufactured and sold by him under said Letters Patent, and has given written notice to defendant of his said infringement.

Wherefore plaintiff demands a preliminary and final injunction against continued infringement, an accounting for damages, and an assessment of interest and costs against defendant.

Form 17.

COMPLAINT FOR INFRINGEMENT OF COPYRIGHT AND UNFAIR COMPETITION

1. Allegation of jurisdiction.

2. Prior to March, 1936, plaintiff, who then was and ever since has been a citizen of the United States, created and wrote an original book, entitled ....

3. This book contains a large amount of material wholly original with plaintiff and is copyrightable subject matter under the laws of the United States.

4. Between March 2, 1936, and March 10, 1936, plaintiff complied in all respects with the Act of (give citation) and all other laws governing copyright, and secured the exclusive rights and privileges in and to the copyright of said book, and received from the Register of Copyrights a certificate of registration, dated and identified as follows: "March 10, 1936, Class ...., No. ...."

5. Since March 10, 1936, said book has been published by plaintiff and all copies of it made by plaintiff or under his authority or license have been printed, bound, and published in strict conformity with the provisions of the Act of .... and all other laws governing copyright.

6. Since March 10, 1936, plaintiff has been and still is the sole proprietor of all rights, title, and interest in and to the copyright in said book.

7. After March 10, 1936, defendant infringed said copyright by publishing and placing upon the market a book entitled

............, which was copied largely from plaintiff's copyrighted book, entitled ....

8. A copy of plaintiff's copyrighted book is hereto attached as "Exhibit 1"; and a copy of defendant's infringing book is hereto attached as "Exhibit 2."

9. Plaintiff has notified defendant that defendant has infringed the copyright of plaintiff, and defendant has continued to infringe the copyright.

10. After March 10, 1936, and continuously since about ...., defendant has been publishing, selling and otherwise marketing the book entitled ...., and has thereby been engaging in unfair trade practices and unfair competition against plaintiff's irreparable damage.

Wherefore plaintiff demands:

(1) That defendant, his agents, and servants be enjoined during the pendency of this action and permanently from infringing said copyright of said plaintiff in any manner, and from publishing, selling, marketing or otherwise disposing of any copies of the book entitled ....

(2) That defendant be required to pay to plaintiff such damages as plaintiff has sustained in consequence of defendant's infringement of said copyright and said unfair trade practices and unfair competition and to account for

(a) all gains, profits and advantages derived by defendant by said trade practices and unfair competition and

(b) all gains, profits, and advantages derived by defendant by his infringement of plaintiff's copyright or such damages as to the court shall appear proper within the provisions of the copyright statutes, but not less than two hundred and fifty dollars.

(3) That defendant be required to deliver up to be impounded during the pendency of this action all copies of said book entitled .... in his possession or under his control and to deliver up for destruction all infringing copies and all plates, molds, and other matter for making such infringing copies.

(4) That defendant pay to plaintiff the costs of this action and reasonable attorney's fees to be allowed to the plaintiff by the court.

(5) That plaintiff have such other and further relief as is just.

Form 18.

COMPLAINT FOR INTERPLEADER AND DECLARATORY RELIEF

1. Allegation of jurisdiction.

2. On or about June 1, 1935, plaintiff issued to G. H. a policy of life insurance whereby plaintiff promised to pay to K. L. as beneficiary the sum of ...... dollars upon the death of G. H. The policy required the payment by G. H. of a stipulated premium on June 1, 1936, and annually thereafter as a condition precedent to its continuance in force.

3. No part of the premium due June 1, 1936, was ever paid and the policy ceased to have any force or effect on July 1, 1936.

4. Thereafter, on September 1, 1936, G. H. and K. L. died as the result of a collision between a locomotive and the automobile in which G. H. and K. L. were riding.

5. Defendant C. D. is the duly appointed and acting executor of the will of G. H.; defendant E. F. is the duly appointed and acting executor of the will of K. L.; defendant X. Y. claims to have been duly designated as beneficiary of said policy in place of K. L.

6. Each of defendants, C. D., E. F., and X. Y. is claiming that the above-mentioned policy was in full force and effect at the time of the death of G. H.; each of them is claiming to be the only person entitled to receive payment of the amount of the policy and has made demand for payment thereof.

7. By reason of these conflicting claims of the defendants, plaintiff is in great doubt as to which defendant is entitled to be paid the amount of the policy, if it was in force at the death of G. H.

Wherefore plaintiff demands that the court adjudge:

(1) That none of the defendants is entitled to recover from plaintiff the amount of said policy or any part thereof.

(2) That each of the defendants be restrained from instituting any action against plaintiff for the recovery of the amount of said policy or any part thereof.

(3) That, if the court shall determine that said policy was in force at the death of G. H., the defendants be required to interplead and settle between themselves their rights to the money due under said policy, and that plaintiff be discharged from all

liability in the premises except to the person whom the court shall adjudge entitled to the amount of said policy.

(4) That plaintiff recover its costs.

Form 18–A.

NOTICE AND ACKNOWLEDGMENT FOR SERVICE BY MAIL

United States District Court for the Southern District of New York

Civil Action, File Number ......

A. B., Plaintiff v. C. D., Defendant	Notice and Acknowledgment of Receipt of Summons and Complaint

NOTICE

To: (insert the name and address of the person to be served.)

The enclosed summons and complaint are served pursuant to Rule 4(c)(2)(C)(ii) of the Federal Rules of Civil Procedure.

You must complete the acknowledgment part of this form and return one copy of the completed form to the sender within 20 days.

You must sign and date the acknowledgment. If you are served on behalf of a corporation, unincorporated association (including a partnership), or other entity, you must indicate under your signature your relationship to that entity. If you are served on behalf of another person and you are authorized to receive process, you must indicate under your signature your authority.

If you do not complete and return the form to the sender within 20 days, you (or the party on whose behalf you are being served) may be required to pay any expenses incurred in serving a summons and complaint in any other manner permitted by law.

If you do complete and return this form, you (or the party on whose behalf you are being served) must answer the complaint within 20 days. If you fail to do so, judgment by default will be taken against you for the relief demanded in the complaint.

I declare, under penalty of perjury, that this Notice and Acknowledgment of Receipt of Summons and Complaint was mailed on (insert date)

....
Signature

....
Date of Signature

ACKNOWLEDGMENT OF RECEIPT OF SUMMONS AND COMPLAINT

I declare, under penalty of perjury, that I received a copy of the summons and of the complaint in the above-captioned manner at (insert address).

....
Signature

....
Relationship to Entity/Authority to Receive Service of Process

....
Date of Signature

Form 19.

MOTION TO DISMISS, PRESENTING DEFENSES OF FAILURE TO STATE A CLAIM, OF LACK OF SERVICE OF PROCESS, OF IMPROPER VENUE, AND OF LACK OF JURISDICTION UNDER RULE 12 (b)

The defendant moves the court as follows:

1. To dismiss the action because the complaint fails to state a claim against defendant upon which relief can be granted.

2. To dismiss the action or in lieu thereof to quash the return of service of summons on the grounds (a) that the defendant is a corporation organized under the laws of Delaware and was not and is not subject to service of process within the Southern District of New York, and (b) that the defendant has not been properly served with process in this action, all of which more clearly appears in the affidavits of M. N. and X. Y. hereto annexed as Exhibit A and Exhibit B respectively.

3. To dismiss the action on the ground that it is in the wrong district because (a) the jurisdiction of this court is invoked solely on the ground that the action arises under the Constitution and laws of the United States and (b) the defendant is a corporation incorporated under the laws of the State of Delaware and is not licensed to do or doing business in the Southern District of New York, all of which more clearly appears in the affidavits of K. L. and V. W. hereto annexed as Exhibit C and D respectively.

4. To dismiss the action on the ground that the court lacks jurisdiction because the amount actually in controversy is less than ten thousand dollars exclusive of interest and costs.

Signed: ....,
Attorney for Defendant.

Address: ....

Notice of Motion

To: ....

Attorney for Plaintiff.

....

Please take notice, that the undersigned will bring the above motion on for hearing before this Court at Room ...., United States Court House, Foley Square, City of New York, on the .... day of ...., 193.., at 10 o'clock in the forenoon of that day or as soon thereafter as counsel can be heard.

Signed: ....,
Attorney for Defendant.

Address: ....

Explanatory Notes

1. The above motion and notice of motion may be combined and denominated Notice of Motion. See Rule 7(b).

2. As to paragraph 3, see U.S.C., Title 28, § 1391 (Venue generally), subsections (b) and (c).

3. As to paragraph 4, see U.S.C., Title 28, § 1331 (Federal question; amount in controversy; costs), as amended by P.L. 85–554, 72 Stat. 415, July 25, 1958, requiring that the amount in controversy, exclusive of interest and costs, be in excess of $10,000.

Form 20.

ANSWER PRESENTING DEFENSES UNDER RULE 12 (b)

First Defense

The complaint fails to state a claim against defendant upon which relief can be granted.

Second Defense

If defendant is indebted to plaintiffs for the goods mentioned in the complaint, he is indebted to them jointly with G. H. G. H. is alive; is a citizen of the State of New York and a resident of this district, is subject to the jurisdiction of this court, as to both service of process and venue; can be made a party without depriving this court of jurisdiction of the present parties, and has not been made a party.

Third Defense

Defendant admits the allegation contained in paragraphs 1 and 4 of the complaint; alleges that he is without knowledge or information sufficient to form a belief as to the truth of the allegations contained in paragraph 2 of the complaint; and denies each and every other allegation contained in the complaint.

Fourth Defense

The right of action set forth in the complaint did not accrue within six years next before the commencement of this action.

Counterclaim

(Here set forth any claim as a counterclaim in the manner in which a claim is pleaded in a complaint. No statement of the grounds on which the court's jurisdiction depends need be made unless the counterclaim requires independent grounds of jurisdiction.)

Cross-Claim Against Defendant M. N.

(Here set forth the claim constituting a cross-claim against defendant M. N. in the manner in which a claim is pleaded in a complaint. The statement of grounds upon which the court's jurisdiction depends need not be made unless the cross-claim requires independent grounds of jurisdiction.)

Note

The above form contains examples of certain defenses provided for in Rule 12(b). The first defense challenges the legal sufficiency of the complaint. It is a substitute for a general demurrer or a motion to dismiss.

The second defense embodies the old plea in abatement; the decision thereon, however, may well provide under Rules 19 and 21 for the citing in of the party rather than an abatement of the action.

The third defense is an answer on the merits.

The fourth defense is one of the affirmative defenses provided for in Rule 8(c).

The answer also includes a counterclaim and a cross-claim.

Form 21.

ANSWER TO COMPLAINT SET FORTH IN FORM 8, WITH COUNTERCLAIM FOR INTERPLEADER

Defense

Defendant admits the allegations stated in paragraph 1 of the complaint; and denies the allegations stated in paragraph 2 to the extent set forth in the counterclaim herein.

Counterclaim for Interpleader

1. Defendant received the sum of ...... dollars as a deposit from E. F.

2. Plaintiff has demanded the payment of such deposit to him by virtue of an assignment of it which he claims to have received from E. F.

3. E. F. has notified the defendant that he claims such deposit, that the purported assignment is not valid, and that he holds the defendant responsible for the deposit.

Wherefore defendant demands:

(1) That the court order E. F. to be made a party defendant to respond to the complaint and to this counterclaim.[1]

(2) That the court order the plaintiff and E. F. to interplead their respective claims.

(3) That the court adjudge whether the plaintiff or E. F. is entitled to the sum of money.

(4) That the court discharge defendant from all liability in the premises except to the person it shall adjudge entitled to the sum of money.

(5) That the court award to the defendant its costs and attorney's fees.

Form 22.

MOTION TO BRING IN THIRD-PARTY DEFENDANT

[The contents of Form 22 are eliminated down to and including the words "Exhibit A," thus eliminating the motion and notice of motion.] See Forms 22–A and 22–B.

---

1 Rule 13(h) provides for the court ordering parties to a counterclaim, but who are not parties to the original action, to be brought in as defendants.

Form 22-A.

SUMMONS AND COMPLAINT AGAINST THIRD-PARTY DEFENDANT

UNITED STATES DISTRICT COURT FOR THE SOUTHERN DISTRICT OF NEW YORK

Civil Action, File Number ......

A. B., Plaintiff v. C. D., Defendant and Third-Party Plaintiff v. E. F., Third-Party Defendant	Summons

To the above-named Third-Party Defendant:

You are hereby summoned and required to serve upon ...., plaintiff's attorney whose address is ...., and upon ...., who is attorney for C. D., defendant and third-party plaintiff, and whose address is ...., an answer to the third-party complaint which is herewith served upon you within 20 days after the service of this summons upon you exclusive of the day of service. If you fail to do so, judgment by default will be taken against you for the relief demanded in the third-party complaint. There is also served upon you herewith a copy of the complaint of the plaintiff which you may but are not required to answer.

......................,
Clerk of Court.

[Seal of District Court]

Dated ....

UNITED STATES DISTRICT COURT FOR THE SOUTHERN DISTRICT OF NEW YORK

Civil Action, File Number ......

A.B., Plaintiff v. C.D., Defendant and Third-Party Plaintiff v. E.F., Third-Party Defendant	Third-Party Complaint.

1. Plaintiff A.B. has filed against defendant C.D. a complaint, a copy of which is hereto attached as "Exhibit A."

2. (Here state the grounds upon which C.D. is entitled to recover from E.F., all or part of what A.B. may recover from C.D. The statement should be framed as in an original complaint.)

Wherefore C.D. demands judgment against third-party defendant E.F. for all sums [1] that may be adjudged against defendant C.D. in favor of plaintiff A.B.

Signed: ....
Attorney for C. D.,
Third-Party Plaintiff

Address: ....

Form 22-B

MOTION TO BRING IN THIRD-PARTY DEFENDANT

Defendant moves for leave, as third-party plaintiff, to cause to be served upon E.F. a summons and third-party complaint, copies of which are hereto attached as Exhibit X.

Signed: ....
Attorney for Defendant C.D.

Address: ....

---

[1] Make appropriate change where C.D. is entitled to only partial recovery-over against E.F.

Notice of Motion

(Contents the same as in Form 19. The notice should be addressed to all parties to the action.)

Exhibit X

(Contents the same as in Form 22–A.)

Form 23.

MOTION TO INTERVENE AS A DEFENDANT UNDER RULE 24

(Based upon the complaint, Form 16)

United States District Court for the Southern District of New York

Civil Action, File Number ....

A. B., plaintiff *v.* C. D., defendant E. F., applicant for intervention	*Motion to intervene as a defendant*

E. F. moves for leave to intervene as a defendant in this action, in order to assert the defenses set forth in his proposed answer, of which a copy is hereto attached, on the ground that he is the manufacturer and vendor to the defendant, as well as to others, of the articles alleged in the complaint to be an infringement of plaintiff's patent, and as such has a defense to plaintiff's claim presenting both questions of law and of fact which are common to the main action.[1]

Signed: ....,
Attorney for E. F., Applicant for Intervention.
Address: ....

Notice of Motion

(Contents the same as in Form 19)

United States District Court for the Southern District of New York

Civil Action, File Number ....

A. B., plaintiff *v.* C. D., defendant E. F., intervener	*Intervener's Answer*

[1] For other grounds of intervention, either of right or in the discretion of the court, see Rule 24 (a) and (b).

First Defense

Intervener admits the allegations stated in paragraphs 1 and 4 of the complaint; denies the allegations in paragraph 3, and denies the allegations in paragraph 2 in so far as they assert the legality of the issuance of the Letters Patent to plaintiff.

Second Defense

Plaintiff is not the first inventor of the articles covered by the Letters Patent specified in his complaint, since articles substantially identical in character were previously patented in Letters Patent granted to intervener on January 5, 1920.

Signed: ....,
Attorney for E. F., Intervener
Address: ....

Form 24.

REQUEST FOR PRODUCTION OF DOCUMENTS, ETC., UNDER RULE 34

Plaintiff A. B. requests defendant C. D. to respond within ...... days to the following requests:

(1) That defendant produce and permit plaintiff to inspect and to copy each of the following documents:

(Here list the documents either individually or by category and describe each of them.)

(Here state the time, place, and manner of making the inspection and performance of any related acts.)

(2) That defendant produce and permit plaintiff to inspect and to copy, test, or sample each of the following objects:

(Here list the objects either individually or by category and describe each of them.)

(Here state the time, place, and manner of making the inspection and performance of any related acts.)

(3) That defendant permit plaintiff to enter (here describe property to be entered) and to inspect and to photograph, test or sample (here describe the portion of the real property and the objects to be inspected).

(Here state the time, place, and manner of making the inspection and performance of any related acts.)

Signed: ....
Attorney for Plaintiff.
Address: ....

Form 25.

REQUEST FOR ADMISSION UNDER RULE 36

Plaintiff A. B. requests defendant C. D. within .... days after service of this request to make the following admissions for the purpose of this action only and subject to all pertinent objections to admissibility which may be interposed at the trial:

1. That each of the following documents, exhibited with this request, is genuine.

(Here list the documents and describe each document.)

2. That each of the following statements is true.

(Here list the statements.)

Signed: ....,

Attorney for Plaintiff.

Address: ....

Form 26.

ALLEGATION OF REASON FOR OMITTING PARTY

When it is necessary, under Rule 19 (c), for the pleader to set forth in his pleading the names of persons who ought to be made parties, but who are not so made, there should be an allegation such as the one set out below:

John Doe named in this complaint is not made a party to this action [because he is not subject to the jurisdiction of this court]; [because he cannot be made a party to this action without depriving this court of jurisdiction].

Form 27.

NOTICE OF APPEAL TO COURT OF APPEALS UNDER RULE 73 (b)

Abrogated.

Form 28.

NOTICE: CONDEMNATION

United States District Court for the Southern District of New York

Civil Action, File Number ....

UNITED STATES OF AMERICA, PLAINTIFF *v.* 1,000 ACRES OF LAND IN [here insert a general location as "City of ...." or "County of ...."], JOHN DOE ET AL., AND UNKNOWN OWNERS, DEFENDANTS	Notice.

To (here insert the names of the defendants to whom the notice is directed):

You are hereby notified that a complaint in condemnation has heretofore been filed in the office of the clerk of the United States District Court for the Southern District of New York, in the United States Court House in New York City, New York, for the taking (here state the interest to be acquired, as "an estate in fee simple") for use (here state briefly the use, "as a site for a post-office building") of the following described property in which you have or claim an interest.

(Here insert brief description of the property in which the defendants, to whom the notice is directed, have or claim an interest.)

The authority for the taking is (here state briefly, as "the Act of ...., ... Stat. ...., U.S.C.A., Title ...., § ....".)[1]

You are further notified that if you desire to present any objection or defense to the taking of your property you are required to serve your answer on the plaintiff's attorney at the address herein designated within twenty days after ....[2]

Your answer shall identify the property in which you claim to have an interest, state the nature and extent of the interest you claim, and state all of your objections and defenses to the taking of your property. All defenses and objections not so presented are waived. And in case of your failure so to answer the com-

---

[1] And where appropriate add a citation to any applicable Executive Order.

[2] Here insert the words "personal service of this notice upon you," if personal service is to be made pursuant to subdivision (d)(3)(i) of this rule [Rule 71A]; or, insert the date of the last publication of notice, if service by publication is to be made pursuant to subdivision (d)(3)(ii) of this rule.

plaint, judgment of condemnation of that part of the above-described property in which you have or claim an interest will be rendered.

But without answering, you may serve on the plaintiff's attorney a notice of appearance designating the property in which you claim to be interested. Thereafter you will receive notice of all proceedings affecting it. At the trial of the issue of just compensation, whether or not you have previously appeared or answered, you may present evidence as to the amount of the compensation to be paid for your property, and you may share in the distribution of the award.

....

United States Attorney.

Address ....

(Here state an address within the district where the United States Attorney may be served as "United States Court House, New York, N. Y.")

Dated ....

Form 29.

COMPLAINT: CONDEMNATION

United States District Court for the Southern District of New York

Civil Action, File Number ....

UNITED STATES OF AMERICA, PLAINTIFF *v.* 1,000 ACRES OF LAND IN [here insert a general location as "City of .... " or "County of ...."], JOHN DOE, ET AL., AND UNKNOWN OWNERS, DEFENDANTS	Complaint.

1. This is an action of a civil nature brought by the United States of America for the taking of property under the power of eminent domain and for the ascertainment and award of just compensation to the owners and parties in interest.[1]

[1] If the plaintiff is not the United States, but is, for example, a corporation invoking the power of eminent domain delegated to it by the state, then this paragraph 1 of the complaint should be appropriately modified and should be preceded by a paragraph appropriately alleging federal jurisdiction for the action, such as diversity. See Form 2.

2. The authority for the taking is (here state briefly, as "the Act of ...., ... Stat. ...., U.S.C.A., Title ...., § ....").[2]

3. The use for which the property is to be taken is (here state briefly the use, "as a site for a post-office building").

4. The interest to be acquired in the property is (here state the interest as "an estate in fee simple").

5. The property so to be taken is (here set forth a description of the property sufficient for its identification) or (described in Exhibit A hereto attached and made a part hereof).

6. The persons known to the plaintiff to have or claim an interest in the property[3] are:

(Here set forth the names of such persons and the interests claimed.)[4]

7. In addition to the persons named, there are or may be others who have or may claim some interest in the property to be taken, whose names are unknown to the plaintiff and on diligent inquiry have not been ascertained. They are made parties to the action under the designation "Unknown Owners."

Wherefore the plaintiff demands judgment that the property be condemned and that just compensation for the taking be ascertained and awarded and for such other relief as may be lawful and proper.

....
United States Attorney.

Address ....

(Here state an address within the district where the United States Attorney may be served, as "United States Court House, New York, N. Y.").

---

[2] And where appropriate add a citation to any applicable Executive Order.

[3] At the commencement of the action the plaintiff need name as defendants only the persons having or claiming an interest in the property whose names are then known, but prior to any hearing involving the compensation to be paid for a particular piece of property the plaintiff must add as defendants all persons having or claiming an interest in that property whose names can be ascertained by an appropriate search of the records and also those whose names have otherwise been learned. See Rule 71A (c) (2).

[4] The plaintiff should designate, as to each separate piece of property, the defendants who have been joined as owners thereof or of some interest therein. See Rule 71A (c) (2).

Form 30.

SUGGESTION OF DEATH UPON THE RECORD UNDER RULE 25(a) (1)

A.B. [describe as a party, or as executor, administrator, or other representative or successor of C.D., the deceased party] suggests upon the record, pursuant to Rule 25(a) (1), the death of C.D. [describe as party] during the pendency of this action.

Form 31.

JUDGMENT ON JURY VERDICT

UNITED STATES DISTRICT COURT FOR THE SOUTHERN DISTRICT OF NEW YORK

Civil Action, File Number ......

A.B., Plaintiff v. C.D., Defendant	Judgment

This action came on for trial before the Court and a jury, Honorable John Marshall, District Judge, presiding, and the issues having been duly tried and the jury having duly rendered its verdict,

It is Ordered and Adjudged

[that the plaintiff A.B. recover of the defendant C.D. the sum of ......, with interest thereon at the rate of ...... per cent as provided by law, and his costs of action.]

[that the plaintiff take nothing, that the action be dismissed on the merits, and that the defendant C.D. recover of the plaintiff A.B. his costs of action.]

Dated at New York, New York, this ...... day of ......, 19..

....

Clerk of Court

Explanatory Note

1. This Form is illustrative of the judgment to be entered upon the general verdict of a jury. It deals with the cases where there is a general jury verdict awarding the plaintiff money damages or finding for the defendant, but is adaptable to other situations of jury verdicts.

2. The clerk, unless the court otherwise orders, is required forthwith to prepare, sign, and enter the judgment upon a general jury verdict without awaiting any direction by the court. The form of the judgment upon a special verdict or a general verdict accompanied by answers to interrogatories shall be promptly approved by the court, and the clerk shall thereupon enter it. See Rule 58, as amended.

3. The Rules contemplate a simple judgment promptly entered. See Rule 54(a). Every judgment shall be set forth on a separate document. See Rule 58, as amended.

4. Attorneys are not to submit forms of judgment unless directed in exceptional cases to do so by the court. See Rule 58, as amended.

Form 32.

JUDGMENT ON DECISION BY THE COURT

UNITED STATES DISTRICT COURT FOR THE SOUTHERN DISTRICT OF NEW YORK

Civil Action, File Number ......

A.B., Plaintiff
v.
C.D., Defendant } Judgment

This action came on for [trial] [hearing] before the Court, Honorable John Marshall, District Judge, presiding, and the issues having been duly [tried] [heard] and a decision having been duly rendered,

It is Ordered and Adjudged

[that the plaintiff A.B. recover of the defendant C.D. the sum of ......, with interest thereon at the rate of ...... per cent as provided by law, and his costs of action.]

[that the plaintiff take nothing, that the action be dismissed on the merits, and that the defendant C.D. recover of the plaintiff A.B. his costs of action.]

Dated at New York, New York, this ...... day of ......, 19..

....

Clerk of Court

Explanatory Note

1. This Form is illustrative of the judgment to be entered upon a decision of the court. It deals with the cases of decisions by the court awarding a party only money damages or costs, but is adaptable to other decisions by the court.

2. The clerk, unless the court otherwise orders, is required forthwith, without awaiting any direction by the court, to prepare, sign, and enter the judgment upon a decision by the court that a party shall recover only a sum certain or costs or that all relief shall be denied. The form of the judgment upon a decision by the court granting other relief shall be promptly approved by the court, and the clerk shall thereupon enter it. See Rule 58, as amended.

3. See also paragraphs 3-4 of the Explanatory Note to Form 31.

Form 33.

NOTICE OF RIGHT TO CONSENT TO THE EXERCISE OF CIVIL JURISDICTION BY A MAGISTRATE AND APPEAL OPTION

In accordance with the provisions of Title 28, U.S.C. § 636(c), you are hereby notified that the United States magistrates of this district court, in addition to their other duties, upon the consent of all parties in a civil case, may conduct any or all proceedings in a civil case including a jury or nonjury trial, and order the entry of a final judgment.

You should be aware that your decision to consent, or not to consent, to the referral of your case to a United States magistrate must be entirely voluntary. Only if all the parties to the case consent to the reference to a magistrate will either the judge or magistrate to whom the case has been assigned be informed of your decision.

An appeal from a judgment entered by a magistrate may be taken directly to the United States court of appeals for this judicial circuit in the same manner as an appeal from any other judgment of a district court. Alternatively, upon consent of all parties, an appeal from a judgment entered by a magistrate may be taken directly to a district judge. Cases in which an appeal is taken to a district judge may be reviewed by the United States court of appeals for this judicial circuit only by way of petition for leave to appeal.

Copies of the Form for the "Consent to Proceed Before a United States Magistrate" and "Election of Appeal to a District Judge" are available from the clerk of the court.

Form 34.

CONSENT TO PROCEED BEFORE A UNITED STATES MAGISTRATE, ELECTION OF APPEAL TO DISTRICT JUDGE, AND ORDER OF REFERENCE

UNITED STATES DISTRICT COURT FOR THE ....

DISTRICT OF ....

Plaintiff,
vs.
No. .... } Docket
Defendant.

CONSENT TO PROCEED BEFORE A UNITED STATES MAGISTRATE

In accordance with the provisions of Title 28, U.S.C. § 636(c), the parties to the above-captioned civil matter hereby voluntarily waive their rights to proceed before a judge of the United States district court and consent to have a United States magistrate conduct any and all further proceedings in the case, including trial, and order the entry of a final judgment.

....

....

....
Date

ELECTION OF APPEAL TO DISTRICT JUDGE

[Do not execute this portion of the Consent Form if the parties desire that the appeal lie directly to the court of appeals.]

In accordance with the provisions of Title 28, U.S.C. § 636(c)(4), the parties elect to take any appeal in this case to a district judge.

....

....

....
Date

ORDER OF REFERENCE

IT IS HEREBY ORDERED that the above-captioned matter be referred to United States Magistrate .... for all further proceedings and the entry of judgment in accordance with Title 28, U.S.C. § 636(c) and the foregoing consent of the parties.

....
U.S. District Judge

Note

Return this form to the Clerk of the Court only if all parties have consented to proceed before a magistrate.

SUPPLEMENTAL RULES
FOR CERTAIN
ADMIRALTY AND MARITIME CLAIMS

As amended to August 1, 1983

Editorial Note: These Supplemental Rules were included in the amendments of February 28, 1966, 383 U.S. 1031, effective July 1, 1966. The former Rules of Practice in Admiralty and Maritime Cases, promulgated by the Supreme Court on December 6, 1920, effective March 7, 1921, as revised, amended and supplemented thereafter, were rescinded at the same time, 383 U.S. 1031–1032, effective July 1, 1966.

Rule A.

SCOPE OF RULES

These Supplemental Rules apply to the procedure in admiralty and maritime claims within the meaning of Rule 9(h) with respect to the following remedies:

(1) Maritime attachment and garnishment;
(2) Actions in rem;
(3) Possessory, petitory, and partition actions;
(4) Actions for exoneration from or limitation of liability.

These rules also apply to the procedure in statutory condemnation proceedings analogous to maritime actions in rem, whether within the admiralty and maritime jurisdiction or not. Except as otherwise provided, references in these Supplemental Rules to actions in rem include such analogous statutory condemnation proceedings.

The general Rules of Civil Procedure for the United States District Courts are also applicable to the foregoing proceedings except to the extent that they are inconsistent with these Supplemental Rules.

Rule B.
ATTACHMENT AND GARNISHMENT: SPECIAL PROVISIONS

(1) When Available; Complaint, Affidavit, and Process. With respect to any admiralty or maritime claim in personam a verified complaint may contain a prayer for process to attach the defendant's goods and chattels, or credits and effects in the hands of garnishees named in the complaint to the amount sued for, if the defendant shall not be found within the district. Such a complaint shall be accompanied by an affidavit signed by the plaintiff or his attorney that, to the affiant's knowledge, or to the best of his information and belief, the defendant cannot be found within the district. When a verified complaint is supported by such an affidavit the clerk shall forthwith issue a summons and process of attachment and garnishment. In addition, or in the alternative, the plaintiff may, pursuant to Rule 4(e), invoke the remedies provided by state law for attachment and garnishment or similar seizure of the defendant's property. Except for Rule E(8) these Supplemental Rules do not apply to state remedies so invoked.

(2) Notice to Defendant. No judgment by default shall be entered except upon proof, which may be by affidavit, (a) that the plaintiff or the garnishee has given notice of the action to the defendant by mailing to him a copy of the complaint, summons, and process of attachment or garnishment, using any form of mail requiring a return receipt, or (b) that the complaint, summons, and process of attachment or garnishment have been served on the defendant in a manner authorized by Rule 4(d) or (i), or (c) that the plaintiff or the garnishee has made diligent efforts to give notice of the action to the defendant and has been unable to do so.

(3) Answer.

(a) *By Garnishee.* The garnishee shall serve his answer, together with answers to any interrogatories served with the complaint, within 20 days after service of process upon him. Interrogatories to the garnishee may be served with the complaint without leave of court. If the garnishee refuses or neglects to answer on oath as to the debts, credits, or effects of the defendant in his hands, or any interrogatories concerning such debts, credits, and effects that may be propounded by the plaintiff, the court may award compulsory process against him. If he admits any debts, credits, or effects, they shall be held in his hands or paid into the registry of the court, and shall be held in either case subject to the further order of the court.

(b) *By Defendant.* The defendant shall serve his answer within 30 days after process has been executed, whether by attachment of property or service on the garnishee.

Rule C.

ACTIONS IN REM: SPECIAL PROVISIONS

(1) When Available. An action in rem may be brought:

(a) To enforce any maritime lien;

(b) Whenever a statute of the United States provides for a maritime action in rem or a proceeding analogous thereto.

Except as otherwise provided by law a party who may proceed in rem may also, or in the alternative, proceed in personam against any person who may be liable.

Statutory provisions exempting vessels or other property owned or possessed by or operated by or for the United States from arrest or seizure are not affected by this rule. When a statute so provides, an action against the United States or an instrumentality thereof may proceed on in rem principles.

(2) Complaint. In actions in rem the complaint shall be verified on oath or solemn affirmation. It shall describe with reasonable particularity the property that is the subject of the action and state that it is within the district or will be during the pendency of the action. In actions for the enforcement of forfeitures for violation of any statute of the United States the complaint shall state the place of seizure and whether it was on land or on navigable waters, and shall contain such allegations as may be required by the statute pursuant to which the action is brought.

(3) Process. Upon the filing of the complaint the clerk shall forthwith issue a warrant for the arrest of the vessel or other property that is the subject of the action and deliver it to the marshal for service. If the property that is the subject of the action consists in whole or in part of freight, or the proceeds of property sold, or other intangible property, the clerk shall issue a summons directing any person having control of the funds to show cause why they should not be paid into court to abide the judgment.

(4) Notice. No notice other than the execution of the process is required when the property that is the subject of the action has been released in accordance with Rule E(5). If the property is not released within 10 days after execution of process, the plaintiff shall promptly or within such time as may be allowed by the court cause public notice of the action and arrest to be given in a newspaper of general circulation in the district, designated by order of the court. Such notice shall specify the time within which the answer is required to be filed as provided by subdivision (6) of this rule. This rule does not affect the requirements of notice in actions to foreclose a preferred ship mortgage pursuant to the Act of June 5, 1920, ch. 250, § 30, as amended.

(5) Ancillary Process. In any action in rem in which process has been served as provided by this rule, if any part of the property that is the subject of the action has not been brought within the control of the court because it has been removed or sold, or because it is intangible property in the hands of a person who has not been served with process, the court may, on motion, order any person having possession or control of such property or its proceeds to show cause why it should not be delivered into the custody of the marshal or paid into court to abide the judgment; and, after hearing, the court may enter such judgment as law and justice may require.

(6) Claim and Answer; Interrogatories. The claimant of property that is the subject of an action in rem shall file his claim within 10 days after process has been executed, or within such additional time as may be allowed by the court, and shall serve his answer within 20 days after the filing of the claim. The claim shall be verified on oath or solemn affirmation, and shall state the interest in the property by virtue of which the claimant demands its restitution and the right to defend the action. If the claim is made on behalf of the person entitled to possession by an agent, bailee, or attorney, it shall state that he is duly authorized to make the claim. At the time of answering the claimant shall also serve answers to any interrogatories served with the complaint. In actions in rem interrogatories may be so served without leave of court.

Rule D.

POSSESSORY, PETITORY, AND PARTITION ACTIONS

In all actions for possession, partition, and to try title maintainable according to the course of the admiralty practice with respect to a vessel, in all actions so maintainable with respect to the possession of cargo or other maritime property, and in all actions by one or more part owners against the others to obtain security for the return of the vessel from any voyage undertaken without their consent, or by one or more part owners against the others to obtain possession of the vessel for any voyage on giving security for its safe return, the process shall be by a warrant of arrest of the vessel, cargo, or other property, and by notice in the manner provided by Rule B(2) to the adverse party or parties.

Rule E.

ACTIONS IN REM AND QUASI IN REM: GENERAL PROVISIONS

(1) Applicability. Except as otherwise provided, this rule applies to actions in personam with process of maritime attachment and garnishment, actions in rem, and petitory, possessory, and partition actions, supplementing Rules B, C, and D.

(2) Complaint; Security.

(a) Complaint. In actions to which this rule is applicable the complaint shall state the circumstances from which the claim arises with such particularity that the defendant or claimant will be able, without moving for a more definite statement, to commence an investigation of the facts and to frame a responsive pleading.

(b) Security for Costs. Subject to the provisions of Rule 54(d) and of relevant statutes, the court may, on the filing of the complaint or on the appearance of any defendant, claimant, or any other party, or at any later time, require the plaintiff, defendant, claimant, or other party to give security, or additional security, in such sum as the court shall direct to pay all costs and expenses that shall be awarded against him by any interlocutory order or by the final judgment, or on appeal by any appellate court.

(3) Process.

(a) Territorial Limits of Effective Service. Process in rem and of maritime attachment and garnishment shall be served only within the district.

(b) Issuance and Delivery. Issuance and delivery of process in rem, or of maritime attachment and garnishment, shall be held in abeyance if the plaintiff so requests.

(4) Execution of Process; Marshal's Return; Custody of Property.

(a) In General. Upon issuance and delivery of the process, or, in the case of summons with process of attachment and garnishment, when it appears that the defendant cannot be found within the district, the marshal shall forthwith execute the process in accordance with this subdivision (4), making due and prompt return.

(b) Tangible Property. If tangible property is to be attached or arrested, the marshal shall take it into his possession for safe custody. If the character or situation of the property is such that the taking of actual possession is impracticable, the marshal

shall execute the process by affixing a copy thereof to the property in a conspicuous place and by leaving a copy of the complaint and process with the person having possession or his agent. In furtherance of his custody of any vessel the marshal is authorized to make a written request to the collector of customs not to grant clearance to such vessel until notified by the marshal or his deputy or by the clerk that the vessel has been released in accordance with these rules.

(c) Intangible Property. If intangible property is to be attached or arrested the marshal shall execute the process by leaving with the garnishee or other obligor a copy of the complaint and process requiring him to answer as provided in Rules B(3) (a) and C(6); or he may accept for payment into the registry of the court the amount owed to the extent of the amount claimed by the plaintiff with interest and costs, in which event the garnishee or other obligor shall not be required to answer unless alias process shall be served.

(d) Directions with Respect to Property in Custody. The marshal may at any time apply to the court for directions with respect to property that has been attached or arrested, and shall give notice of such application to any or all of the parties as the court may direct.

(e) Expenses of Seizing and Keeping Property; Deposit. These rules do not alter the provisions of Title 28, U.S.C., § 1921, as amended, relative to the expenses of seizing and keeping property attached or arrested and to the requirement of deposits to cover such expenses.

(5) Release of Property.

(a) Special Bond. Except in cases of seizures for forfeiture under any law of the United States, whenever process of maritime attachment and garnishment or process in rem is issued the execution of such process shall be stayed, or the property released, on the giving of security, to be approved by the court or clerk, or by stipulation of the parties, conditioned to answer the judgment of the court or of any appellate court. The parties may stipulate the amount and nature of such security. In the event of the inability or refusal of the parties so to stipulate the court shall fix the principal sum of the bond or stipulation at an amount sufficient to cover the amount of the plaintiff's claim fairly stated with accrued interest and costs; but the principal sum shall in no event exceed (i) twice the amount of the plaintiff's claim or (ii) the value of the property on due appraisement, whichever is smaller. The bond or stipulation shall be conditioned for the payment of the principal sum and interest thereon at 6 per cent per annum.

(b) *General Bond.* The owner of any vessel may file a general bond or stipulation, with sufficient surety, to be approved by the court, conditioned to answer the judgment of such court in all or any actions that may be brought thereafter in such court in which the vessel is attached or arrested. Thereupon the execution of all such process against such vessel shall be stayed so long as the amount secured by such bond or stipulation is at least double the aggregate amount claimed by plaintiffs in all actions begun and pending in which such vessel has been attached or arrested. Judgments and remedies may be had on such bond or stipulation as if a special bond or stipulation had been filed in each of such actions. The district court may make necessary orders to carry this rule into effect, particularly as to the giving of proper notice of any action against or attachment of a vessel for which a general bond has been filed. Such bond or stipulation shall be indorsed by the clerk with a minute of the actions wherein process is so stayed. Further security may be required by the court at any time.

If a special bond or stipulation is given in a particular case, the liability on the general bond or stipulation shall cease as to that case.

(c) *Release by Consent or Stipulation; Order of Court or Clerk; Costs.* Any vessel, cargo, or other property in the custody of the marshal may be released forthwith upon his acceptance and approval of a stipulation, bond, or other security, signed by the party on whose behalf the property is detained or his attorney and expressly authorizing such release, if all costs and charges of the court and its officers shall have first been paid. Otherwise no property in the custody of the marshal or other officer of the court shall be released without an order of the court; but such order may be entered as of course by the clerk, upon the giving of approved security as provided by law and these rules, or upon the dismissal or discontinuance of the action; but the marshal shall not deliver any property so released until the costs and charges of the officers of the court shall first have been paid.

(d) *Possessory, Petitory, and Partition Actions.* The foregoing provisions of this subdivision (5) do not apply to petitory, possessory, and partition actions. In such cases the property arrested shall be released only by order of the court, on such terms and conditions and on the giving of such security as the court may require.

(6) Reduction or Impairment of Security. Whenever security is taken the court may, on motion and hearing, for good cause shown, reduce the amount of security given; and if the surety shall be or become insufficient, new or additional sureties may be required on motion and hearing.

(7) Security on Counterclaim. Whenever there is asserted a counterclaim arising out of the same transaction or occurrence with respect to which the action was originally filed, and the defendant or claimant in the original action has given security to respond in damages, any plaintiff for whose benefit such security has been given shall give security in the usual amount and form to respond in damages to the claims set forth in such counterclaim, unless the court, for cause shown, shall otherwise direct; and proceedings on the original claim shall be stayed until such security is given, unless the court otherwise directs. When the United States or a corporate instrumentality thereof as defendant is relieved by law of the requirement of giving security to respond in damages it shall nevertheless be treated for the purposes of this subdivision E(7) as if it had given such security if a private person so situated would have been required to give it.

(8) Restricted Appearance. An appearance to defend against an admiralty and maritime claim with respect to which there has issued process in rem, or process of attachment and garnishment whether pursuant to these Supplemental Rules or to Rule 4(e), may be expressly restricted to the defense of such claim, and in that event shall not constitute an appearance for the purposes of any other claim with respect to which such process is not available or has not been served.

(9) Disposition of Property; Sales.

(a) Actions for Forfeitures. In any action in rem to enforce a forfeiture for violation of a statute of the United States the property shall be disposed of as provided by statute.

(b) Interlocutory Sales. If property that has been attached or arrested is perishable, or liable to deterioration, decay, or injury by being detained in custody pending the action, or if the expense of keeping the property is excessive or disproportionate, or if there is unreasonable delay in securing the release of property, the court, on application of any party or of the marshal, may order the property or any portion thereof to be sold; and the proceeds, or so much thereof as shall be adequate to satisfy any judgment, may be ordered brought into court to abide the event of the action; or the court may, on motion of the defendant or claimant, order delivery of the property to him, upon the giving of security in accordance with these rules.

(c) Sales; Proceeds. All sales of property shall be made by the marshal or his deputy, or other proper officer assigned by the court where the marshal is a party in interest; and the proceeds of sale shall be forthwith paid into the registry of the court to be disposed of according to law.

Rule F.

LIMITATION OF LIABILITY

(1) Time for Filing Complaint; Security. Not later than six months after his receipt of a claim in writing, any vessel owner may file a complaint in the appropriate district court, as provided in subdivision (9) of this rule, for limitation of liability pursuant to statute. The owner (a) shall deposit with the court, for the benefit of claimants, a sum equal to the amount or value of his interest in the vessel and pending freight, or approved security therefor, and in addition such sums, or approved security therefor, as the court may from time to time fix as necessary to carry out the provisions of the statutes as amended; or (b) at his option shall transfer to a trustee to be appointed by the court, for the benefit of claimants, his interest in the vessel and pending freight, together with such sums, or approved security therefor, as the court may from time to time fix as necessary to carry out the provisions of the statutes as amended. The plaintiff shall also give security for costs and, if he elects to give security, for interest at the rate of 6 per cent per annum from the date of the security.

(2) Complaint. The complaint shall set forth the facts on the basis of which the right to limit liability is asserted, and all facts necessary to enable the court to determine the amount to which the owner's liability shall be limited. The complaint may demand exoneration from as well as limitation of liability. It shall state the voyage, if any, on which the demands sought to be limited arose, with the date and place of its termination; the amount of all demands including all unsatisfied liens or claims of lien, in contract or in tort or otherwise, arising on that voyage, so far as known to the plaintiff, and what actions and proceedings, if any, are pending thereon; whether the vessel was damaged, lost, or abandoned, and, if so, when and where; the value of the vessel at the close of the voyage or, in case of wreck, the value of her wreckage, strippings, or proceeds, if any, and where and in whose possession they are; and the amount of any pending freight recovered or recoverable. If the plaintiff elects to transfer his interest in the vessel to a trustee, the complaint must further show any prior paramount liens thereon, and what voyages or trips, if any, she has made since the voyage or trip on which the claims sought to be limited arose, and any existing liens arising upon any such subsequent voyage or trip, with the amounts and causes thereof, and the names and addresses of the lienors, so far as known; and whether the vessel sustained any injury upon or by reason of such subsequent voyage or trip.

(3) Claims Against Owner; Injunction. Upon compliance by the owner with the requirements of subdivision (1) of this rule all claims and proceedings against the owner or his property with respect to the matter in question shall cease. On application of the plaintiff the court shall enjoin the further prosecution of any action or proceeding against the plaintiff or his property with respect to any claim subject to limitation in the action.

(4) Notice to Claimants. Upon the owner's compliance with subdivision (1) of this rule the court shall issue a notice to all persons asserting claims with respect to which the complaint seeks limitation, admonishing them to file their respective claims with the clerk of the court and to serve on the attorneys for the plaintiff a copy thereof on or before a date to be named in the notice. The date so fixed shall not be less than 30 days after issuance of the notice. For cause shown, the court may enlarge the time within which claims may be filed. The notice shall be published in such newspaper or newspapers as the court may direct once a week for four successive weeks prior to the date fixed for the filing of claims. The plaintiff not later than the day of second publication shall also mail a copy of the notice to every person known to have made any claim against the vessel or the plaintiff arising out of the voyage or trip on which the claims sought to be limited arose. In cases involving death a copy of such notice shall be mailed to the decedent at his last known address, and also to any person who shall be known to have made any claim on account of such death.

(5) Claims and Answer. Claims shall be filed and served on or before the date specified in the notice provided for in subdivision (4) of this rule. Each claim shall specify the facts upon which the claimant relies in support of his claim, the items thereof, and the dates on which the same accrued. If a claimant desires to contest either the right to exoneration from or the right to limitation of liability he shall file and serve an answer to the complaint unless his claim has included an answer.

(6) Information to Be Given Claimants. Within 30 days after the date specified in the notice for filing claims, or within such time as the court thereafter may allow, the plaintiff shall mail to the attorney for each claimant (or if the claimant has no attorney to the claimant himself) a list setting forth (a) the name of each claimant, (b) the name and address of his attorney (if he is known to have one), (c) the nature of his claim, i.e., whether property loss, property damage, death, personal injury, etc., and (d) the amount thereof.

(7) Insufficiency of Fund or Security. Any claimant may by motion demand that the funds deposited in court or the security given by the plaintiff be increased on the ground that they are less than the value of the plaintiff's interest in the vessel and pending freight. Thereupon the court shall cause due appraisement to be made of the value of the plaintiff's interest in the vessel and pending freight; and if the court finds that the deposit or security is either insufficient or excessive it shall order its increase or reduction. In like manner any claimant may demand that the deposit or security be increased on the ground that it is insufficient to carry out the provisions of the statutes relating to claims in respect of loss of life or bodily injury; and, after notice and hearing, the court may similarly order that the deposit or security be increased or reduced.

(8) Objections to Claims: Distribution of Fund. Any interested party may question or controvert any claim without filing an objection thereto. Upon determination of liability the fund deposited or secured, or the proceeds of the vessel and pending freight, shall be divided pro rata, subject to all relevant provisions of law, among the several claimants in proportion to the amounts of their respective claims, duly proved, saving, however, to all parties any priority to which they may be legally entitled.

(9) Venue; Transfer. The complaint shall be filed in any district in which the vessel has been attached or arrested to answer for any claim with respect to which the plaintiff seeks to limit liability; or, if the vessel has not been attached or arrested, then in any district in which the owner has been sued with respect to any such claim. When the vessel has not been attached or arrested to answer the matters aforesaid, and suit has not been commenced against the owner, the proceedings may be had in the district in which the vessel may be, but if the vessel is not within any district and no suit has been commenced in any district, then the complaint may be filed in any district. For the convenience of parties and witnesses, in the interest of justice, the court may transfer the action to any district; if venue is wrongly laid the court shall dismiss or, if it be in the interest of justice, transfer the action to any district in which it could have been brought. If the vessel shall have been sold, the proceeds shall represent the vessel for the purposes of these rules.

RULES OF PROCEDURE

OF THE

JUDICIAL PANEL ON MULTIDISTRICT LITIGATION

As amended to August 1, 1983

Editorial Note: Pursuant to 28 U.S.C. § 1407(f), the Judicial Panel on Multidistrict Litigation prescribed rules of procedure that became effective September 1, 1970. Substantial amendments became effective February 14, 1975. The rules, as amended, are set forth below.

TABLE OF RULES

Rule 1.

DEFINITIONS

As used in these Rules "Panel" means all available but not less than four members of the Judicial Panel on Multidistrict Litigation appointed by the Chief Justice of the United States pursuant to Section 1407, Title 28, United States Code.

"Clerk" means the official appointed by the Panel to act as Clerk of the Panel and shall include those deputized by the Clerk to perform or assist in the performance of the duties of the Clerk of the Panel.

"Chairman" means the Chairman of the Judicial Panel on Multidistrict Litigation appointed by the Chief Justice of the United States pursuant to Section 1407, or the member of the Panel designated by the Panel to act as Chairman in the Absence or inability of the appointed Chairman.

A "tag-along action" refers to a civil action apparently sharing common questions of fact with actions previously transferred under Section 1407.

Rule 2.

PLACE OF KEEPING RECORDS AND FILES

The records and files of the Panel shall be kept by the Clerk of the Panel at the offices of the Panel. Records and files may be temporarily or permanently removed to such places at such times as the Panel or the Chairman of the Panel shall direct. The Clerk of the Panel may release records or files for a limited time for the purpose of duplicating.

Rule 3.

ADMISSION TO PRACTICE BEFORE THE PANEL AND REPRESENTATION IN TRANSFERRED ACTIONS

Every member in good standing of the Bar of any district court of the United States is entitled without condition to practice before the Judicial Panel on Multidistrict Litigation. Any Attorney of record in any action transferred under Section 1407 may continue to represent his client in any district court of the United States to which such action is transferred. Parties to any action transferred under Section 1407 are not required to obtain local counsel in the district to which such action is transferred.

Rule 4.

PLACE AND MANNER OF THE FILING OF PAPERS

(a) All papers filed for consideration by the Panel shall be filed with the Clerk of the Panel by mailing or delivering to:

Clerk of the Panel
Judicial Panel on Multidistrict Litigation
1030 15th Street, N.W.
320 Executive Building
Washington, D. C. 20005

No papers shall be left with or mailed to a Judge of the Panel or his chamber for filing.

(b) An original and ten copies of each paper, other than an application for extension of time, a proof of service or a notice of opposition pursuant to Rules 9 and 11 of these Rules, shall be filed with the Clerk of the Panel. The Clerk of the Panel may require that additional copies also be filed.

(c) When papers are submitted for filing in compliance with the provisions of these Rules, the Clerk of the Panel shall endorse thereon the date of filing.

(d) Copies of motions for transfer of an action or actions pursuant to 28 U.S.C. § 1407 shall be filed in each district court in which an action is pending that will be affected by the motion.

Rule 5.
SERVICE OF PAPERS FILED

(a) All papers filed with Clerk of the Panel shall be accompanied by proof of service on all other parties in all actions involved in the litigation. Service and proof of service shall be made as provided in Rules 5 and 6 of the Federal Rules of Civil Procedure. The proof of service shall indicate the name and address of each person served and shall indicate the party represented by each. If a party is not represented by counsel, the proof of service shall indicate the name of the party and his last known address. The original proof of service shall be filed with the Clerk of the Panel and copies thereof shall be sent to each person included within the proof of service.

(b) The proof of service pertaining to motions for the transfer of actions pursuant to 28 U.S.C. § 1407 shall certify that copies of the motions have been mailed or otherwise delivered for filing to the clerk of each district court in which an action is pending that will be affected by the motion.

(c) Within ten days of filing of a motion to transfer, an order to show cause or a conditional transfer order, each party or designated attorney shall notify the Clerk of the Panel, in writing, of the name and address of the attorney designated to receive service of all pleadings, notices, orders and other papers relating to practice before the Judicial Panel on Multidistrict Litigation. Only one attorney shall be designated for each party. Any party not represented by counsel will be served by mailing such pleadings to that party's last known address.

(d) In order to facilitate compliance with subsection (a) of this Rule, the Clerk of the Panel will prepare and serve on all counsel and parties not represented by counsel a "Panel Service List" containing the names and addresses of the designated attorneys and the party or parties they represent and the names and addresses of the parties not represented by counsel.

(e) If following transfer of any group of multidistrict litigation, the transferee court appoints liaison counsel, this Rule will be satisfied by serving each party in each affected action and all liaison counsel. Liaison counsel designated by the transferee court will receive copies of all Panel orders concerning their particular litigation and shall be responsible for distribution to the parties for whom he serves as liaison counsel.

Rule 6.

FORM OF PAPERS FILED

(a) Averments in any motion seeking action by the Panel shall be made in numbered paragraphs, each of which shall be limited, as far as practicable, to a statement of a single factual averment. Responses to averments in motions shall be made in numbered paragraphs, each of which shall correspond to the number of the paragraph of the motion to which the responsive paragraph is directed. Each responsive paragraph shall admit or deny wholly or in part the averment of the motion, and shall contain the respondent's version of the subject matter when the averment or the motion is not wholly admitted.

(b) Each document filed shall be flat and unfolded, shall be plainly written, typed in double space, printed or prepared by means of a duplicating process, without erasures or interlineations which materially deface it, on opaque, unglazed, white paper approximately $8\frac{1}{2}$ x 11 inches in size, and shall be secured on the left margin. Each document shall bear the identification "MDL Docket No. ______" and the appropriate descriptive title of the litigation involved, and on the final page thereof shall contain the name, address and telephone number of the attorney in active charge of the case.

Rule 7.

MOTION PRACTICE

All requests for action by the panel shall be made by written motion. Every motion shall be accompanied by (1) a brief in support thereof in which the background of the litigation and the factual and legal contentions of the movant shall be concisely stated in separate portions of the brief with citation of applicable authorities; and (2) a schedule giving complete captions of each action involved, noting the district court in which each action is pending, the civil action number of each, and the name of the judge assigned each action, if known. Within fifteen days after filing of a motion, all other parties shall file a response thereto. The movant may, within five days after the lapse of the time period for filing responsive briefs, file a single brief in reply to any opposition. Failure of a party to respond to a motion shall be deemed as that party's acquiescence to the action requested in the motion. Motions, responses, and replies shall also be governed by Rules 4, 5 and 6 of these Rules.

Rule 8.

SHOW CAUSE ORDERS

When transfer of multidistrict litigation is being considered on the initiative of the Panel pursuant to 28 U.S.C. § 1407(c)(i) an order will be filed by the Clerk of the Panel directing the parties to show cause why the action or actions should not be transferred for coordinated or consolidated pretrial proceedings. Any party may file a response to the show cause order within fifteen days of the filing of said order unless otherwise provided for in the order. Within five days after the lapse of the time period for filing a response, any party may file a reply limited to new matters. Responses and replies shall be filed and served in conformity with Rules 4, 5, 6 and 7 of these Rules.

Rule 9.

CONDITIONAL TRANSFER ORDERS FOR "TAG-ALONG ACTIONS"

(a) Upon learning of the pendency of a "tag-along action," an order may be entered by the Clerk of the Panel transferring that "tag-along action" to the previously designated transferee court on the basis of the prior hearing or hearings and for the reasons expressed in previous opinions and orders of the Panel in the litigation. The Clerk of the Panel shall serve this order on each party to the litigation but, in order to afford all parties the opportunity to oppose transfer, shall not send the order to the clerk of the transferee court for fifteen days from the entry thereof.

(b) Any party opposing the transfer shall file a Notice of Opposition with the Clerk of the Panel within the fifteen-day period. If a Notice of Opposition is received by the Clerk of the Panel within this fifteen-day period, the Clerk of the Panel shall not transmit said order to the clerk of the transferee court until further order of the Panel.

(c) Within fifteen days of the filing of its Notice of Opposition, the party opposing transfer shall file a motion to vacate the conditional transfer order and brief in support thereof. The Clerk of the Panel shall set the motion for hearing at the next appropriate session of the Panel. Failure to file and serve a motion and brief shall be deemed withdrawal of the opposition and the Clerk of the Panel shall forthwith transmit the order to the clerk of the transferee court.

(d) Conditional transfer orders do not become effective unless and until they are filed with the clerk of the transferee court.

(e) Notices of opposition and motions to vacate orders of the Panel and responses thereto shall be governed by Rules 4, 5, 6 and 7 of these Rules.

Rule 10.

MISCELLANEOUS PROVISIONS CONCERNING "TAG-ALONG ACTIONS"

(a) "Tag-along actions" filed in the transferee district require no action on the part of the Panel and requests for assignment of such actions to the Section 1407 transferee judge should be made in accordance with local rules for the assignment of related actions.

(b) Upon learning of the pendency of a "tag-along action" and having reasonable anticipation of opposition to transfer of that action, the Panel may direct the Clerk of the Panel to file a show cause order, in accordance with Rule 8 of these Rules, instead of a conditional transfer order.

(c) Failure to serve one or more of the defendants in a "tag-along action" with the complaint and summons as required by Rule 4 of the Federal Rules of Civil Procedure does not preclude transfer of such action under Section 1407. Such failure, however, may be submitted by such a defendant as a basis for opposing the proposed transfer. The inability of the Clerk of the Panel to serve a conditional transfer order on all defendants or their counsel shall not render the transfer of the action void but can be submitted by such a defendant as a basis for moving to remand as to such defendant.

(d) A civil action apparently sharing common questions of fact with actions under consideration by the Panel for transfer under Section 1407, which was filed or came to the attention of the Panel either after the initial hearing before it or too late to be included in the initial hearing, will be treated by the Panel as a potential "tag-along action."

Rule 11.

TERMINATION AND REMAND

In the absence of unusual circumstances—

(a) Actions terminated in the transferee court by valid judgment, including but not limited to summary judgment, judgment of dismissal and judgment upon stipulation, shall not be remanded by the Panel and shall be dismissed by the transferee court. The clerk of the transferee court shall send a copy of the order terminating the action to the Clerk of the Panel and to the clerk of the transferor court but shall retain the original files and records unless otherwise directed by the transferee judge or by the Panel.

(b) Each transferred action that has not been terminated in the transferee court will be remanded by the Panel to the transferor district for trial, unless ordered transferred by the transferee judge to the transferee or other district under 28 U.S.C. § 1404(a) or 28 U.S.C. § 1406. In the event that the transferee judge transfers an action under 28 U.S.C. §§ 1404(a) or 1406, no further action of the Panel shall be necessary to authorize further proceedings including trial.

(c) The Panel shall consider remand of each transferred action or any separable claim, cross-claim or third-party claim at or before the conclusion of coordinated or consolidated pretrial proceedings on

(i) motion of any party,

(ii) suggestion of the transferee court, or

(iii) its own initiative, by entry of an order to show cause, a conditional remand order or other appropriate order.

(d) If remand is sought by motion of a party, the motion shall be accompanied by:

(i) an affidavit reciting that all common discovery and other pretrial proceedings have been completed in the action sought to be remanded and that all orders of the transferee court have been satisfactorily complied with or that remand is otherwise appropriate; and

(ii) a copy of the transferee court's final pretrial order, where such order has been entered.

Motions to remand and responses thereto shall be governed by Rules 4, 5, 6, and 7 of these Rules.

(e) When an order to show cause why an action or actions should not be remanded is entered pursuant to subsection (c), paragraph (iii) of this Rule, any party may file a response within fifteen days of the filing of said order unless otherwise provided for in the order. Within five days of filing of a party's response, any party may file a reply brief limited to new matters. Responses and replies shall be filed and served in conformity with Rules 4, 5, 6 and 7 of these Rules.

(f) Conditional Remand Orders

(i) When the Panel has been advised by the transferee judge that pretrial proceedings in the litigation assigned to him are concluded or that remand of an action or actions is otherwise appropriate, an order may be entered by the Clerk of the Panel remanding the action or actions to the transferor court. The Clerk of the Panel shall serve this order on each party to the litigation but, in order to afford all parties the opportunity to oppose remand, shall not send the order to the clerk of the transferee court for fifteen days from the entry thereof.

(ii) Any party opposing the remand shall file a Notice of Opposition with the Clerk of the Panel within the fifteen-day period. If a Notice of Opposition is received by the Clerk of the Panel within this fifteen-day period, the Clerk of the Panel shall not transmit said order to the clerk of the transferee court until further order of the Panel.

(iii) Within fifteen days of the filing of its Notice of Opposition, the party opposing remand shall file a motion to vacate the conditional remand order and brief in support thereof. The Clerk of the Panel shall set the motion for hearing at the next appropriate session of the Panel. Failure to file and serve a motion and brief shall be deemed a withdrawal of the opposition and the Clerk of the Panel shall forthwith transmit the order to the clerk of the transferee court.

(iv) Conditional remand orders do not become effective unless and until they are filed with the clerk of the transferee court.

(v) Notices of opposition and motions to vacate such orders of the Panel and responses thereto shall be governed by Rules 4, 5, 6 and 7 of these Rules.

(g) Upon receipt of an order to remand from the Clerk of the Panel, the parties shall furnish forthwith to the transferee clerk a stipulation or designation of the contents of the record or part thereof to be remanded and furnish the transferee clerk all necessary copies of any pleading or other matter filed so as to enable the transferee clerk to comply with the order of remand.

Rule 12.

APPLICATIONS FOR EXTENSIONS OF TIME

Any application for an extension of time to file a pleading or perform an act required by these Rules may be acted upon by the Clerk of the Panel. Any party aggrieved by the Clerk's action or such application may submit its objections to the Panel for consideration.

Rule 13.

HEARINGS

(a) Hearings shall be held as ordered by the Panel. The Panel shall convene whenever and wherever desirable or necessary in the judgment of the Chairman. The Chairman shall determine which matters shall be set for hearing at each session and the Clerk of the Panel shall give notice to counsel for all parties involved in the litigation of the time, place, and subject matter of such hearing.

(b) No action shall be ordered transferred or remanded by the Panel over the objections of any party unless a hearing has been held or unless the matter has been submitted on the briefs in accordance with Rule 14 of these Rules. Unless otherwise ordered by the Panel, all other requests for action by the Panel shall be considered and determined upon the basis of the papers filed.

(c) Except for leave of the Panel on a showing of good cause, only those parties who have filed a motion or written response to a motion or order shall be permitted to appear before the Panel and present argument.

(d) Counsel for those supporting transfer or remand under Section 1407 and counsel for those opposing such transfer or remand are to confer separately prior to the hearing for the purpose of organizing their arguments and selecting spokesmen to present all views without duplication.

(e) Unless otherwise ordered by the Panel, a maximum of one hour will be allotted for argument in each new group of actions being considered for Section 1407 treatment and a maximum of one-half hour will be allotted for arguments in all other matters. The time shall be divided equally among those with varying viewpoints. Counsel for the moving party or parties will generally be heard first.

(f) So far as practicable and consistent with the purposes of Section 1407 the offering of oral testimony before the Panel shall be avoided. Accordingly, oral testimony shall not be received except upon notice, motion and order of the Panel expressly providing for it. Proof may be submitted as provided in the Federal Rules of Civil Procedure.

(g) After an action or group of actions has been set for hearing, it may only be continued by order of the Panel on good cause shown.

Rule 14.

MATTERS SUBMITTED ON THE BRIEFS

When the Panel has set a matter for hearing and a party intends to waive oral argument, it must communicate this fact, in writing, to the Clerk of the Panel in advance of the date of hearing. If all parties to the matter to be heard decided to waive oral argument, the matter will be submitted for decision by the Panel on the basis of the papers filed. Likewise, if a matter is scheduled to be heard and none of the parties is present when the matter is called at the hearing, the matter will not be re-scheduled and will be deemed submitted for decision by the Panel on the basis of the papers filed, unless otherwise ordered by the Panel.

Rule 15.

FAILURE TO COMPLY WITH RULES

The Clerk of the Panel may, when a paper submitted for filing is not in compliance with the provisions of these Rules, refuse to file such paper until full compliance is accomplished.

Rule 16.

EFFECT OF THE PENDENCY OF AN ACTION BEFORE THE PANEL

The pendency of a motion or order to show cause before the Panel concerning transfer of an action pursuant to 28 U.S.C. § 1407 does not affect or suspend orders and pretrial proceedings in the district court in which the action is pending and does not in any way limit the pretrial jurisdiction of that court. A transfer shall be effective when the transfer order is filed in the office of the clerk of the district court of the transferee district.

Rule 17.

TRANSFER OF FILES

(a) Upon receipt of a certified copy of a transfer order from the clerk of the transferee court, the clerk of the transferor court shall forward to the clerk of the transferee court the complete original file and a certified copy of the docket sheet for each transferred action.

(b) If an appeal is pending, or a notice of appeal has been filed, or leave to appeal has been sought under 28 U.S.C. § 1292 (b) or a petition for an extraordinary writ is pending, in any action included in an order of transfer, and the original file or parts thereof have been forwarded to the court of appeals, the clerk of the transferor court shall notify the clerk of the court of appeals of the order of transfer and secure the original file long enough to prepare and transmit to the clerk of the transferee court a certified copy of all papers contained in the original file and a certified copy of the docket sheet.

(c) If the transfer order provides for the separation and simultaneous remand of any claim, cross-claim, counterclaim, or third-party claim, the clerk of the transferor court shall retain the original file and shall prepare and transmit to the clerk of the transferee court a certified copy of the docket sheet and copies of all papers except those relating exclusively to separated and remanded claims.

(d) Upon receipt of an order to remand from the Clerk of the Panel, the transferee court shall prepare and send to the clerk of the transferor court the following:

(i) a certified copy of the individual docket sheet for action being remanded;

(ii) a certified copy of the master docket sheet, if applicable;

(iii) the entire file for each action being remanded;

(iv) a certified copy of the final pretrial order, if applicable; and

(v) a "record on remand" to be composed of those parts of the files and records produced during coordinated or consolidated pretrial proceedings which have been stipulated to or designated by counsel as being necessary for any or all proceedings to be conducted following remand. It shall be the responsibility of counsel originally preparing or filing any document to be included in the "record on remand" to furnish on request sufficient copies to the clerk of the transferee court.

(e) The Clerk of the Panel shall be notified when any files have been transmitted pursuant to this Rule.

Rule 18.

PRACTICE

Where not fixed by statute or rule, the practice shall be that heretofore customarily followed by the Panel.

FEDERAL RULES

OF

CRIMINAL PROCEDURE

FOR THE

UNITED STATES DISTRICT COURTS

AS AMENDED TO AUGUST 1, 1983

Editorial Note: The Federal Rules of Criminal Procedure became effective on March 21, 1946. Like the rules of civil procedure, they were adopted by the Supreme Court after extensive study and recommendations by an advisory committee.

The authority to prescribe the rules was conferred by various statutes.

Rules 32 to 39 were issued pursuant to the Act of February 24, 1933, 47 Stat. 904, as amended by the Act of March 8, 1934, 48 Stat. 399; the Act of June 7, 1934, 48 Stat. 926; and the Act of June 25, 1936, 49 Stat. 1921. They superseded rules first issued by the Court on May 7, 1934. See 292 U.S. 661. As amended, the Act of February 24, 1933, provided:

> "* * * That the Supreme Court of the United States shall have the power to prescribe, from time to time, rules of practice and procedure with respect to any or all proceedings after verdict, or finding of guilt by the court if a jury has been waived, or plea of guilty, in criminal cases in district courts of the United States, including the District Courts of Alaska, Hawaii, Puerto Rico, Canal Zone, District of Columbia, and Virgin Islands, in the Supreme Courts of Hawaii, and Puerto Rico, in the United States Court for China, in the United States Circuit Courts of Appeals, in the United States Court of Appeals for the District of Columbia, and in the Supreme Court of the United States: *Provided,* That nothing herein contained shall be construed to give the Supreme Court the power to abridge the right of the accused to apply for withdrawal of a plea of guilty, if such application be made within ten days after entry of such plea, and before sentence is imposed.
>
> "Sec. 2. The right of appeal shall continue in those cases in which appeals are now authorized by law, but the rules made as herein authorized may prescribe the times

for and manner of taking appeals and applying for writs of certiorari and preparing records and bills of exceptions and the conditions on which supersedeas or bail may be allowed.

"Sec. 3. The Supreme Court may fix the dates when such rules shall take effect and the extent to which they shall apply to proceedings then pending, and after they become effective all laws in conflict therewith shall be of no further force."

Rules 1 to 31 and Rules 40 to 60 were authorized by the Act of June 29, 1940, 54 Stat. 688. That Act provided:

"That the Supreme Court of the United States shall have the power to prescribe, from time to time, rules of pleading, practice, and procedure with respect to any or all proceedings prior to and including verdict, or finding of guilty or not guilty by the court if a jury has been waived, or plea of guilty, in criminal cases in district courts of the United States, including the district courts of Alaska, Hawaii, Puerto Rico, Canal Zone, and the Virgin Islands, in the Supreme Courts of Hawaii and Puerto Rico, in the United States Court for China, and in proceedings before United States commissioners. Such rules shall not take effect until they shall have been reported to Congress by the Attorney General at the beginning of a regular session thereof and until after the close of such session, and thereafter all laws in conflict therewith shall be of no further force and effect."

The rules promulgated under the 1933 Act were modified and merged into the rules issued under the 1940 Act and comprehensively entitled the Federal Rules of Criminal Procedure. (See 327 U.S. 821). They became effective March 21, 1946.

The 1940 Act was extended to proceedings to punish for criminal contempt by the Act of November 21, 1941, 55 Stat. 779, and to appeals by the United States in criminal cases by the Act of May 9, 1942, Section 1, 56 Stat. 271. By a special rule effective also on March 21, 1946, the Supreme Court provided that rules promulgated from time to time pursuant to the Act of February 24, 1933, should be applicable to appeals by the United States under the Act of May 9, 1942, 56 Stat. 271, "except that the time for taking such appeals shall be as prescribed by the said Act of May 9, 1942." (323 U.S. 824).

Following the enactment of Revised Titles 18 and 28, the Court adopted a series of amendments making formal changes necessary to conform the rules to the revision. The amendments authorized by the 1933 Act (now Title 18, U.S.C., § 3772) became effective January 1, 1949. Those adopted pursuant to the 1940 Act (now Title 18, U.S.C. § 3771) became effective "on the day following the final adjournment of the first regular session of the 81st Congress." (335 U.S. 949). By order of April 12, 1954, effective July 1, 1954 (346 U.S. 941), the Court revised Rule 37 on appeals to conform to the concurrent revision of its own rules. Further amendments to Rules 41, 46, and 54 were made by order of April 9, 1956, effective July 8, 1956 (350 U.S. 1017).

Subsequent changes in the rules, effective July 1, 1966 (383 U.S. 1087), July 1, 1968 (389 U.S. 1125), July 1, 1971, and October 1, 1972 (406 U.S. 979), were made in accordance with the procedure established pursuant to the Act of July 11, 1958, amending 28 U.S.C. § 331, described in the editorial note introducing the Rules of Civil Procedure, p. 314, *supra*.

Former Chapter VIII, entitled Appeal, was abrogated by the Supreme Court, effective July 1, 1968, the subject being covered by the new Federal Rules of Appellate Procedure, except for Rule 38(a), which is preserved (389 U.S. 1065).

Amendments to Rules 41 and 50, prescribed by the Supreme Court on March 18, 1974, became effective July 1, 1974.

Amendments to Rules 26, 26.1 and 28, necessitated by the proposed Federal Rules of Evidence, were prescribed November 20, 1972, to become effective July 1, 1973. The controversy about the Rules of Evidence led to the enactment of Pub.L. 93–12 of March 30, 1973, postponing the effective date of the amendments until Congress should "expressly approve" them. The Act of January 2, 1975, Pub.L. 93–595, 88 Stat. 1926, enacting rules of evidence in statutory form, provided that "Congress expressly approves" these amendments, fixing their effective date in 180 days.

On April 22, 1974, the Supreme Court prescribed and the Chief Justice transmitted to Congress important amendments of the Rules of Criminal Procedure, to take effect on August 1, 1974. 416 U.S. 1005. The amendments consisted of new Rules 12.1, 12.2 and 29.1 and modifications in Rules 4, 9(a), 11, 12, 15, 16, 17(f), 20, 32(a), 32(c), 32(e) and 43. On July 30, 1974, Pub.L. 93–361, 88 Stat. 397, postponed the effective date of the amendments to August 1, 1975. On July 31, 1975, Congress enacted the Federal Rules of Criminal Procedure Amendments Act of 1975, Pub.L. 94–64, 89 Stat. 370. That Act "approved" the amendments embraced in the Supreme Court's order of April 22, 1975, except as otherwise provided in the Act, which then proceeded to enact revised amendments to Rules 4, 9(a), 11(c), 11(e), 12(e), 12(h), 12.1, 12.2(c), 15(a), 15(b), 15(c), 15(e), 15(g), 15(h), 16(a), 16(b), 16(c), 16(d), 17(f), 20(d),

32(a), 32(c) and 43(b). The Act prescribed December 1, 1975, as the effective date of the amendments, except for Rule 11(e)(6), which was made effective August 1. Minor technical amendments were made by Pub.L. 94–149, December 12, 1975.

On April 26, 1976, the Supreme Court prescribed and transmitted to Congress several amendments, to become effective August 1, 1976. Congress first postponed the effective date to August 1, 1977, then by Act of July 30, 1977, Pub.L. 95–78, 91 Stat. 319, enacted them with some changes.

On April 30, 1979, the Chief Justice submitted to Congress several amendments and additions, to become effective August 1, 1979. Congress, however, by Pub.L. 96–42, July 31, 1979, 93 Stat. 326, provided that the proposed amendments affecting Rules 11(e)(6), 17(h), 32(f) and 44(c), and adding new Rules 26.2 and 32.1 "shall not take effect until December 1, 1980, or until and then only to the extent approved by Act of Congress, whichever is earlier." Congress took no action and the amendments became effective as submitted.

Further amendments (to Rules 1, 5(b), 9(a), 9(b)(1), 9(b)(2), 9(c)(1), 9(c)(2), 11(c)(1), 11(c)(4), 11(c)(5), 20(b), 40(d)(2), 45(a), 54(a), 54(b)(4) and 54(c)), submitted April 28, 1982, became effective August 1, 1982. The most recent amendments took effect August 1, 1983.

TABLE OF RULES

I. SCOPE, PURPOSE, AND CONSTRUCTION

Rule 1.

SCOPE

These rules govern the procedure in all criminal proceedings in the courts of the United States, as provided in Rule 54(a); and, whenever specifically provided in one of the rules, to preliminary, supplementary, and special proceedings before United States magistrates and at proceedings before state and local judicial officers.

Rule 2.

PURPOSE AND CONSTRUCTION

These rules are intended to provide for the just determination of every criminal proceeding. They shall be construed to secure simplicity in procedure, fairness in administration and the elimination of unjustifiable expense and delay.

II. PRELIMINARY PROCEEDINGS

Rule 3.

THE COMPLAINT

The complaint is a written statement of the essential facts constituting the offense charged. It shall be made upon oath before a magistrate.

Rule 4.

ARREST WARRANT OR SUMMONS UPON COMPLAINT

(a) Issuance. If it appears from the complaint, or from an affidavit or affidavits filed with the complaint, that there is probable cause to believe that an offense has been committed and that the defendant has committed it, a warrant for the arrest of the defendant shall issue to any officer authorized by law to execute it. Upon the request of the attorney for the government a summons instead of a warrant shall issue. More than one warrant or summons may issue on the same complaint. If a defendant fails to appear in response to the summons, a warrant shall issue.

(b) Probable Cause. The finding of probable cause may be based upon hearsay evidence in whole or in part.

(c) Form.

(1) Warrant. The warrant shall be signed by the magistrate and shall contain the name of the defendant or, if his name is unknown, any name or description by which he can be identified with reasonable certainty. It shall describe the offense charged in the complaint. It shall command that the defendant be arrested and brought before the nearest available magistrate.

(2) Summons. The summons shall be in the same form as the warrant except that it shall summon the defendant to appear before a magistrate at a stated time and place.

(d) Execution or Service; and Return.

(1) By Whom. The warrant shall be executed by a marshal or by some other officer authorized by law. The summons may be served by any person authorized to serve a summons in a civil action.

(2) Territorial Limits. The warrant may be executed or the summons may be served at any place within the jurisdiction of the United States.

(3) Manner. The warrant shall be executed by the arrest of the defendant. The officer need not have the warrant in his possession at the time of the arrest, but upon request he shall show the warrant to the defendant, as soon as possible. If the officer does not have the warrant in his possession at the time of the arrest, he shall then inform the defendant of the offense charged and of the fact that a warrant has been issued. The summons shall be served upon a defendant by delivering a copy to him personally, or by leaving it at his dwelling house or usual place of abode with some person of suitable age and discretion then residing therein and by mailing a copy of the summons to the defendant's last known address.

(4) Return. The officer executing a warrant shall make return thereof to the magistrate or other officer before whom the defendant is brought pursuant to Rule 5. At the request of the attorney for the government any unexecuted warrant shall be returned to the magistrate by whom it was issued and shall be cancelled by him. On or before the return day the person to whom a summons was delivered for service shall make return thereof to the magistrate before whom the summons is returnable. At the request of the attorney for the government made at any time while the complaint is pending, a warrant returned unexecuted and not cancelled or a summons returned unserved or a duplicate thereof may be delivered by the magistrate to the marshal or other authorized person for execution or service.

Rule 5.

INITIAL APPEARANCE BEFORE THE MAGISTRATE

(a) In General. An officer making an arrest under a warrant issued upon a complaint or any person making an arrest without a warrant shall take the arrested person without unnecessary delay before the nearest available federal magistrate or, in the event that a federal magistrate is not reasonably available, before a state or local judicial officer authorized by 18 U.S.C. § 3041. If a person arrested without a warrant is brought before a magistrate, a complaint shall be filed forthwith which shall comply with the requirements of Rule 4(a) with respect to the showing of probable cause. When a person, arrested with or without a warrant or given a summons, appears initially before the magistrate, the magistrate shall proceed in accordance with the applicable subdivisions of this rule.

(b) Misdemeanors. If the charge against the defendant is a misdemeanor triable by a United States magistrate under 18 U.S.C. § 3401, the United States magistrate shall proceed in accordance with the Rules of Procedure for the Trial of Misdemeanors Before United States Magistrates.

(c) Offenses Not Triable by the United States Magistrate. If the charge against the defendant is not triable by the United States magistrate, the defendant shall not be called upon to plead. The magistrate shall inform the defendant of the complaint against him and of any affidavit filed therewith, of his right to retain counsel, of his right to request the assignment of counsel if he is unable to obtain counsel, and of the general circumstances under which he may secure pretrial release. He shall inform the defendant that he is not required to make a statement and that any statement made by him may be used against him. The magistrate shall also inform the defendant of his right to a preliminary examination. He shall allow the defendant reasonable time and opportunity to consult counsel and shall admit the defendant to bail as provided by statute or in these rules.

A defendant is entitled to a preliminary examination, unless waived, when charged with any offense, other than a petty offense, which is to be tried by a judge of the district court. If the defendant waives preliminary examination, the magistrate shall forthwith hold him to answer in the district court. If the defendant does not waive the preliminary examination, the magistrate shall schedule a preliminary examination. Such examination shall be held within a reasonable time but in any event not later than 10 days following the initial appearance if the defendant is in custody and no later than 20 days if he is not in custody, provided, however, that the preliminary examination shall not be held if the defendant is indicted or if an information against the defendant is filed in district court before the date set for the preliminary examination. With the consent of the defendant and upon a showing of good cause, taking into account the public interest in the prompt disposition of criminal cases, time limits specified in this subdivision may be extended one or more times by a federal magistrate. In the absence of such consent by the defendant, time limits may be extended by a judge of the United States only upon a showing that extraordinary circumstances exist and that delay is indispensable to the interests of justice.

Rule 5.1.

PRELIMINARY EXAMINATION

(a) Probable Cause Finding. If from the evidence it appears that there is probable cause to believe that an offense has been committed and that the defendant committed it, the federal magistrate shall forthwith hold him to answer in district court. The finding of probable cause may be based upon hearsay evidence in whole or in part. The defendant may cross-examine witnesses against him and may introduce evidence in his own behalf. Objections to evidence on the ground that it was acquired by unlawful means are not properly made at the preliminary examination. Motions to suppress must be made to the trial court as provided in Rule 12.

(b) Discharge of Defendant. If from the evidence it appears that there is no probable cause to believe that an offense has been committed or that the defendant committed it, the federal magistrate shall dismiss the complaint and discharge the defendant. The discharge of the defendant shall not preclude the government from instituting a subsequent prosecution for the same offense.

(c) Records. After concluding the proceeding the federal magistrate shall transmit forthwith to the clerk of the district court all papers in the proceeding. The magistrate shall promptly make or cause to be made a record or summary of such proceeding.

(1) On timely application to a federal magistrate, the attorney for a defendant in a criminal case may be given the opportunity to have the recording of the hearing on preliminary examination made available for his information in connection with any further hearing or in connection with his preparation for trial. The court may, by local rule, appoint the place for and define the conditions under which such opportunity may be afforded counsel.

(2) On application of a defendant addressed to the court or any judge thereof, an order may issue that the federal magistrate make available a copy of the transcript, or of a portion thereof, to defense counsel. Such order shall provide for prepayment of costs of such transcript by the defendant unless the defendant makes a sufficient affidavit that he is unable to pay or to give security therefor, in which case the expense shall be paid by the Director of the Administrative Office of the United States Courts from available appropriated funds. Counsel for the government may move also that a copy of the transcript, in whole or in part, be made available to it, for good cause shown, and an order may be entered granting such motion in whole or in part, on appropriate terms, except that the government need not prepay costs nor furnish security therefor.

III. INDICTMENT AND INFORMATION

Rule 6.

THE GRAND JURY

(a) Summoning Grand Juries. The court shall order one or more grand juries to be summoned at such times as the public interest requires. The grand jury shall consist of not less than 16 nor more than 23 members. The court shall direct that a sufficient number of legally qualified persons be summoned to meet this requirement.

(b) Objections to Grand Jury and to Grand Jurors.

(1) **Challenges.** The attorney for the government or a defendant who has been held to answer in the district court may challenge the array of jurors on the ground that the grand jury was not selected, drawn or summoned in accordance with law, and may challenge an individual juror on the ground that the

juror is not legally qualified. Challenges shall be made before the administration of the oath to the jurors and shall be tried by the court.

(2) **Motion to Dismiss.** A motion to dismiss the indictment may be based on objections to the array or on the lack of legal qualification of an individual juror, if not previously determined upon challenge. It shall be made in the manner prescribed in 28 U.S.C. § 1867(e) and shall be granted under the conditions prescribed in that statute. An indictment shall not be dismissed on the ground that one or more members of the grand jury were not legally qualified if it appears from the record kept pursuant to subdivision (c) of this rule that 12 or more jurors, after deducting the number not legally qualified, concurred in finding the indictment.

(c) Foreman and Deputy Foreman. The court shall appoint one of the jurors to be foreman and another to be deputy foreman. The foreman shall have power to administer oaths and affirmations and shall sign all indictments. He or another juror designated by him shall keep a record of the number of jurors concurring in the finding of every indictment and shall file the record with the clerk of the court, but the record shall not be made public except on order of the court. During the absence of the foreman, the deputy foreman shall act as foreman.

(d) Who May Be Present. Attorneys for the government, the witness under examination, interpreters when needed and, for the purpose of taking the evidence, a stenographer or operator of a recording device may be present while the grand jury is in session, but no person other than the jurors may be present while the grand jury is deliberating or voting.

(e) Recording and Disclosure of Proceedings.

(1) Recording of Proceedings. All proceedings, except when the grand jury is deliberating or voting, shall be recorded stenographically or by an electronic recording device. An unintentional failure of any recording to reproduce all or any portion of a proceeding shall not affect the validity of the prosecution. The recording or reporter's notes or any transcript prepared therefrom shall remain in the custody or control of the attorney for the government unless otherwise ordered by the court in a particular case.

(2) General Rule of Secrecy. A grand juror, an interpreter, a stenographer, an operator of a recording device, a typist who transcribes recorded testimony, an attorney for the government, or any person to whom disclosure is made under paragraph (3)(A)(ii) of this subdivision shall not disclose matters occurring before the grand jury, except as otherwise provided for in these rules. No obligation of secrecy may be imposed on any person except in accordance with this rule. A knowing violation of Rule 6 may be punished as a contempt of court.

(3) Exceptions.

(A) Disclosure otherwise prohibited by this rule of matters occurring before the grand jury, other than its deliberations and the vote of any grand juror, may be made to—

(i) an attorney for the government for use in the performance of such attorney's duty; and

(ii) such government personnel as are deemed necessary by an attorney for the government to assist an attorney for the government in the performance of such attorney's duty to enforce federal criminal law.

(B) Any person to whom matters are disclosed under subparagraph (A)(ii) of this paragraph shall not utilize that grand jury material for any purpose other than assisting the attorney for the government in the performance of such attorney's duty to enforce federal criminal law. An attorney for the government shall promptly provide the district court before which was impaneled the grand jury whose material has been so disclosed, with the names of the persons to whom such disclosure has been made.

(C) Disclosure otherwise prohibited by this rule of matters occurring before the grand jury may also be made—

(i) when so directed by a court preliminary to or in connection with a judicial proceeding;

(ii) when permitted by a court at the request of the defendant, upon a showing that grounds may exist for a motion to dismiss the indictment because of matters occurring before the grand jury; or

(iii) when the disclosure is made by an attorney for the government to another federal grand jury.

If the court orders disclosure of matters occurring before the grand jury, the disclosure shall be made in such manner, at such time, and under such conditions as the court may direct.
If the court orders disclosure of matters occurring before the grand jury, the disclosure shall be made in such manner, at such time, and under such conditions as the court may direct.

(D) A petition for disclosure pursuant to subdivision (e)(3)(C)(i) shall be filed in the district where the grand jury convened. Unless the hearing is ex parte, which it may be when the petitioner is the government, the petitioner shall serve written notice of the petition upon (i) the attorney for the government, (ii) the parties to the judicial proceeding if disclosure is sought in connection with such a proceeding, and (iii) such other persons as the court may direct. The court shall afford those persons a reasonable opportunity to appear and be heard.

(E) If the judicial proceeding giving rise to the petition is in a federal district court in another district, the court shall transfer the matter to that court unless it can reasonably obtain sufficient knowledge of the proceeding to determine whether disclosure is proper. The court shall order transmitted to the court to which the matter is transferred the material sought to be disclosed, if feasible, and a written evaluation of the need for continued grand jury secrecy. The court to which the matter is transferred shall afford the aforementioned persons a reasonable opportunity to appear and be heard.

(4) Sealed Indictments. The federal magistrate to whom an indictment is returned may direct that the indictment be kept secret until the defendant is in custody or has been released pending trial. Thereupon the clerk shall seal the indictment and no person shall disclose the return of the indictment except when necessary for the issuance and execution of a warrant or summons.

(5) Closed hearing. Subject to any right to an open hearing in contempt proceedings, the court shall order a hearing on matters affecting a grand jury proceeding to be closed to the extent necessary to prevent disclosure of matters occurring before a grand jury.

(6) Sealed records. Records, orders and subpoenas relating to grand jury proceedings shall be kept under seal to the extent and for such time as is necessary to prevent disclosure of matters occurring before a grand jury.

(f) Finding and Return of Indictment. An indictment may be found only upon the concurrence of 12 or more jurors. The indictment shall be returned by the grand jury to a federal magistrate in open court. If the defendant is in custody or has given bail and 12 jurors do not concur in finding an indictment, the foreman shall so report to the federal magistrate in writing forthwith.

(g) Discharge and Excuse. A grand jury shall serve until discharged by the court, but no grand jury may serve more than 18 months unless the court extends the service of the grand jury for a period of six months or less upon a determination that such extension is in the public interest. At any time for cause shown the court may excuse a juror either temporarily or permanently, and in the latter event the court may impanel another person in place of the juror excused.

Rule 7.

THE INDICTMENT AND THE INFORMATION

(a) Use of Indictment or Information. An offense which may be punished by death shall be prosecuted by indictment. An offense which may be punished by imprisonment for a term exceeding one year or at hard labor shall be prosecuted by indictment or, if indictment is waived, it may be prosecuted by information. Any other offense may be prosecuted by indictment or by information. An information may be filed without leave of court.

(b) Waiver of Indictment. An offense which may be punished by imprisonment for a term exceeding one year or at hard labor may be prosecuted by information if the defendant, after he has been advised of the nature of the charge and of his rights, waives in open court prosecution by indictment.

(c) Nature and Contents.

(1) In General. The indictment or the information shall be a plain, concise and definite written statement of the essential facts constituting the offense charged. It shall be signed by the attorney for the government. It need not contain a formal commencement, a formal conclusion or any other matter not necessary to such statement. Allegations made in one count may be incorporated by reference in another count. It may be alleged in a single count that the means by which the defendant committed the offense are unknown or that he committed it by one or more specified means. The indictment or information shall state for each count the official or customary citation of the statute, rule, regulation or other provision of law which the defendant is alleged therein to have violated.

(2) Criminal Forfeiture. No judgment of forfeiture may be entered in a criminal proceeding unless the indictment or the information shall allege the extent of the interest or property subject to forfeiture.

(3) Harmless Error. Error in the citation or its omission shall not be ground for dismissal of the indictment or information or for reversal of a conviction if the error or omission did not mislead the defendant to his prejudice.

(d) Surplusage. The court on motion of the defendant may strike surplusage from the indictment or information.

(e) Amendment of Information. The court may permit an information to be amended at any time before verdict or finding if no additional or different offense is charged and if substantial rights of the defendant are not prejudiced.

(f) Bill of Particulars. The court may direct the filing of a bill of particulars. A motion for a bill of particulars may be made before arraignment or within ten days after arraignment or at such later time as the court may permit. A bill of particulars may be amended at any time subject to such conditions as justice requires.

Rule 8.

JOINDER OF OFFENSES AND OF DEFENDANTS

(a) Joinder of Offenses. Two or more offenses may be charged in the same indictment or information in a separate count for each offense if the offenses charged, whether felonies or misdemeanors or both, are of the same or similar character or are based on the same act or transaction or on two or more acts or transactions connected together or constituting parts of a common scheme or plan.

(b) Joinder of Defendants. Two or more defendants may be charged in the same indictment or information if they are alleged to have participated in the same act or transaction or in the same series of acts or transactions constituting an offense or offenses. Such defendants may be charged in one or more counts together or separately and all of the defendants need not be charged in each count.

Rule 9.

WARRANT OR SUMMONS UPON INDICTMENT OR INFORMATION

(a) Issuance. Upon the request of the attorney for the government the court shall issue a warrant for each defendant named in an information supported by a showing of probable cause under oath as is required by Rule 4(a), or in an indictment. Upon the request of the attorney for the government a summons instead of a warrant shall issue. If no request is made, the court may issue either a warrant or a summons in its discretion. More than one warrant or summons may issue for the same defendant. The clerk shall deliver the warrant or summons to the marshal or other person authorized by law to execute or serve it. If a defendant fails to appear in response to the summons, a warrant shall issue. When a defendant arrested with a warrant or given a summons appears initially before a magistrate, the magistrate shall proceed in accordance with the applicable subdivisions of Rule 5.

(b) Form.

(1) Warrant. The form of the warrant shall be as provided in Rule 4(c)(1) except that it shall be signed by the clerk, it shall describe the offense charged in the indictment or information and it shall command that the defendant be arrested and brought before the nearest available magistrate. The amount of bail may be fixed by the court and endorsed on the warrant.

(2) Summons. The summons shall be in the same form as the warrant except that it shall summon the defendant to appear before a magistrate at a stated time and place.

(c) Execution or Service; and Return.

(1) Execution or Service. The warrant shall be executed or the summons served as provided in Rule 4(d)(1), (2) and (3). A summons to a corporation shall be served by delivering a copy to an officer or to a managing or general agent or to any other agent authorized by appointment or by law to receive service of process and, if the agent is one authorized by statute to receive service and the statute so requires, by also mailing a copy to the corporation's last known address within the district or at its principal place of business elsewhere in the United States. The officer executing the warrant shall bring the arrested person without unnecessary delay before the nearest available federal magistrate or, in the event that a federal magistrate is not reasonably available, before a state or local judicial officer authorized by 18 U.S.C. § 3041.

(2) Return. The officer executing a warrant shall make return thereof to the magistrate or other officer before whom the defendant is brought. At the request of the attorney for the government any unexecuted warrant shall be returned and cancelled. On or before the return day the person to whom a summons was delivered for service shall make return thereof. At the request of the attorney for the government made at any time while the indictment or information is pending, a warrant returned unexecuted and not cancelled or a summons returned unserved or a duplicate thereof may be delivered by the clerk to the marshal or other authorized person for execution or service.

IV. ARRAIGNMENT AND PREPARATION FOR TRIAL

Rule 10.

ARRAIGNMENT

Arraignment shall be conducted in open court and shall consist of reading the indictment or information to the defendant or stating to him the substance of the charge and calling on him to plead thereto. He shall be given a copy of the indictment or information before he is called upon to plead.

Rule 11.

PLEAS

(a) Alternatives.

(1) In General. A defendant may plead not guilty, guilty, or nolo contendere. If a defendant refuses to plead or if a defendant corporation fails to appear, the court shall enter a plea of not guilty.

(2) Conditional pleas. With the approval of the court and the consent of the government, a defendant may enter a conditional plea of guilty or nolo contendere, reserving in writing the right, on appeal from the judgment, to review of the adverse determination of any specified pretrial motion. If the defendant prevails on appeal, he shall be allowed to withdraw his plea.

(b) Nolo Contendere. A defendant may plead nolo contendere only with the consent of the court. Such a plea shall be accepted by the court only after due consideration of the views of the parties and the interest of the public in the effective administration of justice.

(c) Advice to Defendant. Before accepting a plea of guilty or nolo contendere, the court must address the defendant personally in open court and inform him of, and determine that he understands, the following:

(1) the nature of the charge to which the plea is offered, the mandatory minimum penalty provided by law, if any, and the maximum possible penalty provided by law including the effect of any special parole term; and

(2) if the defendant is not represented by an attorney, that he has the right to be represented by an attorney at every stage of the proceeding against him and, if necessary, one will be appointed to represent him; and

(3) that he has the right to plead not guilty or to persist in that plea if it has already been made, and that he has the right to be tried by a jury and at that trial has the right to the assistance of counsel, the right to confront and cross-examine witnesses against him, and the right not to be compelled to incriminate himself; and

(4) that if his plea of guilty or nolo contendere is accepted by the court there will not be a further trial of any kind, so that by pleading guilty or nolo contendere he waives the right to a trial; and

(5) if the court intends to question the defendant under oath, on the record, and in the presence of counsel about the offense to which he has pleaded, that his answers may later be used against him in a prosecution for perjury or false statement.

(d) Insuring That the Plea is Voluntary. The court shall not accept a plea of guilty or nolo contendere without first, by addressing the defendant personally in open court, determining that the plea is voluntary and not the result of force or threats or of promises apart from a plea agreement. The court shall also inquire as to whether the defendant's willingness to plead guilty or nolo contendere results from prior discussions between the attorney for the government and the defendant or his attorney.

(e) Plea Agreement Procedure.

(1) In General. The attorney for the government and the attorney for the defendant or the defendant when acting pro se may engage in discussions with a view toward reaching an agreement that, upon the entering of a plea of guilty or nolo contendere to a charged offense or to a lesser or related offense, the attorney for the government will do any of the following:

(A) move for dismissal of other charges; or

(B) make a recommendation, or agree not to oppose the defendant's request, for a particular sentence, with the understanding that such recommendation or request shall not be binding upon the court; or

(C) agree that a specific sentence is the appropriate disposition of the case.

The court shall not participate in any such discussions.

(2) Notice of Such Agreement. If a plea agreement has been reached by the parties, the court shall, on the record, require the disclosure of the agreement in open court, or on a showing of good cause, in camera, at the time the plea is offered. If the agreement is of the type specified in subdivision (e)(1)(A) or (C), the court may accept or reject the agreement, or may defer its decision as to the acceptance or rejection until there has been an opportunity to consider the presentence report. If the agreement is of the type specified in subdivision (e)(1)(B), the court shall advise the defendant that if the court does not accept the recommendation or request the defendant nevertheless has no right to withdraw his plea.

(3) Acceptance of a Plea Agreement. If the court accepts the plea agreement, the court shall inform the defendant that it will embody in the judgment and sentence the disposition provided for in the plea agreement.

(4) Rejection of a Plea Agreement. If the court rejects the plea agreement, the court shall, on the record, inform the parties of this fact, advise the defendant personally in open court or, on a showing of good cause, in camera, that the court is not bound by the plea agreement, afford the defendant the opportunity to then withdraw his plea, and advise the defendant that if he persists in his guilty plea or plea of nolo contendere the disposition of the case may be less favorable to the defendant than that contemplated by the plea agreement.

(5) Time of Plea Agreement Procedure. Except for good cause shown, notification to the court of the existence of a plea agreement shall be given at the arraignment or at such other time, prior to trial, as may be fixed by the court.

(6) Inadmissibility of Pleas, Plea Discussions, and Related Statements. Except as otherwise provided in this paragraph, evidence of the following is not, in any civil or criminal proceeding, admissible against the defendant who made the plea or was a participant in the plea discussions:

(A) a plea of guilty which was later withdrawn;

(B) a plea of nolo contendere;

(C) any statement made in the course of any proceedings under this rule regarding either of the foregoing pleas; or

(D) any statement made in the course of plea discussions with an attorney for the government which do not result in a plea of guilty or which result in a plea of guilty later withdrawn.

However, such a statement is admissible (i) in any proceeding wherein another statement made in the course of the same plea or plea discussions has been introduced and the statement ought in fairness be considered contemporaneously with it, or (ii) in a criminal proceeding for perjury or false statement if the statement was made by the defendant under oath, on the record, and in the presence of counsel.

(f) Determining Accuracy of Plea. Notwithstanding the acceptance of a plea of guilty, the court should not enter a judgment upon such plea without making such inquiry as shall satisfy it that there is a factual basis for the plea.

(g) Record of Proceedings. A verbatim record of the proceedings at which the defendant enters a plea shall be made and, if there is a plea of guilty or nolo contendere, the record shall include, without limitation, the court's advice to the defendant, the inquiry into the voluntariness of the plea including any plea agreement, and the inquiry into the accuracy of a guilty plea.

(h) Harmless Error. Any variance from the procedures required by this rule which does not affect substantial rights shall be disregarded.

Rule 12.

PLEADINGS AND MOTIONS BEFORE TRIAL; DEFENSES AND OBJECTIONS

(a) Pleadings and Motions. Pleadings in criminal proceedings shall be the indictment and the information, and the pleas of not guilty, guilty and nolo contendere. All other pleas, and demurrers and motions to quash are abolished, and defenses and objections raised before trial which heretofore could have been raised by one or more of them shall be raised only by motion to dismiss or to grant appropriate relief, as provided in these rules.

(b) Pretrial Motions. Any defense, objection, or request which is capable of determination without the trial of the general issue may be raised before trial by motion. Motions may be written or oral at the discretion of the judge. The following must be raised prior to trial:

(1) Defenses and objections based on defects in the institution of the prosecution; or

(2) Defenses and objections based on defects in the indictment or information (other than that it fails to show jurisdiction in the court or to charge an offense which objections shall be noticed by the court at any time during the pendency of the proceedings); or

(3) Motions to suppress evidence; or

(4) Requests for discovery under Rule 16; or

(5) Requests for a severance of charges or defendants under Rule 14.

(c) Motion Date. Unless otherwise provided by local rule, the court may, at the time of the arraignment or as soon thereafter as practicable, set a time for the making of pretrial motions or requests and, if required, a later date of hearing.

(d) Notice by the Government of the Intention to Use Evidence.

(1) At the Discretion of the Government. At the arraignment or as soon thereafter as is practicable, the government may give notice to the defendant of its intention to use specified evidence at trial in order to afford the defendant an opportunity to raise objections to such evidence prior to trial under subdivision (b)(3) of this rule.

(2) At the Request of the Defendant. At the arraignment or as soon thereafter as is practicable the defendant may, in order to afford an opportunity to move to suppress evidence under subdivision (b)(3) of this rule, request notice of the government's intention to use (in its evidence in chief at trial) any evidence which the defendant may be entitled to discover under Rule 16 subject to any relevant limitations prescribed in Rule 16.

(e) Ruling on Motion. A motion made before trial shall be determined before trial unless the court, for good cause, orders that it be deferred for determination at the trial of the general issue or until after verdict, but no such determination shall be deferred if a party's right to appeal is adversely affected. Where factual issues are involved in determining a motion, the court shall state its essential findings on the record.

(f) Effect of Failure to Raise Defenses or Objections. Failure by a party to raise defenses or objections or to make requests which must be made prior to trial, at the time set by the court pursuant to subdivision (c), or prior to any extension thereof made by the court, shall constitute waiver thereof, but the court for cause shown may grant relief from the waiver.

(g) Records. A verbatim record shall be made of all proceedings at the hearing, including such findings of fact and conclusions of law as are made orally.

(h) Effect of Determination. If the court grants a motion based on a defect in the institution of the prosecution or in the indictment or information, it may also order that the defendant be continued in custody or that his bail be continued for a specified time pending the filing of a new indictment or information. Nothing in this rule shall be deemed to affect the provisions of any Act of Congress relating to periods of limitations.

(i) Production of Statements at Suppression Hearing. Except as herein provided, rule 26.2 shall apply at a hearing on a motion to suppress evidence under subdivision (b)(3) of this rule. For purposes of this subdivision, a law enforcement officer shall be deemed a witness called by the government, and upon a claim of privilege the court shall excise the portions of the statement containing privileged matter.

Rule 12.1

NOTICE OF ALIBI

(a) Notice by Defendant. Upon written demand of the attorney for the government stating the time, date, and place at which the alleged offense was committed, the defendant shall serve within ten days, or at such different time as the court may direct, upon the attorney for the government a written notice of his intention to offer a defense of alibi. Such notice by the defendant shall state the specific place or places at which the defendant claims to have been at the time of the alleged offense and the names and addresses of the witnesses upon whom he intends to rely to establish such alibi.

(b) Disclosure of Information and Witness. Within ten days thereafter, but in no event less than ten days before trial, unless the court otherwise directs, the attorney for the government shall serve upon the defendant or his attorney a written notice stating the names and addresses of the witnesses upon whom the government intends to rely to establish the defendant's presence at the scene of the alleged offense and any other witnesses to be relied on to rebut testimony of any of the defendant's alibi witnesses.

(c) Continuing Duty to Disclose. If prior to or during trial, a party learns of an additional witness whose identity, if known, should have been included in the information furnished under subdivision (a) or (b), the party shall promptly notify the other party or his attorney of the existence and identity of such additional witness.

(d) Failure to Comply. Upon the failure of either party to comply with the requirements of this rule, the court may exclude the testimony of any undisclosed witness offered by such party as to the defendant's absence from or presence at, the scene of the alleged offense. This rule shall not limit the right of the defendant to testify in his own behalf.

(e) Exceptions. For good cause shown, the court may grant an exception to any of the requirements of subdivisions (a) through (d) of this rule.

(f) Inadmissibility of Withdrawn Alibi. Evidence of an intention to rely upon an alibi defense, later withdrawn, or of statements made in connection with such intention, is not admissible in any civil or criminal proceeding against the person who gave notice of the intention.

Rule 12.2

NOTICE OF INSANITY DEFENSE OR EXPERT TESTIMONY OF DEFENDANT'S MENTAL CONDITION

(a) Defense of Insanity. If a defendant intends to rely upon the defense of insanity at the time of the alleged crime, he shall, within the time provided for the filing of pretrial motions or at such later time as the court may direct, notify the attorney for the government in writing of such intention and file a copy of such notice with the clerk. If there is a failure to comply with the requirements of this subdivision, insanity may not be raised as a defense. The court may for cause shown allow late filing of the notice or grant additional time to the parties to prepare for trial or make such other order as may be appropriate.

(b) Expert Testimony of Defendant's Mental Condition. If a defendant intends to introduce expert testimony relating to a mental disease or defect or any other mental condition of the defendant bearing upon the issue of his guilt, he shall, within the time provided for the filing of pretrial motions or at such later time as the court may direct, notify the attorney for the government in writing of such intention and file a copy of such notice with the clerk. The court may for cause shown allow late filing of the notice or grant additional time to the parties to prepare for trial or make such other order as may be appropriate.

(c) Mental Examination of Defendant. In an appropriate case the court may, upon motion of the attorney for the government, order the defendant to submit to a mental examination by a psychiatrist or other expert designated for this purpose in the order of the court. No statement made by the defendant in the course of any examination provided for by this rule, whether the examination be with or without the consent of the defendant, no testimony by the expert based upon such statement, and no other fruits of the statement shall be admitted in evidence against the defendant in any criminal proceeding except on an issue respecting mental condition on which the defendant has introduced testimony.

(d) Failure to Comply. If there is a failure to give notice when required by subdivision (b) of this rule or to submit to an examination when ordered under subdivision (c) of this rule, the court may exclude the testimony of any expert witness offered by the defendant on the issue of his mental condition.

(e) Inadmissibility of Withdrawn Intention. Evidence of an intention as to which notice was given under subdivision (a) or (b), later withdrawn, is not admissible in any civil or criminal proceeding against the person who gave notice of the intention.

Rule 13.

TRIAL TOGETHER OF INDICTMENTS OR INFORMATIONS

The court may order two or more indictments or informations or both to be tried together if the offenses, and the defendants if there is more than one, could have been joined in a single indictment or information. The procedure shall be the same as if the prosecution were under such single indictment or information.

Rule 14.

RELIEF FROM PREJUDICIAL JOINDER

If it appears that a defendant or the government is prejudiced by a joinder of offenses or of defendants in an indictment or information or by such joinder for trial together, the court may order an election or separate trials of counts, grant a severance of defendants or provide whatever other relief justice requires. In ruling on a motion by a defendant for severance the court may order the attorney for the government to deliver to the court for inspection *in camera* any statements or confessions made by the defendants which the government intends to introduce in evidence at the trial.

Rule 15.

DEPOSITIONS

(a) When Taken. Whenever due to exceptional circumstances of the case it is in the interest of justice that the testimony of a prospective witness of a party be taken and preserved for use at trial, the court may upon motion of such party and notice to the parties order that testimony of such witness be taken by deposition and that any designated book, paper, document, record, recording, or other material not privileged, be produced at the same time and place. If a witness is committed for failure to give bail to appear to testify at a trial or hearing, the court on written motion of the witness and upon notice to the parties may direct that his deposition be taken. After the deposition has been subscribed the court may discharge the witness.

(b) Notice of Taking. The party at whose instance a deposition is to be taken shall give to every party reasonable written notice of the time and place for taking the deposition. The notice shall state the name and address of each person to be examined. On motion of a party upon whom the notice is served, the court for cause shown may extend or shorten the time or change the place for taking the deposition. The officer having custody of a defendant shall be notified of the time and place set for the examination and shall, unless the defendant waives in writing the right to be present, produce him at the examination and keep him in the presence of the witness during the examination, unless, after being warned by the court that disruptive conduct will cause him to be removed from the place of the taking of the deposition, he persists in conduct which is such as to justify his being excluded from that place. A defendant not in custody shall have the right to be present at the examination upon request subject to such terms as may be fixed by the court, but his failure, absent good cause shown, to appear after notice and tender of expenses in accordance with subdivision (c) of this rule shall constitute a waiver of that right and of any objection to the taking and use of the deposition based upon that right.

(c) Payment of Expenses. Whenever a deposition is taken at the instance of the government, or whenever a deposition is taken at the instance of a defendant who is unable to bear the expenses of the taking of the deposition, the court may direct that the expense of travel and subsistence of the defendant and his attorney for attendance at the examination and the cost of the transcript of the deposition shall be paid by the government.

(d) How Taken. Subject to such additional conditions as the court shall provide, a deposition shall be taken and filed in the manner provided in civil actions except as otherwise provided in these rules, provided that (1) in no event shall a deposition be taken of a party defendant without his consent, and (2) the scope and manner of examination and cross-examination shall be such as would be allowed in the trial itself. The government shall make available to the defendant or his counsel for examination and use at the taking of the deposition any statement of the witness being deposed which is in the possession of the government and to which the defendant would be entitled at the trial.

(e) Use. At the trial or upon any hearing, a part or all of a deposition, so far as otherwise admissible under the rules of evidence, may be used as substantive evidence if the witness is unavailable, as unavailability is defined in Rule 804(a) of the Federal Rules of Evidence, or the witness gives testimony at the trial or hearing inconsistent with his deposition. Any deposition may also be used by any party for the purpose of contradicting or impeaching the testimony of the deponent as a witness. If only a part of a deposition is offered in evidence by a party, an adverse party may require him to offer all of it which is relevant to the part offered and any party may offer other parts.

(f) Objections to Deposition Testimony. Objections to deposition testimony or evidence or parts thereof and the grounds for the objection shall be stated at the time of the taking of the deposition.

(g) Deposition by Agreement Not Precluded. Nothing in this rule shall preclude the taking of a deposition, orally or upon written questions, or the use of a deposition, by agreement of the parties with the consent of the court.

Rule 16.

DISCOVERY AND INSPECTION

(a) Disclosure of Evidence by the Government.

(1) Information Subject to Disclosure.

(A) Statement of Defendant. Upon request of a defendant the government shall permit the defendant to inspect and copy or photograph: any relevant written or recorded statements made by the defendant, or copies thereof, within the possession, custody or control of the government, the existence of which is known, or by the exercise of due diligence may become known, to the attorney for the government; the substance of any oral statement which the government intends to offer in evidence at the trial made by the defendant whether before or after arrest in response to interrogation by any person then known to the defendant to be a government agent; and recorded testimony of the defendant before a grand jury which relates to the offense charged. Where the defendant is a corporation, partnership, association or labor union, the court may grant the defendant, upon its motion, discovery of relevant recorded testimony of any witness before a grand jury who (1) was, at the time of his testimony, so situated as an officer or employee as to have been able legally to bind the defendant in respect to conduct constituting the offense, or (2) was, at the time of the offense, personally involved in the alleged conduct constituting the offense and so situated as an officer or employee as to have been able legally to bind the defendant in respect to that alleged conduct in which he was involved.

(B) Defendant's Prior Record. Upon request of the defendant, the government shall furnish to the defendant such copy of his prior criminal record, if any, as is within the possession, custody, or control of the government, the existence of which is known, or by the exercise of due diligence may become known, to the attorney for the government.

(C) Documents and Tangible Objects. Upon request of the defendant the government shall permit the defendant to inspect and copy or photograph books, papers, documents, photographs, tangible objects, buildings or places, or copies or portions thereof, which are within the possession, custody or control of the government, and which are material to the preparation of his defense or are intended for use by the government as evidence in chief at the trial, or were obtained from or belong to the defendant.

(D) Reports of Examinations and Tests. Upon request of a defendant the government shall permit the defendant to inspect and copy or photograph any results or reports of physical or mental examinations, and of scientific tests or experiments, or copies thereof, which are within the possession, custody, or control of the government, the existence of which is known, or by the exercise of due diligence may become known, to the attorney for the government, and which are material to the preparation of the defense or are intended for use by the government as evidence in chief at the trial.

(2) Information Not Subject to Disclosure. Except as provided in paragraphs (A), (B), and (D) of subdivision (a)(1), this rule does not authorize the discovery or inspection of reports, memoranda, or other internal government documents made by the attorney for the government or other government agents in connection with the investigation or prosecution of the case, or of statements made by government witnesses or prospective government witnesses except as provided in 18 U.S.C. § 3500.

(3) Grand Jury Transcripts. Except as provided in Rules 6, 12(i) and 26.2, and subdivision (a)(1)(A) of this rule, these rules do not relate to discovery or inspection of recorded proceedings of a grand jury.

(b) Disclosure of Evidence by the Defendant.

(1) Information Subject to Disclosure.

(A) Documents and Tangible Objects. If the defendant requests disclosure under subdivision (a)(1)(C) or (D) of this rule, upon compliance with such request by the government, the defendant, on request of the government, shall permit the government to inspect and copy or photograph books, papers, documents, photographs, tangible objects, or copies or portions thereof, which are within the possession, custody, or control of the defendant and which the defendant intends to introduce as evidence in chief at the trial.

(B) Reports of Examinations and Tests. If the defendant requests disclosure under subdivision (a)(1)(C) or (D) of this rule, upon compliance with such request by the government, the defendant, on request of the government, shall permit the government to inspect and copy or photograph any results or reports of physical or mental examinations and of scientific tests or experiments made in connection with the particular case, or copies thereof, within the possession or control of the defendant, which the defendant intends to introduce as evidence in chief at the trial or which were prepared by a witness whom the defendant intends to call at the trial when the results or reports relate to his testimony.

(2) Information Not Subject to Disclosure. Except as to scientific or medical reports, this subdivision does not authorize the discovery or inspection of reports, memoranda, or other internal defense documents made by the defendant, or his attorneys or agents in connection with the investigation or defense of the case, or of statements made by the defendant, or by government or defense witnesses, or by prospective government or defense witnesses, to the defendant, his agents or attorneys.

(c) Continuing Duty to Disclose. If, prior to or during trial, a party discovers additional evidence or material previously requested or ordered, which is subject to discovery or inspection under this rule, he shall promptly notify the other party or his attorney or the court of the existence of the additional evidence or material.

(d) Regulation of Discovery.

(1) Protective and Modifying Orders. Upon a sufficient showing the court may at any time order that the discovery or inspection be denied, restricted, or deferred, or make such other order as is appropriate. Upon motion by a party, the court may permit the party to make such showing, in whole or in part, in the form of a written statement to be inspected by the judge alone. If the court enters an order granting relief following such an ex parte showing, the entire text of the party's statement shall be sealed and preserved in the records of the court to be made available to the appellate court in the event of an appeal.

(2) Failure to Comply with a Request. If at any time during the course of the proceedings it is brought to the attention of the court that a party has failed to comply with this rule, the court may order such party to permit the discovery or inspection, grant a continuance, or prohibit the party from introducing evidence not disclosed, or it may enter such other order as it deems just under the circumstances. The court may specify the time, place and manner of making the discovery and inspection and may prescribe such terms and conditions as are just.

(e) Alibi Witnesses. Discovery of alibi witnesses is governed by Rule 12.1.

Rule 17.
SUBPOENA

(a) For Attendance of Witnesses; Form; Issuance. A subpoena shall be issued by the clerk under the seal of the court. It shall state the name of the court and the title, if any, of the proceeding, and shall command each person to whom it is directed to attend and give testimony at the time and place specified therein. The clerk shall issue a subpoena, signed and sealed but otherwise in blank to a party requesting it, who shall fill in the blanks before it is served. A subpoena shall be issued by a United States magistrate in a proceeding before him, but it need not be under the seal of the court.

(b) Defendants Unable to Pay. The court shall order at any time that a subpoena be issued for service on a named witness upon an *ex parte* application of a defendant upon a satisfactory showing that the defendant is financially unable to pay the fees of the witness and that the presence of the witness is necessary to an adequate defense. If the court orders the subpoena to be issued the costs incurred by the process and the fees of the witness so subpoenaed shall be paid in the same manner in which similar costs and fees are paid in case of a witness subpoenaed in behalf of the government.

(c) For Production of Documentary Evidence and of Objects. A subpoena may also command the person to whom it is directed to produce the books, papers, documents or other objects designated therein. The court on motion made promptly may quash or modify the subpoena if compliance would be unreasonable or oppressive. The court may direct that books, papers, documents or objects designated in the subpoena be produced before the court at a time prior to the trial or prior to the time when they are to be offered in evidence and may upon their production permit the books, papers, documents or objects or portions thereof to be inspected by the parties and their attorneys.

(d) Service. A subpoena may be served by the marshal, by his deputy or by any other person who is not a party and who is not less than 18 years of age. Service of a subpoena shall be made by delivering a copy thereof to the person named and by tendering to him the fee for 1 day's attendance and the mileage allowed by law. Fees and mileage need not be tendered to the witness upon service of a subpoena issued in behalf of the United States or an officer or agency thereof.

(e) **Place of Service.**

(1) **In United States.** A subpoena requiring the attendance of a witness at a hearing or trial may be served at any place within the United States.

(2) **Abroad.** A subpoena directed to a witness in a foreign country shall issue under the circumstances and in the manner and be served as provided in Title 28, U.S.C. § 1783.

(f) **For Taking Deposition; Place of Examination.**

(1) **Issuance.** An order to take a deposition authorizes the issuance by the clerk of the court for the district in which the deposition is to be taken of subpoenas for the persons named or described therein.

(2) **Place.** The witness whose deposition is to be taken may be required by subpoena to attend at any place designated by the trial court, taking into account the convenience of the witness and the parties.

(g) **Contempt.** Failure by any person without adequate excuse to obey a subpoena served upon him may be deemed a contempt of the court from which the subpoena issued or of the court for the district in which it issued if it was issued by a United States magistrate.

(h) **Information not Subject to Subpoena.** Statements made by witnesses or prospective witnesses may not be subpoenaed from the government or the defendant under this rule, but shall be subject to production only in accordance with the provisions of Rule 26.2.

Rule 17.1.

PRETRIAL CONFERENCE

At any time after the filing of the indictment or information the court upon motion of any party or upon its own motion may order one or more conferences to consider such matters as will promote a fair and expeditious trial. At the conclusion of a conference the court shall prepare and file a memorandum of the matters agreed upon. No admissions made by the defendant or his attorney at the conference shall be used against the defendant unless the admissions are reduced to writing and signed by the defendant and his attorney. This rule shall not be invoked in the case of a defendant who is not represented by counsel.

V. VENUE

Rule 18.

PLACE OF PROSECUTION AND TRIAL

Except as otherwise permitted by statute or by these rules, the prosecution shall be had in a district in which the offense was committed. The court shall fix the place of trial within the district with due regard to the convenience of the defendant and the witnesses and the prompt administration of justice.

Rule 19.

TRANSFER WITHIN THE DISTRICT

Rescinded.

Rule 20.

TRANSFER FROM THE DISTRICT FOR PLEA AND SENTENCE

(a) Indictment or Information Pending. A defendant arrested, held, or present in a district other than that in which an indictment or information is pending against him may state in writing that he wishes to plead guilty or nolo contendere, to waive trial in the district in which the indictment or information is pending, and to consent to disposition of the case in the district in which he was arrested, held, or present, subject to the approval of the United States attorney for each district. Upon receipt of the defendant's statement and of the written approval of the United States attorneys, the clerk of the court in which the indictment or information is pending shall transmit the papers in the proceeding or certified copies thereof to the clerk of the court for the district in which the defendant is arrested, held, or present, and the prosecution shall continue in that district.

(b) Indictment or Information Not Pending. A defendant arrested, held, or present in a district other than the district in which a complaint is pending against him may state in writing that he wishes to plead guilty or nolo contendere, to waive venue and trial in the district in which the warrant was issued, and to consent to disposition of the case in the district in which he was arrested, held, or present subject to the approval of the United States attorney for each district. Upon filing the written waiver of venue in the district in which the defendant is present, the prosecution may proceed as if venue were in such district.

(c) Effect of Not Guilty Plea. If after the proceeding has been transferred pursuant to subdivision (a) or (b) of this rule the defendant pleads not guilty, the clerk shall return the papers to the court in which the prosecution was commenced, and the proceeding shall be restored to the docket of that court. The defendant's statement that he wishes to plead guilty or nolo contendere shall not be used against him.

(d) Juveniles. A juvenile (as defined in 18 U.S.C. § 5031) who is arrested, held, or present in a district other than that in which he is alleged to have committed an act in violation of a law of the United States not punishable by death or life imprisonment may, after he has been advised by counsel and with the approval of the court and the United States attorney for each district, consent to be proceeded against as a juvenile delinquent in the district in which he is arrested, held, or present. The consent shall be given in writing before the court but only after the court has apprised the juvenile of his rights, including the right to be returned to the district in which he is alleged to have committed the act, and of the consequences of such consent.

Rule 21.

TRANSFER FROM THE DISTRICT FOR TRIAL

(a) For Prejudice in the District. The court upon motion of the defendant shall transfer the proceeding as to him to another district whether or not such district is specified in the defendant's motion if the court is satisfied that there exists in the district where the prosecution is pending so great a prejudice against the defendant that he cannot obtain a fair and impartial trial at any place fixed by law for holding court in that district.

(b) Transfer in Other Cases. For the convenience of parties and witnesses, and in the interest of justice, the court upon motion of the defendant may transfer the proceeding as to him or any one or more of the counts thereof to another district.

(c) Proceedings on Transfer. When a transfer is ordered the clerk shall transmit to the clerk of the court to which the proceeding is transferred all papers in the proceeding or duplicates thereof and any bail taken, and the prosecution shall continue in that district.

Rule 22.

TIME OF MOTION TO TRANSFER

A motion to transfer under these rules may be made at or before arraignment or at such other time as the court or these rules may prescribe.

VI. TRIAL

Rule 23.

TRIAL BY JURY OR BY THE COURT

(a) Trial by Jury. Cases required to be tried by jury shall be so tried unless the defendant waives a jury trial in writing with the approval of the court and the consent of the government.

(b) Jury of Less than Twelve. Juries shall be of 12 but at any time before verdict the parties may stipulate in writing with the approval of the court that the jury shall consist of any number less than 12 or that a valid verdict may be returned by a jury of less than 12 should the court find it necessary to excuse one or more jurors for any just cause after trial commences. Even absent such stipulation, if the court finds it necessary to excuse a juror for just cause after the jury has retired to consider its verdict, in the discretion of the court a valid verdict may be returned by the remaining 11 jurors.

(c) Trial Without a Jury. In a case tried without a jury the court shall make a general finding and shall in addition, on request made before the general finding, find the facts specially. Such findings may be oral. If an opinion or memorandum of decision is filed, it will be sufficient if the findings of fact appear therein.

Rule 24.

TRIAL JURORS

(a) Examination. The court may permit the defendant or his attorney and the attorney for the government to conduct the examination of prospective jurors or may itself conduct the examination. In the latter event the court shall permit the defendant or his attorney and the attorney for the government to supplement the examination by such further inquiry as it deems proper or shall itself submit to the prospective jurors such additional questions by the parties or their attorneys as it deems proper.

(b) Peremptory Challenges. If the offense charged is punishable by death, each side is entitled to 20 peremptory challenges. If the offense charged is punishable by imprisonment for more than one year, the government is entitled to 6 peremptory challenges and the defendant or defendants jointly to 10 peremptory challenges. If the offense charged is punishable by imprisonment for not more than one year or by fine or both, each side is entitled to 3 peremptory challenges. If there is more than one defendant, the court may allow the defendants additional peremptory challenges and permit them to be exercised separately or jointly.

(c) Alternate Jurors. The court may direct that not more than 6 jurors in addition to the regular jury be called and impanelled to sit as alternate jurors. Alternate jurors in the order in which they are called shall replace jurors who, prior to the time the jury retires to consider its verdict, become or are found to be unable or disqualified to perform their duties. Alternate jurors shall be drawn in the same manner, shall have the same qualifications, shall be subject to the same examination and challenges, shall take the same oath and shall have the same functions, powers, facilities and privileges as the regular jurors. An alternate juror who does not replace a regular juror shall be discharged after the jury retires to consider its verdict. Each side is entitled to 1 peremptory challenge in addition to those otherwise allowed by law if 1 or 2 alternate jurors are to be impanelled, 2 peremptory challenges if 3 or 4 alternate jurors are to be impanelled, and 3 peremptory challenges if 5 or 6 alternate jurors are to be impanelled. The additional peremptory challenges may be used against an alternate juror only, and the other peremptory challenges allowed by these rules may not be used against an alternate juror.

Rule 25.

JUDGE; DISABILITY

(a) During Trial. If by reason of death, sickness or other disability the judge before whom a jury trial has commenced is unable to proceed with the trial, any other judge regularly sitting in or assigned to the court, upon certifying that he has familiarized himself with the record of the trial, may proceed with and finish the trial.

(b) After Verdict or Finding of Guilt. If by reason of absence, death, sickness or other disability the judge before whom the defendant has been tried is unable to perform the duties to be performed by the court after a verdict or finding of guilt, any other judge regularly sitting in or assigned to the court may perform those duties; but if such other judge is satisfied that he cannot perform those duties because he did not preside at the trial or for any other reason, he may in his discretion grant a new trial.

Rule 26.

TAKING OF TESTIMONY

In all trials the testimony of witnesses shall be taken orally in open court, unless otherwise provided by an Act of Congress or by these rules, the Federal Rules of Evidence, or other rules adopted by the Supreme Court.

Rule 26.1

DETERMINATION OF FOREIGN LAW

A party who intends to raise an issue concerning the law of a foreign country shall give reasonable written notice. The court, in determining foreign law, may consider any relevant material or source, including testimony, whether, or not submitted by a party or admissible under the Federal Rules of Evidence. The court's determination shall be treated as a ruling on a question of law.

Rule 26.2

PRODUCTION OF STATEMENTS OF WITNESSES

(a) Motion for Production. After a witness other than the defendant has testified on direct examination, the court, on motion of a party who did not call the witness, shall order the attorney for the government or the defendant and his attorney, as the case may be, to produce, for the examination and use of the moving party, any statement of the witness that is in their possession and that relates to the subject matter concerning which the witness has testified.

(b) Production of Entire Statement. If the entire contents of the statement relate to the subject matter concerning which the witness has testified, the court shall order that the statement be delivered to the moving party.

(c) Production of Excised Statement. If the other party claims that the statement contains matter that does not relate to the subject matter concerning which the witness has testified, the court shall order that it be delivered to the court in camera. Upon inspection, the court shall excise the portions of the statement that do not relate to the subject matter concerning which the witness has testified, and shall order that the statement, with such material excised, be delivered to the moving party. Any portion of the statement that is withheld from the defendant over his objection shall be preserved by the attorney for the government, and, in the event of a conviction and an appeal by the defendant, shall be made available to the appellate court for the purpose of determining the correctness of the decision to excise the portion of the statement.

(d) Recess for Examination of Statement. Upon delivery of the statement to the moving party, the court, upon application of that party, may recess proceedings in the trial for the examination of such statement and for preparation for its use in the trial.

(e) Sanction for Failure to Produce Statement. If the other party elects not to comply with an order to deliver a statement to the moving party, the court shall order that the testimony of the witness be stricken from the record and that the trial proceed, or, if it is the attorney for the government who elects not to comply, shall declare a mistrial if required by the interest of justice.

(f) Definition. As used in this rule, a "statement" of a witness means:

(1) a written statement made by the witness that is signed or otherwise adopted or approved by him;

(2) a substantially verbatim recital of an oral statement made by the witness that is recorded contemporaneously with the making of the oral statement and that is contained in a stenographic, mechanical, electrical, or other recording or a transcription thereof; or

(3) a statement, however taken or recorded, or a transcription thereof, made by the witness to a grand jury.

Rule 27.

PROOF OF OFFICIAL RECORD

An official record or an entry therein or the lack of such a record or entry may be proved in the same manner as in civil actions.

Rule 28.

INTERPRETERS

The court may appoint an interpreter of its own selection and may fix the reasonable compensation of such interpreter. Such compensation shall be paid out of funds provided by law or by the government, as the court may direct.

Rule 29.

MOTION FOR JUDGMENT OF ACQUITTAL

(a) Motion Before Submission to Jury. Motions for directed verdict are abolished and motions for judgment of acquittal shall be used in their place. The court on motion of a defendant or of its own motion shall order the entry of judgment of acquittal of one or more offenses charged in the indictment or information after the evidence on either side is closed if the evidence is insufficient to sustain a conviction of such offense or offenses. If a defendant's motion for judgment of acquittal at the close of the evidence offered by the government is not granted, the defendant may offer evidence without having reserved the right.

(b) Reservation of Decision on Motion. If a motion for judgment of acquittal is made at the close of all the evidence, the court may reserve decision on the motion, submit the case to the jury and decide the motion either before the jury returns a verdict or after it returns a verdict of guilty or is discharged without having returned a verdict.

(c) Motion After Discharge of Jury. If the jury returns a verdict of guilty or is discharged without having returned a verdict, a motion for judgment of acquittal may be made or renewed within 7 days after the jury is discharged or within such further time as the court may fix during the 7-day period. If a verdict of guilty is returned the court may on such motion set aside the verdict and enter judgment of acquittal. If no verdict is returned the court may enter judgment of acquittal. It shall not be necessary to the making of such a motion that a similar motion has been made prior to the submission of the case to the jury.

Rule 29.1

CLOSING ARGUMENT

After the closing of evidence the prosecution shall open the argument. The defense shall be permitted to reply. The prosecution shall then be permitted to reply in rebuttal.

Rule 30.

INSTRUCTIONS

At the close of the evidence or at such earlier time during the trial as the court reasonably directs, any party may file written requests that the court instruct the jury on the law as set forth in the requests. At the same time copies of such requests shall be furnished to adverse parties. The court shall inform counsel of its proposed action upon the requests prior to their arguments to the jury, but the court shall instruct the jury after the arguments are completed. No party may assign as error any portion of the charge or omission therefrom unless he objects thereto before the jury retires to consider its verdict, stating distinctly the matter to which he objects and the grounds of his objection. Opportunity shall be given to make the objection out of the hearing of the jury and, on request of any party, out of the presence of the jury.

Rule 31.

VERDICT

(a) Return. The verdict shall be unanimous. It shall be returned by the jury to the judge in open court.

(b) Several Defendants. If there are two or more defendants, the jury at any time during its deliberations may return a verdict or verdicts with respect to a defendant or defendants as to whom it has agreed; if the jury cannot agree with respect to all, the defendant or defendants as to whom it does not agree may be tried again.

(c) Conviction of Less Offense. The defendant may be found guilty of an offense necessarily included in the offense charged or of an attempt to commit either the offense charged or an offense necessarily included therein if the attempt is an offense.

(d) Poll of Jury. When a verdict is returned and before it is recorded the jury shall be polled at the request of any party or upon the court's own motion. If upon the poll there is not unanimous concurrence, the jury may be directed to retire for further deliberations or may be discharged.

(e) Criminal Forfeiture. If the indictment or the information alleges that an interest or property is subject to criminal forfeiture, a special verdict shall be returned as to the extent of the interest or property subject to forfeiture, if any.

VII. JUDGMENT

Rule 32.

SENTENCE AND JUDGMENT

(a) Sentence.

(1) Imposition of Sentence. Sentence shall be imposed without unreasonable delay. Before imposing sentence the court shall

(A) determine that the defendant and his counsel have had the opportunity to read and discuss the presentence investigation report made available pursuant to subdivision (c) (3) (A) or summary thereof made available pursuant to subdivision (c) (3) (B);

(B) afford counsel an opportunity to speak on behalf of the defendant; and

(C) address the defendant personally and ask him if he wishes to make a statement in his own behalf and to present any information in mitigation of punishment.

The attorney for the government shall have an equivalent opportunity to speak to the court.

(2) Notification of Right to Appeal. After imposing sentence in a case which has gone to trial on a plea of not guilty, the court shall advise the defendant of his right to appeal and of the right of a person who is unable to pay the cost of an appeal to apply for leave to appeal in forma pauperis. There shall be no duty on the court to advise the defendant of any right of appeal after sentence is imposed following a plea of guilty or nolo contendere. If the defendant so requests, the clerk of the court shall prepare and file forthwith a notice of appeal on behalf of the defendant.

(b) Judgment.

(1) In General. A judgment of conviction shall set forth the plea, the verdict or findings, and the adjudication and sentence. If the defendant is found not guilty or for any other reason is entitled to be discharged, judgment shall be entered accordingly.

The judgment shall be signed by the judge and entered by the clerk.

(2) Criminal Forfeiture. When a verdict contains a finding of property subject to a criminal forfeiture, the judgment of criminal forfeiture shall authorize the Attorney General to seize the interest or property subject to forfeiture, fixing such terms and conditions as the court shall deem proper.

(c) Presentence Investigation.

(1) When Made. The probation service of the court shall make a presentence investigation and report to the court before the imposition of sentence or the granting of probation unless, with the permission of the court, the defendant waives a presentence investigation and report, or the court finds that there is in the record information sufficient to enable the meaningful exercise of sentencing discretion, and the court explains this finding on the record.

The report shall not be submitted to the court or its contents disclosed to anyone unless the defendant has pleaded guilty or nolo contendere or has been found guilty, except that a judge may, with the written consent of the defendant, inspect a presentence report at any time.

(2) Report.—The presentence report shall contain—

(A) any prior criminal record of the defendant;

(B) a statement of the circumstances of the commission of the offense and circumstances affecting the defendant's behavior;

(C) information concerning any harm, including financial, social, psychological, and physical harm, done to or loss suffered by any victim of the offense; and

(D) any other information that may aid the court in sentencing, including the restitution needs of any victim of the offense.

(3) Disclosure.

(A) At a reasonable time before imposing sentence the court shall permit the defendant and his counsel to read the report of the presentence investigation exclusive of any recommendation as to sentence, but not to the extent that in the opinion of the court the report contains diagnostic opinions which, if disclosed, might seriously disrupt a program of rehabilitation; or sources of information obtained upon a promise of confidentiality; or any other information which, if disclosed, might result in harm, physical or otherwise, to the defendant or other persons. The court shall afford the defendant and his counsel an opportunity to comment on the report and, in the discretion of the court, to introduce testimony or other information relating to any alleged factual inaccuracy contained in it.

(B) If the court is of the view that there is information in the presentence report which should not be disclosed under subdivision (c) (3) (A) of this rule, the court in lieu of making the report or part thereof available shall state orally or in writing a summary of the factual information contained therein to be relied on in determining sentence, and shall give the defendant and his counsel an opportunity to comment thereon. The statement may be made to the parties in camera.

(C) Any material which may be disclosed to the defendant and his counsel shall be disclosed to the attorney for the government.

(D) If the comments of the defendant and his counsel or testimony or other information introduced by them allege any factual inaccuracy in the presentence investigation report or the summary of the report or part thereof, the court shall, as to each matter controverted, make (i) a finding as to the allegation, or (ii) a determination that no such finding is necessary because the matter controverted will not be taken into account in sentencing. A written record of such findings and determinations shall be appended to and accompany any copy of the presentence investigation report thereafter made available to the Bureau of Prisons or the Parole Commission.

(E) Any copies of the presentence investigation report made available to the defendant and his counsel and the attorney for the government shall be returned to the probation officer immediately following the imposition of sentence or the granting of probation, unless the court, in its discretion, otherwise directs.

(F) The reports of studies and recommendations contained therein made by the Director of the Bureau of Prisons or the Parole Commission pursuant to 18 U.S.C. §§ 4205(c), 4252, 5010(e), or 5037(c) shall be considered a presentence investigation within the meaning of subdivision (c) (3) of this rule.

(d) Plea Withdrawal. If a motion for withdrawal of a plea of guilty or nolo contendere is made before sentence is imposed, imposition of sentence is suspended, or disposition is had under 18 U.S.C. § 4205(c), the court may permit withdrawal of the plea upon a showing by the defendant of any fair and just reason. At any later time, a plea may be set aside only on direct appeal or by motion under 28 U.S.C. § 2255.

(e) **Probation.** After conviction of an offense not punishable by death or by life imprisonment, the defendant may be placed on probation if permitted by law.

Rule 32.1

REVOCATION OR MODIFICATION OF PROBATION

(a) Revocation of Probation.

(1) Preliminary Hearing. Whenever a probationer is held in custody on the ground that he has violated a condition of his probation, he shall be afforded a prompt hearing before any judge, or a United States magistrate who has been given authority pursuant to 28 U.S.C. § 636 to conduct such hearings, in order to determine whether there is probable cause to hold the probationer for a revocation hearing. The probationer shall be given

(A) notice of the preliminary hearing and its purpose and of the alleged violation of probation;

(B) an opportunity to appear at the hearing and present evidence in his own behalf;

(C) upon request, the opportunity to question witnesses against him unless, for good cause, the federal magistrate decides that justice does not require the appearance of the witness; and

(D) notice of his right to be represented by counsel.

The proceedings shall be recorded stenographically or by an electronic recording device. If probable cause is found to exist, the probationer shall be held for a revocation hearing. The probationer may be released pursuant to Rule 46(c) pending the revocation hearing. If probable cause is not found to exist, the proceeding shall be dismissed.

(2) Revocation Hearing. The revocation hearing, unless waived by the probationer, shall be held within a reasonable time in the district of probation jurisdiction. The probationer shall be given

(A) written notice of the alleged violation of probation;

(B) disclosure of the evidence against him;

(C) an opportunity to appear and to present evidence in his own behalf;

(D) the opportunity to question witnesses against him; and

(E) notice of his right to be represented by counsel.

(b) Modification of Probation. A hearing and assistance of counsel are required before the terms or conditions of probation can be modified, unless the relief granted to the probationer upon his request or the court's own motion is favorable to him.

Rule 33.

NEW TRIAL

The court on motion of a defendant may grant a new trial to him if required in the interest of justice. If trial was by the court without a jury the court on motion of a defendant for a new trial may vacate the judgment if entered, take additional testimony and direct the entry of a new judgment. A motion for a new trial based on the ground of newly discovered evidence may be made only before or within two years after final judgment, but if an appeal is pending the court may grant the motion only on remand of the case. A motion for a new trial based on any other grounds shall be made within 7 days after verdict or finding of guilty or within such further time as the court may fix during the 7-day period.

Rule 34.

ARREST OF JUDGMENT

The court on motion of a defendant shall arrest judgment if the indictment or information does not charge an offense or if the court was without jurisdiction of the offense charged. The motion in arrest of judgment shall be made within 7 days after verdict or finding of guilty, or after plea of guilty or *nolo contendere,* or within such further time as the court may fix during the 7-day period.

Rule 35.

CORRECTION OR REDUCTION OF SENTENCE

(a) Correction of Sentence. The court may correct an illegal sentence at any time and may correct a sentence imposed in an illegal manner within the time provided herein for the reduction of sentence.

(b) Reduction of Sentence. The court may reduce a sentence within 120 days after the sentence is imposed or probation is revoked, or within 120 days after receipt by the court of a mandate issued upon affirmance of the judgment or dismissal of the appeal, or within 120 days after entry of any order or judgment of the Supreme Court denying review of, or having the effect of upholding, a judgment of conviction or probation revocation. Changing a sentence from a sentence of incarceration to a grant of probation shall constitute a permissible reduction of sentence under this subdivision.

Rule 36.

CLERICAL MISTAKES

Clerical mistakes in judgments, orders or other parts of the record and errors in the record arising from oversight or omission may be corrected by the court at any time and after such notice, if any, as the court orders.

VIII. APPEAL

Rule 37.

TAKING APPEAL, AND PETITION FOR WRIT OF CERTIORARI

[Abrogated.]

Rule 38.

STAY OF EXECUTION, AND RELIEF PENDING REVIEW

(a) Stay of Execution.

(1) Death. A sentence of death shall be stayed if an appeal is taken.

(2) Imprisonment. A sentence of imprisonment shall be stayed if an appeal is taken and the defendant is released pending disposition of appeal pursuant to Rule 9(b) of the Federal Rules of Appellate Procedure. If not stayed, the court may recommend to the Attorney General that the defendant be retained at, or transferred to, a place of confinement near the place of trial or the place where his appeal is to be heard, for a period reasonably necessary to permit the defendant to assist in the preparation of his appeal to the court of appeals.

(3) Fine. A sentence to pay a fine or a fine and costs, if an appeal is taken, may be stayed by the district court or by the court of appeals upon such terms as the court deems proper. The court may require the defendant pending appeal to deposit the whole or any part of the fine and costs in the registry of the district court, or to give bond for the payment thereof, or to submit to an examination of assets, and it may make any appropriate order to restrain the defendant from dissipating his assets.

(4) Probation. An order placing the defendant on probation may be stayed if an appeal is taken. If not stayed, the court shall specify when the term of probation shall commence. If the order is stayed the court shall fix the terms of the stay.

[**(b) Bail.** Abrogated.]

(c) Application for Relief Pending Review. Abrogated.

Rule 39.

SUPERVISION OF APPEAL

[Abrogated.]

IX. SUPPLEMENTARY AND SPECIAL PROCEEDINGS

Rule 40.

COMMITMENT TO ANOTHER DISTRICT; REMOVAL

(a) Appearance Before Federal Magistrate. If a person is arrested in a district other than that in which the offense is alleged to have been committed, he shall be taken without unnecessary delay before the nearest available federal magistrate. Preliminary proceedings concerning the defendant shall be conducted in accordance with Rules 5 and 5.1, except that if no preliminary examination is held because an indictment has been returned or an information filed or because the defendant elects to have the preliminary examination conducted in the district in which the prosecution is pending, the person shall be held to answer upon a finding that he is the person named in the indictment, information or warrant. If the defendant is held to answer, he shall be held to answer in the district court in which the prosecution is pending, provided that a warrant is issued in that district if the arrest was made without a warrant, upon production of the warrant or a certified copy thereof.

(b) Statement by Federal Magistrate. In addition to the statements required by Rule 5, the federal magistrate shall inform the defendant of the provisions of Rule 20.

(c) Papers. If a defendant is held or discharged, the papers in the proceeding and any bail taken shall be transmitted to the clerk of the district court in which the prosecution is pending.

(d) Arrest of Probationer. If a person is arrested for a violation of his probation in a district other than a district having probation jurisdiction, he shall be taken without unnecessary delay before the nearest available federal magistrate. The federal magistrate shall:

(1) Proceed under Rule 32.1 if jurisdiction over the probationer is transferred to that district pursuant to 18 U.S.C. § 3653;

(2) Hold a prompt preliminary hearing if the alleged violation occurred in that district, and either (i) hold the probationer to answer in the district court of the district having probation jurisdiction or (ii) dismiss the proceedings and so notify that court; or

(3) Otherwise order the probationer held to answer in the district court of the district having probation jurisdiction upon production of certified copies of the probation order, the warrant, and the application for the warrant, and upon a finding that the person before him is the person named in the warrant.

(e) Arrest for Failure to Appear. If a person is arrested on a warrant in a district other than that in which the warrant was issued, and the warrant was issued because of the failure of the person named therein to appear as required pursuant to a subpoena or the terms of his release, the person arrested shall be taken without unnecessary delay before the nearest available federal magistrate. Upon production of the warrant or a certified copy thereof and upon a finding that the person before him is the person named in the warrant, the federal magistrate shall hold the person to answer in the district in which the warrant was issued.

(f) Bail. If bail was previously fixed in another district where a warrant, information or indictment issued, the federal magistrate shall take into account the amount of bail previously fixed and the reasons set forth therefor, if any, but will not be bound by the amount of bail previously fixed. If the federal magistrate fixes bail different from that previously fixed, he shall set forth the reasons for his action in writing.

Rule 41.
SEARCH AND SEIZURE

(a) Authority to Issue Warrant. A search warrant authorized by this rule may be issued by a federal magistrate or a judge of a state court of record within the district wherein the property or person sought is located, upon request of a federal law enforcement officer or an attorney for the government.

(b) Property or Persons Which May be Seized with a Warrant. A warrant may be issued unde this rule to search for and seize any (1) property that constitutes evidence of the commission of a criminal offense; or (2) contraband, the fruits of crime, or things otherwise criminally possessed; or (3) property designed or intended for use or which is or has been used as the means of committing a criminal offense; or (4) person for whose arrest there is probable cause, or who is unlawfully restrained.

(c) Issuance and Contents.

(1) Warrant Upon Affidavit. A warrant other than a warrant upon oral testimony under paragraph (2) of this subdivision shall issue only on an affidavit or affidavits sworn to before the federal magistrate or state judge and establishing the grounds for issuing the warrant. If the federal magistrate or state judge is satisfied that grounds for the application exist or that there is probable cause to believe that they exist, he shall issue a warrant identifying the property or person to be seized and naming or describing the person or place to be searched. The finding of probable cause may be based upon hearsay evidence in whole or in part. Before ruling on a request for a warrant the federal magistrate or state judge may require the affiant to appear personally and may examine under oath the affiant and any witnesses he may produce, provided that such proceeding shall be taken down by a court reporter or recording equipment and made part of the affidavit. The warrant shall be directed to a civil officer of the United States authorized to enforce or assist in enforcing any law thereof or to a person so authorized by the President of the United States. It shall command the officer to search, within a specified period of time not to exceed 10 days, the person or place named for the property or person specified. The warrant shall be served in the daytime, unless the issuing authority, by appropriate provision in the warrant, and for reasonable cause shown, authorizes its execution at times other than daytime. It shall designate a federal magistrate to whom it shall be returned.

(2) Warrant Upon Oral Testimony.

(A) General Rule. If the circumstances make it reasonable to dispense with a written affidavit, a Federal magistrate may issue a warrant based upon sworn oral testimony communicated by telephone or other appropriate means.

(B) Application. The person who is requesting the warrant shall prepare a document to be known as a duplicate original warrant and shall read such duplicate original warrant, verbatim, to the Federal magistrate. The Federal magistrate shall enter, verbatim, what is so read to such magistrate on a document to be known as the original warrant. The Federal magistrate may direct that the warrant be modified.

(C) Issuance. If the Federal magistrate is satisfied that the circumstances are such as to make it reasonable to dispense with a written affidavit and that grounds for the application exist or that there is probable cause to believe that they exist, the Federal magistrate shall order the issuance of a warrant by directing the person requesting the warrant to sign the Federal magistrate's name on the duplicate original warrant. The Federal magistrate shall immediately sign the original warrant and enter on the face of the original warrant the exact time when the warrant was ordered to be issued. The finding of probable cause for a warrant upon oral testimony may be based on the same kind of evidence as is sufficient for a warrant upon affidavit.

(D) Recording and Certification of Testimony. When a caller informs the Federal magistrate that the purpose of the call is to request a warrant, the Federal magistrate shall immediately place under oath each person whose testimony forms a basis of the application and each person applying for that warrant. If a voice recording device is available, the Federal magistrate shall record by means of such device all of the call after the caller informs the Federal magistrate that the purpose of the call is to request a warrant. Otherwise a stenographic or longhand verbatim record shall be made. If a voice recording device is used or a stenographic record made, the Federal magistrate shall have the record transcribed, shall certify the accuracy of the transcription, and shall file a copy of the original record and the transcription with the court. If a longhand verbatim record is made, the Federal magistrate shall file a signed copy with the court.

(E) Contents. The contents of a warrant upon oral testimony shall be the same as the contents of a warrant upon affidavit.

(F) Additional Rule for Execution. The person who executes the warrant shall enter the exact time of execution on the face of the duplicate original warrant.

(G) Motion to Suppress Precluded. Absent a finding of bad faith, evidence obtained pursuant to a warrant issued under this paragraph is not subject to a motion to suppress on the ground that the circumstances were not such as to make it reasonable to dispense with a written affidavit.

(d) Execution and Return with Inventory. The officer taking property under the warrant shall give to the person from whom or from whose premises the property was taken a copy of the warrant and a receipt for the property taken or shall leave the copy and receipt at the place from which the property was taken. The return shall be made promptly and shall be accompanied by a written inventory of any property taken. The inventory shall be made in the presence of the applicant for the warrant and the person from whose possession or premises the property was taken, if they are present, or in the presence of at least one credible person other than the applicant for the warrant or the person from whose possession or premises the property was taken, and shall be verified by the officer. The federal magistrate shall upon request deliver a copy of the inventory to the person from whom or from whose premises the property was taken and to the applicant for the warrant.

(e) Motion for Return of Property. A person aggrieved by an unlawful search and seizure may move the district court for the district in which the property was seized for the return of the property on the ground that he is entitled to lawful possession of the property which was illegally seized. The judge shall receive evidence on any issue of fact necessary to the decision of the motion. If the motion is granted the property shall be restored and it shall not be admissible in evidence at any hearing or trial. If a motion for return of property is made or comes on for hearing in the district of trial after an indictment or information is filed, it shall be treated also as a motion to suppress under Rule 12.

(f) Motion to Suppress. A motion to suppress evidence may be made in the court of the district of trial as provided in Rule 12.

(g) Return of Papers to Clerk. The federal magistrate before whom the warrant is returned shall attach to the warrant a copy of the return, inventory and all other papers in connection therewith and shall file them with the clerk of the district court for the district in which the property was seized.

(h) Scope and Definition. This rule does not modify any act, inconsistent with it, regulating search, seizure and the issuance and execution of search warrants in circumstances for which special provision is made. The term "property" is used in this rule to include documents, books, papers and any other tangible objects. The term "daytime" is used in this rule to mean the hours from 6:00 a. m. to 10:00 p. m. according to local time. The phrase "federal law enforcement officer" is used in this rule to mean any government agent, other than an attorney for the government as defined in Rule 54(c), who is engaged in the enforcement of the criminal laws and is within any category of officers authorized by the Attorney General to request the issuance of a search warrant.

Rule 42.

CRIMINAL CONTEMPT

(a) Summary Disposition. A criminal contempt may be punished summarily if the judge certifies that he saw or heard the conduct constituting the contempt and that it was committed in the actual presence of the court. The order of contempt shall recite the facts and shall be signed by the judge and entered of record.

(b) Disposition Upon Notice and Hearing. A criminal contempt except as provided in subdivision (a) of this rule shall be prosecuted on notice. The notice shall state the time and place of hearing, allowing a reasonable time for the preparation of the defense, and shall state the essential facts constituting the criminal contempt charged and describe it as such. The notice shall be given orally by the judge in open court in the presence of the defendant or, on application of the United States attorney or of an attorney appointed by the court for that purpose, by an order to show cause or an order of arrest. The defendant is entitled to a trial by jury in any case in which an act of Congress so provides. He is entitled to admission to bail as provided in these rules. If the contempt charged involves disrespect to or criticism of a judge, that judge is disqualified from presiding at the trial or hearing except with the defendant's consent. Upon a verdict or finding of guilt the court shall enter an order fixing the punishment.

X. GENERAL PROVISIONS

Rule 43.

PRESENCE OF THE DEFENDANT

(a) Presence Required. The defendant shall be present at the arraignment, at the time of the plea, at every stage of the trial including the impaneling of the jury and the return of the verdict, and at the imposition of sentence, except as otherwise provided by this rule.

(b) Continued Presence Not Required. The further progress of the trial to and including the return of the verdict shall not be prevented and the defendant shall be considered to have waived his right to be present whenever a defendant, initially present,

(1) voluntarily absents himself after the trial has commenced (whether or not he has been informed by the court of his obligation to remain during the trial), or

(2) after being warned by the court that disruptive conduct will cause him to be removed from the courtroom, persists in conduct which is such as to justify his being excluded from the courtroom.

(c) Presence Not Required. A defendant need not be present in the following situations:

(1) A corporation may appear by counsel for all purposes.

(2) In prosecutions for offenses punishable by fine or by imprisonment for not more than one year or both, the court, with the written consent of the defendant, may permit arraignment, plea, trial, and imposition of sentence in the defendant's absence.

(3) At a conference or argument upon a question of law.

(4) At a reduction of sentence under Rule 35.

Rule 44.

RIGHT TO AND ASSIGNMENT OF COUNSEL

(a) Right to Assigned Counsel. Every defendant who is unable to obtain counsel shall be entitled to have counsel assigned to represent him at every stage of the proceedings from his initial appearance before the federal magistrate or the court through appeal, unless he waives such appointment.

(b) Assignment Procedure. The procedures for implementing the right set out in subdivision (a) shall be those provided by law and by local rules of court established pursuant thereto.

(c) Joint Representation. Whenever two or more defendants have been jointly charged pursuant to Rule 8(b) or have been joined for trial pursuant to Rule 13, and are represented by the same retained or assigned counsel or by retained or assigned counsel who are associated in the practice of law, the court shall promptly inquire with respect to such joint representation and shall personally advise each defendant of his right to the effective assistance of counsel, including separate representation. Unless it appears that there is good cause to believe no conflict of interest is likely to arise, the court shall take such measures as may be appropriate to protect each defendant's right to counsel.

Rule 45.

TIME

(a) Computation. In computing any period of time the day of the act or event from which the designated period of time begins to run shall not be included. The last day of the period so computed shall be included, unless it is a Saturday, a Sunday, or a legal holiday, or, when the act to be done is the filing of some paper in court, a day on which weather or other conditions have made the office of the clerk of the district court inaccessible, in which event the period runs until the end of the next day which is not one of the aforementioned days. When a period of time prescribed or allowed is less than 7 days, intermediate Saturdays, Sundays and legal holidays shall be excluded in the computation. As used in these rules, "legal holiday" includes New Year's Day, Washington's Birthday, Memorial Day, Independence Day, Labor Day, Columbus Day, Veterans Day, Thanksgiving Day, Christmas Day, and any other day appointed as a holiday by the President or the Congress of the United States, or by the state in which the district court is held.

(b) Enlargement. When an act is required or allowed to be done at or within a specified time, the court for cause shown may at any time in its discretion (1) with or without motion or notice, order the period enlarged if request therefor is made before the expiration of the period originally prescribed or as extended by a previous order or (2) upon motion made after the expiration of the specified period permit the act to be done if the failure to act was the result of excusable neglect; but the court may not extend the time for taking any action under Rules 29, 33, 34 and 35, except to the extent and under the conditions stated in them.

[(c) **Unaffected by Expiration of Term.** Rescinded.]

(d) **For Motions; Affidavits.** A written motion, other than one which may be heard *ex parte,* and notice of the hearing thereof shall be served not later than 5 days before the time specified for the hearing unless a different period is fixed by rule or order of the court. For cause shown such an order may be made on *ex parte* application. When a motion is supported by affidavit, the affidavit shall be served with the motion; and opposing affidavits may be served not less than 1 day before the hearing unless the court permits them to be served at a later time.

(e) **Additional Time After Service by Mail.** Whenever a party has the right or is required to do an act within a prescribed period after the service of a notice or other paper upon him and the notice or other paper is served upon him by mail, 3 days shall be added to the prescribed period.

Rule 46.

RELEASE FROM CUSTODY

(a) **Release Prior to Trial.** Eligibility for release prior to trial shall be in accordance with 18 U.S.C. § 3146, § 3148, or § 3149.

(b) **Release During Trial.** A person released before trial shall continue on release during trial under the same terms and conditions as were previously imposed unless the court determines that other terms and conditions or termination of release are necessary to assure his presence during the trial or to assure that his conduct will not obstruct the orderly and expeditious progress of the trial.

(c) **Pending Sentence and Notice of Appeal.** Eligibility for release pending sentence or pending notice of appeal or expiration of the time allowed for filing notice of appeal, shall be in accordance with 18 U.S.C. § 3148. The burden of establishing that the defendant will not flee or pose a danger to any other person or to the community rests with the defendant.

(d) **Justification of Sureties.** Every surety, except a corporate surety which is approved as provided by law, shall justify by affidavit and may be required to describe in the affidavit the property by which he proposes to justify and the encumbrances thereon, the number and amount of other bonds and undertakings for bail entered into by him and remaining undischarged and all his other liabilities. No bond shall be approved unless the surety thereon appears to be qualified.

(e) Forfeiture.

(1) Declaration. If there is a breach of condition of a bond, the district court shall declare a forfeiture of the bail.

(2) Setting Aside. The court may direct that a forfeiture be set aside, upon such conditions as the court may impose, if it appears that justice does not require the enforcement of the forfeiture.

(3) Enforcement. When a forfeiture has not been set aside, the court shall on motion enter a judgment of default and execution may issue thereon. By entering into a bond the obligors submit to the jurisdiction of the district court and irrevocably appoint the clerk of the court as their agent upon whom any papers affecting their liability may be served. Their liability may be enforced on motion without the necessity of an independent action. The motion and such notice of the motion as the court prescribes may be served on the clerk of the court, who shall forthwith mail copies to the obligors to their last known addresses.

(4) Remission. After entry of such judgment, the court may remit it in whole or in part under the conditions applying to the setting aside of forfeiture in paragraph (2) of this subdivision.

(f) Exoneration. When the condition of the bond has been satisfied or the forfeiture thereof has been set aside or remitted, the court shall exonerate the obligors and release any bail. A surety may be exonerated by a deposit of cash in the amount of the bond or by a timely surrender of the defendant into custody.

(g) Supervision of Detention Pending Trial. The court shall exercise supervision over the detention of defendants and witnesses within the district pending trial for the purpose of eliminating all unnecessary detention. The attorney for the government shall make a biweekly report to the court listing each defendant and witness who has been held in custody pending indictment, arraignment or trial for a period in excess of ten days. As to each witness so listed the attorney for the government shall make a statement of the reasons why such witness should not be released with or without the taking of his deposition pursuant to Rule 15(a). As to each defendant so listed the attorney for the government shall make a statement of the reasons why the defendant is still held in custody.

Rule 47.

MOTIONS

An application to the court for an order shall be by motion. A motion other than one made during a trial or hearing shall be in writing unless the court permits it to be made orally. It shall state the grounds upon which it is made and shall set forth the relief or order sought. It may be supported by affidavit.

Rule 48.

DISMISSAL

(a) By Attorney for Government. The Attorney General or the United States attorney may by leave of court file a dismissal of an indictment, information or complaint and the prosecution shall thereupon terminate. Such a dismissal may not be filed during the trial without the consent of the defendant.

(b) By Court. If there is unnecessary delay in presenting the charge to a grand jury or in filing an information against a defendant who has been held to answer to the district court, or if there is unnecessary delay in bringing a defendant to trial, the court may dismiss the indictment, information or complaint.

Rule 49.

SERVICE AND FILING OF PAPERS

(a) Service: When Required. Written motions other than those which are heard *ex parte*, written notices, designations of record on appeal and similar papers shall be served upon each of the parties.

(b) Service: How Made. Whenever under these rules or by an order of the court service is required or permitted to be made upon a party represented by an attorney, the service shall be made upon the attorney unless service upon the party himself is ordered by the court. Service upon the attorney or upon a party shall be made in the manner provided in civil actions.

(c) Notice of Orders. Immediately upon the entry of an order made on a written motion subsequent to arraignment the clerk shall mail to each party a notice thereof and shall make a note in the docket of the mailing. Lack of notice of the entry by the clerk does not affect the time to appeal or relieve or authorize the court to relieve a party for failure to appeal within the time allowed, except as permitted by Rule 4(b) of the Federal Rules of Appellate Procedure.

(d) Filing. Papers required to be served shall be filed with the court. Papers shall be filed in the manner provided in civil actions.

Rule 50.

CALENDARS; PLAN FOR PROMPT DISPOSITION

(a) Calendars. The district courts may provide for placing criminal proceedings upon appropriate calendars. Preference shall be given to criminal proceedings as far as practicable.

(b) Plans for Achieving Prompt Disposition of Criminal Cases. To minimize undue delay and to further the prompt disposition of criminal cases, each district court shall conduct a continuing study of the administration of criminal justice in the district court and before United States magistrates of the district and shall prepare plans for the prompt disposition of criminal cases in accordance with the provisions of Chapter 208 of Title 18, United States Code.

Rule 51.

EXCEPTIONS UNNECESSARY

Exceptions to rulings or orders of the court are unnecessary and for all purposes for which an exception has heretofore been necessary it is sufficient that a party, at the time the ruling or order of the court is made or sought, makes known to the court the action which he desires the court to take or his objection to the action of the court and the grounds therefor; but if a party has no opportunity to object to a ruling or order, the absence of an objection does not thereafter prejudice him.

Rule 52.

HARMLESS ERROR AND PLAIN ERROR

(a) Harmless Error. Any error, defect, irregularity or variance which does not affect substantial rights shall be disregarded.

(b) Plain Error. Plain errors or defects affecting substantial rights may be noticed although they were not brought to the attention of the court.

Rule 53.

REGULATION OF CONDUCT IN THE COURT ROOM

The taking of photographs in the court room during the progress of judicial proceedings or radio broadcasting of judicial proceedings from the court room shall not be permitted by the court.

Rule 54.

APPLICATION AND EXCEPTION

(a) Courts. These rules apply to all criminal proceedings in the United States District Courts; in the District Court of Guam; in the District Court for the Northern Mariana Islands, except as otherwise provided in articles IV and V of the covenant provided by the Act of March 24, 1976 (90 Stat. 263); in the District Court of the Virgin Islands; and (except as otherwise provided in the Canal Zone Code) in the United States District Court for the District of the Canal Zone; in the United States Courts of Appeals; and in the Supreme Court of the United States; except that all offenses shall continue to be prosecuted in the District Court of Guam and in the District Court of the Virgin Islands by information as heretofore except such as may be required by local law to be prosecuted by indictment by grand jury.

(b) Proceedings.

(1) Removed Proceedings. These rules apply to criminal prosecutions removed to the United States district courts from state courts and govern all procedure after removal, except that dismissal by the attorney for the prosecution shall be governed by state law.

(2) Offenses Outside a District or State. These rules apply to proceedings for offenses committed upon the high seas or elsewhere out of the jurisdiction of any particular state or district, except that such proceedings may be had in any district authorized by 18 U.S.C. § 3238.

(3) Peace Bonds. These rules do not alter the power of judges of the United States or of United States magistrates to hold to security of the peace and for good behavior under 18

U.S.C. § 3043, and under Revised Statutes, § 4069, 50 U.S.C. § 23, but in such cases the procedure shall conform to these rules so far as they are applicable.

(4) Proceedings Before United States Magistrates. Proceedings involving misdemeanors before the United States Magistrates, are governed by the Rules of Procedure for the Trial of Misdemeanors before United States Magistrates.

(5) Other Proceedings. These rules are not applicable to extradition and rendition of fugitives; civil forfeiture of property for violation of a statute of the United States; or the collection of fines and penalties. Except as provided in Rule 20(d) they do not apply to proceedings under 18 U.S.C., Chapter 403—Juvenile Delinquency—so far as they are inconsistent with that chapter. They do not apply to summary trials for offenses against the navigation laws under Revised Statutes §§ 4300–4305, 33 U.S.C. §§ 391–396, or to proceedings involving disputes between seamen under Revised Statutes, §§ 4079–4081, as amended, 22 U.S.C. §§ 256–258, or to proceedings for fishery offenses under the Act of June 28, 1937, c. 392, 50 Stat. 325–327, 16 U.S.C. §§ 772–772i, or to proceedings against a witness in a foreign country under 28 U.S.C. § 1784.

(c) Application of Terms. As used in these rules the following terms have the designated meanings.

"Act of Congress" includes any act of Congress locally applicable to and in force in the District of Columbia, in Puerto Rico, in a territory or in an insular possession.

"Attorney for the government" means the Attorney General, an authorized assistant of the Attorney General, a United States Attorney, an authorized assistant of a United States Attorney, when applicable to cases arising under the laws of Guam the Attorney General of Guam or such other person or persons as may be authorized by the laws of Guam to act therein, and when applicable to cases arising under the laws of the Northern Mariana Islands the Attorney General of the Northern Mariana Islands or any other person or persons as may be authorized by the laws of the Northern Marianas to act therein.

"Civil action" refers to a civil action in a district court.

The words "demurrer," "motion to quash," "plea in abatement," "plea in bar" and "special plea in bar," or words to the same effect, in any act of Congress shall be construed to mean the motion raising a defense or objection provided in Rule 12.

"District court" includes all district courts named in subdivision (a) of this rule.

"Federal magistrate" means a United States magistrate as defined in 28 U.S.C. §§ 631–639, a judge of the United States or another judge or judicial officer specifically empowered by statute in force in any territory or possession, the Commonwealth of Puerto Rico, or the District of Columbia, to perform a function to which a particular rule relates.

"Judge of the United States" includes a judge of a district court, court of appeals, or the Supreme Court.

"Law" includes statutes and judicial decisions.

"Magistrate" includes a United States magistrate as defined in 28 U.S.C. §§ 631–639, a judge of the United States, another judge or judicial officer specifically empowered by statute in force in any territory or possession, the Commonwealth of Puerto Rico, or the District of Columbia, to perform a function to which a particular rule relates, and a state or local judicial officer, authorized by 18 U.S.C. § 3041 to perform the functions prescribed in Rules 3, 4, and 5.

"Oath" includes affirmations.

"Petty offense" is defined in 18 U.S.C. § 1(3).

"State" includes District of Columbia, Puerto Rico, territory and insular possession.

"United States magistrate" means the officer authorized by 28 U.S.C. §§ 631–639.

Rule 55.

RECORDS

The clerk of the district court and each United States magistrate shall keep records in criminal proceedings in such form the Director of the Administrative Office of the United States Courts may prescribe. The clerk shall enter in the records each order or judgment of the court and the date such entry is made.

Rule 56.

COURTS AND CLERKS

The district court shall be deemed always open for the purpose of filing any proper paper, of issuing and returning process and of making motions and orders. The clerk's office with the clerk or a deputy in attendance shall be open during business hours on all days except Saturdays, Sundays, and legal holidays, but a court may provide by local rule or order that its clerk's office shall be open for specified hours on Saturdays or particular legal holidays other than New Year's Day, Washington's Birthday, Memorial Day, Independence Day, Labor Day, Columbus Day, Veterans Day, Thanksgiving Day, and Christmas Day.

Rule 57.

RULES OF COURT

(a) Rules by District Courts. Rules made by district courts for the conduct of criminal proceedings shall not be inconsistent with these rules. Copies of all rules made by a district court shall upon their promulgation be furnished to the Administrative Office of the United States Courts. The clerk shall make appropriate arrangements, subject to the approval of the Director of the Administrative Office of the United States Courts, to the end that all rules made as provided herein be published promptly and that copies of them be available to the public.

(b) Procedure Not Otherwise Specified. If no procedure is specifically prescribed by rule, the court may proceed in any lawful manner not inconsistent with these rules or with any applicable statute.

Rule 58.

[Abrogated]

Rule 59.

EFFECTIVE DATE

These rules take effect on the day which is 3 months subsequent to the adjournment of the first regular session of the 79th Congress, but if that day is prior to September 1, 1945, then they take effect on September 1, 1945. They govern all criminal proceedings thereafter commenced and so far as just and practicable all proceedings then pending.

[Note: For effective dates of subsequent amendments, see Editorial Note, *supra*, pp. 535–538.]

Rule 60.

TITLE

These rules may be known and cited as the Federal Rules of Criminal Procedure.

[APPENDIX OF FORMS ABROGATED]

RULES AND FORMS GOVERNING PROCEEDINGS IN THE UNITED STATES DISTRICT COURTS UNDER SECTION 2254 AND SECTION 2255 OF TITLE 28, UNITED STATES CODE

As amended to August 1, 1983

Editorial Note: By order of April 26, 1976, the Supreme Court prescribed rules governing petitions for post-conviction review and relief filed under § 2254 of Title 28 by persons in state custody and under § 2255 by persons in federal custody, the rules to take effect August 1, 1976. They were approved by the Judicial Conference of the United States and transmitted to Congress pursuant to § 2072 of Title 28 and §§ 3771 and 3772 of Title 18, United States Code. By Act of July 8, 1976, Pub.L. 94–349, 90 Stat. 822, Congress postponed the effective date of these rules indefinitely. By Act of Sept. 28, 1976, Pub.L. 94–426, 90 Stat. 1334, and Act of Oct. 21, 1976, Pub.L. 94–577, 90 Stat. 2730, the rules were approved with certain amendments, and made effective with respect to petitions under § 2254 and motions under § 2255 of Title 28 filed on or after February 1, 1977. Minor amendments to certain of these rules were submitted to Congress on April 30, 1979, and took effect on August 1, 1979. Additional amendments were transmitted to Congress on April 28, 1982, and became effective on August 1, 1982. The rules appear here as in effect on August 1, 1983.

The forms set forth below differ in some respects from those originally promulgated by the Supreme Court. According to the Committee on Rules of Practice and Procedure of the Judicial Conference of the United States, the changes in the forms were made "to conform to Congressional comments contained in Report No. 94–1471" of the Committee on the Judiciary of the House of Representatives (Sept. 2, 1976).

RULES GOVERNING SECTION 2254 CASES IN THE UNITED STATES DISTRICT COURTS

Table of Contents

RULES GOVERNING SECTION 2255 PROCEEDINGS FOR THE UNITED STATES DISTRICT COURTS

Table of Contents

RULES GOVERNING SECTION 2254 CASES IN THE UNITED STATES DISTRICT COURTS

Rule 1.

SCOPE OF RULES

(a) Applicable to cases involving custody pursuant to a judgment of a state court.—These rules govern the procedure in the United States district courts on applications under 28 U.S.C. § 2254:

(1) by a person in custody pursuant to a judgment of a state court, for a determination that such custody is in violation of the Constitution, laws, or treaties of the United States; and

(2) by a person in custody pursuant to a judgment of either a state or a federal court, who makes application for a determination that custody to which he may be subject in the future under a judgment of a state court will be in violation of the Constitution, laws, or treaties of the United States.

(b) Other situations.—In applications for habeas corpus in cases not covered by subdivision (a), these rules may be applied at the discretion of the United States district court.

Rule 2.

PETITION

(a) Applicants in present custody.—If the applicant is presently in custody pursuant to the state judgment in question, the application shall be in the form of a petition for a writ of habeas corpus in which the state officer having custody of the applicant shall be named as respondent.

(b) Applicants subject to future custody.—If the applicant is not presently in custody pursuant to the state judgment against which he seeks relief but may be subject to such custody in the future, the application shall be in the form of a petition for a writ of habeas corpus with an added prayer for appropriate relief against the judgment which he seeks to attack. In such a case the officer having present custody of the applicant and the attorney general of the state in which the judgment which he seeks to attack was entered shall each be named as respondents.

(c) Form of petition.—The petition shall be substantially in the form annexed to these rules, except that any district court may by local rule require that petitions filed with it shall be in a form prescribed by the local rule. Blank petitions in the prescribed form shall be made available without charge by the clerk of the district court to applicants upon their request. It shall specify all the grounds for relief which are available to the petitioner and of which he has or by the exercise of reasonable diligence should have knowledge and shall set forth in summary form the facts supporting each of the grounds thus specified. It shall also state the relief requested. The petition shall be typewritten or legibly handwritten and shall be signed under penalty of perjury by the petitioner.

(d) Petition to be directed to judgments of one court only.—A petition shall be limited to the assertion of a claim for relief against the judgment or judgments of a single state court (sitting in a county or other appropriate political subdivision). If a petitioner desires to attack the validity of the judgments of two or more state courts under which he is in custody or may be subject to future custody, as the case may be, he shall do so by separate petitions.

(e) Return of insufficient petition.—If a petition received by the clerk of a district court does not substantially comply with the requirements of rule 2 or rule 3, it may be returned to the petitioner, if a judge of the court so directs, together with a statement of the reason for its return. The clerk shall retain a copy of the petition.

Rule 3.

FILING PETITION

(a) Place of filing; copies; filing fee.—A petition shall be filed in the office of the clerk of the district court. It shall be accompanied by two conformed copies thereof. It shall also be accompanied by the filing fee prescribed by law unless the petitioner applies for and is given leave to prosecute the petition in forma pauperis. If the petitioner desires to prosecute the petition in forma pauperis, he shall file the affidavit required by 28 U.S.C. § 1915. In all such cases the petition shall also be accompanied by a certificate of the warden or other appropriate officer of the institution in which the petitioner is confined as to the amount of money or securities on deposit to the petitioner's credit in any account in the institution, which certificate may be considered by the court in acting upon his application for leave to proceed in forma pauperis.

(b) **Filing and service.**—Upon receipt of the petition and the filing fee, or an order granting leave to the petitioner to proceed in forma pauperis, and having ascertained that the petition appears on its face to comply with rules 2 and 3, the clerk of the district court shall file the petition and enter it on the docket in his office. The filing of the petition shall not require the respondent to answer the petition or otherwise move with respect to it unless so ordered by the court.

Rule 4.

PRELIMINARY CONSIDERATION BY JUDGE

The original petition shall be presented promptly to a judge of the district court in accordance with the procedure of the court for the assignment of its business. The petition shall be examined promptly by the judge to whom it is assigned. If it plainly appears from the face of the petition and any exhibits annexed to it that the petitioner is not entitled to relief in the district court, the judge shall make an order for its summary dismissal and cause the petitioner to be notified. Otherwise the judge shall order the respondent to file an answer or other pleading within the period of time fixed by the court or to take such other action as the judge deems appropriate. In every case a copy of the petition and any order shall be served by certified mail on the respondent and the attorney general of the state involved.

Rule 5.

ANSWER; CONTENTS

The answer shall respond to the allegations of the petition. In addition it shall state whether the petitioner has exhausted his state remedies including any post-conviction remedies available to him under the statutes or procedural rules of the state and including also his right of appeal both from the judgment of conviction and from any adverse judgment or order in the post-conviction proceeding. The answer shall indicate what transcripts (of pretrial, trial, sentencing, and post-conviction proceedings) are available, when they can be furnished, and also what proceedings have been recorded and not transcribed. There shall be attached to the answer such portions of the transcripts as the answering party deems relevant. The court on its own motion or upon request of the petitioner may order that further portions of the existing transcripts be furnished or that certain portions of the non-transcribed proceedings be transcribed and furnished. If a transcript is neither available nor procurable, a narrative summary of the evidence may be submitted. If the petitioner appealed from the judgment of conviction or from an adverse judgment or order in a post-conviction proceeding, a copy of the petitioner's brief on appeal and of the opinion of the appellate court, if any, shall also be filed by the respondent with the answer.

Rule 6.

DISCOVERY

(a) Leave of court required.—A party shall be entitled to invoke the processes of discovery available under the Federal Rules of Civil Procedure if, and to the extent that, the judge in the exercise of his discretion and for good cause shown grants leave to do so, but not otherwise. If necessary for effective utilization of discovery procedures, counsel shall be appointed by the judge for a petitioner who qualifies for the appointment of counsel under 18 U.S.C. § 3006A(g).

(b) Requests for discovery.—Requests for discovery shall be accompanied by a statement of the interrogatories or requests for admission and a list of the documents, if any, sought to be produced.

(c) Expenses.—If the respondent is granted leave to take the deposition of the petitioner or any other person the judge may as a condition of taking it direct that the respondent pay the expenses of travel and subsistence and fees of counsel for the petitioner to attend the taking of the deposition.

Rule 7.

EXPANSION OF RECORD

(a) Direction for expansion.—If the petition is not dismissed summarily the judge may direct that the record be expanded by the parties by the inclusion of additional materials relevant to the determination of the merits of the petition.

(b) Materials to be added.—The expanded record may include, without limitation, letters predating the filing of the petition in the district court, documents, exhibits, and answers under oath, if so directed, to written interrogatories propounded by the judge. Affidavits may be submitted and considered as a part of the record.

(c) Submission to opposing party.—In any case in which an expanded record is directed, copies of the letters, documents, exhibits, and affidavits proposed to be included shall be submitted to the party against whom they are to be offered, and he shall be afforded an opportunity to admit or deny their correctness.

(d) Authentication.—The court may require the authentication of any material under subdivision (b) or (c).

Rule 8.

EVIDENTIARY HEARING

(a) Determination by court.—If the petition is not dismissed at a previous stage in the proceeding, the judge, after the answer and the transcript and record of state court proceedings are filed, shall, upon a review of those proceedings and of the expanded record, if any, determine whether an evidentiary hearing is required. If it appears that an evidentiary hearing is not required, the judge shall make such disposition of the petition as justice shall require.

(b) Function of the magistrate.—

(1) When designated to do so in accordance with 28 U.S.C. § 636(b), a magistrate may conduct hearings, including evidentiary hearings, on the petition, and submit to a judge of the court proposed findings of fact and recommendations for disposition.

(2) The magistrate shall file proposed findings and recommendations with the court and a copy shall forthwith be mailed to all parties.

(3) Within ten days after being served with a copy, any party may serve and file written objections to such proposed findings and recommendations as provided by rules of court.

(4) A judge of the court shall make a de novo determination of those portions of the report or specified proposed findings or recommendations to which objection is made. A judge of the court may accept, reject, or modify in whole or in part any findings or recommendations made by the magistrate.

(c) Appointment of counsel; time for hearing.—If an evidentiary hearing is required the judge shall appoint counsel for a petitioner who qualifies for the appointment of counsel under 18 U.S.C. § 3006A(g) and the hearing shall be conducted as promptly as practicable, having regard for the need of counsel for both parties for adequate time for investigation and preparation. These rules do not limit the appointment of counsel under 18 U.S.C. § 3006A at any stage of the case if the interest of justice so requires.

Rule 9.

DELAYED OR SUCCESSIVE PETITIONS

(a) Delayed petitions.—A petition may be dismissed if it appears that the state of which the respondent is an officer has been prejudiced in its ability to respond to the petition by delay in its filing unless the petitioner shows that it is based on grounds of which he could not have had knowledge by the exercise of reasonable diligence before the circumstances prejudicial to the state occurred.

(b) Successive petitions.—A second or successive petition may be dismissed if the judge finds that it fails to allege new or different grounds for relief and the prior determination was on the merits or, if new and different grounds are alleged, the judge finds that the failure of the petitioner to assert those grounds in a prior petition constituted an abuse of the writ.

Rule 10.

POWERS OF MAGISTRATES

The duties imposed upon the judge of the district court by these rules may be performed by a United States magistrate pursuant to 28 U.S.C. § 636.

Rule 11.

FEDERAL RULES OF CIVIL PROCEDURE; EXTENT OF APPLICABILITY

The Federal Rules of Civil Procedure, to the extent that they are not inconsistent with these rules, may be applied, when appropriate, to petitions filed under these rules.

MODEL FORM FOR USE IN APPLICATIONS FOR HABEAS CORPUS UNDER 28 U.S.C. § 2254

Name ....
Prison number ....
....
Place of confinement ....
United States District Court .... District of ....
Case No. ....
(To be supplied by Clerk of U. S. District Court)

...., PETITIONER
(Full name) (Include name under which you were convicted)

v.

...., RESPONDENT

(Name of Warden, Superintendent, Jailor, or authorized person having custody of petitioner)

and

THE ATTORNEY GENERAL OF THE STATE OF ....
.........................., ADDITIONAL RESPONDENT.

(If petitioner is attacking a judgment which imposed a sentence to be served in the *future*, petitioner must fill in the name of the state where the judgment was entered. If petitioner has a sentence to be served in the *future* under a federal judgment which he wishes to attack, he should file a motion under 28 U.S. C. § 2255, in the federal court which entered the judgment.)

PETITION FOR WRIT OF HABEAS CORPUS BY A PERSON IN STATE CUSTODY

INSTRUCTIONS—READ CAREFULLY

(1) This petition must be legibly handwritten or typewritten, and signed by the petitioner under penalty of perjury. Any false statement of a material fact may serve as the basis for prosecution and conviction for perjury. All questions must be answered concisely in the proper space on the form. Where more room is needed to answer any question, use reverse side of sheet.

(2) Additional pages are not permitted. No citation of authorities need be furnished. If briefs or arguments are submitted, they should be submitted in the form of a separate memorandum.

(3) Upon receipt of a fee of $5 your petition will be filed if it is in proper order.

(4) If you do not have the necessary filing fee, you may request permission to proceed *in forma pauperis*, in which event you must execute the declaration on the last page, setting forth information establishing your inability to prepay the fees and costs or give security therefor. If you wish to proceed *in forma pauperis*, you must have an authorized officer at the penal institution complete the certificate as to the amount of money and securities on deposit to your credit in any account in the institution. If your prison account exceeds $......, you must pay the filing fee as required by the rule of the district court.

(5) Only judgments entered by one court may be challenged in a single petition. If you seek to challenge judgments entered by different courts either in the same state or in

different states, you must file separate petitions as to each court.

(6) Your attention is directed to the fact that you must include all grounds for relief and all facts supporting such grounds for relief in the petition you file seeking relief from any judgment of conviction.

(7) When the petition is fully completed, *the original and two copies must be* mailed to the Clerk of the United States District Court whose address is ....

....

(8) Petitions which do not conform to these instructions will be returned with a notation as to the deficiency.

PETITION

1. Name and location of court which entered the judgment of conviction under attack ....

2. Date of judgment of conviction ....

3. Length of sentence ....

Sentencing judge ....

4. Nature of offense or offenses for which you were convicted: ....

....

....

....

5. What was your plea? (Check one)

(a) Not guilty ☐

(b) Guilty ☐

(c) Nolo contendere ☐

If you entered a guilty plea to one count or indictment, and a not guilty plea to another count or indictment, give details: ....

....

....

6. Kind of trial: (Check one)

(a) Jury ☐

(b) Judge only ☐

7. Did you testify at the trial?

Yes ☐ No ☐

8. Did you appeal from the judgment of conviction?

   Yes ☐ No ☐

9. If you did appeal, answer the following:

   (a) Name of court ....

   (b) Result ....

   (c) Date of result ....

   If you filed a second appeal or filed a petition for certiorari in the Supreme Court, give details: ....

   ....

   ....

10. Other than a direct appeal from the judgment of conviction and sentence, have you previously filed any petitions, applications, or motions with respect to this judgment in any court, state or federal?

    Yes ☐ No ☐

11. If your answer to 10 was "yes," give the following information:

    (a) (1) Name of court ....

    (2) Nature of proceeding ....

    ....

    (3) Grounds raised ....

    ....

    ....

    ....

    (4) Did you receive an evidentiary hearing on your petition, application or motion?

    Yes ☐ No ☐

    (5) Result ....

    (6) Date of result ....

    (b) As to any second petition, application or motion give the same information:

    (1) Name of court ....

    (2) Nature of proceeding ....

    ....

    (3) Grounds raised ....

    ....

    ....

    ....

(4) Did you receive an evidentiary hearing on your petition, application or motion?

Yes ☐ No ☐

(5) Result ....

(6) Date of result ....

(c) As to any third petition, application or motion, give the same information:

(1) Name of court ....

(2) Nature of proceeding ....

....

(3) Grounds raised ....

....

....

....

(4) Did you receive an evidentiary hearing on your petition, application or motion?

Yes ☐ No ☐

(5) Result ....

(6) Date of result ....

(d) Did you appeal to the highest state court having jurisdiction the result of action taken on any petition, application or motion?

(1) First petition, etc. Yes ☐ No ☐

(2) Second petition, etc. Yes ☐ No ☐

(3) Third petition, etc. Yes ☐ No ☐

(e) If you did *not* appeal from the adverse action on any petition, application or motion, explain briefly why you did not:

....

....

12. State *concisely* every ground on which you claim that you are being held unlawfully. Summarize *briefly* the *facts* supporting each ground.

CAUTION: In order to proceed in the federal court, you must ordinarily first exhaust your state court remedies as to each ground on which you request action by the federal court. As to all grounds on which you have previously exhausted state court remedies, you should set them forth in this petition if you wish to seek federal relief. If you fail to set forth all such grounds in this petition, you may be barred from presenting them at a later date.

For your information, the following is a list of the most frequently raised grounds for relief in habeas corpus proceedings. Each statement preceded by a letter constitutes a separate ground for possible relief. You may raise any grounds which you may have other than those listed if you have exhausted all your state court remedies with respect to them. However, *you should raise in this petition all available grounds* (relating to this conviction) on which you base your allegations that you are being held in custody unlawfully.

If you select one or more of these grounds for relief, you must allege facts in support of the ground or grounds which you choose. Do not check any of the grounds listed below. The petition will be returned to you if you merely check (a) through (j) or any one of these grounds.

(a) Conviction obtained by plea of guilty which was unlawfully induced or not made voluntarily with understanding of the nature of the charge and the consequences of the plea.

(b) Conviction obtained by use of coerced confession.

(c) Conviction obtained by use of evidence gained pursuant to an unconstitutional search and seizure [where the state has not provided a full and fair hearing on the merits of the Fourth Amendment claim].

(d) Conviction obtained by use of evidence obtained pursuant to an unlawul arrest [where the state has not provided a full and fair hearing on the merits of the Fourth Amendment claim].

(e) Conviction obtained by a violation of the privilege against self-incrimination.

(f) Conviction obtained by the unconstitutional failure of the prosecution to disclose to the defendant evidence favorable to the defendant.

(g) Conviction obtained by a violation of the protection against double jeopardy.

(h) Conviction obtained by action of a grand or petit jury which was unconstitutionally selected and impanelled.

(i) Denial of effective assistance of counsel.

(j) Denial of right of appeal.

A. Ground one: ....

....

Supporting FACTS (tell your story *briefly* without citing cases or law): ....

....

....

....

....

....

B. Ground two: ....

....

Supporting FACTS (tell your story *briefly* without citing cases or law): ....

....

....

....

....

....

C. Ground three: ....

....

Supporting FACTS (tell your story *briefly* without citing cases or law): ....

....

....

....

....

D. Ground four: ....

....

Supporting FACTS (tell your story *briefly* without citing cases or law): ....

....

....

....

....

....

....

13. If any of the grounds listed in 12A, B, C, and D were not previously presented in any other court, state or federal, state *briefly* what grounds were not so presented, and give your reasons for not presenting them: ....

....

....

....

14. Do you have any petition or appeal now pending in any court, either state or federal, as to the judgment under attack?

Yes ☐ No ☐

15. Give the name and address, if known, of each attorney who represented you in the following stages of the judgment attacked herein:

(a) At preliminary hearing ....

....

(b) At arraignment and plea ....

....

(c) At trial ....

....

(d) At sentencing ....

....

(e) On appeal ....

....

(f) In any post-conviction proceeding ....

....

....

(g) On appeal from any adverse ruling in a post-conviction proceeding ....

....

....

16. Were you sentenced on more than one count of an indictment, or on more than one indictment, in the same court and at the same time?

Yes ☐ No ☐

17. Do you have any future sentence to serve after you complete the sentenced imposed by the judgment under attack?

Yes ☐ No ☐

(a) If so, give name and location of court which imposed sentence to be served in the future: ....

....

(b) And give date and length of sentence to be served in the future: ....

....

(c) Have you filed, or do you contemplate filing, any petition attacking the judgment which imposed the sentence to be served in the future?

Yes ☐ No ☐

Wherefore, petitioner prays that the Court grant petitioner relief to which he may be entitled in this proceeding.

....

Signature of Attorney (if any)

I declare (or certify, verify, or state) under penalty of perjury that the foregoing is true and correct. Executed on ....
(date)

....

Signature of Petitioner

IN FORMA PAUPERIS DECLARATION

....

[Insert appropriate court]

.... (Petitioner) v. .... (Respondent(s))	DECLARATION IN SUPPORT OF REQUEST TO PROCEED IN FORMA PAUPERIS

I, ..., declare that I am the petitioner in the above entitled case; that in support of my motion to proceed without being required to prepay fees, costs or give security therefor, I state that because of my poverty I am unable to pay the costs of said proceeding or to give security therefor; that I believe I am entitled to relief.

1. Are you presently employed? Yes ☐ No ☐

   a. If the answer is "yes," state the amount of your salary or wages per month, and give the name and address of your employer.

   ....

   ....

   b. If the answer is "no," state the date of last employment and the amount of the salary and wages per month which you received.

   ....

   ....

2. Have you received within the past twelve months any money from any of the following sources?

   a. Business, profession or form of self-employment? Yes ☐ No ☐

   b. Rent payments, interest or dividends? Yes ☐ No ☐

   c. Pensions, annuities or life insurance payments? Yes ☐ No ☐

   d. Gifts or inheritances? Yes ☐ No ☐

   e. Any other sources? Yes ☐ No ☐

   If the answer to any of the above is "yes," describe each source of money and state the amount received from each during the past twelve months. ....

   ....

   ....

   ....

3. Do you own cash, or do you have money in a checking or savings account?

   Yes ☐ No ☐ (Include any funds in prison accounts.)

   If the answer is "yes," state the total value of the items owned. ....

   ....

   ....

   ....

4. Do you own any real estate, stocks, bonds, notes, automobiles, or other valuable property (excluding ordinary household furnishings and clothing)?

   Yes ☐ No ☐

If the answer is "yes," describe the property and state its approximate value. ....

....

....

5. List the persons who are dependent upon you for support, state your relationship to those persons, and indicate how much you contribute toward their support. ....

....

....

I declare (or certify, verify, or state) under penalty of perjury that the foregoing is true and correct. Executed on

....
(date)

....
Signature of Petitioner

CERTIFICATE

I hereby certify that the petitioner herein has the sum of $...... on account to his credit at the .... institution where he is confined. I further certify that petitioner likewise has the following securities to his credit according to the records of said .... institution: ....

....

....

....

....
Authorized Officer of Institution

MODEL FORM FOR USE IN 28 U.S.C. § 2254 CASES INVOLVING A RULE 9 ISSUE

United States District Court,
. . . . District of . . . .

Case No. . . . . . .

. . . ., PETITIONER

v.

. . . ., RESPONDENT

and

. . . ., ADDITIONAL RESPONDENT

Petitioner's Response as to Why His Petition Should Not Be Barred Under Rule 9

EXPLANATION AND INSTRUCTIONS—READ CAREFULLY

(I) **Rule 9. Delayed or successive petitions.**

(a) Delayed petitions.—A petition may be dismissed if it appears that the state of which the respondent is an officer has been prejudiced in its ability to respond to the petition by delay in its filing unless the petitioner shows that it is based on grounds of which he could not have had knowledge by the exercise of reasonable diligence before the circumstances prejudicial to the state occurred.

(b) Successive petitions.—A second or successive petition may be dismissed if the judge finds that it fails to allege new or different grounds for relief and the prior determination was on the merits or, if new and different grounds are alleged, the judge finds that the failure of the petitioner to assert those grounds in a prior petition constituted an abuse of the writ.

(II) Your petition for habeas corpus has been found to be subject to dismissal under rule 9( ) for the following reason(s): . . . .

. . . .

. . . .

. . . .

(III) This form has been sent so that you may explain why your petition contains the defect(s) noted in (II) above. It is required that you fill out this form and send it back to the court within . . . . . . days.

Failure to do so will result in the automatic dismissal of your petition.

(IV) When you have fully completed this form, the original and two copies must be mailed to the Clerk of the United States District Court whose address is

....

....

(V) This response must be legibly handwritten or typewritten, and signed by the petitioner, under penalty of perjury. Any false statement of a material fact may serve as the basis for prosecution and conviction for perjury. All questions must be answered concisely in the proper space on the form.

(VI) Additional pages are not permitted except with respect to the *facts* which you rely upon in item 4 or 5 in the response. Any citation of authorities should be kept to an absolute minimum and is only appropriate if there has been a change in the law since the judgment you are attacking was rendered.

(VII) Respond to 4 *or* 5 below, not to both, unless (II) above indicates that you must answer both sections.

RESPONSE

1. Have you had the assistance of an attorney, other law-trained personnel, or writ writers since the conviction your petition is attacking was entered?

   Yes ☐ No ☐

2. If you checked "yes" above, specify as precisely as you can the period(s) of time during which you received such assistance, up to and including the present. ....

   ....

3. Describe the nature of the assistance, including the names of those who rendered it to you. ....

   ....

   ....

   ....

   ....

4. If your petition is in jeopardy because of delay prejudicial to the state under rule 9(a), explain why you feel the de-

lay has not been prejudicial and/or why the delay is excusable under the terms of 9(a). This should be done by relying upon FACTS, not your opinions or conclusions.

....

....

....

....

....

5. If your petition is in jeopardy under rule 9(b) because it asserts the same grounds as a previous petition, explain why you feel it deserves a reconsideration. If its fault under rule 9(b) is that it asserts new grounds which should have been included in a prior petition, explain why you are raising these grounds now rather than previously. Your explanation should rely on FACTS, not your opinions or conclusions. ....

....

....

....

....

....

....

....

....

I declare (or certify, verify, or state) under penalty of perjury that the foregoing is true and correct. Executed on

....

(date)

....

Signature of Petitioner

RULES GOVERNING SECTION 2255 PROCEEDINGS FOR THE UNITED STATES DISTRICT COURTS

Rule 1

SCOPE OF RULES

These rules govern the procedure in the district court on a motion under 28 U.S.C. § 2255:

(1) by a person in custody pursuant to a judgment of that court for a determination that the judgment was imposed in violation of the Constitution or laws of the United States, or that the court was without jurisdiction to impose such judgment, or that the sentence was in excess of the maximum authorized by law, or is otherwise subject to collateral attack; and

(2) by a person in custody pursuant to a judgment of a state or other federal court and subject to future custody under a judgment of the district court for a determination that such future custody will be in violation of the Constitution or laws of the United States, or that the district court was without jurisdiction to impose such judgment, or that the sentence was in excess of the maximum authorized by law, or is otherwise subject to collateral attack.

Rule 2

MOTION

(a) Nature of application for relief.—If the person is presently in custody pursuant to the federal judgment in question, or if not presently in custody may be subject to such custody in the future pursuant to such judgment, the application for relief shall be in the form of a motion to vacate, set aside, or correct the sentence.

(b) Form of motion.—The motion shall be in substantially the form annexed to these rules, except that any district court may by local rule require that motions filed with it shall be in a form prescribed by the local rule. Blank motions in the prescribed form shall be made available without charge by the clerk of the district court to applicants upon their request. It shall specify all the grounds for relief which are available to the movant and of which he has or, by the exercise of reasonable diligence, should have knowledge and shall set forth in summary form the facts supporting each of the grounds thus specified.

It shall also state the relief requested. The motion shall be typewritten or legibly handwritten and shall be signed under penalty of perjury by the petitioner.

(c) Motion to be directed to one judgment only.—A motion shall be limited to the assertion of a claim for relief against one judgment only of the district court. If a movant desires to attack the validity of other judgments of that or any other district court under which he is in custody or may be subject to future custody, as the case may be, he shall do so by separate motions.

(d) Return of insufficient motion.—If a motion received by the clerk of a district court does not substantially comply with the requirements of rule 2 or rule 3, it may be returned to the movant, if a judge of the court so directs, together with a statement of the reason for its return. The clerk shall retain a copy of the motion.

Rule 3

FILING MOTION

(a) Place of filing; copies.—A motion under these rules shall be filed in the office of the clerk of the district court. It shall be accompanied by two conformed copies thereof.

(b) Filing and service.—Upon receipt of the motion and having ascertained that it appears on its face to comply with rules 2 and 3, the clerk of the district court shall file the motion and enter it on the docket in his office in the criminal action in which was entered the judgment to which it is directed. He shall thereupon deliver or serve a copy of the motion together with a notice of its filing on the United States Attorney of the district in which the judgment under attack was entered. The filing of the motion shall not require said United States Attorney to answer the motion or otherwise move with respect to it unless so ordered by the court.

Rule 4

PRELIMINARY CONSIDERATION BY JUDGE

(a) Reference to judge; dismissal or order to answer.—The original motion shall be presented promptly to the judge of the district court who presided at the movant's trial and sentenced him, or, if the judge who imposed sentence was not the trial judge, then it shall go to the judge who was in charge of that part of the proceedings being attacked by the movant. If the appropriate judge is unavailable to consider the motion, it shall be presented to another judge of the district in accordance with the procedure of the court for the assignment of its business.

(b) **Initial consideration by judge.**—The motion, together with all the files, records, transcripts, and correspondence relating to the judgment under attack, shall be examined promptly by the judge to whom it is assigned. If it plainly appears from the face of the motion and any annexed exhibits and the prior proceedings in the case that the movant is not entitled to relief in the district court, the judge shall make an order for its summary dismissal and cause the movant to be notified. Otherwise, the judge shall order the United States Attorney to file an answer or other pleading within the period of time fixed by the court or to take such other action as the judge deems appropriate.

Rule 5

ANSWER; CONTENTS

(a) **Contents of answer.**—The answer shall respond to the allegations of the motion. In addition it shall state whether the movant has used any other available federal remedies including any prior post-conviction motions under these rules or those existing previous to the adoption of the present rules. The answer shall also state whether an evidentiary hearing was accorded the movant in a federal court.

(b) **Supplementing the answer.**—The court shall examine its files and records to determine whether it has available copies of transcripts and briefs whose existence the answer has indicated. If any of these items should be absent, the government shall be ordered to supplement its answer by filing the needed records. The court shall allow the government an appropriate period of time in which to do so, without unduly delaying the consideration of the motion.

Rule 6

DISCOVERY

(a) **Leave of court required.**—A party may invoke the processes of discovery available under the Federal Rules of Criminal Procedure or the Federal Rules of Civil Procedure or elsewhere in the usages and principles of law if, and to the extent that, the judge in the exercise of his discretion and for good cause shown grants leave to do so, but not otherwise. If necessary for effective utilization of discovery procedures, counsel shall be appointed by the judge for a movant who qualifies for appointment of counsel under 18 U.S.C. § 3006A(g).

(b) Requests for discovery.—Requests for discovery shall be accompanied by a statement of the interrogatories or requests for admission and a list of the documents, if any, sought to be produced.

(c) Expenses.—If the government is granted leave to take the deposition of the movant or any other person, the judge may as a condition of taking it direct that the government pay the expenses of travel and subsistence and fees of counsel for the movant to attend the taking of the deposition.

Rule 7

EXPANSION OF RECORD

(a) Direction for expansion.—If the motion is not dismissed summarily, the judge may direct that the record be expanded by the parties by the inclusion of additional materials relevant to the determination of the merits of the motion.

(b) Materials to be added.—The expanded record may include, without limitation, letters predating the filing of the motion in the district court, documents, exhibits, and answers under oath, if so directed, to written interrogatories propounded by the judge. Affidavits may be submitted and considered as a part of the record.

(c) Submission to opposing party.—In any case in which an expanded record is directed, copies of the letters, documents, exhibits, and affidavits proposed to be included shall be submitted to the party against whom they are to be offered, and he shall be afforded an opportunity to admit or deny their correctness.

(d) Authentication.—The court may require the authentication of any material under subdivision (b) or (c).

Rule 8

EVIDENTIARY HEARING

(a) Determination by court.—If the motion has not been dismissed at a previous stage in the proceeding, the judge, after the answer is filed and any transcripts or records of prior court actions in the matter are in his possession, shall, upon a review of those proceedings and of the expanded record, if any, determine whether an evidentiary hearing is required. If it appears that an evidentiary hearing is not required, the judge shall make such disposition of the motion as justice dictates.

(b) Function of the magistrate.—(1) When designated to do so in accordance with 28 U.S.C. § 636(b), a magistrate may conduct hearings, including evidentiary hearings, on the motion, and submit to a judge of the court proposed findings and recommendations for disposition.

(2) The magistrate shall file proposed findings and recommendations with the court and a copy shall forthwith be mailed to all parties.

(3) Within ten days after being served with a copy, any party may serve and file written objections to such proposed findings and recommendations as provided by rules of court.

(4) A judge of the court shall make a de novo determination of those portions of the report or specified proposed findings or recommendations to which objection is made. A judge of the court may accept, reject, or modify in whole or in part any findings or recommendations made by the magistrate.

(c) Appointment of counsel; time for hearing.—If an evidentiary hearing is required, the judge shall appoint counsel for a movant who qualifies for the appointment of counsel under 18 U.S.C. § 3006A(g) and the hearing shall be conducted as promptly as practicable, having regard for the need of counsel for both parties for adequate time for investigation and preparation. These rules do not limit the appointment of counsel under § 3006A at any stage of the proceeding if the interest of justice so requires.

Rule 9

DELAYED OR SUCCESSIVE MOTIONS

(a) Delayed motions.—A motion for relief made pursuant to these rules may be dismissed if it appears that the government has been prejudiced in its ability to respond to the motion by delay in its filing unless the movant shows that it is based on grounds of which he could not have had knowledge by the exercise of reasonable diligence before the circumstances prejudicial to the government occurred.

(b) Successive motions.—A second or successive motion may be dismissed if the judge finds that it fails to allege new or different grounds for relief and the prior determination was on the merits or, if new and different grounds are alleged, the judge finds that the failure of the movant to assert those grounds in a prior motion constituted an abuse of the procedure governed by these rules.

Rule 10

POWERS OF MAGISTRATES

The duties imposed upon the judge of the district court by these rules may be performed by a United States magistrate pursuant to 28 U.S.C. § 636.

Rule 11

TIME FOR APPEAL

The time for appeal from an order entered on a motion for relief made pursuant to these rules is as provided in Rule 4(a) of the Federal Rules of Appellate Procedure. Nothing in these rules shall be construed as extending the time to appeal from the original judgment of conviction in the district court.

Rule 12

FEDERAL RULES OF CRIMINAL AND CIVIL PROCEDURE; EXTENT OF APPLICABILITY

If no procedure is specifically prescribed by these rules, the district court may proceed in any lawful manner not inconsistent with these rules, or any applicable statute, and may apply the Federal Rules of Criminal Procedure or the Federal Rules of Civil Procedure, whichever it deems most appropriate, to motions filed under these rules.

MODEL FORM FOR MOTIONS UNDER 28 U.S.C. § 2255

Name ....

Prison Number ....

Place of Confinement ....

United States District Court .... District of ....

Case No. ...... (to be supplied by Clerk of Court) United States,

v.

....

(full name of movant) (Include name under which you were convicted)

(If movant has a sentence to be served in the *future* under a federal judgment which he wishes to attack, he should file a motion in the federal court which entered the judgment.)

MOTION TO VACATE, SET ASIDE, OR CORRECT SENTENCE BY A PERSON IN FEDERAL CUSTODY

INSTRUCTIONS—READ CAREFULLY

(1) This motion must be legibly handwritten or typewritten, and signed by the movant under penalty of perjury. Any false statement of a material fact may serve as the basis for prosecution and conviction for perjury. All questions must be answered concisely in the proper space on the form. Where more room is needed to answer any question use reverse side of sheets.

(2) Additional pages are not permitted. No citation of authorities need be furnished. If briefs or arguments are submitted, they should be submitted in the form of a separate memorandum.

(3) Upon receipt, your motion will be filed if it is in proper order. No fee is required with this motion.

(4) If you do not have the necessary funds for transcripts, counsel, appeal, and other costs connected with a motion of this type, you may request permission to proceed *in forma pauperis*, in which event you must execute the declaration on the last page, setting forth information establishing your inability to pay the costs. If you wish to proceed *in forma pauperis,* you must have an authorized officer at the penal institution complete the certificate as to the amount of money and securities on deposit to your credit in any account in the institution.

(5) Only judgments entered by one court may be challenged in a single motion. If you seek to challenge judgments entered by different judges or divisions either in the same district or in different districts, you must file separate motions as to each judgment.

(6) Your attention is directed to the fact that you must include all grounds for relief and all facts supporting such grounds for relief in the motion you file seeking relief from any judgment of conviction.

(7) When the motion is fully completed, the *original and two copies* must be mailed to the Clerk of the United States District Court whose address is ....
....

(8) Motions which do not conform to these instructions will be returned with a notation as to the deficiency.

MOTION

1. Name and location of court which entered the judgment of conviction under attack ....
2. Date of judgment of conviction ....
3. Length of sentence ....
   Sentencing Judge ....
4. Nature of offense or offenses for which you were convicted
   ....
   ....
   ....
5. What was your plea? (Check one)
   (a) Not guilty ☐
   (b) Guilty ☐
   (c) Nolo contendere ☐

If you entered a guilty plea to one count or indictment, and a not guilty plea to another count or indictment, give details:
....
....
....

6. Kind of trial: (Check one)
   (a) Jury ☐
   (b) Judge only ☐
7. Did you testify at the trial?
   Yes ☐ No ☐
8. Did you appeal from the judgment of conviction?
   Yes ☐ No ☐
9. If you did appeal, answer the following:
   (a) Name of court ....
   (b) Result ....
   (c) Date of result ....
10. Other than a direct appeal from the judgment of conviction and sentence, have you previously filed any petitions, applications or motions with respect to this judgment in any federal court?
    Yes ☐ No ☐

11. If your answer to 10 was "yes," give the following information:

(a) (1) Name of court ....

(2) Nature of proceeding ....

....

(3) Grounds raised ....

....

....

....

....

(4) Did you receive an evidentiary hearing on your petition, application or motion?

Yes ☐ No ☐

(5) Result ....

(6) Date of result ....

(b) As to any second petition, application or motion give the same information:

(1) Name of court ....

(2) Nature of proceeding ....

....

(3) Grounds raised ....

....

....

....

....

(4) Did you receive an evidentiary hearing on your petition, application or motion?

Yes ☐ No ☐

(5) Result ....

(6) Date of result ....

(c) As to any third petition, application or motion, give the same information:

(1) Name of court ....

(2) Nature of proceeding ....

....

(3) Grounds raised ....

....

....

....

....

(4) Did you receive an evidentiary hearing on your petition, application or motion?

Yes ☐ No ☐

(d) Did you appeal, to an appellate federal court having jurisdiction, the result of action taken on any petition, application or motion?

(1) First petition, etc. Yes ☐ No ☐

(2) Second petition, etc. Yes ☐ No ☐

(3) Third petition, etc. Yes ☐ No ☐

(e) If you did *not* appeal from the adverse action on any petition, application or motion, explain briefly why you did not:

....

....

....

12. State *concisely* every ground on which you claim that you are being held unlawfully.

CAUTION: If you fail to set forth all grounds in this motion, you may be barred from presenting additional grounds at a later date.

For your information, the following is a list of the most frequently raised grounds for relief in these proceedings. Each statement preceded by a letter constitutes a separate ground for possible relief. You may raise any grounds which you have other than those listed. However, *you should raise in this motion all available grounds* (relating to this conviction) on which you based your allegations that you are being held in custody unlawfully.

If you select one or more of these grounds for relief, you must allege facts in support of the ground or grounds which you choose. Do not check any of the grounds listed below. The petition will be returned to you if you merely check (a) through (j) or any one of these grounds.

(a) Conviction obtained by plea of guilty which was unlawfully induced or not made voluntarily or with understanding of the nature of the charge and the consequences of the plea.

(b) Conviction obtained by use of coerced confession.

(c) Conviction obtained by use of evidence gained pursuant to an unconstitutional search and seizure.

(d) Conviction obtained by use of evidence obtained pursuant to an unlawful arrest.

(e) Conviction obtained by a violation of the privilege against self-incrimination.

(f) Conviction obtained by the unconstitutional failure of the prosecution to disclose to the defendant evidence favorable to the defendant.

(g) Conviction obtained by a violation of the protection against double jeopardy.

(h) Conviction obtained by action of a grand or petit jury which was unconstitutionally selected and impanelled.

(i) Denial of effective assistance of counsel.

(j) Denial of right of appeal.

A. Ground one: ....

....

Supporting FACTS (tell your story *briefly* without citing cases or law): ....

....

....

....

....

....

....

B. Ground two: ....

....

Supporting FACTS (tell your story *briefly* without citing cases or law): ....

....

....

....

....

....

....

C. Ground three: ....

....

Supporting FACTS (tell your story *briefly* without citing cases or law): ....

....

....

....

....

....

....

D. Ground four: ....

....

Supporting FACTS (tell your story *briefly* without citing cases or law): ....

....

....

....

....

....

....

13. If any of the grounds listed in 12A, B, C, and D were not previously presented, state *briefly* what grounds were not so presented, and give your reasons for not presenting them: ....

....

....

....

....

14. Do you have any petition or appeal now pending in any court as to the judgment under attack?

Yes ☐ No ☐

15. Give the name and address, if known, of each attorney who represented you in the following stages of the judgment attacked herein:

(a) At preliminary hearing ....

....

(b) At arraignment and plea ....

....

(c) At trial ....

....

(d) At sentencing ....

....

(e) On appeal ....

....

(f) In any post-conviction proceeding ....

....

(g) On appeal from any adverse ruling in a post-conviction proceeding ....

....

16. Were you sentenced on more than one count of an indictment, or on more than one indictment, in the same court and at approximately the same time?

Yes ☐ No ☐

17. Do you have any future sentence to serve after you complete the sentence imposed by the judgment under attack?

Yes ☐ No ☐

(a) If so, give name and location of court which imposed sentence to be served in the future: ......

....

....

(b) And give date and length of sentence to be served in the future: ....

....

(c) Have you filed, or do you contemplate filing, any petition attacking the judgment which imposed the sentence to be served in the future?

Yes ☐ No ☐

Wherefore, movant prays that the Court grant him all relief to which he may be entitled in this proceeding.

....
Signature of Attorney (if any)

I declare (or certify, verify, or state) under penalty of perjury that the foregoing is true and correct. Executed on

....
(date)

....
Signature of Movant

IN FORMA PAUPERIS DECLARATION

. . . .

[Insert appropriate court]

United States v. . . . . (Movant)	DECLARATION IN SUPPORT OF REQUEST TO PROCEED *IN FORMA PAUPERIS*

I, ..., declare that I am the movant in the above entitled case; that in support of my motion to proceed without being required to prepay fees, costs or give security therefor, I state that because of my poverty, I am unable to pay the costs of said proceeding or to give security therefor; that I believe I am entitled to relief.

1. Are you presently employed? Yes ☐ No ☐
   a. If the answer is "yes," state the amount of your salary or wages per month, and give the name and address of your employer. . . . .

      . . . .

      . . . .

   b. If the answer is "no," state the date of last employment and the amount of the salary and wages per month which you received.

      . . . .

      . . . .

2. Have you received within the past twelve months any money from any of the following sources?
   a. Business, profession or form of self-employment? Yes ☐ No ☐
   b. Rent payments, interest or dividends? Yes ☐ No ☐
   c. Pensions, annuities or life insurance payments? Yes ☐ No ☐
   d. Gifts or inheritances? Yes ☐ No ☐
   e. Any other sources? Yes ☐ No ☐

   If the answer to any of the above is "yes," describe each source of money and state the amount received from each during the past twelve months. . . . .

   . . . .

   . . . .

3. Do you own any cash, or do you have money in a checking or savings account?

   Yes ☐ No ☐ (Include any funds in prison accounts)

   If the answer is "yes," state the total value of the items owned. ....

   ....

   ....

4. Do you own real estate, stocks, bonds, notes, automobiles, or other valuable property (excluding ordinary household furnishings and clothing)?

   Yes ☐ No ☐

   If the answer is "yes," describe the property and state its approximate value. ....

   ....

   ....

5. List the persons who are dependent upon you for support, state your relationship to those persons, and indicate how much you contribute toward their support. ....

   ....

   ....

I declare (or certify, verify, or state) under penalty of perjury that the foregoing is true and correct. Executed on

....
(date)

....
Signature of Movant

CERTIFICATE

I hereby certify that the movant herein has the sum of $...... on account to his credit at the .... institution where he is confined. I further certify that movant likewise has the following securities to his credit according to the records of said .... institution:

....

....

....

....

....
Authorized Officer of Institution

MODEL FORM FOR USE IN 28 U.S.C. § 2255 CASES INVOLVING A RULE 9 ISSUE

FORM NO. 9

United States District Court
.... District of ....

Case No. ......

United States
v.

....
(Name of Movant)

Movant's Response as to Why His Motion Should Not Be Barred Under Rule 9

EXPLANATION AND INSTRUCTIONS—READ CAREFULLY

(I) **Rule 9. Delayed or successive motions.**

(a) Delayed motions.—A motion for relief made pursuant to these rules may be dismissed if it appears that the government has been prejudiced in its ability to respond to the motion by delay in its filing unless the movant shows that it is based on grounds of which he could not have had knowledge by the exercise of reasonable diligence before the circumstances prejudicial to the government occurred.

(b) Successive motions.—A second or successive motion may be dismissed if the judge finds that it fails to allege new or different grounds for relief and the prior determination was on the merits or, if new and different grounds are alleged, the judge finds that the failure of the movant to assert those grounds in a prior motion constituted an abuse of the procedure governed by these rules.

(II) Your motion to vacate, set aside, or correct sentence has been found to be subject to dismissal under rule 9( ) for the following reason(s): ....
....
....
....
....

(III) This form has been sent so that you may explain why your motion contains the defect(s) noted in (II) above.

It is required that you fill out this form and send it back to the court within ...... days. Failure to do so will result in the automatic dismissal of your motion.

(IV) When you have fully completed this form, the original and two copies must be mailed to the Clerk of the United States District Court whose address is ....

....

....

(V) This response must be legibly handwritten or typewritten, and signed by the movant, under penalty of perjury. Any false statement of a material fact may serve as the basis for prosecution and conviction for perjury. All questions must be answered concisely in the proper space on the form.

(VI) Additional pages are not permitted except with respect to the *facts* which you rely upon in item 4 or 5 in the response. Any citation of authorities should be kept to an absolute minimum and is only appropriate if there has been a change in the law since the judgment you are attacking was rendered.

(VII) Respond to 4 *or* 5, not to both, unless (II) above indicates that you must answer both sections.

RESPONSE

1. Have you had the assistance of an attorney, other law-trained personnel, or writ writers since the conviction your motion is attacking was entered?

   Yes ☐ No ☐

2. If you checked "yes" above, specify as precisely as you can the period(s) of time during which you received such assistance, up to and including the present. ....

   ....

3. Describe the nature of the assistance, including the names of those who rendered it to you. ....

   ....

   ....

   ....

4. If your motion is in jeopardy because of delay prejudicial to the government under rule 9(a), explain why you feel the delay has not been prejudicial and/or why the delay

is excusable under the terms of 9(a). This should be done by relying upon FACTS, not your opinions or conclusions.

....

....

....

....

....

....

5. If your motion is in jeopardy under rule 9(b) because it asserts the same grounds as a previous motion, explain why you feel it deserves a reconsideration. If its fault under rule 9(b) is that it asserts new grounds which should have been included in a prior motion, explain why you are raising these grounds now rather than previously. Your explanation should rely on FACTS, not your opinions or conclusions. ....

....

....

....

....

....

....

....

....

I declare (or certify, verify, or state), under penalty of perjury that the foregoing is true and correct. Executed on

....
(date)

....
Signature of Movant

RULES OF PROCEDURE

FOR THE

TRIAL OF MISDEMEANORS

BEFORE

UNITED STATES MAGISTRATES

As amended to August 1, 1983

Editorial Note: Rules, made necessary by the enactment of the Federal Magistrates Act (Oct. 17, 1968, 82 Stat. 1107) 28 U.S.C. §§ 631–639, were prescribed by the Supreme Court on May 19, 1969 (395 U.S. 989), pursuant to the direction contained in 18 U.S.C. § 3402, *supra.* They became effective the same day. By order of January 27, 1971, the initial rules were superseded, and again superseded by order of April 14, 1980. Pursuant to that order, the rules set forth below became effective on June 1, 1980.

TABLE OF RULES

Rules of Procedure for the Trial of Misdemeanors before United States Magistrates

Rule

Rule 1.

SCOPE

(a) In General. These rules govern the procedure and practice for the conduct of proceedings in misdemeanor cases, including petty offenses, before United States magistrates under 18 U.S.C. § 3401, and for appeals in such cases to judges of the district courts.

(b) Applicability of Federal Rules of Criminal Procedure. Except as specifically provided by these rules, the Federal Rules of Criminal Procedure govern all proceedings except those concerning petty offenses for which no sentence of imprisonment will be imposed. Proceedings concerning petty offenses for which no sentence of imprisonment will be imposed are not governed by the Federal Rules of Criminal Procedure, except as specifically provided therein or by these rules. However, to the extent they are not inconsistent with these rules, a magistrate may follow such provisions of the Federal Rules of Criminal Procedure as he deems appropriate.

(c) Definition. The term "petty offenses for which no sentence of imprisonment will be imposed," as used in these rules, means any petty offenses, regardless of the penalty authorized by law, as to which the magistrate determines that, in the event of conviction, no sentence of imprisonment will actually be imposed in the particular case.

Rule 2.

PRETRIAL PROCEDURES

(a) Trial Document. The trial of a misdemeanor may proceed on an indictment, information, or complaint or, if it be a petty offense, on a citation or violation notice. The district court, by order or local rule, may make provision for the reference of such cases to a magistrate.

(b) Initial Appearance. At the defendant's initial appearance on a misdemeanor charge, the magistrate shall inform the defendant of the following:

(1) the charge against him, and the maximum possible penalty provided by law;

(2) his right to retain counsel;

(3) unless he is charged with a petty offense for which appointment of counsel is not required, his right to request the assignment of counsel if he is unable to obtain counsel;

(4) that he is not required to make a statement and that any statement made by him may be used against him;

(5) that he has a right to trial, judgment and sentencing before a judge of the district court;

(6) unless the offense charged is a petty offense, that he has a right to trial by jury before either a magistrate or a judge of the district court;

(7) if the prosecution is not on an indictment or information and is for a misdemeanor other than a petty offense, that he has a right to have a preliminary examination unless he consents to be tried before the magistrate; and

(8) if he is in custody, of the general circumstances under which he may secure pretrial release.

(c) Consent and Arraignment. If the defendant signs a written consent to be tried before the magistrate which specifically waives trial before a judge of the district court, the magistrate shall take the defendant's plea to the misdemeanor charge. The defendant may plead not guilty, guilty or, with the consent of the magistrate, *nolo contendere.* If the defendant pleads not guilty, the magistrate shall either conduct the trial within 30 days upon written consent of the defendant or fix a later time for the trial, giving due regard to the needs of the parties to consult with counsel and prepare for trial.

Rule 3.

ADDITIONAL PROCEDURES APPLICABLE ONLY TO PETTY OFFENSES FOR WHICH NO SENTENCE OF IMPRISONMENT WILL BE IMPOSED

(a) Failure to Consent. If the defendant charged with a petty offense for which no sentence of imprisonment will be imposed does not consent to trial before the magistrate, he shall be ordered to appear before a judge of the district court for further proceedings on notice. The file shall be transmitted forthwith to the clerk of the district court.

(b) Plea of Guilty or Nolo Contendere. No plea of guilty or *nolo contendere* to a petty offense for which no sentence of imprisonment will be imposed shall be accepted unless the magistrate is satisfied that the defendant understands the nature of the charge and the maximum possible penalty provided by law.

(c) Waiver of Venue for Plea and Sentence. A defendant charged with a petty offense for which no sentence of imprisonment will be imposed who is arrested, held, or present in a district other than that in which an indictment, information, complaint, citation or violation notice is pending against him may state in writing that he wishes to plead guilty or *nolo contendere*, to waive venue and trial in the district in which the proceeding against him is pending, and to consent to disposition of the case in the district in which he was arrested, is held, or is present. Unless the defendant thereafter pleads not guilty, the prosecution shall be had as if venue were in such district, and notice of same shall be given to the magistrate in the district where the proceeding was originally commenced. The defendant's statement that he wishes to plead guilty or *nolo contendere* shall not be used against him.

(d) Sentence. If the defendant charged with a petty offense for which no sentence of imprisonment will be imposed pleads guilty or *nolo contendere* or is found guilty after trial, the magistrate shall afford him an opportunity to be heard in mitigation. The magistrate shall then immediately proceed to sentence the defendant, except that in the discretion of the magistrate sentencing may be continued to allow an investigation by the probation service or the submission of additional information by either party.

(e) Notification of Right to Appeal. After imposing sentence in a case which has gone to trial on a plea of not guilty, the magistrate shall advise the defendant of his right to appeal.

Rule 4.

SECURING DEFENDANT'S APPEARANCE; PAYMENT IN LIEU OF APPEARANCE

(a) Forfeiture of Collateral. When authorized by local rules of the district court, payment of a fixed sum may be accepted in suitable types of misdemeanor cases in lieu of appearance and as authorizing the termination of the proceedings. Such local rules may make provision for increases in such fixed sums not to exceed the maximum fine which could be imposed upon conviction.

(b) Notice to Appear. If a defendant fails to pay a fixed sum, request a hearing, or appear in response to a citation or violation notice, the clerk of the district court or a magistrate may issue a notice for the defendant to appear before a magistrate on a date certain. The notice may also afford the defendant an additional opportunity to pay a fixed sum in lieu of appearance, and shall be served upon the defendant by mailing a copy to his last known address.

(c) Summons or Warrant. Upon an indictment or a showing by one of the other documents specified in Rule 2(a) of probable cause to believe that a misdemeanor has been committed and that the defendant has committed it, a magistrate may issue an arrest warrant or, if no warrant is requested by the attorney for the government, a summons. The showing shall be made in writing upon oath or under penalty of perjury, but the affiant need not appear before the magistrate. If the defendant fails to appear before the magistrate in response to a summons, the magistrate may summarily issue a warrant for his immediate arrest and appearance before the magistrate.

Rule 5.

RECORD

Proceedings under these rules shall be taken down by a reporter or recorded by suitable sound recording equipment. In the discretion of the magistrate or, in the case of a misdemeanor other than a petty offense, on timely request of either party as provided by local rule, the proceedings shall be taken down by a reporter. With the written consent of the defendant, the keeping of a verbatim record may be waived in petty offense cases.

Rule 6.

NEW TRIAL

The magistrate, on motion of a defendant, may grant a new trial if required in the interest of justice. The magistrate may vacate the judgment if entered, take additional testimony, and direct the entry of a new judgment. A motion for a new trial based on the ground of newly discovered evidence may be made only before or within two years after final judgment, but if an appeal is pending the magistrate may grant the motion only on remand of the case. A motion for a new trial based on any other grounds shall be made within 7 days after a finding of guilty or within such further time as the magistrate may fix during the 7-day period.

Rule 7.

APPEAL

(a) Interlocutory Appeal. A decision or order by a magistrate which, if made by a judge of the district court, could be appealed by the government or defendant under any provision of law, shall be subject to an appeal to a judge of the district court provided such appeal is taken within 10 days of the entry of the decision or order. An appeal shall be taken by filing with the clerk of the district court a statement specifying the decision or order from which an appeal is taken, and by serving a copy of the statement upon the adverse party, personally or by mail, and by filing a copy with the magistrate.

(b) Appeal from Conviction. An appeal from a judgment of conviction by a magistrate to a judge of the district court shall be taken within 10 days after entry of the judgment. An appeal shall be taken by filing with the clerk of the district court a statement specifying the judgment from which an appeal is taken, and by serving a copy of the statement upon the United States Attorney, personally or by mail, and by filing a copy with the magistrate.

(c) Record. The record shall consist of the original papers and exhibits in the case together with any transcript, tape, or other recording of the proceedings and a certified copy of the docket entries which shall be transmitted promptly by the magistrate to the clerk of the district court. For purposes of the appeal, a copy of the record of such proceedings shall be made available at the expense of the United States to a person who establishes by affidavit that he is unable to pay or give security therefor, and the expense of such copy shall be paid by the Director of the Administrative Office of the United States Courts.

(d) Stay of Execution; Release Pending Appeal. The provisions of Rule 38(a) of the Federal Rules of Criminal Procedure relating to stay of execution shall be applicable to a judgment of conviction entered by a magistrate. The defendant may be released pending appeal by the magistrate or a district judge in accordance with the provisions of law relating to release pending appeal from a judgment of conviction of a district court.

(e) Scope of Appeal. The defendant shall not be entitled to a trial *de novo* by a judge of the district court. The scope of appeal shall be the same as on an appeal from a judgment of a district court to a court of appeals.

Rule 8.

LOCAL RULES

Rules adopted by a district court for the conduct of trials before magistrates shall not be inconsistent with these rules. Copies of all rules made by a district court shall, upon their promulgation, be filed with the clerk of the district court and furnished to the Administrative Office of the United States Courts.

FEDERAL RULES
OF
APPELLATE PROCEDURE

As amended to August 1, 1983

Editorial Note: The Federal Rules of Appellate Procedure were prescribed by the Supreme Court on December 4, 1967, pursuant to 18 U.S.C.A. §§ 3771 and 3772 and 28 U.S.C.A. §§ 2072 and 2075. They were transmitted to Congress on the same date and resubmitted January 15, 1968, becoming effective July 1, 1968 (389 U.S. 1063). A few minor amendments were submitted to Congress on March 30, 1970, becoming effective July 1, 1970 (398 U.S. 971); on March 1, 1971, effective July 1, 1971 (401 U.S. 1029); on April 24, 1972, effective October 1, 1972 (406 U.S. 1005); and on April 30, 1979, effective August 1, 1979 (441 U.S. 971).

As previously noted, these rules supersede Chapter IX of the Rules of Civil Procedure for the United States District Courts, containing former Rules 72–76, and Form 27. They similarly supersede Chapter VIII of the Rules of Criminal Procedure for the United States District Courts, containing former Rules 37–39, and Forms 26 and 27, except that Rule 38(a) is preserved.

Under Rule 47, the rules of the various courts of appeals are superseded only to the extent that they are inconsistent with these rules.

TABLE OF RULES

Title I. Applicability of Rules

Title II. Appeals from Judgments and Orders of District Courts

Title II. Appeals from Judgments and Orders of District Courts—Continued

Title III. Review of Decisions of the Tax Court of the United States

Title IV. Review and Enforcement of Orders of Administrative Agencies, Boards, Commissions and Officers

Title V. Extraordinary Writs

Title VI. Habeas Corpus; Proceedings in Forma Pauperis

Title VII. General Provisions

TITLE I. APPLICABILITY OF RULES

Rule 1.

SCOPE OF RULES

(a) Scope of Rules. These rules govern procedure in appeals to United States courts of appeals from the United States district courts and the United States Tax Court; in proceedings in the courts of appeals for review or enforcement of orders of administrative agencies, boards, commissions and officers of the United States; and in applications for writs or other relief which a court of appeals or a judge thereof is competent to give. When these rules provide for the making of a motion or application in the district court, the procedure for making such motion or application shall be in accordance with the practice of the district court.

(b) Rules Not to Affect Jurisdiction. These rules shall not be construed to extend or limit the jurisdiction of the courts of appeals as established by law.

Rule 2.

SUSPENSION OF RULES

In the interest of expediting decision, or for other good cause shown, a court of appeals may, except as otherwise provided in

Rule 26(b), suspend the requirements or provisions of any of these rules in a particular case on application of a party or on its own motion and may order proceedings in accordance with its direction.

TITLE II. APPEALS FROM JUDGMENTS AND ORDERS OF DISTRICT COURTS

Rule 3.

APPEAL AS OF RIGHT—HOW TAKEN

(a) Filing the Notice of Appeal. An appeal permitted by law as of right from a district court to a court of appeals shall be taken by filing a notice of appeal with the clerk of the district court within the time allowed by Rule 4. Failure of an appellant to take any step other than the timely filing of a notice of appeal does not affect the validity of the appeal, but is ground only for such action as the court of appeals deems appropriate, which may include dismissal of the appeal. Appeals by permission under 28 U.S.C. § 1292(b) and appeals by allowance in bankruptcy shall be taken in the manner prescribed by Rule 5 and Rule 6 respectively.

(b) Joint or Consolidated Appeals. If two or more persons are entitled to appeal from a judgment or order of a district court and their interests are such as to make joinder practicable, they may file a joint notice of appeal, or may join in appeal after filing separate timely notices of appeal, and they may thereafter proceed on appeal as a single appellant. Appeals may be consolidated by order of the court of appeals upon its own motion or upon motion of a party, or by stipulation of the parties to the several appeals.

(c) Content of the Notice of Appeal. The notice of appeal shall specify the party or parties taking the appeal; shall designate the judgment, order or part thereof appealed from; and shall name the court to which the appeal is taken. Form 1 in the Appendix of Forms is a suggested form of a notice of appeal. An appeal shall not be dismissed for informality of form or title of the notice of appeal.

(d) Service of the Notice of Appeal. The clerk of the district court shall serve notice of the filing of a notice of appeal by mailing a copy thereof to counsel of record of each party other than the appellant, or, if a party is not represented by counsel, to the party at his last known address; and the clerk shall transmit forthwith a copy of the notice of appeal and of the docket entries to the clerk of the court of appeals named in the notice. When an appeal is taken by a defendant in a criminal case, the clerk shall also serve a copy of the notice of appeal upon him, either by personal service or by mail addressed to him. The clerk shall note on each copy served the date on which the notice of appeal was filed. Failure of the clerk to serve notice shall not affect the validity of the appeal. Service shall be sufficient notwithstanding the death of a party or his counsel. The clerk shall note in the docket the names of the parties to whom he mails copies, with the date of mailing.

(e) Payment of Fees. Upon the filing of any separate or joint notice of appeal from the district court, the appellant shall pay to the clerk of the district court such fees as are established by statute, and also the docket fee prescribed by the Judicial Conference of the United States, the latter to be received by the clerk of the district court on behalf of the court of appeals.

Rule 4.

APPEAL AS OF RIGHT—WHEN TAKEN

(a) Appeals in Civil Cases.

(1) In a civil case in which an appeal is permitted by law as of right from a district court to a court of appeals the notice of appeal required by Rule 3 shall be filed with the clerk of the district court within 30 days after the date of entry of the judgment or order appealed from; but if the United States or an officer or agency thereof is a party, the notice of appeal may be filed by any party within 60 days after such entry. If a notice of appeal is mistakenly filed in the court of appeals, the clerk of the court of appeals shall note thereon the date on which it was received and transmit it to the clerk of the district court and it shall be deemed filed in the district court on the date so noted.

(2) Except as provided in (a)(4) of this Rule 4, a notice of appeal filed after the announcement of a decision or order but before the entry of the judgment or order shall be treated as filed after such entry and on the day thereof.

(3) If a timely notice of appeal is filed by a party, any other party may file a notice of appeal within 14 days after the date on which the first notice of appeal was filed, or within the time otherwise prescribed by this Rule 4(a), whichever period last expires.

(4) If a timely motion under the Federal Rules of Civil Procedure is filed in the district court by any party: (i) for judgment under Rule 50(b); (ii) under Rule 52(b) to amend or

make additional findings of fact, whether or not an alteration of the judgment would be required if the motion is granted; (iii) under Rule 59 to alter or amend the judgment; or (iv) under Rule 59 for a new trial, the time for appeal for all parties shall run from the entry of the order denying a new trial or granting or denying any other such motion. A notice of appeal filed before the disposition of any of the above motions shall have no effect. A new notice of appeal must be filed within the prescribed time measured from the entry of the order disposing of the motion as provided above. No additional fees shall be required for such filing.

(5) The district court, upon a showing of excusable neglect or good cause, may extend the time for filing a notice of appeal upon motion filed not later than 30 days after the expiration of the time prescribed by this Rule 4(a). Any such motion which is filed before expiration of the prescribed time may be *ex parte* unless the court otherwise requires. Notice of any such motion which is filed after expiration of the prescribed time shall be given to the other parties in accordance with local rules. No such extension shall exceed 30 days past such prescribed time or 10 days from the date of entry of the order granting the motion, whichever occurs later.

(6) A judgment or order is entered within the meaning of this Rule 4(a) when it is entered in compliance with Rules 58 and 79(a) of the Federal Rules of Civil Procedure.

(b) Appeals in Criminal Cases. In a criminal case the notice of appeal by a defendant shall be filed in the district court within 10 days after the entry of the judgment or order appealed from. A notice of appeal filed after the announcement of a decision, sentence or order but before entry of the judgment or order shall be treated as filed after such entry and on the day thereof. If a timely motion in arrest of judgment or for a new trial on any ground other than newly discovered evidence has been made, an appeal from a judgment of conviction may be taken within 10 days after the entry of an order denying the motion. A motion for a new trial based on the ground of newly discovered evidence will similarly extend the time for appeal from a judgment of conviction if the motion is made before or within 10 days after entry of the judgment. When an appeal by the government is authorized by statute, the notice of appeal shall be filed in the district court within 30 days after the entry of the judgment or order appealed from. A judgment or order is entered within the meaning of this subdivision when it is entered in the criminal docket. Upon a showing of excusable neglect the district court may, before or after the time has expired, with or without motion and notice, extend the time for filing a notice of appeal for a period not to exceed 30 days from the expiration of the time otherwise prescribed by this subdivision.

Rule 5.

APPEALS BY PERMISSION UNDER 28 U.S.C. § 1292(b)

(a) Petition for Permission to Appeal. An appeal from an interlocutory order containing the statement prescribed by 28 U.S.C. § 1292(b) may be sought by filing a petition for permission to appeal with the clerk of the court of appeals within 10 days after the entry of such order in the district court with proof of service on all other parties to the action in the district court. An order may be amended to include the prescribed statement at any time, and permission to appeal may be sought within 10 days after entry of the order as amended.

(b) Content of Petition; Answer. The petition shall contain a statement of the facts necessary to an understanding of the controlling question of law determined by the order of the district court; a statement of the question itself; and a statement of the reasons why a substantial basis exists for a difference of opinion on the question and why an immediate appeal may materially advance the termination of the litigation. The petition shall include or have annexed thereto a copy of the order from which appeal is sought and of any findings of fact, conclusions of law and opinion relating thereto. Within 7 days after service of the petition an adverse party may file an answer in opposition. The application and answer shall be submitted without oral argument unless otherwise ordered.

(c) Form of Papers; Number of Copies. All papers may be typewritten. Three copies shall be filed with the original, but the court may require that additional copies be furnished.

(d) Grant of Permission; Cost Bond; Filing of Record. Within 10 days after the entry of an order granting permission to appeal the appellant shall (1) pay to the clerk of the district court the fees established by statute and the docket fee prescribed by the Judicial Conference of the United States and (2) file a bond for costs if required pursuant to Rule 7. The clerk of the district court shall notify the clerk of the court of appeals of the payment of the fees. Upon receipt of such notice the clerk of the court of appeals shall enter the appeal upon the docket. The record shall be transmitted and filed in accordance with Rules 11 and 12(b). A notice of appeal need not be filed.

Rule 6.

APPEALS BY ALLOWANCE IN BANKRUPTCY PROCEEDINGS

(a) Petition for Allowance. Allowance of an appeal under section 24 of the Bankruptcy Act (11 U.S.C. § 47) from orders, decrees, or judgments of a district court involving less than $500, or from an order making or refusing to make allowances of compensation or reimbursement under sections 250 or 498 thereof (11 U.S.C. § 650, § 898) shall be sought by filing a petition for allowance with the clerk of the court of appeals within the time provided by Rule 4(a) for filing a notice of appeal, with proof of service on all parties to the action in the district court. A notice of appeal need not be filed.

(b) Content of Petition; Answer. The petition shall contain a statement of the facts necessary to an understanding of the questions to be presented by the appeal; a statement of those questions and of the relief sought; a statement of the reasons why in the opinion of the petitioner the appeal should be allowed; and a copy of the order, decree or judgment complained of and of any opinion or memorandum relating thereto. Within 7 days after service of the petition an adverse party may file an answer in opposition. The petition and answer shall be submitted without oral argument unless otherwise ordered.

(c) Form of Papers; Number of Copies. All papers may be typewritten. Three copies shall be filed with the original, but the court may require that additional copies be furnished.

(d) Allowance of the Appeal; Fees; Cost Bond; Filing of Record. Within 10 days after the entry of an order granting permission to appeal the appellant shall (1) pay to the clerk of the district court the fees established by statute and the docket fee prescribed by the Judicial Conference of the United States and (2) file a bond for costs if required pursuant to Rule 7. The clerk of the district court shall notify the clerk of the court of appeals of the payment of the fees. Upon receipt of such notice the clerk of the court of appeals shall enter the appeal upon the docket. The record shall be transmitted and filed in accordance with Rules 11 and 12(b). A notice of appeal need not be filed.

Rule 7.

BOND FOR COSTS ON APPEAL IN CIVIL CASES

The district court may require an appellant to file a bond or provide other security in such form and amount as it finds necessary to ensure payment of costs on appeal in a civil case. The provisions of Rule 8(b) apply to a surety upon a bond given pursuant to this rule.

Rule 8.

STAY OR INJUNCTION PENDING APPEAL

(a) Stay Must Ordinarily Be Sought in the First Instance in District Court; Motion for Stay in Court of Appeals. Application for a stay of the judgment or order of a district court pending appeal, or for approval of a supersedeas bond, or for an order suspending, modifying, restoring or granting an injunction during the pendency of an appeal must ordinarily be made in the first instance in the district court. A motion for such relief may be made to the court of appeals or to a judge thereof, but the motion shall show that application to the district court for the relief sought is not practicable, or that the district court has denied an application, or has failed to afford the relief which the applicant requested, with the reasons given by the district court for its action. The motion shall also show the reasons for the relief requested and the facts relied upon, and if the facts are subject to dispute the motion shall be supported by affidavits or other sworn statements or copies thereof. With the motion shall be filed such parts of the record as are relevant. Reasonable notice of the motion shall be given to all parties. The motion shall be filed with the clerk and normally will be considered by a panel or division of the court, but in exceptional cases where such procedure would be impracticable due to the requirements of time, the application may be made to and considered by a single judge of the court.

(b) Stay May Be Conditioned upon Giving of Bond; Proceedings Against Sureties. Relief available in the court of appeals under this rule may be conditioned upon the filing of a bond or other appropriate security in the district court. If security is given in the form of a bond or stipulation or other undertaking with one or more sureties, each surety submits himself to the jurisdiction of the district court and irrevocably appoints the clerk of the district court as his agent upon whom any papers affecting his liability on the bond or undertaking may be served. His liability may be enforced on motion in the district court without the necessity of an independent action. The motion and such notice of the motion as the district court prescribes may be served on the clerk of the district court, who shall forthwith mail copies to the sureties if their addresses are known.

(c) Stays in Criminal Cases. Stays in criminal cases shall be had in accordance with the provisions of Rule 38(a) of the Federal Rules of Criminal Procedure.

Rule 9.

RELEASE IN CRIMINAL CASES

(a) Appeals from Orders Respecting Release Entered Prior to a Judgment of Conviction. An appeal authorized by law from an order refusing or imposing conditions of release shall be determined promptly. Upon entry of an order refusing or imposing conditions of release, the district court shall state in writing the reasons for the action taken. The appeal shall be heard without the necessity of briefs after reasonable notice to the appellee upon such papers, affidavits, and portions of the record as the parties shall present. The court of appeals or a judge thereof may order the release of the appellant pending the appeal.

(b) Release Pending Appeal from a Judgment of Conviction. Application for release after a judgment of conviction shall be made in the first instance in the district court. If the district court refuses release pending appeal, or imposes conditions of release, the court shall state in writing the reasons for the action taken. Thereafter, if an appeal is pending, a motion for release, or for modification of the conditions of release, pending review may be made to the court of appeals or to a judge thereof. The motion shall be determined promptly upon such papers, affidavits, and portions of the record as the parties shall present and after reasonable notice to the appellee. The court of appeals or a judge thereof may order the release of the appellant pending disposition of the motion.

(c) Criteria for Release. The decision as to release pending appeal shall be made in accordance with Title 18, U.S.C. § 3148. The burden of establishing that the defendant will not flee or pose a danger to any other person or to the community rests with the defendant.

Rule 10.

THE RECORD ON APPEAL

(a) Composition of the Record on Appeal. The original papers and exhibits filed in the district court, the transcript of proceedings, if any, and a certified copy of the docket entries prepared by the clerk of the district court shall constitute the record on appeal in all cases.

(b) The Transcript of Proceedings; Duty of Appellant to Order; Notice to Appellee if Partial Transcript is Ordered.

(1) Within 10 days after filing the notice of appeal the appellant shall order from the reporter a transcript of such parts of the proceedings not already on file as he deems necessary, subject to local rules of the courts of appeals. The order shall be in writing and within the same period a copy shall be filed with the clerk of the district court. If funding is to come from the United States under the Criminal Justice Act, the order shall so state. If no such parts of the proceedings are to be ordered, within the same period the appellant shall file a certificate to that effect.

(2) If the appellant intends to urge on appeal that a finding or conclusion is unsupported by the evidence or is contrary to the evidence, he shall include in the record a transcript of all evidence relevant to such finding or conclusion.

(3) Unless the entire transcript is to be included, the appellant shall, within the 10 days time provided in (b)(1) of this Rule 10, file a statement of the issues he intends to present on the appeal and shall serve on the appellee a copy of the order or certificate and of the statement. If the appellee deems a transcript of other parts of the proceedings to be necessary, he shall, within 10 days after the service of the order or certificate and the statement of the appellant, file and serve on the appellant a designation of additional parts to be included. Unless within 10 days after service of such designation the appellant has ordered such parts, and has so notified the appellee, the appellee may within the following 10 days either order the parts or move in the district court for an order requiring the appellant to do so.

(4) At the time of ordering, a party must make satisfactory arrangements with the reporter for payment of the cost of the transcript.

(c) Statement of the Evidence or Proceedings When no Report Was Made or When the Transcript Is Unavailable. If no report of the evidence or proceedings at a hearing or trial was made, or if a transcript is unavailable, the appellant may prepare a statement of the evidence or proceedings from the best available means, including his recollection. The statement shall be served on the appellee, who may serve objections or propose amendments thereto within 10 days after service. Thereupon the statement and any objections or proposed amendments shall be submitted to the district court for settlement and approval and as settled and approved shall be included by the clerk of the district court in the record on appeal.

(d) Agreed Statement as the Record on Appeal. In lieu of the record on appeal as defined in subdivision (a) of this rule, the parties may prepare and sign a statement of the case showing how the issues presented by the appeal arose and were decided in the district court and setting forth only so many of the facts averred and proved or sought to be proved as are essential to a decision of the issues presented. If the statement conforms to the truth, it, together with such additions as the court may consider necessary fully to present the issues raised by the appeal, shall be approved by the district court and shall then be certified to the court of appeals as the record on appeal and transmitted thereto by the clerk of the district court within the time provided by Rule 11. Copies of the agreed statement may be filed as the appendix required by Rule 30.

(e) Correction or Modification of the Record. If any difference arises as to whether the record truly discloses what occurred in the district court, the difference shall be submitted to and settled by that court and the record made to conform to the truth. If anything material to either party is omitted from the record by error or accident or is misstated therein, the parties by stipulation, or the district court, either before or after the record is transmitted to the court of appeals, or the court of appeals, on proper suggestion or of its own initiative, may direct that the omission or misstatement be corrected, and if necessary that a supplemental record be certified and transmitted. All other questions as to the form and content of the record shall be presented to the court of appeals.

Rule 11.

TRANSMISSION OF THE RECORD

(a) Duty of Appellant. After filing the notice of appeal the appellant, or in the event that more than one appeal is taken, each appellant, shall comply with the provisions of Rule 10(b) and shall take any other action necessary to enable the clerk to assemble and transmit the record. A single record shall be transmitted.

(b) Duty of Reporter to Prepare and File Transcript; Notice to Court of Appeals; Duty of Clerk to Transmit the Record. Upon receipt of an order for a transcript, the reporter shall acknowledge at the foot of the order the fact that he has received it and the date on which he expects to have the transcript completed and shall transmit the order, so endorsed, to the clerk of the court of appeals. If the transcript cannot be completed within 30 days of receipt of the order the reporter shall request an extension of time from the clerk of the court of appeals and the action of the clerk of the court of appeals shall be entered on the docket and the parties notified. In the event of the failure of the reporter to file the transcript within the time allowed, the clerk of the court of appeals shall notify the district judge and take such other steps as may be directed by the court of appeals. Upon completion of the transcript the reporter shall file it with the clerk of the district court and shall notify the clerk of the court of appeals that he has done so.

When the record is complete for purposes of the appeal, the clerk of the district court shall transmit it forthwith to the clerk of the court of appeals. The clerk of the district court shall number the documents comprising the record and shall transmit with the record a list of documents correspondingly numbered and identified with reasonable definiteness. Documents of unusual bulk or weight, physical exhibits other than documents, and such other parts of the record as the court of appeals may designate by local rule, shall not be transmitted by the clerk unless he is directed to do so by a party or by the clerk of the court of appeals. A party must make advance arrangements with the clerks for the transportation and receipt of exhibits of unusual bulk or weight.

(c) Temporary Retention of Record in District Court for Use in Preparing Appellate Papers. Notwithstanding the provisions of (a) and (b) of this Rule 11, the parties may stipulate, or the district court on motion of any party may order, that the clerk of the district court shall temporarily retain the record for use by the parties in preparing appellate papers. In that event the clerk of the district court shall certify to the clerk of the court of appeals that the record, including the transcript or parts thereof designated for inclusion and all necessary exhibits, is complete for purposes of the appeal. Upon receipt of the brief of the appellee, or at such earlier time as the parties may agree or the court may order, the appellant shall request the clerk of the district court to transmit the record.

(d) [Abrogated.]

(e) Retention of the Record in the District Court by Order of Court. The court of appeals may provide by rule or order that a certified copy of the docket entries shall be transmitted in lieu of the entire record, subject to the right of any party to request at any time during the pendency of the appeal that designated parts of the record be transmitted.

If the record or any part thereof is required in the district court for use there pending the appeal, the district court may make an order to that effect, and the clerk of the district court shall retain the record or parts thereof subject to the request of the court of appeals, and shall transmit a copy of the order and of the docket entries together with such parts of the original record as the district court shall allow and copies of such parts as the parties may designate.

(f) Stipulation of Parties That Parts of the Record Be Retained in the District Court. The parties may agree by written stipulation filed in the district court that designated parts of the record shall be retained in the district court unless thereafter the court of appeals shall order or any party shall request their transmittal. The parts thus designated shall nevertheless be a part of the record on appeal for all purposes.

(g) Record for Preliminary Hearing in the Court of Appeals. If prior to the time the record is transmitted a party desires to make in the court of appeals a motion for dismissal, for release, for a stay pending appeal, for additional security on the bond on appeal or on a supersedeas bond, or for any intermediate order, the clerk of the district court at the request of any party shall transmit to the court of appeals such parts of the original record as any party shall designate.

Rule 12.

DOCKETING THE APPEAL; FILING OF THE RECORD

(a) Docketing the Appeal. Upon receipt of the copy of the notice of appeal and of the docket entries, transmitted by the clerk of the district court pursuant to Rule 3(d), the clerk of the court of appeals shall thereupon enter the appeal upon the docket. An appeal shall be docketed under the title given to the action in the district court, with the appellant identified as such, but if such title does not contain the name of the appellant, his name, identified as appellant, shall be added to the title.

(b) Filing the Record, Partial Record, or Certificate. Upon receipt of the record transmitted pursuant to Rule 11(b), or the partial record transmitted pursuant to Rule 11(e), (f), or (g), or the clerk's certificate under Rule 11(c), the clerk of the court of appeals shall file it and shall immediately give notice to all parties of the date on which it was filed.

TITLE III. REVIEW OF DECISIONS OF THE TAX COURT OF THE UNITED STATES

Rule 13.

REVIEW OF DECISIONS OF THE TAX COURT

(a) How Obtained; Time for Filing Notice of Appeal. Review of a decision of the United States Tax Court shall be obtained by filing a notice of appeal with the clerk of the Tax Court within 90 days after the decision of the Tax Court is entered. If a timely notice of appeal is filed by one party, any other party may take an appeal by filing a notice of appeal within 120 days after the decision of the Tax Court is entered.

The running of the time for appeal is terminated as to all parties by a timely motion to vacate or revise a decision made pursuant to the Rules of Practice of the Tax Court. The full time for appeal commences to run and is to be computed from the entry of an order disposing of such motion, or from the entry of decision, whichever is later.

(b) Notice of Appeal—How Filed. The notice of appeal may be filed by deposit in the office of the clerk of the Tax Court in the District of Columbia or by mail addressed to the clerk. If a notice is delivered to the clerk by mail and is received after expiration of the last day allowed for filing, the postmark date shall be deemed to be the date of delivery, subject to the provisions of § 7502 of the Internal Revenue Code of 1954, as amended, and the regulations promulgated pursuant thereto.

(c) Content of the Notice of Appeal; Service of the Notice; Effect of Filing and Service of the Notice. The content of the notice of appeal, the manner of its service, and the effect of the filing of the notice and of its service shall be as prescribed by Rule 3. Form 2 in the Appendix of Forms is a suggested form of the notice of appeal.

(d) The Record on Appeal; Transmission of the Record; Filing of the Record. The provisions of Rules 10, 11 and 12 respecting the record and the time and manner of its transmission and filing and the docketing of the appeal in the court of appeals in cases on appeal from the district courts shall govern in cases on appeal from the Tax Court. Each reference in those rules and in Rule 3 to the district court and to the clerk of the district court shall be read as a reference to the Tax Court and to the clerk of the Tax Court respectively. If appeals are taken from a decision of the Tax Court to more than one court of appeals, the original record shall be transmitted to the court of appeals named in the first notice of appeal filed. Provision for the record in any other appeal shall be made upon appropriate application by the appellant to the court of appeals to which such other appeal is taken

Rule 14.

APPLICABILITY OF OTHER RULES TO REVIEW OF DECISIONS OF THE TAX COURT

All provisions of these rules are applicable to review of a decision of the Tax Court, except that Rules 4–9, Rules 15–20, and Rules 22 and 23 are not applicable.

TITLE IV. REVIEW AND ENFORCEMENT OF ORDERS OF ADMINISTRATIVE AGENCIES, BOARDS, COMMISSIONS AND OFFICERS

Rule 15.

REVIEW OR ENFORCEMENT OF AGENCY ORDERS—HOW OBTAINED; INTERVENTION

(a) Petition for Review of Order; Joint Petition. Review of an order of an administrative agency, board, commission or officer (hereinafter, the term "agency" shall include agency, board, commission or officer) shall be obtained by filing with the clerk of a court of appeals which is authorized to review such order, within the time prescribed by law, a petition to enjoin, set aside, suspend, modify or otherwise review, or a notice of appeal, whichever form is indicated by the applicable statute (hereinafter, the term "petition for review" shall include a petition to enjoin, set aside, suspend, modify or otherwise review, or a notice of appeal). The petition shall specify the parties seeking review and shall designate the respondent and the order or part thereof to be reviewed. Form 3 in the Appendix of Forms is a suggested form of a petition for review. In each case the agency shall be named respondent. The United States shall also be deemed a respondent if so required by statute, even though not so designated in the petition. If two or more persons are entitled to petition the same court for review of the same order and their interests are such as to make joinder practicable, they may file a joint petition for review and may thereafter proceed as a single petitioner.

(b) Application for Enforcement of Order; Answer; Default; Cross-Application for Enforcement. An application for enforcement of an order of an agency shall be filed with the clerk of a court of appeals which is authorized to enforce the order. The application shall contain a concise statement of the proceedings in which the order was entered, the facts upon which venue is based, and the relief prayed. Within 20 days after the application is filed, the respondent shall serve on the petitioner and file with the clerk an answer to the application. If the respondent fails to file an answer within such time, judgment will be awarded for the relief prayed. If a petition is filed for review of an order which the court has jurisdiction to enforce, the respondent may file a cross-application for enforcement.

(c) Service of Petition or Application. A copy of a petition for review or of an application or cross-application for enforcement of an order shall be served by the clerk of the court of appeals on each respondent in the manner prescribed by Rule 3(d), unless a different manner of service is prescribed by an applicable statute. At the time of filing, the petitioner shall furnish the clerk with a copy of the petition or application for each respondent. At or before the time of filing a petition for review, the petitioner shall serve a copy thereof on all parties who shall have been admitted to participate in the proceedings before the agency other than respondents to be served by the clerk, and shall file with the clerk a list of those so served.

(d) Intervention. Unless an applicable statute provides a different method of intervention, a person who desires to intervene in a proceeding under this rule shall serve upon all parties to the proceeding and file with the clerk of the court of appeals a motion for leave to intervene. The motion shall contain a concise statement of the interest of the moving party and the grounds upon which intervention is sought. A motion for leave to intervene or other notice of intervention authorized by an applicable statute shall be filed within 30 days of the date on which the petition for review is filed.

Rule 16.

THE RECORD ON REVIEW OR ENFORCEMENT

(a) Composition of the Record. The order sought to be reviewed or enforced, the findings or report on which it is based, and the pleadings, evidence and proceedings before the agency shall constitute the record on review in proceedings to review or enforce the order of an agency.

(b) Omissions from or Misstatements in the Record. If anything material to any party is omitted from the record or is misstated therein, the parties may at any time supply the omission or correct the misstatement by stipulation, or the court may at any time direct that the omission or misstatement be corrected and, if necessary, that a supplemental record be prepared and filed.

Rule 17.

FILING OF THE RECORD

(a) Agency to File; Time for Filing; Notice of Filing. The agency shall file the record with the clerk of the court of appeals within 40 days after service upon it of the petition for review unless a different time is provided by the statute authorizing review. In enforcement proceedings the agency shall file the record within 40 days after filing an application for enforcement, but the record need not be filed unless the respondent has filed an answer contesting enforcement of the order, or unless the court otherwise orders. The court may shorten or extend the time above prescribed. The clerk shall give notice to all parties of the date on which the record is filed.

(b) Filing—What Constitutes. The agency may file the entire record or such parts thereof as the parties may designate by stipulation filed with the agency. The original papers in the agency proceeding or certified copies thereof may be filed. Instead of filing the record or designated parts thereof, the agency may file a certified list of all documents, transcripts of testimony, exhibits and other material comprising the record, or a list of such parts thereof as the parties may designate, adequately describing each, and the filing of the certified list shall constitute filing of the record. The parties may stipulate that neither the record nor a certified list be filed with the court. The stipulation shall be filed with the clerk of the court of appeals and the date of its filing shall be deemed the date on which the record is filed. If a certified list is filed, or if the parties designate only parts of the record for filing or stipulate that neither the record nor a certified list be filed, the agency shall retain the record or parts thereof. Upon request of the court or the request of a party, the record or any part thereof thus retained shall be transmitted to the court notwithstanding any prior stipulation. All parts of the record retained by the agency shall be a part of the record on review for all purposes.

Rule 18.

STAY PENDING REVIEW

Application for a stay of a decision or order of an agency pending direct review in the court of appeals shall ordinarily be made in the first instance to the agency. A motion for such relief may be made to the court of appeals or to a judge thereof, but the motion shall show that application to the agency for the relief sought is not practicable, or that application has been made to the agency and denied, with the reasons given by it for denial, or that the action of the agency did not afford the relief which the applicant had requested. The motion shall also show the reasons for the relief requested and the facts relied upon, and if the facts are subject to dispute the motion shall be supported by affidavits or other sworn statements or copies thereof. With the motion shall be filed such parts of the record as are relevant to the relief sought. Reasonable notice of the motion shall be given to all parties to the proceeding in the court of appeals. The court may condition relief under this rule upon the filing of a bond or other appropriate security. The motion shall be filed with the clerk and normally will be considered by a panel or division of the court, but in exceptional cases where such procedure would be impracticable due to the requirements of time, the application may be made to and considered by a single judge of the court.

Rule 19.

SETTLEMENT OF JUDGMENTS ENFORCING ORDERS

When an opinion of the court is filed directing the entry of a judgment enforcing in whole or in part the order of an agency, the agency shall within 14 days thereafter serve upon the respondent and file with the clerk a proposed judgment in conformity with the opinion. If the respondent objects to the proposed judgment as not in conformity with the opinion, he shall within 7 days thereafter serve upon the agency and file with the clerk a proposed judgment which he deems to be in conformity with the opinion. The court will thereupon settle the judgment and direct its entry without further hearing or argument.

Rule 20.

APPLICABILITY OF OTHER RULES TO REVIEW OR ENFORCEMENT OF AGENCY ORDERS

All provisions of these rules are applicable to review or enforcement of orders of agencies, except that Rules 3–14 and Rules 22 and 23 are not applicable. As used in any applicable rule, the term "appellant" includes a petitioner and the term "appellee" includes a respondent in proceedings to review or enforce agency orders.

TITLE V. EXTRAORDINARY WRITS

Rule 21.

WRITS OF MANDAMUS AND PROHIBITION DIRECTED TO A JUDGE OR JUDGES AND OTHER EXTRAORDINARY WRITS

(a) Mandamus or Prohibition to a Judge or Judges; Petition for Writ; Service and Filing. Application for a writ of mandamus or of prohibition directed to a judge or judges shall be made by filing a petition therefor with the clerk of the court of appeals with proof of service on the respondent judge or judges and on all parties to the action in the trial court. The petition shall contain a statement of the facts necessary to an understanding of the issues presented by the application; a statement of the issues presented and of the relief sought; a statement of the reasons why the writ should issue; and copies of any order or opinion or parts of the record which may be essential to an understanding of the matters set forth in the petition. Upon receipt of the prescribed docket fee, the clerk shall docket the petition and submit it to the court.

(b) Denial; Order Directing Answer. If the court is of the opinion that the writ should not be granted, it shall deny the petition. Otherwise, it shall order that an answer to the petition be filed by the respondents within the time fixed by the order. The order shall be served by the clerk on the judge or judges named respondents and on all other parties to the action in the trial court. All parties below other than the petitioner shall also be deemed respondents for all purposes. Two or more respondents may answer jointly. If the judge or judges named respondents do not desire to appear in the proceeding, they may so advise the clerk and all parties by letter, but the petition shall not thereby be taken as admitted. The clerk shall advise the parties of the dates on which briefs are to be filed, if briefs are required, and of the date of oral argument. The proceeding shall be given preference over ordinary civil cases.

(c) Other Extraordinary Writs. Application for extraordinary writs other than those provided for in subdivisions (a) and (b) of this rule shall be made by petition filed with the clerk of the court of appeals with proof of service on the parties named as respondents. Proceedings on such application shall conform, so far as is practicable, to the procedure prescribed in subdivisions (a) and (b) of this rule.

(d) Form of Papers; Number of Copies. All papers may be typewritten. Three copies shall be filed with the original, but the court may direct that additional copies be furnished.

TITLE VI. HABEAS CORPUS; PROCEEDINGS IN FORMA PAUPERIS

Rule 22.

HABEAS CORPUS PROCEEDINGS

(a) Application for the Original Writ. An application for a writ of habeas corpus shall be made to the appropriate district court. If application is made to a circuit judge, the application will ordinarily be transferred to the appropriate district court. If an application is made to or transferred to the district court and denied, renewal of the application before a circuit judge is not favored; the proper remedy is by appeal to the court of appeals from the order of the district court denying the writ.

(b) Necessity of Certificate of Probable Cause for Appeal. In a habeas corpus proceeding in which the detention complained of arises out of process issued by a state court, an appeal by the applicant for the writ may not proceed unless a district or a circuit judge issues a certificate of probable cause. If an appeal is taken by the applicant, the district judge who rendered the judgment shall either issue a certificate of probable cause or state the reasons why such a certificate should not issue. The certificate or the statement shall be forwarded to the court of appeals with the notice of appeal and the file of the proceedings in the district court. If the district judge has denied the certificate, the applicant for the writ may then request issuance of the certificate by a circuit judge. If such a request is addressed to the court of appeals, it shall be deemed addressed to the judges thereof and shall be considered by a circuit judge or judges as the court deems appropriate. If no express request for a certificate is filed, the notice of appeal shall be deemed to constitute a request addressed to the judges of the court of appeals. If an appeal is taken by a state or its representative, a certificate of probable cause is not required.

Rule 23.

CUSTODY OF PRISONERS IN HABEAS CORPUS PROCEEDINGS

(a) Transfer of Custody Pending Review. Pending review of a decision in a habeas corpus proceeding commenced before a court, justice or judge of the United States for the release of a prisoner, a person having custody of the prisoner shall not transfer custody to another unless such transfer is directed in accordance with the provisions of this rule. Upon application of a custodian showing a need therefor, the court, justice or judge rendering the decision may make an order authorizing transfer and providing for the substitution of the successor custodian as a party.

(b) Detention or Release of Prisoner Pending Review of Decision Failing to Release. Pending review of a decision failing or refusing to release a prisoner in such a proceeding, the prisoner may be detained in the custody from which release is sought, or in other appropriate custody, or may be enlarged upon his recognizance, with or without surety, as may appear fitting to the court or justice or judge rendering the decision, or to the court of appeals or to the Supreme Court, or to a judge or justice of either court.

(c) Release of Prisoner Pending Review of Decision Ordering Release. Pending review of a decision ordering the release of a prisoner in such a proceeding, the prisoner shall be enlarged upon his recognizance, with or without surety, unless the court or justice or judge rendering the decision, or the court of appeals or the Supreme Court, or a judge or justice of either court shall otherwise order.

(d) Modification of Initial Order Respecting Custody. An initial order respecting the custody or enlargement of the prisoner and any recognizance or surety taken, shall govern review in the court of appeals and in the Supreme Court unless for special reasons shown to the court of appeals or to the Supreme Court, or to a judge or justice of either court, the order shall be modified, or an independent order respecting custody, enlargement or surety shall be made.

Rule 24.

PROCEEDINGS IN FORMA PAUPERIS

(a) Leave to Proceed on Appeal in Forma Pauperis from District Court to Court of Appeals. A party to an action in a district court who desires to proceed on appeal in forma pauperis shall file in the district court a motion for leave so to proceed, together with an affidavit showing, in the detail prescribed by Form 4 of the Appendix of Forms, his inability to pay fees and costs or to give security therefor, his belief that he is entitled to redress, and a statement of the issues which he intends to present on appeal. If the motion is granted, the party may proceed without further application to the court of appeals and without prepayment of fees or costs in either court or the giving of security therefor. If the motion is denied, the district court shall state in writing the reasons for the denial.

Notwithstanding the provisions of the preceding paragraph, a party who has been permitted to proceed in an action in the district court in forma pauperis, or who has been permitted to proceed there as one who is financially unable to obtain an adequate defense in a criminal case, may proceed on appeal in forma pauperis without further authorization unless, before or after the notice of appeal is filed, the district court shall certify that the appeal is not taken in good faith or shall find that the party is otherwise not entitled so to proceed, in which event the district court shall state in writing the reasons for such certification or finding.

If a motion for leave to proceed on appeal in forma pauperis is denied by the district court, or if the district court shall certify that the appeal is not taken in good faith or shall find that the party is otherwise not entitled to proceed in forma pauperis, the clerk shall forthwith serve notice of such action. A motion for leave so to proceed may be filed in the court of appeals within 30 days after service of notice of the action of the district court. The motion shall be accompanied by a copy of the affidavit filed in the district court, or by the affidavit prescribed by the first paragraph of this subdivision if no affidavit has been filed in the district court, and by a copy of the statement of reasons given by the district court for its action.

(b) Leave to Proceed on Appeal or Review in Forma Pauperis in Administrative Agency Proceedings. A party to a proceeding before an administrative agency, board, commission or officer (including, for the purpose of this rule, the United States Tax Court) who desires to proceed on appeal or review in a court of appeals in forma pauperis, when such appeal or review may be had directly in a court of appeals, shall file in the court of appeals a motion for leave so to proceed, together with the affidavit prescribed by the first paragraph of (a) of this Rule 24.

(c) Form of Briefs, Appendices and Other Papers. Parties allowed to proceed in forma pauperis may file briefs, appendices and other papers in typewritten form, and may request that the appeal be heard on the original record without the necessity of reproducing parts thereof in any form.

TITLE VII. GENERAL PROVISIONS

Rule 25.

FILING AND SERVICE

(a) Filing. Papers required or permitted to be filed in a court of appeals shall be filed with the clerk. Filing may be accomplished by mail addressed to the clerk, but filing shall not be timely unless the papers are received by the clerk within the time fixed for filing, except that briefs and appendices shall be deemed filed on the day of mailing if the most expeditious form of delivery by mail, excepting special delivery, is utilized. If a motion requests relief which may be granted by a single judge, the judge may permit the motion to be filed with him, in which event he shall note thereon the date of filing and shall thereafter transmit it to the clerk.

(b) Service of all Papers Required. Copies of all papers filed by any party and not required by these rules to be served by the clerk shall, at or before the time of filing, be served by a party or person acting for him on all other parties to the appeal or review. Service on a party represented by counsel shall be made on counsel.

(c) Manner of Service. Service may be personal or by mail. Personal service includes delivery of the copy to a clerk or other responsible person at the office of counsel. Service by mail is complete on mailing.

(d) Proof of Service. Papers presented for filing shall contain an acknowledgment of service by the person served or proof of service in the form of a statement of the date and manner of service and of the names of the person served, certified by the person who made service. Proof of service may appear on or be affixed to the papers filed. The clerk may permit papers to be filed without acknowledgment or proof of service but shall require such to be filed promptly thereafter.

Rule 26.

COMPUTATION AND EXTENSION OF TIME

(a) Computation of Time. In computing any period of time prescribed by these rules, by an order of court, or by any applicable statute, the day of the act, event, or default from which the designated period of time begins to run shall not be included. The last day of the period shall be included, unless it is a Saturday, a Sunday, or a legal holiday, in which event the period extends until the end of the next day which is not a Saturday, a Sunday, or a legal holiday. When the period of time prescribed or allowed is less than 7 days, intermediate Saturdays, Sundays, and legal holidays shall be excluded in the computation. As used in this rule "legal holiday" includes New Year's Day, Washington's Birthday, Memorial Day, Independence Day, Labor Day, Columbus Day, Veterans Day, Thanksgiving Day, Christmas Day, and any other day appointed as a holiday by the President or the Congress of the United States. It shall also include a day appointed as a holiday by the state wherein the district court which rendered the judgment or order which is or may be appealed from is situated, or by the state wherein the principal office of the clerk of the court of appeals in which the appeal is pending is located.

(b) Enlargement of Time. The court for good cause shown may upon motion enlarge the time prescribed by these rules or by its order for doing any act, or may permit an act to be done after the expiration of such time; but the court may not enlarge the time for filing a notice of appeal, a petition for allowance, or a petition for permission to appeal. Nor may the court enlarge the time prescribed by law for filing a petition to enjoin, set aside, suspend, modify, enforce or otherwise review, or a notice of appeal from, an order of an administrative agency, board, commission or officer of the United States, except as specifically authorized by law.

(c) Additional Time After Service by Mail. Whenever a party is required or permitted to do an act within a prescribed period after service of a paper upon him and the paper is served by mail, 3 days shall be added to the prescribed period.

Rule 27.

MOTIONS

(a) Content of Motions; Response; Reply. Unless another form is elsewhere prescribed by these rules, an application for an order or other relief shall be made by filing a motion for such order or relief with proof of service on all other parties. The motion shall contain or be accompanied by any matter required by a specific provision of these rules governing such a motion, shall state with particularity the grounds on which it is based, and shall set forth the order or relief sought. If a motion is supported by briefs, affidavits or other papers, they shall be served and filed with the motion. Any party may file a response in opposition to a motion other than one for a procedural order [for which see subdivision (b)] within 7 days after service of the motion, but motions authorized by Rules 8, 9, 18 and 41 may be acted upon after reasonable notice, and the court may shorten or extend the time for responding to any motion.

(b) Determination of Motions for Procedural Orders. Notwithstanding the provisions of (a) of this Rule 27 as to motions generally, motions for procedural orders, including any motion under Rule 26(b), may be acted upon at any time, without awaiting a response thereto, and pursuant to rule or order of the court, motions for specified types of procedural orders may be disposed of by the clerk. Any party adversely affected by such action may by application to the court request consideration, vacation or modification of such action.

(c) Power of a Single Judge to Entertain Motions. In addition to the authority expressly conferred by these rules or by law, a single judge of a court of appeals may entertain and may grant or deny any request for relief which under these rules may properly be sought by motion, except that a single judge may not dismiss or otherwise determine an appeal or other proceeding, and except that a court of appeals may provide by order or rule that any motion or class of motions must be acted upon by the court. The action of a single judge may be reviewed by the court.

(d) Form of Papers; Number of Copies. All papers relating to motions may be typewritten. Three copies shall be filed with the original, but the court may require that additional copies be furnished.

Rule 28.

BRIEFS

(a) Brief of the Appellant. The brief of the appellant shall contain under appropriate headings and in the order here indicated:

(1) A table of contents, with page references, and a table of cases (alphabetically arranged), statutes and other authorities cited, with references to the pages of the brief where they are cited.

(2) A statement of the issues presented for review.

(3) A statement of the case. The statement shall first indicate briefly the nature of the case, the course of proceedings, and its disposition in the court below. There shall follow a statement of the facts relevant to the issues presented for review, with appropriate references to the record (see subdivision (e)).

(4) An argument. The argument may be preceded by a summary. The argument shall contain the contentions of the appellant with respect to the issues presented, and the reasons therefor, with citations to the authorities, statutes and parts of the record relied on.

(5) A short conclusion stating the precise relief sought.

(b) Brief of the Appellee. The brief of the appellee shall conform to the requirements of subdivision (a) (1)–(4), except that a statement of the issues or of the case need not be made unless the appellee is dissatisfied with the statement of the appellant.

(c) Reply Brief. The appellant may file a brief in reply to the brief of the appellee, and if the appellee has cross-appealed, the appellee may file a brief in reply to the response of the appellant to the issues presented by the cross appeal. No further briefs may be filed except with leave of court.

(d) References in Briefs to Parties. Counsel will be expected in their briefs and oral arguments to keep to a minimum references to parties by such designations as "appellant" and "appellee". It promotes clarity to use the designations used in the lower court or in the agency proceedings, or the actual names of parties, or descriptive terms such as "the employee," "the injured person," "the taxpayer," "the ship," "the stevedore," etc.

(e) References in Briefs to the Record. References in the briefs to parts of the record reproduced in the appendix filed with the brief of the appellant (see Rule 30(a)) shall be to the pages of the appendix at which those parts appear. If the appendix is prepared after the briefs are filed, references in the briefs to the record shall be made by one of the methods allowed by Rule 30(c). If the record is reproduced in accordance with the provisions of Rule 30(f), or if references are made in the briefs to parts of the record not reproduced, the references shall be to the pages of the parts of the record involved; e. g., Answer p. 7, Motion for Judgment p. 2, Transcript p. 231. Intelligible abbreviations may be used. If reference is made to evidence the admissibility of which is in controversy, reference shall be made to the pages of the appendix or of the transcript at which the evidence was identified, offered, and received or rejected.

(f) Reproduction of Statutes, Rules, Regulations, Etc. If determination of the issues presented requires the study of statutes, rules, regulations, etc. or relevant parts thereof, they shall be reproduced in the brief or in an addendum at the end, or they may be supplied to the court in pamphlet form.

(g) Length of Briefs. Except by permission of the court, or as specified by local rule of the court of appeals, principal briefs shall not exceed 50 pages, and reply briefs shall not exceed 25 pages, exclusive of pages containing the table of contents, tables of citations and any addendum containing statutes, rules, regulations, etc.

(h) Briefs in Cases Involving Cross Appeals. If a cross appeal is filed, the plaintiff in the court below shall be deemed the appellant for the purposes of this rule and Rules 30 and 31, unless the parties otherwise agree or the court otherwise orders. The brief of the appellee shall contain the issues and argument involved in his appeal as well as the answer to the brief of the appellant.

(i) Briefs in Cases Involving Multiple Appellants or Appellees. In cases involving more than one appellant or appellee, including cases consolidated for purposes of the appeal, any number of either may join in a single brief, and any appellant or appellee may adopt by reference any part of the brief of another. Parties may similarly join in reply briefs.

(j) Citation of Supplemental Authorities. When pertinent and significant authorities come to the attention of a party after his brief has been filed, or after oral argument but before decision, a party may promptly advise the clerk of the court, by letter, with a copy to all counsel, setting forth the citations. There shall be a reference either to the page of the brief or to a point argued orally to which the citations pertain, but the letter shall without argument state the reasons for the supplemental citations. Any response shall be made promptly and shall be similarly limited.

Rule 29.

BRIEF OF AN AMICUS CURIAE

A brief of an amicus curiae may be filed only if accompanied by written consent of all parties, or by leave of court granted on motion or at the request of the court, except that consent or leave shall not be required when the brief is presented by the United States or an officer or agency thereof, or by a State, Territory or Commonwealth. The brief may be conditionally filed with the motion for leave. A motion for leave shall identify the interest of the applicant and shall state the reasons why a brief of an amicus curiae is desirable. Save as all parties otherwise consent, any amicus curiae shall file its brief within the time allowed the party whose position as to affirmance or reversal the amicus brief will support unless the court for cause shown shall grant leave for later filing, in which event it shall specify within what period an opposing party may answer. A motion of an amicus curiae to participate in the oral argument will be granted only for extraordinary reasons.

Rule 30.

APPENDIX TO THE BRIEFS

(a) Duty of Appellant to Prepare and File; Content of Appendix; Time for Filing; Number of Copies. The appellant shall prepare and file an appendix to the briefs which shall contain: (1) the relevant docket entries in the proceeding below; (2)

any relevant portions of the pleadings, charge, findings or opinion; (3) the judgment, order or decision in question; and (4) any other parts of the record to which the parties wish to direct the particular attention of the court. The fact that parts of the record are not included in the appendix shall not prevent the parties or the court from relying on such parts.

Unless filing is to be deferred pursuant to the provisions of subdivision (c) of this rule, the appellant shall serve and file the appendix with his brief. Ten copies of the appendix shall be filed with the clerk, and one copy shall be served on counsel for each party separately represented, unless the court shall by rule or order direct the filing or service of a lesser number.

(b) Determination of Contents of Appendix; Cost of Producing. The parties are encouraged to agree as to the contents of the appendix. In the absence of agreement, the appellant shall, not later than 10 days after the date on which the record is filed, serve on the appellee a designation of the parts of the record which he intends to include in the appendix and a statement of the issues which he intends to present for review. If the appellee deems it necessary to direct the particular attention of the court to parts of the record not designated by the appellant, he shall, within ten days after receipt of the designation, serve upon the appellant a designation of those parts. The appellant shall include in the appendix the parts thus designated. In designating parts of the record for inclusion in the appendix, the parties shall have regard for the fact that the entire record is always available to the court for reference and examination and shall not engage in unnecessary designation.

Unless the parties otherwise agree, the cost of producing the appendix shall initially be paid by the appellant, but if the appellant considers that parts of the record designated by the appellee for inclusion are unnecessary for the determination of the issues presented he may so advise the appellee and the appellee shall advance the cost of including such parts. The cost of producing the appendix shall be taxed as costs in the case, but if either party shall cause matters to be included in the appendix unnecessarily the court may impose the cost of producing such parts on the party.

(c) Alternative Method of Designating Contents of the Appendix; How References to the Record May Be Made in the Briefs When Alternative Method Is Used. If the court shall so provide by rule for classes of cases or by order in specific cases, preparation of the appendix may be deferred until after the briefs have been filed, and the appendix may be filed 21 days after service of the brief of the appellee. If the preparation and filing of the appendix is thus deferred, the provisions of subdivision (b) of this Rule 30 shall apply, except that the designations referred to therein shall be made by each party at the time his brief is served, and a statement of the issues presented shall be unnecessary.

If the deferred appendix authorized by this subdivision is employed, references in the briefs to the record may be to the pages of the parts of the record involved, in which event the original paging of each part of the record shall be indicated in the appendix by placing in brackets the number of each page at the place in the appendix where that page begins. Or if a party desires to refer in his brief directly to pages of the appendix, he may serve and file typewritten or page proof copies of his brief within the time required by Rule 31(a), with appropriate references to the pages of the parts of the record involved. In that event, within 14 days after the appendix is filed he shall serve and file copies of the brief in the form prescribed by Rule 32(a) containing references to the pages of the appendix in place of or in addition to the initial references to the pages of the parts of the record involved. No other changes may be made in the brief as initially served and filed, except that typographical errors may be corrected.

(d) Arrangement of the Appendix. At the beginning of the appendix there shall be inserted a list of the parts of the record which it contains, in the order in which the parts are set out therein, with references to the pages of the appendix at which each part begins. The relevant docket entries shall be set out following the list of contents. Thereafter, other parts of the record shall be set out in chronological order. When matter contained in the reporter's transcript of proceedings is set out in the appendix, the page of the transcript at which such matter may be found shall be indicated in brackets immediately before the matter which is set out. Omissions in the text of papers or of the transcript must be indicated by asterisks. Immaterial formal matters (captions, subscriptions, acknowledgments, etc.) shall be omitted. A question and its answer may be contained in a single paragraph.

(e) Reproduction of Exhibits. Exhibits designated for inclusion in the appendix may be contained in a separate volume, or volumes, suitably indexed. Four copies thereof shall be filed with the appendix and one copy shall be served on counsel for each party separately represented. The transcript of a proceeding before an administrative agency, board, commission or officer used in an action in the district court shall be regarded as an exhibit for the purpose of this subdivision.

(f) Hearing of Appeals on the Original Record Without the Necessity of an Appendix. A court of appeals may by rule applicable to all cases, or to classes of cases, or by order in specific cases, dispense with the requirement of an appendix and permit appeals to be heard on the original record, with such copies of the record, or relevant parts thereof, as the court may require.

Rule 31.

FILING AND SERVICE OF BRIEFS

(a) Time for Serving and Filing Briefs. The appellant shall serve and file his brief within 40 days after the date on which the record is filed. The appellee shall serve and file his brief within 30 days after service of the brief of the appellant. The appellant may serve and file a reply brief within 14 days after service of the brief of the appellee, but, except for good cause shown, a reply brief must be filed at least 3 days before argument. If a court of appeals is prepared to consider cases on the merits promptly after briefs are filed, and its practice is to do so, it may shorten the periods prescribed above for serving and filing briefs, either by rule for all cases or for classes of cases, or by order for specific cases.

(b) Number of Copies to Be Filed and Served. Twenty-five copies of each brief shall be filed with the clerk, unless the court by order in a particular case shall direct a lesser number, and two copies shall be served on counsel for each party separately represented. If a party is allowed to file typewritten ribbon and carbon copies of the brief, the original and three legible copies shall be filed with the clerk, and one copy shall be served on counsel for each party separately represented.

(c) Consequence of Failure to File Briefs. If an appellant fails to file his brief within the time provided by this rule, or within the time as extended, an appellee may move for dismissal of the appeal. If an appellee fails to file his brief, he will not be heard at oral argument except by permission of the court.

Rule 32.

FORM OF BRIEFS, THE APPENDIX AND OTHER PAPERS

(a) Form of Briefs and the Appendix. Briefs and appendices may be produced by standard typographic printing or by any duplicating or copying process which produces a clear black image on white paper. Carbon copies of briefs and appendices may not be submitted without permission of the court, except in behalf of parties allowed to proceed in forma pauperis. All printed matter must appear in at least 11 point type on opaque, unglazed paper. Briefs and appendices produced by the standard typographic process shall be bound in volumes having pages 6⅛ by 9¼ inches and type matter 4⅙ by 7⅙ inches. Those produced by any other process shall be bound in volumes having pages not exceeding 8½ by 11 inches and type matter not exceeding 6½ by 9½ inches, with double spacing between each line of text. In patent cases the pages of briefs and appendices may be of such size as is necessary to utilize copies of patent documents. Copies of the reporter's transcript and other papers reproduced in a manner authorized by this rule may be inserted in the appendix; such pages may be informally renumbered if necessary.

If briefs are produced by commercial printing or duplicating firms, or, if produced otherwise and the covers to be described are available, the cover of the brief of the appellant should be blue; that of the appellee, red; that of an intervenor or amicus curiae, green; that of any reply brief, gray. The cover of the appendix, if separately printed, should be white. The front covers of the briefs and of appendices, if separately printed, shall contain: (1) the name of the court and the number of the case; (2) the title of the case (see Rule 12(a)); (3) the nature of the proceeding in the court (e. g., Appeal; Petition for Review) and the name of the court, agency, or board below; (4) the title of the document (e. g., Brief for Appellant, Appendix); and (5) the names and addresses of counsel representing the party on whose behalf the document is filed.

(b) Form of Other Papers. Petitions for rehearing shall be produced in a manner prescribed by subdivision (a). Motions and other papers may be produced in like manner, or they may be typewritten upon opaque, unglazed paper 8½ by 11 inches in size. Lines of typewritten text shall be double spaced. Consecutive sheets shall be attached at the left margin. Carbon copies may be used for filing and service if they are legible.

A motion or other paper addressed to the court shall contain a caption setting forth the name of the court, the title of the case, the file number, and a brief descriptive title indicating the purpose of the paper.

Rule 33.

PREHEARING CONFERENCE

The court may direct the attorneys for the parties to appear before the court or a judge thereof for a prehearing conference to consider the simplification of the issues and such other matters as may aid in the disposition of the proceeding by the court. The court or judge shall make an order which recites the action taken at the conference and the agreements made by the parties as to any of the matters considered and which limits the issues to those not disposed of by admissions or agreements of counsel, and such order when entered controls the subsequent course of the proceeding, unless modified to prevent manifest injustice.

Rule 34.

ORAL ARGUMENT

(a) In General; Local Rule. Oral argument shall be allowed in all cases unless pursuant to local rule a panel of three judges, after examination of the briefs and record, shall be unanimously of the opinion that oral argument is not needed. Any such local rule shall provide any party with an opportunity to file a statement setting forth the reasons why, in his opinion, oral argument should be heard. A general statement of the criteria employed in the administration of such local rule shall be published in or with the rule and such criteria shall conform substantially to the following minimum standard:

Oral argument will be allowed unless

(1) the appeal is frivolous; or

(2) the dispositive issue or set of issues has been recently authoritatively decided; or

(3) the facts and legal arguments are adequately presented in the briefs and record and the decisional process would not be significantly aided by oral argument.

(b) Notice of Argument; Postponement. The clerk shall advise all parties whether oral argument is to be heard, and if so, of the time and place therefor, and the time to be allowed each side. A request for postponement of the argument or for allowance of additional time must be made by motion filed reasonably in advance of the date fixed for hearing.

(c) Order and Content of Argument. The appellant is entitled to open and conclude the argument. The opening argument shall include a fair statement of the case. Counsel will not be permitted to read at length from briefs, records or authorities.

(d) Cross and Separate Appeals. A cross or separate appeal shall be argued with the initial appeal at a single argument, unless the court otherwise directs. If a case involves a cross-appeal, the plaintiff in the action below shall be deemed the appellant for the purpose of this rule unless the parties otherwise agree or the court otherwise directs. If separate appellants support the same argument, care shall be taken to avoid duplication of argument.

(e) Non-Appearance of Parties. If the appellee fails to appear to present argument, the court will hear argument on behalf of the appellant, if present. If the appellant fails to appear, the court may hear argument on behalf of the appellee, if his counsel is present. If neither party appears, the case will be decided on the briefs unless the court shall otherwise order.

(f) Submission on Briefs. By agreement of the parties, a case may be submitted for decision on the briefs, but the court may direct that the case be argued.

(g) Use of Physical Exhibits at Argument; Removal. If physical exhibits other than documents are to be used at the argument, counsel shall arrange to have them placed in the court room before the court convenes on the date of the argument. After the argument counsel shall cause the exhibits to be removed from the court room unless the court otherwise directs. If exhibits are not reclaimed by counsel within a reasonable time after notice is given by the clerk, they shall be destroyed or otherwise disposed of as the clerk shall think best.

Rule 35.

DETERMINATION OF CAUSES BY THE COURT IN BANC

(a) When Hearing or Rehearing in Banc Will Be Ordered. A majority of the circuit judges who are in regular active service may order that an appeal or other proceeding be heard or reheard by the court of appeals in banc. Such a hearing or rehearing is not favored and ordinarily will not be ordered except (1) when consideration by the full court is necessary to secure or maintain uniformity of its decisions, or (2) when the proceeding involves a question of exceptional importance.

(b) Suggestion of a Party for Hearing or Rehearing in Banc. A party may suggest the appropriateness of a hearing or rehearing in banc. No response shall be filed unless the court shall so order. The clerk shall transmit any such suggestion to the members of the panel and the judges of the court who are in regular active service but a vote need not be taken to determine whether the cause shall be heard or reheard in banc unless a judge in regular active service or a judge who was a member of the panel that rendered a decision sought to be reheard requests a vote on such a suggestion made by a party.

(c) Time for Suggestion of a Party for Hearing or Rehearing in Banc; Suggestion Does Not Stay Mandate. If a party desires to suggest that an appeal be heard initially in banc, the suggestion must be made by the date on which the appellee's brief is filed. A suggestion for a rehearing in banc must be made within the time prescribed by Rule 40 for filing a petition for rehearing, whether the suggestion is made in such petition or otherwise. The pendency of such a suggestion whether or not included in a petition for rehearing shall not affect the finality of the judgment of the court of appeals or stay the issuance of the mandate.

Rule 36.

ENTRY OF JUDGMENT

The notation of a judgment in the docket constitutes entry of the judgment. The clerk shall prepare, sign and enter the judgment following receipt of the opinion of the court unless the opinion directs settlement of the form of the judgment, in which event the clerk shall prepare, sign and enter the judgment following final settlement by the court. If a judgment is rendered without an opinion, the clerk shall prepare, sign and enter the judgment following instruction from the court. The clerk shall, on the date judgment is entered, mail to all parties a copy of the opinion, if any, or of the judgment if no opinion was written, and notice of the date of entry of the judgment.

Rule 37.

INTEREST ON JUDGMENTS

Unless otherwise provided by law, if a judgment for money in a civil case is affirmed, whatever interest is allowed by law shall be payable from the date the judgment was entered in the district court. If a judgment is modified or reversed with a direction that a judgment for money be entered in the district court, the mandate shall contain instructions with respect to allowance of interest.

Rule 38.

DAMAGES FOR DELAY

If a court of appeals shall determine that an appeal is frivolous, it may award just damages and single or double costs to the appellee.

Rule 39.

COSTS

(a) To Whom Allowed. Except as otherwise provided by law, if an appeal is dismissed, costs shall be taxed against the appellant unless otherwise agreed by the parties or ordered by the court; if a judgment is affirmed, costs shall be taxed against the appellant unless otherwise ordered; if a judgment is reversed, costs shall be taxed against the appellee unless otherwise ordered; if a judgment is affirmed or reversed in part, or is vacated, costs shall be allowed only as ordered by the court.

(b) Costs For and Against the United States. In cases involving the United States or an agency or officer thereof, if an award of costs against the United States is authorized by law, costs shall be awarded in accordance with the provisions of subdivision (a); otherwise, costs shall not be awarded for or against the United States.

(c) Costs of Briefs, Appendices, and Copies of Records. Unless otherwise provided by local rule, the cost of printing, or otherwise producing necessary copies of briefs, appendices, and copies of records authorized by Rule 30(f) shall be taxable in the court of appeals at rates not higher than those generally charged for such work in the area where the clerk's office is located.

(d) Bill of Costs; Objections; Costs to be Inserted in Mandate or Added Later. A party who desires such costs to be taxed shall state them in an itemized and verified bill of costs which he shall file with the clerk, with proof of service, within 14 days after the entry of judgment. Objections to the bill of costs must be filed within 10 days of service on the party against whom costs are to be taxed unless the time is extended by the court. The clerk shall prepare and certify an itemized statement of costs taxed in the court of appeals for insertion in the mandate, but the issuance of the mandate shall not be delayed for taxation of costs and if the mandate has been issued before final determination of costs, the statement, or any amendment thereof, shall be added to the mandate upon request by the clerk of the court of appeals to the clerk of the district court.

(e) Costs on Appeal Taxable in the District Courts. Costs incurred in the preparation and transmission of the record, the cost of the reporter's transcript, if necessary for the determination of the appeal, the premiums paid for cost of supersedeas bonds or other bonds to preserve rights pending appeal, and the fee for filing the notice of appeal shall be taxed in the district court as costs of the appeal in favor of the party entitled to costs under this rule.

Rule 40.

PETITION FOR REHEARING

(a) Time for Filing; Content; Answer; Action by Court if Granted. A petition for rehearing may be filed within 14 days after entry of judgment unless the time is shortened or enlarged by order or by local rule. The petition shall state with particularity the points of law or fact which in the opinion of the petitioner the court has overlooked or misapprehended and shall contain such argument in support of the petition as the petitioner desires to present. Oral argument in support of the petition will not be permitted. No answer to a petition for rehearing will be received unless requested by the court, but a petition for rehearing will ordinarily not be granted in the absence of such a request. If a petition for rehearing is granted the court may make a final disposition of the cause without reargument or may restore it to the calendar for reargument or resubmission or may make such other orders as are deemed appropriate under the circumstances of the particular case.

(b) Form of Petition; Length. The petition shall be in a form prescribed by Rule 32(a), and copies shall be served and filed as prescribed by Rule 31(b) for the service and filing of briefs. Except by permission of the court, or as specified by local rule of the court of appeals, a petition for rehearing shall not exceed 15 pages.

Rule 41.

ISSUANCE OF MANDATE; STAY OF MANDATE

(a) Date of Issuance. The mandate of the court shall issue 21 days after the entry of judgment unless the time is shortened or enlarged by order. A certified copy of the judgment and a copy of the opinion of the court, if any, and any direction as to costs shall constitute the mandate, unless the court directs that a formal mandate issue. The timely filing of a petition for rehearing will stay the mandate until disposition of the petition unless otherwise ordered by the court. If the petition is denied, the mandate shall issue 7 days after entry of the order denying the petition unless the time is shortened or enlarged by order.

(b) Stay of Mandate Pending Application for Certiorari. A stay of the mandate pending application to the Supreme Court for a writ of certiorari may be granted upon motion, reasonable notice of which shall be given to all parties. The stay shall not exceed 30 days unless the period is extended for cause shown. If during the period of the stay there is filed with the clerk of the court of appeals a notice from the clerk of the Supreme Court that the party who has obtained the stay has filed a petition for the writ in that court, the stay shall continue until final disposition by the Supreme Court. Upon the filing of a copy of an order of the Supreme Court denying the petition for writ of certiorari the mandate shall issue immediately. A bond or other security may be required as a condition to the grant or continuance of a stay of the mandate.

Rule 42.

VOLUNTARY DISMISSAL

(a) Dismissal in the District Court. If an appeal has not been docketed, the appeal may be dismissed by the district court upon the filing in that court of a stipulation for dismissal signed by all the parties, or upon motion and notice by the appellant.

(b) Dismissal in the Court of Appeals. If the parties to an appeal or other proceeding shall sign and file with the clerk of the court of appeals an agreement that the proceeding be dismissed, specifying the terms as to payment of costs, and shall pay whatever fees are due, the clerk shall enter the case dismissed, but no mandate or other process shall issue without an order of the court. An appeal may be dismissed on motion of the appellant upon such terms as may be agreed upon by the parties or fixed by the court.

Rule 43.

SUBSTITUTION OF PARTIES

(a) Death of a Party. If a party dies after a notice of appeal is filed or while a proceeding is otherwise pending in the court of appeals, the personal representative of the deceased party may be substituted as a party on motion filed by the representative or by any party with the clerk of the court of appeals. The motion of a party shall be served upon the representative in accordance with the provisions of Rule 25. If the deceased party has no representative, any party may suggest the death on the record and proceedings shall then be had as the court of appeals may direct. If a party against whom an appeal may be taken dies after entry of a judgment or order in the district court but before a notice of appeal is filed, an appellant may proceed as if death had not occurred. After the notice of appeal is filed substitution shall be effected in the court of appeals in accordance with this subdivision. If a party entitled to appeal shall die before filing a notice of appeal, the notice of appeal may be filed by his personal representative, or, if he has no personal representative, by his attorney of record within the time prescribed by these rules. After the notice of appeal is filed substitution shall be effected in the court of appeals in accordance with this subdivision.

(b) Substitution for Other Causes. If substitution of a party in the court of appeals is necessary for any reason other than death, substitution shall be effected in accordance with the procedure prescribed in subdivision (a).

(c) Public Officers; Death or Separation from Office.

(1) When a public officer is a party to an appeal or other proceeding in the court of appeals in his official capacity and during its pendency dies, resigns or otherwise ceases to hold office, the action does not abate and his successor is automatically substituted as a party. Proceedings following the substitution shall be in the name of the substituted party, but any misnomer not affecting the substantial rights of the parties shall be disregarded. An order of substitution may be entered at any time, but the omission to enter such an order shall not affect the substitution.

(2) When a public officer is a party to an appeal or other proceeding in his official capacity he may be described as a party by his official title rather than by name; but the court may require his name to be added.

Rule 44.

CASES INVOLVING CONSTITUTIONAL QUESTIONS WHERE UNITED STATES IS NOT A PARTY

It shall be the duty of a party who draws in question the constitutionality of any Act of Congress in any proceeding in a court of appeals to which the United States, or any agency thereof, or any officer or employee thereof, as such officer or employee, is not a party, upon the filing of the record, or as soon thereafter as the question is raised in the court of appeals, to give immediate notice in writing to the court of the existence of said question. The clerk shall thereupon certify such fact to the Attorney General.

Rule 45.

DUTIES OF CLERKS

(a) General Provisions. The clerk of a court of appeals shall take the oath and give the bond required by law. Neither the clerk nor any deputy clerk shall practice as an attorney or counselor in any court while he continues in office. The court of appeals shall be deemed always open for the purpose of filing any proper paper, of issuing and returning process and of making motions and orders. The office of the clerk with the clerk or a deputy in attendance shall be open during business hours on all days except Saturdays, Sundays, and legal holidays, but a court may provide by local rule or order that the office of its clerk shall be open for specified hours on Saturdays or on particular legal holidays other than New Year's Day, Washington's Birthday, Memorial Day, Independence Day, Labor Day, Columbus Day, Veterans Day, Thanksgiving Day and Christmas Day.

(b) The Docket; Calendar; Other Records Required. The clerk shall keep a book known as the docket, in such form and style as may be prescribed by the Director of the Administrative Office of the United States Courts with the approval of the Judicial Conference of the United States, and shall enter therein each case. Cases shall be assigned consecutive file numbers. The file number of each case shall be noted on the folio of the docket whereon the first entry is made. All papers filed with the clerk and all process, orders and judgments shall be entered chronologically in the docket on the folio assigned to the case. Entries shall be brief but shall show the nature of each paper filed or judgment or order entered. The entry of an order or judgment shall show the date the entry is made. The clerk shall keep a suitable index of cases contained in the docket.

The clerk shall prepare, under the direction of the court, a calendar of cases awaiting argument. In placing cases on the calendar for argument, he shall give preference to appeals in criminal cases and to appeals and other proceedings entitled to preference by law.

The clerk shall keep such other books and records as may be required from time to time by the Director of the Administrative Office of the United States Courts with the approval of the Judicial Conference of the United States, or as may be required by the court.

(c) Notice of Orders or Judgments. Immediately upon the entry of an order or judgment the clerk shall serve a notice of entry by mail upon each party to the proceeding together with a copy of any opinion respecting the order or judgment, and shall make a note in the docket of the mailing. Service on a party represented by counsel shall be made on counsel.

(d) Custody of Records and Papers. The clerk shall have custody of the records and papers of the court. He shall not permit any original record or paper to be taken from his custody except as authorized by the orders or instructions of the court.

Original papers transmitted as the record on appeal or review shall upon disposition of the case be returned to the court or agency from which they were received. The clerk shall preserve copies of briefs and appendices and other printed papers filed.

Rule 46.

ATTORNEYS

(a) Admission to the Bar of a Court of Appeals; Eligibility; Procedure for Admission. An attorney who has been admitted to practice before the Supreme Court of the United States, or the highest court of a state, or another United States court of appeals, or a United States district court (including the district courts for the Canal Zone, Guam and the Virgin Islands), and who is of good moral and professional character, is eligible for admission to the bar of a court of appeals.

An applicant shall file with the clerk of the court of appeals, on a form approved by the court and furnished by the clerk, an application for admission containing his personal statement showing his eligibility for membership. At the foot of the application the applicant shall take and subscribe to the following oath or affirmation:

> I, ..., do solemnly swear (or affirm) that I will demean myself as an attorney and counselor of this court, uprightly and according to law; and that I will support the Constitution of the United States.

Thereafter, upon written or oral motion of a member of the bar of the court, the court will act upon the application. An applicant may be admitted by oral motion in open court, but it is not necessary that he appear before the court for the purpose of being admitted, unless the court shall otherwise order. An applicant shall upon admission pay to the clerk the fee prescribed by rule or order of the court.

(b) Suspension or Disbarment. When it is shown to the court that any member of its bar has been suspended or disbarred from practice in any other court of record, or has been guilty of conduct unbecoming a member of the bar of the court, he will be subject to suspension or disbarment by the court. The member shall be afforded an opportunity to show good cause, within such time as the court shall prescribe, why he should not be suspended or disbarred. Upon his response to the rule to show cause, and after hearing, if requested, or upon expiration of the time prescribed for a response if no response is made, the court shall enter an appropriate order.

(c) Disciplinary Power of the Court over Attorneys. A court of appeals may, after reasonable notice and an opportunity to show cause to the contrary, and after hearing, if requested, take any appropriate disciplinary action against any attorney who practices before it for conduct unbecoming a member of the bar or for failure to comply with these rules or any rule of the court.

Rule 47.

RULES BY COURTS OF APPEALS

Each court of appeals by action of a majority of the circuit judges in regular active service may from time to time make and amend rules governing its practice not inconsistent with these rules. In all cases not provided for by rule, the courts of appeals may regulate their practice in any manner not inconsistent with these rules. Copies of all rules made by a court of appeals shall upon their promulgation be furnished to the Administrative Office of the United States Courts.

Rule 48.

TITLE

These rules may be known and cited as the Federal Rules of Appellate Procedure.

APPENDIX OF FORMS

Form 1.

NOTICE OF APPEAL TO A COURT OF APPEALS FROM A JUDGMENT OR ORDER OF A DISTRICT COURT

United States District Court for the .... District of ....

File Number ....

A. B., Plaintiff v. C. D., Defendant	Notice of Appeal

Notice is hereby given that C. D., defendant above named, hereby appeals to the United States Court of Appeals for the .... Circuit (from the final judgment) (from the order (describing it)) entered in this action on the .... day of ....

.........., 19....

(S) ....

....
(Address)
Attorney for C. D.

Form 2.

NOTICE OF APPEAL TO A COURT OF APPEALS FROM A DECISION OF THE TAX COURT

Tax Court of the United States
Washington, D. C.

A. B., Petitioner v. Commissioner of Internal Revenue, Respondent	Docket No. ....

Notice of Appeal

Notice is hereby given that A. B. hereby appeals to the United States Court of Appeals for the .... Circuit from [that part of] the decision of this court entered in the above captioned proceeding on the .... day of ...., 19... [relating to ....].

(S) ....

....
(Address)
Counsel for A. B.

Form 3.

PETITION FOR REVIEW OF ORDER OF AN AGENCY, BOARD, COMMISSION OR OFFICER

United States Court of Appeals for the .... Circuit

A. B. Petitioner v. XYZ Commission, Respondent	Petition for Review

A. B. hereby petitions the court for review of the Order of the XYZ Commission (describe the order) entered on ...., 19....

....
Attorney for Petitioner
Address: ....

Form 4.

AFFIDAVIT TO ACCOMPANY MOTION FOR LEAVE TO APPEAL IN FORMA PAUPERIS

United States District Court for the .... District of ....

United States of America v. A. B.	No. ....

Affidavit in Support of Motion to Proceed on Appeal in Forma Pauperis

I, ... being first duly sworn, depose and say that I am the ...., in the above-entitled case; that in support of my motion to proceed on appeal without being required to prepay fees, costs or give security therefor, I state that because of my poverty I am unable to pay the costs of said proceeding or to give security therefor; that I believe I am entitled to redress; and that the issues which I desire to present on appeal are the following:

I further swear that the responses which I have made to the questions and instructions below relating to my ability to pay the cost of prosecuting the appeal are true.

1. Are you presently employed?
   a. If the answer is yes, state the amount of your salary or wages per month and give the name and address of your employer.
   b. If the answer is no, state the date of your last employment and the amount of the salary and wages per month which you received.
2. Have you received within the past twelve months any income from a business, profession or other form of self-employment, or in the form of rent payments, interest, dividends, or other source?
   a. If the answer is yes, describe each source of income, and state the amount received from each during the past twelve months.
3. Do you own any cash or checking or savings account?
   a. If the answer is yes, state the total value of the items owned.
4. Do you own any real estate, stocks, bonds, notes, automobiles, or other valuable property (excluding ordinary household furnishings and clothing)?
   a. If the answer is yes, describe the property and state its approximate value.
5. List the persons who are dependent upon you for support and state your relationship to those persons.

I understand that a false statement or answer to any questions in this affidavit will subject me to penalties for perjury.

SUBSCRIBED AND SWORN To before me this .... day of ...., 19...

Let the applicant proceed without prepayment of costs or fees or the necessity of giving security therefor.

....

District Judge

RULES OF THE SUPREME COURT OF THE UNITED STATES

AS AMENDED TO AUGUST 1, 1983

Editorial Note: The contemporary Rules of the Supreme Court were adopted by the Court on April 14, 1980, effective June 30, 1980 and amended by order dated Oct. 21, 1980, effective Nov. 21, 1980. In organization and in major content they derive from a general re-examination of the earlier rules, effective July 1, 1954 (346 U.S. 949). Subsequent revisions were effective October 2, 1967 (388 U.S. 931) and July 1, 1970 (398 U.S. 1009), with minor amendments on October 12, 1970 (400 U.S. 1027) and November 12, 1971 (404 U.S. 1066).

Table of Rules

PART I. THE COURT

Rule 1.

CLERK

1. The Clerk shall have custody of all the records and papers of the Court and shall not permit any of them to be taken from his custody except as authorized by the Court. After the conclusion of the proceedings in this Court, any original records and papers transmitted as the record on appeal or certiorari will be returned to the court from which they were received. Pleadings, papers, and briefs filed with the Clerk may not be withdrawn by litigants.

2. The office of the Clerk will be open, except on a federal legal holiday, from 9 a. m. to 5 p. m. Monday through Friday, and from 9 a. m. to noon Saturday.

3. The Clerk shall not practice as an attorney or counselor while holding his office. See 28 U.S.C. § 955.

Rule 2.

LIBRARY

1. The Bar library will be open to the appropriate personnel of this Court, members of the Bar of this Court, Members of Congress, members of their legal staffs, and attorneys for the United States, its departments and agencies.

2. The library will be open during such times as the reasonable needs of the Bar require and shall be governed by regulations made by the Librarian with the approval of the Chief Justice or the Court.

3. Books may not be removed from the building, except by a Justice or a member of his legal staff.

Rule 3.

TERM

1. The Court will hold an annual Term commencing on the first Monday in October, and may hold a special term whenever necessary. See 28 U.S.C. § 2.

2. The Court at every Term will announce the date after which no case will be called for argument at that Term unless otherwise ordered for special cause shown.

3. At the end of each Term, all cases on the docket will be continued to the next Term.

Rule 4.

SESSIONS, QUORUM, AND ADJOURNMENTS

1. Open sessions of the Court will be held at 10 a. m. on the first Monday in October of each year, and thereafter as announced by the Court. Unless otherwise ordered, the Court will sit to hear arguments from 10 a. m. until noon and from 1 p. m. until 3 p. m.

2. Any six Members of the Court shall constitute a quorum. See 28 U.S.C. § 1. In the absence of a quorum on any day appointed for holding a session of the Court, the Justices attending, or if no Justice is present the Clerk or a Deputy Clerk, may announce that the Court will not meet until there is a quorum.

3. The Court in appropriate circumstances may direct the Clerk or the Marshal to announce recesses and adjournments.

PART II. ATTORNEYS AND COUNSELORS

Rule 5.

ADMISSION TO THE BAR

1. It shall be requisite to the admission to practice in this Court that the applicant shall have been admitted to practice in the highest court of a State, Territory, District, Commonwealth, or Possession for the three years immediately preceding the date of application, and that the applicant appears to the Court to be of good moral and professional character.

2. Each applicant shall file with the Clerk (1) a certificate from the presiding judge, clerk, or other duly authorized official of the proper court evidencing the applicant's admission to practice there and present good standing, and (2) an executed copy of the form approved by the Court and furnished by the Clerk containing (i) the applicant's personal statement and (ii) the statement of two sponsors (who must be members of the Bar of this Court and must personally know, but not be related to, the applicant) endorsing the correctness of the applicant's statement, stating that the applicant possesses all the qualifications

required for admission, and affirming that the applicant is of good moral and professional character.

3. If the documents submitted by the applicant demonstrate that the applicant possesses the necessary qualifications, the Clerk shall so notify the applicant. Upon the applicant's signing the oath or affirmation and paying the fee required under Rule 45(e), the Clerk shall issue a certificate of admission. If the applicant desires, however, the applicant may be admitted in open court on oral motion by a member of the Bar, provided that the requirements for admission have been satisfied.

4. Each applicant shall take or subscribe the following oath or affirmation:

I, ______, do solemnly swear (or affirm) that as an attorney and as a counselor of this Court I will conduct myself uprightly and according to law, and that I will support the Constitution of the United States.

Rule 6.

ARGUMENT PRO HAC VICE

1. An attorney admitted to practice in the highest court of a State, Territory, District, Commonwealth, or Possession who has not been such for three years, but who is otherwise eligible for admission to practice in this Court under Rule 5.1, may be permitted to present oral argument *pro hac vice* in a particular case.

2. An attorney, barrister, or advocate who is qualified to practice in the courts of a foreign state may be permitted to present oral argument *pro hac vice* in a particular case.

3. Oral argument *pro hac vice* shall be allowed only on motion of the attorney of record for the party on whose behalf leave is sought. Such motion must briefly and distinctly state the appropriate qualifications of the attorney for whom permission to argue orally is sought; it must be filed with the Clerk, in the form prescribed by Rule 42, no later than the date on which the appellee's or respondent's brief on the merits is due to be filed and it must be accompanied by proof of service as prescribed by Rule 28.

Rule 7.

PROHIBITION AGAINST PRACTICE

No one serving as a law clerk or secretary to a Justice of this Court and no other employee of this Court shall practice as an attorney or counselor in any court or before any agency of Government while holding that position; nor shall such person after separating from that position participate, by way of any form of professional consultation or assistance, in any case before this Court until two years have elapsed after such separation; nor shall such person ever participate, by way of any form of professional consultation or assistance, in any case that was pending in this Court during the tenure of such position.

Rule 8.

DISBARMENT

Where it is shown to the Court that any member of its Bar has been disbarred or suspended from practice in any court of record, or has engaged in conduct unbecoming a member of the Bar of this Court, such member forthwith may be suspended from practice before this Court. Such member thereupon will be afforded the opportunity to show good cause, within 40 days, why disbarment should not be effectuated. Upon his response, or upon the expiration of the 40 days if no response is made, the Court will enter an appropriate order.

PART III. ORIGINAL JURISDICTION

Rule 9.

PROCEDURE IN ORIGINAL ACTIONS

1. This Rule applies only to actions within the Court's original jurisdiction under Article III of the Constitution of the United States. Original applications for writs in aid of the Court's appellate jurisdiction are governed by Part VII of these Rules.

2. The form of pleadings and motions in original actions shall be governed, so far as may be, by the Federal Rules of Civil Procedure, and in other respects those Rules, where their application is appropriate, may be taken as a guide to procedure in original actions in this Court.

3. The initial pleading in any original action shall be prefaced by a motion for leave to file such pleading, and both shall be printed in conformity with Rule 33. A brief in support of the motion for leave to file, which shall comply with Rule 33, may be filed with the motion and pleading. Sixty copies of each document, with proof of service as prescribed by Rule 28, are required, except that, when an adverse party is a State,

service shall be made on the Governor and Attorney General of such State. See Rule 28.1

4. The case will be placed upon the original docket when the motion for leave to file is filed with the Clerk. The docket fee must be paid at that time, and the appearance of counsel for the plaintiff entered.

5. Within 60 days after receipt of the motion for leave to file and allied documents, any adverse party may file, with proof of service as prescribed by Rule 28, 60 printed copies of a brief in opposition to such motion. The brief shall conform to Rule 33. When such brief in opposition has been filed, or when the time within which it may be filed has expired, the motion, pleading, and briefs will be distributed to the Court by the Clerk. The Court may thereafter grant or deny the motion, set it down for argument, or take other appropriate action.

6. Additional pleadings may be filed, and subsequent proceedings had, as the Court may direct. See Rule 28.1

7. A summons issuing out of this Court in any original action shall be served on the defendant 60 days before the return day set out therein; and if the defendant, on such service, shall not respond by the return day, the plaintiff shall be at liberty to proceed *ex parte*.

8. Any process against a State issued from the Court in an original action shall be served on the Governor and Attorney General of such State.

PART IV. JURISDICTION ON APPEAL

Rule 10.

APPEAL—HOW TAKEN—PARTIES—CROSS-APPEAL

1. An appeal to this Court permitted by law shall be taken by filing a notice of appeal in the form, within the time, and at the place prescribed by this Rule, and shall be perfected by docketing the case in this Court as provided in Rule 12.

2. The notice of appeal shall specify the parties taking the appeal, shall designate the judgment or part thereof appealed from, giving the date of its entry, and shall specify the statute or statutes under which the appeal to this Court is taken. A copy of the notice of appeal shall be served on all parties to the proceeding in the court where the judgment appealed from was issued, in the manner prescribed by Rule 28, and proof of service shall be filed with the notice of appeal.

3. If the appeal is taken from a federal court, the notice of appeal shall be filed with the clerk of that court. If the appeal is taken from a state court, the notice of appeal shall be filed with the clerk of the court from whose judgment the appeal is taken, and a copy of the notice of appeal shall be filed with the court possessed of the record.

4. All parties to the proceeding in the court from whose judgment the appeal is being taken shall be deemed parties in this Court, unless the appellant shall notify the Clerk of this Court in writing of appellant's belief that one or more of the parties below has no interest in the outcome of the appeal. A copy of such notice shall be served on all parties to the proceeding below and a party noted as no longer interested may remain a party here by notifying the Clerk, with service on the other parties, that he has an interest in the appeal. All parties other than appellants shall be appellees, but any appellee who supports the position of an appellant shall meet the time schedule for filing papers which is provided for that appellant, except that any response by such appellee to a jurisdictional statement shall be filed within 20 days after receipt of the statement

5. The Court may permit an appellee, without filing a cross-appeal, to defend a judgment on any ground that the law and record permit and that would not expand the relief he has been granted.

6. Parties interested jointly, severally, or otherwise in a judgment may join in an appeal therefrom; or any one or more of them may appeal separately; or any two or more of them may join in an appeal. Where two or more cases that involve identical or closely related questions are appealed from the same court, it will suffice to file a single jurisdictional statement covering all the issues.

7. An appellee may take a cross-appeal by perfecting an appeal in the normal manner or, without filing a notice of appeal, by docketing the cross-appeal within the time permitted by Rule 12.4.

Rule 11.

APPEAL, CROSS–APPEAL—TIME FOR TAKING

1. An appeal to review the judgment of a state court in a criminal case shall be in time when the notice of appeal prescribed by Rule 10 is filed with the clerk of the court from whose judgment the appeal is taken within 90 days after the

entry of such judgment and the case is docketed within the time provided in Rule 12. See 28 U.S.C. § 2101(d).

2. An appeal in all other cases shall be in time when the notice of appeal prescribed by Rule 10 is filed with the clerk of the appropriate court within the time allowed by law for taking such appeal and the case is docketed within the time provided in Rule 12. See 28 U.S.C. §§ 2101(a), (b), and (c).

3. The time for filing the notice of appeal runs from the date the judgment or decree sought to be reviewed is rendered, and not from the date of the issuance of the mandate (or its equivalent under local practice). However, if a petition for rehearing is timely filed by any party in the case, the time for filing the notice of appeal for all parties (whether or not they requested rehearing or joined in the petition for rehearing, or whether or not the petition for rehearing relates to an issue the other parties would raise) runs from the date of the denial of rehearing or the entry of a subsequent judgment.

4. The time for filing a notice of appeal may not be extended.

5. A cross-appeal shall be in time if it complies with this Rule or if it is docketed as provided in Rule 12.4.

Rule 12.

DOCKETING CASES

1. Not more than 90 days after the entry of the judgment appealed from, it shall be the duty of the appellant to docket the case in the manner set forth in paragraph 3 of this Rule, except that in the case of appeals pursuant to 28 U.S.C. §§ 1252 or 1253, the time limit for docketing shall be 60 days from the filing of the notice of appeal. See 28 U.S.C. § 2101(a). The Clerk will refuse to receive any jurisdictional statement in a case in which the notice of appeal has obviously not been timely filed.

2. For good cause shown, a Justice of this Court may extend the time for docketing a case for a period not exceeding 60 days. An application for extension of time within which to docket a case must set out the grounds on which the jurisdiction of this Court is invoked, must identify the judgment sought to be reviewed, must have appended a copy of the opinion, must specify the date and place of filing of the notice of appeal and append a copy thereof, and must set forth with specificity the reasons why the granting of an extension of time is thought justified.

For the time and manner of presenting such an application, see Rules 29, 42.2, and 43. Such applications are not favored.

3. Counsel for the appellant shall enter an appearance, pay the docket fee, and file, with proof of service as prescribed by Rule 28, 40 copies of a printed statement as to jurisdiction, which shall comply in all respects with Rule 15. The case then will be placed on the docket. It shall be the duty of counsel for appellant to notify all appellees, on a form supplied by the Clerk, of the date of docketing and of the docket number of the case. Such notice shall be served as required by Rule 28.

4. Not more than 30 days after receipt of the statement of jurisdiction, counsel for an appellee wishing to cross-appeal shall enter an appearance, pay the docket fee, and file, with proof of service as prescribed by Rule 28, 40 copies of a printed statement as to jurisdiction on cross-appeal, which shall comply in all respects with Rule 15. The cross-appeal will then be placed on the docket. The issues tendered by a timely cross-appeal docketed under this paragraph may be considered by the Court only in connection with a separate and duly perfected appeal over which this Court has jurisdiction without regard to this paragraph. It shall be the duty of counsel for the cross-appellant to notify the cross-appellee on a form supplied by the Clerk of the date of docketing and of the docket number of the cross-appeal. Such notice shall be served as required by Rule 28. A statement of jurisdiction on cross-appeal may not be joined with any other pleading. The Clerk shall not accept any pleadings so joined. The time for filing a cross-appeal may not be extended.

Rule 13.

CERTIFICATION OF THE RECORD

1. An appellant at any time prior to action by this Court on the jurisdictional statement, may request the clerk of the court possessed of the record to certify it, or any part of it, and to provide for its transmission to this Court, but the filing of the record in this Court is not required for the docketing of an appeal. If the appellant has not done so, the appellee may request such clerk to certify and transmit the record or any part of it. Thereafter, the Clerk of this Court or any party to the appeal may request that additional parts of the record be certified and transmitted to this Court. Copies of all requests for certification and transmission shall be sent to all parties. Such requests to certify the record prior to action by the Court on the jurisdictional statement, however, shall not be made as

a matter of course but only when the record is deemed essential to a proper understanding of the case by this Court.

2. When requested to certify and transmit the record, or any part of it, the clerk of the court possessed of the record shall number the documents to be certified and shall transmit with the record a numbered list of the documents, identifying each with reasonable definiteness.

3. The record may consist of certified copies. But whenever it shall appear necessary or proper, in the opinion of the presiding judge of the court from which the appeal is taken, that original papers of any kind should be inspected in this Court in lieu of copies, the presiding judge may make any rule or order for safekeeping, transporting, and return of the original papers as may seem proper to him. If the record or stipulated portions thereof have been printed for the use of the court below, this printed record plus the proceedings in the court below may be certified as the record unless one of the parties or the Clerk of this Court otherwise requests.

4. When more than one appeal is taken to this Court from the same judgment, it shall be sufficient to prepare a single record containing all the matter designated by the parties or the Clerk of this Court, without duplication.

Rule 14.

DISMISSING APPEALS

1. After a notice of appeal has been filed, but before the case has been docketed in this Court, the parties may dismiss the appeal by stipulation filed in the court whose judgment is the subject of the appeal, or that court may dismiss the appeal upon motion and notice by the appellant. For dismissal after the case has been docketed, see Rule 53.

2. If a notice of appeal has been filed but the case has not been docketed in this Court within the time for docketing, plus any enlargement thereof duly granted, the court whose judgment is the subject of the appeal may dismiss the appeal upon motion of the appellee and notice to the appellant, and may make such order thereon with respect to costs as may be just.

3. If a notice of appeal has been filed but the case has not been docketed in this Court within the time for docketing, plus any enlargement thereof duly granted, and the court whose judgment is the subject of the appeal has denied for any reason an appellee's motion to dismiss the appeal, made as provided in the foregoing paragraph, the appellee may have the

cause docketed and may seek to have the appeal dismissed in this Court, by producing a certificate, whether in term or vacation, from the clerk of the court whose judgment is the subject of the appeal, establishing the foregoing facts, and by filing a motion to dismiss, which shall conform to Rule 42 and be accompanied by proof of service as prescribed by Rule 28. The clerk's certificate shall be attached to the motion, but it shall not be necessary for the appellee to file the record. In the event that the appeal is thereafter dismissed, the Court may give judgment for costs against the appellant and in favor of appellee. The appellant shall not be entitled to docket the cause after the appeal shall have been dismissed under this paragraph, except by special leave of Court.

Rule 15.

JURISDICTIONAL STATEMENT

1. The jurisdictional statement required by Rule 12 shall contain, in the order here indicated:

(a) The questions presented by the appeal, expressed in the terms and circumstances of the case but without unnecessary detail. The statement of the questions should be short and concise and should not be argumentative or repetitious. The statement of a question presented will be deemed to comprise every subsidiary question fairly included therein. Only the questions set forth in the jurisdictional statement or fairly included therein will be considered by the Court.

(b) A list of all parties to the proceeding in the court whose judgment is sought to be reviewed, except where the caption of the case in this Court contains the names of all such parties. This listing may be done in a footnote. See Rule 28.1

(c) A table of contents and table of authorities, if required by Rule 33.5.

(d) A reference to the official and unofficial reports of any opinions delivered in the courts or administrative agency below.

(e) A concise statement of the grounds on which the jurisdiction of this Court is invoked, showing:

(i) The nature of the proceeding and, if the appeal is from a federal court, the statutory basis for federal jurisdiction.

(ii) The date of the entry of the judgment or decree sought to be reviewed, the date of any order respecting a rehearing, the date the notice of appeal was filed, and the court in which it was filed. In the case of a cross-appeal docketed under Rule 12.4, reliance upon that Rule shall be expressly noted, and the date of receipt of the appellant's jurisdictional statement by the appellee-cross-appellant shall be stated.

(iii) The statutory provision believed to confer jurisdiction of the appeal on this Court, and, if deemed necessary, the cases believed to sustain jurisdiction.

(f) The constitutional provisions, treaties, statutes, ordinances, and regulations that the case involves, setting them out verbatim, and giving the appropriate citation therefor. If the provisions involved are lengthy, their citation alone will suffice at this point, and their pertinent text then shall be set forth in the appendix referred to in subparagraph 1(j) of this Rule.

(g) A *concise* statement of the case containing the facts material to consideration of the questions presented. The statement of the case shall also specify the stage in the proceedings (both in the court of first instance and in the appellate court) at which the questions sought to be reviewed were raised; the method or manner of raising them; and the way in which they were passed upon by the court.

(h) A statement of the reasons why the questions presented are so substantial as to require plenary consideration, with briefs on the merits and oral argument, for their resolution.

(i) If the appeal is from a decree of a district court granting or denying a preliminary injunction, a showing of the matters in which it is contended that the court has abused its discretion by such action. See United States v. Corrick, 298 U.S. 435 (1936); Mayo v. Lakeland Highlands Canning Co., 309 U.S. 310 (1940).

(j) An appendix containing, in the following order:

(i) Copies of any opinions, orders, findings of fact, and conclusions of law, whether written or oral (if recorded and transcribed), delivered upon the rendering of the judgment or decree by the court whose decision is sought to be reviewed.

(ii) Copies of any other such opinions, orders, findings of fact, and conclusions of law rendered by courts or administrative agencies in the case, and, if reference thereto is necessary to ascertain the grounds of the judgment or decree, of those in companion cases. Each of these documents shall include the caption showing the name of the issuing court or agency, the title and number of the case, and the date of its entry.

(iii) A copy of the judgment or decree appealed from and any order on rehearing, including in each the caption showing the name of the issuing court or agency, the title and number of the case, and the date of entry of the judgment, decree, or order on rehearing.

(iv) A copy of the notice of appeal showing the date it was filed and the name of the court where it was filed.

(v) Any other appended materials.

If what is required by this paragraph to be appended to the statement is voluminous, it may, if more convenient, be separately presented.

2. The jurisdictional statement shall be produced in conformity with Rule 33. The Clerk shall not accept any jurisdictional statement that does not comply with this Rule and with Rule 33, except that a party proceeding *in forma pauperis* may proceed in the manner provided in Rule 46.

3. The jurisdictional statement shall be as short as possible, but may not exceed 30 pages, excluding the subject index, table of authorities, any verbatim quotations required by subparagraph 1(f) of this Rule, and the appendices.

Rule 16.

MOTION TO DISMISS OR AFFIRM—REPLY—SUPPLEMENTAL BRIEFS

1. Within 30 days after receipt of the jurisdictional statement, unless the time is enlarged by the Court or a Justice thereof, or by the Clerk under the provisions of Rule 29.4, the appellee may file a motion to dismiss, or a motion to affirm. Where appropriate, a motion to affirm may be united in the alternative with a motion to dismiss, provided that a motion to affirm or dismiss shall not be joined with any other pleading. The Clerk shall not accept any motion so joined.

(a) The Court will receive a motion to dismiss an appeal on the ground that the appeal is not within this Court's jurisdiction, or because not taken in conformity with statute or with these Rules.

(b) The Court will receive a motion to dismiss an appeal from a state court on the ground that it does not present a substantial federal question; or that the federal question sought to be reviewed was not timely or properly raised and was not expressly passed on; or that the judgment rests on an adequate non-federal basis.

(c) The Court will receive a motion to affirm the judgment sought to be reviewed on appeal from a federal court on the ground that it is manifest that the questions on which the decision of the cause depends are so unsubstantial as not to need further argument.

(d) The Court will receive a motion to dismiss or affirm on any other ground the appellee wishes to present as a reason why the Court should not set the case for argument.

2. A motion to dismiss or affirm shall comply in all respects with Rules 33 and 42. Forty copies, with proof of service as prescribed by Rule 28, shall be filed with the Clerk. The Clerk shall not accept a motion or brief that does not comply with this Rule and with Rules 33 and 42, except that a party proceeding *in forma pauperis* may proceed in the manner provided in Rule 46. See Rule 28.1

3. A motion to dismiss or affirm shall be as short as possible and may not, either separately or cumulatively, exceed 30 pages, excluding the subject index, table of authorities, any verbatim quotations included in accordance with Rule 34.1(f), and any appendix.

4. Upon the filing of such motion, or the expiration of the time allowed therefor, or express waiver of the right to file, the jurisdictional statement and the motion, if any, will be distributed by the Clerk to the Court for its consideration. However, if a jurisdictional statement on cross-appeal has been docketed under Rule 12.4, distribution of both it and the jurisdictional statement on appeal will be delayed until the filing of a motion to dismiss or affirm by the cross-appellee, or the expiration of the time allowed therefor, or express waiver of the right to file.

5. A brief opposing a motion to dismiss or affirm may be filed by any appellant, but distribution of the jurisdictional statement and consideration thereof by this Court will not be delayed pending the filing of any such brief. Such brief shall be as short as possible but may not exceed 10 pages. Forty

copies of any such brief, prepared in accordance with Rule 33 and served as prescribed by Rule 28, shall be filed.

6. Any party may file a supplemental brief at any time while a jurisdictional statement is pending, calling attention to new cases or legislation or other intervening matter not available at the time of the party's last filing. A supplemental brief, restricted to such new matter, may not exceed 10 pages. Forty copies of any such brief, prepared in accordance with Rule 33 and served as prescribed by Rule 28, shall be filed.

7. After consideration of the papers distributed pursuant to this Rule, the Court will enter an appropriate order. The order may be a summary disposition on the merits. If the order notes probable jurisdiction or postpones consideration of jurisdiction to the hearing on the merits, the Clerk forthwith shall notify the court below and counsel of record of the noting or postponement. The case then will stand for briefing and oral argument. If the record has not previously been filed, the Clerk of this Court shall request the clerk of the court possessed of the record to certify it and transmit it to this Court.

8. If consideration of jurisdiction is postponed, counsel, at the outset of their briefs and oral argument, shall address the question of jurisdiction.

PART V. JURISDICTION ON WRIT OF CERTIORARI

Rule 17.

CONSIDERATIONS GOVERNING REVIEW ON CERTIORARI

1. A review on writ of certiorari is not a matter of right, but of judicial discretion, and will be granted only when there are special and important reasons therefor. The following, while neither controlling nor fully measuring the Court's discretion, indicate the character of reasons that will be considered.

(a) When a federal court of appeals has rendered a decision in conflict with the decision of another federal court of appeals on the same matter; or has decided a federal question in a way in conflict with a state court of last resort; or has so far departed from the accepted and usual course of judicial proceedings, or so far sanctioned such a departure by a lower court, as to call for an exercise of this Court's power of supervision.

(b) When a state court of last resort has decided a federal question in a way in conflict with the decision of another state court of last resort or of a federal court of appeals.

(c) When a state court or a federal court of appeals has decided an important question of federal law which has not been, but should be, settled by this Court, or has decided a federal question in a way in conflict with applicable desions of this Court.

2. The same general considerations outlined above will control in respect of petitions for writs of certiorari to review judgments of the Court of Claims, of the Court of Customs and Patent Appeals, and of any other court whose judgments are reviewable by law on writ of certiorari.

Rule 18.

CERTIORARI TO A FEDERAL COURT OF APPEALS BEFORE JUDGMENT

A petition for writ of certiorari to review a case pending in a federal court of appeals, before judgment is given in such court, will be granted only upon a showing that the case is of such imperative public importance as to justify the deviation from normal appellate practice and to require immediate settlement in this Court. See 28 U.S.C. § 2101(e); see also, United States v. Bankers Trust Co., 294 U.S. 240 (1935); Railroad Retirement Board v. Alton R. Co., 295 U.S. 330 (1935); Rickert Rice Mills v. Fontenot, 297 U.S. 110 (1936); Carter v. Carter Coal Co., 298 U.S. 238 (1936); Ex parte Quirin, 317 U.S. 1 (1942); United States v. Mine Workers, 330 U.S. 258 (1947); Youngstown Sheet & Tube Co. v. Sawyer, 343 U.S. 579 (1952); Wilson v. Girard, 354 U.S. 524 (1957); United States v. Nixon, 418 U.S. 683 (1974).

Rule 19.

REVIEW ON CERTIORARI—HOW SOUGHT—PARTIES

1. A party intending to file a petition for certiorari, prior to filing the case in this Court or at any time prior to action by this Court on the petition, may request the clerk of the court possessed of the record to certify it, or any part of it, and to provide for its transmission to this Court, but the filing of the record in this Court is not a requisite for docketing the petition. If the petitioner has not done so, the respondent may request

such clerk to certify and transmit the record or any part of it. Thereafter, the Clerk of this Court or any party to the case may request that additional parts of the record be certified and transmitted to this Court. Copies of all requests for certification and transmission shall be sent to all parties to the proceeding. Such requests to certify the record prior to action by the Court on the petition for certiorari, however, should not be made as a matter of course but only when the record is deemed essential to a proper understanding of the case by this Court.

2. When requested to certify and transmit the record, or any part of it, the clerk of the court possessed of the record shall number the documents to be certified and shall transmit with the record a numbered list of the documents, identifying each with reasonable definiteness. If the record, or stipulated portions thereof, has been printed for the use of the court below, such printed record plus the proceedings in the court below may be certified as the record unless one of the parties or the Clerk of this Court otherwise requests. The provisions of Rule 13.3 with respect to original papers shall apply to all cases sought to be reviewed on writ of certiorari.

3. Counsel for the petitioner shall enter an appearance, pay the docket fee, and file, with proof of service as provided by Rule 28, 40 copies of a petition which shall comply in all respects with Rule 21. The case then will be placed on the docket. It shall be the duty of counsel for the petitioner to notify all respondents, on a form supplied by the Clerk, of the date of filing and of the docket number of the case. Such notice shall be served as required by Rule 28.

4. Parties interested jointly, severally, or otherwise in a judgment may join in a petition for a writ of certiorari therefrom; or any one or more of them may petition separately; or any two or more of them may join in a petition. When two or more cases are sought to be reviewed on certiorari to the same court and involve identical or closely related questions, it will suffice to file a single petition for writ of certiorari covering all the cases.

5. Not more than 30 days after receipt of the petition for certiorari, counsel for a respondent wishing to file a cross-petition that would otherwise be untimely shall enter an appearance, pay the docket fee, and file, with proof of service as prescribed by Rule 28, 40 copies of a cross-petition for certiorari, which shall comply in all respects with Rule 21. The cross-petition will then be placed on the docket subject, however, to the provisions of Rule 20.5. It shall be the duty of counsel for the cross-petitioner to notify the cross-respondent on a form

supplied by the Clerk of the date of docketing and of the docket number of the cross-petition. Such notice shall be served as required by Rule 28. A cross-petition for certiorari may not be joined with any other pleading. The Clerk shall not accept any pleadings so joined. The time for filing a cross-petition may not be extended.

6. All parties to the proceeding in the court whose judgment is sought to be reviewed shall be deemed parties in this Court, unless the petitioner shall notify the Clerk of this Court in writing of petitioner's belief that one or more of the parties below has no interest in the outcome of the petition. A copy of such notice shall be served on all parties to the proceeding below and a party noted as no longer interested may remain a party here by notifying the Clerk, with service on the other parties, that he has an interest in the petition. All parties other than petitioners shall be respondents, but any respondent who supports the position of a petitioner shall meet the time schedule for filing papers which is provided for that petitioner, except that any response by such respondent to the petition shall be filed within 20 days after receipt of the petition. The time for filing such response may not be extended.

Rule 20.

REVIEW ON CERTIORARI—TIME FOR PETITIONING

1. A petition for writ of certiorari to review the judgment in a criminal case of a state court of last resort or of a federal court of appeals shall be deemed in time when it is filed with the Clerk within 60 days after the entry of such judgment. A Justice of this Court, for good cause shown, may extend the time for applying for a writ of certiorari in such cases for a period not exceeding 30 days.

2. A petition for writ of certiorari in all other cases shall be deemed in time when it is filed with the Clerk within the time prescribed by law. See 28 U.S.C. § 2101(c).

3. The Clerk will refuse to receive any petition for a writ of certiorari which is jurisdictionally out of time.

4. The time for filing a petition for writ of certiorari runs from the date the judgment or decree sought to be reviewed is rendered, and not from the date of the issuance of the mandate (or its equivalent under local practice). However, if a petition for rehearing is timely filed by any party in the case, the time for filing the petition for writ of certiorari for all parties (whether or not they requested rehearing or joined in the

petition for rehearing) runs from the date of the denial of rehearing or of the entry of a subsequent judgment entered on the rehearing.

5. A cross-petition for writ of certiorari shall be deemed in time when it is filed as provided in paragraphs 1, 2, and 4 of this Rule or in Rule 19.5. However, no cross-petition filed untimely except for the provision of Rule 19.5 shall be granted unless a timely petition for writ of certiorari of another party to the case is granted.

6. An application for extension of time within which to file a petition for writ of certiorari must set out, as in a petition for certiorari (see Rule 21.1, subparagraphs (e) and (h)), the grounds on which the jurisdiction of this Court is invoked, must identify the judgment sought to be reviewed and have appended thereto a copy of the opinion, and must set forth with specificity the reasons why the granting of an extension of time is thought justified. For the time and manner of presenting such an application, see Rules 29, 42, and 43. Such applications are not favored.

Rule 21.

THE PETITION FOR CERTIORARI

1. The petition for writ of certiorari shall contain, in the order here indicated:

(a) The questions presented for review, expressed in the terms and circumstances of the case but without unnecessary detail. The statement of the questions should be short and concise and should not be argumentative or repetitious. The statement of a question presented will be deemed to comprise every subsidiary question fairly included therein. Only the questions set forth in the petition or fairly included therein will be considered by the Court.

(b) A list of all parties to the proceeding in the court whose judgment is sought to be reviewed, except where the caption of the case in this Court contains the names of all parties. This listing may be done in a footnote. See Rule 28.1.

(c) A table of contents and table of authorities, if required by Rule 33.5.

(d) A reference to the official and unofficial reports of any opinions delivered in the courts or administrative agency below.

(e) A concise statement of the grounds on which the jurisdiction of this Court is invoked showing:

(i) The date of the judgment or decree sought to be reviewed, and the time of its entry;

(ii) The date of any order respecting a rehearing, and the date and terms of any order granting an extension of time within which to petition for certiorari; and

(iii) Where a cross-petition for writ of certiorari is filed under Rule 19.5, reliance upon that Rule shall be expressly noted and the cross-petition shall state the date of receipt of the petition for certiorari in connection with which the cross-petition is filed.

(iv) The statutory provision believed to confer on this Court jurisdiction to review the judgment or decree in question by writ of certiorari.

(f) The constitutional provisions, treaties, statutes, ordinances, and regulations which the case involves, setting them out verbatim, and giving the appropriate citation therefor. If the provisions involved are lengthy, their citation alone will suffice at this point, and their pertinent text then shall be set forth in the appendix referred to in subparagraph 1(k) of this Rule.

(g) A *concise* statement of the case containing the facts material to the consideration of the questions presented.

(h) If review of the judgment of a state court is sought, the statement of the case shall also specify the stage in the proceedings, both in the court of first instance and in the appellate court, at which the federal questions sought to be reviewed were raised; the method or manner of raising them and the way in which they were passed upon by the court; such pertinent quotation of specific portions of the record, or summary thereof, with specific reference to the places in the record where the matter appears (*e. g.*, ruling on exception, portion of court's charge and exception thereto, assignment of errors) as will show that the federal question was timely and properly raised so as to give this Court jurisdiction to review the judgment on writ of certiorari.

Where the portions of the record relied upon under this subparagraph are voluminous, they shall be included in the appendix referred to in subparagraph 1(k) of this Rule.

(i) If review of the judgment of a federal court is sought, the statement of the case shall also show the basis for federal jurisdiction in the court of first instance.

(j) A direct and concise argument amplifying the reasons relied on for the allowance of the writ. See Rule 17.

(k) An appendix containing, in the following order:

(i) Copies of any opinions, orders, findings of fact, and conclusions of law, whether written or oral (if recorded and transcribed), delivered upon the rendering of the judgment or decree by the court whose decision is sought to be reviewed.

(ii) Copies of any other such opinions, orders, findings of fact, and conclusions of law rendered by courts or administrative agencies in the case, and, if reference thereto is necessary to ascertain the grounds of the judgment or decree, of those in companion cases. Each of these documents shall include the caption showing the name of the issuing court or agency and the title and number of the case, and the date of its entry.

(iii) A copy of the judgment or decree sought to be reviewed and any order on rehearing, including in each the caption showing the name of the issuing court or agency, the title and number of the case, and the date of entry of the judgment, decree, or order on rehearing.

(iv) Any other appended materials.

If what is required by this paragraph or by subparagraphs 1(f) and (h) of this Rule, to be included in the petition is voluminous, it may, if more convenient, be separately presented.

2. The petition for writ of certiorari shall be produced in conformity with Rule 33. The Clerk shall not accept any petition for writ of certiorari that does not comply with this Rule and with Rule 33, except that a party proceeding *in forma pauperis* may proceed in the manner provided in Rule 46.

3. All contentions in support of a petition for writ of certiorari shall be set forth in the body of the petition, as provided in subparagraph 1(j) of this Rule. No separate brief in support of a petition for a writ of certiorari will be received, and the Clerk will refuse to file any petition for a writ of certiorari to which is annexed or appended any supporting brief.

4. The petition for writ of certiorari shall be as short as possible, but may not exceed 30 pages, excluding the subject in-

dex, table of authorities, any verbatim quotations required by subparagraph 1(f) of this Rule, and the appendix.

5. The failure of a petitioner to present with accuracy, brevity, and clearness whatever is essential to a ready and adequate understanding of the points requiring consideration will be a sufficient reason for denying his petition.

Rule 22.

BRIEF IN OPPOSITION—REPLY—SUPPLEMENTAL BRIEFS

1. Respondent shall have 30 days (unless enlarged by the Court or a Justice thereof or by the Clerk pursuant to Rule 29.4) after receipt of a petition, within which to file 40 printed copies of an opposing brief disclosing any matter or ground why the cause should not be reviewed by this Court. See Rule 17. Such brief in opposition shall comply with Rule 33 and with the requirements of Rule 34 governing a respondent's brief, and shall be served as prescribed by Rule 28. The Clerk shall not accept a brief which does not comply with this Rule and with Rule 33, except that a party proceeding *in forma pauperis* may proceed in the manner provided in Rule 46.

2. A brief in opposition shall be as short as possible and may not, in any single case, exceed 30 pages, excluding the subject index, table of authorities, any verbatim quotations included in accordance with Rule 34.1(f), and any appendix. See Rule 28.1

3. No motion by a respondent to dismiss a petition for writ of certiorari will be received. Objections to the jurisdiction of the Court to grant the writ of certiorari may be included in the brief in opposition.

4. Upon the filing of a brief in opposition, or the expiration of the time allowed therefor, or express waiver of the right to file, the petition and brief, if any, will be distributed by the Clerk to the Court for its consideration. However, if a cross-petition for certiorari has been filed, distribution of both it and the petition for certiorari will be delayed until the filing of a brief in opposition by the cross-respondent, or the expiration of the time allowed therefor, or express waiver of the right to file.

5. A reply brief addressed to arguments first raised in the brief in opposition may be filed by any petitioner but distribution under paragraph 4 hereof will not be delayed pending the filing of any such brief. Such brief shall be as short as possible,

but may not exceed 10 pages. Forty copies of any such brief, prepared in accordance with Rule 33 and served as prescribed by Rule 28, shall be filed.

6. Any party may file a supplemental brief at any time while a petition for writ of certiorari is pending calling attention to new cases or legislation or other intervening matter not available at the time of the party's last filing. A supplemental brief, restricted to such new matter, may not exceed 10 pages. Forty copies of any such brief, prepared in accordance with Rule 33 and served as prescribed by Rule 28, shall be filed.

Rule 23.

DISPOSITION OF PETITION FOR CERTIORARI

1. After consideration of the papers distributed pursuant to Rule 22, the Court will enter an appropriate order. The order may be a summary disposition on the merits.

2. Whenever a petition for writ of certiorari to review a decision of any court is granted, an order to that effect shall be entered, and the Clerk forthwith shall notify the court below and counsel of record. The case then will stand for briefing and oral argument. If the record has not previously been filed, the Clerk of this Court shall request the clerk of the court possessed of the record to certify it and transmit it to this Court. A formal writ shall not issue unless specially directed.

3. Whenever a petition for writ of certiorari to review a decision of any court is denied, an order to that effect will be entered and the Clerk forthwith will notify the court below and counsel of record. The order of denial will not be suspended pending disposition of a petition for rehearing except by order of the Court or a Justice thereof.

PART VI. JURISDICTION OF CERTIFIED QUESTIONS

Rule 24.

QUESTIONS CERTIFIED BY A COURT OF APPEALS OR BY THE COURT OF CLAIMS

1. When a federal court of appeals or the Court of Claims shall certify to this Court a question or proposition of law concerning which it desires instruction for the proper decision of a cause (see 28 U.S.C. §§ 1254(3), 1255(2)), the certificate shall contain a statement of the nature of the cause and the facts on which such question or proposition of law arises. Questions

of fact cannot be certified. Only questions or propositions of law may be certified, and they must be distinct and definite.

2. When a question is certified by a federal court of appeals, and if it appears that there is special reason therefor, this Court, on application or on its own motion, may consider and decide the entire matter in controversy. See 28 U.S.C. § 1254(3).

Rule 25.

PROCEDURE IN CERTIFIED CASES

1. When a case is certified, the Clerk will notify the respective parties and shall docket the case. Counsel shall then enter their appearances.

2. After docketing, the certificate shall be submitted to the Court for a preliminary examination to determine whether the case shall be briefed, set for argument, or the certificate dismissed. No brief may be filed prior to the preliminary examination of the certificate.

3. If the Court orders that the case be briefed or set down for argument, the parties shall be notified and permitted to file briefs. The Clerk of this Court shall request the clerk of the court from which the case comes to certify the record and transmit it to this Court. Any portion of the record to which the parties wish to direct the Court's particular attention shall be printed in a joint appendix prepared by the appellant or plaintiff in the court below under the procedures provided in Rule 30, but the fact that any part of the record has not been printed shall not prevent the parties or the Court from relying on it.

4. Briefs on the merits in a case on certificate shall comply with Rules 33, 34, and 35, except that the brief of the party who was appellant or plaintiff below shall be filed within 45 days of the order requiring briefs or setting the case down for argument. See Rule 28.1

PART VII. JURISDICTION TO ISSUE EXTRAORDINARY WRITS

Rule 26.

CONSIDERATIONS GOVERNING ISSUANCE OF EXTRAORDINARY WRITS

The issuance by the Court of any extraordinary writ authorized by 28 U.S.C. § 1651(a) is not a matter of right, but of discretion sparingly exercised. To justify the granting of any writ under that provision, it must be shown that the writ will be in aid of the Court's appellate jurisdiction, that there are present exceptional circumstances warranting the exercise of the Court's discretionary powers, and that adequate relief cannot be had in any other form or from any other court.

Rule 27.

PROCEDURE IN SEEKING AN EXTRAORDINARY WRIT

1. The petition in any proceeding seeking the issuance by this Court of a writ authorized by 28 U.S.C. §§ 1651(a), 2241, or 2254(a), shall comply in all respects with Rule 33, except that a party proceeding *in forma pauperis* may proceed in the manner provided in Rule 46. The petition shall be captioned "In re (name of petitioner)." All contentions in support of the petition shall be included in the petition. The case will be placed upon the docket when 40 copies, with proof of service as prescribed by Rule 28 (subject to paragraph 3(b) of this Rule), are filed with the Clerk and the docket fee is paid. The appearance of counsel for the petitioner must be entered at this time. The petition shall be as short as possible, and in any event may not exceed 30 pages.

2. (a) If the petition seeks issuance of a writ of prohibition, a writ of mandamus, or both in the alternative, it shall identify by names and office or function all persons against whom relief is sought and shall set forth with particularity why the relief sought is not available in any other court. There shall be appended to such petition a copy of the judgment or order in respect of which the writ is sought, including a copy of any opinion rendered in that connection, and such other papers as may be essential to an understanding of the petition.

(b) The petition shall follow, insofar as applicable, the form for the petition for writ of certiorari prescribed by Rule 21. The petition shall be served on the judge or judges to whom the writ is sought to be directed, and shall also be served on every other party to the proceeding in respect of which relief is desired. The judge or judges, and the other parties, within 30 days after receipt of the petition, may file 40 copies of a brief or briefs in opposition thereto, which shall comply fully with Rules 22.1 and 22.2, including the 30-page limit. If the judge or judges concerned do not desire to respond to the petition, they shall so advise the Clerk and all parties by letter. All persons served pursuant to this paragraph shall be deemed respondents for all purposes in the proceedings in this Court.

3. (a) If the petition seeks issuance of a writ of habeas corpus, it shall comply with the requirements of 28 U.S.C. § 2242, and in particular with the requirement in the last paragraph thereof that it state the reasons for not making application to the district court of the district in which the petitioner is held. If the relief sought is from the judgment of a state court, the petition shall set forth specifically how and wherein the petitioner has exhausted his remedies in the state courts or otherwise comes within the provisions of 28 U.S.C. § 2254(b). To justify the granting of a writ of habeas corpus, it must be shown that there are present exceptional circumstances warranting the exercise of the Court's discretionary powers and that adequate relief cannot be had in any other form or from any other court. Such writs are rarely granted.

(b) Proceedings under this paragraph 3 will be *ex parte*, unless the Court requires the respondent to show cause why the petition for a writ of habeas corpus should not be granted. If a response is ordered, it shall comply fully with Rules 22.1 and 22.2, including the 30-page limit. Neither denial of the petition, without more, nor an order of transfer under authority of 28 U.S.C. § 2241(b), is an adjudication on the merits, and the former action is to be taken as without prejudice to a further application to any other court for the relief sought.

4. If the petition seeks issuance of a common-law writ of certiorari under 28 U.S.C. § 1651(a), there may also be filed, at the time of docketing, a certified copy of the record, including all proceedings in the court to which the writ is sought to be directed. However, the filing of such record is not required. The petition shall follow, insofar as applicable, the form for a petition for certiorari prescribed by Rule 21, and shall set forth with particularity why the relief sought is not available in any other court, or cannot be had through other appellate process. The respondent, within 30 days after receipt of the petition, may file 40 copies of a brief in opposition, which shall comply fully with Rules 22.1 and 22.2, including the 30-page limit.

5. When a brief in opposition under paragraphs 2 and 4 has been filed, or when a response under paragraph 3 has been ordered and filed, or when the time within which it may be filed has expired, or upon an express waiver of the right to file, the papers will be distributed to the Court by the Clerk.

6. If the Court orders the cause set down for argument, the Clerk will notify the parties whether additional briefs are required, when they must be filed, and, if the case involves a petition for common-law certiorari, that the parties shall proceed to print a joint appendix pursuant to Rule 30.

PART VIII. PRACTICE

Rule 28.

FILING AND SERVICE—SPECIAL RULE FOR SERVICE WHERE CONSTITUTIONALITY OF ACT OF CONGRESS OR STATE STATUTE IS IN ISSUE

1. Pleadings, motions, notices, briefs, or other documents or papers required or permitted to be presented to this Court or to a Justice shall be filed with the Clerk. Any document filed by or on behalf of counsel of record whose appearance has not previously been entered must be accompanied by an entry of appearance. Any document, except a joint appendix or a brief *amicus curiae*, filed by or on behalf of one or more corporations, shall include a listing naming all parent companies, subsidiaries (except wholly owned subsidiaries) and affiliates of each such corporation. This listing may be done in a footnote. If such listing has been included in a document filed earlier in the particular case, reference may be made to the earlier document and only amendments to the listing to make it currently accurate need be included in the document currently being filed.

2. To be timely filed, a document must be received by the Clerk within the time specified for filing, except that any document shall be deemed timely filed if it has been deposited in a United States post office or mailbox, with first-class postage prepaid, and properly addressed to the Clerk of this Court, within the time allowed for filing, and if there is filed with the Clerk a notarized statement by a member of the Bar of this Court, setting forth the details of the mailing, and stating that to his knowledge the mailing took place on a particular date within the permitted time.

3. Whenever any pleading, motion, notice, brief, or other document is required by these Rules to be served, such service may be made personally or by mail on each party to the proceeding at or before the time of filing. If the document has been produced under Rule 33, three copies shall be served on each other party separately represented in the proceeding. If the document is typewritten, service of a single copy on each other party separately represented shall suffice. If personal service is made, it may consist of delivery, at the office of counsel of record, to counsel or an employee therein. If service is by mail, it shall consist of depositing the document in a United States post office or mailbox, with first-class postage prepaid, addressed to counsel of record at his post office address. Where a par-

ty is not represented by counsel, service shall be upon the party, personally or by mail.

4. (a) If the United States or any department, office, agency, officer, or employee thereof is a party to be served, service must be made upon the Solicitor General, Department of Justice, Washington, D. C. 20530; and if a response is required or permitted within a prescribed period after service, the time does not begin to run until the document actually has been received by the Solicitor General's office. Where an agency of the United States is authorized by law to appear in its own behalf as a party, or where an officer or employee of the United States is a party, in addition to the United States, such agency, officer, or employee also must be served, in addition to the Solicitor General; and if a response is required or permitted within a prescribed period, the time does not begin to run until the document actually has been received by both the agency, officer, or employee and the Solicitor General's office.

(b) In any proceeding in this Court wherein the constitutionality of an Act of Congress is drawn in question, and the United States or any department, office, agency, officer, or employee thereof is not a party, the initial pleading, motion, or paper in this Court shall recite that 28 U.S.C. § 2403(a) may be applicable and shall be served upon the Solicitor General, Department of Justice, Washington, D. C. 20530. In proceedings from any court of the United States, as defined by 28 U.S.C. § 451, the initial pleading, motion, or paper shall state whether or not any such court, pursuant to 28 U.S.C. § 2403(a), has certified to the Attorney General the fact that the constitutionality of such Act of Congress was drawn in question.

(c) In any proceeding in this Court wherein the constitutionality of any statute of a State is drawn in question, and the State or any agency, officer, or employee thereof is not a party, the initial pleading, motion, or paper in this Court shall recite that 28 U.S.C. § 2403(b) may be applicable and shall be served upon the Attorney General of the State. In proceedings from any court of the United States as defined by 28 U.S.C. § 451, the initial pleading, motion, or paper shall state whether or not any such court, pursuant to 28 U.S.C. § 2403(b), has certified to the State Attorney General the fact that the constitutionality of such statute of the State was drawn in question.

5. Whenever proof of service is required by these Rules, it must accompany or be endorsed upon the document in question at the time the document is presented to the Clerk for filing. Proof of service shall be shown by any one of the methods set forth below, and it must contain or be accompanied by a state-

ment that all parties required to be served have been served, together with a list of the names and addresses of those parties; it is not necessary that service on each party required to be served be made in the same manner or evidenced by the same proof:

(a) By an acknowledgment of service of the document in question, signed by counsel of record for the party served.

(b) By a certificate of service of the document in question, reciting the facts and circumstances of service in compliance with the appropriate paragraph or paragraphs of this Rule, and signed by a member of the Bar of this Court representing the party on whose behalf such serice has been made. (If counsel certifying to such service has not yet entered an appearance in this Court in respect of the cause in which such service is made, an entry of appearance shall accompany the certificate of service.)

(c) By an affidavit of service of the document in question, reciting the facts and circumstances of service in compliance with the appropriate paragraph or paragraphs of this Rule, whenever such service is made by any person not a member of the Bar of this Court.

Rule 29.

COMPUTATION AND ENLARGEMENT OF TIME

1. In computing any period of time prescribed or allowed by these Rules, by order of Court, or by an applicable statute, the day of the act, event, or default after which the designated period of time begins to run is not to be included. The last day of the period so computed is to be included, unless it is a Sunday or a federal legal holiday, in which event the period runs until the end of the next day which is neither a Sunday nor a federal legal holiday.

2. Whenever any Justice of this Court or the Clerk is empowered by law or under any provision of these Rules to extend the time for filing any document or paper, an application seeking such extension must be presented to the Clerk within the period sought to be extended. However, an application for extension of time to docket an appeal or to file a petition for certiorari shall be submitted at least 10 days before the specified final filing date and will not be granted, except in the most extraordinary circumstances, if filed less than 10 days before that date.

3. An application to extend the time within which a party may docket an appeal or file a petition for a writ of certiorari shall be presented in the form prescribed by Rules 12.2 and 20.6, respectively. An application to extend the time within which to file any other document or paper may be presented in the form of a letter to the Clerk setting forth with specificity the reasons why the granting of an extension of time is thought justified. Any application seeking an extension of time must be presented and served upon all other parties as provided in Rule 43, and any such application, if once denied, may not be renewed.

4. Any application for extension of time to file a brief, motion, joint appendix, or other paper, to designate parts of a record for printing in the appendix, or otherwise to comply with a time limit provided by these Rules (except an application for extension of time to docket an appeal, to file a petition for certiorari, to file a petition for rehearing, or to issue a mandate) shall in the first instance be acted upon by the Clerk, whether addressed to him, to the Court, or to a Justice. Any party aggrieved by the Clerk's action on such application may request that it be submitted to a Justice or to the Court. The Clerk's action under this Rule shall be reported by him to the Court in accordance with the instructions that may be issued to him by the Court.

Rule 30.

THE JOINT APPENDIX

1. Unless the parties agree to use the deferred method allowed in paragraph 4 of this Rule, or the Court so directs, the appellant or petitioner, within 45 days after the order noting or postponing probable jurisdiction or granting the writ of certiorari, shall file 40 copies of a joint appendix, duplicated in the manner prescribed by Rule 33, which shall contain: (1) the relevant docket entries in the courts below; (2) any relevant pleading, jury instruction, finding, conclusion, or opinion; (3) the judgment, order, or decision in question; and (4) any other parts of the record to which the parties wish to direct the Court's attention. However, any of the foregoing items which have already been reproduced in a jurisdictional statement or the petition for certiorari complying with Rule 33.1 need not be reproduced again in the joint appendix. The appellant or petitioner shall serve at least three copies of the joint appendix on each of the other parties to the proceeding.

2. The parties are encouraged to agree to the contents of the joint appendix. In the absence of agreement, the appellant or petitioner, not later than 10 days after the order noting or postponing jurisdiction or granting the writ of certiorari, shall serve on the appellee or respondent a designation of the parts of the record which he intends to include in the joint appendix. If in the judgment of the appellee or respondent the parts of the record so designated are not sufficient, he, within 10 days after receipt of the designation, shall serve upon the appellant or petitioner a designation of additional parts to be included in the joint appendix, and the appellant or petitioner shall include the parts so designated, unless, on his motion in a case where the respondent has been permitted by this Court to proceed *in forma pauperis*, he is excused from supplementing the record.

In making these designations, counsel should include only those materials the Court should examine. Unnecessary designations should be avoided. The record is on file with the Clerk and available to the Justices, and counsel may refer in their briefs and oral argument to relevant portions of the record that have not been printed.

3. At the time that the joint appendix is filed or promptly thereafter, the appellant or petitioner shall file with the Clerk a statement of the costs of preparing the same, and shall serve a copy thereof on each of the other parties to the proceeding. Unless the parties otherwise agree, the cost of producing the joint appendix shall initially be paid by the appellant or petitioner; but if he considers that parts of the record designated by the appellee or respondent are unnecessary for the determination of the issues presented, he may so advise the appellee or respondent who then shall advance the cost of including such parts unless the Court or a Justice otherwise fixes the initial allocation of the costs. The cost of producing the joint appendix shall be taxed as costs in the case, but if a party shall cause matter to be included in the joint appendix unnecessarily, the Court may impose the cost of producing such matter on that party.

4. (a) If the parties agree or if the Court shall so order, preparation of the joint appendix may be deferred until after the briefs have been filed, and in that event the appellant or petitioner shall file the joint appendix within 14 days after receipt of the brief of the appellee or respondent. The provisions of paragraphs 1, 2, and 3 of this Rule shall be followed except that the designations referred to therein shall be made by each party at the time his brief is served.

(b) If the deferred method is used, reference in the briefs to the record may be to the pages of the parts of the record involved, in which event the original paging of each part of the record shall be indicated in the joint appendix by placing in brackets the number of each page at the place in the joint appendix where that page begins. Or if a party desires to refer in his brief directly to pages of the joint appendix, he may serve and file typewritten or page-proof copies of his brief within the time required by Rule 35, with appropriate references to the pages of the parts of the record involved. In that event, within 10 days after the joint appendix is filed he shall serve and file copies of the brief in the form prescribed by Rule 33 containing references to the pages of the joint appendix in place of or in addition to the initial references to the pages of the parts of the record involved. No other change may be made in the brief as initially served and filed, except that typographical errors may be corrected.

5. At the beginning of the joint appendix there shall be inserted a table of the parts of the record which it contains, in the order in which the parts are set out therein, with references to the pages of the joint appendix at which each part begins. The relevant docket entries shall be set out following the table of contents. Thereafter, the other parts of the record shall be set out in chronological order. When matter contained in the reporter's transcript of proceedings is set out in the joint appendix, the page of the transcript at which such matter may be found shall be indicated in brackets immediately before the matter which is set out. Omissions in the text of papers or of the transcript must be indicated by asterisks. Immaterial formal matters (captions, subscriptions, acknowledgments, etc.) shall be omitted. A question and its answer may be contained in a single paragraph.

6. Exhibits designated for inclusion in the joint appendix may be contained in a separate volume, or volumes, suitably indexed. The transcript of a proceeding before an administrative agency, board, commission, or officer used in an action in a district court or a court of appeals shall be regarded as an exhibit for the purpose of this paragraph.

7. The Court by order may dispense with the requirement of a joint appendix and may permit a case to be heard on the original record (with such copies of the record, or relevant parts thereof, as the Court may require), or on the appendix used in the court below, if it conforms to the requirements of this Rule.

8. For good cause shown, the time limits specified in this Rule may be shortened or enlarged by the Court, by a Justice thereof, or by the Clerk under the provisions of Rule 29.4.

Rule 31.

TRANSLATIONS

Whenever any record transmitted to this Court contains any document, paper, testimony, or other proceeding in a foreign language without a translation made under the authority of the lower court or admitted to be correct, the clerk of the court transmitting the record shall report the fact immediately to the Clerk of this Court, to the end that this Court may order that a translation be supplied and, if necessary, printed as a part of the joint appendix.

Rule 32.

MODELS, DIAGRAMS, AND EXHIBITS OF MATERIAL

1. Models, diagrams, and exhibits of material forming part of the evidence taken in a case, and brought up to this Court for its inspection, shall be placed in the custody of the Clerk at least two weeks before the case is heard or submitted.

2. All such models, diagrams, and exhibits of material placed in the custody of the Clerk must be taken away by the parties within 40 days after the case is decided. When this is not done, it shall be the duty of the Clerk to notify counsel to remove the articles forthwith; and if they are not removed within a reasonable time after such notice, the Clerk shall destroy them, or make such other disposition of them as to him may seem best.

Rule 33.

FORM OF JURISDICTIONAL STATEMENTS, PETITIONS, BRIEFS, APPENDICES, MOTIONS, AND OTHER DOCUMENTS FILED WITH THE COURT

1. (a) Except for typewritten filings permitted by Rules 42.2(c), 43, and 46, all jurisdictional statements, petitions, briefs, appendices, and other documents filed with the Court shall be produced by standard typographic printing, which is preferred, or by any photostatic or similar process which produces a clear, black image on white paper; but ordinary carbon copies may not be used.

(b) The text of documents produced by standard typographic printing shall appear in print as 11-point or larger type with 2-point or more leading between lines. Footnotes shall appear in print as 9-point or larger type with 2-point or more leading between lines. Such documents shall be printed on both sides of the page.

(c) The text of documents produced by a photostatic or similar process shall be done in pica type at no more than 10 characters per inch with the lines double-spaced, except that indented quotations and footnotes may be single-spaced. In footnotes, elite type at no more than 12 characters per inch may be used. Such documents may be duplicated on both sides of the page, if practicable. They shall not be reduced in duplication.

(d) Whether duplicated under subparagraph (b) or (c) of this paragraph, documents shall be produced on opaque, unglazed paper 6⅛ by 9¼ inches in size, with type matter approximately 4⅛ by 7⅛ inches, and margins of at least ¾ inch on all sides. The paper shall be firmly bound in at least two places along the left margin so as to make an easily opened volume, and no part of the text shall be obscured by the binding. However, appendices in patent cases may be duplicated in such size as is necessary to utilize copies of patent documents.

2. (a) All documents filed with the Court must bear on the cover, in the following order, from the top of the page: (1) the number of the case or, if there is none, a space for one; (2) the name of this Court; (3) the Term; (4) the caption of the case as appropriate in this Court; (5) the nature of the proceeding and the name of the court from which the action is brought (*e. g.*, On Appeal from the Supreme Court of California; On Writ of Certiorari to the United States Court of Appeals for the Fifth Circuit); (6) the title of the paper (*e. g.*, Jurisdictional Statement, Brief for Respondent, Joint Appendix); (7) the name, post office address, and telephone number of the member of the Bar of this Court who is counsel of record for the party concerned, and upon whom service is to be made. The individual names of other members of the Bar of this Court or of the Bar of the highest court in their respective states and, if desired, their post office addresses, may be added, but counsel of record shall be clearly identified. The foregoing shall be displayed in an appropriate typographic manner and, except for the identification of counsel, may not be set in type smaller than 11-point or in upper case pica.

(b) The following documents shall have a suitable cover consisting of heavy paper in the color indicated: (1) jurisdictional statements and petitions for writs of certiorari, white; (2)

motions, briefs, or memoranda filed in response to jurisdictional statements or petitions for certiorari, light orange; (3) briefs on the merits for appellants or petitioners, light blue; (4) briefs on the merits for appellees or respondents, light red; (5) reply briefs, yellow; (6) intervenor or *amicus curiae* briefs (or motions for leave to file, if bound with brief), green; (7) joint appendices, tan; (8) documents filed by the United States, by any department, office, or agency of the United States, or by any officer or employee of the United States, represented by the Solicitor General, gray. All other documents shall have a tan cover. Counsel shall be certain that there is adequate contrast between the printing and the color of the cover.

3. All documents produced by standard typographic printing or its equivalent shall comply with the page limits prescribed by these Rules. See Rules 15.3; 16.3, 16.5, and 16.6; 21.4; 22.2, 22.5, and 22.6; 27.1, 27.2(b), 27.3(b), and 27.4; 34.3 and 34.4; 36.1 and 36.2. Where documents are produced by photostatic or similar process, the following page limits shall apply:

Jurisdictional Statement (Rule 15.3)	65 pages;
Motion to Dismiss or Affirm (Rule 16.3)	65 pages;
Brief Opposing Motion to Dismiss or Affirm (Rule 16.5)	20 pages;
Supplemental Brief (Rule 16.6)	20 pages;
Petition for Certiorari (Rule 21.4)	65 pages;
Brief in Opposition (Rule 22.2)	65 pages;
Reply Brief (Rule 22.5)	20 pages;
Supplemental Brief (Rule 22.6)	20 pages;
Petition Seeking Extraordinary Writ (Rule 27.1)	65 pages;
Brief in Opposition (Rule 27.2(b))	65 pages;
Response to Petition for Habeas Corpus (Rule 27.3(b))	65 pages;
Brief in Opposition (Rule 27.4)	65 pages;
Brief on the Merits (Rule 34.3)	110 pages;
Reply Brief (Rule 34.4)	45 pages;
Brief of *Amicus Curiae* (Rule 36.2)	65 pages.

4. The Court or a Justice, for good cause shown, may grant leave for the filing of a document in excess of the page limits, but such an application is not favored. An application for such leave shall comply in all respects with Rule 43; and it must be submitted at least 15 days before the filing date of the document in question, except in the most extraordinary circumstances.

5. (a) All documents filed with the Court which exceed five pages, regardless of method of duplication (other than joint

appendices, which in this respect are governed by Rule 30), shall be preceded by a table of contents, unless the document contains only one item.

(b) All documents which exceed three pages, regardless of method of duplication, shall contain, following the table of contents, a table of authorities (*i. e.*, cases (alphabetically arranged), constitutional provisions, statutes, textbooks, etc.) with correct references to the pages where they are cited.

6. The body of all documents at their close shall bear the name of counsel of record and such other counsel identified on the cover of the document in conformity with Rule 33.2(a) as may be desired. One copy of every motion and application (other than one to dismiss or affirm under Rule 16) in addition must bear at its close the manuscript signature of counsel of record.

7. The Clerk shall not accept for filing any document presented in a form not in compliance with this Rule, but shall return it indicating to the defaulting party wherein he has failed to comply: the filing, however, shall not thereby be deemed untimely provided that new and proper copies are promptly substituted. If the Court shall find that the provisions of this Rule have not been adhered to, it may impose, in its discretion, appropriate sanctions including but not limited to dismissal of the action, imposition of costs, or disciplinary sanction upon counsel. See also Rule 38 respecting oral argument.

Rule 34.

BRIEFS ON THE MERITS—IN GENERAL

1. A brief of an appellant or petitioner on the merits shall comply in all respects with Rule 33, and shall contain in the order here indicated:

(a) The questions presented for review, stated as required by Rule 15.1(a) or Rule 21.1(a), as the case may be. The phrasing of the questions presented need not be identical with that set forth in the jurisdictional statement or the petition for certiorari, but the brief may not raise additional questions or change the substance of the questions already presented in those documents. At its option, however, the Court may consider a plain error not among the questions presented but evident from the record and otherwise within its jurisdiction to decide.

(b) A list of all parties to the proceeding in the court whose judgment is sought to be reviewed, except where the caption of the case in this Court contains the names of all such parties. This listing may be done in a footnote. See Rule 28.1.

(c) The table of contents and table of authorities, as required by Rule 33.5.

(d) Citations to the opinions and judgments delivered in the courts below.

(e) A concise statement of the grounds on which the jurisdiction of this Court is invoked, with citation to the statutory provision and to the time factors upon which such jurisdiction rests.

(f) The constitutional provisions, treaties, statutes, ordinances, and regulations which the case involves, setting them out verbatim, and giving the appropriate citation therefor. If the provisions involved are lengthy, their citation alone will suffice at this point, and their pertinent text, if not already set forth in the jurisdictional statement or petition for certiorari, shall be set forth in an appendix to the brief.

(g) A concise statement of the case containing all that is material to the consideration of the questions presented, with appropriate references to the Joint Appendix, *e. g.* (J.A. 12) or to the record, *e. g.* (R. 12).

(h) A summary of argument, suitably paragraphed, which should be a succinct, but accurate and clear, condensation of the argument actually made in the body of the brief. It should not be a mere repetition of the headings under which the argument is arranged.

(i) The argument, exhibiting clearly the points of fact and of law being presented, citing the authorities and statutes relied upon.

(j) A conclusion, specifying with particularity the relief to which the party believes himself entitled.

2. The brief filed by an appellee or respondent shall conform to the foregoing requirements, except that no statement of the case need be made beyond what may be deemed necessary in correcting any inaccuracy or omission in the statement by the other side, and except that items (a), (b), (d), (e), and (f) need not be included unless the appellee or respondent is dissatisfied with their presentation by the other side. See Rule 28.1.

3. A brief on the merits shall be as short as possible, but, in any event, shall not exceed 50 pages in length.

4. A reply brief shall conform to such portions of the Rule as are applicable to the brief of an appellee or respondent, but need not contain a summary of argument, if appropriately divided by topical headings. A reply brief shall not exceed 20 pages in length.

5. Whenever, in the brief of any party, a reference is made to the Joint Appendix or the record, it must be accompanied by the appropriate page number. If the reference is to an exhibit, the page numbers at which the exhibit appears, at which it was offered in evidence, and at which it was ruled on by the judge must be indicated, *e. g.* (Pl.Ex. 14; R. 199, 2134).

6. Briefs must be compact, logically arranged with proper headings, concise, and free from burdensome, irrelevant, immaterial, and scandalous matter. Briefs not complying with this paragraph may be disregarded and stricken by the Court.

Rule 35.

BRIEFS ON THE MERITS—TIME FOR FILING

1. Counsel for the appellant or petitioner shall file with the Clerk 40 copies of the printed brief on the merits within 45 days of the order noting or postponing probable jurisdiction, or of the order granting the writ of certiorari.

2. Forty printed copies of the brief of the appellee or respondent shall be filed with the Clerk within 30 days after the receipt by him of the brief filed by the appellant or petitioner.

3. A reply brief will be received no later than one week before the date of oral argument, and only by leave of Court thereafter.

4. The periods of time stated in paragraphs 1 and 2 of this Rule may be enlarged as provided in Rule 29, upon application duly made; or, if a case is advanced for hearing, the time for filing briefs may be abridged as circumstances require, pursuant to order of the Court on its own or a party's application.

5. Whenever a party desires to present late authorities, newly enacted legislation, or other intervening matters that were not available in time to have been included in his brief in chief, he may file 40 printed copies of a supplemental brief, restricted to such new matter and otherwise in conformity with these Rules, up to the time the case is called for hearing, or, by leave of Court, thereafter.

6. No brief will be received through the Clerk or otherwise after a case has been argued or submitted, except from a party and upon leave of the Court.

7. No brief will be received by the Clerk unless the same shall be accompanied by proof of service as required by Rule 28.

Rule 36.

BRIEF OF AN AMICUS CURIAE

1. A brief of an *amicus curiae* prior to consideration of the jurisdictional statement or of the petition for writ of certiorari, accompanied by written consent of the parties, may be filed only if submitted within the time allowed for the filing of the motion to dismiss or affirm or the brief in opposition to the petition for certiorari. A motion for leave to file such a brief when consent has been refused is not favored. Any such motion must be filed within the time allowed for filing of the brief and must be accompanied by the proposed brief. In any event, no such brief shall exceed 20 pages in length.

2. A brief of an *amicus curiae* in a case before the Court for oral argument may be filed when accompanied by written consent of all parties to the case and presented within the time allowed for the filing of the brief of the party supported and if in support of neither party, within the time allowed for filing appellant's or petitioner's brief. Any such brief must identify the party supported, shall be as concise as possible, and in no event shall exceed 30 pages in length. No reply brief of an *amicus curiae* will be received.

3. When consent to the filing of a brief of an *amicus curiae* in a case before the Court for oral argument is refused by a party to the case, a motion for leave to file, accompanied by the proposed brief, complying with the 30-page limit, may be presented to the Court. No such motion shall be received unless submitted within the time allowed for the filing of an *amicus* brief on written consent. The motion shall concisely state the nature of the applicant's interest, set forth facts or questions of law that have not been, or reasons for believing that they will not adequately be, presented by the parties, and their relevancy to the disposition of the case; and it shall in no event exceed five pages in length. A party served with such motion may seasonably file an objection concisely stating the reasons for withholding consent.

4. Consent to the filing of a brief of an *amicus curiae* need not be had when the brief is presented for the United States sponsored by the Solicitor General; for any agency of the United States authorized by law to appear in its own behalf, spon-

sored by its appropriate legal representative; for a State, Territory, or Commonwealth sponsored by its attorney general; or for a political subdivision of a State, Territory, or Commonwealth sponsored by the authorized law officer thereof.

5. All briefs, motions, and responses filed under this Rule shall comply with the applicable provisions of Rules 33, 34, and 42 (except that it shall be sufficient to set forth the interest of the *amicus curiae*, the argument, the summary of argument, and the conclusion); and shall be accompanied by proof of service as required by Rule 28.

Rule 37.

CALL AND ORDER OF THE CALENDAR

1. The Clerk, at the commencement of each Term, and periodically thereafter, shall prepare a calendar consisting of cases available for argument. Cases will be calendared so that they will not normally be called for argument less than two weeks after the brief of the appellee or respondent is due. The Clerk shall keep the calendar current throughout the Term, adding cases as they are set down for argument, and making rearrangements as required.

2. Unless otherwise ordered, the Court, on the first Monday of each Term, will commence calling cases for argument in the order in which they stand on the calendar, and proceed from day to day during the Term in the same order, except that the arrangement of cases on the calendar shall be subject to modification in the light of the availability of appendices, extensions of time to file briefs, orders advancing, postponing or specially setting arguments, and other relevant factors. The Clerk will advise counsel seasonably when they are required to be present in the Court. He shall periodically publish hearing lists in advance of each argument session, for the convenience of counsel and the information of the public.

3. On the Court's own motion, or on motion of one or more parties, the Court may order that two or more cases, involving what appear to be the same or related questions, be argued together as one case, or on such terms as may be prescribed.

Rule 38.

ORAL ARGUMENT

1. Oral argument should undertake to emphasize and clarify the written argument appearing in the briefs theretofore filed.

Counsel should assume that all Members of the Court have read the briefs in advance of argument. *The Court looks with disfavor on any oral argument that is read from a prepared text.* The Court is also reluctant to accept the submission of briefs, without oral argument, of any case in which jurisdiction has been noted or postponed to the merits or certiorari has been granted. Notwithstanding any such submission, the Court may require oral argument by the parties.

2. The appellant or petitioner is entitled to open and conclude the argument. When there is a cross-appeal or a cross-writ of certiorari it shall be argued with the initial appeal or writ as one case and in the time of one case, and the Court will advise the parties which one is to open and close.

3. Unless otherwise directed, one-half hour on each side is allowed for argument. Counsel is not required to use all the allotted time. Any request for additional time shall be presented by motion to the Court filed under Rule 42 not later than 15 days after service of appellant's or petitioner's brief on the merits, and shall set forth with specificity and conciseness why the case cannot be presented within the half-hour limitation.

4. Only one counsel will be heard for each side, except by special permission granted upon a request presented not later than 15 days after service of the petitioner's or appellant's brief on the merits. Such request shall be by a motion to the Court under Rule 42, and shall set forth with specificity and conciseness why more than one counsel should be heard. Divided arguments are not favored.

5. In any case, and regardless of the number of counsel participating, counsel having the opening will present his case fairly and completely and not reserve points of substance for rebuttal.

6. Oral argument will not be heard on behalf of any party for whom no brief has been filed.

7. By leave of Court, and subject to paragraph 4 of this Rule, counsel for an *amicus curiae* whose brief has been duly filed pursuant to Rule 36 may, with the consent of a party, argue orally on the side of such party. In the absence of such consent, argument by counsel for an *amicus curiae* may be made only by leave of Court, on motion particularly setting forth why such argument is thought to provide assistance to the Court not otherwise available. Any such motion will be granted only in the most extraordinary circumstances.

Rule 39.

FORM OF TYPEWRITTEN PAPERS

1. All papers specifically permitted by these Rules to be presented to the Court without being printed shall, subject to Rule 46.3, be typewritten or otherwise duplicated upon opaque, unglazed paper, 8½ by 13 inches in size (legal cap), and shall be stapled or bound at the upper left-hand corner. The typed matter, except quotations, must be double-spaced. All copies presented to the Court must be legible.

2. The original of any such motion or application, except a motion to dismiss or affirm, must be signed in manuscript by the party or by counsel of record.

Rule 40.

DEATH, SUBSTITUTION, AND REVIVOR—PUBLIC OFFICERS, SUBSTITUTION AND DESCRIPTION

1. Whenever any party shall die after filing a notice of appeal to this Court or a petition for writ of certiorari, the proper representative of the deceased may appear and, upon motion, may be substituted in an appropriate case as a party to the proceeding. If such representative shall not voluntarily become a party, the other party may suggest the death on the record, and on motion obtain an order that, unless such representative shall become a party within a designated time, the party moving for such an order, if appellee or respondent, shall be entitled to have the appeal or petition for writ of certiorari dismissed or the judgment vacated for mootness, as may be appropriate. The party so moving, if an appellant or petitioner, shall be entitled to proceed as in other cases of nonappearance by appellee or respondent. Such substitution, or, in default thereof, such suggestion, must be made within six months after the death of the party, or the case shall abate.

2. Whenever, in the case of a suggestion made as provided in paragraph 1 of this Rule, the case cannot be revived in the court whose judgment is sought to be reviewed because the deceased party has no proper representative within the jurisdiction of that court, but does have a proper representative elsewhere, proceedings then shall be had as this Court may direct.

3. When a public officer is a party to a proceeding here in his official capacity and during its pendency dies, resigns, or otherwise ceases to hold office, the action does not abate and his successor is automatically substituted as a party. Proceed-

ings following the substitution shall be in the name of the substituted party, but any misnomer not affecting the substantial rights of the parties shall be disregarded. An order of substitution may be entered at any time, but the omission to enter such an order shall not affect the substitution.

4. When a public officer is a party in a proceeding here in his official capacity, he may be described as a party by his official title rather than by name; but the Court may require his name to be added.

Rule 41.

CUSTODY OF PRISONERS IN HABEAS CORPUS PROCEEDINGS

1. Pending review in this Court of a decision in a habeas corpus proceeding commenced before a court, Justice, or judge of the United States for the release of a prisoner, a person having custody of the prisoner shall not transfer custody to another unless such transfer is directed in accordance with the provisions of this Rule. Upon application of a custodian showing a need therefor, the court, Justice, or judge rendering the decision under review may make an order authorizing transfer and providing for the substitution of the successor custodian as a party.

2. Pending such review of a decision failing or refusing to release a prisoner, the prisoner may be detained in the custody from which release is sought, or in other appropriate custody, or may be enlarged upon his recognizance, with or without surety, as may appear fitting to the court, Justice, or judge rendering the decision, or to the court of appeals or to this Court or to a judge or Justice of either court.

3. Pending such review of a decision ordering release, the prisoner shall be enlarged upon his recognizance, with or without surety, unless the court, Justice, or judge rendering the decision, or the court of appeals or this Court, or a judge or Justice of either court, shall otherwise order.

4. An initial order respecting the custody or enlargement of the prisoner, and any recognizance or surety taken, shall govern review in the court of appeals and in this Court unless for reasons shown to the court of appeals or to this Court, or to a judge or Justice of either court, the order shall be modified or an independent order respecting custody, enlargement, or surety shall be made.

Rule 42.

MOTIONS TO THE COURT

1. Every motion to the Court shall state clearly its object, the facts on which it is based, and (except for motions under Rule 27) may present legal argument in support thereof. No separate briefs may be filed. All motions shall be as short as possible, and shall comply with any other applicable page limit. For an application or motion addressed to a single Justice, see Rule 43.

2. (a) A motion in any action within the Court's original jurisdiction shall comply with Rule 9.3.

(b) A motion to dismiss or affirm made under Rule 16, a motion to dismiss as moot (or a suggestion of mootness), a motion for permission to file a brief *amicus curiae*, any motion the granting of which would be dispositive of the entire case or would affect the final judgment to be entered (other than a motion to docket or dismiss under Rule 14, or a motion for voluntary dismissal under Rule 53), and any motion to the Court longer than five pages, shall be duplicated as provided in Rule 33, and shall comply with all other requirements of that Rule. Forty copies of the motion shall be filed.

(c) Any other motion to the Court may be typewritten in accordance with Rule 39, but the Court may subsequently require any such motion to be duplicated by the moving party in the manner provided by Rule 33.

3. A motion to the Court shall be filed with the Clerk, with proof of service as provided by Rule 28, unless *ex parte* in nature. No motion shall be presented in open court, other than a motion for admission to the Bar, except when the proceeding to which it refers is being argued. Oral argument will not be heard on any motion unless the Court so directs.

4. A response to a motion shall be made as promptly as possible considering the nature of the relief asked and any asserted need for emergency action, and, in any event, shall be made within 10 days of receipt, unless otherwise ordered by the Court or a Justice, or by the Clerk under the provisions of Rule 29.4. A response to a printed motion shall be printed if time permits. However, in appropriate cases, the Court in its discretion may act on a motion without waiting for a response.

Rule 43.

MOTIONS AND APPLICATIONS TO INDIVIDUAL JUSTICES

1. Any motion or application addressed to an individual Justice shall normally be submitted to the Clerk, who will promptly transmit it to the Justice concerned. If oral argument on the application is deemed imperative, request therefor shall be included in the application.

2. Any motion or application addressed to an individual Justice shall be filed in the form prescribed by Rule 39, and shall be accompanied by proof of service on all other parties. See Rule 28.1.

3. The Clerk in due course will advise all counsel concerned, by means as speedy as may be appropriate, of the time and place of the hearing, if any, and of the disposition made of the motion or application.

4. The motion or application will be addressed to the Justice allotted to the Circuit within which the case arises. When the Circuit Justice is unavailable, for any reason, a motion or application addressed to that Justice shall be distributed to the Justice then available who is next junior to the Circuit Justice; the turn of the Chief Justice follows that of the most junior Justice.

5. A Justice denying a motion or application made to him will note his denial thereon. Thereafter, unless action thereon is restricted by law to the Circuit Justice or is out of time under Rule 29.3, the party making the motion or application, except in the case of an application for extension of time, may renew it to any other Justice, subject to the provisions of this Rule. Except where the denial has been without prejudice, any such renewed motion or application is not favored.

6. Any Justice to whom a motion or application for a stay or for bail is submitted may refer it to the Court for determination.

Rule 44.

STAYS

1. A stay may be granted by a Justice of this Court as permitted by law; and a writ of injunction may be granted by any Justice in a case where it might be granted by the Court.

2. Whenever a party desires a stay pending review in this Court, he may present for approval to a judge of the court

whose decision is sought to be reviewed, or to such court when action by that court is required by law, or to a Justice of this Court, a motion to stay the enforcement of the judgment of which review is sought. If the stay is to act as a supersedeas, a supersedeas bond shall accompany the motion and shall have such surety or sureties as said judge, court, or Justice may require. The bond shall be conditioned on satisfaction of the judgment in full, together with costs, interest, and damages for delay, if for any reason the appeal is dismissed or if the judgment is affirmed, and on full satisfaction of any modified judgment and such costs, interest, and damages as this Court may adjudge and award. When the judgment is for the recovery of money not otherwise secured, the amount of bond shall be fixed at such sum as will cover the whole amount of the judgment remaining unsatisfied, costs, interest, and damages for delay, unless the judge, court, or Justice, after notice and hearing and for good cause shown, fixes a different amount or orders security other than the bond. When the judgment determines the disposition of the property in controversy, as in a real action, replevin, or an action to foreclose a mortgage, or when the property is in the custody of the court, or when the proceeds of such property or a bond for its value is in the custody or control of any court wherein the proceeding appealed from was had, the amount of the bond shall be fixed at such sum as will secure only the amount recovered for the use and detention of the property, costs, interest, and damages for delay.

3. A petitioner entitled thereto may present to a Justice of this Court an application to stay the enforcement of the judgment sought to be reviewed on certiorari. 28 U.S.C. § 2101(f).

4. An application for a stay or injunction to a Justice of this Court shall not be entertained, except in the most extraordinary circumstances, unless application for the relief sought first has been made to the appropriate court or courts below, or to a judge or judges thereof. Any application must identify the judgment sought to be reviewed and have appended thereto a copy of the order and opinion, if any, and a copy of the order, if any, of the court or judge below denying the relief sought, and must set forth with specificity the reasons why the granting of a stay or injunction is deemed justified. Any such application is governed by Rule 43.

5. If an application for a stay addressed to the Court is received in vacation, the Clerk will refer it pursuant to Rule 43.4.

Rule 45.

FEES

In pursuance of 28 U.S.C. § 1911, the fees to be charged by the Clerk are fixed as follows:

(a) For docketing a case on appeal (except a motion to docket and dismiss under Rule 14.3, wherein the fee is $50) or on petition for writ of certiorari, or docketing any other proceeding, except cases involving certified questions, $200, to be increased to $300 in a case on appeal, or writ of certiorari, or in other circumstances when oral argument is permitted.

(b) For filing a petition for rehearing, $50.

(c) For a photographic reproduction and certification of any record or paper, $1 per page; and for comparing with the original thereof any photographic reproduction of any record or paper, when furnished by the person requesting its certification, 5 cents per page.

(d) For a certificate and seal, $10.

(e) For admission to the Bar and certificate under seal, $100.

(f) For a duplicate certificate of an admission to the Bar under seal, $10.

PART IX. SPECIAL PROCEEDINGS

Rule 46.

PROCEEDINGS IN FORMA PAUPERIS

1. A party desiring to proceed in this Court *in forma pauperis* shall file a motion for leave so to proceed, together with his affidavit in the form prescribed in Fed. Rules App.Proc., Form 4 (as adapted, if the party is seeking a writ of certiorari), setting forth with particularity facts showing that he comes within the statutory requirements. See 28 U.S.C. § 1915. However, the affidavit need not state the issues to be presented, and if the district court or the court of appeals has appointed counsel under the Criminal Justice Act of 1964, as amended, the party need not file an affidavit. See 18 U.S.C. § 3006A(d)(6). The motion shall also state whether or not leave to proceed *in forma pauperis* was sought in any court below and, if so, whether leave was granted.

2. With the motion, and affidavit if required, there shall be filed the appropriate substantive document—jurisdictional statement, petition for writ of certiorari, or motion for leave to file, as the case may be—which shall comply in every respect with the Rules governing the same, except that it shall be sufficient to file a single copy thereof.

3. All papers and documents presented under this Rule shall be clearly legible and should, whenever possible, comply with Rule 39. While making due allowance for any case presented under this Rule by a person appearing *pro se*, the Clerk will refuse to receive any document sought to be filed that does not comply with the substance of these Rules, or when it appears that the document is obviously and jurisdictionally out of time.

4. When the papers required by paragraphs 1 and 2 of this Rule are presented to the Clerk, accompanied by proof of service as prescribed by Rule 28, he, without payment of any docket or other fees, will file them, and place the case on the docket.

5. The appellee or respondent in a case *in forma pauperis* may respond in the same manner and within the same time as in any other case of the same nature, except that the filing of a single response, typewritten or otherwise duplicated, with proof of service as required by Rule 28, will suffice whenever petitioner or appellant has filed typewritten papers. The appellee or respondent, in such response or in a separate document filed earlier, may challenge the grounds for the motion to proceed *in forma pauperis*.

6. Whenever the Court appoints a member of the Bar to serve as counsel for an indigent party in a case set for oral argument, the briefs prepared by such counsel, unless he requests otherwise, will be printed under the supervision of the Clerk. The Clerk also will reimburse such counsel for necessary travel expenses to Washington, D. C., and return, in connection with the argument.

7. Where this Court has granted certiorari or noted or postponed probable jurisdiction in a federal case involving the validity of a federal or state criminal judgment, and where the defendant in the original criminal proceeding is financially unable to obtain adequate representation or to meet the necessary expenses in this Court, the Court will appoint counsel who may be compensated, and whose necessary expenses may be repaid, to the extent provided by the Criminal Justice Act of 1964, as amended (18 U.S.C. § 3006A).

Rule 47.

VETERANS' AND SEAMEN'S CASES

1. A veteran suing to establish reemployment rights under 38 U.S.C. § 2022, or under similar provisions of law exempting veterans from the payment of fees or court costs, may proceed upon typewritten papers as under Rule 46, except that the motion shall ask leave to proceed as a veteran, and the affidavit shall set forth the moving party's status as a veteran.

2. A seaman suing pursuant to 28 U.S.C. § 1916 may proceed without prepayment of fees or costs or furnishing security therefor, but he is not relieved of printing costs nor entitled to proceed on typewritten papers except by separate motion, or unless, by motion and affidavit, he brings himself within Rule 46.

PART X. DISPOSITION OF CASES

Rule 48.

OPINIONS OF THE COURT

1. All opinions of the Court shall be handed to the Clerk immediately upon delivery thereof. He shall deliver copies to the Reporter of Decisions and shall cause the opinions to be issued in slip form. The opinions shall be filed by the Clerk for preservation.

2. The Reporter of Decisions shall prepare the opinions for publication in preliminary prints and bound volumes of the United States Reports.

Rule 49.

INTEREST AND DAMAGES

1. Unless otherwise provided by law, if a judgment for money in a civil case is affirmed, whatever interest is allowed by law shall be payable from the date the judgment below was entered. If a judgment is modified or reversed with a direction that a judgment for money be entered below, the mandate shall contain instructions with respect to allowance of interest. Interest will be allowed at the same rate that similar judgments bear interest in the courts of the State where the judgment was entered or was directed to be entered.

2. When an appeal or petition for writ of certiorari is frivolous, the Court may award the appellee or the respondent appropriate damages.

Rule 50.

COSTS

1. In a case of affirmance of any judgment or decree by this Court, costs shall be paid by appellant or petitioner, unless otherwise ordered by the Court.

2. In a case of reversal or vacating of any judgment or decree by this Court, costs shall be allowed to appellant or petitioner, unless otherwise ordered by the Court.

3. The fees of the Clerk and the costs of serving process and printing the joint appendix in this Court are taxable items. The costs of the transcript of record from the court below is also a taxable item, but shall be taxable in that court as costs in the case. The expenses of printing briefs, motions, petitions, or jurisdictional statements are not taxable.

4. In a case where a question has been certified, including a case where the certificate is dismissed, costs shall be equally divided unless otherwise ordered by the Court; but where a decision is rendered on the whole matter in controversy (see Rule 24.2), costs shall be allowed as provided in paragraphs 1 and 2 of this Rule.

5. In a civil action commenced on or after July 18, 1966, costs under this Rule shall be allowed for or against the United States, or an officer or agent thereof, unless expressly waived or otherwise ordered by the Court. See 28 U.S.C. § 2412. In any other civil action, no such costs shall be allowed, except where specifically authorized by statute and directed by the Court.

6. When costs are allowed in this Court, it shall be the duty of the Clerk to insert the amount thereof in the body of the mandate or other proper process sent to the court below, and annex to the same the bill of items taxed in detail. The prevailing side in such a case is not to submit to the Clerk any bill of costs.

7. In an appropriate instance, the Court may adjudge double costs.

Rule 51.

REHEARINGS

1. A petition for rehearing of any judgment or decision other than one on a petition for writ of certiorari, shall be filed within 25 days after the judgment or decision, unless the time

is shortened or enlarged by the Court or a Justice. Forty copies, produced in conformity with Rule 33, must be filed (except where the party is proceeding *in forma pauperis* under Rule 46), accompanied by proof of service as prescribed by Rule 28. Such petition must briefly and distinctly state its grounds. Counsel must certify that the petition is presented in good faith and not for delay; one copy of the certificate shall bear the manuscript signature of counsel. A petition for rehearing is not subject to oral argument, and will not be granted except at the instance of a Justice who concurred in the judgment or decision and with the concurrence of a majority of the Court. See also Rule 52.2.

2. A petition for rehearing of an order denying a petition for writ of certiorari shall comply with all the form and filing requirements of paragraph 1, but its grounds must be limited to intervening circumstances of substantial or controlling effect or to other substantial grounds not previously presented. Counsel must certify that the petition is restricted to the grounds specified in this paragraph and that it is presented in good faith and not for delay; one copy of the certificate shall bear the manuscript signature of counsel or of the party when not represented by counsel. A petition for rehearing without such certificate shall be rejected by the Clerk. Such petition is not subject to oral argument.

3. No response to a petition for rehearing will be received unless requested by the Court, but no petition will be granted without an opportunity to submit a response.

4. Consecutive petitions for rehearings, and petitions for rehearing that are out of time under this Rule, will not be received.

Rule 52.

PROCESS; MANDATES

1. All process of this Court shall be in the name of the President of the United States, and shall contain the given names, as well as the surnames, of the parties.

2. In a case coming from a state court, mandate shall issue as of course after the expiration of 25 days from the day the judgment is entered, unless the time is shortened or enlarged by the Court or a Justice, or unless the parties stipulate that it be issued sooner. The filing of a petition for rehearing, unless otherwise ordered, will stay the mandate until disposition of such petition, and if the petition is then denied, the mandate

shall issue forthwith. When, however, a petition for rehearing is not acted upon prior to adjournment, or is filed after the Court adjourns, the judgment or mandate of the Court will not be stayed unless specifically ordered by the Court or a Justice.

3. In a case coming from a federal court, a formal mandate will not issue, unless specially directed; instead, the Clerk will send the proper court a copy of the opinion or order of the Court and a certified copy of the judgment (which shall include provisions for the recovery of costs, if any are awarded). In all other respects, the provisions of paragraph 2 apply.

Rule 53.

DISMISSING CAUSES

1. Whenever the parties thereto, at any stage of the proceedings, file with the Clerk an agreement in writing that any cause be dismissed, specifying the terms with respect to costs, and pay to the Clerk any fees that may be due, the Clerk, without further reference to the Court, shall enter an order of dismissal.

2. (a) Whenever an appellant or petitioner in this Court files with the Clerk a motion to dismiss a cause to which he is a party, with proof of service as prescribed by Rule 28, and tenders to the Clerk any fees and costs that may be due, the adverse party, within 15 days after service thereof, may file an objection, limited to the quantum of damages and costs in this Court alleged to be payable, or, in a proper case, to a showing that the moving party does not represent all appellants or petitioners if there are more than one. The Clerk will refuse to receive any objection not so limited.

(b) Where the objection goes to the standing of the moving party to represent the entire side, the party moving for dismissal, within 10 days thereafter, may file a reply, after which time the matter shall be laid before the Court for its determination.

(c) If no objection is filed, or if upon objection going only to the quantum of damages and costs in this Court, the party moving for dismissal, within 10 days thereafter, shall tender the whole of such additional damages and costs demanded, the Clerk, without further reference to the Court, shall enter an order of dismissal. If, after objection as to quantum of damages and costs in this Court, the moving party does not respond with such a tender within 10 days, the Clerk shall report the matter to the Court for its determination.